ETHICAL ISSUES IN BUSINESS

Eighth Edition

ETHICAL ISSUES IN BUSINESS

A Philosophical Approach

Edited by

Thomas Donaldson
University of Pennsylvania

Patricia H. Werhane
University of Virginia
DePaul University

With contributions from
Joseph D. Van Zandt

PEARSON
Prentice
Hall

Upper Saddle River, New Jersey 07458

Library of Congress Cataloging-in-Publication Data

Ethical issues in business : a philosophical approach / [edited by]
Thomas Donaldson, Patricia H. Werhane, Joseph Van Zandt. — 8th ed.
  p. cm.
  Includes bibliographical references.
  ISBN–13: 978–0–13–184619–7
  ISBN–10: 0–13–184619–1
  1. Business ethics—Case studies.   2. Social responsibility of business—Case studies.
I. Donaldson, Thomas,   II. Werhane, Patricia Hogue.   III. Van Zandt, Joseph.
  HF5387.E8 2008
  174' .4—dc22

                                                                    2007013459

Editor-in-Chief: Sarah Touborg
Senior Acquisitions Editor: Mical Moser
Editorial Assistant: Carla Worner
Director of Marketing: Brandy Dawson
Senior Managing Editor: Joanne Riker
Production Liaison: Joanne Hakim
Manufacturing Buyer: Christina Amato
Cover Art Director: Jayne Conte
Cover Design: Bruce Kenselaar
Manager, Cover Visual Research & Permissions: Karen Sanatar
Cover Image: Al Cohen/Taxi/Getty Images
Full-Service Project Management: Bruce Hobart/Pine Tree Composition, Inc.
Composition: Laserwords Private Limited
Printer/Binder: R. R. Donnelley & Sons Company
Cover Printer: R. R. Donnelley & Sons Company

Credits and acknowledgments borrowed from other sources and reproduced, with
permission, in this textbook appear on appropriate page within text.

Pearson Education LTD., London
Pearson Education Singapore, Pte. Ltd
Pearson Education, Canada, Ltd
Pearson Education—Japan
Pearson Education Australia PTY, Limited
Pearson Education North Asia Ltd
Pearson Educación de Mexico, S.A. de C.V.
Pearson Education Malaysia, Pte. Ltd
Pearson Education, Upper Saddle River, New Jersey

10 9 8 7 6 5 4 3 2 1
ISBN-13: 978-0-13-184619-7
ISBN-10:   0-13-184619-1

Contents

• PART 2 •
Property, Profit, and Justice

• PART 3 •
Corporations, Persons, and Morality

• PART 4 •
International Business

• PART 5 •
Contemporary Business Themes

Preface

The first edition of *Ethical Issues in Business* was published nearly three decades ago in 1979. Since then the awareness of business ethics issues has mushroomed, not only in universities but corporations and the public media. Textbooks, courses, and research in business ethics have multiplied, with more articles, cases, classes, and journals appearing each year. In corporations, training programs for managers, codes of ethics and "ethics officers" are now commonplace. And in newspapers, television reporting, and Internet blogs, accounts of scandals involving Enron, WorldCom, Tyco, Merrill Lynch, Parmalat, the New York Stock Exchange, and AIG ushered in a new era of corporate regulation and governance. The Sarbanes-Oxley legislation, passed in 2002 by the U.S. Congress in the wake of the Enron era scandals, represents the most sweeping change in the regulation of business since the creation of the SEC (Securities Exchange Commission) in the 1930s.

In this, the eighth edition of *Ethical Issues in Business*, we reflect these dramatic social and intellectual changes. To be sure, some of the foundational theoretical perspectives present in the earlier editions of our book are retained. The insights of Adam Smith and John Locke about markets and human rights or the radical claims made by Karl Marx that capitalism distorts the thinking of its participants are no less relevant today than they were decades ago.

Yet other issues are more time-bound and require new material. Since the publication of the seventh edition, striking events have shaped the ethical mindset toward business. Ethical challenges for the pharmaceutical industry, the Enron scandal, Sarbanes-Oxley Congressional legislation, pension plan abandonment by companies, newly emerging women's issues, oil companies drilling in developing countries, and issues about how to market to the poor in these countries—all these emerging issues have prompted new material in the current edition.

This edition, like earlier ones, owes heavily to people whose suggestions, criticism, and editorial assistance made it a better book. We want to especially thank Margaret Cording at Rice University for her excellent editing of the Seventh Edition during a time of personal crisis for both of us. This edition is better thanks to her work. We thank Prentice Hall's reviewers Mark A. Michael, Austin Peay State University; Ralph P. Forsberg, Delta College; and Regina Hobaugh, Holy Family University for their constructive comments, and we owe a great debt to Dr. Joseph D. Van Zandt for his excellent editorial work on this edition. We also want to thank R. Edward Freeman for his input into this edition, Emily Mead for her case work and bibliographical help, and Karen Musselman and Summer Brown for secretarial assistance. Most importantly, we thank the Wharton School, the Darden

School, and DePaul University for their ongoing support of business ethics and this publication.

This edition is dedicated to the memory of Jean Donaldson and Charles Werhane.

T. D.

P. H. W.

Introduction to Ethical Reasoning

THOMAS DONALDSON • PATRICIA H. WERHANE

What is the basis for making ethical decisions? Should Joan challenge Fred the next time he cracks a sexist joke? Should John refrain from lying on his job application despite his temptation to do so? What, if anything, should make Hillary decide that eating meat is corrupting, whereas vegetarianism is uplifting? It is obvious that the kind of evidence required for an ethical decision is different from that needed to make a nonethical one, but what is the nature of the difference? These questions give rise to a search for a method of ethical justification and decision making, a method that will specify the conditions that any good ethical decision should meet.

To see how such questions arise concretely, consider the following case.[1]

Some years ago, a large German chemical firm, BASF, decided to follow the lead of many other European firms and build a factory in the United States. BASF needed land, lots of it (1,800 acres), an inexpensive labor pool, almost five million gallons of fresh water every day, a surrounding area free of import taxes, and a nearby railroad and ocean port. Obviously, only a handful of locations could meet all these requirements. The spot the company finally picked seemed perfect, an area near the coast of South Carolina called Beaufort County. It purchased 1,800 acres.

South Carolina and Beaufort County were pleased with BASF's decision. The surrounding area, from which the company would pick its workers, was economically depressed and per capita income stood well below the national average. Jobs of any kind were desperately needed. Even the governor of South Carolina and his staff were eager for BASF to build in South Carolina, and although BASF had not yet finalized its exact production plans, the State Pollution Central Authority saw no problems with meeting the state pollution laws. BASF itself said that although it would dump chemical byproducts into the local Colleton River, it planned not to lower the river's quality.

But trouble started immediately. To see why, one needs to know that Beaufort County is the home of the internationally famous resort area called Hilton Head. Hilton Head attracts thousands of vacationers every year—most of them with plenty of money—and its developers worried that the scenic splendor of the area might be marred by the air and water pollution. Especially concerned about water pollution, resort developers charged that the proposed chemical plant would pollute the Colleton River. They argued that BASF plants in Germany had polluted the Rhine and, in Belgium, the Schelde River. Further, they noted that on BASF's list of proposed expenditures, pollution control was allocated only one million dollars.

The citizens of Beaufort County, in contrast to the Hilton Head Developers, welcomed BASF. They presented the company with a petition bearing over 7,000 signatures endorsing the new plant. As one local businessman commented, "I would say 80 percent of the people in Beaufort County are in favor of BASF. Those who aren't rich." (William D. McDonald, "Youth Corps Looking for Jobs," *The State*, February 23, 1970.)

The manager of BASF's U.S. operations was clearly confronted by an economic and moral dilemma. He knew that preventing massive pollution was virtually impossible and, in any case, outrageously expensive. The eagerness of South Carolina officials for new industry suggested that pollution standards might be "relaxed" for BASF. If it decided to go ahead and build, was the company to push for the minimum pollution control it could get away with under the law? Such a policy might maximize corporate profits and the financial interests of the shareholders, while at the same time it would lower the aesthetic quality of the environment. It might make jobs available to Beaufort County while ignoring the resort industry and the enjoyment of vacationers. Moreover, the long-term effects of dumping chemicals was hard to predict, but past experience did not give the manager a feeling of optimism. Pollution seemed to be not only a business issue, but also a moral one. But how should the manager sort out, and eventually decide upon, such a moral issue?

To solve his moral problem, BASF's manager might try a variety of strategies. He might, for example, begin by assuming that he has three basic options: (1) Build with minimal pollution control, (2) build with maximal pollution control, or (3) do not build.

Then, he might reason:

> The consequences of option 1 will be significant but tolerable water pollution, hostility from the Hilton Head developers, high short-term corporate profits, and satisfied shareholders.

> The consequences of option 2 will be unnoticeable pollution, no complaints from the Hilton Head developers, high pollution-control costs, low profits, and unsatisfied stockholders.

> The consequences of option 3 will be approval from the Hilton Head developers, low short-term profits (while a search for a new location is under way), and strong disapproval from the local townspeople.

> My job from a moral perspective is to weigh these consequences and consider which of the alternatives constitutes a maximization of good. Who will benefit from each decision? How many people will be adversely affected and in what ways?

Or the manager might reason:

> Both BASF Corporation and I are confronted with a variety of duties, rights, and obligations. First there is the company's obligation to its stockholders, and my duty as manager is to protect the economic interests and rights of our stockholders. Next there are the rights of those Beaufort residents and visitors in the area to clean air and water. Finally there are the rights of other property owners in the area, including the Hilton Head developers, not to be harmed unreasonably by other industries. There is an implied obligation to future generations to protect the river. And finally, there are broader considerations: Is this an act I would want others to undertake? What kind of moral example will I be setting?

> My job from a moral perspective is to balance and assess these duties, rights, and obligations, and determine which have priority.

Notice how different each of these approaches is. The first focuses on the concept of consequences; the second on duties, rights, and obligations. Of course, the two methods may overlap. Reflecting carefully on the consequences of a given action may include considering the impact that the action will have on how seriously people take their duties in the future. And the duty of a manager may include attempting to bring about a certain set of consequences, such as maximizing financial returns to shareholders. Even so, the approaches reflect two fundamentally distinct methods of ethical decision making, each of which is well represented in the history of philosphy. Each has been championed by a well-known traditional philosopher. Moreover, most ethical theories articulated by ethical theorists throughout history can be categorized under one of the two headings. The first may be called "consequentialism"; the second, "deontology."

UTILITARIANISM: A FORM OF CONSEQUENTIALISM

As its name implies, a consequentialist theory of ethical reasoning concentrates on the consequences of human actions, and all actions are evaluated in terms of the extent to which they achieve desirable results. Such theories are also frequently labeled *teleological*, a term derived from the Greek word *telos*, which means "end" or "purpose." According to consequential theories, the concepts of right, wrong, and duty are subordinated to the concept of the end or purpose of an action.

There are at least two types of consequential theory. The first—advocated by only a few consequentialists—is a version of what philosophers call ethical egoism. It construes right action as action whose consequences, considered among all the alternatives, maximizes *my* good—that is, action that benefits *me* the most or harms *me* the least. The second type—advocated by most consequentialists—denies that right action concerns only me. Rather, right action must maximize *overall* good; that is, it must maximize good (or minimize bad) from the standpoint of the entire human community. The best-accepted label for this type of consequentialism is *utilitarianism*. This term was coined by the eighteenth-century philosopher Jeremy Bentham, although its best-known proponent was the nineteenth-century English philosopher John Stuart Mill. As Bentham formulated it, the principle of utility states that an action is right if it produces the greatest balance of pleasure or happiness and unhappiness in light of alternative actions. Mill supported a similar principle, using what he called the "proof" of the principle of utility—namely, the recognition that the only proof for something's being desirable is that someone actually desires it. Since everybody desires pleasure or happiness, it follows, according to Mill, that happiness is the most desirable thing. The purpose of moral action is to achieve greatest overall happiness, and actions are evaluated in terms of the extent to which they contribute to this end. The most desirable state of affairs, the greatest good and the goal of morality, said Mill, is the "greatest happiness for the greatest number."

While later utilitarians accept the general framework of Mill's argument, not all utilitarians are hedonists. That is, not all utilitarians equate the "good" with pleasure or happiness. Some utilitarians have argued that in maximizing the "good," one must be concerned not only with maximizing pleasure, but with maximizing other things, such as knowledge, moral maturity, and friendship. Although it could be claimed that such goods also bring pleasure and happiness to their possessor, it is arguable whether their goodness is ultimately reducible to whatever pleasure they bring. These philosophers are sometimes called pluralistic utilitarians. Still other philosophers have adapted utilitarianism to modern methods of economic theory by championing what is known as preference utilitarianism. Instead of referring to the maximization of specific goods, such as pleasure or knowledge, preference utilitarians understand the ultimate foundation of goodness to be the set of preferences people actually possess. One person prefers oysters to strawberries; another prefers rock music to Mozart. Each person has a set of preferences, and so long as the set is internally consistent, it makes no sense to label one set morally superior to another. Preference utilitarianism thus interprets right action as that which is optimal among alternatives in terms of everyone's preferences. Disputes, however, rage among preference utilitarians and their critics over how to specify the meaning of optimal.

Bentham and Mill thought that utilitarianism was a revolutionary theory, both because it accurately reflected human motivation and because it had clear application to the political and social problems of their day. If one could measure the benefit or harm of any action, rule, or law, they believed, one could sort out good and bad social and political legislation as well as good and bad individual actions.

But how, specifically, does one apply the traditional principle of utility? To begin with, one's race, religion, intelligence, or condition of birth is acknowledged to be irrelevant in calculating one's ultimate worth. Each person counts for "one," and no more than "one." Second, in evaluating happiness, one must take into account not only present generations, but ones in the future. In calculating the effects of pollution, for instance, one must measure the possible effects pollution might have on health, genetics, and the supply of natural resources for future generations. Third, pleasure or happiness is measured in a manner that recognizes that some pleasures are stronger than others, so that the thesis does not reduce to the idea that "one ought to do what makes the most persons happy." Utilitarianism does not reduce to a dictatorship of majority interests. One person's considerable unhappiness might outweigh the minor pleasures of many other persons added together. Utilitarians also consider the long-term consequences for single individuals. For instance, it might be pleasurable to drink a full bottle of wine every evening, but the long-term drawbacks of such a habit might well outweigh its temporary pleasures.

Finally, according to many utilitarians (such as Mill), some pleasures are qualitatively better than others. Intellectual pleasure, for example, is said to be higher than physical pleasure. "Better to be Socrates unsatisfied," writes Mill, "than a pig satisfied." The reasons that drove Mill to formulate this qualitative distinction among pleasures are worth noting. Since Mill believed that the optimal situation was one of "greatest happiness for the greatest number," then what had he to say about a world of people living at the zenith of merely physical happiness? If science could invent a wonder drug, like the "soma" in Aldous Huxley's *Brave New World*, that provided a permanent state of drugged happiness (without even a hangover), would the consequence be a perfect world? Mill believed not, and to remedy this difficulty in his theory he introduced qualitative levels of happiness. For example, he said that the happiness of understanding Plato is "higher" than that of drinking three martinis. But how was Mill to say which pleasures were higher? Here he retreated to an ingenious proposal: When deciding which of two pleasures is higher, one should poll the group of persons who are experienced—that is, who know both pleasures. Their decision will indicate which is the higher pleasure. Ah, but might the majority decision not be wrong? Here Mill provides no clear answer.

Modern-day utilitarians divide themselves roughly into two groups: *act utilitarians* and *rule utilitarians.* An act utilitarian believes that the principle of utility should be applied to individual acts. Thus one measures the consequences of each individual action according to whether it maximizes good. For example, suppose a certain community were offered the opportunity to receive a great deal of wealth in the form of a gift. The only stipulation was that the community force some of its citizens with ugly, deteriorated homes to repair and beautify them. Next, suppose the community held an election to decide whether to accept the gift. An act utilitarian would analyze the problem of whether to vote for or against the proposal from the standpoint of the individual voter. Would an individual's vote to accept the gift be more likely to maximize the community's overall good than would a vote to the contrary?

A *rule utilitarian,* on the other hand, believes that instead of considering the results of specific actions, one must weigh the consequences of adopting a general rule exemplified by that action. According to the rule utilitarian, one should act according to a general rule that, if adopted, would maximize good. For example, in the hypothetical case of the community deciding whether to accept a gift, a rule utilitarian might adopt the rule "Never vote in a way that lowers the self-respect of a given class of citizens." She might accept this rule because of the general unhappiness that would ensue if society systematically treated some persons as second-class citizens. Here the focus is on the general rule and not on the individual act.

Critics raise objections to utilitarianism. Perhaps the most serious objection is that it is unable to account for justice. Because the utilitarian concentrates on the consequences of an action for a majority, the employment of the principle of utility can be argued to allow injustice for a small minority. For example, if overall goodness were maximized in the long run by making slaves of 2 percent of the population, utilitarianism seemingly is forced to condone slavery. But clearly this is unjust. Utilitarianism's obvious response is that such slavery will not, as a matter of empirical fact, maximize goodness. Rule utilitarians, as we have seen, can argue that society should embrace the rule "Never enslave others," because following such a principle will, in the long run, maximize goodness. Even so, the battle continues between utilitarians and their critics. Can utilitarianism account for the widely held moral conviction that injustice to a minority is wrong *regardless* of the consequences? The answer is hotly contested.

Another criticism concerns the determination of the good to be maximized. Any consequentialist has the problem of identifying and ranking whatever is to be maximized. For a utilitarian such as Mill, as we have seen, the problem involves distinguishing between higher and lower pleasures. But for pluralistic utilitarians, a similar problem exists: What is the basis for selecting, for example, friendship and happiness as goods to be maximized and not, say, aesthetic sensitivity? And even granted that this problem can be solved, there is the future problem of arbitrating tradeoffs between goods such as happiness and friendship when they conflict. When one is forced to choose between enhancing happiness and enhancing friendship, which gets priority? And under what conditions?

An interesting fact about consequentialist reasoning is that most of us employ it to some degree in ordinary decisions. We weigh the consequences of alternatives in choosing colleges, in deciding on a career, in hiring and promoting others, and in many other judgments. We frequently weigh good consequences over bad ones and predict the long- and short-term effects of our choices. We often even cite consequentialist-style principles—for example, "No one should choose a college where he or she will be unhappy," or, "No one should pollute the environment."

However, for a variety of reasons, including the objections to utilitarianism mentioned earlier, some philosophers refuse to acknowledge consequentialism as an adequate theory of ethics. They argue that the proper focus for ethical judgments should not be consequences, but moral *precepts*—that is, the rules, norms, and principles we use to guide our actions. Such philosophers are known as deontologists, and the next section will examine their views.

KANTIAN ETHICS AND SOCIAL CONTRACT THEORY: FORMS OF DEONTOLOGY

The term *deontological* comes from the Greek word for "duty," and what is crucial according to the deontologist are the rules and principles that guide actions. We shall discuss here two approaches to deontological ethical reasoning that have profoundly influenced ethics. The first is that of the eighteenth-century philosopher Immanuel Kant and his followers. This approach focuses on duty and universal rules to determine right actions. The second—actually a subspecies of deontological reasoning—is known as the "social contract" approach. It focuses not on individual decision making, but rather on the general social principles that rational persons in certain ideal situations would agree upon and adopt.

Kantian Deontology

Kant believed that ethical reasoning should concern activities that are rationally motivated and should utilize precepts that apply universally to all human actions. To this end, he opens his treatise on ethics by declaring:

> It is impossible to conceive anything at all in the world, . . . which can be taken as good without qualification except a good will.[2]

This statement sums up much of what Kant wants to say about ethics and is worth unraveling. What Kant means is that the only thing that can be good or worthwhile without any provisos or stipulations is an action of the will freely motivated for the right reasons. Other goods such as wealth, beauty, and intelligence are certainly valuable, but they are not good without qualification because they have the potential to create both good and bad effects. Wealth, beauty, and intelligence can be bad when they are used for purely selfish ends. Even human happiness—which Mill held as the highest good—can, according to Kant, create complacency, disinterest, and excessive self-assurance under certain conditions. According to Kant, reason is the faculty that can aid in the discovery of correct moral principles; thus it is reason, not inclination, that should guide the will. When reason guides the will, Kant calls the resulting actions ones done from "duty." Kant's use of the term *duty* turns out to be less formidable than it first appears. Kant is simply saying that a purely good and free act of the will is one done not merely because you have an inclination to do it, but because you have the right reasons for doing it. For example, suppose you discover a wallet belonging to a stranger. Kant would say that despite one's inclination to keep the money (which the stranger may not even need), one should return it. This is an act you know is right despite your inclinations. Kant also believes you should return the wallet even when you believe the consequences of not returning it are better. Here his views are at sharp odds with consequentialism. Suppose that the stranger is known for her stinginess, and you plan to donate the money to a children's hospital. No matter. For Kant, you must return the wallet. Thus the moral worth lies in the act itself and not in either your happiness or the consequences brought about by the act. Acts are good because they are done for the sake of what is right and not because of the consequences they might produce.

But how do I know what my duty is? While it may be clear that one should return a wallet, there are other circumstances in which one's duty is less evident. Suppose you are in a six-person lifeboat at sea with five others and a seventh person swims up? What is one's duty here? And how does one even know that what one thinks is right is indeed right? To settle such problems, Kant claims that duty is more than doing merely what you "feel" is right. Duty is acting with respect for other rational beings. It almost goes without saying, then, that "acting from duty" is not to be interpreted as action done in obedience to local, state, or national laws, since these can be good or bad. Instead, duty is linked to the idea of universal principles that should govern all our actions.

Is there any principle that can govern all human beings? Kant believes the answer is yes, and he calls the highest such principle the "categorical imperative." He formulates the categorical imperative in three ways (although we shall consider only two formulations here). The first formulation, roughly translated, is

> One ought only to act such that the principle of one's act could become a universal law of human action in a world in which one would hope to live.

For example, one would want to live in a world where people followed the principle "Return property that belongs to others." Therefore one should return the stranger's wallet. We do not, however, want to live in a world where everyone lies. Therefore, one should not adopt the principle "Lie whenever it seems helpful."

The second formulation of the categorical imperative is:

> One ought to treat others as having intrinsic value in themselves, and not merely as means to achieve one's ends.

In other words, one should respect every person as a rational and free being. Hitler treated one group of persons as nonpersons in order to achieve his own ends, and thus he acted contrary to the categorical imperative. Another instance of treating persons as means would occur if a teacher looked up the grade records of new students to determine how to assign grades in her own class. She would be treating students as if they had no control over their destinies. Such actions are immoral according to Kant because they fail to respect the inherent dignity of rational beings.

Ethical reasoning for Kant implies adopting principles of action and evaluating one's actions in terms of those principles. Even Kant grants that the evaluation is sometimes difficult. For example, there is the problem of striking the proper level of generality in choosing a principle. A principle that read, "If one is named John Doe and attends Big State University and has two sisters, then he should borrow 50 dollars without intending to repay it" is far too specific. On the other hand, the principle "You should always pay your debts" might be too general, since it would require that a starving man give the only money he possesses to buy a loaf of bread. Because of the problem of striking the proper degree of generality, many modern deontologists have reformulated Kant's basic question to read: "Could I wish that everyone in the world would follow this principle under relevantly similar conditions?"

As with utilitarianism, critics challenge deontological reasoning. Some assert that fanatics such as Hitler could at least believe that the rule "Persecute Jews whenever possible" is one that the world should live by. Similarly, a thief might universalize the principle "Steal whenever you have a good opportunity." Moreover, a strict interpretation of deontological ethical reasoning is said to allow no exceptions to a universal principle. Such strict adherence to universal principles might encourage moral rigidity and might fail to reflect the diversity of responses required by complex moral situations. Finally, critics argue that, in a given case, two principles may conflict without there being a clear way to decide which principle or rule should take precedence. Jean-Paul Sartre tells of his dilemma during World War II when he was forced to choose between staying to comfort his ill and aging mother and fighting for the freedom of France. Two principles seemed valid: "Give aid to your father and mother" and "Contribute to the cause of freedom." But with conflicting principles, how is one to choose? Nevertheless, deontological ethical reasoning represents a well-respected and fundamentally distinctive mode of ethical reasoning, one that, like consequentalism, appears in the deliberation of ordinary persons as well as philosophers. We have all heard actions condemned by the comment, "What would it be like if everyone did that?"

The Contractarian Alternative

Kant assumes that the categorical imperative is something all rational individuals can discover and agree upon. A different version of deontology is offered by many philosophers who focus less on the actions of individuals and more on the principles that govern society at large. These include two philosophers whose writings appear in our book: the seventeenth-century political philosopher John Locke and the twentieth-century U.S. philosopher John Rawls. They and others try to establish universal principles of a just society through what might be called "social contract thought experiments." They ask us to imagine what it would be like to live in a situation where there are no laws, no social conventions, and no political state. In this so-called state of nature, we imagine that rational persons gather to formulate principles or rules to govern political and social communities. Such rules would resemble principles derived through the categorical imperative in that they would presumably be principles to which every rational person would agree and that would hold universally.

Locke and Rawls differ in their approach to establishing rules or principles of justice, and the difference illustrates two distinct forms of contractarian reasoning. Locke argues from a "natural rights" position, while Rawls argues from a "reasonable person" position. Locke claims that every person is born with, and possesses, certain basic rights that are "natural." These rights are inherent to a person's nature, and they are possessed by every one equally. Like other inherent traits, they cannot be taken away. They are, in the words of the U.S. Declaration of Independence, "inalienable." When rational persons meet to formulate principles to govern the formation of social and political communities, they construct a social contract that is the basis for an agreement between themselves and their government, and whose rules protect natural rights. Rights, then, become deontological precepts by which one forms and evaluates rules, constitutions, government, and socioeconomic systems. While many philosophers disagree with Locke's view that each of us has inherent or natural rights, many do utilize a theory of human rights as the basis for justifying and evaluating political institutions.

Rawls adopts a different perspective. He does not begin from a natural-rights position. Instead, he asks which principles of justice rational persons would formulate if they were behind a "veil of ignorance"—if each person knew nothing about who he or she was. That is, one would not know whether one were old or young, male or female, rich or poor, highly motivated or lazy, or anything about one's personal status in society. Unable to predict which principles, if picked, will favor them personally, Rawls argues, persons will be forced to choose principles that are fair to all.

Rawls and Locke are not in perfect agreement about which principles would be adopted in such hypothetical situations, and more will be said about their views later in the book. For now it is important to remember simply that the social-contract approach maintains a deontological character. It is used to formulate principles of justice that apply universally. Some philosophers note, however, that from an original position in a "state of nature" or behind a "veil of ignorance," rational persons could adopt consequentialist principles as rules for a just society. Thus, while the social contract approach is deontological in style, the principles it generates are not necessarily ones that are incompatible with consequentialism.

In the moral evaluations of business, all deontologists—contractarians included—would ask questions such as the following:

1. Are the rules fair to everyone?
2. Do the rules hold universally even with the passage of time?
3. Is every person treated with equal respect?

What may be missing from a deontological approach to ethical reasoning is a satisfactory means of coping with valid exceptions to general rules. Under what circumstances, if any, are exceptions allowed? Deontologists believe that they can answer this question, but their solutions vary. Suffice it to say that deontologists, just as utilitarians, have not convinced everyone.

Virtue Theory Ethics

According to many contemporary philosophers, the preceding two modes of ethical reasoning exhaust all possible modes. That is to say, they believe that any kind of ethical reasoning can be classified as either consequential or deontological. Whether this is true cannot be settled now, but a brief introduction to what some philosophers consider to be a third category, namely "virtue ethics," will be helpful.

To understand why some theorists consider the preceding two methods incomplete, consider the following hypothetical business situation. Imagine that Mr. Johns is the CEO and chairman of a large pharmaceutical company, called Health-Is-First, Inc. Suppose further that Health-Is-First, Inc. manufactures and sells medicines that aid in the treatment and prevention of cancer. The company's motto is "The health of our customers is first; it comes before anything else." Mr. Johns appears to be a model CEO. He delivers moving, emotional speeches to customers, employees, and the media about the passion with which Health-Is-First, Inc. approaches the treatment of cancer. He often talks with groups of employees about their personal problems and takes steps to alleviate those problems whenever he can. What is more, he astutely looks after the interests of shareholders, making sure that the company efficiently allocates its resources in ways that deliver shareholders excellent financial value. Shareholders have done well, indeed, under Mr. Johns.

But now suppose that Mr. Johns himself cares not at all for customers, employees, or shareholders. He does *all* of what he does for the sake of his high, multimillion-dollar income. To be sure, he does the "right" things; but then, isn't something missing in this picture of Mr. Johns? Isn't it important that someone like Mr. Johns embody an underlying character that reflects compassion rather than greed? Isn't ethical behavior more than simply following the right rules and getting the right results? Doesn't someone also need to do the right things and get the right results *because* one is the right sort of person? In short, isn't a person's *character* critical in evaluating his or her actions?

In the latter part of the twentieth century a growing number of ethical philosophers introduced concerns about the role of character in ethics and prompted a growing philosophical movement known as virtue ethics. With roots in the writings of the Greek philosophers, especially Aristotle, the virtue ethics philosophical movement has criticized traditional deontological and consequential modes of reasoning and has argued that both overlook the most fundamental aspects of moral behavior, namely a person's underlying moral character. According to Aristotle, persons are "social" by nature and cannot be understood apart from the larger communities in which they participate. "The person," Aristotle wrote, is a "social animal." For Aristotle, then, fulfilling one's natural constitution implies developing certain virtue or traits of character, including wisdom, generosity, and self-restraint, all of which help to make one a good member of the community. Moral virtue, crucial in Aristotle theory, involves the rational control of one's desires. In action where a choice is possible, one exercises moral virtue by restraining harmful desires and cultivating beneficial ones. According to Aristotle, the development of virtue requires the cultivation of good habits, and this turn leads him or her to emphasize the importance of good upbringing and a good education.

When linking virtue to business ethics, it helps to note that business, like other social phenomena, is a set of *social* practices. Managers play a special role in society by virtue of their role in business organizations, and their role in these organizations requires that they cultivate the kind of organizational excellence appropriate to managers. Ethical excellence and social excellence are thus intertwined.

Of course, virtue ethics adherents are frequently criticized, in turn, by deontologists and consequentialists. Such critics allege that virtue ethics is often hard to use in practical situations, since it lacks clear-cut rules and decision-making procedures. Consequentialists might argue that ethical decision making in business includes the minimum requirement that managers and companies do not create net harms, whatever their personal moral character. Kantian ethicists allege that their own theory already takes full account of the motivation for action, even though they may acknowledge that Kant's theory says little about moral character *per se.* As we have already seen, Kant's categorical imperative insists that an action's motivation is crucial for its evaluation. Hence, Kantian theorists would argue that Mr. Johns is not an exemplar of moral behavior, even though he may have acted consistently with the rules prescribed by the categorical imperative. In short, Mr. Johns did the right thing for the wrong reason.

In light of these objections, it follows that any well-argued virtue-ethics system will take pains to spell out the aspects of human character that when actualized constitute the ultimate ground for moral judgments, and will, further, explain the need for emphasizing character in addition to mere motivation. Robert Solomon's essay, included in this book, illustrates this approach.

CONCLUSION

The two major approaches to ethical reasoning that we have discussed—consequentialism and deontology—both present theories of ethical reasoning distinguished in terms of their basic methodological elements. Each represents a type of moral reasoning that is applicable to practical decisions in concrete situations. Consider, for example, the case study with which we began our discussion, involving BASF and its proposed new plant. As it happened, BASF chose option 3 and decided to build elsewhere. In making his decision, did the BASF manager actually use any or all of the methods described above? Although we cannot know the answer to this question, it is clear, as we saw earlier, that each method *was* applicable to his problem and might have contributed to a different answer. Indeed, the two methods of moral reasoning are sufficiently broad that each is applicable to the full range of problems confronting human moral experience. The question of which method, if any, is superior to the others cannot be settled here. The intention of this essay is not a substitute for a thorough study of traditional ethical theories—something for which there is no substitute—but to introduce the reader to basic modes of ethical reasoning that will help him or her to analyze the ethical problems in business that arise in the remainder of the book.

Notes

1. "BASF Corporation vs. The Hilton Head Island Developers," in *Business and Society*, Robert D. Hay, et al., eds. (Cincinnati: South-Western Publishing Co., 1984), pp. 100–12.
2. Immanuel Kant, *Groundwork of the Metaphysic of Morals*, trans. H. J. Paton (New York: Harper & Row, 1948, 1956), p. 61

PART

1

General Issues in Business Ethics

INTRODUCTION

What do business and ethics have in common? Is "ethical" behavior expected and rewarded in the business world? Or do different ethical principles apply to business activities than those that apply in other social interactions? As a businessperson, is it sufficient to manage one's firm such that it operates within the confines of the law? In its most basic sense, what is the purpose of a large business organization?

These are some of the questions that this book helps to address. Selections from moral philosophers, contemporary business writers, and case studies combine to provoke the reader's thinking about the role of a business organization in a free society. The study of ethics concerns itself not with what people do, but with what people ought to do. But on what basis do we justify our beliefs about what people ought to do? Moral philosophies attempt to provide the basis on which we can make ethical decisions.

The application of these moral theories to the business environment is not without controversy. Some argue that ethics has nothing to do with business, nor business with ethics. For example, the obligation of a firm that generates pollution as a byproduct to its manufacturing processes is only to comply with pollution-control laws; it is up to the government to set these standards such that the public welfare is protected. Others claim that because business involves people, by definition it involves ethical considerations. In determining the amount of corporate funds to spend on pollution control and abatement, they argue, firms must consider the damage their actions may have on innocent people. Both sides of this argument are presented throughout the text.

Part 1 covers three topics. Chapter 1 provides an overview of the differing perspectives concerning the role of ethics in business. An application of classic ethical theories and perspectives to business organizations follows in Chapter 2. Part 1 concludes with Chapter 3, an examination of the obligation to tell the truth—one of philosophy's traditional ethical concerns—and of the role of trust in an efficient economy.

CHAPTER 1 BUSINESS ETHICS: THE CONTROVERSY

One of the most outspoken critics of broad corporate obligations to society is the economist Milton Friedman. In his article "The Social Responsibility of Business Is to Increase Its Profits," Friedman denies the claim that businesses have obligations to society over and above their obligation to their shareholders, an obligation that usually entails making a profit, so long as managers obey laws and respect the mores of society. Society is best served, states Friedman, when businesses have the opportunity to compete for consumer dollars by running efficient and innovative organizations that seek to maximize profits. Society, in turn, prospers under this free market system. Friedman's argument rests on one key assumption: The shareholders of a corporation have profit making as their one primary goal. Corporate executives, as these shareholders' employees, have an obligation to their employers to accomplish that objective. Spending corporate resources to meet non-profit-oriented goals represents a "tax" on these owners and is fundamentally unjust. Persons acting in their individual capacity should be free to spend their own money on whatever "causes" they choose to endorse; the corporation should play no role advocating social priorities. Hence, Friedman views the business corporation solely as an agent of economic activity.

R. Edward Freeman's article, "Stakeholder Theory of the Modern Corporation," presents a direct challenge to Friedman's views. Advocating an increasingly popular concept in both business ethics and strategy literature, Freeman defines a stakeholder group as any group or individual who can affect or is affected by a business. More narrowly conceived, stakeholders are individuals or groups of individuals who have defined role relationships with the corporation in question. Under this more restricted definition, ordinarily primary stakeholders include stockholders, employees, and customers. Suppliers, other individuals or groups, and/or the community play a primary or secondary role, depending upon the particular firm and context. Notice that the stakeholder concept conflicts with the assumption that the moral responsibility of business is nothing other than profit maximization for shareholders. It assumes, rather, that the firm has, or should have, equal responsibilities to all its primary stakeholders. Thus the job of the manager is to weigh and balance the interests of a variety of stakeholders including, but not limited to, those of investors. Moreover, accountability relationships between an organization and its stakeholders are reciprocal; that is, "each can affect the other in terms of harms and benefits as well as rights and duties." So stakeholder relationships are ethical or "normative" relationships that entail, at a minimum, mutual respect between both parties.

One of the inevitable questions that arise in stakeholder theory is whether, or how, or on what grounds one evaluates stakeholder relationships. Freeman argues that stakeholder relationships entail a normative core—a set of normative theories that spell out how corporations should be governed and how managers should act. While refusing to commit himself to one set of moral considerations, Freeman acknowledges that respect for individuals and value creation are part of the normative core of all stakeholder relationships.

The case study "H.B. Fuller in Honduras" illustrates these issues. H.B. Fuller, a Minneapolis-based multinational corporation, is a well-managed company with the highest ethical standards. In 1995 it received a Forbes award for corporate ethics. But when what Fuller thought was an innocent product, glue, that it manufactures and sells in Honduras became the "sniffing drug of choice" by street children there, they were challenged, as a company, to reconsider their moral and social responsibilities.

CHAPTER 2 ETHICAL REASONING IN PRACTICE

Confronting and dealing with ethical dilemmas is common in the business world. How are we to frame and think about the often complex and subtle issues involved in these situations?

In his article, "A Kantian Approach to Business Ethics," Norman Bowie outlines a deontological approach to ethical reasoning in the context of a business organization. Kant believed that the intention behind an action is paramount. "Good" actions are those performed out of duty, not due to instrumental reasons (i.e., being honest to earn a good reputation). Certain duties are required *per se*, which Kant called a "categorical imperative." He formulated three versions of this imperative: (1) Act only on maxims that you can will to be universal laws of nature; (2) always treat other people as ends in themselves, never as merely a means to an end; and (3) act as if you were both subject and sovereign of an ideal kingdom of ends.

An application of these principles to a business firm results in a number of requirements that must be met in order for the firm to be ethical in a Kantian sense. The first formulation helps to identify decisions that are morally permissible. The businessperson who can will her decision to be a universal principle without contradiction will know that it is an ethical decision. For instance, if a businessperson is considering breaking a contract to obtain more favorable terms, can the practice of contract breaking be universalized in a coherent way? Clearly not, because business as we know it would cease to exist if contracts were widely broken. Therefore, breaking a contract is not a moral act under a Kantian view.

The second formulation requires that all stakeholders be treated as persons, with respect for their individual dignity. While this formulation should not be viewed as prohibiting commercial transactions, it does place some moral constraints around those relationships. No one is used as a means in a voluntary exchange in which both parties benefit. People do, however, deserve to be free of coercion and deception. When this criterion is met, actions such as layoffs can morally occur.

Another important element of this principle is Kant's belief that people should be free to develop their rational and moral capabilities. This gives rise, Bowie argues, to the obligation of the business firm to provide an environment in which people can thrive. Meaningful work, stakeholder participation in the decision-making process, and the democratization of the workplace are all elements of a Kantian ethical business organization.

Kant's third formulation of the categorical imperative focuses on the community. A business organization represents a community and is therefore subject to this formulation. Each member of the community deserves the right to express his or her views, agree to the rules and procedures governing the community, have his or her interests considered in any relevant decision, and not have his or her interests subordinated to the interests of another stakeholder group.

In an age in which technological systems and complex organizational structures dominate business activity, what role should the integrity of the individual manager play? Large conglomerates, transnational corporations, and worldwide trading systems appear to mask the importance of the single businessperson, even though he or she is the final focal point of all business activities. Finding inspiration in the philosophy of the ancient Greek thinker, Aristotle, Robert Solomon argues, in "Corporate Roles, Personal Virtues: An Aristotelean Approach to Business Ethics," that individual character and virtue do matter in business. He asserts that the personal and community aspects of business are no less relevant today than they were centuries ago. To neglect personal virtues, in turn, is to condemn business ethics to sterile irrelevance. In so doing, he reflects the late-twentieth-century trend toward what has been called virtue ethics. Solomon's approach, however, is not merely an exposition of personal virtues that, ideally, every manager should exemplify. Solomon recognizes that each of us develops out of a set of communities, so who we are is created from and found only within a community or society. Solomon then locates the manager within the community of the corporation, which in turn is part of a larger set of communities: the local community, the culture, the state, and ultimately the world. Thus, the Aristotelean virtues Solomon expounds are community, excellence, role identity, holism, integrity, and judgment, all virtues that involve relationships with others and with communities.

Solomon lays out a matrix for managerial moral excellence that takes into account the moral community of business. This approach has been criticized as being too contextual because it does not provide a moral framework for evaluating role responsibilities, excellence, business judgments, or community values; such evaluations are usually made from a Kantian or utilitarian perspective. But Solomon's project may be of a different order. He is not merely extolling managerial virtues; he is also challenging each of us to rethink the way in which we often depict business as a separate, morally mute, community-independent enterprise of self-interested managers and entrepreneurs.

A third perspective is that of utilitarianism, particularly the philosophy of John Stuart Mill, the well-known nineteenth-century philosopher. Mill argued, in brief, that the best moral decisions are those that on balance produce a balance of pleasure over pain, happiness instead of suffering, or benefits that outweigh costs. Cost/benefit analysis is standard procedure in management decision making, and it has normative dimensions as well. Mill, however, as Andrew Gustafson reminds us, pushes us to think beyond merely calculating benefits versus costs. He argues that there is a hierarchy of pleasures and that human beings, as opposed to other animals, are able to enjoy the highest pleasures of the intellect, of art and music, of poetry and politics.

John McVea offers a more practical view of moral reasoning that derives from the well-known American philosopher, John Dewey (1859–1952). Dewey and his colleagues defended a theory called "pragmatism" they believed restored commonsense to philosophy. On his view, ethics is not about proving what is good or right but about an ever-changing process that we engage in to discover a more enlightened way of living. Each person, Dewey believed, should undertake a journey toward higher self-realization, and toward a better understanding of the meaning of her actions in society. Dewey viewed traditional moral systems such as utilitarianism and deontology as static. They lay out a conception of the good such as "greatest happiness for the greatest number" as if we could never change our ideas. We should give up the idea that there are static answers to moral questions and consider each question in its own time and context.

CHAPTER 3 TRUTH TELLING

- As the newly appointed controller of a small family-held company, you are asked to approve a year-end financial statement that does not accurately represent the company's finances. The external auditors have approved the financial statement package. What should you do?
- If you were operating a branch of a U.S. company in a foreign country, would you follow that country's tax procedures if they conflicted with procedures in the United States and even required falsifying earnings reports?
- Suppose you were a manager of a corporation doing business in a country where bribery and extortion were acceptable practices in getting business contracts. Would you participate in that activity? Would you condone such activities by your foreign national managers?
- As an account executive, you think that one of the advertisements for which you are responsible presents misleading information about the product. Would you request a change in the advertisement?
- In seeking employment do you always tell the whole truth in an interview? Does your resume accurately represent you, even your weaknesses?

Each of these vignettes is drawn from an actual business situation, and, in fact, such dilemmas arise more frequently than one might expect. Understanding their ethical implications requires not only an awareness of concrete situations but also the ability to subsume business problems under categories of more general ethical concern. Cynthia Cooper, the head of internal audit at WorldCom, faced such issues when she was asked to overlook audit irregularities so that WorldCom's executives could rescue the company before it failed. She was faced with the concerns: What obligations, if any, exist for individuals and organizations to communicate honestly? When, if ever, is not telling the truth justified?

The concept of truth telling can be used to investigate a wide variety of issues, including those relating to nondeceptive advertising, the accuracy of consumer information, and the responsibilities a business has to communicate honestly with its employees and stockholders. A philosopher well known for his vigorous defense of truth telling is the eighteenth-century German philosopher Immanuel Kant. In this section, a selection from his *Lectures on Ethics* is presented in which Kant claims that truth telling is an essential feature of morally right communication. Kant equates honesty with both frankness and reserve and supports the principle of never telling a lie on three grounds. First, the principle of truth telling is one that each of us would like everyone else to follow. In other words, it is a principle that philosophers call "universalizable," meaning that each of us would like to see it universally followed by all human beings. Second, truth telling is a necessary element for society because all societies depend on mutual bonds of honesty and truthfulness to enforce their unity and orderly continuation. Finally, lying undermines one of the major sources of human development—knowledge acquisition—since, without underlying trust in the veracity of research, experimentation, reporting, and fact-gathering, it would be impossible to discover or evaluate truth claims in any field. Kant's famous example of an enemy trying to extort information challenges us to wonder whether there are extreme cases where it is morally permissible to lie. Kant argues that lies in these cases are not violations of trust between oneself and the enemy, since such an understanding does not exist. Nevertheless, even lying to an enemy violates a universal principle. It is "contrary to the general right of mankind" not to be deceived.

Questioning Kant's strict prohibitions on lying, Albert Carr, in his lively article, "Is Business Bluffing Ethical?" suggests that the moral requirement of telling the truth depends on the context in which the activity takes place. For example, in advertising, although few advertisers lie about their products, most engage in puffery or make unfair comparisons between their products and the competition. This is all right, according to Carr, because everyone understands the "game" of advertising, and no one is really fooled by the claims.

Similarly, according to Carr, in applying for a job, one does not tell a prospective employer all of one's past, nor detail one's weaknesses. It is part of the "game" of the hiring process and full disclosure is not expected or warranted. Hiring is a form of negotiation, and like other negotiating practices in business the "game" is more akin to poker than to full disclosure. Because perfect market information—or in Kantian terms, the whole truth—is never obtainable, market imperfections are often to the advantage of business. Moreover, it is not always to the economic advantage of business to reveal the "whole truth" about a product or service, and it is often unprofitable not to engage in competitive bluffing in bargaining processes when other businesses are doing so.

Despite Carr's persuasive arguments, many advertisers as well as other business persons and philosophers are worried about the impact of the "game" analogy in business, and in particular its effect on those of us not "playing the game" or those of us who are unaware of its rules. Is bluffing or puffery justified when some persons affected by them do not understand the game and are deceived or misled? Moreover, business is part of our social life. Businesses cannot exist or thrive except in communities thus the basic moral standards of those communities apply to business dealings as well. The convention of truth telling and the standard of trust are part of basic community mores. To question those conventions and standards is to separate business from the community and to invite regulation and restriction.

Sissela Bok supports that view. One of the reasons to blow the whistle, Cynthia Cooper's challenge, is exactly so that deceptive practices are made public. Recognizing that this is difficult, in practice, she argues that there are usually other avenues to clear up these practices in many companies, such as hot lines, anonymous complaint mechanisms, and ombudspersons. When these avenues are exhausted, then whistle blowing is the only option, since deceptive practices hurt companies, their employees, and their shareholders.

This discussion of truth telling leads one to think about the role of trust in business. Can commercial transactions occur without some fundamental level of trust between the parties? George Brenkert's article, "Trust, Morality and International Business," argues that some form of trust underlies all business activities. Because trust is a fundamental aspect of business morality, and because trust is valued in all cultures and societies, Brenkert suggests that it can play a substantial foundational role in developing an international business ethic. Brenkert identifies four morally relevant aspects of trust: communication of self-understanding to others, the voluntary exposure of one's vulnerabilities to others, voluntary restriction of self-interested behavior, and a reciprocity that fosters autonomy. Clearly, trust is not exclusively about self-interest or economic rationality. Something deeper, and moral, goes on in a trusting relationship.

Trust is not a moral principle, but rather an attitude or disposition to act in a certain way: to accept risks of harm or injury on the belief that the other person does not intend harm. It also involves a commonality of values or purposes and the assumption that the other person has goodwill and good intentions. Brenkert focuses particularly on international business relations because developing morally worthy trust in a global context presents some problems that are not necessarily present at a national level. Each party to the relationship may have values and motives that differ significantly, making the ability to begin trusting the other person or organization more difficult. Differences in ethnocentric and egocentric tendencies, histories, and the willingness to be open with others may also impede trusting relations. Despite these difficulties, given the crucial role trust plays in all business activities and the increasing globalization of business, trusting relationships can and do exist, although they evolve gradually and incrementally. Trust-enhancing mechanisms such as laws, trade associations, and global oversight can facilitate the development of trust.

A business ethic founded (in part) on trust recognizes that trusting relationships help form other practical moral norms and principles, which become widely held. Viewing trust as the correct starting point for the derivation of ethical behavior enables the construction of practical ethics in business and other contexts.

Chapter 1

Business Ethics: The Controversy

Case Study

H. B. Fuller in Honduras: Street Children and Substance Abuse

Norman E. Bowie   ●   Stefanie Ann Lenway

In the summer of 1985 the following news story was brought to the attention of an official of the H. B. Fuller Company in St. Paul, Minnesota.

Glue Sniffing Among Honduran Street Children in Honduras: Children Sniffing Their Lives Away

An Inter Press Service Feature
By Peter Ford

Tegucigalpa July 16, 1985 (IPS)—They lie senseless on doorsteps and pavements, grimy and loose limbed, like discarded rag dolls.

Some are just five or six years old. Others are already young adults, and all are addicted to sniffing a commonly sold glue that is doing them irreversible brain damage.

Roger, 21, has been sniffing "Resistol" for eight years. Today, even when he is not high, Roger walks with a stagger, his motor control wrecked. His scarred face puckers with concentration, his right foot taps nervously, incessantly, as he talks.

Since he was 11, when he ran away from the aunt who raised him, Roger's home has been the streets of the capital of Honduras, the second poorest nation in the western hemisphere after Haiti.

Roger spends his time begging, shining shoes, washing car windows, scratching together a few pesos a day, and sleeping in doorways at night.

Sniffing glue, he says, "makes me feel happy, makes me feel big. What do I care if my family does not love me? I know it's doing me damage, but it's a habit I have got, and a habit's a habit. I can not give it up, even though I want to."

Norman Bowie and Stefanie Ann Lenway, University of Minnesota. All rights reserved by Graduate School of Business, Columbia University. The authors express their deep appreciation to the H. B. Fuller Company for providing access to company documents and personnel relevant to this case. Reprinted by permission.

No one knows how many of Tegucigalpa's street urchins seek escape from the squalor and misery of their daily existence through the hallucinogenic fumes of "Resistol." No one has spent the time and money needed to study the question.

But one thing is clear, according to Dr. Rosalio Zavala, Head of the Health Ministry's Mental Health Department, "these children come from the poorest slums of the big cities. They have grown up as illegal squatters in very disturbed states of mental health, tense, depressed, aggressive.

"Some turn that aggression on society, and start stealing. Others turn it on themselves, and adopt self destructive behavior . . ."

But, he understands the attraction of the glue, whose solvent, toluene, produces feelings of elation. "It gives you delusions of grandeur, you feel powerful, and that compensates these kids for reality, where they feel completely worthless, like nobodies."

From the sketchy research he has conducted, Dr. Zavala believes that most boys discover Resistol for the first time when they are about 11, though some children as young as five are on their way to becoming addicts.

Of a small sample group of children interviewed in reform schools here, 56 percent told Zavala that friends introduced them to the glue, but it is easy to find on the streets for oneself.

Resistol is a contact cement glue, widely used by shoe repairers, and available at household goods stores everywhere . . .

In some states of the United States, glue containing addictive narcotics such as toluene must also contain oil of mustard—the chemical used to produce poisonous mustard gas—which makes sniffing the glue so painful it is impossible to tolerate. There is no federal U.S. law on the use of oil of mustard, however . . .

But even for Dr. Zavala, change is far more than a matter of just including a chemical compound, such as oil of mustard, in a contact cement.

"This is a social problem," he acknowledges. "What we need is a change in philosophy, a change in social organization."

Resistol is manufactured by H. B. Fuller S.A., a subsidiary of Kativo Chemical Industries, S.A. which in turn is a wholly owned subsidiary of the H. B. Fuller Company of St. Paul, Minnesota.[1] Kativo sells more than a dozen different adhesives under the Resistol brand name in several countries in Latin America for a variety of industrial and commercial applications. In Honduras the Resistol products have a strong market position.

Three of the Resistol products are solvent-based adhesives designed with certain properties that are not possible to attain with a water-based formula. These properties include rapid set, strong adhesion, and water resistance. These products are similar to airplane glue or rubber cement and are primarily intended for use in shoe manufacturing and repair, leatherwork, and carpentry.

Even though the street children of each Central American country may have a different choice of a drug for substance abuse, and even though Resistol is not the only glue that Honduran street children use as an inhalant, the term "Resistolero" stuck and has become synonymous with all street children, whether they use inhalants or not. In Honduras Resistol is identified as the abused substance.

Edward Sheehan writes in *Agony in the Garden*:

Resistol. I had heard about Resistol. It was a glue, the angel dust of Honduran orphans. . . . In Tegucigalpa, their addiction had become so common they were known as los Resistoleros. (p. 32)

CONTEXT

HONDURAS[2]

The social problems that contribute to widespread inhalant abuse among street children can be attributed to the depth of poverty in Honduras. In 1989, 65 percent of all households and 40 percent of urban households in Honduras were living in poverty, making it one of the poorest countries in Latin America. Between 1950 and 1988, the increase in the Honduran gross domestic product (GDP) was 3.8 percent, only slightly greater than the average yearly increase in population growth. In 1986, the Honduran GDP was about U.S. $740 per capita and has only grown slightly since. Infant and child mortality rates are high, life expectancy for adults is 64 years, and the adult literacy rate is estimated to be about 60 percent.

Honduras has faced several economic obstacles in its efforts to industrialize. First, it lacks abundant natural resources. The mountainous terrain has restricted agricultural productivity and growth. In addition, the small domestic market and competition from more industrially advanced countries has prevented the manufacturing sector from progressing much beyond textiles, food processing, and assembly operations.

The key to the growth of the Honduran economy has been the production and export of two commodities—bananas and coffee. Both the vagaries in the weather and the volatility of commodity markets had made the foreign exchange earned from these products very unstable. Without consistently strong export sales, Honduras has not been able to buy sufficient fuel and other productive input to allow the growth of its manufacturing sector. It also had to import basic grains (corn and rice) because the country's traditional staples are produced inefficiently by small farmers using traditional technologies with poor soil.

In the 1970s the Honduran government relied on external financing to invest in physical and social infrastructures and to implement development programs intended to diversify the economy. Government spending increased 10.4 percent a year from 1973. By 1981, the failure of many of these development projects led the government to stop financing state-owned industrial projects. The public sector failures were attributed to wasteful administration, mismanagement, and corruption. Left with little increase in productivity to show for these investments, Honduras continues to face massive budgetary deficits and unprecedented levels of external borrowing.

The government deficit was further exacerbated in the early 1980s by increasing levels of unemployment. By 1983, unemployment reached 20–30 percent of the economically active population, with an additional 40 percent of the population underemployed, primarily in agriculture. The rising unemployment, falling real wages, and low level of existing social infrastructure in education and health care contributed to the low level of labor productivity. Unemployment benefits were very limited and only about 7.3 percent of the population was covered by social security.

Rural-to-urban migration has been a major contributor to urban growth in Honduras. In the 1970s the urban population grew at more than twice as fast a rate as the rural population. This migration has increased in part as a result of a high birth rate among the rural population, along with a move by large landholders to convert forest and fallow land, driving off subsistence farmers to use the land for big-scale cotton and beef farming. As more and more land was enclosed, an increasing number of landless sought the cities for a better life.

Tegucigalpa, the capital, has had one of the fastest population increases among Central American cities. . . .

The slow growth in the industrial and commercial sectors has not been adequate to provide jobs for those moving to the city. The migrants to the urban areas typically move first to cuarterias (rows) of connected rooms. The rooms are generally constructed of wood with dirt floors, and they are usually windowless. The average household contains about seven persons, who live together in a single room. For those living in the rooms facing an alley, the narrow passageway between buildings serves both as sewage and waste disposal area and as a courtyard for as many as 150 persons.

Although more than 70 percent of the families living in these cuarterias had one member with a permanent salaried job, few could survive on that income alone. For stable extended families, salaried income is supplemented by entrepreneurial activities, such as selling tortillas. Given migratory labor, high unemployment, and income insecurity many family relationships are unstable. Often the support of children is left to mothers. Children are frequently forced to leave school, helping support the family through shining shoes, selling newspapers, or guarding cars; such help often is essential income. If a lone mother has become sick or dies, her children may be abandoned to the streets.

KATIVO CHEMICAL INDUSTRIES S.A.[3]

Kativo celebrated its 40th anniversary in 1989. It is now one of the 500 largest private corporations in Latin America. In 1989, improved sales in most of Central America were partially offset by a reduction of its sales in Honduras.

Walter Kissling, chairman of Kativo's board and senior vice president for H. B. Fuller's international operations, has the reputation of giving the company's local managers a high degree of autonomy. Local managers often have to respond quickly because of unexpected currency fluctuations. He comments that, "In Latin America, if you know what you are doing, you can make more money managing your balance sheet than by selling products." The emphasis on managing the balance sheet in countries with high rates of inflation has led Kativo managers to develop a distinctive competence in finance.

In spite of the competitive challenge of operating under unstable political and economic conditions Kativo managers emphasized in the annual report the importance of going beyond the bottom line:

> Kativo is an organization with a profound philosophy and ethical conduct, worthy of the most advanced firms. It carries out business with the utmost respect for ethical and legal principles and its orientation is not solely directed to the customer, who has the highest priority, but also to the shareholders, and communities where it operates.

In the early 1980s the managers of Kativo, which was primarily a paint company, decided to enter the adhesive market in Latin America. Their strategy was to combine their marketing experience with H. B. Fuller's products. Kativo found the adhesive market potentially profitable in Latin America because it lacked strong competitors. Kativo's initial concern was to win market share. Resistol was the brand name for all adhesive products including the water-based school glue.

KATIVO AND THE STREET CHILDREN

In 1983, Honduran newspapers carried articles about police arrests of "Resistoleros"—street children drugging themselves by sniffing glue. In response to these newspaper articles, Kativo's Honduras advertising agency, Calderon Publicidad, informed the newspapers that Resistol was not the only substance abused by street children and that the image of the manufacturer was being damaged by using a prestigious trademark as a synonym for drug abusers. Moreover glue sniffing was not caused by something inherent in the product but was a social problem. For example, on one occasion the company complained to the editor, requesting that he "make the necessary effort to recommend to the editorial staff that they abstain from using the brand name Resistol as a synonym for the drug, and the adjective Resistolero as a synonym for the drug addict."

The man on the spot was Kativo's Vice President, Humberto Larach ("Beto"), a Honduran, who headed Kativo's North Adhesives Division. Managers in nine countries including all of Central America, Mexico, the Caribbean and two South American countries, Ecuador and Colombia, reported to him. He had become manager of the adhesive division after demonstrating his entrepreneurial talents managing Kativo's paint business in Honduras.

Beto had proven his courage and his business creativity when he was among 105 taken hostage in the Chamber of Commerce building in downtown San Pedro Sula by guerrillas from the Communist Popular Liberation Front. Despite fire fights between the guerrillas and government troops, threats of execution, and being used as a human shield, Beto had sold his product to two clients (fellow hostages) who had previously been buying products from Kativo's chief competitor! Beto also has a reputation for emphasizing the importance of "Making the bottom line," as a part of Kativo corporate culture.

By summer 1985, more than corporate image was at stake. As a solution to the glue sniffing problem social activists working with street children suggested that oil of mustard, allyl isothiocyanate, could be added to the product to prevent its abuse. They argued that a person attempting to sniff glue with oil of mustard added would find it too powerful to tolerate. Sniffing it has been described like getting an "overdose of horseradish." An attempt to legislate the addition of oil of mustard received a boost when Honduran Peace Corps volunteer, Timothy Bicknell, convinced a local group called the "Committee for the Prevention of Drugs at the National Level," of the necessity of adding oil of mustard to Resistol. All members of the committee were prominent members of Honduran society.

Beto, in response to the growing publicity about the "Resistoleros," requested staff members of H. B. Fuller's U.S. headquarters to look into the viability of oil of mustard as a solution with special attention to side effects and whether it was required or used in the U.S. H. B. Fuller's corporate industrial hygiene staff found 1983 toxicology reports that oil of mustard was a cancer-causing agent in tests run with rats. A 1986 toxicology report from the Aldrich Chemical Company described the health hazard data of allyl isothiocyanate as:

Acute Effects

May be fatal if inhaled, swallowed, or absorbed through skin.

Carcinogen.

Causes burns.

Material is extremely destructive to tissue of the mucous membranes and upper respiratory tract, eyes and skin.

Prolonged Contact Can Cause:

Nausea, dizziness and headache.

Severe irritation or burns.

Lung irritation, chest pain and edema which may be fatal.

Repeated exposure may cause asthma.

In addition the product had a maximum shelf-life of six months. To the best of our knowledge, the chemical, physical and toxicological properties have not been thoroughly investigated.

In 1986, Beto contacted Hugh Young, president of Solvent Abuse Foundation for Education (SAFE), and gathered information on programs SAFE had developed in Mexico. Young, who believed that there was no effective deterrent, took the position that the only viable approach to substance abuse was education, not product modification. He argued that reformulating the product was an exercise in futility because "nothing is available in the solvent area that is not abusable." With these reports in hand, Beto attempted to persuade Resistol's critics, relief agencies, and government officials that adding oil of mustard to Resistol was not the solution to the glue sniffing problem.

During the summer of 1986 Beto had his first success in changing the mind of one journalist. Earlier in the year Mary Kawas, an independent writer, wrote an article sympathetic to the position of Timothy Bicknell and the Committee for the Prevention of Drugs in Honduras. In June, Beto met with her and explained how both SAFE and Kativo sought a solution that was not product-oriented but that was directed at changing human behavior.

She was also informed of the research on the dangers of oil of mustard (about which additional information had been obtained). Kawas then wrote an article:

Education Is the Solution for Drug Addiction

La Ceiba (by Marie J. Kawas)

. . . A lot of people have been interested in combating drug addiction amng youths and children, but few have sought solutions, and almost no one looks into the feasibility of the alternative that are so desperately proposed . . .

Oil of mustard (allyl isothiocynate) may well have been an irresponsible solution in the United States of America during the sixties and seventies, and the Hondurans want to adopt this as a panacea without realizing that their information sources are out of date. Through scientific progress, it has been found that the inclusion of oil of mustard in products which contain solvents, in order to prevent their perversion into use as an addictive drug, only causes greater harm to the consumers and workers involved in their manufacture . . .

Education is a primordial instrument for destroying a social cancer. An effort of this magnitude requires the cooperation of different individuals and organizations . . .

Future generations of Hondurans will be in danger of turning into human parasites, without a clear awareness of what is harmful to them. But if drugs and ignorance are to blame, it is even more harmful to sin by indifference before those very beings who are growing up in an environment without the basic advantages for a healthy physical and mental existence. Who will be the standard bearer in the philanthropic activities which will provide Honduras with the education necessary to combat drug addiction? Who will be remiss in their duty in the face of the nation's altruism?

At first, Beto did not have much success at the governmental level. In September 1986, Dr. Rosalio Zavala, Head of the Mental Health Division of the Honduran Ministry of Health, wrote an article attacking the improper use of Resistol by youth. Beto was unsuccessful in his attempt to contact Dr. Zavala. He had better luck with Mrs. Norma Castro, Governor of the State of Cortes, who after a conversation with Beto became convinced that oil of mustard had serious dangers and that glue sniffing was a social problem.

Beto's efforts continued into the new year. Early in 1987, Kativo began to establish Community Affairs Councils, as a planned expansion of the worldwide company's philosophy of community involvement. These employee committees had already been in place in the U.S. since 1978.

A company document gave the purpose of Community Affairs Councils:

To educate employees about community issues.

To develop understanding of, and be responsive to the communities near our facilities.

To contribute to Kativo/H. B. Fuller's corporate presence in the neighborhoods and communities we are a part of.

To encourage and support employee involvement in the community.

To spark a true interest in the concerns of the communities in which we live and work.

The document goes on to state, "We want to be more than just bricks, mortar, machines and people. We want to be a company with recognized values, demonstrating involvement, and commitment to the betterment of the communities we are a part of." Later that year, the Honduran community affairs committees went on to make contributions to several organizations working with street children.

In May 1987, Beto visited Jose Oqueli, Vice-Minister of Public Health, to explain the philosophy behind H. B. Fuller's Community Affairs program. He also informed him of the health hazards of oil of mustard; they discussed the cultural, family and economic roots of the problem of glue-sniffing among street children.

In June 1987, Parents Resource Institute for Drug Education (PRIDE) set up an office in San Pedro Sula. PRIDE's philosophy was that through adequate parental education on the drug problem, it would be possible to deal with the problems of inhalant use. PRIDE was a North American organization that had taken international Nancy Reagan's "just say no" approach to inhalant abuse. Like SAFE, PRIDE took the position that oil of mustard was not the solution to glue-sniffing.

Through PRIDE, Beto was introduced to Wilfredo Alvarado, the new Head of the Mental Health Division in the Ministry of Health. Dr. Alvarado, an advisor to the Congressional Committee on Health, was in charge of preparing draft legislation and evaluating legislation received by Congress. Together with Dr. Alvarado, the Kativo staff worked to prepare draft legislation addressing the problem of inhalant addicted children. At the same time, five Congressmen drafted a proposed law that required the use of oil of mustard in locally produced or imported solvent based adhesives.

In June 1988, Dr. Alvarado asked the Congressional Committee on Health to reject the legislation proposed by the five congressmen. Alvarado was given 60 days to present a complete draft of legislation. In August 1988, however, he retired from his position and Kativo lost its primary communication channel with the Committee. This was critical because Beto was relying on Alvarado to help insure that the legislation reflected the technical information that he had collected.

The company did not have an active lobbying or government monitoring function in Tegucigalpa, the capital, which tends to be isolated from the rest of the country. (In fact, the company's philosophy has generally been not to lobby on behalf of its own narrow self-interest.) Beto, located in San Pedro Sula, had no staff support to help him monitor political developments. Monitoring, unfortunately, was an addition to his regular, daily responsibilities. His ability to keep track of political developments was made more difficult by the fact that he traveled about 45 percent of the time outside of Honduras. It took over two months for Beto to learn of Alvarado's departure from government. When the legislation was passed in March, he was completely absorbed in reviewing strategic plans for the nine-country divisions which report to him.

On March 30, 1989, the Honduran Congress approved the legislation drafted by the five congressmen.

After the law's passage Beto spoke to the press about the problems with the legislation. He argued:

> This type of cement is utilized in industry, in crafts, in the home, schools, and other places where it has become indispensable; thus by altering the product, he said, not only will the drug addiction problem not be solved, but rather, the country's development would be slowed.

> In order to put an end to the inhalation of Resistol by dozens of people, various products which are daily necessities would have to be eliminated from the marketplace. This is impossible, he added, since it would mean a serious setback to industry at several levels . . .

> There are studies that show that the problem is not the glue itself, but rather the individual. The mere removal of this substance would immediately be substituted by some other, to play the same hallucinogenic trip for the person who was sniffing it.

H. B. FULLER: THE CORPORATE RESPONSE

In late April 1986, Elmer Andersen, H. B. Fuller Chairman of the Board, received the following letter:

4/21/86

Elmer L. Anderson
H. B. Fuller Co.

I heard part of your talk on public radio recently, and was favorable impressed with your philosophy that business should not be primarily for profit. This was consistent with my previous impression of H. B. Fuller Co. since I am a public health nurse and have been aware of your benevolence to the nursing profession.

However, on a recent trip to Honduras, I spent some time at a new home for chemically dependent "street boys" who are addicted to glue sniffing. It was estimated that there are 600 of these children still on the streets in Pan Pedro Sula alone. The glue is sold for repairing *tennis shoes* and I am told it is made by H. B. Fuller in *Costa Rica*. These children also suffer toxic effects of liver and brain damage from the glue . . .

Hearing you on the radio, I immediately wondered how this condemnation of H. B. Fuller Company could be consistent with the company as I knew it before and with your business philosophy.

Are you aware of this problem in Honduras, and, if so, how are you dealing with it?

That a stockholder should write the 76-year-old Chairman of the Board directly is significant. Elmer Andersen is a legendary figure in Minnesota. He is responsible for the financial success of H. B. Fuller from 1941–1971 and his values reflected in his actions as CEO are embodied in H. B. Fuller's mission statement.

H. B. FULLER MISSION STATEMENT

The H. B. Fuller corporate mission is to be a leading and profitable worldwide formulator, manufacturer, and marketer of quality specialty chemicals, emphasizing service to customers and managed in accordance with a strategic plan.

H. B. Fuller Company is committed to its responsibilities, in order of priority, to its customers, employees and shareholders. H. B. Fuller will conduct business legally and ethically, support the activities of its employees in their communities, and be a responsible corporate citizen.

It was also Elmer Andersen who, as President and CEO, made the decision that foreign acquisitions should be managed by locals. Concerning the 1967 acquisition of Kativo Chemical Industries Ltd. Elmer Andersen said:

We had two objectives in mind. One was directly business related and one was altruistic. Just as we had expanded in America, our international business strategy was to pursue markets where our competitors were not active. We were convinced that we had something to offer Latin America that the region did not have locally. In our own small way, we also wanted to be of help to that part of the world. We believed that by producing adhesives in Latin America and by employing only local people, we would create new jobs and help elevate the standard of living. We were convinced that the way to aid world peace was to help Latin America become more prosperous.

Three years later a stockholder dramatically raised the Resistol issue, the second time it was raised directly by a stockholder. On June 7, 1989, Vice President for Corporate Relations, Dick Johnson, received a call from a stockholder whose daughter was in the Peace Corps in Honduras. She asked, "How can a company like H. B. Fuller claim to have a social conscience and continue to sell Resistol which is 'literally burning out the brains' of children in Latin America?"

Johnson was galvanized into action. This complaint was of special concern because he was about to meet with a national group of socially responsible investors who were considering including H. B. Fuller's stock in their portfolio. Fortunately Karen Muller, Director of Community Affairs, had been keeping a file on the glue-sniffing problem. Within 24 hours of receiving the call, Dick had written a memo to CEO Tony Andersen.

In that memo he set forth the basic values to be considered as H. B. Fuller wrestled with the problem. Among them were the following:

1. H. B. Fuller's explicitly stated public concern about substance abuse.
2. H. B. Fuller's "Concern for Youth" focus in its community affairs projects.
3. H. B. Fuller's reputation as a socially responsible company.
4. H. B. Fuller's history of ethical conduct.
5. H. B. Fuller's commitment to the intrinsic value of each individual.

Whatever "solution" was ultimately adopted would have to be consistent with these values. In addition, Dick suggested a number of options including the company's withdrawal from the market or perhaps altering the formula to make Resistol a water-based product, eliminating sniffing as an issue.

Tony responded by suggesting that Dick create a task force to find a solution and a plan to implement it. Dick decided to accept Beto's invitation to travel to Honduras to view the situation first hand. He understood that the problem crossed functional and divisional responsibilities. Given H. B. Fuller's high visibility as a socially responsible corporation, the glue-sniffing problem had the potential for becoming a public relations nightmare. The brand name of one of H. B. Fuller's products had become synonymous with a serious social problem. Additionally, Dick understood that there was an issue larger than product misuse involved, and it had social and community ramifications. The issue was substance abuse by children, whether the substance is a H. B. Fuller product or not. As a part of the solution, a community relations response was required. Therefore, he invited Karen to join him on his trip to Honduras.

Karen recalled a memo she had written about a year earlier directed to Beto. In it she had suggested a community relations approach rather than Beto's government relations approach. In that memo Karen wrote:

> This community relations process involves developing a community-wide coalition from all those with a vested interest in solving the community issue—those providing services in dealing with the street children and drug users, other businesses, and the government. It does require leadership over the long-term both with a clear set of objectives and a commitment on the part of each group represented to share in the solution . . .

In support of the community relations approach Karen argued that:

1. It takes the focus and pressure off H. B. Fuller as one individual company.
2. It can educate the broader community and focus on the best solution, not just the easiest ones.
3. It holds everyone responsible, the government, educators, H. B. Fuller's customers, legitimate consumers of our product, social service workers and agencies.
4. It provides H. B. Fuller with an expanded good image as a company that cares and will stay with the problem—that we are willing to go the second mile.
5. It can de-politicize the issue.
6. It offers the opportunity to counterbalance the negative impact of the use of our product named Resistol by re-identifying the problem.

Karen and Dick left on a four-day trip to Honduras September 18. Upon arriving they were joined by Beto, Oscar Sahuri, General Manager for Kativo's adhesives business in Honduras, and Jorge Walter Bolanos, Vice-President Director of Finance, Kativo. Karen had also asked Mark Connelly, a health consultant from an international agency working with street children, to join the group. They began the process of looking at all aspects of the situation. Visits to two different small shoe manufacturing shops and a shoe supply distributor helped to clarify the issues around pricing, sales, distribution, and the packaging of the product.

A visit to a well-run shelter for street children provided them with some insight into the dynamics of substance abuse among this vulnerable population in the streets of Tegucigalpa and San Pedro Sula. At a meeting with the officials at the Ministry of Health, they reviewed the issue of implementing the oil-of-mustard law, and the Kativo managers offered to assist the committee as it reviewed the details of the law. In both Tegucigalpa and San Pedro Sula, the National Commission for Technical Assistance to Children in Irregular Situations (CONATNSI), a county-wide association of private and public agencies working with street children, organized meetings of its members at which the Kativo managers offered an explanation of the company's philosophy and the hazards involved in the use of oil of mustard.

As they returned from their trip to Honduras, Karen and Dick had the opportunity to reflect on what they had learned. They agreed that removing Resistol from the market would not resolve the problem. However, the problem was extremely complex. The use of inhalants by street children was a symptom of Honduras' underlying economic problems—problems with social, cultural, and political aspects as well as economic dimensions.

Honduran street children come from many different circumstances. Some are true orphans while others are abandoned. Some are runaways, while others are working the streets to help support their parents. Children working at street jobs or begging usually earn more than the minimum wage. Nevertheless, they are often punished if they bring home too little. This creates a vicious circle; they would rather be on the street than take punishment at home—a situation that increases the likelihood they will fall victim to drug addiction. The street children's problems are exacerbated by the general lack of opportunities and a lack of enforcement of school attendance laws. In addition, the police sometimes abuse street children.

Karen and Dick realized that Resistol appeared to be the drug of choice for young street children, and children were able to obtain it in a number of different ways. There was no clear pattern, and hence the solution could not be found in simply changing some features of the distribution system. Children might obtain the glue from legitimate customers, small shoe repair stalls, by theft, from "illegal" dealers or from third parties who purchased it from legitimate stores and then sold it to children. For some sellers the sale of Resistol to children could be profitable. The glue was available in small packages, which made it more affordable, but the economic circumstances of the typical legitimate customer made packaging in small packages economically sensible.

The government had long been unstable. As a result there was a tendency for people working with the government to hope that new policy initiatives would fade away within a few months. Moreover there was a large continuing turnover of government, so that any knowledge of H. B. Fuller and its corporate philosophy soon disappeared. Government officials usually had to settle for a quick fix, for they were seldom around long enough to manage any other kind of policy. Although it was on the books for six months by the time of their trip, the oil-of-mustard law had not yet been implemented, and national elections were to be held in three months. During meetings with government officials, it appeared to Karen and Dick that no further actions would be taken as current officials waited for the election outcome.

Kativo company officers, Jorge Walter Bolanos and Humberto Larach discussed continuing the government relations strategy, hoping that the law might be repealed or modified. They were also concerned with the damage done to H. B. Fuller's image. Karen and Dick thought the focus should be on community relations. From their perspective, efforts directed toward changing the law seemed important but would do nothing to help with the long-term solution to the problems of the street children who abused glue.

Much of the concern for street children was found in private agencies. The chief coordinating association was CONATNSI, created as a result of a seminar sponsored by UNICEF in 1987. CONATNSI was under the direction of a general assembly and a Board of Directors elected by the General Assembly. It began its work in 1988; its objectives included a) improving the quality of services, b) promoting interchange of experiences, c) coordinating human and material resources, d) offering technical support, and e) promoting research. Karen and others believe that CONATNSI had a shortage of both financial and human resources, but it appeared to be well-organized and was a potential intermediary for the company.

As a result of their trip, they knew that a community relations strategy would be complex and risky. H. B. Fuller was committed to a community relations approach, but what would a community relations solution look like in Honduras? The mission statement did not provide a complete answer. It indicated the company had responsibilities to its Honduran customers and employees, but exactly what kind? Were there other responsibilities beyond that directly involving its product? What effect can a single company have in solving an intractable social problem? How should the differing emphases in perspective of Kativo and its parent, H. B. Fuller, be handled? What does corporate citizenship require in situations like this?

References

Acker, Alison, *The Making of a Banana Republic* (Boston: South End Press, 1988).

H. B. Fuller Company, *A Fuller Life: The Story of H. B. Fuller Company: 1887–1987* (St. Paul: H. B. Fuller Company, 1986).

Rudolph, James D., ed., *Honduras: A Country Study*, 2nd ed. (Washington, DC: Department of the Army, 1984).

Schinc, Eric, "Preparing for Banana Republic U.S." *Corporate Finance* (December, 1987).

Sheehan, Edward, *Agony in the Garden: A Stranger in Central America* (Boston: Houghton Mifflin, 1989).

Notes

1. The Subsidiaries of the North Adhesives Division of Kativo Chemical Industries, S.A. go by the name "H. B. Fuller (Country of Operation)," e.g., H. B. Fuller S.A. Honduras. To prevent confusion with the parent company we will refer to H. B. Fuller S.A. Honduras by the name of its parent, "Kativo."
2. The following discussion is based on *Honduras: A Country Study*, 2nd ed., James D. Rudolph, ed. (Washington, DC: Department of the Army, 1984).
3. Unless otherwise indicated all references and quotations regarding H. B. Fuller and its subsidiary Kativo Chemical Industries S.A. are from company documents.

The Social Responsibility of Business Is to Increase Its Profits

MILTON FRIEDMAN

When I hear businessmen speak eloquently about the "social responsibilities of business in a free-enterprise system," I am reminded of the wonderful line about the Frenchman who discovered at the age of 70 that he had been speaking prose all his life. The businessmen believe that they are defending free enterprise when they declaim that business is not concerned "merely" with profit but also with promoting desirable "social" ends; that business has a "social conscience" and takes seriously its responsibilities for providing employment, eliminating discrimination, avoiding pollution and whatever else may be the catchwords of the contemporary crop of reformers. In fact they are—or would be if they or anyone else took them seriously—preaching pure and unadulterated socialism. Businessmen who talk this way are unwitting puppets of the intellectual forces that have been undermining the basis of a free society these past decades. The discussions of the "social responsibilities of business" are notable for their analytical looseness and lack of rigor. What does it mean to say that "business" has responsibilities? Only people can have responsibilities. A corporation is an artificial person and in this sense may have artificial responsibilities, but "business" as a whole cannot be said to have responsibilities, even in this vague sense. The first step toward clarity to examining the doctrine of the social responsibility of business is to ask precisely what it implies for whom.

Presumably, the individuals who are to be responsible are businessmen, which means individual proprietors or corporate executives. Most of the discussion of social responsibility is directed at corporations, so in what follows I shall mostly neglect the individual proprietors and speak of corporate executives.

In a free-enterprise, private-property system, a corporate executive is an employee of the owners of the business. He has direct responsibility to his employers. That responsibility is to conduct the business in accordance with their desires, which generally will be to make as much money as possible while conforming to the basic rules of the society, both those embodied in law and those embodied in ethical custom. Of course, in some cases his employers may have a different objective. A group of persons might establish a corporation for an eleemosynary purpose—for example, a hospital or a school. The manager of such a corporation will not have money profit as his objectives but the rendering of certain services.

In either case, the key point is that, in his capacity as a corporate executive, the manager is the agent of the individuals who own the corporation or establish the eleemosynary institution, and his primary responsibility is to them.

Needless to say, this does not mean that it is easy to judge how well he is performing his task. But at least the criterion of performance is straightforward, and the persons among whom a voluntary contractual arrangement exists are clearly defined.

Of course, the corporate executive is also a person in his own right. As a person, he may have many other responsibilities that he recognizes or assumes voluntarily—to his family, his conscience, his feelings of charity, his church, his clubs, his city, his country. He may feel impelled by these responsibilities to devote part of his income to causes he regards as worthy, to refuse to work for particular corporations, even to leave his job, for example, to join his country's armed forces. If we wish, we may refer to some of these responsibilities as "social responsibilities." But in these respects he is acting as a principal, not an agent; he is spending his own money or time or energy, not the money of his employers or the time or energy he has contracted to devote to their purposes. If these are "social responsibilities," they are the social responsibilities of individuals, not of business.

What does it mean to say that the corporate executive has a "social responsibility" in his capacity as businessman? If this statement is not pure rhetoric, it must mean that he is to act in some way that is not in the interest of his employers. For example, that he is to refrain from increasing the price of the product in order to contribute to the social objective of preventing inflation, even though a price increase would be in the best interests of the corporation. Or that he is to make expenditures on reducing pollution beyond the amount that is in the best interests of the corporation or that is required by law in order to contribute to the social objective of improving the environment. Or that, at the expense of corporate profits, he is to hire "hard-core" unemployed instead of better qualified available workmen to contribute to the social objective of reducing poverty.

In each of these cases, the corporate executive would be spending someone else's money for a general social interest. Insofar as his actions in accord with his "social responsibility" reduce returns to stockholders, he is spending their money. Insofar as his actions raise the price to customers, he is spending customers' money. Insofar as his actions lower the wages of some employees, he is spending their money.

The stockholders or the customers or the employees could separately spend their own money on the particular action if they wished to do so. The executive is exercising a distinct "social responsibility," rather than serving as an agent of the stockholders or the customers or the employees, only if he spends the money in a different way than they would have spent it.

But if he does this, he is in effect imposing taxes, on the one hand, and deciding how the tax proceeds shall be spent, on the other.

This process raises political questions on two levels: principle and consequences. On the level of political principle, the imposition of taxes and the expenditure of tax proceeds are governmental functions. We have established elaborate constitutional, parliamentary and judicial provisions to control these functions, to assure that taxes are imposed so far as possible in accordance with the preferences and desires of the public—after all, "taxation without representation" was one of the battle cries of the American Revolution. We have a system of checks and balances to separate the legislative function of imposing taxes and enacting expenditures from the executive function of collecting taxes and administering expenditure programs and from the judicial function of mediating disputes and interpreting the law.

Here the businessman—self-selected or appointed directly or indirectly by stockholders—is to be simultaneously legislator, executive and jurist. He is to decide whom to tax by how much and for what purpose, and he is to spend the proceeds—all this guided only by general exhortations from on high to restrain inflation, improve the environment, fight poverty and so on and on.

The whole justification for permitting the corporate executive to be selected by the stockholders is that the executive is an agent serving the interests of his principal. This justification disappears when the corporate executive imposes taxes and spends the proceeds for "social" purposes. He becomes in effect a public employee, a civil servant, even though he remains in name an employee of a private enterprise. On grounds of political principle, it is intolerable that such civil servants—insofar as their actions in the name of social responsibility are real and not just window dressing—should be selected as they are now. If they are to be civil servants, then they must be elected through a political process. If they are to impose taxes and make expenditures to foster "social" objectives, then political machinery must be set up to make the assessment of taxes and to determine through a political process the objectives to be served.

This is the basic reason why the doctrine of "social responsibility" involves the acceptance of the socialist view that political mechanisms, not market mechanisms, are the appropriate way to determine the allocation of scarce resources to alternative uses.

On the grounds of consequences, can the corporate executive in fact discharge his alleged "social responsibilities"? On the one hand, suppose he could get away with spending the stockholders' or customers' or employees' money. How is he to know how to spend it? He is told that he must contribute to fighting inflation. How is he to know what action of his will contribute to that end? He is presumably an expert in running his company—in producing a product or selling it or financing it. But nothing about his selection makes him an expert on inflation. Will his holding down the price of his product reduce inflationary pressure? Or, by leaving more spending power in the hands of his customers, simply divert it elsewhere? Or, by forcing him to produce less because of the lower price, will it simply contribute to shortages? Even if he could answer these questions, how much cost is he justified in imposing on his stockholders, customers, and employees for this social purpose? What is his appropriate share and what is the appropriate share of others?

And, whether he wants to or not, can he get away with spending his stockholders', customers' or employees' money? Will not the stockholders fire him? (Either the present ones or those who take over when his actions in the name of social responsibility have reduced the corporation's profits and the price of its stock.) His customers and his employees can desert him for other producers and employers less scrupulous in exercising their social responsibilities.

This facet of "social responsibility" doctrine is brought into sharp relief when the doctrine is used to justify wage restraint by trade unions. The conflict of interest is naked and clear when union officials are asked to subordinate the interest of their members to some more general purpose. If union officials try to enforce wage restraint, the consequence is likely to be wildcat strikes, rank-and-file revolts and the emergence of strong competitors for their jobs. We thus have the ironic phenomenon that union leaders—at least in the U.S.—have objected to Government interference with the market far more consistently and courageously than have business leaders. The difficulty of exercising "social responsibility" illustrates, of course, the great virtue of private competitive enterprise—it forces people to be responsible for their own actions and makes it difficult for them to "exploit" other people for either selfish or unselfish purposes. They can do good—but only at their own expense.

Many a reader who has followed the argument this far may be tempted to remonstrate that it is all well and good to speak of Government's having the responsibility to impose taxes and determine expenditures for such "social" purposes as controlling pollution or training the hard-core unemployed, but that the problems are too urgent to wait on the slow course of political processes, that the exercise of social responsibility by businessmen is a quicker and surer way to solve pressing current problems.

Aside from the question of fact—I share Adam Smith's skepticism about the benefits that can be expected from "those who affect to trade for the public good"—this argument must be rejected on the grounds of principle. What it amounts to is an assertion that those who favor the taxes and expenditures in question have failed to persuade a majority of their fellow citizens to be of like mind and that they are seeking to attain by undemocratic procedures what they cannot attain by democratic procedures. In a free society it is hard for "evil" people to do "evil," especially since one man's good is another's evil.

I have, for simplicity, concentrated on the special case of the corporate executive, except only for the brief digression on trade unions. But precisely the same argument applies to the newer phenomenon of calling upon stockholders to require corporations to exercise social responsibility (the recent GM crusade for example). In most of these cases, what is in effect involved is some stockholders trying to get other stockholders (or customers or employees) to contribute against their will to "social" causes favored by the activists. Insofar as they succeed, they are again imposing taxes and spending the proceeds.

The situation of the individual proprietor is somewhat different. If he acts to reduce the returns of his enterprise in order to exercise his "social responsibility," he is spending his own money, not someone else's. If he wishes to spend his money on such purposes, that is his right, and I cannot see that there is any objection to his doing so. In the process, he, too, may impose costs on employees and customers. However, because he is far less likely than a large corporation or union to have monopolistic power, any such side effects will tend to be minor.

Of course, in practice the doctrine of social responsibility is frequently a cloak for actions that are justified on other grounds rather than a reason for those actions.

To illustrate, it may well be in the long-run interest of a corporation that is a major employer in a small community to devote resources to providing amenities to that community or to improving its government. That may make it easier to attract desirable employees, it may reduce the wage bill or lessen losses from pilferage and sabotage or have other worthwhile effects. Or it may be that, given the laws about the deductibility of corporate charitable contributions, the stockholders can contribute more to charities they favor by having the corporation make the gift than by doing it themselves, since they can in that way contribute an amount that would otherwise have been paid as corporate taxes.

In each of these—and many similar—cases, there is a strong temptation to rationalize these actions as an exercise of "social responsibility." In the present climate of opinion, with its widespread aversion to "capitalism," "profits," and the "soulless corporation" and so on, this is one way for a corporation to generate goodwill as a by-product of expenditures that are entirely justified in its own self-interest.

It would be inconsistent of me to call on corporate executives to refrain from this hypocritical window-dressing because it harms the foundations of a free society. That would be to call on them to exercise a "social responsibility"! If our institutions, and the attitudes of the public make it in their self-interest to cloak their actions in this way, I cannot summon much indignation to renounce them. At the same time, I can express admiration for those individual proprietors or owners of closely held corporations or stockholders of more broadly held corporations who disdain such tactics as approaching fraud.

Whether blameworthy or not, the use of the cloak of social responsibility, and the nonsense spoken in its name by influential and prestigious businessmen, does clearly harm the foundations of a free society. I have been impressed time and again by the schizophrenic character of many businessmen. They are capable of being extremely far-sighted and clearheaded in matters that are internal to their businesses. They are incredibly short-sighted and muddle-headed in matters that are outside their businesses but affect the possible survival of business in general. This short-sightedness is strikingly exemplified in the calls from many businessmen for wage and price guidelines or controls or income policies. There is nothing that could do more in a brief period to destroy a market system and replace it by a centrally controlled system than effective governmental control of prices and wages.

The short-sightedness is also exemplified in speeches by businessmen on social responsibility. This may gain them kudos in the short run. But it helps to strengthen the already too prevalent view that the pursuit of profits is wicked and immoral and must be curbed and controlled by external forces. Once this view is adopted, the external forces that curb the market will not be the social consciences, however highly developed, of the pontificating executives; it will be the iron fist of Government bureaucrats. Here, as with price and wage controls, businessmen seem to me to reveal a suicidal impulse.

The political principle that underlies the market mechanism is unanimity. In an ideal free market resting on private property, no individual can coerce any other, all cooperation is voluntary, all parties to such cooperation benefit or they need not participate. There are no values, no "social" responsibilities in any sense other than the shared values and responsibilities of individuals. Society is a collection of individuals and of the various groups they voluntarily form.

The political principle that underlies the political mechanism is conformity. The individual must serve a more general social interest—whether that be determined by a church or a dictator or a majority. The individual may have a vote and say in what is to be done, but if he is overruled, he must conform. It is appropriate for some to require others to contribute to a general social purpose whether they wish to or not.

Unfortunately, unanimity is not always feasible. There are some respects in which conformity appears unavoidable, so I do not see how one can avoid the use of the political mechanism altogether.

But the doctrine of "social responsibility" taken seriously would extend the scope of the political mechanism to every human activity. It does not differ in philosophy from the most explicitly collectivist doctrine. It differs only by professing to believe that collectivist ends can be attained without collectivist means. That is why, in my book *Capitalism and Freedom*, I have called it a "fundamentally subversive doctrine" in a free society, and I have said that in such a society, "there is one and only one social responsibility of business—to use its resources and engage in activities designed to increase its profits so long as it stays within the rules of the game, which is to say, engages in open and free competition without deception or fraud."

Managing for Stakeholders[1]

R. EDWARD FREEMAN

I. INTRODUCTION

The purpose of this essay is to outline an emerging view of business that we shall call "managing for stakeholders."[2] This view has emerged over the past thirty years from a group of scholars in a diverse set of disciplines, from finance to philosophy.[3] The basic idea is that businesses, and the executives who manage them, actually do and should create value for customers, suppliers, employees, communities, and financiers (or shareholders). And, that we need to pay careful attention to how these relationships are managed and how value gets created for these stakeholders. We contrast this idea with the dominant model of business activity; namely, that businesses are to be managed solely for the benefit of shareholders. Any other benefits (or harms) that are created are incidental.[4]

Simple ideas create complex questions, and we proceed as follows. In the next section we examine why the dominant story or model of business that is deeply embedded in our culture is no longer workable. It is resistant to change, not consistent with the law, and for the most part, simply ignores matters of ethics. Each of these flaws is fatal in business world of the 21st Century.

We then proceed to define the basic ideas of "managing for stakeholders" and why it solves some of the problems of the dominant model. In particular we pay attention to how using "stakeholder" as a basic unit of analysis

"Managing for Stakeholders" first appeared in *Ethical Theory in Business, 8th ed.*, Tom L. Beauchamp, Norman R. Bowie, and Denis G. Arnold, eds., (Upper Saddle River, NJ: Pearson Prentice Hall, 2007). R. Edward Freeman is Professor of Business at the Darden School at the University of Virginia. Reprinted by permission of the author.

makes it more difficult to ignore matters of ethics. We argue that the primary responsibility of the executive is to create as much value for stakeholders as possible, and that no stakeholder interest is viable in isolation of the other stakeholders. We sketch three primary arguments from ethical theory for adopting "managing for stakeholders." We conclude by outlining a fourth "pragmatist argument" that suggests we see managing for stakeholders as a new narrative about business that lets us improve the way we currently create value for each other. Capitalism is on this view a system of social cooperation and collaboration, rather than primarily a system of competition.

II. THE DOMINANT STORY: MANAGERIAL CAPITALISM WITH SHAREHOLDERS AT THE CENTER

The modern business corporation has emerged during the 20th Century as one of the most important innovations in human history. Yet the changes that we are now experiencing call for its reinvention. Before we suggest what this revision, "managing for stakeholders" or "stakeholder capitalism," is, first we need to understand how the dominant story came to be told.

Somewhere in the past, organizations were quite simple and "doing business" consisted of buying raw materials from suppliers, converting it to products, and selling it to customers. For the most part owner-entrepreneurs founded such simple businesses and worked at the business along with members of their families. The development of new production processes, such as the assembly line, meant that jobs could be specialized and more work could be accomplished. New technologies and sources of power became readily available. These and other social and political forces combined to require larger amounts of capital, well beyond the scope of most individual owner-manager-employees. Additionally, "workers" or non-family members began to dominate the firm and were the rule rather than the exception.

Ownership of the business became more dispersed, as capital was raised from banks, stockholders, and other institutions. Indeed, the management of the firm became separated from the ownership of the firm. And, in order to be successful, the top managers of the business had to simultaneously satisfy the owners, the employees and their unions, suppliers and customers. This system of organization of businesses along the lines set forth here was known as managerial capitalism or laissez faire capitalism, or more recently, shareholder capitalism.[5]

As businesses grew, managers developed a means of control via the divisionalized firm. Led by Alfred Sloan at General Motors, the divisionalized firm with a central headquarters staff was widely adapted.[6] The dominant model for managerial authority was the military and civil service bureaucracy. By creating rational structures and processes, the orderly progress of business growth could be well-managed.

Thus, managerialism, hierarchy, stability, and predictability all evolved together, in the United States and Europe, to form the most powerful economic system in the history of humanity. The rise of bureaucracy and managerialism was so strong, that the economist Joseph Schumpeter predicted that it would wipe out the creative force of capitalism, stifling innovation in its drive for predictability and stability.

During the last 50 years this "Managerial Model" has put "shareholders" at the center of the firm as the most important group for managers to worry about. This mindset has dealt with the increasing complexity of the business world by focusing more intensely on "shareholders" and "creating value for shareholders." It has become common wisdom to "increase shareholder value," and many companies have instituted complex incentive compensation plans aimed at aligning the interests of executives with the interests of shareholders. These incentive plans are often tied to the price of a company's stock which is affected by many factors not the least of which is the expectations of Wall Street analysts about earnings per share each quarter. Meeting Wall Street targets, and forming a stable and predictable base of quarter over quarter increases in earnings per share has become the standard for measuring company performance. Indeed, all of the recent scandals at Enron, WorldCom, Tyco, Arthur Anderson and others are in part due to executives trying to increase shareholder value, sometimes in opposition to accounting rules and law. Unfortunately, the world has changed so that the stability and predictability required by the shareholder approach can no longer be assured.

The Dominant Model Is Resistant to Change

The Managerial View of business with shareholders at the center is inherently resistant to change. It puts shareholders' interests over and above the interests of customers, suppliers, employees, and others, as if these interests must conflict with each other. It understands a business as an essentially hierarchical organization fastened together with authority to act in the shareholders' interests. Executives often speak in the language of hierarchy as "working for shareholders," "shareholders are the boss," and "you have to do what the shareholders want." On this interpretation, change should occur only when the shareholders are unhappy, and as long as executives can produce a series of incrementally better financial results there is no problem. According to this view the only change that counts is change oriented toward shareholder value. If customers are unhappy, if accounting rules have been compromised, if product quality is bad, if environmental disaster looms, even if competitive forces threaten, the only interesting questions are whether and how these forces for change affect shareholder value, measured by the price of the stock every day. Unfortunately in today's world there is just too much uncertainty and complexity to rely on such a single criterion. Business in the 21st Century is global and multi-faceted, and shareholder value may not capture that dynamism. Or, if it does, as the theory suggests it must eventually, it will be too late for executives to do anything about it. The dominant story may work for how things turn out in the long run on Wall Street, but managers have to act with an eye to Main Street as well, to anticipate change to try and take advantage of the dynamism of business.[7]

The Dominant Model Is Not Consistent with the Law

In actual fact the clarity of putting shareholders' interests first, above that of customers, suppliers, employees, and communities, flies in the face of the reality the law. The law has evolved to put constraints on the kinds of trade-offs that can be made. In fact the law of corporations gives a less clear answer to the question of in whose interest and for whose benefit the corporation should be governed. The law has evolved over the years to give *de facto* standing to the claims of groups other than stockholders. It has in effect, required that the claims of customers, suppliers, local communities, and employees be taken into consideration.

For instance, the doctrine of "privity of contract," as articulated in *Winterbottom v. Wright* in 1842, has been eroded by recent developments in products liability law. *Greenman v. Yuba Power* gives the manufacturer strict liability for damage caused by its products, even though the seller has exercised all possible care in the preparation and sale of the product and the consumer has not bought the product from nor entered into any contractual arrangement with the manufacturer. *Caveat emptor* has been replaced, in large part, with *caveat venditor*. The Consumer Product Safety Commission has the power to enact product recalls, essentially leading to an increase in the number of voluntary product recalls by companies seeking to mitigate legal damage awards. Some industries are required to provide information to customers about a product's ingredients, whether or not the customers want and are willing to pay for this information. Thus, companies must take the interests of customers into account, by law.

A similar story can be told about the evolution of the law forcing management to take the interests of employees into account. The National Labor Relations Act gave employees the right to unionize and to bargain in good faith. It set up the National Labor Relations Board to enforce these rights with management. The Equal Pay Act of 1963 and Title VII of the Civil Rights Act of 1964 constrain management from discrimination in hiring practices; these have been followed with the Age Discrimination in Employment Act of 1967, and recent extensions affecting people with disabilities. The emergence of a body of administrative case law arising from labor–management disputes and the historic settling of discrimination claims with large employers have caused the emergence of a body of management practice that is consistent with the legal guarantee of the rights of employees.

The law has also evolved to try and protect the interests of local communities. The Clean Air Act and Clean Water Act, and various amendments to these classic pieces of legislation, have constrained management from "spoiling the commons." In an historic case, *Marsh v. Alabama*, the Supreme Court ruled that a company-owned town was subject to the provisions of the U.S. Constitution, thereby guaranteeing the rights of local citizens and negating the "property rights" of the firm. Current issues center around protecting local businesses, forcing companies to pay the health care costs of their employees, increases in minimum wages, environmental standards, and the effects of business development on the lives of local community members. These issues fill the local political landscapes and executives and their companies must take account of them.

Some may argue that the constraints of the law, at least in the U.S., have become increasingly irrelevant in a world where business is global in nature. However, globalization simply makes this argument stronger. The laws that are relevant to business have evolved differently around the world, but they have evolved nonetheless to take into account the interests of groups other than just shareholders. Each state in India has a different set of regulations that affect how a company can do business. In China the law has evolved to give business some property rights, but it is far from exclusive.

And, in most of the European Union, laws around "civil society" and the role of "employees" are much more complex than even U.S. law.

"Laissez faire capitalism" is simply a myth. The idea that business is about "maximizing value for stockholders regardless of the consequences to others" is one that has outlived its usefulness. The dominant model simply does not describe how business operates. Another way to see this is that if executives always have to qualify "maximize shareholder value" with exceptions of law, or even good practice, then the dominant story isn't very useful any more. There are just too many exceptions. The dominant story could be saved by arguing that it describes a normative view about how business should operate, despite how actual businesses have evolved.[8] So, we need to look more closely at some of the conceptual and normative problems that the dominant model raises.

The Dominant Model Is Not Consistent with Basic Ethics

Previously we have argued that most theories of business rely on separating "business" decisions from "ethical" decision.[9] This is seen most clearly in the popular joke about "business ethics as an oxymoron." More formally we might suggest that we define:

The Separation Fallacy

It is useful to believe that sentences like "x is a business decision" have no ethical content or any implicit ethical point of view. And, it is useful to believe that sentences like "x is an ethical decision, the best thing to do all things considered" have no content or implicit view about value creation and trade (business).

This fallacy underlies much of the dominant story about business, as well as in other areas in society. There are two implications of rejecting the Separation Fallacy. The first is that almost any business decision has some ethical content. To see that this true one need only ask whether the following questions make sense for virtually any business decision:

The Open Question Argument

1. If this decision is made for whom is value created and destroyed?
2. Who is harmed and/or benefited by this decision?
3. Whose rights are enabled and whose values are realized by this decision (and whose are not)?
4. What kind of person will I (we) become if we make this decision?

Since these questions are always open for most business decisions, it is reasonable to give up the Separation Fallacy, which would have us believe that these questions aren't relevant for making business decisions, or that they could never be answered. We need a theory about business that builds in answers to the "Open Question Argument" above. One such answer would be "Only value to shareholders counts," but such an answer would have to be enmeshed in the language of ethics as well as business. Milton Friedman, unlike most of his expositors, may actually give such a morally rich answer. He claims that the responsibility of the executive is to make profits subject to law and ethical custom. Depending on how "law and ethical custom" is interpreted, the key difference with the stakeholder approach may well be that we disagree about how the world works. In order to create value we believe that it is better to focus on integrating business and ethics within a complex set of stakeholder relationships rather than treating ethics as a side constraint on making profits. In short we need a theory that has as its basis what we might call:

The Integration Thesis

Most business decisions, or sentences about business have some ethical content, or implicit ethical view. Most ethical decisions, or sentences about ethics have some business content or implicit view about business.[10]

One of the most pressing challenges facing business scholars is to tell compelling narratives that have the Integration Thesis at its heart. This is essentially the task that a group of scholars, "business ethicists" and "stakeholder theorists," have begun over the last 30 years. We need to go back to the very basics of ethics. Ethics is about the rules, principles, consequences, matters of character, etc. that we use to live together. These ideas give us a set of open questions that we are constantly searching for better ways to answer in reasonable complete ways.[11] One might define "ethics" as a conversation about how we can reason together and solve our differences, recognize where our interests are joined and need development, so that we can all flourish without resorting to coercion and violence. Some may disagree with such a definition, and we do not intend to privilege definitions, but such a pragmatist approach to ethics entails that we reason and talk together to try and create a better world for all of us.

If our critiques of the dominant model are correct then we need to start over by reconceptualizing the very language that we use to understand how business operates. We want to suggest that something like the following principle is implicit in most reasonably comprehensive views about ethics.

The Responsibility Principle[12]

Most people, most of the time, want to, actually do, and should accept responsibility for the effects of their actions on others.

Clearly the Responsibility Principle is incompatible with the Separation Fallacy. If business is separated from ethics, there is no question of moral responsibility for business decisions; hence, the joke is that "business ethics" is an oxymoron. More clearly still, without something like the Responsibility Principle it is difficult to see how ethics gets off the ground. "Responsibility" may well be a difficult and multi-faceted idea. There are surely many different ways to understand it. But, if we are not willing to accept the responsibility for our own actions (as limited as that may be due to complicated issues of causality and the like), then ethics, understood as how we reason together so we can all flourish, is likely an exercise in bad faith.

If we want to give up the separation fallacy and adopt the integration thesis, if the open question argument makes sense, and if something like the responsibility thesis is necessary, then we need a new model for business. And, this new story must be able to explain how value creation at once deals with economics and ethics, and how it takes account of all of the effects of business action on others. Such a model exists, and has been developing over the last 30 years by management researchers and ethics scholars, and there are many businesses who have adopted this "stakeholder framework" for their businesses.

III. MANAGING FOR STAKEHOLDERS

The basic idea of "managing for stakeholders" is quite simple. Business can be understood as a set of relationships among groups which have a stake in the activities that make up the business. Business is about how customers, suppliers, employees, financiers (stockholders, bondholders, banks, etc.), communities and managers interact and create value. To understand a business is to know how these relationships work. And, the executive's or entrepreneur's job is to manage and shape these relationships, hence the title, "managing for stakeholders."

Figure 1 depicts the idea of "managing for stakeholders" in a variation of the classic "wheel and spoke" diagram.[13] However, it is important to note that the stakeholder idea is perfectly general. Corporations are not the center of the universe, and there are many possible pictures. One might put customers in the center to signal that a company puts customers as the key priority. Another might put employees in the center and link them to customers and shareholders. We prefer the generic diagram because it suggests, pictorially, that "managing for stakeholders" is a theory about management and business; hence, managers and companies in the center. But, there is no larger metaphysical claim here.

Stakeholders and Stakes

Owners of financiers (a better term) clearly have a financial stake in the business in the form of stocks, bonds, and so on, and they expect some kind of financial return from them. Of course, the stakes of financiers will differ by type of owner, preferences for money, moral preferences, and so on, as well as by type of firm. The shareholders of Google may well want returns as well as be supportive of Google's articulated purpose of "Do No Evil." To the extent that it makes sense to talk about the financiers "owning the firm," they have a concomitant responsibility for the uses of their property.

Employees have their jobs and usually their livelihood at stake; they often have specialized skills for which there is usually no perfectly elastic market. In return for their labor, they expect security, wages, benefits and meaningful work. Often, employees are expected to participate in the decision making of the organization, and if the employees are management or senior executives we see them as shouldering a great deal of responsibility for the conduct of the organization as a whole. And, employees are sometimes financiers as well, since many companies have stock ownership plans, and loyal employees who believe in the future of their companies often voluntarily invest. One way to think about the employee relationship is in terms of contracts. Customers and suppliers exchange resources for the products and services of the firm and in return receive the benefits of the products and services. As with financiers and employees, the customer and supplier relationships are enmeshed in ethics. Companies make

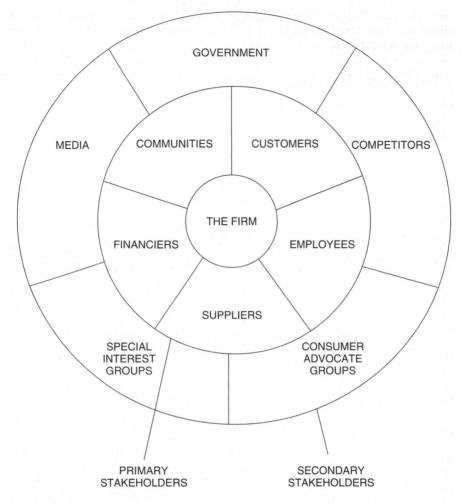

Source: R. Edward Freeman, Jeffrey Harrison, and Andrew Wicks, *Managing for Stakeholders* (New Haven, CT: Yale University Press, forthcoming in 2007).

promises to customers via their advertising, and when products or services don't deliver on these promises then management has a responsibility to rectify the situation. It is also important to have suppliers who are committed to making a company better. If suppliers find a better, faster, and cheaper way of making critical parts or services, then both supplier and company can win. Of course, some suppliers simply compete on price, but even so, there is a moral element of fairness and transparency to the supplier relationship.

Finally, the local community grants the firm the right to build facilities, and in turn, it benefits from the tax base and economic and social contributions of the firm. Companies have a real impact on communities, and being located in a welcoming community helps a company create value for its other stakeholders. In return for the provision of local services, companies are expected to be good citizens, as is any individual person. It should not expose the community to unreasonable hazards in the form of pollution, toxic waste, etc. It should keep whatever commitments it makes to the community, and operate in a transparent manner as far as possible. Of course, companies don't have perfect knowledge, but when management discovers some danger or runs afoul of new competition, it is expected to inform and work with local communities to mitigate any negative effects, as far as possible.

While any business must consist of financiers, customers, suppliers, employees, and communities, it is possible to think about other stakeholders as well. We can define "stakeholder" in a number of ways. First of all we could define the term fairly narrowly to capture the idea that any business, large or small, is about creating value for "those groups without whose support, the business would cease to be viable." The inner circle of Figure 1 depicts this view. Almost every business is concerned at some level with relationships among financiers, customers, suppliers, employees, and communities. We might call these groups "primary" or "definitional." However, it should be noted that as a business starts up, sometimes one particular stakeholder is more important than another. In a new business start up, sometimes there are no suppliers, and paying lots of attention to one or two key customers, as well as to the venture capitalist (financier) is the right approach.

There is also a somewhat broader definition that captures the idea that if a group or individual can affect a business, then the executives must take that group into consideration in thinking about how to create value. Or, a stakeholder is any group or individual that can affect or be affected by the realization of an organization's purpose. At a minimum some groups affect primary stakeholders and we might see these as stakeholders in the outer ring of Figure 1 and call them "secondary" or "instrumental."

There are other definitions that have emerged during the last 30 years, some based on risks and rewards, some based on mutuality of interests. And, the debate over finding the one "true definition" of "stakeholder" is not likely to end. We prefer a more pragmatist approach of being clear of the purpose of using any of the proposed definitions. Business is a fascinating field of study. There are very few principles and definitions that apply to all businesses all over the world. Furthermore, there are many different ways to run a successful business, or if you like, many different flavors of "managing for stakeholders." We see limited usefulness in trying to define one model of business, either based on the shareholder or stakeholder view, that works for all businesses everywhere. We see much value to be gained in examining how the stakes work in the value creation process, and the role of the executive.

IV. THE RESPONSIBILITY OF THE EXECUTIVE IN MANAGING FOR STAKEHOLDERS

Executives play a special role in the activity of the business enterprise. On the one hand, they have a stake like every other employee in terms of an actual or implied employment contract. And, that stake is linked to the stakes of financiers, customers, suppliers, communities, and other employees. In addition, executives are expected to look after the health of the overall enterprise, to keep the varied stakes moving in roughly the same direction, and to keep them in balance.[14]

No stakeholder stands alone in the process of value creation. The stakes of each stakeholder group are multi-faceted, and inherently connected to each other. How could a bondholder recognize any returns without management paying attention to the stakes of customers or employees? How could customers get the products and services they need without employees and suppliers? How could employees have a decent place to live without communities? Many thinkers see the dominant problem of "managing for stakeholders" as how to solve the priority problem, or "Which stakeholders are more important," or "how do we make tradeoffs among stakeholders." We see this as a secondary issue.

First and foremost, we need to see stakeholder interests as joint, as inherently tied together. Seeing stakeholder interests as "joint" rather than opposed is difficult. It is not always easy to find a way to accommodate all stakeholder interests. It is easier to trade off one versus another. Why not delay spending on new products for customers in order to keep earnings a bit higher? Why not cut employee medical benefits in order to invest in a new inventory control system?

Managing for stakeholders suggests that executives try to reframe the questions. How can we invest in new products and create higher earnings? How can we be sure our employees are healthy and happy and are able to work creatively so that we can capture the benefits of new information technology such as inventory control systems? In a recent book reflecting on his experience as CEO of Medtronic, Bill George summarized the managing for stakeholders mindset:[15]

> Serving all your stakeholders is the best way to produce long term results and create a growing, prosperous company . . . Let me be very clear about this: There is no conflict between serving all your stakeholders and providing excellent returns for shareholders. In the long term it is impossible to have one without the other. However, serving all these stakeholder groups requires discipline, vision, and committed leadership.

The primary responsibility of the executive is to create as much value as possible for stakeholders.[16] Where stakeholder interests conflict, the executive must find a way to rethink the problems so that these interests can go together, so that even more value can be created for each. If tradeoffs have to be made, as often happens in the real world, then the executive must figure out how to make the tradeoffs, and immediately begin improving the tradeoffs for all sides. **Managing for stakeholders is about creating as much value as possible for stakeholders, without resorting to tradeoffs.**

We believe that this task is more easily accomplished when a business has a sense of purpose. Furthermore, there are few limits on the kinds of purpose that can drive a business. Wal-Mart may stand for "everyday low price." Merck can stand for "alleviating human suffering." The point is that if an entrepreneur or an executive can find a purpose that speaks to the hearts and minds of key stakeholders, it is more likely that there will be sustained success.

Purpose is complex and inspirational. The Grameen Bank wants to eliminate poverty. Fannie Mae wants to make housing affordable to every income level in society. Tastings (a local restaurant) wants to bring the taste of really good food and wine to lots of people in the community. And, all of these organizations have to generate profits, or else they cannot pursue their purposes. Capitalism works because we can pursue our purpose with others. When we coalesce around a big idea, or a joint purpose evolves from our day to day activities with each other, then great things can happen.

To create value for stakeholders, executives must understand that business is fully situated in the realm of humanity. Businesses are human institutions populated by real live complex human beings. Stakeholders have names and faces and children. They are not mere placeholders for social roles. As such, matters of ethics are routine when one takes a managing for stakeholders approach. Of course this should go without saying, but a part of the dominant story about business is that business people are only in it for their own narrowly defined self interest. One main assumption of the managerial view with shareholders at the center is that shareholders only care about returns, and therefore their agents, managers, should only care about returns. However, this does not fit either our experiences or our aspirations. In the words of one CEO, "The only assets I manage go up and down the elevators everyday."

Most human beings are complicated. Most of us do what we do because we are self-interested and interested in others. Business works in part because of our urge to create things with others and for others. Working on a team, or creating a new product or delivery mechanism that makes customers lives better or happier or more pleasurable all can be contributing factors to why we go to work each day. And, this is not to deny the economic incentive of getting a pay check. The assumption of narrow self-interest is extremely limiting, and can be self-reinforcing—people can begin to act in a narrow self-interested way if they believe that is what is expected of them, as some of the scandals such as Enron, have shown. We need to be open to a more complex psychology—one any parent finds familiar as they have shepherded the growth and development of their children.

V. SOME ARGUMENTS FOR MANAGING FOR STAKEHOLDERS

Once you say stakeholders are persons, then the ideas of ethics are automatically applicable. However you interpret the idea of "stakeholders," you must pay attention to the effects of your actions on others. And, something like the Responsibility Principle suggests that this is a cornerstone of any adequate ethical theory. There are at least three main arguments for adopting a managing for stakeholders approach. Philosophers will see these as connected to the three main approaches to ethical theory that have developed historically. We shall briefly set forth sketches of these arguments, and then suggest that there is a more powerful fourth argument.[17]

The Argument from Consequences

A number of theorists have argued that the main reason that the dominant model of managing for shareholders is a good idea is that it leads to the best consequences for all. Typically these arguments invoke Adam Smith's idea of the invisible hand, whereby each business actor pursues her own self interest and the greatest good of all actually emerges. The problem with this argument is that we now know with modern general equilibrium economics that the argument only works under very specialized conditions that seldom describe the real world. And further, we know that if the economic conditions get very close to those needed to produce the greatest good, there is no guarantee that the greatest good will actually result.

Managing for stakeholders may actually produce better consequences for all stakeholders because it recognizes that stakeholder interests are joint. If one stakeholder pursues its interests at the expense of all the others, then the others will either withdraw their support, or look to create another network of stakeholder value creation. This is not to say that there are not times when one stakeholder will benefit at the expense of others, but if this happens continuously over time, then in a relatively free society, stakeholders will either: (1) exit to form a new stakeholder network that satisfies their needs; (2) use the political process to constrain the offending stakeholder; or, (3) invent some other form of activity to satisfy their particular needs.[18]

Alternatively, if we think about stakeholders engaged in a series of bargains among themselves, then we would expect that as individual stakeholders recognized their joint interests, and made good decisions based on these interests, better consequences would result, than if they each narrowly pursued their individual self interests.[19]

Now it may be objected that such an approach ignores "social consequences" or "consequences to society," and hence, that we need a concept of "corporate social responsibility" to mitigate these effects. This objection is a vestigial limb of the dominant model. Since the only effects, on that view, were economic effects, then we need to think about "social consequences" or "corporate social responsibility." However, if stakeholder relationships are understood to be fully embedded in morality, then there is no need for an idea like corporate social responsibility. We can replace it with "corporate stakeholder responsibility" which is a dominant feature of managing for stakeholders.

The Argument from Rights

The dominant story gives property rights in the corporation exclusively to shareholders, and the natural question arises about the rights of other stakeholders who are affected. One way to understand managing for stakeholders is that it takes this question of rights, seriously. If you believe that rights make sense, and further that if one person has a right to X then all persons have a right to X, it is just much easier to think about these issues using a stakeholder approach. For instance, while shareholders may well have property rights, these rights are not absolute, and should not be seen as such. Shareholders may not use their property to abridge the rights of others. For instance, shareholders and their agents, managers, may not use corporate property to violate the right to life of others. One way to understand managing for stakeholders is that it assumes that stakeholders have some rights. Now it is notoriously difficult to parse the idea of "rights." But, if executives take managing for stakeholders seriously, they will automatically think about what is owed to customers, suppliers, employees, financiers and communities, in virtue of their stake, and in virtue of their basic humanity.

The Argument from Character

One of the strongest arguments for managing for stakeholders is that it asks executives and entrepreneurs to consider the question of what kind of company they want to create and build. The answer to this question will be in large part an issue of character. Aspiration matters. The business virtues of efficiency, fairness, respect, integrity, keeping commitments, and others are all critical in being successful at creating value for stakeholders. These virtues are simply absent when we think only about the dominant model and its sole reliance on a narrow economic logic.

If we frame the central question of management as "how do we create value for shareholders," then the only virtue that emerges is one of loyalty to the interests of shareholders. However, if we frame the central question more broadly as "how do we create and sustain the creation of value for stakeholders" or "how do we get stakeholder interests all going in the same direction," then it is easy to see how many of the other virtues are relevant. Taking a stakeholder approach helps people decide how companies can contribute to their well-being and kinds of lives they want to lead. By making ethics explicit and building it into the basic way we think about business, we avoid a situation of bad faith and self deception.

The Pragmatist's Argument

The previous three arguments point out important reasons for adopting a new story about business. Pragmatists want to know how we can live better, how we can create both ourselves and our communities in a way where values such as freedom and solidarity are present in our everyday lives to the maximal extent. While it is sometimes useful to think about consequences, rights, and character in isolation, in reality our lives are richer if we can have a conversation about how to live together better. There is a long tradition of pragmatist ethics dating to philosophers such as William James and John Dewey. More recently philosopher Richard Rorty has expressed the pragmatist ideal.[20]

> . . . pragmatists . . . hope instead that human beings will come to enjoy more money, more free time, and greater social equality, and also that they will develop more empathy, more ability to put themselves in the shoes of others. We hope that human beings will behave more decently toward one another as their standard of living improves.

By building into the very conceptual framework we use to think about business a concern with freedom, equality, consequences, decency, shared purpose, and paying attention to all of the effects of how we create value for each other, we can make business a human institution, and perhaps remake it in a way that sustains us.

For the pragmatist, business (and capitalism) has evolved as a social practice an important one that we use to create value and trade with each other. On this view, first and foremost, business is about collaboration. Of course, in a free society, stakeholders are free to form competing networks. But, the fuel for capitalism is our desire to create something of value, and to create it for ourselves and others. The spirit of capitalism is the spirit of individual achievement together with the spirit of accomplishing great tasks in collaboration with others. Managing for stakeholders makes this plain so that we can get about the business of creating better selves and better communities.

Notes

1. The ideas in this paper have had a long development time. The ideas here have been reworked from: R. Edward Freeman, *Strategic Management: A Stakeholder Approach* (Boston: Pitman, 1984); R. Edward Freeman, "A Stakeholder Theory of the Modern Corporation," in T. Beauchamp and N. Bowie (eds.), *Ethical Theory and Business*, 7th ed. [Upper Saddle River, NJ: Prentice Hall, 2005], also in earlier editions coauthored with William Evan; Andrew Wicks, R. Edward Freeman, Patricia Werhane, Kirsten Martin, *Business Ethics: A Managerial Approach* (Upper Saddle River, NJ: Prentice Hall, forthcoming in 2008); and R. Edward Freeman, Jeffrey Harrison, and Andrew Wicks, *Managing for Stakeholders* (New Haven: Yale University Press, forthcoming in 2007). I am grateful to editors and coauthors for permission to rework these ideas here.

2. It has been called a variety of things from "stakeholder management," "stakeholder capitalism," "a stakeholder theory of the modern corporation," etc. Our reasons for choosing "managing for stakeholders" will become clearer as we proceed. Many others have worked on these ideas and should not be held accountable for the rather idiosyncratic view outlined here.

3. For a stylized history of the idea, see R. Edward Freeman, "The Development of Stakeholder Theory: An Idiosyncratic Approach," in K. Smith and M. Hitt (eds.), *Great Minds in Management* (Oxford, UK: Oxford University Press, 2005).

4. One doesn't manage "for" these benefits (and harms).

5. The difference between managerial and shareholder capitalism is large. However, the existence of agency theory lets us treat the two identically for our purposes here. Both agree on the view that the modern firm is characterized by the separation of decision making and residual risk bearing. The resulting agency problem is the subject of a vast literature.

6. Alfred Chandler's brilliant book, *Strategy and Structure* (Boston: MIT Press, 1970) chronicles the rise of the divisionalized corporation. For a not-so-flattering account of General Motors during the same time period, see Peter Drucker's classic work, *The Concept of the Corporation*, Reprint Edition (New York: Transaction Publishers, 1993).

7. Executives can take little comfort in the nostrum that in the long run things work out and the most efficient companies survive. Some market theorists suggest that finance theory acts like "universal acid" cutting through every possible management decision, whether or not actual managers are aware of it. Perhaps the real difference between the dominant model and the "managing for stakeholders" model proposed here is that they are simply "about" different things. The dominant model is about the strict and narrow economic logic of markets, and the managing for stakeholders model is about how human beings create value for each other.

8. Often the flavor of the response of finance theorists sounds like this. The world would be better off if, despite all of the imperfections, executives tried to maximize shareholder value. It is difficult to see how any rational being could accept such a view in the face of the recent scandals, where it could be argued that the worst offenders were the most ideologically pure, and the result was the actual destruction of shareholder value (see

Breaking the Short Term Cycle [Charlottesville, VA: Business Roundtable Institute for Corporate Ethics/CFA Center for Financial Market Integrity, 2006]). Perhaps we have a version of Aristotle's idea that happiness is not a result of trying to be happy, or Mill's idea that it does not maximize utility to try and maximize utility. Collins and Porras have suggested that even if executives want to maximize shareholder value, they should focus on purpose instead, that trying to maximize shareholder value does not lead to maximum value (see J. Collins and J. Porras, *Built to Last* [New York: HarperCollins, 2002]).

 9. See R. Edward Freeman, "The Politics of Stakeholder Theory: Some Future Directions," *Business Ethics Quarterly*, vol. 4, October, 1994, 409–422.

10. The second part of the integration thesis is left for another occasion. Philosophers who read this essay may note the radical departure from standard accounts of political philosophy. Suppose we began the inquiry into political philosophy with the question of "How is value creation and trade sustainable over time?" and suppose that the traditional beginning question, "How is the state justified?" was a subsidiary one. We might discover or create some very different answers from the standard accounts of most political theory. See R. Edward Freeman and Robert Phillips, "Stakeholder Theory: A Libertarian Defense," *Business Ethics Quarterly*, vol. 12, No. 3, 2002, pp. 331ff.

11. Here we roughly follow the logic of John Rawls in *Political Liberalism* (New York: Columbia University Press, 1995).

12. There are many statements of this principle. Our argument is that whatever the particular conception of responsibility, there is some underlying concept that is captured like our willingness or our need to justify our lives to others. Note the answer that the dominant view of business must give to questions about responsibility. "Executives are responsible only for the effects of their actions on shareholders, or only in so far as their actions create or destroy shareholder value."

13. The spirit of this diagram is from R. Phillips, *Stakeholder Theory and Organizational Ethics* (San Francisco: Berret- Koehler Publishers, 2003).

14. In earlier versions of this essay in this volume we suggested that the notion of a fiduciary duty to stockholders be extended to "fiduciary duty to stakeholders." We believe that such a move cannot be defended without doing damage to the notion of "fiduciary." The idea of having a special duty to either one or a few stakeholders is not helpful.

15. Bill George, *Authentic Leadership* (San Francisco: Jossey Bass, 2004).

16. This is at least as clear as the directive given by the dominant model: Create as much value as possible for shareholders.

17. Some philosophers have argued that the stakeholder approach is in need of a "normative justification." To the extent that this phrase has any meaning, we take it as a call to connect the logic of managing for stakeholders with more traditional ethical theory. As pragmatists we eschew the "descriptive vs. normative vs. instrumental" distinction that so many business thinkers (and stakeholder theorists) have adopted. Managing for stakeholders is inherently a narrative or story that is at once *descriptive* of how some businesses do act, *aspirational* and *normative* about how they could and should act, *instrumental* in terms of what means lead to what ends, and *managerial* in that it must be coherent on all of these dimensions and actually guide executive action.

18. See S. Venkataraman, "Stakeholder Value Equilibration and the Entrepreneurial Process," *Ethics and Entrepreneurship*, The Ruffin Series, vol. 3, 2002, pp. 45–57; S. R. Velamuri, "Entrepreneurship, Altruism, and the Good Society," *Ethics and Entrepreneurship*, The Ruffin Series, vol. 3, 2002, pp. 125–143; and T. Harting, S. Harmeling, and S. Venkataraman, "Innovative Stakeholder Relations: When 'Ethics Pays' (and When It Doesn't)," *Business Ethics Quarterly*, vol. 16, 2006, pp. 43–68.

19. Sometimes there are tradeoffs and situations that economists would call the "prisoner's dilemma," but these are not the paradigmatic cases, or if they are, we seem to solve them routinely, as Russell Hardin has suggested in *Morality within the Limits of Reason* (Chicago: University of Chicago Press, 1998).

20. E. Mendieta (ed.), *Take Care of Freedom and Truth Will Take Care of Itself: Interviews with Richard Rorty* (Stanford: Stanford University Press, 2006), p. 68.

Chapter 2

Ethical Reasoning in Practice

Case Study

Italian Tax Mores

ARTHUR L. KELLY

The Italian federal corporate tax system has an official, legal tax structure and tax rates just as the U.S. system does. However, all similarity between the two systems ends there.

The Italian tax authorities assume that no Italian corporation would ever submit a tax return which shows its true profits but rather would submit a return which understates actual profits by anywhere between 30 percent and 70 percent; their assumption is essentially correct. Therefore, about six months after the annual deadline for filing corporate tax returns, the tax authorities issue to each corporation an "invitation to discuss" its tax return. The purpose of this notice is to arrange a personal meeting between them and representatives of the corporation. At this meeting, the Italian revenue service states the amount of corporate income tax which it believes is due. Its position is developed from both prior years' taxes actually paid and the current year's return; the amount which the tax authorities claim is due is generally several times that shown on the corporation's return for the current year. In short, the corporation's tax return and the revenue service's stated position are the opening offers for the several rounds of bargaining which will follow.

The Italian corporation is typically represented in such negotiations by its *commercialista*, a function which exists in Italian society for the primary purpose of negotiating corporate (and individual) tax payments with the Italian tax authorities; thus, the management of an Italian corporation seldom, if ever, has to meet directly with the Italian revenue service and probably has a minimum awareness of the details of the negotiation other than the final settlement.

This case, based on an actual occurrence, was prepared by Arthur L. Kelly and was first presented at Loyola University in Chicago in April 1977 at a Mellon Foundation Symposium entitled "Foundations of Corporate Responsibility to Society." Mr. Kelly has served as Vice President—International of the management consulting firm A. T. Kearney, Inc., and as President of LaSalle Steel Company; he is currently Managing Partner of KEL Enterprises Ltd., a Chicago holding and investment company. He serves as a member of the Board of Directors of corporations in the United States and Europe, including Deere & Company and BMW A.G. Copyright 1977. All rights reserved.

Both the final settlement and the negotiation are extremely important to the corporation, the tax authorities, and the *commercialista*. Since the tax authorities assume that a corporation *always* earned more money this year than last year and *never* has a loss, the amount of the final settlement, i.e., corporate taxes which will actually be paid, becomes, for all practical purposes, the floor for the start of next year's negotiations. The final settlement also represents the amount of revenue the Italian government will collect in taxes to help finance the cost of running the country. However, since large amounts of money are involved and two individuals having vested personal interests are conducting the negotiations, the amount of *bustarella*—typically a substantial cash payment "requested" by the Italian revenue agent from the *commercialista*—usually determines whether the final settlement is closer to the corporation's original tax return or to the fiscal authority's original negotiating position.

Whatever *bustarella* is paid during the negotiation is usually included by the *commercialista* in his lump-sum fee "for services rendered" to his corporate client. If the final settlement is favorable to the corporation, and it is the *commercialista's* job to see that it is, then the corporation is not likely to complain about the amount of its *commercialista's* fee, nor will it ever know how much of that fee was represented by *bustarella* and how much remained for the *commercialista* as payment for his negotiating services. In any case, the tax authorities will recognize the full amount of the fee as a tax deductible expense on the corporation's tax return for the following year.

About ten years ago, a leading American bank opened a banking subsidiary in a major Italian city. At the end of its first year of operation, the bank was advised by its local lawyers and tax accountants, both from branches of U.S. companies, to file its tax return "Italian-style," i.e., to understate its actual profits by a significant amount. The American general manager of the bank, who was on his first overseas assignment, refused to do so both because he considered it dishonest and because it was inconsistent with the practices of his parent company in the United States.

About six months after its "American-style" tax return, the bank received an "invitation to discuss" notice for the Italian tax authorities. The bank's general manager consulted with his lawyers and tax accountants who suggested he hire a *commercialista*. He rejected this advice and instead wrote a letter to the Italian revenue service not only stating that his firm's corporate return was correct as filed but also requesting that they inform him of any specific items about which they had questions. His letter was never answered.

About sixty days after receiving the initial "invitation to discuss" notice, the bank received a formal tax assessment notice calling for a tax of approximately three times that shown on the bank's corporate tax return; the tax authorities simply assumed the bank's original return had been based on generally accepted Italian practices, and they reacted accordingly. The bank's general manager again consulted with his lawyers and tax accountants who again suggested he hire a *commercialista* who knew how to handle these matters. Upon learning that the *commercialista* would probably have to pay *bustarella* to his revenue service counterpart in order to reach a settlement, the general manager again chose to ignore his advisors. Instead, he responded by sending the Italian revenue service a check for the full amount of taxes due according to the bank's American-style tax return even though the due date for the payment was almost six months hence; he made no reference to the amount of corporate taxes shown on the formal tax assessment notice.

Ninety days after paying its taxes, the bank received a third notice from the fiscal authorities. This one contained the statement, "We have reviewed your corporate tax return of 19__ and have determined that [the lira equivalent of] $6,000,000 of interest paid on deposits is not an allowable expense for federal tax purposes. Accordingly, the total tax due for 19__ is lira ____." Since interest paid on deposits is any bank's largest single expense item, the new tax assessment was for an amount many times larger than that shown in the initial tax assessment notice and almost fifteen times larger than the taxes which the bank had actually paid.

The bank's general manager was understandably very upset. He immediately arranged an appointment to meet personally with the manager of the Italian revenue service's local office. Shortly after the start of their meeting, the conversation went something like this:

> **General Manager:** "You can't really be serious about disallowing interest paid on deposits as a tax deductible expense."

> **Italian Revenue Service:** "Perhaps. However, we thought it would get your attention. Now that you're here, shall we begin our negotiations?"[1]

Note

1. For readers interested in what happened subsequently, the bank was forced to pay the taxes shown in the initial tax assessment, and the American manager was recalled to the United States and replaced.

A Kantian Approach to Business Ethics

NORMAN E. BOWIE

Even the most cursory foray into business ethics will bring one face to face with Kantianism. Indeed Kant's influence on that branch of ethical theory known as deontology is so strong that some writers simply refer to deontology as Kantianism. Despite the fact that Kant's name is often invoked in business ethics, as of 1997 there was no published book that systematically applied Kantian theory to business. (However, Bowie (1999) fills this gap.) Kant is best known for defending a version of the "respect for persons" principle which implies that any business practice that puts money on a par with people is immoral, but there is much more to a Kantian approach to business ethics than this. In this essay, I focus on some of the implications of Kant's three formulations of the fundamental principle of ethics. I then show why Kant's emphasis on the purity of our intentions in acting morally has created problems for a Kantian theory of business ethics.

From *A Companion to Business Ethics*, ed. Robert E. Fredrick (1999; Blackwell Publishers). Reprinted by permission of the author, Norman E. Bowie, and Blackwell Publishers, Ltd.

BACKGROUND

Kant was born in 1724 in Konigsberg in East Prussia, not far from the Baltic Sea. He spent his entire life within 26 kilometers of Konigsberg and died there in 1804. Today, Konigsberg is located in a small strip of Russian territory between Poland and Lithuania, and is called Kaliningrad. Kant's major writings on ethical theory occurred between 1785 and 1797. Kant argued that the highest good was the good will. To act from a good will is to act from duty. Thus, it is the intention behind an action rather than its consequences that make that action good. For example, for Kant if a merchant is honest so as to earn a good reputation, these acts of being honest are not genuinely moral. The merchant is only truly moral if he or she is honest because being honest is right (one's duty). Persons of good will do their duty because it is their duty and for no other reason. It is this emphasis on duty, and the lack of concern with consequences, that makes Kant the quintessential deontologist.

But what does Kantian morality think our duties are? Kant distinguished between two kinds of duty (imperatives). Sometimes we do something so that we may get something else. We go to work to earn money or study to earn good grades. If you want good grades, you ought to study. Kant referred to this kind of duty as a hypothetical imperative because it is of the form if you want to do *x*, do *y*. The duty to study is dependent on your desire for good grades.

Other duties are required *per se*, with no ifs, ands or buts. Kant described these duties as categorical and referred to the fundamental principle of ethics as the categorical imperative. He believed that reason provided the basis for the categorical imperative, thus the categorical imperatives of morality were requirements of reason. Although Kant spoke of "the" categorical imperative, he formulated it in many ways. Most commentators focus on three formulations:

1. Act only on maxims which you can will to be universal laws of nature.
2. Always treat the humanity in a person as an end, and never as a means merely.
3. So act as if you were a member of an ideal kingdom of ends in which you were both subject and sovereign at the same time.

Kant believed that only human beings can follow laws of their own choosing (i.e., act rationally). Human beings are the only creatures that are free, and it is the fact that we are free that enables us to be rational and moral. Our free will is what gives us our dignity and unconditioned worth.

Kant's ethics then is an ethics of duty rather than an ethics of consequences. The ethical person is the person who acts from the right intentions. We are able to act in this way this because we have free will. The fundamental principle of ethics, the categorical imperative, is a requirement of reason and is binding on all rational beings. These are the essentials of Kant's ethics. Let us see how they apply, specifically, to business ethics.

THE SELF-DEFEATING NATURE OF IMMORAL ACTIONS

Kant's first formulation of the categorical imperative is "Act only on that maxim by which you can at the same time will that it should become a universal law." Although the phrasing is awkward, Kant is providing a test to see if any proposed action, including actions in business, is moral. Since Kant believed that every action has a maxim, we are to ask what would happen if the principle (maxim) of your action were a universal law (one that everyone acted on). Would a world where everyone acted on that principle be possible? One example Kant used to illustrate his theory was a business one.

Suppose you desperately needed money. Should you ask someone to lend you money with a promise to pay the money back but with no intention of paying it back? Do your extreme financial circumstances justify a lying promise? To find out, Kant would require us to universalize the maxim of this action: "It is morally permissible for anyone in desperate financial circumstances to make a lying promise, that is, to promise to repay borrowed money with no intention of doing so." Would such a universalized maxim be logically coherent? Kant (1990, p. 19) answers with a resounding no.

> And could I say to myself that everyone may make a false promise when he is in a difficulty from which he cannot escape? Immediately I see that I could will the lie but not a universal law to lie. For with such a law there would be no promises at all, inasmuch as it would be futile to make a pretense of my intention in regard to future actions to those who would not believe this pretense or—if they over hastily did so—would pay me back in my own coin. Thus my maxim would necessarily destroy itself as soon as it was made a universal law.

Notice what Kant is *not* saying here. He is not saying that if everyone made lying promises, the consequences would be bad—although they would. Rather, Kant is saying that the very concept of lying promises, when adopted as a principle by everyone, is incoherent.

Thus the categorical imperative functions as a test to see if the principles (maxims) upon which an action is based are morally permissible. The action can only be undertaken if the principle on which the action is based passes the test of the categorical imperative. A business manager who accepts Kantian morality would ask for any given decision, does the principle on which the decision is based pass the test of the categorical imperative, that is, can it be willed universally without contradiction? If it can, then the decision would be morally permissible. If it cannot, the action is morally forbidden.

Let us consider two other examples to illustrate Kant's point. First, theft by employees, managers, and customers is a major problem in business. Suppose that an employee, angry at the boss for some justified reason, considers stealing from the firm. Could a maxim which permitted stealing be universalized? It could not. Because goods and services are in limited supply and universal collective ownership is impossible, the institution of private property has developed. If a maxim that permitted stealing were universalized, there could be no private property. If everyone were free to take from everyone else, then nothing could be owned. Given the practical necessity of some form of private property, a universalized maxim that permitted stealing would be self-defeating. Thus, if the employee steals from the boss, the theft is morally wrong.

Another example found in the press concerns companies that try to renegotiate contracts. A favorite ploy of General Motors, especially with Jose Lopez in charge, was to demand price reductions from negotiated contracts with suppliers. In this way, General Motors cut costs and contributed to its bottom line. Would such a tactic pass the test of the categorical imperative?

No, it could not. If a maxim that permitted contract breaking were universalized, there could not be no contracts (and contracts would cease to exist). No one would enter into a contract if he or she believed the other party had no intention of honoring it. A universalized maxim that permitted contract breaking would be self-defeating. . . .

The test of the categorical imperative becomes a principle of fair play. One of the essential features of fair play is that one does not make an exception of oneself. For example, Kant (1990, p. 41) says:

> When we observe ourselves in any transgression of a duty, we find that we do not actually will that our maxim should become a universal law. That is impossible for us; rather the contrary of this maxim should remain as the law generally, and we only take the liberty of making an exception to it for ourselves or for the sake of inclination, and for this one occasion. Consequently, if we weighed everything from one and the same standpoint, namely reason, we would come upon a contradiction in our own will, viz., that a certain principle is objectively necessary as a universal law and yet subjectively does not hold universally but rather admits exceptions.

Thus the categorical imperative captures one of the key features of morality. Unless the principle of your action can be universalized, to make an exception for yourself is immoral.

I have frequently used these arguments with executives who may find them theoretically persuasive but who, nonetheless, think that their practical application is limited in the real world of business. They point out that, in the real world, contracts are often "renegotiated" and yet business people still engage in contract-making.

These executives raise an interesting point. However, an examination of what goes on in the business world does more to vindicate Kant than to refute him. Consider the following real-world situations.

- When on vacation in Ocean City, Maryland, my favorite seafood outlet had a large sign on the wall saying, "We do not cash checks and here is why." Below the sign and nearly covering the entire wall were photocopies of checks that had been returned with "Returned: Insufficient Funds" stamped in large letters. At least in this retail outlet, a threshold had been crossed. A sufficiently large number of customers wrote bad checks so that it was no longer possible to use checks in that retail store. Suppose a maxim permitting writing checks without sufficient funds in the bank to cover them was really universalized. There would be no institution of check writing.
- While lecturing in Poland in 1995, I was informed that, shortly after the fall of communism, there was a bank collapse because people did not pay on their loans. And experts generally agree that one of the impediments to the development of capitalism in Russia is the failure of various parties to pay their bills. A supplier is reluctant to provide a product if it is not known if and when payment will be received.
- Finally, there has been considerable speculation regarding the future of capitalism in Hong Kong now that the Chinese have regained sovereignty there. As business commentators have pointed out, Hong Kong had developed a legal system that enforced business contracts and limited the influence of politics. In China, political influence plays a much greater role. If the tradition of legal enforcement that has been developed is undermined, can Hong Kong survive as a thriving prosperous major center of business practice? A Kantian would agree with the economists here. Hong Kong would lose its premier standing as a commercial center and would suffer economically. . . .

Thus the categorical imperative is not irrelevant in the world of business. If a maxim for an action when universalized is self-defeating, then the contemplated action is not ethical. That is Kant's conceptual point. And when enough people behave immorally in that sense, certain business practices like the use of checks or credit become impossible.

TREATING STAKEHOLDERS AS PERSONS

Since human beings have free will and thus are able to act from laws required by reason, Kant believed they have dignity or a value beyond price. Thus, one human being cannot use another simply to satisfy his or her own interests. This is the core insight behind Kant's second formulation of the categorical imperative: "Always treat the humanity in a person as an end and never as a means merely." What are the implications of this formulation of the categorical imperative for business?

First, it should be pointed out that the "respect for persons" principle, as I shall call it, does not prohibit commercial transactions. No one is used as merely a means in a voluntary economic exchange where both parties benefit. What this formulation of the categorical imperative does is to put some constraints on the nature of economic transactions.

To understand Kant fully here, we need to draw a distinction between negative freedom and positive freedom. Negative freedom is freedom from coercion and deception. Kant scholar Christine Korsgaard (1996, pp. 140–1) has put it this way:

> According to the Formula of Humanity, coercion and deception are the most fundamental forms of wrongdoing to others—the roots of all evil. Coercion and deception violate the conditions of possible assent, and all actions which depend for their nature and efficacy on their coercive or deceptive character are ones that others cannot assent to . . . Physical coercion treats someone's person as a tool, lying treats someone's reason as a tool. That is why Kant finds it so horrifying: it is a direct violation of autonomy.

However, simply refraining from coercive or deceptive acts is not sufficient for respecting the humanity in a person. Additional requirements can be derived from Kant's view of positive freedom. Positive freedom is the freedom to develop one's human capacities. For Kant, that means developing one's rational and moral capacities. In interacting with others, we must not do anything to diminish or inhibit these uniquely human capacities.

Thus, treating the humanity in a person as an end, and not as a means merely, in a business relationship requires two things. First, it requires that people in a business relationship not be used, i.e., they not be coerced or deceived. Second, it means that business organizations and business practices should be arranged so that they contribute to the development of human rational and moral capacities, rather than inhibit the development of these capacities. These requirements, if implemented, would change the nature of business practice. A few examples are in order.

Americans have been deeply concerned about the massive layoffs created by the downsizing of corporations in the early and mid-1990s. Are these layoffs immoral? A naive Kantian response would label them as immoral because, allegedly, the employees are being used as mere means to enhance shareholder wealth. However, that judgment would be premature. What would be required from a Kantian perspective is an examination of the employer/employee relationship, including any contractual agreements. So long as the relationship was neither coercive nor deceptive, there would be nothing immoral about layoffs.

What is highly contested is whether or not the standard employer/employee relationship is coercive and/or deceptive. Employers tend to argue that employees are well aware of the possibility of layoffs when they take a position and, furthermore, that employees have the right, which they frequently exercise, to take positions elsewhere. There is neither deception nor coercion in either standard labor contracts or in the implicit norms governing the employer/employee relationship. On the other hand, many employees argue that, in times of relatively high unemployment and job insecurity, employees really must accept job offers on management terms. You take what you can so as to eat, but you do not accept the threat of a layoff to enhance shareholder wealth freely. Moreover, in many companies, such as IBM, there had been a long tradition of job security in exchange for employee loyalty. The sudden unilateral changing of the rules amounted to both deception and coercion on the part of management, or so it is argued.

An examination of these opposing arguments would take us far beyond the scope of this essay. However, by framing the issue in terms of whether or not coercion and/or deception has occurred, one has adopted a Kantian approach to business ethics.

Another concern about contemporary business practice is the extent to which employees have very limited knowledge about the affairs of the company. In economic terminology, there is high information asymmetry between management and the employees. Wherever one side has information that it keeps from other side, there is a severe temptation for abuse of power and deception. A Kantian would look for ways to reduce the information asymmetry between management and employees.

In practical terms, a Kantian would endorse the practice known as open book management. Open book management was developed by Jack Stack at the Springfield Manufacturing Company. Stack and his company won a prestigious business ethics award for the technique. Under open book management, all employees are given all the financial information about the company on a regular frequent basis. With complete information and the proper incentive, employees behave responsibly without the necessity of layers of supervision.

> How does open book management do what it does? The simplest answer is this. People get a chance to act, to take responsibility, rather than just doing their job. ... No supervisor or department head can anticipate or handle all ... situations. A company that hired enough managers to do so would go broke from the overhead. Open book management gets people on the job doing things right. And it teaches them to make smart decisions ... because they can see the impact of their decisions on the relevant numbers (Case, 1995, pp. 45–46).

The adoption of practices like open book management would go far toward correcting the asymmetrical information that managers possess, a situation that promotes abuse of power and deception. Under open book management, if a firm faced a situation that might involve the layoff of employees, everyone in the firm would have access to the same information.

Deception would be very difficult in such circumstances. Suspicion would be less and, as a result, cooperative efforts to address the problem would be more likely.

Open book management also enhances employee self-respect. Employees at Springfield Manufacturing Company use Kantian "respect for persons" language when describing the impact of open book management on working conditions. Thus, open book management lessens the opportunity for deception and supports negative freedom.

By enhancing employee self-respect, open book management supports positive freedom as well. What are the implications of Kant's theory of positive freedom for business practice? To treat the humanity in a person as an end in itself sometimes requires that we take some positive action to help a person. This is required by the "respect for persons" formulation of the categorical imperative, by some of Kant's own writing on the nature of work, and by the demands of Kant's imperfect duty of beneficence to help others.

The requirement that business practice be supportive of positive freedom has wide implications for business practice. I will focus on only one implication here. I believe Kant's moral philosophy enables business ethicists to develop a useful definition of meaningful work and that Kantian ethics would require companies to provide meaningful work so defined. Although I cannot cite all the Kantian texts in this brief essay, I think the following conditions for meaningful work are consistent with Kant's views. For a Kantian, meaningful work:

- is freely chosen and provides opportunities for the worker to exercise autonomy on the job;
- supports the autonomy and rationality of human beings; work that lessens autonomy or that undermines rationality is immoral;
- provides a salary sufficient to exercise independence and provide for physical well-being and the satisfaction of some of the worker's desires;
- enables a worker to develop rational capacities; and
- does not interfere with a worker's moral development.

(Notice that these requirements are normative in the sense that they spell out what meaningful work ought to be. There is no requirement that workers who are provided meaningful work must themselves subjectively experience it as meaningful.)

A manager taking the Kantian approach to business ethics would regard providing meaningful work as a moral obligation. Some management attitudes and practices are more conducive toward meeting this obligation than others. Thus, Kantian managers need to create a certain kind of organization. A discussion of what a Kantian business firm would look like leads directly to a discussion of the third formulation of the categorical imperative.

THE BUSINESS FIRM AS A MORAL COMMUNITY

Kant's third formulation of the categorical imperative roughly says that you should act as if you were a member of an ideal kingdom of ends in which you were both subject and sovereign at the same time. Organizations are composed of persons and, given the nature of persons, organizational structures must treat the humanity in persons with dignity and respect (as an end). Moreover, the rules that govern an organization must be rules that can be endorsed by everyone in the organization. This universal endorsement by rational persons is what enables Kant to say that everyone is both subject and sovereign with respect to the rules that govern them. I believe a Kantian approach to the organizational design of a business firm would endorse these principles:

1. The business firm should consider the interests of all the affected stakeholders in any decision it makes.
2. The firm should have those affected by the firm's rules and policies participate in the determination of those rules and policies before they are implemented.
3. It should not be the case that, for all decisions, the interests of one stakeholder automatically take priority.
4. When a situation arises where it appears that the interest of one set of stakeholders must be subordinated to the interests of another set of stakeholders, that decision should not be made solely on the grounds that there is a greater number of stakeholders in one group than in another.
5. No business rule or practice can be adopted which is inconsistent with the first two formulations of the categorical imperative.
6. Every profit-making firm has a limited, but genuine, duty of beneficence.
7. Every business firm must establish procedures designed to ensure that relations among stakeholders are governed by rules of justice.

I think the rationale for most of these principles can be derived from the explanation of Kant's ethics already provided. Principle 1 seems like a straightforward requirement for any moral theory that takes respect for persons seriously. Since autonomy is what makes humans worthy of respect, a commitment to principle 2 is required. Principle 3 provides a kind of organizational legitimacy; it ensures that those involved in the firm receive some minimum benefits from being a part of it. Principle 4 rules out utilitarianism as a criterion for decision-making in the moral firm. The justification for principle 6 is based on an extension of the individual's imperfect obligation of beneficence which Kant defended in the Metaphysics of Morals. There Kant (1994, p. 52) says:

> That beneficence is a duty results from the fact that since our self-love cannot be separated from our need to be loved by others (to obtain help from them in the case of need), we thereby make ourselves an end for others . . . hence the happiness of others is an end which is at the same time a duty.

The strategy here is to extend this argument to the corporate level. If corporations have benefited from society, they have a duty of beneficence to society in return. And corporations have benefited. Society protects corporations by providing the means for enforcing business contracts. It provides the infrastructure which allows the corporation to function—such as roads, sanitation facilities, police and fire protection—and, perhaps most importantly, an educated work force with both the skills and attitudes required to perform well in a corporate setting. Few would argue that corporate taxes pay the full cost of these benefits. Finally, principle 7 is a procedural principle designed to ensure that whatever rules the corporation adopts conform to the basic principles of justice.

A Kantian views an organization as a moral community. Each member of the organization stands in a moral relationship to all the others. On one hand, the managers of a business firm should respect the humanity in all the persons in the organization. On the other hand, each individual in a business firm, managed as a Kantian moral community, should view the organization other than purely instrumentally, that is, as merely a means for achieving individual goals. Organizations are created as ways of achieving common goals and shared ends. An individual who views the organization purely instrumentally is acting contrary to the "respect for persons" principle.

A manager who adopts the Kantian principles of a moral firm must also look at human nature in a certain way. In management terms, the theory Y view of human nature must be adopted rather than a theory X views. [The distinction between theory X and theory Y was made prominent by McGregor (1960).] Theory X assumed that people had an inherent dislike of work and would avoid it if possible. It also assumed that the average person seeks to avoid responsibility. Theory Y assumes the opposite: that employees prefer to act imaginatively and creatively and are willing to assume responsibility. Although we can debate about which theory is descriptively more accurate, as a normative matter a Kantian manager should adopt theory Y. For it is theory Y that views human beings as having the dignity Kant thinks they deserve.

Moreover, both theory X and theory Y have the tendency to become self-fulfilling prophecies. By that I mean that people will tend to behave as they are treated. If a manager treats people in accordance with theory X, employees will tend to behave as theory X predicts. Conversely with theory Y. Thus the question becomes what kind of organization should the manager and the employees, working together, create. For the Kantian, the answer is clear. People should try to create an organization where the participants in the organization behave as theory Y would predict. People should seek to create an organization where members develop their rational and moral capacities, including the capacity to take responsibility.

One of the chief implications of Kant's ethics is that it acts as a moral critique of authoritarian hierarchical organizational structures. Principle 2 demands participation in some form by all the corporate stakeholders, especially stockholders and employees. A Kantian would morally object to a hierarchical structure that requires those lower down to carry out the orders of those above, more or less without question.

Kantian moral theory also requires worker participation: indeed, it requires a vast democratization of the work place. Certainly, a necessary condition of autonomy is consent given under non-coercive and non-deceptive conditions. Consent also requires that the individuals in an organization endorse the rules that govern them. As a minimum condition of democratization, Kantian moral philosophy requires that each person in an organization be represented by the stakeholder group to which he or she belongs, and that these various stakeholder groups must consent to the rules and policies which govern the organization.

This requirement for a more democratic work place is not purely utopian: it has some support in management theory and in management practice. Teamwork is almost universally praised, and several corporations have endorsed varieties of the concept of participitative management. Levi Strauss and Singapore Airlines, to name just two examples, have democratic work places.

I hope I have convinced the reader that Kant's moral philosophy has rich implications for business practice. When the three formulations of the categorical imperative are considered together as a coherent whole, they provide guidance to the manager, both in terms of negative injunctions and positive ideals. The negative injunctions prohibit actions like contract breaking, theft, deception, and coercion. The positive ideals include a more democratic work place and a commitment toward meaningful work.

However Kantian ethics is not without its limitations and challenges. Kant had nothing to say about environmental ethics and had little understanding of the suffering of animals and thus held a truncated view of our obligations to animals. But the biggest challenge to the Kantian ethic is that the Kantian ethic is too demanding. Let us consider that objection at greater length.

THE PURITY OF MOTIVE

It is a central tenet of Kant's moral philosophy that an action is only truly moral if it is morally motivated. Truly moral actions cannot be contaminated by motives of self-interest. Since the good acts of even the most enlightened corporations are almost always justified in part on the grounds that such actions are profitable, it appears that even the best actions of the best corporations are not truly moral. Consider the following quotation from J. W. Marriott Jr. (Milbank, 1996, p. A1) describing the decision of the Marriott Corporation to hire welfare recipients.

> We're getting good employees for the long term but we're also helping these communities. If we don't step up in these inner cities and provide work, they'll never pull out of it. But it makes bottom line sense. If it didn't we wouldn't do it.

A strict Kantian could not call Marriott's act of hiring welfare recipients a good act. In Kantian language, the act would be done in conformity with duty but not out of duty. But doesn't that make Kant's theory too austere to apply to business? Several things can be said in response to this question.

We might say that Kant is mistaken about requiring such purity of motive. Yet even if Kant is wrong about the necessity of pure motivation for an act's being moral, he still has a lot to offer the business ethicist. Working out the implications of the three formulations of the categorical imperative provides a rich agenda for the business ethicist. However, a bit more should be said, especially in light of the fact that the general public judges business from a strict Kantian position.

In discussing the issue, people seem to assume that actions that enhance the bottom line are acts of self-interest on the part of the corporation. However, for publicly held corporations and for partnerships, this is not the case. Publicly held corporations have an obligation to make a profit based on their charters of incorporation, legal obligations to shareholders, and an implied contract with the public. It would not be stretching a point too far to say that the managers of a publicly held corporation have promised to strive for profits. If that is so, the position of the Marriott Corporation is a moral one, even for the strict Kantian. The Marriott Corporation is honoring its obligation to realize profits and its obligation of beneficence. Thus, Kant's insistence that an action must be done from a truly moral motive need not undercut acts of corporate beneficence that also contribute to the bottom line.

So far all we have shown is that Kant's insistence on the purity of a moral motive has not made his theory irrelevant to business ethics. But perhaps his insistence on the purity of the moral motive has a positive contribution to make to business ethics and is not simply a barrier to be overcome. Perhaps focusing on issues other than profits, such as meaningful work for employees, a democratic work place, non-deceptive advertising, and a non-coercive relationship with suppliers will actually enhance the bottom line. Many management theorists urge businesses to always focus on the bottom line. However, perhaps paradoxically, profits can be enhanced if we do not focus so exclusively on the bottom line. To put this in more Kantian terms, perhaps profits will be enhanced if the manager focuses on respecting the humanity in the person of all the corporate stakeholders. Perhaps we should view profits as a consequence of good business practices rather than as the goal of business. . . .

References

Bowie, N.E., *Business Ethics: A Kantian Perspective* (Oxford: Blackwell Publishers, 1999).

Case, J. *Open Book Management* (New York: Harper Collins Publishers, 1995).

Kant, I. *Foundations of the Metaphysics of Morals* (1785). Trans. by Lewis White Beck (New York: Macmillan Publishing Company, 1990).

Kant, I. *The Metaphysics of Moral: The Metaphysical Principles of Virtue* (1797). In I. Kant, *Ethical Philosophy*, 2nd ed. Trans. by James W. Ellington (Indianapolis/Cambridge, MA: Hackett Publishing Company, 1994).

Korsgaard, C. *Creating the Kingdom of Ends* (New York: Cambridge University Press, 1996).

McGregor, D. *The Human Side of Enterprise* (New York: McGraw Hill Book Company, 1960).

Millbank, D. "Hiring welfare people, hotel chain finds, is tough but rewarding," *The Wall Street Journal*, October 31, 1996.

Corporate Roles, Personal Virtues: An Aristotelean Approach to Business Ethics

ROBERT C. SOLOMON

Each of us is ultimately lonely. In the end, it's up to each of us and each of us alone to figure out who we are and who we are not, and to act more or less consistently on those conclusions.

TOM PETERS, "The Ethical Debate,"
Ethics Digest, December 1989, p. 2.

THE ARISTOTELEAN APPROACH TO BUSINESS ETHICS

Economists and economic theorists naturally tend to look at systems and theories about systems, while ethicists tend to look at individual behavior, its motives and consequences. Neither of these approaches is suitable for business

Reprinted by permission of the author, Robert C. Solomon, University of Texas at Austin, and *Business Ethics Quarterly, The Journal of the Society for Business Ethics*, July 1992, vol. 2.

ethics. One of the problems in business ethics, accordingly, is the scope and focus of the disciplines and the proper unit of study and discourse. Much of the work in business ethics courses and seminars centers around "case studies," which almost always involve one or several particular people within the realm of a particular corporation in a particular industry facing some particular crisis or dilemma. Individual ethical values are, of course, relevant here, but they are rarely the focus of attention. Economics, of course, is essential to the discussion—since the realm of the corporation is, after all, a business, but the desire to show a profit is virtually taken for granted while our attention is drawn to other values. Insofar as business ethics theories tend to be drawn from either individualistic ethics or economics they remain remote from the case study method which often seems so inadequate with regard to more general implications and conclusions in business and why business ethics theory lags so far behind theory in both ethics and economics. In this paper, I want to begin to develop a more appropriate focus for business ethics theory, one that centers on the individual within the corporation. For reasons that should be evident to anyone who has had the standard Philosophy 102 History of Ethics course, I call this the Aristotelean Approach to Business Ethics. . . .

Aristotle is the philosopher who is best known for this emphasis on the cultivation of the virtues. But isn't it inappropriate if not perverse to couple Aristotle and business ethics? True, he was the first economist. He had much to say about the ethics of exchange and so might well be called the first (known) business ethicist as well. But Aristotle distinguished two different senses of what I call economics, one of them "*oecinomicus*" or household trading, which he approved of and thought essential to the working of any even modestly complex society, and "*chrematisike*," which is trade for profit. Aristotle declared that latter activity wholly devoid of virtue and called those who engaged in such purely selfish practices "parasites." All trade, he believed, was a kind of exploitation. Such was his view of what I call "business." Indeed, Aristotle's attack on the unsavory and unproductive practice of "usury" and the personal vice of avarice held force virtually until the seventeenth century. Only outsiders at the fringe of society, not respectable citizens, engaged in such practices. (Shakespeare's Shylock, in *The Merchant of Venice*, was such an outsider and a usurer, though his idea of a forfeit was a bit unusual.) It can be argued that Aristotle had too little sense of the importance of production and based his views wholly on the aristocratically proper urge for acquisition, thus introducing an unwarranted zero-sum thinking into his economics.[1] And, of course, it can be charged that Aristotle, like his teacher Plato, was too much the spokesman for the aristocratic class and quite unfair to the commerce and livelihoods of foreigners and commoners.[2] It is Aristotle who initiates so much of the history of business ethics as the wholesale attack on business and its practices. Aristotelean prejudices underlie much of business criticism and the contempt for finance that preoccupies so much of Christian ethics even to this day, avaricious evangelicals notwithstanding. Even defenders of business often end up presupposing Aristotelean prejudices in such Pyrrhonian arguments as "business is akin to poker and apart from the ethics of everyday life."[3] (Albert Carr) and "the [only] social responsibility of business is to increase its profits" (Milton Friedman).[4] But if it is just this schism between business and the rest of life that so infuriated Aristotle, for whom life was

supposed to fit together, in a coherent whole, it is the same holistic idea—
that business people and corporations are first of all part of a larger community—that drives business ethics today. I can no longer accept the amoral
idea that "business is business" (not a tautology but an excuse for insensi-
tivity). According to Aristotle, one has to think of oneself as a member of
the larger community, the *Polis*, and strive to excel, to bring out what was
best in ourselves and our shared enterprise. What is best in us—our
virtues—are in turn defined by that larger community, and there is therefore no ultimate split of antagonism between individual self-interest and the
greater public good. Of course, there were no corporations in those days,
but Aristotle would certainly know what I mean when I say that most people in business now identify themselves—if tenuously—in terms of their
companies, and corporate policies, much less corporate codes of ethics, are
not by themselves enough to constitute an ethics. But corporations are not
isolated city-states, not even the biggest and most powerful of the multinationals (contrast the image of "the sovereign state of ITT"). They are part
and parcel of a larger global community. The people that work for them are
thus citizens of two communities at once, and one might think of business
ethics as getting straight about the dual citizenship. What I need to cultivate
is a certain way of thinking about ourselves in and out of the corporate context, and this is the aim of ethical theory in business, as I understand it. It
is not, I insist, anti-individualistic in any sense of "individualism" that is
worth defending. The Aristotelean approach to business ethics rather begins
with the idea that it is individual virtue and integrity that counts: good corporate and social policy will follow: good corporate and social policy are both
the preconditions and the result of careful cultivation and encouragement.

With what is this Aristotelean approach to be contrasted? . . .

It is to be contrasted with that two hundred or so year old obsession in
ethics that takes everything of significance to be a matter of *rational principles*, "morality" as the strict Kantian sense of duty to the moral law. This is
not to say, of course, that Aristotelean ethics dispenses with rationality, or
for that matter with principles or the notion of duty. But Aristotle is quite
clear about the fact that it is cultivation of character that counts, long before we begin to "rationalize" our actions, and the formulation of general
principles (in what he famously but confusingly calls his "practical syllo-
gism") is not an explicit step in correct and virtuous behavior as such but
rather a philosopher's formulation about what it means to act rationally.[5]
And, most important for our purposes here, duties too are defined by our
roles in a community, e.g., a corporation, and not by means of any abstract
ratiocination, principle of contradiction, or *a priori* formulations of the categorical imperative. Kant, magnificent as he was a thinker, has proved to be
a kind of disease in ethics. It's all very elegant, even brilliant, until one walks
into the seminar room with a dozen or so bright, restless corporate managers, waiting to hear what's new and what's relevant to them on the business ethics scene. And then we tell them: don't lie, don't steal, don't
cheat—elaborated and supported by the most gothic non-econometric construction ever allowed in a company training center. But it's not just its impracticality and the fact that we don't actually do ethics that way; the problem
is that the Kantian approach shifts our attention away from just what I would

call the "inspirational" matters of business ethics (its "incentives") and the emphasis on "excellence" (a buzz-word for Aristotle as well as Tom Peters and his millions of readers). It shifts the critical focus from oneself as a full-blooded person occupying a significant role in a productive organization to an abstract role-transcendent morality that necessarily finds itself empty-handed when it comes to most of the matters and many of the motives that we hear so much about in any corporate setting.

The Aristotelean approach is also to be contrasted with that rival ethical theory that goes by the name of "utilitarianism." I have considerably more to say about utilitarianism, its continued vulgarization and its forgotten humanistic focus in John Stuart Mill, but not here. For now, I just want to point out that utilitarianism shares with Kant that special appeal to anal compulsives in its doting over principles and rationalization (in crass calculation) and its neglect of individual responsibility and the cultivation of character. (John Stuart Mill exempted himself from much of this charge in the last chapter of *Utilitarianism,* but I promised not to talk about that here.) But I can imagine a good existentialist complaining quite rightly that the point of all such "decision procedures" in ethics is precisely to neutralize the annoyance of personal responsibility altogether, appealing every decision to "the procedure" rather than taking responsibility oneself. Of course, I am not denying the importance of concern for the public good or the centrality of worrying, in any major policy decision, about the number of people helped and hurt. But I take very seriously the problems of measurement and incommensurability that have been standard criticisms of utilitarianism ever since Bentham, and there are considerations that often are more basic than public utility—if only because, in most of our actions, the impact on public utility is so small in contrast to the significance for our personal sense of integrity and "doing the right thing" that it becomes a negligible factor in our deliberations.

I would also distinguish the Aristotelean approach to business ethics from all of those approaches that primarily emphasize rights, whether the rights of free enterprise as such, the rights of the employee, the customer or the community and even civil rights. Again, I have no wish to deny the relevance of rights to ethics or the centrality of civil rights, but I think that we should remind ourselves that talk about rights was never intended to eclipse talk about responsibilities and I think the emphasis in business ethics should move from *having* rights oneself to *recognizing* the rights of others, but then, I'm not at all sure that all of this couldn't just as well or better be expressed by saying that there are all sorts of things that a virtuous person should or shouldn't ever do to others.[6] Of course, Aristotle's defense of slavery in his *Politics* should be more than enough to convince us that we would still need the language of rights even with a fully developed language of the virtues. The problem with virtue ethics is that it tends to be provincial and ethnocentric. It thereby requires the language of rights and some general sense of utility as a corrective.

It will be evident to most of you that I am arguing—or about to argue—for a version of what has recently been called "virtue ethics," but I do want to distance myself from much of what has been defended recently under that title. . . .

THE SIX DIMENSIONS OF VIRTUE ETHICS

So what defines the Aristotelean approach to business ethics? What are its primary dimensions? There is a great deal of ground to be covered, from the general philosophical questions "what is a virtue?" and "what is the role of the virtues in ethics and the good life?" to quite specific questions about virtues and supposed virtues in business, such as loyalty, dependability, integrity, shrewdness and "toughness." But I can only begin to answer these general questions or speak much of these particular virtues here, but what I want to do first is to very briefly circumscribe the discussion of the virtues in business ethics with a half dozen considerations not usually so highlighted in the more abstract and principle-bound discussions of ethics nor so personalized in the policy discussions that so dominate the field. Those six considerations make up the framework of virtue ethics in business, and for the sake of brevity I simply call them: *community, excellence, role identity, holism, integrity, judgment.*

Community

The Aristotelean approach and, I would argue, the leading question for business in the nineties begins with the idea that the corporation is first of all a community. We are all individuals, to be sure, but we find our identities and our meanings only within communities, and for most of us that means—at work in a company or an institution. The philosophical myth that has grown almost cancerous in many business circles, the neo-Hobbesian view that "it's every man[sic] for himself" and the newer Darwinian view that "it's all a jungle out there" are direct denials of the Aristotelean view that we are all *first of all* members of a community and our self-interest is for the most part identical to the larger interests of the group. Our individuality is socially constituted and socially situated. Furthermore, our seemingly all-important concept of competition presumes, it does not replace, an underlying assumption of mutual interest and cooperation. Whether we do well, whether we like ourselves, whether we lead happy productive lives, depends to a large extent on the companies we choose. As the Greeks used to say, "to live the good life one must live in a great city." To my business students today, who are all too prone to choose a job on the basis of salary and start-up bonus alone, I always say, "to live a decent life choose the right company." In business ethics the corporation is one's community, which is not to deny, of course, that there is always a larger community—as diverse as it may be—that counts even more.

Excellence

The Greek "*arete*" is often translated either "virtue" or "excellence," as opposed to the rather modest and self-effacing notion of "virtue" that we inherited from our Victorian ancestors (indeed, even Kant used the term). The dual translation by itself makes a striking point. It is not enough to do no wrong. "Knowingly do no harm" (*Primus non nocere*) is not the end of business ethics (as Peter Drucker suggests[7]). The hardly original slogan I sometimes use to sell what I do, "ethics and excellence" (the title of the book in which this essay finds its home) is not just a tag-along with Peters and Waterman. Virtue is doing one's best, excelling, and not merely "toeing the line" and "keeping one's nose clean." The virtues that constitute business ethics should not be conceived as purely ethical or moral virtues, as if (to come again) business ethics were nothing other than the general application of moral principles to one specific context (among others). Being a "tough negotiator" is a virtue in business but not in babysitting. It does not follow, however, that the virtues of business are therefore opposed to the ordinary virtues of civilized life—as Albert Carr famously argued in his *Harvard Business Review* polemic of several years ago. The virtues of business ethics are business virtues but they are nonetheless virtues, and the exercise of these virtues is aimed at both "the bottom line" and ethics.

Role Identity

Much has been written, for example, by Norman Bowie in his good little book *Business Ethics*, on the importance of "role morality" and "My Position and its Duties."[8] It is the situatedness of corporate roles that lends them their particular ethical poignancy, the fact that an employee or an executive is not just a person who happens to be in a place and is constrained by no more than the usual ethical prohibitions. To work for a company is to accept a set of particular obligations, to assume a prima facie loyalty to one's employer, to adopt a certain standard of excellence and conscientiousness that is largely defined by the job itself. There may be general ethical rules and guidelines that cut across most positions but as these get more general and more broadly applicable they also become all but useless in concrete ethical dilemmas. Robert Townsend's cute comment that "if a company needs an ethical code, use the Ten Commandments" is thus not only irreverent but irrelevant too.[9] The Aristotelean approach to business ethics presumes concrete situations and particular people and their place in organizations. There is little point to an ethics that tries to transcend all such particularities and embrace the chairman of the board as well as a middle manager, a secretary and a factory worker. All ethics is contextual, and one of the problems with all of those grand theories is that they try to transcend context and end up with vacuity. The problem, of course, is that people in business inevitably play several roles ("wear several hats") at once, and these roles may clash with one another as they may clash with more personal roles based on family, friendship and personal obligation. This, I will argue, is the pervasive problem in micro-business ethics, and it is the legitimacy of roles and their responsibilities, and the structures of the corporation that defines those roles and their responsibilities, that ought to occupy a good deal more of our time and attention.

Integrity

Integrity, accordingly, in the key to Aristotelean ethics, not, perhaps, as a virtue as such but rather as the linchpin of all of the virtues, the key to their unity or, in conflict and disunity, an anchor against personal disintegration. "Integrity" is a word, like "honor"—its close kin—that sometimes seems all but archaic in the modern business world. To all too many business executives, it suggests stubbornness and inflexibility, a refusal to be a "team player." But integrity seems to have at least two divergent meanings, one of them encouraging conformity, the other urging a belligerent independence.[10] Both of these are extreme and potentially dangerous. The very word suggests "wholeness," but insofar as one's identity is not that of an isolated atom but rather the product of a larger social molecule, that wholeness includes—rather than excludes—other people and one's social roles. A person's integrity on the job typically requires him or her to follow the rules and practices that define that job, rather than allow oneself to be swayed by distractions and contrary temptations. And yet, critical encounters sometimes require a show of integrity that is indeed antithetical to one's assigned role and duties. At that point some virtues, notably moral courage, become definitive and others, e.g. loyalty, may be jettisoned. (In other cases, of course, it is loyalty that might require moral courage.) But in harmony or in conflict, integrity represents the integration of one's roles and responsibilities and the virtues defined by them.

Judgment (Phronesis)

The fact that our roles conflict and there are often no singular principles to help us decide on an ethical course of action shifts the emphasis away from our calculative and ratiocinative faculties and back towards an older, often ignored faculty called "judgment." Against the view that ethics consists primarily of general principles that get applied to particular situations, Aristotle thought that it was "good judgment" or *phronesis* that was of the greatest importance in ethics. Good judgment (which centered on "perception" rather than the abstract formulation and interpretation of general principles) was the product of a good up-bringing, a proper education. It was always situated, perhaps something like Joseph Fletcher's still much referred-to notion of a "situation ethics," and took into careful account the particularity of the persons and circumstances involved. But I think the real importance of *phronesis* is not just its priority to ethical deliberation and ratiocination; it has rather to do with the inevitable conflicts of both concerns and principles that define almost every ethical dilemma. Justice, for example, may sound (especially in some philosophers) as if it were a monolithic or hierarchically layered and almost mechanical process. But, as I have argued elsewhere, there are a dozen or more different considerations that enter into most deliberations about justice, including not only rights and prior obligations and the public good but questions of merit (which themselves break down into a variety of sometimes conflicting categories) and responsibility and risk.[11] I won't go into this here but the point is that there is *no* (non-arbitrary) mechanical decision procedure for resolving most disputes about justice, and what is required, in each and every particular case, is the ability to balance and weigh competing concerns and come to a "fair" conclusion. But what's fair is not the outcome of one or several pre-ordained principles of justice; it is (as they say) a "judgment call," always disputable but nevertheless well or badly made. I have often thought that encouraging abstract ethical theory actually discourages and distracts us from the need to make judgments. I have actually heard one of my colleagues say (without qualms) that, since he's been studying ethical theory, he no longer has any sense of ethics. And if this sounds implausible, I urge you to remember your last department or faculty senate meeting, and the inverse relationship between high moral tone of the conversation and ridiculousness of the proposals and decisions that followed.

Holism

It more or less follows from what I've said above that one of the problems of traditional business thinking is our tendency to isolate our business or professional roles from the rest of our lives, a process that Marx, following Schiller, described as "alienation." The good life may have many facets, but they are facets and not mere components, much less isolated aspects despite the tiresome emphasis on tasks, techniques and "objectives," that a manager's primary and ultimate concern is *people*. It's gotten trite, but as I watch our more ambitious students and talk with more and more semi-successful but "trapped" middle managers and executives, I become more and more convinced that the tunnel-vision of business life encouraged by the too narrow business curriculum and the daily rhetoric of the corporate community is damaging and counter-productive. Good employees are good people, and to pretend that the virtues of business stand isolated from the virtues of the rest of our lives—and this is not for a moment to deny the particularity of either our business roles or our lives—is to set up that familiar tragedy in which a pressured employee violates his or her "personal values" because, from a purely business point of view, he or she "didn't really have any choice." It is the integration of our roles—or at least their harmonization—that is our ideal here, and that integration should not be construed as either the personal yielding to the corporate or the corporate giving in to the personal. The name of that integration is ethics, construed in an Aristotelean way.

BUSINESS AND THE VIRTUES

Business ethics is too often conceived as a set of impositions and constraints, obstacles to business behavior rather than the motivating force of that behavior. So conceived, it is no surprise that many people in business look upon ethics and ethicists with suspicion, as antagonistic if not antithetical to their enterprise. But properly understood, ethics does not and should not consist of a set of prohibitive principles or rules, and it is the virtue of an ethics of virtue to be rather an intrinsic part and the driving force of a successful life well lived. Its motivation need not depend on elaborate soul searching and deliberation but in the best companies moves along with the easy flow of interpersonal relations and a mutual sense of mission and accomplishment.

"The virtues" is a short-hand way of summarizing the ideals that define good character. There are a great many virtues that are relevant to business life; in fact, it would be a daunting task to try to even list them all. Just for a start, we have honesty, loyalty, sincerity, courage, reliability, trustworthiness, benevolence, sensitivity, helpfulness, cooperativeness, civility, decency, modesty, openness, cheerfulness, amiability, tolerance, reasonableness, tactfulness, wittiness, gracefulness, liveliness, magnanimity, persistence, prudence, resourcefulness, cool-headedness, warmth and hospitality.[12] Each of these has subtle sub-traits and related virtues, and there are a great many virtues of strength, energy and skill as well as attractiveness, charm and aesthetic appeal that I have not yet mentioned. There are "negative" virtues, that is, virtues that specify the absence of some annoying, inefficient or anti-social trait, such as non-negligence, non-vengefulness, non-vindictiveness and non-pretentiousness, and there are virtues of excess and superiority, such as super-conscientiousness and super-reliability. Then there are those virtues that seem peculiar (though not unique) to business, such as being shrewd and ruthless and "tough," which may well be vices in other aspects of life.

From the variety of virtues, one of the most important conclusions to be drawn immediately is the impoverished nature of ethical language when it limits itself to such terms as "good" and "bad," "right" and "wrong." To be sure, most of the virtues are "good" and lead to "right" action, and most of the contrary vices are "bad" and lead to "wrong"-doing. But not only does such ethical language lead us to ignore most of what is significant and subtle in our ordinary ethical judgments, it tends to lead us away from just that focus on personal character that is most essential to most of our interpersonal decisions, whether it is to trust a colleague, make a new friend, hire or fire a new assistant, respect a superior or invite the boss over to the house for dinner. Ethics is not the study of right and wrong, anymore than art and aesthetics are the study of beauty and ugliness.[13] Ethics (like art and aesthetics) is a colorful, multifaceted appreciation and engagement with other people in the world. In business ethics, it is only the extreme and sinister misdeed that we label simply "wrong"; more often, we invoke an artist's palette of imaginative descriptions such as "sleazy" and "slimy." Even the phrase "good character" (or "good person") strikes us as uninteresting and vacuous; it is the details that count, not the gloss. And there are many, many details, any of which might become more or less significant in some particular situation.

A virtue, according to Aristotle, is an excellence. It is not, however, a very specialized skill or talent (like being good with numbers or a brilliant researcher) but an exemplary way of getting along with other people, a way of manifesting in one's own thoughts, feelings and actions the ideals and aims of the entire community. Thus honesty is a virtue not because it is a skill necessary for any particular endeavor or because it represents the ideal of straight dealing, fair play, common knowledge and open inquiry. What is public is probably approved of and what is hidden is probably dangerous. So, too, courage is a virtue not just because it requires a special talent or because "somebody's got to do it" but because we all believe (with varying degrees of commitment) that a person should stand up for what he or she cares about and what he or she believes in. But not all virtues need to be so serious or so central to our idea of integrity. Aristotle listed charm, wit and a good sense of humor as virtues, and with corporate life in particular I think that we would probably agree. To be sure, the circumstances in which congeniality is a central virtue and in which courage becomes cardinal will be very different, but it is a troubled organization that requires the more heroic virtues all the time and does not have the relative security and leisure to enjoy those virtues that make life worthwhile rather than those that are necessary for mere survival. Indeed, part of the folly of the familiar military, machine and jungle metaphors in business is that they all make business life out to be something threatening and relentless. But the truth (even in the military and in the jungle) is that there are long and sometimes relaxed respites and a need for play and playfulness as well as diligence. There is welcome camaraderie and the virtues of "getting along" are just as important to group survival as the coordination needed for fighting together.

There are reasons why we want to survive—apart from sheer Darwinian obstinacy—and the fact that we relish and enjoy the social harmony of our life and our jobs is one of them. One of the most powerful but most ignored arguments against hostile takeovers and unfriendly mergers is the desire on the part of the members of a corporate community to maintain that community, and this is not the same as executives "fighting to keep their jobs." . . .

If business life was like the brutal and heroic world of Homer's *Iliad*, corporations in mortal conflict with one another, we would expect the business virtues to be those warrior virtues most closely associated with combat, not only strength and prowess but courage, imperviousness to pain or pity, frightfulness (that is, causing fright in others, not being frightened oneself). We would expect the warrior to have an appropriately insensitive personality, rather clumsy social habits, and an enormous ego. Not surprising, these are precisely the virtues often praised and attributed to top business executives, summarized (badly) in the single word, "toughness." But, of course, warrior metaphors depend on a war-like situation, but business ethicists have taken considerable pains to dismiss that picture of corporate business life as pathological and misleading. Most CEOs, however "tough," do not fit this picture at all. Consider, instead, a very different and usually more representative picture of the corporation, the corporation as a wealthy and prosperous "polis," a free and sophisticated city-state with considerable pride in its products, philosophy, and corporate culture. There will still be external threats and an occasional battle, but this is not the day-to-day concern of the community. Courage might still be an important virtue, but most of the other warrior virtues and the typical characteristics of the warrior personality will seem boorish and bullish, inappropriate in most social settings and downright embarrassing in some. The virtues, in such a society, will tend to be the genteel, congenial virtues, those which lubricate a rich, pleasant social life. And these will be just as applicable to the CEO as to the boy at the loading dock or the teller at the check-out window. . . .

One might insist, just to waylay the argument I seem to be developing here, that warrior virtues, congeniality (Aristotelean) virtues and moral virtues are in fact quite compatible, and there is no reason why a James Burke or a Warren Buffett, for example, can't display warrior toughness, Aristotelean gentility and Christian righteousness. And indeed, this is the case. But my argument is not that three sets of virtues are incompatible as such, but rather that they present us with three quite distinct contexts and three different ethical frameworks, and to understand business ethics is to understand the confluence, the priorities and the potential conflicts between these. Excessive attention paid to a corporation may become a screaming alliance of desperation and one's personal sense of integrity can be threatened or fatally damaged. Excessive attention to the congenial virtues may in fact "soften" a company so that it becomes less competitive, and an exaggerated sense of righteousness to the detriment of congeniality and competitiveness may well cause a company to shatter into a thousand rigid little moralists, incapable of working together. But the Aristotelean framework tells us that it is cooperation and not an isolated individual sense of self-worth that defines the most important virtues, in which the warrior virtues play an essential but diminished role, in which the well-being of the community goes hand in hand with individual excellence, not by virtue of any "invisible hand" but precisely because of the social consciousness and public spirit of each and every individual.

Almost all of Aristotle's virtues are recognizable as business virtues, and this is, of course, not surprising. Business is, above all, a social activity, involving dealing with other people in both stressful and friendly situations (and trying to make the former into the latter). Despite our emphasis on hard-headedness and the bottom line, we do not praise and often despise tight-fistedness and we do praise great-souled generosity ("magnificence"). But such virtues may be misleading for us. We would not praise an executive who "gave away the store"; we would rather think that executive mentally unhinged. But the virtues for Aristotle do not involve radical demands on our behavior, and the sort of fanaticism praised if not preached in many religions ("give away all of your worldly goods") is completely foreign to Aristotle's insistence on "moderation." Thus the generous or "magnificent" person gives away only as much of wealth as will increase his or her status in the community. Here we would encounter the familiar charge that such giving is not true generosity, for it involves no personal sacrifice and includes a "selfish" motive, the quest for self-aggrandizement. But Aristotle would refuse to recognize this opposition between enlightened self-interest and virtue, and we continue to enforce it at our peril. The argument here, of course, is exactly the skeptical argument leveled against generous corporations when they give to the arts, to education, to social welfare programs: "They're only doing it for the P.R." But here executives (and everyone else) would be wise to follow Aristotle and reject the notion that "true" generosity is self-sacrifice and self-benefiting generosity is only "P.R." There are occasions that call for self-sacrifice, but to insist that such extreme action is essential to the virtues is to deny the virtues their relevance to business (and most of) life.

This brings us to the perhaps most misunderstood virtue in business life, the virtue of *toughness*. The word "tough" is typically used by way of admiration, though often coupled with a shake of the head and an expression of frustration. Sometimes, it is used as a euphemism, in place of or in conjunction with various synonyms for a nasty or odious human being. Not infrequently, it simply means stubborn, impossible or mean-spirited. But toughness is generally and genuinely perceived as virtue, albeit a virtue that is often misplaced and misconceived. Insofar as business consists of bargaining and dealing with other people, toughness is essential, and its opposite is not so much weakness as incompetence. But much of what is called toughness is neither a virtue nor a vice. It is not a character trait so much as it is a skill, whether cultivated or "natural." In certain central business practices, notably negotiating, toughness is not so much a personal virtue as it is a technique or set of techniques, an acquired manner and an accomplished strategy, "knowing when to hold 'em, knowing when to fold 'em." Toughness includes knowing how to bluff and when to keep silent, when to be cooperative and when not to be. But such a skill is not, contra Carr, unethical or divorced from ordinary morals; it is a legitimate part of a certain kind of obviously legitimate activity. Yet, as a specific skill or set of skills, being a tough negotiator is not sufficiently personal or general to count as a virtue, which is not to say, of course, that it is not therefore admirable or necessary. . . .

Toughness in an executive also has an ethically painful element. Sometimes it is necessary to do something wrong in order to do what is right. Powerful politicians, of course, face such dilemmas all of the time, giving rise to a substantial literature on the controversial virtues of toughness and "ruthlessness" and the allegedly opposed domains of public and private morality.[14] Sometimes, to reach a higher goal, one must do what one otherwise would not and should not even consider. For example, in the face of debts or deficiencies that will very likely capsize the company, a chairman may need to let go perfectly qualified, hard-working loyal employees. Viewed as an action isolated from the circumstances, letting people go for no reason whatever, that is, for no fault of their own, would be the height of injustice. But if it is a matter of saving the company, then this otherwise unjust act may nevertheless be necessary. Toughness is being able and willing to undertake such measures. This is not to say, however—and this cannot be emphasized enough—that such decisions can or should be made without guilt or pain or bad feelings. It does not mean that what one has done is not, despite its necessity, wrong. The chief executive of a large corporation once told me that "down-sizing" his company was the most painful thing he had ever had to do. His toughness lay not in callousness or indifference but in his willingness to do what was necessary and in his insistence on doing it as humanely as possible. Indeed, callousness and indifference are not themselves signs of toughness but the very opposite, indications of that form of weakness that can face moral issues only by denying them. Toughness is a virtue, but callousness and indifference are not, and the two should never be confused. . . .

THE BOTTOM LINE (CONCLUSION)

The bottom line of the Aristotelean approach to business ethics is that we have to get away from both traditional individualistic ethics and "bottom line" thinking. This does not in any way imply that the individual "checks his or her values at the office door" nor does it suggest that, except in the unusual and unfortunate case, there will be any thoroughgoing disharmony or incompatibility between one's personal and professional values. Quite to the contrary, the point of what I am arguing is that we are, as Aristotle famously insisted, social creatures who get our identity from our communities and measure our worth accordingly. And as much as many employees may feel the need to divorce themselves from their work and pretend that what they "do" is not indicative of their true selves, the truth is that most adults spend literally half of their waking adult life on the job, in the office, in the role or position that defines them as a citizen of the corporation. The Aristotelean approach to business ethics ultimately comes down to the idea that, while business life has its specific goals and distinctive practices and people in business have their particular concerns, loyalties, roles and responsibilities, there is no "business world" apart from the people who work in business and the integrity of those people determines the integrity of the organization as well as vice versa. The Aristotelean approach to business ethics is, perhaps, just another way of saying that people come before profits.

Notes

Earlier versions of this essay were presented at a number of conferences, the Ruffin conference at the University of Virginia, the Applied Ethics conference at the University of British Columbia, and (with Nick Imparato) the International Association of Business and Society conference in Sundance, Utah, the Center of Ethics conference at the University of Melbourne. Some parts of this essay have been published in some of the proceedings of those conferences, and I have benefited from comments and criticism from my colleagues there, most notably, from Patricia Werhane, Peter French, R. Edward Freeman, and Tony Coady. Parts of this essay also appear in my book, *Ethics and Excellence* (Oxford, UK: Oxford University Press, 1992).

1. Anthony Flew, "The Profit Motive," in *Ethics*, vol. 86 (July 1976), pp. 312–22.
2. Manuel Velasquez, comment on Joanne Ciulla, Ruffin lectures, 1989.
3. Albert Carr, "Is Business Bluffing Ethical?" *Harvard Business Review* (Jan.–Feb. 1968).
4. Milton Friedman, "The Social Responsibility of Business Is to Increase Its Profits," *New York Times Magazine* (1971).
5. This has been the topic of considerable debate. See, notably, G. E. M. Anscombe, *Intention*, Cambridge University Press, 1957 and John Cooper, *Reason and Human Good in Aristotle* (Cambridge, 1975).
6. Elizabeth Wolgast, *A Grammar of Justice* (Ithaca, NY: Cornell University Press, 1989).
7. Peter Drucker, *Management* (New York: Harper and Row, 1973), pp. 366f.
8. Norman Bowie, *Business Ethics* (Englewood Cliffs, NJ: Prentice-Hall, 1982), pp. 1–16.
9. Robert Townsend, *Up the Organization* (New York: Knopf, 1970).
10. Lynne McFall, "Integrity," *Ethics* Vol. 98, p. 5 (October 1987).
11. Robert C. Solomon, *A Passion for Justice* (New York: Addison-Wesley, 1989), Chapter 2.
12. A complex taxonomy of the virtues is in Edmund Pincoffs, *Quandries and Virtues* (University of Press Kansas, 1986), p. 84.
13. See Frithjof Bergmann, "The Experience of Values," in S. Hauerwas and A. MacIntyre, eds., *Revisions* (South Bend, IN: Notre Dame University Press, 1983), pp. 127–59.
14. See, for example, Stuart Hampshire, ed., *Public and Private Morality* (Cambridge, UK: Cambridge University Press, 1978) and Stuart Hampshire, *Innocence and Experience* (Cambridge, MA: Harvard University Press, 1989). See also Bernard Williams, "Politics and Moral Character" in *Moral Luck* (Cambridge, UK; Cambridge University Press, 1981) and Thomas Nagel, "Ruthlessness in Public Life" in Stuart Hampshire, *Public and Private Morality* (Cambridge, UK: Cambridge University Press, 1989).

Utilitarianism and Business Ethics

ANDREW GUSTAFSON

*... the creed which accepts as the foundation of morals, Utility, or the Greatest Happiness Principle, holds that actions are right in proportion as they tend **to promote happiness**, wrong as they tend to produce the reverse of happiness. By happiness is intended **pleasure**, and the absence of pain; by unhappiness, pain, and the privation of pleasure.*

Andrew Gustafson is an Associate Professor of Business Ethics and Society at the Creighton University School of Business. Used by permission of the author.

It would appear that business would be *the* arena most likely to appropriate Mill's utilitarian ethics. Utilitarianism is outcome-oriented, its goal is to bring about the greatest happiness—i.e., the greatest social benefit—something many companies would like to believe that they do promote alongside their goal of making a profit. In addition, those familiar with Herbert Simon's concept of 'satisficing' or the abundance of publications on 'happiness economics' may find that the earlier utilitarians have fruitful things to add to the discussion. Despite this alignment, strangely, there are only a few articles written attempting to apply utilitarianism as an ethical theory to business.[2]

What does utilitarianism have to say to business? Utilitarianism is often referred to casually and even in business literature as a method of making decisions which are essentially expedient and concerned with making the most money possible. But utilitarians actually have much more to offer business ethics than this. Utilitarians offer an ethical theory to business which helps calculate happiness, but does so with full awareness of the importance of sponsoring the higher sentiments. A society which does not support higher aspirations will become an animal-like society where the capacity for better levels of happiness become less possible. Business, it will be seen, can have some important power in preserving these higher capacities in society. Further, I will suggest some business decision-making questions rooted in utilitarianism. Our goal is a utilitarian business-ethic which evaluates business in terms of its contributions towards higher-pleasure capacities in society.

JEREMY BENTHAM

Jeremy Bentham, an eighteenth-century British philosopher and political reformer, was one of the early founders of utilitarianism. He frequently visited John Stuart Mill's house, as he was a close friend and confidant of James Mill, John Stuart Mill's father. Bentham was not religious, was very practical in his considerations, and thought that pleasure is the only good, and pain is the only evil—we seek pleasure, and avoid pain, because we believe this to be our good. His utilitarian ethics was based on a principle which all people in their hearts agreed to, namely, the greatest happiness principle. This utilitarian principle is simply that the right thing to do is to do whatever brings the most pleasure to the most people. We determine what to do by calculating what will bring the most pleasure, and avoid pain. Utilitarians argue that we must make our decisions based on what we forecast to be the most pleasurable and least painful outcome. This is why utilitarianism is referred to as a *consequentialist* theory, for consequences are what we consider in making a decision. It is also referred to as a *eudaimonianistic* theory, meaning that happiness is the ultimate goal of ethics—not merely sensual happiness from simple pleasures like eating an ice cream cone, but happiness which comes from staying healthy by jogging, or the reward of success after years of work on a project, or the satisfaction of a good marriage after years of fidelity. Since pleasure is the specific form of happiness which is sought after, it is also frequently referred to as a *hedonistic* theory, meaning that its goal is pleasure. Of course pleasure can come from many sources, including acquiring land, friendships, community, or even intellectual pursuits, as well as sheer sensual pleasures of taste, touch, and smell. For Bentham, there is

no hierarchy of pleasures, all are equal qualitatively, and it is up to us to calculate the quantitative pleasure-value of one act over another in making our
moral decisions. Bentham says that, if the quantity of pleasure derived from
one is as much as the other, then 'pushpin is as good as poetry.' Pushpin is
a child's game, and it is of no less value than poetry, provided that they provide the same amount of pleasure.

This hedonistic calculus is done by determining which act is likely to result in the greatest maximization or happiness overall for the most people.
At times, this may mean I need to sacrifice for the good of the many, for example, by stepping down from a position for the good of the company, or
staying late so the project is completed on time. At other times this may
mean that one person's good may outweigh the relatively small pain of a
group—for example when we give an arrested man a fair trial at the expense
of the many taxpayers—because the relative significance of the taxes used for
the trial are insignificant in comparison with the good of his fair trial.

Bentham provides us seven categories of consideration that should be
taken into account in deciding the relative happiness-value of each act as we
perform this hedonistic calculus.

1. **Intensity**: How intense will the pleasure be from this action?
2. **Duration**: How long will this pleasure last?
3. **Certainty:** How likely is it that this pleasure will actually take place?
4. **Remoteness**: How far away is the hoped-for pleasure outcome?
5. **Repeatability**: How likely is it that this will be a repeatable pleasure?
6. **Purity:** How much pain will accompany the pleasure produced?
7. **Extent** (number): How many will be affected with either pleasure or pain?

These principles are quite practical. We do consider how extensive the
return is when we evaluate an investment possibility (intensity). We consider
how long the benefit will last (duration). We consider 'how sure of a bet'
this investment is (certainty). We often disregard unlikely scenarios, consequences hundreds of years from now, etc. (remoteness). We consider the potential repeatability of our actions—for example, if I steal, I may never work
here again, or anywhere for that matter (repeatability). We consider the
negative consequences along with the benefits (purity), and we finally consider the overall benefits for the many (extent).

Consider an example: Suppose I am considering embellishing my expense report after a particularly tiring company trip. I would need to consider first, the intensity of the pleasure derived from it—how much pleasure
would I receive from the additional funds? How much pain (perhaps from
conscience, possible punishments, etc.)? Then I need to consider how long
that pleasure or pain would last. Third, how certain is it that I could actually achieve that pleasure—will I get caught? Will I feel guilty once I do it
so that I won't enjoy it? Will this bring about further problems? Fourth, I
should consider how far away the hoped for pleasure is—suppose that I
must file similar expense reports on my next trips in order to cover my mistakes? Fifth, is this something which I could repeat? What if I get caught?
Then I would not be able to repeat it. Doing it often might make it more
likely for my actions to be found out. Sixth, will pain accompany this pleasure? Will I experience pangs of guilt? Will I get fired? And seventh, how
will this affect others with regard to their pleasure or pain? This seventh
consideration must not be forgotten. If Bentham was a mere egoist—

someone who thinks right and wrong are based simply on what benefits me alone—then he would not have this final consideration, but in fact part of the Greatest Happiness Principle is that I accept responsibility to bring about the greatest happiness for the most, not just for me.

To those familiar with the term 'satisficing' or the recent explosion of literature on 'happiness economics,' this may sound familiar. In his 1957 work *Models of Man* Nobel Prize winner Herbert A. Simon first introduced the concept of 'satisficing.'[3] On this model, instead of achieving the optimal-maximum result, one aims for a satisfying result—one which will provide satisfactory happiness, if not maximal happiness. In many cases it seems that it would be more rational to achieve a satisfying result resulting in actual happiness, rather than not being satisfied until the optimal result occurs. Why be dissatisfied that you could not achieve perfection when you can achieve something quite pleasing and completely satisfying, despite its not being the best of all possible results? We see the problem of maximal-oriented decision making practically in many work situations where a perfectionist has difficulties finishing a project because there is always 'just one more thing to adjust' to make the project better. In such cases we realize that it is better (and will bring about more happiness) to achieve the closer-at-hand satisfying result rather than perpetually put off the maximal result. We almost always have limited timeframes for our decision-making, and limited resources to learn the consequences of our actions sometimes. But we must make our decisions within these bounds. This was what Simon referred to as 'bounded rationality'—we have limits within which we must strive for the most satisfying solution possible (given our situated limits). This relativization of the framework of decision making is more practical. If one waits until all possible data is received, it may be too late to make a decision. So we must often simply make decisions based on the information we have. To make a decision with limited information is better than to not make a decision at all.

Bentham's hedonistic calculus can be seen to be a precursor to this upsurge in 'happiness economics.' But while much of this makes good sense, it appears that there are some problems with Bentham-style utilitarianism as an ethical theory.

Perhaps the most damning criticism is that utilitarianism doesn't appear to adequately support principles of justice, fairness, truth telling, etc. If it would bring more happiness to the majority to not provide a fair or just trial, then the interest of the many might override the interest of the one. If our company signs a contract with a dealer, but later finds that honoring that contract would cause a great deal of pain for the company, its customers and employees, and other stakeholders, then the right thing to do would be to break promises made in the contract, due to the new information. One can imagine scenarios where it would appear to bring more happiness in the end if a company or individual lies, cheats, steals, acts unfairly, etc.

Another criticism may be that even on this hedonistic calculus, sometimes the bad consequences don't nearly outweigh the benefits of what would appear to be wrong conduct. This we see in cases where a company happily pays a fine for doing immoral and illegal activities since committing those illegal acts nets it hundreds of times more money than the cost of the fine. As a method of decision making seems to face similar criticisms—compromise becomes always the better choice, and sacrificing for the sake of principle becomes irrelevant. In short, a pursuit of will always choose what will suffice, rather than sacrifice.

The question, then, for the utilitarian, is: how can utilitarianism provide a basis for ethical behavior when its consequentialism seems to undermine the very moral principles (such as justice, fairness and truth telling) which we normally consider to be moral starting points?

I. MILL'S REVISED UTILITARIAN PRINCIPLE

Like Bentham, utilitarianism, Mill stated, "holds that actions are right in proportion as they tend to promote happiness, wrong as they tend to produce the reverse of happiness."[4] But despite this initial agreement, Mill saw problems in Bentham's utilitarianism. Mill, in contrast to Bentham, claims that there are two classes of pleasures—higher and lower. Human beings have capacities for higher and lower pleasures. We desire food, sleep, breathing, and sensual pleasures, and these are not bad. But lower pleasures have a lower quality and are lower in the sense that they are not unique to us, but are shared with squirrels, dogs, rats, etc. To live for lower pleasures would be to live like a dog. Mill says "a beast's pleasures do not satisfy a human being's conceptions of happiness."[5] Its not that we shouldn't like to eat, or that we should despise these sorts of pleasures we share with animals. The point is rather, that we shouldn't have these as our higher aspirations and meaning for being. If your meaning in life is eating, you have a problem. If you meaning in life is to sleep, you are depressed. If your sole purpose in life is to have sex, most would say you have a shallow existence. Human beings should have higher goals and higher pleasure capacities than that of animals.

Critics frequently attack Mill's higher-lower pleasure distinction with objections like: if I am extremely hungry, by Mill's principle, I would have to choose an ounce of Roquefort cheese over a pound of cheap mild cheddar, or if I was thirsty, I should choose a small amount of a top-quality bottled water over a gallon jug of low-cost grocery-store fill-it-up-yourself water. These sorts of criticisms are irrelevant, and misunderstand Mill. These examples, it is easy to see, refer to differences in quality between the same kinds of things. Here the distinction is between higher and lower quality food, etc. On this logic, I would choose a bumper of a Rolls Royce, over a complete Hyundai with a 100,000 mile warranty, etc. But that is not Mill's point at all. He is talking about distinguishing higher-types from lower types, but he is not suggesting this for making inner-type distinctions necessarily.

But Mill is also not suggesting that one should always choose the higher over the lower. Sometimes it is good to sleep, sometimes one should eat. Mill is not advocating people starving to death at the opera house, or suffering from sleep-deprivation in order to read the encyclopedia.

Higher Pleasure Capacities

But what are these higher-pleasure capacities? Mill mentions these four[6]:

1. Pleasures of the *intellect:* literacy, logic, emotional intelligence, etc.
2. Pleasures of the *noble feelings*: sympathy, heroism, empathy, humility, courage.
3. Pleasures of *imagination*: moral imagination, creativity, innovative thinking.
4. Pleasures of the *moral sentiments*: justice, honesty, fairness.

Certainly we might be content with the bestial pleasures alone—but no one would really agree that such a life was better than the non-bestial life.

If people in society lose their higher capacities, the overall societal possibility for pleasure is lost. In other words, societal pleasure-maximization rating goes down. Consider the consequences of a loss of moral sentiments: Think, for example, of a society in which one cannot trust that others will act decently—a society in which one person may decide to shoot another, or where one person might decide to strap a bomb to herself and kill a group of others. We value sentiments like justice, fairness, and honesty because to do so will ultimately lead to a greater happiness potential for all. Mill says that we value virtue as we value money—for what it will DO for us. But, just as we often forget why we want money, we forget why we want justice—*we just do want it.* But the reason we want justice, says Mill, is because a society in which we want justice is better able to make us more satisfied.

Consider the happiness which is brought about by noble feelings like heroism: This feeling, when nurtured in society, brings about bravery in the face of danger, the kind of bravery which leads firefighters and policemen to risk their lives, or leads a parent to provide and sacrifice for her family. If these sentiments are lost, then society as a whole suffers and loses important happiness-possibilities. In the movie *Blackhawk Down* the marines had a motto, and it was "never leave a man behind." That was something they followed, even when it meant risking men's lives to try to save injured soldiers. They had this principle which put others in harm's way. But the reason that they had this principle was that maintaining that motto preserved morale among the men. Knowing their fellow soldiers would come to rescue them if they went down gave them courage. Similarly, maintaining particular ethical principles at work, even when not immediately convenient, will in many cases bring about greater capacity for happiness in the company, and also society at large.

Consider the loss of intellectual or imaginative capacities. A society which loses its ability to think and dream cannot be as happy as a society which educates people to think for themselves and to creatively respond to life situations and opportunities which arise. In the same way, a company which does not empower its employees by nurturing their intellectual and imaginative capacities is likely to be less competitive, less capable of dealing with change, and less able to maintain a positive future.

On Losing Higher Capacities

Now if higher pleasures are so very important, then how or why do we lose them? The very capacity we have for higher pleasures may be lost, according to Mill, and often is in our day-to-day living which often neglects pursuits of the higher pleasures. One must be careful to maintain the higher capacities, like a gardener caring for a plant. Most don't lose them intentionally, but only inadvertently. First, we don't take time or opportunity to indulge and strengthen those higher pleasures, and second, we addict ourselves to lower pleasures. Our business culture may either foster or hamper these capacities. Insofar as we discourage the higher capacities, or simply sponsor neglect of those capacities, we are undermining the very possibility for those higher pleasures in ourselves and others. We need to consider how our work situations nourish or diminish the higher capacities. We need to maintain work environments which are favorable to keeping the higher capacities in exercise. This is not merely the responsibility of management—all employees should be nurturing their higher capacities as well—but there is some degree of responsibility which management must take to nurture these capacities, and certainly to try not to undermine them.

Today business can become all-consuming, and when this happens, one is left with little energy for ethical concerns or pursuit of the higher pleasure capacities. The less that our work demands allow us to pursue higher pleasures, the less likely we are to be concerned about such matters. Mill saw this in his own day:

> Instead of great energies guided by vigorous reason, and strong feelings strongly controlled by a conscientious will, its result is weak feelings and weak energies, which therefore can be kept in outward conformity to rule without any strength either of will or of reason. . . . There is now scarcely any outlet for energy in this country except business. . . . What little is left from that employment is expanded on some hobby, . . . and generally a thing of small dimensions.[7]

It is widely held that many business scandals happen not because of one or two bad-apple employees, but because of the entire work-culture of certain corporations. When particular moral sentiments and noble feelings are lost, the net result will ultimately be the creation of a less satisfactory corporate culture that breeds questionable practices. When we lose the capacity for moral imagination, and stupefy ourselves to numb our conscious from the real consequences of our actions, we are acting against the greater happiness principle, and our behavior is unethical.

The Loss of Higher Capacities and the Loss of Moral Conscience

A common objection to the claim that some pleasures are higher is, if they are so much more pleasurable, then why is it that so many people neglect them? Mill raises this question to himself when he says, "It may be objected, that many who are capable of the higher pleasures, occasionally, under the influence of temptation, postpone them to the lower."[8] His answer is clear: "Men often, from infirmity of character, make their election for the nearer good, though they know it to be the less valuable; and this no less when the choice is between two bodily pleasures, than when it is between bodily and mental. They pursue sensual indulgences to the injury of health, though perfectly aware that health is the greater good."[9] In such a situation, one has it on good authority that they should choose the higher good, but they don't but rather postpone it, because it is easier in the short run to do so. In Mill's opinion, they are either lazy or shortsighted. People generally do immoral things not because they enjoy the wrong they do, and the harm it does, but because they try not to think through the consequences of their actions. The people harmed by their action are at a comfortable distance, so those effects seem quite remote to the immediate personal pleasure of ill-gotten gain. The company thinks only of the quarterly report, not considering the long-range effects of repeatedly misrepresenting earnings over the course of two or three years, for example.

We make wrong decisions all the time—choosing the worse of two options, knowing in our heart that they are wrong. In business I may choose to report accurately, or choose to make my numbers look better than reality. These questionable choices are eventually habituated after repeated practice, insofar as I act almost as if out of instinct when I make them. Soon I am by habit doing that which is not in my or the company's long-term best interest. Thus I am not functioning to my highest ability.

The Social Nature of Utilitarianism

It is one thing to know that you should do what is in the best interest of the many. It is quite another thing to actually want to do that right thing. Mill understands that, and writes extensively about the importance of education, particularly education of the sentiments through poetry and art to help us develop social sympathy. Mill thinks that when we are functioning properly we will both be socially concerned and be happier for that social concern. An increase in public affections, social concern, and a cultivation of the mind lead to an increase in happiness, or at least the potential for happiness, according to Mill. But such a society can exist only when we are mutually brought up to respect one another's value and to consider others as having equal worth to our own. From a very young age, people learn cooperation, and think in terms of corporate and collective goals. The self-regarding interests are there, but they are alongside some very strong sympathies for others, according to Mill.[10]

The Conscience

People generally do the right thing and don't do the wrong thing because of their conscience, but what is the origin of this conscience? According to Mill, conscience is not only motivated by threats of external sanctions—punishment, disfavor, or disgrace; rather, conscience is the compiled collections of inner feelings, desires, and sentiments which themselves constitute a motivating power within us, apart from any outside responsibility. These feelings which constitute the inner sanctions are sponsored by our upbringing and community, but these feelings are desires which I eventually take on as my own. So while perhaps as a child I am polite to the elderly for fear of retribution or disgrace from my family, when I am older I am kind to the elderly because of desires which I have developed through nurturing over time. This education of the feelings and sentiments is not academic, but habitual. It is more like training in the sense of piano playing or sports than in terms of being educated in history or geography. The end result of such training is a general sense of duty which I have, not from fear of outside retribution, but a desire to fulfill my self-imposed obligations. Fulfilling these obligations makes me pleased, while not fulfilling those obligations makes me displeased.

But rarely does one experience feelings which are purely dutiful. Instead, I find that I do have feelings of duty, but they are,

> . . . in general all encrusted over with collateral associations, derived from sympathy, from love, and still more from fear, from the forms of religious feeling; from the recollections of childhood and all our past life; from self-esteem, desire of the esteem of others, and occasionally self-abasement.[11]

In other words, most of our actions are guided not simply by internal motives of duty, but by motives of passion, fear, or other such feelings. But this complex web of reasons which under gird our moral behavior is a very powerful, if mysterious, force.

Most of us feel compelled to not act immorally, or one is repelled from immorality, by this thick and complex firewall of multiple motives provided from relationships with others, a concept of divine retribution, and one's own desires and affections. And even when I do act immorally, we are later 'punished' by the internal guilt and shame which follows immoral behavior. On the other hand, I often find that I have a variety of internal and external sanctions which motivate me towards moral action. For example, I may resist the temptation to embezzle money for a variety of internal and external sanctions, both positive and negative. I may not want the negative external sanctions of possible shame in the public eye or possible prison. I may also not want to face the personal guilt which would follow such an act. Positively, I may want the enjoyable sense of knowing I did the right thing, and I may enjoy the positive external sanction of the affirmation I will receive from my colleague or friend when I tell them of my successful resistance to temptation.

Mill emphasizes the positive power and drive of our desires more than our fears. One is not likely to be made moral through fear. This is worth considering when we are attempting to figure out how to encourage compliance with particular codes of ethics. Punitive threats may be of some help in thwarting unethical behavior, but positive encouragement towards good acts and the development of moral conscience is even more powerful at times. A love of virtue and a vision of the ideal lives which are presented to us through stories and other means will sustain our moral desires, and help instantiate moral action. As my imagination is directed towards beauty and a desire and even reverence for the higher pleasures, I will become more and more 'naturally' inclined towards right actions. This happens as my feelings are directed appropriately, or when my conscientious feelings are nurtured and strongest in me. Mill says that one's sense of moral obligation arises from such feelings:

> [Moral obligation's] binding force, however, consists in the existence of a mass of feeling which must be broken through in order to do what violates our standard of right, and which, if we do nevertheless violate that standard, will probably have to be encountered afterwards in the form of remorse. Whatever theory we have of the nature or origin of conscience, this is what essentially constitutes it.[12]

It is essential in business that we nurture and build up this mass of feeling in favor of the principles which will ultimately bring about a greater potential for happiness in society. Of course most will agree that the 'right' thing to do is to do what will benefit the most—but what people lack is the motivation to do the right thing. People often criticize utilitarianism for being untenable, because there is no motive for the one to be willing to sacrifice for the many—a requirement which seems to follow from the utilitarian principle. Those who pursue the higher pleasures will be capable of such a sacrifice. This, then, is why Mill says, "Utilitarianism, therefore, could only attain its end by the general cultivation of nobleness of character, even if each individual were only benefited by the nobleness of others, and his own, so far as happiness is concerned, were a sheer deduction from the benefit."[13]

Distinguishing Higher from Lower Pleasures

A question often asked is, how can one distinguish higher from lower pleasures? Mill provides at least four different criteria in his writings. These four principles can be written shorthand as follows:

P1: If a person who is competently acquainted with two pleasures prefers one to the other even though a) they will be attended with a greater amount of discontent and b) they would not resign it for any quantity of the other pleasure which their nature is capable of—then the pleasure preferred in this way is a higher pleasure than the other.

One would not, for example, be willing to sacrifice one's literacy (one aspect of one's capacity for intellectual pleasure) for one's ability to enjoy bratwurst (one aspect of one's capacity for sensory pleasure). We would respect a family who denied themselves one meal per week and set aside the savings in order to buy a computer or encyclopedia, for example. Someone who doesn't know how to read may not understand this sort of choice, but that proves Mill's point.

P2: Only those pleasures which arise from faculties unique to human beings are higher pleasures.

Sensual pleasures including eating, sleeping, breathing, or any physical pleasure would not be unique to humans. Those which involve the use of our intelligence, imagination, our noble feelings or moral sentiments would be unique to humans.

P3: Higher pleasures will be those which can be chosen without a loss of pride, liberty, or dignity by the one who chooses it, provided that the one who is choosing has some admirable degree of pride, liberty, and dignity.

Of course if one is shameless, then this principle has little use. But for one who has a degree of dignity, shameful behaviors will spark a healthy degree of a sense of loss of dignity. We know we have many 'guilty pleasures'—things from which we gain pleasure of which we are ashamed. These are likely not higher pleasures. Behaviors which ennoble the spirit and which one would model shamelessly are key candidates for higher pleasures.

P4: If X is a higher pleasure, then it will stimulate our imagination to rise above known reality towards ideals beyond the regular world, and it will also be limitless.

Mill is certainly not talking about anything religious here. But he is saying that higher pleasures help us to rise above ourselves, to be motivated by ideals—things which are only dreams today, which we hope for. Higher pleasures are also unique in that, the more we use them, the more we are able to enjoy them. The more you read, the more you enjoy reading. The more you think about things, the more you enjoy thinking about things. It is not a desire which is fulfilled temporarily, like eating or sex—it grows more as you use it.

How Does Mill's Qualitative Utilitarianism Apply to Business Ethics?

The question now is: how can business use this utilitarianism of Mill? In what concrete ways can we apply this to Business? We might begin by trying to apply Mill's pleasure criteria to particular actions of business. Mill's basic ethical principle is: do whatever would bring about the greatest happiness. But we have now seen that this is qualified considerably. Mill is concerned not just with whether or not we achieve short term base (ignoble) pleasure, but he is concerned with helping foster the possibility and reality of the most excellent pleasures, and guarding the capacities which are necessary for maintaining the highest degrees of happiness for the many. The question then is, how can we develop a business ethic or practical application of this greatest happiness principle to business practice?

We might start with the above-mentioned principles for distinguishing higher from lower pleasures. With slight adjustment, we could derive the following principles for choosing the higher pleasures when faced with alternative options:

1. Which option would one well-acquainted with both most likely choose?
2. Which option is unique to humans, and not a mere animal pleasure?
3. Which option can be chosen without loss of pride, dignity, or liberty?
4. Which option inspires the imagination to noble ideals and higher goals?

These principles could be used as basic principles giving direction to business decisions. When we make a business decision, we might consult these general rules to help us sort out between viable alternatives. For example, if I am going to advertise a product, I could use these criteria to help me decide what sort of advertising I think is more or less moral by attempting to decide which advertising is more or less harmful to the higher sentiments in society.

We can also derive some like-minded principles from what we have earlier in the essay learned from Mill. I think we can derive the following series of questions from what we have seen in Mill, and these questions could be referred to when making a decision:

1. Does this decision nurture or undermine the higher social sentiments of society?
2. Is this decision going to have an impact on people's conscience? If so, would it tend to undermine or nurture the conscience of people?
3. Through this decision, am I encouraging people to be selfish or socially minded?

There is no doubt that answering such questions requires a degree of judgment—an ability to decide, and a character which is functioning well—a character whose higher sentiments are being nurtured.

DRAWING SOME CONCLUSIONS

In Mill's utilitarianism, the development of social feelings and sentiments is essential for the morality of individuals. External sanctions are not enough, and internal sanction of duty along with the other internal feelings of social sympathy provide the necessary foundation for authentic moral behavior. It is essential that the individual understand himself as being within a social matrix web, and essential for business to see how it has an effect on that social matrix. Habits of thinking and feeling this way are to be nurtured through a variety of educational means.

It is often said that business is 'utilitarian' in nature. If companies adopt Mill's utilitarianism, it will begin to be concerned not only with outcome with regard to bottom line financial gain, but the effects which its practices have upon the happiness-achievement capacities of society. This is Mill's vision of utilitarianism, and it provides an interesting and exciting model for business ethics, when properly understood.

Notes

1. Special thanks to Patricia Werhane, Kevin Gibson, and students at Bethel University for their encouragement and support of my work on Mill and review of various sections and ideas contained in this essay.
2. Herbert Simon published many works along these lines including the original 1957 *Models of Man*. More recent work includes that of Andrew J. Oswald and David G. Blanchflower (*The Wage Curve*).
3. One of the earliest attempts to apply the concept of ethics to business is R.M Cyert and J.G. March's *A Behavioral Theory of the Firm* (Prentice-Hall, 1963). Other more recent literature on measuring happiness in general include *Well Being: The Foundations of Hedonic Psychology* by Kahneman, Diener, and Schwarz (1999).
4. J.S. Mill, *Utilitarianism*, ed. by Roger Crisp (New York: Oxford, 1998), 2.2.1.
5. Mill, *Utilitarianism*, 2.4.9 [Chapter 2, Section 4, Line 9].
6. Mill, *Utilitarianism*, 2.4.17.
7. Mill, *On Liberty*, J.S. Mill, *On Liberty* London, J.W. Parker and Son, 1859, 135.
8. Mill, *Utilitarianism*, 2.7.1.
9. Mill, *Utilitarianism*, 2.7.4.
10. Mill, *Utilitarianism*, 3.10.30-57.
11. Mill, *Utilitarianism*, 1.4.8.
12. Mill, *Utilitarianism*, 3.4.19.
13. Mill, *Utilitarianism*, 2.9.

Ethics and Pragmatism: John Dewey's Deliberative Approach

JOHN MCVEA

THE NATURE OF ETHICS—A PROCESS OF INQUIRY

One of the most arresting aspects of pragmatism, at least as it is represented in the work of the American philosopher, John Dewey, is the fundamentally different nature of a pragmatist approach to ethics compared with more traditional approaches. Ethics is not about proving what is good or right. Rather, ethics is a way of living that enables enlightened conduct. In some ways we could say that the pragmatists revert back to classical notions of ethics as a description of the good life. However, this would be deceptive, at least in the way Dewey thinks about pragmatism and ethics, because Dewey incorporates into ethics the continuous discovery and reinvention of good ways to live that contrasts with the striving for eternal Aristotelian virtues.

John McVea is an Assistant Professor in the School of Business at St. Thomas College in Minneapolis, specializing in entrepreneurial decision and ethical deliberation and decision making, among other areas of research. Reprinted by permission.

What is most distinctive about Dewey's pragmatist approach to ethics? First, ethics is a process, or an enlightened way of living. Second, ethics grows out of our concrete everyday experience; it is not a metaphysical abstraction that must be applied to our lives. Third, ethics should liberate our intelligence, our analysis, and our imaginations, rather than constrain these abilities through blind observance of rules or principles. Fourth, ethics should, first and foremost, be a process of self-realization. "*The best hope for the common good is in each person being aware of the implications of his own conduct, especially the meaning of his conduct in the context of social action.*" (Dewey, MW.)

This pragmatic approach to ethics can be contrasted with more conventional approaches. Two forms of ethical theory tend to dominate discussion of ethics: "the ethics of what is good" or "the ethics of what is right." Normally these consequential and deontological perspectives are contrasted as polar extremes. The former is most commonly associated with the utilitarianism of Bentham and Mill. According to this approach, we should determine what we ought to do by calculating the costs and benefits of the alternatives and selecting whichever results in the 'greatest good for the greatest number.' The alternative deontological approach is most commonly associated with Kant. According to this approach, we should determine what we ought to do by considering the fundamental duties or principles that reason tells us must apply at all times. There are two important ways in which Dewey's pragmatism differs from these conventional approaches.

First, there is the issue of incommensurability. Despite their differences, deontological and consequential approaches actually have something in common. Both approaches use a single criterion to determine moral action. On the one hand, we determine what we ought to do because it would result in the most good, regardless of other principles of what is right. On the other hand, we determine what we ought to do based on what is right, regardless of the consequences. However, for Dewey, ethical problems can never be reduced to a single dimension. Indeed, the incommensurability of the interests involved is the essence of an ethical problem (Dewey, 1957,112)

Second, there is the issue of whether ethical systems should be static or dynamic. Both consequential and deontological approaches are static to the extent that moral action is guided by a fixed conception of what is good or what is right. Of course, both approaches allow for error and revision of our deliberations. However, even when we revise an ethical decision, we would still look back and say that "what was right" or "what was good" has not changed, simply that our perception was mistaken.

Dewey takes a radically different approach. From this perspective, traditional ethical frameworks fail to rise to the challenge of the modern world. For Dewey, a fundamental requirement of the transition from *feudalism* to the *modern* world was seeing the world as a dynamic, rather than as a static, system. However, according to Dewey, the modern revolution is still incomplete; ethics remains the last bastion of feudalism. Dewey argued that we should abandon these feudal myths of morality and start pursuing the dynamic and scientific approaches that we successfully apply in every other aspect of life. Thus, we should abandon the idea that there are fixed answers to moral questions and thus, we should consider each situation in its own time and context. We should apply intelligent analysis to each situation in order to establish an ethical path. We should become actively engaged in the process of choosing, rather than appealing to a set of enduring rules and principles. Once we see morality as a process of inquiry, or a *way of living*, rather than as a *masterplan to discover*, our focus can shift from metaphysical speculation to how to resolve and remove persistent ills.

Having urged us to abandon the dogma of using higher ends to provide ethical guidance, Dewey must then explain precisely how we can live ethically by focusing on concrete and particular problems. At one level his ethical approach is quite simple—we should simply apply our intelligence to the problems that we face. On the other hand, to fully understand the content and implications of this approach requires us to accept two assumptions in Dewey's work. First, because of the complex nature of the natural world in which human beings live and interact, our actions are highly constrained and modified by complex interactions from within the natural world, lessening the need for a metaphysical or spiritual constraint or explanation. Second, Dewey approaches the process of ethics and ethical decision from a holistic, or more precisely, creature-focused, approach to inquiry. Rather than study the concepts of stimulus and response, we would be better served by studying whole creatures which are taking actions in pursuit of particular ends.

HARMONY WITH OUR LOCAL ENVIRONMENT

From a natural and holistic perspective the only appropriate way to conduct human inquiry is as a natural phenomenon within an evolving world. Human beings should be considered just as particular creatures without special powers or associations. Thus, from this perspective, certain facts of nature need no particular explanation beyond empirical observation. For instance, humans are born, they live in social groups, and they die. As human beings have never been observed or recorded living successfully as isolated individuals, and as extended isolation seems to cause a breakdown in human psyche, there is no need to puzzle over the roots, the foundations or the justification of society. Humans also have impulses and desires. Once again, there is no need to puzzle greatly over this. We simply have to observe a human infant to confirm that this is true. Infants do not lie passively waiting for stimulation; they enter the world with impact, energy, and uncoordinated responses. What distinguishes human life is not just physical evolution of the species, but evolution of ways of living and ways of believing. Thus, ethics is integral to human life at the most basic of levels.

Habits and customs are both moral and a natural social response to our environment. Thus, the evolution of habits plays a central role in Dewey's understanding of ethics. Acquiring habits is a social process. Habits are most successfully passed on from the mature to the immature through a shared experience, from the parent to the child, from the teacher to the pupil. However, once acquired, a habit is more like a disposition than a tool in a box. Habits link our impulse, our actions, and our environment. As such, a habit is like a hammer that is actively looking for a nail. If, for some reason we find that we cannot follow our habits, we feel an emotional frustration or craving. Equally, even when we have good reason to act otherwise, we can find it hard to resist our habits. For this reason, Dewey is careful to distinguish between two types of habits, passive and active. Passive habits, or habituations, are routine, fixed modes of behaviour that fit our surroundings. We use these habits to take care of the background conditions of life where we do not feel impelled to grow. Thus, on the way to work we can walk, drive, drink coffee, smoke and chew gum only vaguely being aware of our actions. On the other hand, active habits "involve thought, invention, and initiative in applying capacities to new aims. They are opposed to routine, which marks an arrest of growth" (Dewey, 1944, 53). Through passive habits we ensure continuity with our past experience and take account of lessons learned. Through active habits we unleash the possibilities of the future and use our intelligence to project and create.

To remain in harmony habits must be continuously be reformed, resulting in a continuity of character. As developed so far, we use habits to assimilate certain aspects of our environment so that it supports rather than destroys us. However, the environment is uncertain and is forever changing. Thus, over time a healthy organism must adapt its habits in order to stay in harmony within the world. The driving forces behind this process are the emotions. We feel discomfort when we fall out of harmony with our surroundings or when we find that previously successful habits no longer yield successful results expected. Thus, emotions provide a trigger for us to challenge our existing habits and use our intelligence to develop new ones.

Habits are not just the routines that we tend to follow. Habits include our physical interactions with the world, our social interactions, the way we think and how we make sense to the world. Indeed, according to Dewey, the very conception of the self is a collection of evolving habits. Thus, our character is determined by the habits that we follow and how these habits evolve, and the concept of "the self" can be thought of as a dynamic construct that consists of a stable, but evolving, collection of habits through which we extract meaning from the world.

THE ROLE OF INTELLIGENCE

Having laid out the role of emotion, experience, and habit we are now in a position to explore in more detail the role of intelligence, and deliberation in our ethical lives. For Dewey intelligence is not a natural gift or a particular aptitude. Intelligence is a way of living that maintains the organism in harmony with its environment over the long run. Intelligence is the process of bringing our impulses, our habits and our environment into harmony. Thus, at its core, intelligence has an aesthetic dimension. Harmony, balance, symmetry, and fit are goals through which intelligent action can be differentiated from unintelligent action. However, every decision, every habit, will have unforeseen consequences. Furthermore, this task of revising and readjusting cannot be done by impulse and habit alone. What is needed is a process of deliberation, and intelligent analysis.

THE NATURE OF DELIBERATION IN ETHICAL DECISION-MAKING

For Dewey, ethical decision-making is no more and no less than intelligent decision-making. Intelligence springs to action when we find our habits and instincts blocked. Suppose that I come home at night and find that the electricity in my house has failed. If I acted habitually I would breeze through the front door and march swiftly through the living room into the kitchen, open the refrigerator and start to prepare my tea. This approach would require little effort in terms of thought, however, it might also result in my breaking a limb, as I trip in the dark, or poisoning myself with spoiled food. Thus, sticking to my habit, in this case, would be far from intelligent. To the contrary, intelligence is the process of adaptation that allows us to develop new approaches that are more in harmony with changes to the environment. For instance, I might crawl through the dark house on hands and knees to avoid falling; I might postpone all other activities until I can find a flashlight; I might return to my car and eat out, hoping that the power cut will soon be resolved. Clearly, there are numerous ways that we can approach a problematic situation, but they all involve adapting the meanings and habits by which we have operated in the past to the new environment. Thus, from Dewey's perspective, intelligent decision-making is not mere attribute of an individual; it is a process of adaptation between the environment and ourselves. Furthermore, intelligent decision-making is an inherently ethical process as only through this way of living can we move towards harmony between the individual and the social and physical environment.

In reassessing our situation we consider three different aspects—we recollect previous actions and situations, we observe the context of the current situation, and we make plans for future actions. This "trinity of forecasts, perceptions and remembrances" (Dewey, MW, Volume 14:1922, 127) is the starting point of deliberation, which is central to the ethical decision-making process.

CONTEXTUAL DISCOVERY

Contextual discovery is critical to Dewey's ethical approach. However, contextual facts do not simply exist, we must interpret them. Critical analysis of the context of a problematic situation is the first stage in finding meaning in an environment. Furthermore, unlike traditional ethical frameworks, from a pragmatist approach ethical facts do not exist in advance of a context. Even the oldest and most reliable ethical principles have grown out of experiences in particular contexts. They are not pre-existing answers that exist independently of our experience.

It would be a misinterpretation to assume from this that Dewey saw no role for principles. Principles and generalizations play a significant role in Dewey's ethical framework. However, for Dewey's perspective, principles are simply general summaries of lessons that have been useful in the past. They might serve as useful temporary hypotheses or placeholders until we have had the opportunity to fully analyze the issue at hand. But principles cannot establish ethical facts on their own. Only experimentation and subsequent verification can uncover discover ethical "facts." For Dewey, to live according to principles is to live solely under the guidance of the past and to give no weighting to our own intelligence and ability to reason in the present.

DRAMATIC REHEARSAL

Before we make moral judgments we need to gather the evidence. Dewey called this process of empirical discovery dramatic rehearsal. We use our imagination to discover the options that might be available to us. We rehearse potential actions in our mind to establish not only the consequences, but also how we feel about the potential outcomes. Rationally based traditional approaches leave no role for emotions or feelings in the process of ethical deliberation. However, through dramatic rehearsal can we engage our emotions from the very start of the deliberative process. Indeed, the feelings of satisfaction that we experience when we dramatically rehearse an option are signs that this alternative might be prima facia good. Equally, imaginative rehearsal might raise negative feelings or doubts. In either case it is important to note that prima facia value of an alternative is fixed by a visceral reaction to the imaginative process. Thus, in situations of moral choice we feel discomfort because, through rehearsal, we feel torn between incompatible ends that feel good for different reasons. The next obvious question is "How do we choose between these competing ends?"

MORAL JUDGMENT IS ULTIMATELY AN AESTHETIC EXPERIENCE OF CHARACTER

For Dewey, the only way to establish 'truth' in a dynamic world is to use the principles of scientific inquiry. Thus, we will only be able to establish the best alternative by acting on a hypothesis and assessing whether the empirical evidence supports or denies the claim. Since, in moral situations, dramatic rehearsal has established a number of prima facia good and bad alternatives, moral judgment involves developing a hypothesis about which alternative is best. However, from Dewey's perspective, we should abandon the search for universal ethical criteria to discriminate between alternatives. "When ends are genuinely incompatible, no common denominator can be found except by deciding what sort of character is most highly prized" (Dewey, MW Volume 14, 1922, 103). Thus, the only way to develop an ethical hypothesis, especially in demanding situations, is to analyze the situation and to try to determine what sort of person that you want to be. Our character grows out of the difficult ethical decisions that we made. This view stands in contrast to the more conventional view that we start with our character, defined by abiding principles, and apply it to situations in order to derive an ethical solution. For Dewey, ethics is a process of inquiry into our experiences through which we form and amend our beliefs and out of which our character emerges.

This self-actualizing approach could be criticized as a form of hedonism; that is, we choose what is best depending on how good it makes us feel about ourselves. However, although we can only discover ethical facts about ourselves within situations, we cannot reinvent ourselves *ex nihilo* every time we morally reason. The development of habits and the formation of character are very important to Dewey's scheme. Intelligent and reflective beings must have some consistency of character as well as an ability to adapt. Thus, Dewey proposes that there is a set of minimum criteria that we can use to provisionally differentiate between good and bad dispositions. To be human beings capable of reflection and choice we must have characters that are harmonious, flexible and stable in the face of changing circumstances. Thus when we make initial moral judgments we are forming hypotheses about which sorts of person it is more desirable to be. Our initial hypotheses are about choices that are likely to lead to a character that is flexible, stable and harmonious.

At this point it may seem that Dewey has slipped in some *a priori* principles that run counter to his belief in empirically driven ethics. But we must remember that at this stage in moral reasoning we are only establishing a reasonable hypothesis of an ethical alternative that will only gain its credibility through empirical testing. The selection according to principles of harmony and continuity is simply a holding place for an empirically driven choice. Furthermore, he does not propose that the habits of good character are lasting, fixed, or prior to our experience. Rather, character grows out of past experience and it persists and adapts in the light of future experience.

EXPERIMENTAL ETHICS?

Dewey argues that continuous experimentation and observation of consequences provides the ultimate justification in ethics. His reasons are as follows. Warranted ethical facts can be tested. One important arena for the testing of ethical facts is the field of social science. However, this is not the only possibility. Sometimes experiments are not possible. Sometimes tests might be irreversible or potentially catastrophic. From this perspective, experimental ethics can sound like an extremely alarming idea. Should we try a little murder for a while, see how it goes, and then review our observations about the consequences? What about marketing small portable nuclear devices to advocates of the right of citizens to arm themselves? What about trying to crossbreed a human with a sheep? Obviously, such extreme examples illustrate an ethically unacceptable interpretation of the idea of experimental ethics. However, there are alternative ways of testing warranted ethical facts. Many different types of experiments can be carried out. We might test hypotheses by making predictions about past events or by studying tragedies that have already occurred. We might consider small-scale trials or case studies or parallel cases. We might build models, use analogies, and create an experimental, but controllable, "laboratory" in which to test the ideas. There are numerous ways in which we can use our imagination to invent ways to test warranted facts, even in difficult circumstances.

Despite our ingenuity and creativity, sometimes it will still be impossible to carry out an experiment. Does this mean a failure for experimental ethics? To the contrary, experimental ethics is a continuous process. If it is truly impossible to carry out an experiment that has any validity, then we can still go ahead and carry out our action based on the initially warranted choice. However, in this case our actual action is an experiment. We are still obliged to search for confirming evidence once we have gone ahead. If the evidence indicates that the initially warranted hypothesis was wrong then we can change it, if the evidence confirms our hypothesis then we can assume that we did indeed act morally.

DRAMATIC REHEARSAL AND MANAGERIAL DECISION-MAKING

Managers trying to make decisions in ethically pioneering situations face considerable practical and intellectual challenges. Traditional ethical frameworks have tended to emphasize the use of either ethical principles or the evaluation of consequences in order to resolve ethical problems. However, ethically pioneering situations are precisely the sort of situation where there is no social consensus on clear ethical principles, and where the consequences are both uncertain and ambiguous. Furthermore, most conventional theories of decision-making place either ignore the role of ethics and values or place them outside the scope of the decision-making process. Equally most conventional views of ethics place the practical challenges of decision-making outside the scope of their inquiry. These challenges emphasize the importance of trying to understand how managers and scientists, in these ethically exposed circumstances, actually make their decisions. Progress in this field will require both empirical study and theoretical development in a number of areas that overlap the fields of decision theory, strategic decision-making and ethics.

THE ROLE OF DELIBERATION IN ETHICAL DECISION-MAKING

Deliberation plays an important role in many ethical frameworks. For example, the path to Rawls' reflective equilibrium (Rawls, 1999) is through a deliberative process that brings our considered judgments and our principles into alignment. However, Rawls says very little about the process itself. Management theory is equally silent on the subject of deliberation. Freeman's stakeholder approach to strategic management is probably the closest thing to a strategic theory that incorporates ethical decision-making. However, having established the importance of uncovering and considering a wide range of stakeholder interests, Freeman tells us little about the process of distilling these, perhaps conflicting, interests into a coherent strategy. Once again deliberation is seen as critical to ethical decision-making, but the process of deliberation remains a mystery.

According to Dewey, deliberation is a dramatic rehearsal carried out in our imagination. It is a series of imaginary experiments carried out in order to discover what various possibilities are really like. The power of dramatic rehearsal is that it allows us to experience various possibilities that may, or may not, help us solve the problem at hand, without yet committing us to action or consequences. This process is a reversal of the conventional view that deliberation is a process of applying our preferences to a set of alternatives. In contrast, according to Dewey, we start with a mass of competing and conflicting preferences and emotions. The emotions arise from the frustrating impasse before us, and the preferences arise from the persistent desire to maintain our tried and trusted habits. We deliberate *in order to develop* a course of action that best satisfies these competing interests.

Therefore, deliberation is not a process of comparison of outcomes. It is not centered on outcomes; it is centered on action. It is the creative discovery of a new way of doing things. It is the search for a new way to proceed that resolves the problem at hand. In other words, it is the process of developing strategies for life.

In order to develop the concept of deliberation as dramatic rehearsal more fully it is useful to compare and contrast it with a more traditional approach—utilitarian calculation.

Dramatic rehearsal emphasizes the journey rather than the destination. Alternatives are imagined as a series of lived-through strategies rather than as ultimate outcomes possessing certain attributes. Decision-making is the evaluation of future ways of living. Dewey notes that, just as we can only meaningfully describe a road by describing the landmarks we see along the way, we can only evaluate an alternative by imagining what our lives would be like if we select that course of action. This is a view of decision-making that focuses on evaluating strategies, not outcomes. Second, dramatic rehearsal does not assume either that we already have a set of preferences. Indeed, one of the purposes of the deliberative process is to discover what we prefer or what is really of value. Thus, preferences and values are an integral part of the decision-making process. Preferences and values emerge and are shaped by the process of dramatic rehearsal. This is not to say that there can be no consistency of preferences and values over time. It is simply not to assume that this is so, and to suggest that, such consistency, as it occurs, is derived from a consistence in our social environment. Third, from a Deweyan perspective, one of the characteristics of an ethical decision is that it has interests and aspects that are truly incommensurable. If all problems could be broken down into attributes that could be quantified, ranked, added and offset with ease, then there would be no ethical dilemma. Thus, through dramatic rehearsal we should consider the incommensurable and unquantifiable aspects of the problem at hand. There are aspects of all situations that are unique, the richness of which can be lost by a rush to evaluate alternatives solely by the tradable values of the outcomes. The objective is not to force all alternatives into an ordered ranking by the best available measures. Rather, it is to imagine strategies that bring conflicting interests into harmony, ways of transcending conflicts, or at least ways of minimizing conflict. Fourth, dramatic rehearsal does not view decision-making purely from a rational perspective. Emotions and impulse play a role throughout the decision-making process. For instance, the initial recognition of the existence of a problem that must be solved happens at the emotional level. Emotions also play a role in the process of dramatic rehearsal. Deliberation does not involve us removing ourselves from our biases, rather it is the search for a way of harnessing our, initially, incompatible, preferences and emotions.

Finally, dramatic rehearsal involves contextual rather than abstract deliberation. It is carried out within the unique context of the current situation. Thus, rather than consider possible courses of action in isolation, the decision-maker can explore how these alternatives interplay with other activities. Rather than considering the character of the decision-maker as being independent of the decision dramatic rehearsal allows us to explore how decisions might actually change the decision-maker. Exploration of these rich interactions gives imagination, creativity and discovery a much more significant role in the deliberative process.

CAN DRAMATIC REHEARSAL HAVE ANY ETHICAL TEETH, OR IS THIS JUST HOLLOW ETHICS?

A common criticism of a pragmatic approach to ethics, like Deweyan dramatic rehearsal, is that such a system can never be more than a hollow framework. For sure, dramatic rehearsal might generate more information, creative alternatives and richer analysis, but without a set of central principles to adjudicate between irreducible conflicts the system has no ethical, or indeed decision-making, teeth. According to this account, a Deweyan ethical decision-making process is no different than sophisticated brainstorming, scenario analysis or, by some accounts, extensive stakeholder analysis. What is needed is a normative core to carry the real ethical load (for example, the work of Phillips in trying to establish a normative core for stakeholder theory). A full Deweyan response to this criticism would require much greater exposition than is available here. However, what follows is a brief outline of an argument that must be completed in another forum.

First, there is an element of truth to the statement that dramatic rehearsal cannot provide full ethical justification of action. From a pragmatist perspective, ethical justification lies in the ultimate consequences of action, which are, by definition, inaccessible to the decision-maker at the point of decision. Thus, the results of dramatic rehearsal will always be tentative, fallible and subject to revision. However, there seems little doubt that, short of being able to travel in time, Dewey intended that a thoughtful and intelligent conclusion, drawn from dramatic rehearsal and careful deliberation, should have provisional moral standing, subject to empirical results. Thus, there is a procedural justification to tentative action.

This still leaves us with the issues of how tensions and conflicts, which cannot be transcended by the imagination of new alternatives, can be resolved without access to fundamental principles. Dewey responds to this challenge with three, probably interrelated, and perhaps contradictory, bases for moral judgment: continuity of character, aesthetics and democracy.

Deliberation through dramatic rehearsal encourages a very different view of character. Dramatic rehearsal not only aids us in resolving the problems that we face, it also helps us take account of issues of character in our decision-making. When we consider a problem through dramatic rehearsal we develop an understanding for our potential actions beyond the simple pleasure and pain, profits and loss, caused by the outcomes. Through dramatic rehearsal, we can consider our decisions within the context of the continuity of our lives. Decisions ultimately result in actions that have an impact not only on the problems before us, but on ourselves. Our future actions amend our habits, and our habits interact with each other in ways that form our character. However, our character evolves over time as some habits persevere and others are replaced.

In ethically pioneering situations the question is not how to adjudicate between two differentially advantageous alternatives, but rather the question is "What will I become?" When we deliberate we consider how possible actions will mesh or jar with our "style" or character. We consider what sort of new habits these actions will encourage, what sort of habits they will force us to adapt or adopt. Thus, currently irresolvable tensions and conflicts are resolved by a choice of character, not a choice of outcomes.

In sum, the starting point of any deliberation is a frustration. There is problem that must be solved, a path that is blocked and interests that conflict and confuse. Of course, possible actions must be evaluated to the extent that they solve the problem, resolve the conflicts, and open the way to action. Dramatic rehearsal allows us to explore these possibilities in our mind in a rich, inclusive and creative way. However, dramatic rehearsal is more than rich, imaginative brainstorming. Dramatic rehearsal changes the nature of what is being considered through deliberation. Dramatic rehearsal integrates the character of the decision-maker into the process of deliberation. Dramatic rehearsal allows us to create inclusive strategies that fit our environment. It has both ethical and decision-making teeth because it forces us to choose what values we really value most, what sort of preferences we prefer and what sort of character we value.

IMPLICATIONS FOR MANAGERIAL DECISION-MAKING

Dewey's approach to ethical decision-making through intelligent deliberation sheds light on both the process of deliberation and the role of values and ethics in the practice of managerial decision-making. First, and most controversially, firms should consider ethical decision-making as no different from thoughtful, intelligent decision-making. This statement cuts two ways. Intelligent decision-making should have a central role for ethics and values, rather than seeing them as either behavioral constraints or as societal and personal decisions that must be dealt with outside the context of business strategy. Equally, ethical analysis should be carried out by those intimately involved with the practical and contextual details, rather than by "independent" ethical experts or committees.

Second, a deliberative approach would describe decision-making as the art of crafting strategies of action that are harmonious and fit with the strategic environment surrounding the firm. While accepting the great value brought to decision-making by scientific and mathematical tools, at the extreme, particularly the ethical extreme, decision-making retains elements that are a form of art. Thus, the craft of decision-making requires a mixture of skills, competencies and experience. Crafts are passed on not simply by abstract instruction, but also through experience shared in the unique context of the firm. For example, discussions of business cases developed from actual firm experience, regular discussion of decision-making procedures between experienced and inexperienced personnel may be even more valuable than academic seminars or training course.

Third, careful deliberation should be seen as central to the decision-making task—requiring creativity and imagination as well as the mobilization of not only reason, but also the emotions and impulses. Managers should become comfortable with the presentation of decision strategies, which are couched in terms other than just "the numbers," or the creation of measurable financial value.

Fourth, the deliberative process should be thought of as an inclusive consideration of all the interests and consequences, both qualitative and quantitative, of the surrounding environment. Such an approach is reminiscent of the stakeholder approach to strategic management. However, the deliberative process requires considerable investment in the dramatic rehearsal of possibilities, engaging the imagination to develop strategies that harmonize the conflicting demands of the problem at hand. This element of the approach is reminiscent of some of the scenario analysis literature, based on strategy development tools developed at Shell.

Fifth, deliberation requires more than just developing inclusive scenarios. The question of "who or what character do we want to epitomize" is also central to the deliberative process. Intelligent deliberation requires managers to imagine what it would be like to "live through" the scenarios. How would it feel? How would it feel for others affected? What would than say about you as a manager/ what would it say about you as a firm?

Finally, pragmatic deliberation would emphasize that all principles, norms, strategies, and even "core" values are always tentative—subject to revision by a new and demanding ethically pioneering situation. Continuity requires than we change and challenge only certain aspects of these systems at a time, however progress demands that we challenge them on a regular basis.

References

Dewey, John. Many citations are from The Collected Works (SIU Press, ed. Jo Ann Boydston), indicated by series (Early Works EW; Middle Works MW; Later Works, LW, volume, page number) Carbondale, Southern Illinois University Press.

_____ 1957. *Reconstruction in Philosophy*, Boston, Beacon Press.

_____ 1944. *Democracy and Education*, New York, Free Press.

Rawls, John. 1999. *A Theory of Justice (Revised Edition)*. Cambridge, Massachusetts: Belknap Press of Harvard University Press.

Freeman, R. E. 1984. Strategic management: A stakeholder approach. Boston: Pitman.

Chapter 3

Truth Telling

Case Study

Cynthia Cooper and WorldCom

EMILY MEAD ● PATRICIA H. WERHANE

In late May of 2002, Cynthia Cooper, the 38-year-old Vice-President of Internal Audit for WorldCom, the second largest telecommunications company in the United States behind AT&T, faced an extremely difficult decision. After months of sleuthing, initially not sure what they were seeking, she and two of her employees at the Clinton, Mississippi WorldCom headquarters had discovered almost $4 billion in questionable accounting entries. The specter of the Enron collapse in the fall of 2001 still loomed large and Cooper realized that the situation at WorldCom might even be a far greater financial debacle. Enron's case was complex: the company had devised a number of partnerships and specific entities to hide debt and create the illusion of income. At WorldCom, however, the fraudulent entries Cooper and her coworkers had discovered seemed pretty straightforward. If this fraud were revealed, much was at stake: the company's credibility, never mind its existence as well as that of its many subsidiaries, the fate of thousands of employees, and pension funds, full of WorldCom stock. WorldCom, the only Fortune 500 company in Mississippi, had long been the pride of the state. Cooper also worried about her and her sleuthing co-workers' reputations being muddied should they assume the role of "whistleblower." Nonetheless, Cooper knew she had to do something; the apparent fraud they suspected they had uncovered was too large and glaring. The logical next step was to meet with the board's audit committee, but Cooper had to decide whether she wanted to take that step.

UNTANGLING A WEB

Bernard Ebbers resigned as CEO of WorldCom on April 29, 2002 after a $400 million personal loan to him from the company came to light. Then WorldCom COO John Sidgmore succeeded him and immediately asked for a complete examination and assessment of the books in every division of the company. Cynthia Cooper was happy to comply because, after a series of small tips, she and auditor Gene Morse, one of her 24 employees, had begun to suspect that WorldCom might be "cooking the books."[1] In one disturbing conversation in March of that year, John Stupka, head of World-Com's wireless division, complained to Cooper that CFO Scott Sullivan had yanked $400 million from Stupka's division to use as an income boost for the company. Stupka had specifically set aside this money to make up for potential shortfalls; now, his division would have to report a tremendous loss in the coming quarter. He had approached two Arthur Anderson auditors who backed Sullivan's decision. Stupka and Cooper were skeptical of this decision, however; "under accounting rules, if a company knows it isn't going to collect on a debt, it has to set up a reserve to cover it in order to avoid reflecting on its books too high a value for that business."[2] Cooper herself tried approaching Arthur Anderson again with no success; the auditors there said that they only answered to Sullivan in WorldCom's accounting issues. Rather than drop the matter—WorldCom's CFO and two of the outside accountants had okayed the wireless division transaction, anyway—Cooper persevered in her investigation. In early March, Cooper presented her concerns about reserves to the company's board audit committee, headed by Max Bobbitt. Although Sullivan did not defend himself in this meeting, he later tracked down Cooper at her appointment with a hairdresser and angrily warned her not to interfere in John Stupka's business affairs. Certain that she was about to lose her job, Cooper packed up her personal belongings in her office. At the same time, Cooper's curiosity was piqued by Sullivan's rage. "When someone is hostile, my instinct is to find out why," she said.[3]

In the meantime, the Securities and Exchange Commission (SEC)—suspicious because in 2001, a notoriously difficult year for telecommunications companies, only WorldCom had a successful year financially—submitted a "Request for Information," giving them access to the company's financial data unavailable through public sources. Startled by this request and in preparation, Cynthia Cooper and her staff began to compile pertinent information. Cooper had also become concerned about Arthur Anderson after the accounting firm's involvement, including document shredding, with the 2001 Enron debacle.

Although it was not the internal audit department's duty, Cooper decided that she and several others in her division would investigate the company's financials on their own, performing what essentially would be a series of mini-audits. She did not mention this task to any of the higher-ups at WorldCom; instead, she and her staff worked long hours, often through the night, as they carefully pored over the books. Cooper was then alarmed when she heard that a WorldCom auditor in Texas had been fired for questioning the accounting method for some capital expenditures. The subject of capital expenditures had already piqued Cooper's interest. She and her team had unearthed a questionable $2 billion that in 2001 WorldCom had ascribed to capital expenditure when, upon further research, it had not been authorized. To Cooper's dismay, she realized that WorldCom had probably shifted operating expenses to the capital expenditure category, an illegal and deceptive accounting practice that made the company look far more profitable than it actually was.

On the evening of May 28, Gene Morse brought Cooper's attention to a rather startling accounting computer expenses entry for $500 million, with no corresponding invoices. These were recorded as capital expenditures. When they tried to follow up on this and on the concept of "prepaid capacity," a vague term that one of WorldCom's financial planners had used when Cooper questioned him about capital expenditures, they were stymied. Cooper and Morse realized that they needed to scrutinize the company's computerized accounting system and Morse figured out a way to access it. Using a new software program that the information-technology staff was testing, Morse examined the debit and credit sides of all transactions. Since the number of transactions was huge and his requests began to slow down the system, Morse started working at night when there was far less demands on the computer system and when there would be less scrutiny by other employees. Within a few weeks, he discovered $2 billion in suspicious accounting entries.

Cooper was unclear as how to proceed. In the meantime, Scott Sullivan, who knew that her department had been doing some investigation, asked Cooper and Glyn Smith, a senior manager who had worked with Cooper and Morse on the investigation, to explain what they had been doing. Without going into the details of what they found, the two told Sullivan about the audit they had been conducting themselves. Sullivan asked them to hold off on continuing the audit or revealing its results, explaining that he planned to take care of the problems the following quarter. Refusing to stall, Cooper met again with Max Bobbitt, who urged her to double-check her findings and to work with the company's new auditors, KPMG, on this problem. As part of their double-checking, Cooper and Smith talked to a number of employees, including Betty Vinson, director of management reporting, and Buford Yates, the company's director of general accounting. The path eventually led to WorldCom's controller, David Myers. Cooper and Smith explained their findings: that WorldCom was capitalizing what should have been ordinary operating expenses, and consequently reflecting less cost on a daily basis than the company was actually incurring against income. Myers admitted that the entries did not have back-up, the accounting practices used were wrong and that while he had been uncomfortable with the practice when it started in 2001, it was hard to stop once started. He also said that he hoped it didn't become a focus of investigation for the SEC.

CYNTHIA COOPER

Cynthia Cooper was born and raised in Clinton, Mississippi, in a neighborhood not far from the WorldCom company headquarters. Growing up, Cooper was well aware that money was tight and consequently began working as a teenager at places like McDonald's, Morrow's Nut House, and Golden Corral. According to her family, her determination was legendary. Unable to compete with veteran waitresses who could carry five food trays at once and in danger of being fired, Cooper did weight training and exercises until she could carry just as many. After several weeks, her manager told her "I did everything I could to make you quit. You were the worst waitress I ever had. . . . And now you're the best."[4] A top student at Clinton High School, Cooper earned an undergraduate accounting degree from the University of Alabama in 1987. Classmates remembered her as "ferocious" in class as "she would proceed to pepper the professor with questions, oblivious to her classmates' disdain."[5] Her first marriage, which landed her in Atlanta, ended in divorce and in 1991, Cooper returned to Clinton with her 2-year-old daughter. She subsequently married a high school crush, Lance Cooper, a former computer consultant who was a stay-at-home dad, and they had another daughter together.

. Now in her late 30s and a regular churchgoer, Cooper had worked at WorldCom for ten years, since being hired in the early 1990s to start an internal audit division. When she started the internal audit division in 1994, Cooper was overjoyed. "These guys were entrepreneurs," she said about Ebbers and his cronies. "There was a need to prove ourselves and the value of internal auditing," she remembers. "I loved it. It was a very exciting place to be. We were moving and shaking and acquiring companies."[6] Eight years later, Cooper remained proud of working at WorldCom and often gave tours of the facility to family and friends. The responsibilities of her department included setting budget standards, increasing efficiency, and evaluating performance; the department did not, however, have complete oversight of the company's finances. WorldCom's outside accountants, Arthur Anderson, performed the financial audits. In the presence of Bernie Ebbers, who was known to be difficult with employees not in his inner circle, Cooper was known to hold her ground even when presenting information that Ebbers did not like. Once again, Cooper's determination to succeed with this new department showed. In one of her first meetings with Ebbers and top management—a meeting that many employees remembered long afterwards—Cooper kept her cool when Ebbers arrived late. One WorldCom worker described the encounter:

> Cooper refused to start without him. After 30 painful minutes, he finally strode in, wearing his trademark sweat suit and holding a cigar. . . . "What the hell is the purpose of this meeting?" Ebbers demanded to know. Cooper, in her low, serious voice, asked him to have a seat and turned to her first slide, which defined the purpose. "He wanted to know where his next dollar was coming from," Cooper says. And she told him. Her division could find millions of dollars in wasteful operations with the use of internal controls. And indeed, over the years that followed, Cooper says, "we paid for ourselves many times over." Ebbers ended up being the last person to leave the meeting.[7]

WORLDCOM ROOTS

WorldCom began in 1983 as Long Distance Discount Services (LDDS), a small Arkansas-based long distance service broker. After the 1984 court-ordered breakup of AT&T Bell System and subsequent de-regulation of the long distance market, LDDS—like many other companies—began buying the excess capacity of the larger long-distance companies at reduced rates and reselling that time to individuals at a slight mark up over its cost. Since the re-seller owned no capacity and had no operating cost, its only risk was whether it would be able to sell its purchased time at a price in excess of the price it committed to pay. LDDS did that well and, at a time when the business community had become obsessed with telecommunications opportunities, LDDS's stock rose quickly. (See Exhibit 3.1 for a chronology of WorldCom history)

EXHIBIT 3.1. WorldCom Chronology through May 2002

1983

- Businessmen Murry Waldron and William Rector create Long Distance Discount Services (LDDS).

1985

- Bernard Ebbers, an early investor in LDDS, becomes CEO.

1989

- LDDS goes public through the acquisition of Advantage Companies, Inc.

1993

- LDDS acquires two other long-distance providers, making it the fourth largest long-distance network in the U.S.

1995

- LDDS changes its name to WorldCom Inc. after the acquisition of Williams Telecommunications Group Inc. for $2.5 billion.

1998

- WorldCom completes a merger with MCI Communications Corp. for $37 billion, the largest takeover in history at that time. Also complete merger with Brooks Fiber Properties, Inc., for $1.2 billion, and Compuserve Corp. for $1.3 billion.

1999

- June 21—WorldCom stock hits an all-time high of $64.50.

2000

- June—WorldCom's proposed $115 billion merger with Sprint is blocked by the Department of Justice on antitrust grounds.

2001

- January 2—WorldCom stock closes at $15.93.

- February 28—Struggling with depressed stock price and troublesome debt, WorldCom cuts about 6,000 jobs nationwide.

2002

- January 2—WorldCom stock closes at $14.50.
- March 11—The SEC begins an investigation of WorldCom regarding its accounting procedures and loans to officers. Over the next week World-Com stock drops 22% to $7.06.
- April 3—WorldCom announces that it is cutting 3,700 jobs (four percent of the telecom's 75,000 work staff) in the U.S.
- WorldCom stock closes at $6.51.
- April 22—Standard & Poor's cuts WorldCom's long-term and short-term credit ratings.
- April 23—Moody's Investors Service and Fitch cut WorldCom's rating.
- April 29—WorldCom CEO Bernard Ebbers resigns, potentially in connection with the SEC inquiry into the controversial $408 million in loans extended to him by WorldCom. WorldCom stock closes at $2.35.
- April 30—Vice Chairman John Sidgmore succeeds Ebbers who resigned as CEO in the midst of an SEC probe of his personal loans.
- May 9—Moody's Investor Service downgrades WorldCom's long-term debt rating three notches to 'junk' status.
- May 13—The S&P 500 drops WorldCom. WorldCom stock closes at $1.44.
- May 15—WorldCom says that it will draw down a $2.65 billion bank credit line, while it attempts to secure $5 billion more in funding from its lenders.
- May 21—Company announces that it is eliminating dividend payments and its two tracking stocks, one of which reflects internet business and the other residential telephone service.
- May 23—WorldCom secures $1.5 billion in new funding to replace the $2 billion credit line.

Although in the 1990s long-time CEO Bernard J. "Bernie" Ebbers became practically synonymous with WorldCom, as LDDS eventually became known, he was not one of the founders. Rather, he was one of the initial investors, coming on board in 1983 after a series of careers that included high school coaching and hotel management. After two years in operation, LDDS was deeply in debt and Ebbers took over as CEO, beginning a long stretch of acquisitions that, by the late 1990s, would make WorldCom one of the largest and most powerful telecommunications companies. Under Ebbers, LDDS used its increasingly valuable stock to acquire other resellers and eventually other telephone companies both in the United States and overseas.

BERNIE EBBERS

Born in Edmonton, Alberta in 1941, Ebbers traveled to Mississippi to attend college; he "arrived at a Jackson train station 32 years ago," a reporter wrote in 1997, "too broke to hire a cab. He had to hitch a ride to a college in nearby Clinton."[8] Ebbers graduated from Mississippi College in 1967 with a degree in physical education, and coached basketball for several years at Hazlehurst High School. From coaching, he went into distribution for a garment manufacturing company then became a hotelier. At six feet, four inches, Ebbers kept himself trim and healthy, and often berated WorldCom employees who did not. Despite the fabulous growth of the company and its financial status, Ebbers moved the company in 1999 to Clinton, Mississippi, home of his alma mater.

Although Ebbers had a rather tyrannical reputation within the World-Com corridors, most of the community, particularly those who knew him personally, admired and liked him, even after his resignation in 2002. Ebbers, "Bernie" to most people, faithfully attended the First Baptist Church of Bookhaven, where he taught Sunday school, had a folksy, farm- and home-grown demeanor, and often wore leather vests and cowboy hats. He was generous and donated money regularly to non-profits, including his college, the Mississippi Children's Home Society, CARES Center Inc., and the Baptist Children's Village. He was known for personal kindnesses, including flying an ill woman on a church mission trip back to the hospital in Mississippi. After his resignation, many locals still supported him. The Clinton country club golf pro and country club manager echoed many others' sentiments when he said "I am 100 percent behind Bernie, and anyone who knows what kind of man he is would be too. . . . He is a good guy, who cares for the community, a regular, nice guy."9

ACQUISITIONS PILE UP AND WORLDCOM GROWS

After taking the helm at LDDS in 1985, Ebbers began a series of acquisitions: ReTel Communications and TPC, both in Tennessee. By the end of 1986, LDDS was doing extremely well, with year-end revenues of $8.6 million. Acquisitions continued through the next several years, and in 1989, LDDS became a public company after acquiring Advantage Companies, Inc. LDDS's stock sold for approximately 84 cents per share, and the company hired Arthur Anderson as an independent auditor. LDDS acquisitions continue through the mid-1990s and, in 1995, Ebbers renamed the company WorldCom and brought Michael Jordan onboard as a spokesperson. World-Com finished out the year with 19.4 billion billed minutes and annual revenues of $3.9 billion. There were 7,000 employees and 160 offices worldwide. In 1996, the *Wall Street Journal* ranked the company number one among 1,000 corporations in returns to shareholders, the company was added to the S&P 500 index, and Ebbers earned the moniker "rising star" from *Fortune Magazine*.10 By 1997, WorldCom was the fourth largest telecommunications company in the United States. (See Exhibit 3.2 for WorldCom financials through 1997.)

WorldCom's biggest acquisitions were UUnet and MCI in 1998, the latter of which WorldCom virtually stole, at a price tag of $40 billion, from under the nose of British Telecom. This acquisition shocked the business world, since MCI was three times the size of WorldCom. In 1999, WorldCom and Sprint agreed to merge, but U.S. and European regulators stopped the merger in 2000. This was, according to one analyst, a "major stumble" for WorldCom. "Ebbers had grown WorldCom's revenues principally through acquisitions of other telecom companies, rather than through growth in operations. Now there were no other large telecommunications companies available for merger, and without mergers the company's phenomenal

EXHIBIT 3.2. WorldCom Financials, 1988–1997

WORLDCOM, INC.

This record provides a historical snapshot of the company as it appeared before Hoover's discontinued active coverage.

Historical Financials & Employees

Income Statement

Year	Revenue ($ mil.)	Net Income ($ mil.)	Net Profit Margin	Employees
Dec 97	7,351.4	383.7	5.2%	20,300
Dec 96	4,485.1	(2,213.3)	—	13,000
Dec 95	3,639.9	267.7	7.4%	7,500
Dec 94	2,220.8	(122.3)	—	4,379
Dec 93	1,144.7	104.2	9.1%	2,440
Dec 92	801.0	(8.0)	—	901
Dec 91	263.0	18.0	6.8%	516
Dec 90	154.0	10.0	6.5%	360
Dec 89	110.0	1.0	0.9%	—
Dec 88	53.0	2.0	3.8%	—

Stock History

	Stock Price ($)			P/E		Per Share ($)		
Year	FY High	FY Low	FY Close	High	Low	Earns.	Div.	Book Value
Dec 97	39.88	21.25	30.25	—	—	0.40	0.00	148.59
Dec 96	28.88	16.25	26.06	—	—	(5.56)	0.00	146.43
Dec 95	17.94	9.56	17.63	—	—	0.64	0.00	56.59
Dec 94	14.75	7.00	9.72	—	—	(0.48)	0.00	57.23
Dec 93	13.19	10.06	12.06	—	—	0.38	0.00	67.99

Source: http://premium.hoovers.com/subscribe/co/boneyard/fin/history.xhtml?ID=15160

revenue growth would come to a halt."[11] Also hurting WorldCom was the overall slowdown in the telecommunications industry growth. Growth had outpaced demand, and 1999 saw a softening of prices overall in this industry.

By the 21st century, WorldCom was a "fully integrated communications company," providing "switched and dedicated long distance and local telephone services, dedicated and broadband data services, debit cards, conference calling, advanced billing systems, enhanced fax and data connections, high speed data communications, facilities management, Web server hosting, integration services, connection via Network Access Points to Internet service providers, and resale of cellular services."[12]

Like Ebbers, WorldCom retained a wild and woolly cowboy-like culture. By 2002, WorldCom had 70,000 employees and was $28 billion in debt. At its peak, the company's market cap was $175 billion. There were 70,000 miles of wire, and lots of entities strung from Mississippi to Bermuda and the Caymans. All of the companies acquired by WorldCom continued to operate as they had before and many WorldCom employees reported chaos despite the company's proud acclaim of "synergy." However, many of WorldCom's employees had no idea whether it was profitable, in large part because the accounting methods were described as "backpocket." Concerns cropped up. A manager in London was troubled when his costs went down—after he had closed the books for his unit. When he questioned local Andersen auditors about this, he was told by Myers, the Chief Accounting officer in Mississippi, to stop asking questions.

Ebbers faced trouble in the spring of 2002 when it was revealed that he had borrowed $400 million from the company, collateralized by his World-Com stock, causing some employees to refer to the company as WorldRon, a nod to Kenneth Lay and his borrowing from the now defunct Enron. Shortly afterwards, in April, Ebbers was forced to resign.

CONCLUSION

Cynthia Cooper had an important decision to make. A lot was at stake. She loved her job and the entrepreneurial spirit at WorldCom and was very loyal to the company. Cooper did not want to damage WorldCom's reputation, nor did she relish the role of whistleblower, a word she hated and which she likened to "tattletale." The events of that spring and her sleuthing efforts had taken a physical and emotional toll on Cooper; family members had seen the strain on her face. Cooper remembered the words her mother used to say repeatedly: "Never allow yourself to be intimidated. Always think about the consequences of your actions."[13] With this in mind, Cooper pondered her choices. Should she report her additional findings once again to the audit board? Should she take steps to make sure this information became public?

Notes

1. Information taken from Susan Pulliam and Deborah Solomon, "How 3 Unlikely Sleuths Uncooked WorldCom's Books; Company's Own Auditors Sniffed Out Cryptic Clues, Followed Their Hunches," *The Wall Street Journal Europe*, October 31, 2002, p. A8.
2. Ibid.
3. Ripley, Amanda, "Cynthia Cooper: The Night Detective," *Time Magazine*, vol. 160, Iss. 27, December 30, 2002, p. 44.
4. Ibid.
5. Ibid.
6. Ibid.
7. Ibid.
8. Colvin, Geoffrey, "Bernie Ebbers' Foolish Faith," *Fortune Magazine*, November 25, 2002, vol. 146, Iss. 11, p. 52.
9. Charles Laurence, "It's Those Damn Yankees," *The Sunday Telegraph* (London, England), June 30, 2002, p. 19.

10. Jeter, Lynne W., *Disconnected: Deceit and Betrayal at WorldCom* Hoboken, NJ: John Wiley & Sons, 2003), p. 59.
11. Cochran, Kenneth, "WorldCom—A Case Study," University of Texas at Dallas, 2004, http://www. utdallas. edu/ ~billdent/ 6334—WorldCom%20Case%20Study. htm
12. Healy, Paul M., and Jacob Cohen J.D., *The MCI-WorldCom Combination (A)* (#9-101-027) (Cambridge, MA: the President and Fellows of Harvard College, Harvard Business School Publishing, September 12, 2000), p. 2.
13. Ripley, op. cit.

Ethical Duties Towards Others: "Truthfulness"

Immanuel Kant

The exchange of our sentiments is the principal factor in social intercourse, and truth must be the guiding principle herein. Without truth social intercourse and conversation become valueless. We can only know what a man thinks if he tells us his thoughts, and when he undertakes to express them he must really do so, or else there can be no society of men. Fellowship is only the second condition of society, and a liar destroys fellowship. Lying makes it impossible to derive any benefit from conversation. Liars are, therefore, held in general contempt. Man is inclined to be reserved and to pretend. . . . Man is reserved in order to conceal his faults and shortcomings which he has; he pretends in order to make others attribute to him merits and virtues which he has not. Our proclivity to reserve and concealment is due to the will of Providence that the defects of which we are full should not be too obvious. Many of our propensities and peculiarities are objectionable to others, and if they became patent we should be foolish and hateful in their eyes. Moreover, the parading of these objectionable characteristics would so familiarize men with them that they would themselves acquire them. Therefore we arrange our conduct either to conceal our faults or to appear other than we are. We possess the art of simulation. In consequence, our inner weakness and error is revealed to the eyes of men only as an appearance of well-being, while we ourselves develop the habit of dispositions which are conducive to good conduct. No man in his true senses, therefore, is candid. Were man candid, were the request of Momus[1] to be complied with that Jupiter should place a mirror in each man's heart so that his disposition might be visible to all, man would have to be better constituted and possess good principles. If all men were good there would be no need for any of us to be reserved; but since they are not, we have to keep the shutters closed. Every house keeps its dustbin in a place of its own. We do not press our friends to come into our water-closet, although they know that we have one just like themselves. Familiarity in such things is the ruin of good taste. In the same way we make no exhibition of our defects, but try to conceal them. We try to conceal our mistrust by affecting a courteous demeanor and so accustom ourselves to courtesy that at last it becomes a reality and we set a good example by it. If that were not so, if there were none who were better than we, we should become neglectful. Accordingly, the endeavour to appear good ultimately makes us really good. If all men were good, they could be candid, but as things are they cannot be. To be reserved is to be restrained in expressing one's mind. We can, of course, keep absolute silence. This is the readiest and most absolute method of reserve, but it is unsociable, and a silent man is not only unwanted in social circles but is also suspected; every one thinks him deep and disparaging, for if when asked for his opinion he remains silent people think that he must be taking the worst view or he would not be averse from expressing it. Silence, in fact, is always a treacherous ally, and therefore it is not even prudent to be completely reserved. Yet there is such a thing as prudent reserve, which requires not silence but careful deliberation; a man who is wisely reserved weighs his words carefully and speaks his mind about every thing excepting only those things in regard to which he deems it wise to be reserved.

We must distinguish between reserve and secretiveness, which is something entirely different. There are matters about which one has no desire to speak and in regard to which reserve is easy. We are, for instance, not naturally tempted to speak about and to betray our own misdemeanours. Everyone finds it easy to keep a reserve about some of his private affairs, but there are times about which it requires an effort to be silent. Secrets have a way of coming out, and strength is required to prevent ourselves betraying them. Secrets are always matters deposited with us by other people and they ought not to be placed at the disposal of third parties. But man has a great liking for conversation, and the telling of secrets adds much to the interest of conversation; a secret told is like a present given; how then are we to keep secrets? Men who are not very talkative as a rule keep secrets well, but good conversationalists, who are at the same time clever, keep them better. The former might be induced to betray something, but the latter's gift of repartee invariably enables them to invent on the spur of the moment something non-committal.

The person who is as silent as a mute goes to one extreme; the person who is loquacious goes to the opposite. Both tendencies are weaknesses. Men are liable to the first, women to the second. Someone has said that women are talkative because the training of infants is their special charge, and their talkativeness soon teaches a child to speak, because they can chatter to it all day long. If men had the care of the child, they would take much longer to learn to talk. However that may be, we dislike anyone who will not speak: he annoys us; his silence betrays his pride. On the other hand, loquaciousness in men is contemptible and contrary to the strength of the male. All this by the way; we shall now pass to more weighty matters.

If I announce my intention to tell what is in my mind, ought I knowingly to tell everything, or can I keep anything back? If I indicate that I mean to speak my mind, and instead of doing so make false declaration, what I say is an untruth, a *falsiloquium*. But there can be *falsiloquium* even when people have no right to assume that we are expressing our thoughts. It is possible to deceive without making any statement whatever. I can make believe, make a demonstration from which others will draw the conclusion I want, though they have no right to expect that my action will express my real mind. In that case I have not lied to them, because I had not undertaken to express my mind. I may, for instance, wish people to think that I am off on a journey, and so I pack my luggage; people draw the conclusion I want them to draw; but others have no right to demand a declaration of my will from me.

. . . Again, I may make a false statement (*falsiloquium*), when my purpose is to hide from another what is in my mind and when the latter can assume that such is my purpose, his own purpose being to make a wrong use of the truth. Thus, for instance, if my enemy takes me by the throat and asks where I keep my money, I need not tell him the truth, because he will abuse it; and my untruth is not a lie (*mendacium*) because the thief knows full well that I will not, if I can help it, tell him the truth and that he has no right to demand it of me. But let us assume that I really say to the fellow, who is fully aware that he has no right to demand it, because he is a swindler, that I will tell him the truth, and I do not, am I then a liar? He has deceived me and I deceive him in return; to him, as an individual, I have done no injustice and he cannot complain; but I am none the less a liar in that my conduct is an infringement of the rights of humanity. It follows that a f*alsiloquium* can be a *mendacium*—a lie—especially when it contravenes the right of an individual. Although I do a man no injustice by lying to him when he has lied to me, yet I act against the right of mankind, since I set myself in opposition to the condition and means through which any human society is possible. If one country breaks the peace this does not justify the other in doing likewise in revenge, for if it did no peace would ever be secure. Even though a statement does not contravene any particular human right it is nevertheless a lie if it is contrary to the general right of mankind. If a man spreads false news, though he does no wrong to anyone in particular, he offends against mankind, because if such a practice were universal man's desire for knowledge would be frustrated. For, apart from speculation, there are only two ways in which I can increase my fund of knowledge, by experience or by what others tell me. My own experience must necessarily be limited, and if what others told me was false, I could not satisfy my craving for knowledge.

. . . Not every untruth is a lie; it is a lie only if I have expressly given the other to understand that I am willing to acquaint him with my thought. Every lie is objectionable and contemptible in that we purposely let people think that we are telling them our thoughts and do not do so. We have broken our pact and violated the right of mankind. But if we were to be at all times punctiliously truthful we might often become victims of the wickedness of others who were ready to abuse our truthfulness. If all men were well-intentioned it would not only be a duty not to lie, but no one would do so because there would be no point in it. But as men are malicious, it cannot be denied that to be punctiliously truthful is often dangerous. This has given rise to the conception of a white lie, the lie enforced upon us by necessity—a difficult point for moral philosophers. For if necessity is urged as an excuse it might be urged to justify stealing, cheating, and killing, and the whole basis of morality goes by the board. Then, again, what is a case of necessity? Everyone will interpret it in his own way. And, as there is then no definite standard to judge by, the application of moral rules becomes uncertain. Consider, for example, the following case. A man who knows that I have money asks me: "Have you any money on you?" If I fail to reply, he will conclude that I have; if I reply in the affirmative he will take it from me; if I reply in the negative, I tell a lie. What am I to do? If force is used to extort a confession from me, if any confession is improperly used against me, and if I cannot save myself by maintaining silence, then my lie is a weapon of defence. The misuse of a declaration extorted by force justifies me in defending myself. For whether it is my money or a confession that is extorted makes no difference. The forcing of a statement from me under conditions which convince me that improper use would be made of it is the only case in which I can be justified in telling a white lie. But if a lie does no harm to anyone and no one's interests are affected by it, is it a lie? Certainly, I undertake to express my mind, and if I do not really do so, though my statement may not be to the prejudice of the particular individual to whom it was made, it is none the less in *praejudicium humanitatis*. Then, again, there are lies which cheat. To cheat is to make a lying promise, while a breach of faith is a true promise which is not kept. A lying promise is an insult to the person to whom it is made, and even if this is not always so, yet there is always something mean about it. If, for instance, I promise to send someone a bottle of wine, and afterwards make a joke of it, I really swindle him. It is true that he had no right to demand the present of me, but in Idea it is already a part of his own property.

   . . . If a man tries to extort the truth from us and we cannot tell it [to] him and at the same time do not wish to lie, we are justified in resorting to equivocation in order to reduce him to silence and put a stop to his questionings. If he is wise, he will leave it at that. But if we let it be understood that we are expressing our sentiments and we proceed to equivocate, we are in a different case; for our listeners might then draw wrong conclusions from our statements and we should have deceived them. . . . But a lie is a lie, and is in itself intrinsically base whether it be told with good or bad intent. For formally a lie is always evil; though if it is evil materially as well, it is a much meaner thing. There are no lies which may not be the source of evil. A liar is a coward; he is a man who has recourse to lying because he is unable to help himself and gain his ends by any other means. But a stouthearted man will love truth and will not recognize a *casus necessitatis*. All expedients which take us off our guard are thoroughly mean. Such are lying, assassination, and poisoning. To attack a man on the highway is less vile than to attempt to poison him. In the former case he can at least defend himself, but, as he must eat, he is defenseless against the poisoner. A flatterer is not always a liar; he is merely lacking in self-esteem; he has no scruple in reducing his own worth and raising that of another in order to gain something by it. But there exists a form of flattery which springs from kindness of heart. Some kind souls flatter people whom they hold in high esteem. There are thus two kinds of flattery, kindly and treacherous; the first is weak, while the second is mean. People who are not given to flattery are apt to be fault-finders.

   If a man is often the subject of conversation, he becomes a subject of criticism. If he is our friend, we ought not invariably to speak well of him or else we arouse jealousy and grudge against him; for people, knowing that he is only human, will not believe that he has only good qualities. We must, therefore, concede a little to the adverse criticism of our listeners and point out some of our friend's faults; if we allow him faults which are common and unessential, while extolling his merits, our friend cannot take it in ill part. Toadies are people who praise others in company in hope of gain. Men are meant to form opinions regarding their fellows and to judge them. Nature has made us judges of our neighbors so that things which are false but are outside the scope of the established legal authority should be arraigned before the court of social opinion. Thus, if a man dishonours someone, the authorities do not punish him, but his fellows judge and punish him, though only so far as it is within their right to punish him and without doing violence to him. People shun him, and that is punishment enough. If that were not so, conduct not punished by the authorities would go altogether unpunished. What then is meant by the enjoinder that we ought not to judge others? As we are ignorant of their dispositions we cannot tell whether they are punishable before God or not, and we cannot, therefore, pass an adequate moral judgment upon them. The moral dispositions of others are for God to judge, but we are competent judges of our own. We cannot judge the inner core of morality; no man can do that; but we are competent to judge its outer manifestations. In matters of morality we are not judges of our fellows, but nature has given us the right to form judgments about others and she also has ordained that we should judge ourselves in accordance with judgments that others form about us. The man who turns a deaf ear to other people's opinion of him is base and reprehensible. There is nothing that happens in this world about which we ought not to form an opinion, and we show considerable subtlety in judging conduct. Those who judge our conduct with exactness are our best friends. Only friends can be quite candid and open with each other. But in judging a man a further question arises. In what terms are we to judge him? Must we pronounce him either good or evil? We must proceed from the assumption that humanity is lovable, and, particularly in regard to wickedness, we ought never to pronounce a verdict either of condemnation or of acquittal. We pronounce such a verdict whenever we judge from his conduct that a man deserves to be condemned or acquitted. But though we are entitled to form opinions about our fellows, we have no right to spy upon them. Everyone has a right to prevent others from watching and scrutinizing his actions. The spy arrogates to himself the right to watch the doings of strangers; no one ought to presume to do such a thing. If I see two people whispering to each other so as to not be heard, my inclination ought to be to get farther away so that no sound may reach my ears. Or if I am left alone in a room and I see a letter lying open on the table, it would be contemptible to try to read it; a right-thinking man would not do so; in fact, in order to avoid suspicion and distrust he will endeavour not to be left alone in a room where money is left lying about, and he will be averse from learning other people's secrets in order to avoid the risk of the suspicion that he has betrayed them; other people's secrets trouble him, for even between the most intimate of friends suspicion might arise. A man who will let his inclination or appetite drive him to deprive his friend of anything, of his fiancée, for instance, is contemptible beyond a doubt. If he can cherish a passion for my sweetheart, he can equally well cherish a passion for my purse. It is very mean to lie in wait and spy upon a friend, or on anyone else, and to elicit information about him from menials by lowering ourselves to the level of our inferiors, who will thereafter not forget to regard themselves as our equals. Whatever militates against frankness lowers the dignity of man. Insidious, underhand conduct uses means which strike at the roots of society because they make frankness impossible; it is far viler than violence; for against violence we can defend ourselves, and a violent man who spurns meanness can be tamed to goodness, but the mean rogue, who has not the courage to come out into the open with his roguery, is devoid of every vestige of nobility of character. For that reason a wife who attempts to poison her husband in England is burnt at the stake, for if such conduct spread, no man would be safe from his wife.

As I am not entitled to spy upon my neighbour, I am equally not entitled to point out his faults to him; and even if he should ask me to do so he would feel hurt if I complied. He knows his faults better than I, he knows that he has them, but he likes to believe that I have not noticed them, and if I tell him of them he realizes that I have. To say, therefore, that friends ought to point out each other's faults, is not sound advice. My friend may know better than I whether my gait or deportment is proper or not, but if I will only examine myself, who can know me better than I can know myself? To point out his faults to a friend is sheer impertinence; and once fault finding begins between friends their friendship will not last long. We must turn a blind eye to the faults of others, lest they conclude that they have lost our respect and we lose theirs. Only if placed in positions of authority over others should we point out to them their defects. Thus a husband is entitled to teach and correct his wife, but his corrections must be well-intentioned and kindly and must be dominated by respect, for if they be prompted only by displeasure they result in mere blame and bitterness. If we must blame, we must temper the blame with a sweetening of love, good-will, and respect. Nothing else will avail to bring about improvement.

Note

1. CF. *Babrii fabulae Aesopeae*, ed. O. Cousins, 1897, Fable 59, p. 54.

Trust, Morality, and International Business

GEORGE G. BRENKERT

I. INTRODUCTION

The expanding globalization of business has brought with it the increased importance of an international business ethics. We need answers to a multitude of questions concerning an international business community in which commerce would occur in accordance with justified moral standards. This ethics would tell us when workers in developing nations were being exploited, which dangerous products should not be shipped across national

Reprinted by permission of the author, George G. Brenkert, and *Business Ethics Quarterly*, vol. 8, Issue 2, 1998.

borders to be sold, and when the offer of cash or gifts amounted to bribes or were being extorted by members of another society. It would speak to the managers of multinationals about transfer pricing, the use of child labor, and attempts to economically develop people living in tribal conditions. It would provide moral guidance for those considering the development of large industrial plants, electrical plants, dams, etc., in developing nations.

However, if we are to speak productively of an international business ethics, we must seek an ethics that can be a morality. By this I mean, among other things, an ethics whose rules, principles, and values are capable of being taught and communicated to others; one for which there are forces that lead to its renewal; and one that will be stable across different societies. An important part, then, of defending an international business ethics is the identification of its practical conditions. . . .

The following paper maintains that trust is one of the important background bases of an international business ethics. Though the role of trust has been examined recently from a number of directions, e.g., its role in the production of national prosperity (Fukuyama, 1995); in competitive advantage (Barney and Hansen, 1994; Jones, 1995); and even as part of morality itself (Hosmer, 1995), it has not, as far as I know, been considered in the role of providing a basic condition for an international business morality. To do so carries important and interesting implications for an international business morality. To do so carries important and interesting implications for an international business ethics. As such, a central aim of this paper is to spell out the conditions surrounding trust and an international business morality.[1] More generally, this paper is an exploration of the relation of trust and morality on the international level between commercial agents. . . .

II. TRUST AND MORALITY

There are several important characteristics of . . . trust which influence the role it can play in an international business ethics.

First, trust is not a principle, let alone a moral principle, but an attitude or disposition to behave and respond in certain ways, viz., to accept certain risks of harm or injury from another agent on the basis of a belief (for which there is some degree of uncertainty) that the other does not intend to do harm to one (or those one cares about), even though he/she could (cf. Solomon, 1992: 213).[2] It is not surprising, then, that Rawls calls trust a natural attitude (Rawls, 1972: 497). Solomon calls trust a business virtue, due to its dispositional nature and because it involves acting in admirable ways (Solomon, 1992: 107f). . . .

Second, trust involves a commonality of values or aims (real or perceived) in terms of which the trust relationship is built. This commonality need not be complete or even extensive. People with very different values can trust each other. Still, there must be some common aims or values in light of which the trust relationship is established and maintained. Such values might include those of consistency, non-maleficence, certain forms of expertise, as well as appreciation of similar activities and forms of success. In short, both moral and nonmoral values and aims might be part of this commonality. The role of these common values and aims is to foster the development of trusting attitudes inasmuch as they may give one reasons to believe that the trusted party will not act contrary to, or harm, vulnerable interests one deems important. Such reasons may take the form of various explicit expectations or predictions of the other's future behavior. They may also take more implicit intuitive forms of confidence in the trusted individual. Her wants are compatible with ours; they value the same things we do; we enjoy a strong sense of mutual sympathy. In these situations, we may trust each other, not because we are thinking about predicting future behaviors, but because we are responding to present mutual connections. . . .

Third, trust may involve judgment in at least two ways. On the one hand, one may make certain judgments about the trustworthiness of someone else. And this may play an important role in entering a trusting relation with that other individual or firm.[3] On the other hand, trust involves allowing some discretion on the part of the person or agent trusted. Thus, Baier comments that ". . . To trust is to give discretionary powers to the trusted, to let the trusted decide how, on a given matter, one's welfare is best advanced, to delay the account for a while, to wait to see how the trusted has advanced one's welfare" (Baier, 1995: 136).[4] That is, each member of the relation is granted some leeway to make various judgments and decisions which are not themselves prescribed by a contract or other set of rules. Rather, the good will and intentions of each member are assumed. It is assumed that they will competently make certain judgments as to what is to be done for the well-being of both parties in the relationship.

Fourth, trust must be distinguished from trustworthiness. Trust is an attitude or disposition to place oneself under certain circumstances in a situation where one is vulnerable to harm which may come from others on whose good will one depends. As an attitude or disposition, trust tends to be open-ended; it need not be specific to a particular, single situation. Hence, it tends to concern longer-term relationships than simply brief, limited ones. The temporal extendedness of trust variously depends upon a number of factors, including the mutuality of the interests that bring those that trust together, the degree and kind of trust, the non-violation of vulnerabilities, and the continuing fulfillment of the conditions of trust.

Trustworthiness, however, is not an attitude, but the evaluative appraisal that an individual is worthy of trust, i.e., that another person might reasonably place his or her trust in that individual. As such, trustworthiness cannot be equated with an individual (or firm) being one that others ought to trust (cf. Horsburgh, 1960: 28) or with simply not being opportunistic (Jones, 1995: 421). The fact that a person or business is trustworthy does not imply that others ought to trust them, since other firms or people may have no reason to form a relationship with them at all. Further, if "opportunism" is understood as "pursuing self-interest with guile," then a person might not be opportunistic and still not trustworthy. This might occur when a person wished only the best for someone else, but could not be considered trustworthy because he was incompetent, not able to keep promises, or unwilling to listen to what others really wanted. Instead, one's trustworthiness betokens the reasonableness with which others might trust one. . . .

Fifth, the conflicted relation of trust to morality deserves notice. On the one hand, trust is widely accepted as an important value. Part of the importance of trust is that it is valued by individuals and cultures around the globe even though they are divided on a variety of other values and principles. For example, Puffer and McCarthy note that "maintaining trust" is one value which both Americans and Russians share and on which they can build mutual relationships (Puffer and McCarthy, 1995: 35). In contrast, they claim, "maximizing profits" though viewed as ethical in the U.S. is considered unethical in Russia, whereas "price fixing" is deemed to be unethical in the U.S. but ethical in Russia (Puffer and McCarthy, 1995: 35). However, "maintaining trust" is ethically esteemed by both societies. This result may well be replicated with other countries (e.g., Japan). Thus, trust may constitute a common value to which people and organizations across different cultures may (and must) appeal.

This is not to say, however, that certain instances of trust may not serve immoral ends. When some are able, because they trust each other, to engage in an enterprise that dumps toxic chemicals in the ocean, overbills a government, colludes against other firms, or misappropriates funds intended for villages affected by their manufacturing plants, then immoral ends are served. Accordingly, Baier comments that "there are immoral as well as moral trust relationships, and trustbusting can be a morally proper goal" (Baier, 1995: 95). Consequently, trust is not an unconditional value. Its value in particular instances depends upon the context within which it is exercised. If trust is employed concerning morally worthy projects, then such trust is valuable. On the other hand, when it is formed around morally unworthy projects trust may lack moral value. Without a good will, as Kant might say, trust can be extremely bad or harmful. What this implies is that trust cannot be a sufficient condition for moral business relations, though it is a necessary condition. As we shall see below, trust involves various forms of interaction which are essential to moral systems and upon which a business ethics may draw. Consequently, it is mistaken to think that trust has no relation to morality or ethics at all because it does not guarantee moral action. People may dispute over whether a glass of water filled to the middle is half empty or half full, but it would be hasty for those who decide it is half empty to proceed to conclude that there is no water in the glass at all.

Still, it would appear that trust is not simply something of instrumental value, but also of intrinsic value. Trust is like courage in that even when it occurs in conjunction with immoral ends we can appreciate the value of the trusting (or the courage) itself. Trust, in this sense, is a kind of attitude and behavior which is distinguishable from instances in which people are unable or unwilling ever to render themselves vulnerable to others, as well as those who recklessly place themselves in the hands of others. The former end up recluses, isolated from others. In the latter case, when people simply place themselves in the hands of others whom everyone else can see are utterly untrustworthy, what might be a valuable form of trusting behavior may be viewed as simply a case of foolhardiness and recklessness. . . .

III. TRUST WITHIN THE BUSINESS CONTEXT

We may portray the role of trust within business by distinguishing three different forms of trust. These are distinguished in terms of the particular contexts in which trust plays a role. Accordingly, we may distinguish Basic Trust,

Guarded Trust and Extended Trust. A complete account of trust and of business ethics needs to address these forms of trust.[5]

Basic trust is the trust that individual agents have that other moral agents, with whom they have only impersonal, systematic relations, will act in certain kinds of standard ways not to take advantage of their vulnerabilities. This is a general form of trust which might be said to be "coextensive with the very existence of a social order" such as the market or morality itself (Gellner, 1988: 142; Thomas, 1978: 90). Sable speaks of such trust as being a precondition of social life (Sable, 1993: 1136). Thus, DeGeorge comments that "if there were not some minimum level of trust between buyer and seller on the international level, just as on the national level, business transactions would prove impossible" (DeGeorge, 1993: 21). And Baier says that ". . . as anything more than a law within, [morality] itself requires trust in order to thrive . . ." (Baier, 1986: 232). Accordingly, trust is a background condition, or part of the background environment (Brenkert, 1994; Dasgupta, 1988: 49; DeGeorge, 1993). In this sense of trust, we must trust strangers. Hence this is an underlying, impersonal, and systematic form of trust. . . .

Basic trust is a background form of trust for this more specialized case of trust. If we did not regularly trust in this basic manner, but distrusted each other or doubted each other's sincerity, cooperation, and good intentions, more elaborate forms of trust would be difficult if not impossible. It is in this sense then that H. B. Acton is said to have held that "trust and mutual confidence are the norm in social life, and that deception and wrongdoing are to be regarded as abnormalities" (Thomas, 1978: 90). This does not mean that social life cannot tolerate distrust. However, as D. O. Thomas argues, "the more violations of trust there are and the greater the reluctance to trust, the more impoverished does social life become and the fewer the benefits that men derive from it" (Thomas, 1978: 92). Basic trust need not be, and most generally is not, articulated or made explicit. However, when it is violated, those involved are made painfully aware that they had indeed trusted that the violator would not act in the way in which he/she did. Basic trust within the market system assumes that others will play by recognized, generally accepted rules, customs, or standards, not that they won't use those rules and their abilities to try to get an advantage over one's firm.

Guarded trust is necessary when agents invoke various explicit contracts to protect their vulnerabilities and specify penalties for injury to those vulnerabilities and their interests. Trust is required here to maintain the relation in the face of unclarities in contracts. "In fact no contract, even if it is scrutinized by sharp lawyers, can detail every eventuality, if for no other reason than that no language can cope with unlimited refinement in distinguishing continuities. Trust covers expectations about what others will do or have done . . . in circumstances that are not explicitly covered in the agreement" (Dasgupta, 1988: 52–53). Thus, guarded trust makes contracts possible. As such, it is singularly important for business. Sako refers to this as contractual trust, i.e., when each partner adheres to agreements and keeps promises (Sako, 1991, 1992). However, "guarded trust" does not require, as does Sako's contractual trust, that those who engage in this form of trust are involved in "upholding a universalistic ethical standard, namely that of keeping promises" (Sako, 1991: 451). Of course, they might be doing this. On the other hand, they might be appealing to some other moral standard(s) or simply to some nonmoral values or aims which motivate and justify their maintenance of the contract. Sako's view overly moralizes this form of trust. Barney and Hansen refer to this trust as "semi-strong form trust." When significant exchange vulnerabilities exist, but the parties can protect themselves through various governance devices, semi-strong trust can exist (Barney and Hansen, 1994: 177). Both market based and contractual governance devices are relevant to guarded trust (Barney and Hansen, 1994: 178).

In contrast to basic trust, guarded trust holds only between those firms and individuals who set up specific contracts and monitoring practices. Hence it is limited in time. In addition, the monitoring devices and restricted range of guarded trust limit the flexibility of the partners and involve various transaction costs. . . .

Extended trust involves firms and individuals acting to trust one another beyond basic and guarded forms of trust. It develops within special relations which involve trusting other firms and individuals when contracts and monitoring devices are not in place or have been significantly reduced. It is in this sense of trust that we are taught as children not to trust strangers, but only certain special individuals. Extended trust requires that firms and individuals expose their vulnerabilities to one another when there is clear uncertainty and risk that harm could come to the firm, or individuals in the firm, from those who are trusted. It is part of an ongoing relationship which is not necessarily temporally limited to a particular contract, but arises out of the value structures of the firms which permit this greater exposure of each firm's vulnerabilities to the other firms so as to create a relation which is mutually desired. To the extent that firms and individuals can trust in this manner they will be able to act with greater flexibility and freedom in their relations with those whom they so trust (cf. Barney and Hansen, 1994; Jones, 1995). This relation may exist not only between firms, but also between firms and their stakeholders (e.g., employees, stockholders, and members of the community). . . . Extended trust, then, differs from guarded trust in the lack of monitoring devices, formal contracts, and special sanctions that are required for guarded trust, as well as in its dependence on the value structures of the participants which permit greater openness to each other through their restriction of their self-interested actions (cf. Barney and Hansen, 1994). Those who trust in this extended fashion may well go on to engage in special initiatives. But firms may also engage in extended trust relations with each other without each partner doing so. It would be sufficient that they engage in various forms of exchange and interchange within a present set of activities, which lack the protections of contracts, etc.

Accordingly, basic trust and guarded trust are important for sustaining the social, economic, and moral systems within which business acts. Without these forms of trust, these systems would collapse. Extended trust is important for the flexibility and independence which it may afford particular businesses which can engage in it as well as for the morally richer relationships which it permits. In addition, one might maintain that if there is extended trust between a firm and its subsidiaries, then the subsidiary will be allowed to make a wider range of decisions involving product differentiation, etc. which permits a fuller moral agency of the subsidiary. If we assume that, all things being equal, a person or group which is accorded full moral agency will respond favorably, then we might expect not only a higher level of morality, but also greater efficiency from such a unit (cf. Horng, 1993). Consequently, a business ethics which does not take these forms of trust into account or provide for their development cannot be complete or a sustainable business ethics. However, since trust may also be involved in nefarious relationships, we must now look more closely at trust within the context of an international business morality.

IV. TRUST AND INTERNATIONAL BUSINESS

Different conditions are required to produce each of the preceding forms of trust. By considering these conditions, we may also see the problems which trust within an international business context faces. We can also identify difficulties which an international business ethics must confront.

Basic trust rests upon two underlying conditions: a) the commonality of motives associated with mutual acceptance of common basic norms, values and customs; and b) the consistency of behavior of those acting on those motives. Individuals tend to trust each other the greater the similarity and mutuality of their motives, values and ends. Accordingly, basic trust rests on several assumptions: that others do not have motives to harm them; that if they do have such motives, they have other overriding motives which keep the former in check; or, finally, that if they have motives which may lead to their harm, these motives are exercised within certain widely recognized and accepted forms of behavior such that they may be anticipated or avoided. Consequently, if one business simply outcompetes another business, this is not a reason to abandon one's basic trust in the market system or in other individuals more generally.

The consistency of the behavior of others is also crucial for basic trust. Obviously, in cases of trust, there is uncertainty by the nature of the case. However, if an individual or firm acted simply arbitrarily or inconsistently, it would not be one that would readily be trusted.[6] It is for this reason that reputation is also so important in establishing the trustworthiness of a firm or individual (Dasgupta, 1988).

Guarded trust requires both of the preceding two conditions regarding common motives and consistency of behavior, as well as knowledge of the competence of the other party, i.e., that the other party is capable of carrying out the contract. If a firm is prepared to commit itself to doing certain things, but is perceived not to be able or competent to do those things, then trust is less likely in such cases. Such competence might include categories which Gabarro has identified: a) functional or specific competence: competence in the specialized knowledge and skills required to do a particular job; and b) interpersonal competence: people skills and knowing how to work with people (Gabarro, 1978).

Finally, extended trust requires the preceding three conditions (common motives, consistency of behavior and acknowledged competence) as well as a fourth condition, openness. Individuals or firms may engage in extended trust depending upon whether each is prepared to open up to the other so as to reveal private or confidential information. Openness may also involve being physically available to the other, e.g., opening the doors of one's plant to the trusted partner. Finally, openness may involve levelling with another, as well as not creating or permitting misleading expectations to be generated in the other (cf. Gabarro, 1978).

Thus, as we move from simpler to more complex forms of trust, the conditions required for earlier forms of trust are added to those required for later forms of trust. Extended trust, the most developed form of trust, requires commonality of motives (or ends), consistency of behavior, acknowledged competence, and openness.

It is immediately obvious that the creation of morally worthy trust within international contexts faces special problems that it does not face on the national level. A partial list of obstacles include the following:

Values and motives may differ dramatically. For example, attitudes towards and evaluations of individualism, uncertainty, and aggressive competition may impede trusting relationships (cf. Hofstede, 1979).[7] It is not surprising then that it is frequently claimed that trust is more likely developed in circumstances where there is a common history, belief in the same god, and dedication to the same political ends (Sable, 1993: 1135). Thus Shell comments that "similarity of backgrounds and tastes also helps smooth the way to trusting relations" (Shell, 1991: 258). And Baier agrees that "awareness of what is customary . . . affects one's ability to trust" (Baier, 1986: 245). Since it is not possible internationally, to rely on joint customs, traditions, language, or histories, much of the common basis upon which trust may develop within a national culture is missing. In addition, similar institutions and social structures such as those regarding property also help in the production of trust. But where there exist significant differences, for example, over intellectual property, obstacles to trust will again be perceived.

Ethnocentric and egocentric tendencies will also impede trusting relations internationally. For example, the tendency of an egocentric fairness bias, "which is a tendency for people to see arrangements that favour themselves over others as fairer than arrangements that favour others" will acerbate other ethnocentric biases (Messick et al., 1985: 624).[8] Michalos notes studies which show that "most people think most [other] people are not as nice as they are themselves and, therefore, cannot be trusted to behave as well" (Michalos, 1990: 627). These tendencies will be particularly acute internationally, where people look, talk, and behave differently.

Due to past colonialism and imperialism, past histories may stand in the way of trusting relationships. Further, due to racism (or suspicions of racism) trusting relations will also be hampered. Similarly, different economic histories of capitalism, socialism, and communism will also play a role in restricting such trusting relations between various MNCs and Third World Nations. Further, some cultures may have different tolerances for inconsistency or standards for competence and different time frames within which performance of various activities may be expected.

Finally, individuals in some cultural contexts might find it more difficult to be open in the same manner as those from other cultures. Their concern might not be with openness so much as not hurting another's feelings or with, perhaps, saving face and not embarrassing themselves or others. When circumstances exist in which these different responses arise, the trust between partners might be jeopardized. One member of the relation might feel that he or she can never "really" know what the others are thinking, because they will not speak their minds. Similarly, if Fukuyama is correct, the social structures within societies differ with respect to the extensiveness of trust which members of those societies may "naturally" engage in (Fukuyama, 1995). These differences will also inhibit the development of trusting relations both within certain societies and between societies.

In short, the obstacles to trust within an international market are substantial. Further, these are also obstacles to the ready acceptance of, and adherence to, systems of international business ethics. Suppose, for instance, that we invoke our earlier distinction between ethics, as a theoretical statement of principles, rules, values, and ideals by which individuals, business, and countries ought to live and act, and morality which (for present purposes) we may take to be an embedded or lived form of an ethics. A morality, then, is an embodied or lived ethics. As such, an embodied ethics must be capable of being taught and communicated to others; it must not be radically inconsistent; it must have forces which lead to its renewal; it must be something that can be stable. If we are to speak of an international business ethics, then surely we seek an ethics that can be a morality. But to speak of such an ethics as being a morality, we must seek to identify the conditions for this transformation of the theoretical into the practical.[9] Trust, as we have seen, is one of these conditions.

Hence, any international business ethics which does not give significant place to the commonality of values or motives, consistency of behavior, reputation, competency determinations, and openness will be an ethics which does not allow for basic conditions which promote its own stability and efficacy as a morality. It is these factors which the preceding identifies as necessary conditions for the various forms of trust. And these forms of trust are crucial as background or supporting conditions for the development and maintenance of morality. Without them an international business ethics will not become a morality.

Now the obstacles to trust can be met only gradually and incrementally. The instruction of managers and participants in international business in ethics will be important (Noreen, 1988), but clearly not be sufficient. Instead, a complicated pattern of interaction among individuals, firms, industries international organizations, and governmental structures and mechanisms will be required to overcome the obstacles briefly noted above. They will require various trust enhancing mechanisms including the law, trade associations, various third parties, and the like (Arrighetti, Bachmann, and Deakin, 1997). Periods of adjustment with gradual increments of trust formation are obviously required. This will involve confidence building measures (Bluhm, 1987). For example, extended trust might be enhanced by an exchange of personnel at home and abroad so that all sides may keep in touch and different interpretations or understanding are recognized. Guarded trust will be enhanced through various market-based and contractual governance devices (Barney and Hansen, 1994). Basic trust will be enhanced by other background institutions, frequency of contact, etc. Accordingly, we must look to both informal and formal means to overcome obstacles to trust.

What this suggests is a shift in the practical basis for business morality as we move from the national to the international arena. We move from a basis which includes common histories, customs, languages, etc. to more external and formal mechanisms (Sellerberg, 1982). On this view, personal relations continue to be crucial for international trust, since it is the individuals from different businesses and different cultures who gain knowledge of and form trust with each other. It is for this reason that business executives travel with the presidents, prime ministers and commerce secretaries of their national states. "Face-to-face interaction with very senior people . . . [overseas and in the company of national leaders] sends a powerful symbolic message. It helps establish trust."[10] This implies the importance of the time and circumstances to allow such relations to develop. Still, inter- and intra-institutional structures are required to support and sustain such personal trust, and to transform it into the organizational trust which could support an international business morality (Dodgson, 1993; Zucker, 1986).

V. MORALLY RELEVANT FEATURES OF TRUST

Finally, though specific cases of trust are not necessarily moral, the fact that firms and people can and do trust in the preceding ways means that something morally important happens in trust. This 'something' is the fact that trust goes beyond simple self-seeking behavior. This is not to deny that individuals and firms form various relations involving trust for self-interest reasons. Obviously they do. However, it does not follow from this when these relations include the different forms of trust distinguished above, that these forms of trust can be understood simply in terms of self-interest. They cannot. Self-interest may be the occasion for seeking or desiring relations with some other person or firm which require trust. Further, one's self-interests may also be met through those trusting relations. But, again, this does not imply that such trust does not include features important for morality. It is an overly rigorous, if not misguided, morality which demands that self-interest and morality be wholly separate. Still, self-interest does not itself provide an account of the nature or justification of the trust that they may develop between individuals and firms. For this, we have seen that (depending upon the kind of trust) we must look to one's preparedness to refrain from taking advantage of another's vulnerabilities or weaknesses, the consistency of one's behavior, the appropriateness of one's competencies and one's readiness to be open regarding knowledge of one's self or firm to others. All these conditions may restrict action on behalf of one's self-interests. Further, social (and industry) norms and expectations, which are part of the commonality of values and beliefs crucial to trust, play a role in constituting forms of behavior, as well as individuals and firms themselves, which are not simply self-seeking. Finally, in trust there is a consideration of the interests of others, beyond one's own present interests. There are, that is, various inherent aspects of trust that might be exploited to promote moral forms of trust. I wish to explore these in the following.

First, to the extent people mutually and consciously trust each other (for example, especially in guarded and extended trust), they must be in communication with, and have a mutual understanding of, each other. They must seek and share knowledge about each other as well as make judgments about the fitness of each other. As we have seen, this mutual understanding involves knowing and assessing each other's motives, consistency, competency and openness. Such knowledge of others (and oneself) has, traditionally, been held to be important for morality.

Second, trust involves a morally significant exposure of oneself to others in the sense that one permits the exposure of one's vulnerabilities to others. With mutual trust there is a sharing of one's vulnerabilities. In this manner a dependence (possibly a mutual dependence) is developed whereby one is expected not only not to harm the other but also to act in ways which promote the well-being of the other. The fact that trust exposes one's vulnerabilities to others and creates certain expectations about the future behavior of those who trust may open firms and individuals up to other more obviously moral relations. For example, to the extent that one trusts others one treats them "as being able and willing to act in accord with the rules without inducement or threats" (Thomas, 1978: 92). Accordingly, Thomas has claimed that trust is involved in respecting the moral dignity of each person. As such, trust creates a potential for morality between those who share in the trust.

Third, trust involves the restriction of self-interested behavior; the interests of the other are not harmed, and may be promoted, even though doing so might not be in one's immediate self-interest. This may involve various preventative forms of behavior as well. For example, to the extent that individuals share such a relation they do not manipulate each other ". . . by deliberately raising false expectations in them about how one will respond to something one wants them to do" (Baier, 1995: 134).[11] Similarly, they ". . . take due care not to lead others to form reasonable but false expectations about what one will do, where they would face significant loss if they relied on such false expectations" (Baier, 1995: 134). Finally, they ". . . take steps to prevent any loss that others would face through reliance on expectations about one's future behavior, expectations that one has either intentionally or negligently led them to form" (Baier, 1995: 134). In short, those engaged in trust relations avoid certain standard negotiating tactics which result in zero-sum games with one's negotiating partner.

Fourth, mutual trust involves a reciprocity between members of the trusting relation which fosters their autonomy. Guarded and extended trust relationships usually only develop slowly, after initial experiences and probing of each other's intentions and reliability. When the other responds positively and in a trusting manner, one may oneself (further) respond in a positive and trusting manner. As such relationships develop, particularly extended ones, it may be that something one does may give the other a one-sided benefit, which one then trusts he or she will not take advantage of. It may even occur that the trust one has bestowed on another is not fulfilled, or not fulfilled in the manner expected. This need not result, however, in a "tit for tat" response, if the trust relationship is healthy and firm. Indeed, when there is trust between individuals, each person will allow the other a wider range of decisions and actions than when distrust characterizes their relationships. If we may then assume that morality is bound up with some form of autonomy or self-determination, trust will promote the realization of this basic condition for morality. In this way, trust is not indifferent to morality, but is positively linked with it. This is in harmony with the connection Horsburgh draws between trust and moral agency in his view that for a person to be a moral agent he or she cannot hold an attitude of systematic and pervasive distrust toward all other people (Horsburgh, 1960: 354).

Hence, at least four morally significant phenomena are inherently linked with trust: a) communication of self-understanding to others; b) the voluntary exposure of one's vulnerabilities to others; c) voluntary restriction of self-interested behavior; and d) a reciprocity which fosters autonomy. These inherent features of trust are central to the institution of morality as well and, hence, link these two concepts[12]. . .

References

Arrighetti, A. Bachmann, R., and Deakin, S. 1997. "Contract Law, Social Norms and Inter-firm Cooperation," *Cambridge Journal of Economics* (forthcoming).

Baier, A. 1985. *Postures of the Mind*. Minneapolis: University of Minnesota Press.

———. 1986. "Trust and Antitrust," *Ethics, 96:* 231–260.

———. 1995. *Moral Prejudices*. Cambridge, MA: Harvard University Press.

Barney, J. B., and Hansen, M. H. 1994. "Trustworthiness as a Source of Competitive Advantage," *Strategic Management Journal, 15:* 175–190.

Bluhm L. H. 1987. "Trust, Terrorism, and Technology," *Journal of Business Ethics, 6:* 333–341.

Brenkert, G. 1995. "The Importance of the Structural Features of Moral Systems for International Business Ethics." In *Proceedings of the Fifth Annual Meeting of the International Association For Business and Society,* IABS, Steven Wartick and Denis Collins (eds.), Hilton Head, SC, pp. 101–106.

Dasgupta, P. 1988. "Trust as a Commodity." In D. Gambetta (ed.), *Trust*. Oxford, UK: SC, Basil Blackwell.

DeGeorge, R. 1993. *Competing with Integrity in International Business*. New York: Oxford University Press.

Dodgson, M. 1993. "Learning, Trust and Technological Collaboration," *Human Relations, 46:* 77–95.

Fukuyama, F. 1995. *Trust: The Social Virtues and the Creation of Prosperity*. New York: Macmillan.

Gabarro, J. J. 1978. "The Development of Trust, Influence and Expectations." In *Interpersonal Behavior*. Englewood Cliffs, NJ: Prentice-Hall.

Gellner, E. 1988. "Trust, Cohesion and the Social Order." In D. Gambetta (ed.), *Trust*. Oxford: Basil Blackwell.

Hofstede, G. 1979. "Value Systems in Forty Countries: Interpretation Validation and Consequences for Theory." In L. H. Eckensberger, W. J. Lonner, and Y. H. Poortinga (eds.), *Cross-Cultural Contributions to Psychology* (pp. 389–407). Lisse, Netherlands: Swes & Zeiliner, B. V.

Horng, C. 1993. "Cultural Differences, Trust and Their Relationships to Business Strategy and Control," *Advances in International Comparative Management, 8:* 175–197.

Horsburgh, H. J. N. 1960. "The Ethics of Trust," *Philosophical Quarterly, 10:* 343–354.

Hosmer, L. T. 1995. "Trust: The Connecting Link Between Organizational Theory and Philosophical Ethics." *Academy of Management Review, 20:* 379–403.

Jones, T. M. 1995. "Instrumental Stakeholder Theory: A Synthesis of Ethics and Economics." *Academy of Management Review, 20:* 404–437.

Messick, D. M., Bloom, S., Boldizar, J. P., and Samuelson, C. D. 1985. "Why We Are Fairer than Others?" *Journal of Business Ethics, 9:* 619–638.

Noreen, E. 1988. "The Economics of Ethics: A New Perspective on Agency Theory." *Accounting, Organizations and Society, 13:* 359–369.

Puffer, S. M., and McCarthy, D. J. 1995. "Finding the Common Ground in Russian and American Business Ethics," *California Management Review, 37:* 29–46.

Rawls, J. 1971. *A Theory of Justice*. Cambridge, MA: Harvard University Press.

Sable, C. F. 1993. "Studied Trust: Building New Forms of Cooperation in a Volatile Economy," *Human Relations, 9:* 1133–1170.

Sako, M. 1991. "The Role of 'Trust' in Japanese Buyer-Supplier Relationships." *Ricerche Economiche, 45:* 449–474.

———. 1992. *Prices, Quality and Trust.* Cambridge, UK: Cambridge University Press.

Scanlon, T. 1990. "Promises and Practices," *Philosophy & Public Affairs, 19:* 199–226.

Sellerberg, A. M. 1982. "On Modern Confidence," *Acta Sociological, 25:* 39–48.

Shell, G. R. 1991. "Opportunism and Trust in the Negotiation of Commercial Contracts: Toward a New Cause of Action," *Vanderbilt Law Review, 44:* 221–282

Solomon, R. C. 1992. *Ethics and Excellence.* New York: Oxford University Press.

Thomas, D. O. 1978. "The Duty to Trust," *Proceedings of the Aristotelian Society, 79:* 89–101.

Zucker, L. 1986. "Production of Trust: Institutional Sources of Economic Structure, 1840–1920," *Research in Organizational Behavior, 8:* 53–111.

Notes

1. Some people (including myself, on occasion) use the terms "ethics" and "morality" interchangeably. I am not doing so (obviously) in the present context. In this paper, I use "ethics" to refer to the theoretical study of moral values, standards and ideals by which people ought to live. "Morality" is used here to refer to the moral values or standards a society (or a person) lives by (whether justifiedly or not), rather than the theoretical investigation of them. Sometimes these "lived" values and standards are referred to as a person's "ethics." But in this context I do not follow this practice. Instead, I separate the two in order to emphasize that we need to develop a theoretical account (i.e., an ethics) of the values and standards by which people could actually morally live (i.e., a morality), rather than simply spin out fine theories which might not actually contain standards and values by which people or business could actually live and operate.

2. To the extent that one's belief that the other will not harm one is strongly held either on the basis of much evidence (though not conclusive evidence), or is held such that contrary evidence will not shake it, trust involves a confidence in the other. In those cases when weaker reason or evidence for the benignity of the other's behavior leads to weaker confidence, such trust as remains becomes a reliance on the other. (When there is little rational evidence of the other's benign disposition, we might speak of "blind trust.") Thus, confidence and reliance are not so much different criteria of trust, as markers of the grounds for the attitude or disposition one has towards the other (cf. Horsburgh, 1962: 28). As such, trust is not the same as reliance since, as Baier points out, "we may rely on our fellows' fate of the newly appointed security guards in shops to deter them from injecting poison into the food on the shelves, once we have ceased to trust them" (Baier, 1986: 234). L. Thomas also contends that trust and reliance are different. I may rely on someone I don't trust (cf. Thomas, 1989).

3. What of the "trust" of an infant for a parent? If only those who are aware of the risks may trust, then infants cannot trust. Instead, the infant depends on its parents. D. O. Thomas notes that in learning whom to trust "we need to make judgments on our own account and doing this is not simply a matter of applying current rules and principles" (Thomas, 1978: 94).

4. Cf. Baier, 1986: 237, 240, 253.

5. Others also draw distinctions among different forms of trust. Among such accounts are: Barney and Hansen (1994) and L. Thomas (1989). I believe that my account is importantly different from each of these accounts and serves different purposes than those authors sought to address in their accounts.

6. Gabarro explicitly notes the condition of consistency of behavior. He interprets it in the related senses of reliability and predictability (Gabarro, 1978).

7. Hofstede measures the value differences between cultures in terms of a Power Distance Index, an Uncertainty Index, an Individualism Index, and a Masculinity Index (Hofstede, 1979).

8. In Liebrand et al., they show that "these fairness biases have transcultural generality" (Liebrand et al., 1986: 602).

9. Brandt raises the question of what makes a moral code effective in a society (Brandt, 1979: 180).

10. The quotation is from Robert Bontempo, Associate Professor of International Management at Columbia University Business School. He was cited by Alex Markels, Joann S. Lublin, and Phil Kuntz, in "Why Executives Tour World with Politicians," *The Wall Street Journal* (April 4, 1996), B1.

11. I cite this and the following two passages from Baier, who is rephrasing the work of Thomas Scanlon on promises and the expectations that promises may set up in others (cf. Scanlon, 1990).

12. I am indebted to the comments of Ken Alpern, Reinhard Bachmann, Robbin Derry, John Dienhart, Darryl Koehn, Christel Lane, and Pat Werhane on earlier versions of this paper.

Whistleblowing and Professional Responsibility

SISSELA BOK

"Whistleblowing" is a new label generated by our increased awareness of the ethical conflicts encountered at work. Whistleblowers sound an alarm from within the very organization in which they work, aiming to spotlight neglect or abuses that threaten the public interest.

The stakes in whistleblowing are high. Take the nurse who alleges that physicians enrich themselves in her hospital through unnecessary surgery; the engineer who discloses safety defects in the braking systems of a fleet of new rapid-transit vehicles; the Defense Department official who alerts Congress to military graft and overspending: all know that they pose a threat to those whom they denounce and that their own careers may be at risk.

MORAL CONFLICTS

Moral conflicts on several levels confront anyone who is wondering whether to speak out about abuses or risks or serious neglect. In the first place, he must try to decide whether, other things being equal, speaking out is in fact in the public interest. This choice is often made more complicated by factual uncertainties: Who is responsible for the abuse or neglect? How great is the threat? And how likely is it that speaking out will precipitate changes for the better?

In the second place, a would-be whistleblower must weigh his responsibility to serve the public interest against the responsibility he owes to his colleagues and the institution in which he works. While the professional ethic requires collegial loyalty, the codes of ethics often stress responsibility to the public over and above duties to colleagues and clients. Thus the United States

From Sissela Bok, "Whistleblowing and Professional Responsibility," *New York University Education Quarterly, 11* (Summer, 1980): 2–7. Reprinted with permission. Bok offers more extensive discussion of these issues in her book, *Secrets: On the Ethics of Concealment and Revelation* (Vantage, 1989).

Code of Ethics for Government Servants asks them to "expose corruption wherever uncovered" and to "put loyalty to the highest moral principles and to country above loyalty to persons, party, or government."[1] Similarly, the largest professional engineering association requires members to speak out against abuses threatening the safety, health, and welfare of the public.[2]

A third conflict for would-be whistleblowers is personal in nature and cuts across the first two: even in cases where they have concluded that the facts warrant speaking out, and that their duty to do so overrides loyalties to colleagues and institutions, they often have reason to fear the results of carrying out such a duty. However strong this duty may seem in theory, they know that, in practice, retaliation is likely. As a result, their careers and their ability to support themselves and their families may be unjustly impaired.[3] A government handbook issued during the Nixon era recommends reassigning "undesirables" to places so remote that they would prefer to resign. Whistleblowers may also be downgraded or given work without responsibility or work for which they are not qualified; or else they may be given many more tasks than they can possibly perform. Another risk is that an outspoken civil servant may be ordered to undergo a psychiatric fitness-for-duty examination,[4] declared unfit for service, and "separated" as well as discredited from the point of view of any allegations he may be making. Outright firing, finally, is the most direct institutional response to whistleblowers.

Add to the conflicts confronting individual whistleblowers the claim to self-policing that many professions make, and professional responsibility is at issue in still another way. For an appeal to the public goes against everything that "self-policing" stands for. The question for the different professions, then, is how to resolve, insofar as it is possible, the conflict between professional loyalty and professional responsibility toward the outside world. The same conflicts arise to some extent in all groups, but professional groups often have special cohesion and claim special dignity and privileges.

The plight of whistleblowers has come to be documented by the press and described in a number of books. Evidence of the hardships imposed on those who chose to act in the public interest has combined with a heightened awareness of professional malfeasance and corruption to produce a shift toward greater public support of whistleblowers. Public service law firms and consumer groups have taken up their cause; institutional reforms and legislation have been proposed to combat illegitimate reprisals.[5]

Given the indispensable services performed by so many whistleblowers, strong public support is often merited. But the new climate of acceptance makes it easy to overlook the dangers of whistleblowing: of uses in error or in malice; of work and reputations unjustly lost for those falsely accused; of privacy invaded and trust undermined. There comes a level of internal prying and mutual suspicion at which no institution can function. And it is a fact that the disappointed, the incompetent, the malicious, and the paranoid all too often leap to accusations in public. Worst of all, ideological persecution throughout the world traditionally relies on insiders willing to inform on their colleagues or even on their family members, often through staged public denunciations or press campaigns.

No society can count itself immune from such dangers. But neither can it risk silencing those with a legitimate reason to blow the whistle. How then can we distinguish between different instances of whistleblowing? A society that fails to protect the right to speak out even on the part of those whose warnings turn out to be spurious obviously opens the door to political repression. But from the moral point of view there are important differences between the aims, messages, and methods of dissenters from within.

NATURE OF WHISTLEBLOWING

Three elements, each jarring, and triply jarring when conjoined, lend acts of whistleblowing special urgency and bitterness: dissent, breach of loyalty, and accusation.

Like all dissent, whistleblowing makes public a disagreement with an authority or a majority view. But whereas dissent can concern all forms of disagreement with, for instance, religious dogma or government policy or court decisions, whistleblowing has the narrower aim of shedding light on negligence or abuse, or alerting to a risk, and of assigning responsibility for this risk.

Would-be whistleblowers confront the conflict inherent in all dissent: between conforming and sticking their necks out. The more repressive the authority they challenge, the greater the personal risk they take in speaking out. At exceptional times, as in times of war, even ordinarily tolerant authorities may come to regard dissent as unacceptable and even disloyal.[6]

Furthermore, the whistleblower hopes to stop the game; but since he is neither referee nor coach, and since he blows the whistle on his own team, his act is seen as a violation of loyalty. In holding his position, he has assumed certain obligations to his colleagues and clients. He may even have subscribed to a loyalty oath or a promise of confidentiality. Loyalty to colleagues and to clients comes to be pitted against loyalty to the public interest, to those who may be injured unless the revelation is made.

Not only is loyalty violated in whistleblowing, hierarchy as well is often opposed, since the whistleblower is not only a colleague but a subordinate. Though aware of the risks inherent in such disobedience, he often hopes to keep his job.[7] At times, however, he plans his alarm to coincide with leaving the institution. If he is highly placed, or joined by others, resigning in protest may effectively direct public attention to the wrongdoing at issue.[8] Still another alternative, often chosen by those who wish to be safe from retaliation, is to leave the institution quietly, to secure another post, and then to blow the whistle. In this way, it is possible to speak with the authority and knowledge of an insider without having the vulnerability of that position.

It is the element of accusation, of calling a "foul," that arouses the strongest reactions on the part of the hierarchy. The accusation may be of neglect, of willfully concealed dangers, or of outright abuse on the part of colleagues or superiors. It singles out specific persons or groups as responsible for threats to the public interest. If no one could be held responsible—as in the case of an impending avalanche—the warning would not constitute whistleblowing.

The accusation of the whistleblower, moreover, concerns a present or an imminent threat. Past errors or misdeeds occasion such an alarm only if they still affect current practices. And risks far in the future lack the immediacy needed to make the alarm a compelling one, as well as the close connection to particular individuals that would justify actual accusations. Thus an alarm can be sounded about safety defects in a rapid-transit system that threaten or will shortly threaten passengers, but the revelation of safety defects in a system no longer in use, while of historical interest, would not constitute whistleblowing. Nor would the revelation of potential problems in a system not yet fully designed and far from implemented.[9]

Not only immediacy, but also specificity, is needed for there to be an alarm capable of pinpointing responsibility. A concrete risk must be at issue rather than a vague foreboding or a somber prediction. The act of whistleblowing differs in this respect from the lamentation or the dire prophecy. An immediate and specific threat would normally be acted upon by those at risk. The whistleblower assumes that his message will alert listeners to something they do not know, or whose significance they have not grasped because it has been kept secret.

The desire for openness inheres in the temptation to reveal any secret, sometimes joined to an urge for self-aggrandizement and publicity and the hope for revenge for past slights or injustices. There can be pleasure, too—righteous or malicious—in laying bare the secrets of co-workers and in setting the record straight at last. Colleagues of the whistleblower often suspect his motives: they may regard him as a crank, as publicity-hungry, wrong about the facts, eager for scandal and discord, and driven to indiscretion by his personal biases and shortcomings.

For whistleblowing to be effective, it must arouse its audience. Inarticulate whistleblowers are likely to fail from the outset. When they are greeted by apathy, their message dissipates. When they are greeted by disbelief, they elicit no response at all. And when the audience is not free to receive or to act on the information—when censorship or fear of retribution stifles response—then the message rebounds to injure the whistleblower. Whistleblowing also requires the possibility of concerted public response: the idea of whistleblowing in an anarchy is therefore merely quixotic.

Such characteristics of whistleblowing and strategic considerations for achieving an impact are common to the noblest warnings, the most vicious personal attacks, and the delusions of the paranoid. How can one distinguish the many acts of sounding an alarm that are genuinely in the public interest from all the petty, biased, or lurid revelations that pervade our querulous and gossip-ridden society? Can we draw distinctions between different whistleblowers, different messages, different methods?

We clearly can, in a number of cases. Whistleblowing may be starkly inappropriate when in malice or error, or when it lays bare legitimately private matters having to do, for instance, with political belief or sexual life. It can, just as clearly, be the only way to shed light on an ongoing unjust practice such as drugging political prisoners or subjecting them to electroshock treatment. It can be the last resort for alerting the public to an impending disaster. Taking such clear-cut cases as benchmarks, and reflecting on what it is about them that weighs so heavily for or against speaking out, we can work our way toward the admittedly more complex cases in which whistleblowing is not so clearly the right or wrong choice, or where different points of view exist regarding its legitimacy—cases where there are moral reasons both for concealment and for disclosure and where judgments conflict. Consider the following cases[10]:

    A. As a construction inspector for a federal agency, John Samuels (not his real name) had personal knowledge of shoddy and deficient construction practices by private contractors. He knew his superiors received free vacations and entertainment, had their homes remodeled and found jobs for their relatives—all courtesy of a private contractor. These superiors later approved a multimillion no-bid contract with the same "generous" firm.

Samuels also had evidence that other firms were hiring nonunion laborers at a low wage while receiving substantially higher payments from the government for labor costs. A former superior, unaware of an office dictaphone, had incautiously instructed Samuels on how to accept bribes for overlooking sub-par performance.

As he prepared to volunteer this information to various members of Congress, he became tense and uneasy. His family was scared and the fears were valid. It might cost Samuels thousands of dollars to protect his job. Those who had freely provided Samuels with information would probably recant or withdraw their friendship. A number of people might object to his using a dictaphone to gather information. His agency would start covering up and vent its collective wrath upon him. As for reporters and writers, they would gather for a few days, then move on to the next story. He would be left without a job, with fewer friends, with massive battles looming, and without the financial means of fighting them, Samuels decided to remain silent.

B. Engineers of Company "A" prepared plans and specifications for machinery to be used in a manufacturing process and Company "A" turned them over to Company "B" for production. The engineers of Company "B," in reviewing the plans and specifications, came to the conclusion that they included certain miscalculations and technical deficiencies of a nature that the final product might be unsuitable for the purposes of the ultimate users, and that the equipment, if built according to the original plans and specifications, might endanger the lives of persons in proximity to it. The engineers of Company "B" called the matter to the attention of appropriate officials of their employer who, in turn, advised Company "A." Company "A" replied that its engineers felt that the design and specifications for the equipment were adequate and safe and that Company "B" should proceed to build the equipment as designed and specified. The officials of Company "B" instructed its engineers to proceed with the work.

C. A recently hired assistant director of admissions in a state university begins to wonder whether transcripts of some applicants accurately reflect their accomplishments. He knows that it matters to many in the university community, including alumni, that the football team continue its winning tradition. He has heard rumors that surrogates may be available to take tests for a fee, signing the names of designated applicants for admission, and that some of the transcripts may have been altered. But he has no hard facts. When he brings the question up with the director of admissions, he is told that the rumors are unfounded and asked not to inquire further into the matter.

INDIVIDUAL MORAL CHOICE

What questions might those who consider sounding an alarm in public ask themselves? How might they articulate the problem they see and weigh its injustice before deciding whether or not to reveal it? How can they best try to make sure their choice is the right one? In thinking about these questions it helps to keep in mind the three elements mentioned earlier: dissent, breach of loyalty, and accusation. They impose certain requirements—of accuracy and judgment in dissent; of exploring alternative ways to cope with improprieties that minimize the breach of loyalty; and of fairness in accusation. For each, careful articulation and testing of arguments are needed to limit error and bias.

Dissent by whistleblowers, first of all, is expressly claimed to be intended to benefit the public. It carries with it, as a result, an obligation to consider the nature of this benefit and to consider also the possible harm that may come from speaking out: harm to persons or institutions and, ultimately, to the public interest itself. Whistleblowers must, therefore, begin by making every effort to consider the effects of speaking out versus those of remaining silent. They must assure themselves of the accuracy of their reports, checking and rechecking the facts before speaking out; specify the degree to which there is genuine impropriety; consider how imminent is the threat they see, how serious, and how closely linked to those accused of neglect and abuse.

If the facts warrant whistleblowing, how can the second element—breach of loyalty—be minimized? The most important question here is whether the existing avenues for change within the organization have been explored. It is a waste of time for the public as well as harmful to the institution to sound the loudest alarm first. Whistleblowing has to remain a last alternative because of its destructive side effects: it must be chosen only when other alternatives have been considered and rejected. They may be rejected if they simply do not apply to the problem at hand, or when there is not time to go through routine channels or when the institution is so corrupt or coercive that steps will be taken to silence the whistleblower should he try the regular channels first.

What weight should an oath or a promise of silence have in the conflict of loyalties? One sworn to silence is doubtless under a stronger obligation because of the oath he has taken. He has bound himself, assumed specific obligations beyond those assumed in merely taking a new position. But even such promises can be overridden when the public interest at issue is strong enough. They can be overridden if they were obtained under duress or through deceit. They can be overridden, too, if they promise something that is in itself wrong or unlawful. The fact that one has promised silence is no excuse for complicity in covering up a crime or a violation of the public's trust.

The third element in whistleblowing—accusation—raises equally serious ethical concerns. They are concerns of fairness to the persons accused of impropriety. Is the message one to which the public is entitled in the first place? Or does it infringe on personal and private matters that one has no right to invade? Here, the very notion of what is in the public's best "interest" is at issue: "accusations" regarding an official's unusual sexual or religious experiences may well appeal to the public's interest without being information relevant to "the public interest." Great conflicts arise here. We have witnessed excessive claims to executive privilege and to secrecy by government officials during the Watergate scandal in order to cover up for abuses the public had every right to discover. Conversely, those hoping to profit from prying into private matters have become adept at invoking "the public's right to know." Some even regard such private matters as threats to the public: they voice their own religious and political prejudices in the language of accusation. Such a danger is never stronger than when the accusation is delivered surreptitiously. The anonymous accusations made during the McCarthy period regarding political beliefs and associations often injured persons who did not even know their accusers or the exact nature of the accusations.

From the public's point of view, accusations that are openly made by identifiable individuals are more likely to be taken seriously. And in fairness to those criticized, openly accepted responsibility for blowing the whistle should be preferred to the denunciation or the leaked rumor. What is openly stated can more easily be checked, its source's motives challenged, and the underlying information examined. Those under attack may otherwise be hard put to defend themselves against nameless adversaries. Often they do not even know that they are threatened until it is too late to respond. The anonymous denunciation, moreover, common to so many regimes, places the burden of investigation on government agencies that may thereby gain the power of a secret police.

From the point of view of the whistleblower, on the other hand, the anonymous message is safer in situations where retaliation is likely. But it is also often less likely to be taken seriously. Unless the message is accompanied by indications of how the evidence can be checked, its anonymity, however safe for the source, speaks against it.

During the process of weighing the legitimacy of speaking out, the method used, and the degree of fairness needed, whistleblowers must try to compensate for the strong possibility of bias on their part. They should be scrupulously aware of any motive that might skew their message: a desire for self-defense in a difficult bureaucratic situation, perhaps, or the urge to seek revenge, or inflated expectations regarding the effect their message will have on the situation. (Needless to say, bias affects the silent as well as the outspoken. The motive for holding back important information about abuses and injustice ought to give similar cause for soul-searching.)

Likewise, the possibility of personal gain from sounding the alarm ought to give pause. Once again there is then greater risk of a biased message. Even if the whistleblower regards himself as incorruptible, his profiting from revelations of neglect or abuse will lead others to question his motives and to put less credence in his charges. If, for example, a government employee stands to make large profits from a book exposing the iniquities in his agency, there is danger that he will, perhaps even unconsciously, slant his report in order to cause more of a sensation.

A special problem arises when there is a high risk that the civil servant who speaks out will have to go through costly litigation. Might he not justifiably try to make enough money on his public revelations—say, through books or public speaking—to offset his losses? In so doing he will not strictly speaking have *profited* from his revelations: he merely avoids being financially crushed by their sequels. He will nevertheless still be suspected at the time of revelation, and his message will therefore seem more questionable.

Reducing bias and error in moral choice often requires consultation, even open debate[11]: methods that force articulation of the moral arguments at stake and challenge privately held assumptions. But acts of whistleblowing present special problems when it comes to open consultation. On the one hand, once the whistleblower sounds his alarm publicly, his arguments will be subjected to open scrutiny; he will have to articulate his reasons for speaking out and substantiate his charges. On the other hand, it will then be too late to retract the alarm or to combat its harmful effects, should his choice to speak out have been ill-advised.

For this reason, the whistleblower owes it to all involved to make sure of two things: that he has sought as much and as objective advice regarding his choice as he can *before* going public; and that he is aware of the arguments for and against the practice of whistleblowing in general, so that he can see his own choice against as richly detailed and coherently structured a background as possible. Satisfying these two requirements once again has special problems because of the very nature of whistleblowing: the more corrupt the circumstances, the more dangerous it may be to seek counsultation before speaking out. And yet, since the whistleblower himself may have a biased view of the state of affairs, he may choose not to consult others when in fact it would be not only safe but advantageous to do so; he may see corruption and conspiracy where none exists.

Notes

1. Code of Ethics for Government Service passed by the U.S. House of Representatives in the 85th Congress (1958) and applying to all government employees and office holders.
2. Code of Ethics of the Institute of Electrical and Electronics Engineers, Article IV.
3. For case histories and descriptions of what befalls whistleblowers, see Rosemary Chalk and Frank von Hippel, "Due Process for Dissenting Whistle-Blowers," *Technology Review, 81* (June–July 1979): 48–55; Alan S. Westin and Stephen Salisbury, eds., *Individual Rights in the Corporation* (New York: Pantheon, 1980); Helen Dudar, "The Price of Blowing the Whistle," *New York Times Magazine*, 30 October 1979, pp. 41–54; John Edsall, *Scientific Freedom and Responsibility* (Washington, DC: American Association for the Advancement of Science, 1975), p. 5; David Ewing, *Freedom Inside the Organization* (New York: Dutton, 1979); Ralph Nader, Peter Petkas, and Kate Blackwell, *Whistle Blowing* (New York: Grossman, 1972); Charles Peter and Taylor Branch, *Blowing the Whistle* (New York: Praeger, 1972).
4. Congressional hearings uncovered a growing resort to mandatory psychiatric examinations.
5. For an account of strategies and proposals to support government whistleblowers, see Government Accountability Project, *A Whistleblower's Guide to the Federal Bureaucracy* (Washington, DC: Institute for Policy Studies, 1977).
6. See, e.g., Samuel Eliot Morison, Frederick Merk, and Frank Friedel, *Dissent in Three American Wars* (Cambridge, MA: Harvard University Press, 1970).
7. In the scheme worked out by Albert Hirschmann in *Exit, Voice and Loyalty* (Cambridge, MA: Harvard University Press, 1970), whistleblowing represents "voice" accompanied by a preference not to "exit," though forced "exit" is clearly a possibility and "voice" after or during "exit" may be chosen for strategic reasons.
8. Edward Weisband and Thomas N. Franck, *Resignation in Protest* (New York: Grossman, 1975).
9. Future developments can, however, be the cause for whistleblowing if they are seen as resulting from steps being taken or about to be taken that render them inevitable.
10. Case A is adapted from Louis Clark, "The Sound of Professional Suicide," *Barrister,* Summer 1978, p. 10; Case B is Case 5 in Robert J. Baum and Albert Flores, eds., *Ethical Problems of Engineering* (Troy, NY: Rensselaer Polytechnic Institute, 1978), p. 186.
11. I discuss these questions of consultation and publicity with respect to moral choice in chapter 7 of Sissela Bok, *Lying* (New York: Pantheon, 1978); and in *Secrets* (New York: Pantheon Books, 1982), Ch. IX and XV.

Is Business Bluffing Ethical?

ALBERT CARR

A respected businessman with whom I discussed the theme of this article remarked with some heat, "You mean to say you're going to encourage men to bluff? Why, bluffing is nothing more than a form of lying! You're advising them to lie!"

I agreed that the basis of private morality is a respect for truth and that the closer a businessman comes to the truth, the more he deserves respect. At the same time, I suggested that most bluffing in business might be regarded simply as game strategy—much like bluffing in poker, which does not reflect on the morality of the bluffer.

I quoted Henry Taylor, the British statesman who pointed out that "falsehood ceases to be falsehood when it is understood on all sides that the truth is not expected to be spoken"—an exact description of bluffing in poker, diplomacy, and business. I cited the analogy of the criminal court, where the criminal is not expected to tell the truth when he pleads "not guilty." Everyone from the judge down takes it for granted that the job of the defendant's attorney is to get his client off, not to reveal the truth; and this is considered ethical practice. I mentioned Representative Omar Burleson, the Democrat from Texas, who was quoted as saying, in regard to the ethics of Congress, "Ethics is a barrel of worms"[1]—a pungent summing up of the problem of deciding who is ethical in politics.

I reminded my friend that millions of businessmen feel constrained every day to say yes to their bosses when they secretly believe no and that this is generally accepted as permissible strategy when the alternative might be the loss of a job. The essential point, I said, is that the ethics of business are game ethics, different from the ethics of religion.

He remained unconvinced. Referring to the company of which he is president, he declared: "Maybe that's good enough for some businessmen, but I can tell you that we pride ourselves on our ethics. In 30 years not one customer has ever questioned my word or asked to check our figures. We're loyal to our customers and fair to our suppliers. I regard my handshake on a deal as a contract. I've never entered into price-fixing schemes with my competitors. I've never allowed my salesmen to spread injurious rumors about other companies. Our union contract is the best in our industry. And, if I do say so myself, our ethical standards are of the highest!"

He really was saying, without realizing it, that he was living up to the ethical standards of the business game—which are a far cry from those of private life. Like a gentlemanly poker player, he did not play in cahoots with others at the table, try to smear their reputations, or hold back chips he owed them.

But this same fine man, at that very time, was allowing one of his products to be advertised in a way that made it sound a great deal better than it actually was. Another item in his product line was notorious among dealers for its "built-in-obsolescence." He was holding back from the market a much-improved product because he did not want to interfere with sales of the inferior item it would have replaced. He had joined with certain of his competitors in hiring a lobbyist to push a state legislature, by methods that he preferred not to know too much about, into amending a bill then being enacted.

In his view these things had nothing to do with ethics; they were merely normal business practice. He himself undoubtedly avoided outright falsehood— never lied in so many words. But the entire organization that he ruled was deeply involved in numerous strategies of deception.

PRESSURE TO DECEIVE

Most executives from time to time are almost compelled, in the interests of their companies or themselves, to practice some form of deception when negotiating with customers, dealers, labor unions, government officials, or even other departments of their companies. By conscious misstatements, concealment of pertinent facts, or exaggeration—in short, by bluffing—they seek to persuade others to agree with them. I think it is fair to say that if the individual executive refuses to bluff from time to time—if he feels obligated to tell the truth, the whole truth, and nothing but the truth—he is ignoring opportunities permitted under the rules and is at a heavy disadvantage in his business dealings.

But here and there a businessman is unable to reconcile himself to the bluff in which he plays a part. His conscience, perhaps spurred by religious idealism, troubles him. He feels guilty; he may develop an ulcer or a nervous tic. Before any executive can make profitable use of the strategy of the bluff, he needs to make sure that in bluffing he will not lose self-respect or become emotionally disturbed. If he is to reconcile personal integrity and high standards of honesty with the practical requirements of business, he must feel that his bluffs are ethically justified. The justification rests on the fact that business, as practiced by individuals as well as by corporations, has the impersonal character of a game—a game that demands both special strategy and an understanding of its special ethics.

The game is played at all levels of corporate life, from the highest to the lowest. At the very instant that a man decides to enter business, he may be forced into a game situation, as is shown by the recent experience of a Cornell honor graduate who applied for a job with a large company:

> This applicant was given a psychological test which included the statement, "Of the following magazines, check any that you have read either regularly or from time to time, and double-check those which interest you most. *Reader's Digest, Time, Fortune, Saturday Evening Post, The New Republic, Life, Look, Ramparts, Newsweek, Business Week, U.S. News & World Report, The Nation, Playboy, Esquire, Harper's, Sports Illustrated.*"

His tastes in reading were broad, and at one time or another he had read almost all of these magazines. He was a subscriber to *The New Republic*, an enthusiast for *Ramparts*, and an avid student of the pictures in *Playboy*. He was not sure whether his interest in *Playboy* would be held against him, but he had a shrewd suspicion that if he confessed to an interest in

Ramparts and *The New Republic*, he would be thought a liberal, a radical, or at least an intellectual, and his chances of getting the job, which he needed, would greatly diminish. He therefore checked five of the more conservative magazines. Apparently it was a sound decision, for he got the job.

He had made a game player's decision, consistent with business ethics.

A similar case is that of a magazine space salesman who, owing to a merger, suddenly found himself out of a job:

> This man was 58, and, in spite of a good record, his chances of getting a job elsewhere in a business where youth is favored in hiring practice was not good. He was a vigorous, healthy man, and only a considerable amount of gray in his hair suggested his age. Before beginning his job search he touched up his hair with a black dye to confine the gray to his temples. He knew that the truth about his age might well come out in time, but he calculated that he could deal with that situation when it arose. He and his wife decided that he could easily pass for 45, and he so stated his age on his résumé.

This was a lie; yet within the accepted rules of the business game, no moral culpability attaches to it.

THE POKER ANALOGY

We can learn a good deal about the nature of business by comparing it with poker. While both have a large element of chance, in the long run the winner is the man who plays with steady skill. In both games ultimate victory requires intimate knowledge of the rules, insight into the psychology of the other players, a bold front, a considerable amount of self-discipline and the ability to respond swiftly and effectively to opportunities provided by chance.

No one expects poker to be played on the ethical principles preached in churches. In poker it is right and proper to bluff a friend out of the rewards of being dealt a good hand. A player feels no more than a slight twinge of sympathy, if that, when—with nothing better than a single ace in his hand—he strips a heavy loser, who holds a pair, of the rest of his chips. It was up to the other fellow to protect himself. In the words of an excellent poker player, former President Harry Truman, "If you can't stand the heat, stay out of the kitchen." If one shows mercy to a loser in poker, it is a personal gesture, divorced from the rules of the game.

Poker has its special ethics, and here I am not referring to rules against cheating. The man who keeps an ace up his sleeve or who marks the cards is more than unethical; he is a crook, and can be punished as such—kicked out of the game or, in the Old West, shot.

In contrast to the cheat, the unethical poker player is one who, while abiding by the letter of the rules, finds ways to put the other players at an unfair disadvantage. Perhaps he unnerves them with loud talk. Or he tries to get them drunk. Or he plays in cahoots with someone else at the table. Ethical poker players frown on such tactics.

Poker's own brand of ethics is different from the ethical ideals of civilized human relationships. The game calls for distrust of the other fellow. It ignores the claim of friendship. Cunning deception and concealment of one's strength and intentions, not kindness and openheartedness, are vital in poker.

No one thinks any the worse of poker on that account. And no one should think any the worse of the game of business because its standards of right and wrong differ from the prevailing traditions of morality in our society. . . .

WE DON'T MAKE THE LAWS

Wherever we turn in business, we can perceive the sharp distinction between its ethical standards and those of the churches. Newspapers abound with sensational stories growing out of this distinction:

- We read one day that Senator Philip A. Hart of Michigan has attacked food processors for deceptive packaging of numerous products.[2]
- The next day there is a Congressional to-do over Ralph Nader's book, *Unsafe At Any Speed*, which demonstrates that automobile companies for years have neglected the safety of car-owning families.[3]
- Then another Senator, Lee Metcalf of Montana, and journalist Vic Reinemer show in their book, *Overcharge*, the methods by which utility companies elude regulating government bodies to extract unduly large payments from users of electricity.[4]

These are merely dramatic instances of a prevailing condition; there is hardly a major industry at which a similar attack could not be aimed. Critics of business regard such behavior as unethical, but the companies concerned know that they are merely playing the business game.

Among the most respected of our business institutions are the insurance companies. A group of insurance executives meeting recently in New England was startled when their guest speaker, social critic Daniel Patrick Moynihan, roundly berated them for "unethical" practices. They had been guilty, Moynihan alleged, of using outdated actuarial tables to obtain unfairly high premiums. They habitually delayed the hearings of lawsuits against them in order to tire out the plaintiffs and win cheap settlements. In their employment policies they used ingenious devices to discriminate against certain minority groups.[5]

It was difficult for the audience to deny the validity of these charges. But these men were business game players. Their reaction to Moynihan's attack was much the same as that of the automobile manufacturers to Nader, of the utilities to Senator Metcalf, and of the food processors to Senator Hart. If the laws governing their business change, or if public opinion becomes clamorous, they will make the necessary adjustments. But morally they have in their view done nothing wrong. As long as they comply with the letter of the law, they are within their rights to operate their businesses as they see fit.

The small business is in the same position as the great corporation in this respect. For example:

> In 1967 a key manufacturer was accused of providing master keys for automobiles to mail-order customers, although it was obvious that some of the purchasers might be automobile thieves. His defense was plain and straightforward. If there was nothing in the law to prevent him from selling his keys to anyone who ordered them, it was not up to him to inquire as to his customers' motives. Why was it any worse, he insisted, for him to sell car keys by mail, than for mail-order houses to sell guns that might be used for murder? Until the law was changed, the key manufacturer could regard himself as being just as ethical as any other businessman by the rules of the business game.[6]

Violations of the ethical ideals of society are common in business, but they are not necessarily violations of business practices. Each year the Federal Trade Commission orders hundreds of companies, many of them of the first magnitude, to "cease and desist" from practices which, judged by ordinary standards, are of questionable morality but which are stoutly defended by the companies concerned.

In one case, a firm manufacturing a well-known mouthwash was accused of using a cheap form of alcohol possibly deleterious to health. The company's chief executive, after testifying in Washington, made this comment privately:

> We broke no law. We're in a highly competitive industry. If we're going to stay in business, we have to look for profit wherever the law permits. We don't make up the laws. We obey them. Then why do we have to put up with this 'holier than thou' talk about ethics? It's sheer hypocrisy. We're not in business to promote ethics. Look at the cigarette companies, for God's sake! If the ethics aren't embodied in the laws by the men who made them, you can't expect businessmen to fill the lack. Why, a sudden submission to Christian ethics by businessmen would bring about the greatest economic upheaval in history!

It may be noted that the government failed to prove its case against him.

CAST ILLUSIONS ASIDE

Talk about ethics by businessmen is often a thin decorative coating over the hard realities of the game:

> Once I listened to a speech by a young executive who pointed to a new industry code as proof that his company and its competitors were deeply aware of their responsibilities to society. It was a code of ethics, he said. The industry was going to police itself, to dissuade constituent companies from wrongdoing. His eyes shone with conviction and enthusiasm.

The same day there was a meeting in a hotel room where the industry's top executives met with the "czar" who was to administer the new code, a man of high repute. No one who was present could doubt their common attitude. In their eyes the code was designed primarily to forestall a move by the federal government to impose stern restrictions on the industry. They felt that the code would hamper them a good deal less than new federal laws would. It was, in other words, conceived as a protection for the industry, not for the public.

The young executive accepted the surface explanation of the code; these leaders, all experienced game players, did not deceive themselves for a moment about its purpose.

The illusion that business can afford to be guided by ethics as conceived in private life is often fostered by speeches and articles containing such phrases as, "It pays to be ethical," or, "Sound ethics is good business." Actually this is not an ethical question at all; it is a self-serving calculation in disguise. The speaker is really saying that in the long run a company can make more money if it does not antagonize competitors, suppliers, employees, and customers by squeezing them too hard. He is saying that oversharp policies reduce ultimate gains. That is true, but it has nothing to do with ethics.

The underlying attitude is much like that in the familiar story of the shop-keeper who finds an extra $20 bill in the cash register, debates with himself the ethical problem—should he tell his partner?—and finally decides to share the money because the gesture will give him an edge over the s.o.b. the next time they quarrel.

I think it is fair to sum up the prevailing attitude of businessmen on ethics as follows:

We live in what is probably the most competitive of the world's civilized societies. Our customs encourage a high degree of aggression in the individual's striving for success. Business is our main area of competition, and it has been ritualized into a game of strategy. The basic rules of the game have been set by the government, which attempts to detect and punish business frauds. But as long as a company does not transgress the rules of the game set by law, it has the legal right to shape its strategy without reference to anything but its profits. If it takes a long-term view of its profits, it will preserve amicable relations, so far as possible, with those with whom it deals. A wise businessman will not seek advantage to the point where he generates dangerous hostility among employees, competitors, customers, government, or the public at large. But decisions in this area are, in the final test, decisions of strategy, not of ethics.

PLAYING TO WIN

. . . If a man plans to make a seat in the business game, he owes it to himself to master the principles by which the game is played, including its special ethical outlook. He can then hardly fail to recognize that an occasional bluff may well be justified in terms of the game's ethics and warranted in terms of economic necessity. Once he clears his mind on this point, he is in a good position to match his strategy against that of the other players. He can then determine objectively whether a bluff in a given situation has a good chance of succeeding and can decide when and how to bluff, without a feeling of ethical transgression.

To be a winner, a man must play to win. This does not mean that he must be ruthless, cruel, harsh, or treacherous. On the contrary, the better his reputation for integrity, honesty, and decency, the better his chances of victory will be in the long run. But from time to time every businessman, like every poker player, is offered a choice between certain loss or bluffing within the legal rules of the game. If he is not resigned to losing, if he wants to rise in his company and industry, then in such a crisis he will bluff—and bluff hard.

Every now and then one meets a successful businessman who has conveniently forgotten the small or large deceptions that he practiced on his way to fortune. "God gave me my money," old John D. Rockefeller once piously told a Sunday school class. It would be a rare tycoon in our time who would risk the horse laugh with which such a remark would be greeted.

In the last third of the twentieth century even children are aware that if a man has become prosperous in business, he has sometimes departed from the strict truth in order to overcome obstacles or has practiced the more subtle deceptions of the half-truth or the misleading omission. Whatever the form of the bluff, it is an integral part of the game, and the executive who does not master its techniques is not likely to accumulate much money or power.

Notes

1. *The New York Times*, March 9, 1967.
2. *The New York Times*, November 21, 1966.
3. New York: Grossman Publishers, 1965.
4. New York: David McKay Company, 1967.
5. *The New York Times*, January 17, 1967.
6. Cited by Ralph Nader in "Business Crime," *The New Republic*, July 1, 1967, p. 7.

PART 2

Property, Profit, and Justice

Introduction
Chapter 4 Traditional Theories of Property and Profit
Chapter 5 Contemporary Challenges to Property Rights
Chapter 6 Justice

INTRODUCTION

Issues about money and economics are often connected to those of ethics and values. If a friend borrows five dollars and later refuses to repay it, then the issue quickly becomes an ethical one. Normally, even a friend should repay the money. At all levels of economics, ethics plays an important role. For example, to decide how society should distribute disposable wealth one must know what ethical standards distinguish fair from unfair distributions. Can society distribute money to those who are sick and disabled? If so, why? Because issues of ethical philosophy arise so often in economics, it is not surprising that two well-known economists, Adam Smith and Karl Marx, both of whom are discussed in this section, began their careers as philosophers.

Two of the most volatile issues in economics have ethical implications: the importance of the profit motive and whether restrictions should be placed on private ownership of property. The pursuit of profit and the existence of private property are said by some economists to be the foundations of a free society. The seventeenth-century philosopher John Locke argued that each person has a natural right to own property. However, others argue that the profit motive and private property can induce corruption in society with labor abuses, unfair tax policies, monopolistic practices, and abuse of the environment. Technological advances sometimes require society to rethink its notion of property rights. For instance, what principles and systems should guide our interpretation of "intellectual property" in the age of the online commerce?

A third issue involving both ethics and economics is the nature of justice. For example, is there such a thing as a just or fair distribution of wealth, resources, and opportunities in society? If so, what does a just distribution look like? Is it fair or just that one person buys yachts and racehorses while another lacks food? But what if it is true that any time government attempts to ensure "fairness" by interfering with the free accumulation of wealth, its attempt to redistribute wealth creates injustice by limiting the freedom of those who have fairly earned power, position, or property?

The Profit Motive

Questions about the role of the profit motive arise every day and no more so than in the instance of pharmaceutical companies. In the case study, "How Drug's Rebirth as Treatment for Cancer Fueled Price Rises," managers of the Celgene company wonder how they should price a drug that helps cancer patients. Does Celgene have special responsibilities to accept less than a maximization of its profits because its drug treats a deadly disease, i.e., cancer? If so, what are they? Is it ever possible to charge too high a price for a drug in a context where the highest price is expected to maximize long-term financial benefit to investors?

It is common today to hear a person or corporation condemned for being greedy. Such an attitude, which questions the morality of emphasizing profit, is not new. If anything, people today are more accepting of the profit motive than at any other time in history. Especially prior to the nineteenth century, pursuing wealth, and sometimes even lending money, were targets of intense criticism. One of the great defenders of the profit motive was the eighteenth-century economist Adam Smith. Today, nearly two hundred years after Smith presented his ideas in *The Wealth of Nations* (excerpts of which are presented in this section), his name is almost synonymous with the defense of the free market economic system. Smith asserted that the pursuit of profit, even for one's self-interest, is not always bad. In a famous quotation from *The Wealth of Nations* he writes, "It is not from the benevolence of the butcher, the brewer, or the baker that we expect our dinner, but from their regard of their own interest. We address ourselves not to their humanity, but to their self-love and never talk to them of our own necessities, but of their advantage."

However, Smith did not believe that economic gain was our most noble goal; rather, he claimed that justice and benevolence were the crowning virtues of humanity. Without endorsing selfishness as a virtue, Smith emphasized how pursuing one's own economic interests could actually enhance public welfare so long as one's actions were in the context of a free marketplace (although he also noted that one should also act with prudence and respect for fair play and the rights of others. Smith believed that a viable political economy could function such that people's pursuing their own economic ends could generate, in the absence of government intervention, great public economic good.

Criticisms of the Invisible Hand

By the time the industrial revolution was under way in the early nineteenth century, Smith's ideas dominated economic theory, and interestingly, many of the emerging social patterns of that era were justified by appealing to his philosophy. The increased specialization, the reduction of quotas and tariffs, and the decreased roles of government in business were all justified by appealing to a reading of Smith's *The Wealth of Nations*. Smith himself, however, did not live to see the changes or the human miseries rampant during the industrial revolution, and his worries about the poor pay of workers indicate that he would not have approved of the treatment of labor as a result of industrialization. In fact, labor was poorly paid, working conditions were deplorable, and working hours were long. One of the most depressing sights of all was children working in factories for 16 hours a day, six days a week. For these children, such work was necessary to supplement their family's meager income.

Many witnesses to the industrial revolution were persuaded that the real villain was the economic system. The German philosopher and economist Karl Marx argued that the "free market" Smith championed was little more than a convenient fiction for capitalist property owners. Whereas Smith had praised the competitive market because of its ability to generate better products at lower prices, Marx argued that in the marketplace workers were mere commodities, available to the factory owners at the lowest possible wages. Indeed, he thought the pressures of the marketplace would force workers, who could not refuse to work without starving, to accept wages barely above a subsistence level. Meanwhile, the owners of the means of production, the capitalists, could exploit workers by using their labor and then selling the resulting product at a profit. Marx identified the difference between the costs of production, including wages, and the selling price of products as "surplus value." For Marx, then, profits always meant exploitation of the worker by the capitalist. He added that whenever technology develops, the economic gap between the capitalist and the workers widens further, since technology allows products to be manufactured with less human labor and thus creates unemployment and lower wages.

In the selections taken from the *Economic and Philosophic Manuscripts of 1844*, Marx outlines his influential theory of alienation, in which he asserts that workers in a capitalistic society are separated from, and deprived of, their own labor. When forced to work for the capitalist, workers are also forced to give the capitalist what most belongs to them: their own work. Factory employees toil away producing products that the factory owner will eventually sell, and they feel no connection to those products; rather, they have been alienated from the effects of their labor. Thus, through the concept of alienation, Marx offers a fundamental condemnation of the treatment of labor in early modern capitalism, a condemnation that was enormously influential in improving labor conditions, although less effective in its more revolutionary implications.

At the same time that Marx was developing his criticism of capitalism, there was another equally dramatic development occurring. In 1859 the English naturalist Charles Darwin published his monumental work on evolution, *On the Origin of Species*. Darwin argued, in short, that in the process of natural selection (1) organisms in the biological kingdom had evolved from simple to more complex species; and (2) during this process, organisms less adaptable to the environment failed to survive, while the more adaptable ones flourished. Darwin himself expressly stated that his ideas applied only to the biological kingdom, but many thinkers extended them to social and economic issues. The resulting theory of society, popularized by Herbert Spencer and industrialists such as Andrew Carnegie (whose article "Wealth" is reproduced in this section), was known as social Darwinism. Social

Darwinism impacted issues dealt with by Adam Smith and Karl Marx, but in point of fact it agreed with neither. The Darwinists argued that the industrial revolution exemplified social evolution from simple to complex societies. In the evolution of free market capitalistic industrial systems then, some individuals may suffer, but the system itself enhances human welfare, since it weeds out the unsuccessful, weak competitors while allowing the tougher ones to flourish. Thus, both the marketplace and nature operate according to the same "natural" laws. Those who can, survive; those who cannot, perish. In this way the thesis of social Darwinism came to view the profit motive in business as the essential motivating force in the struggle for economic survival. Unfortunately, social Darwinism was also touted by a few wealthy tycoons in the nineteenth century as a justification for deplorable working conditions and massive economic inequalities.

The key issues of Part 2—human motivation, human nature, and which economic system is preferable—are interrelated. For example, the ethical question of when, if at all, it is best for people to be motivated by profit is directly connected to the question of whether there is a dominant element of selfishness in human nature. If, as some have argued, people almost always will pursue their own self-interest, then it becomes difficult to criticize all self-interested pursuit of wealth. If this is true, then we should seek an economic system that will best harness self-interest and direct it towards the common good. On the other hand, if one is more optimistic about human nature, believing that people are capable of sustained cooperation and benevolence, then we may be able to enjoy a form of economic system that promise a kinder, gentler society.

Private Ownership

Debates about which economic system is best often turn on the question of public versus private ownership. A common argument used by those who criticize private property asserts that the elimination of private property makes it impossible for people to strive to accumulate wealth and thus discourages them from acting from a bad motive—that is, the profit motive. Defenders of the institution of private property disagree, citing the incentive for hard work and creativity that private property provides. By far the most ingenious argument in favor of private property is the classical one offered by the seventeenth-century English philosopher John Locke. Locke believed that human beings have a fundamental right to own private property, and the basic premises that establish this right can be found in the selection from his *Second Treatise on Government.* Even today his "social contract" argument is commonly used in defending the right to own property. Locke asserted what he claimed to be a truism: In the absence of a formally structured society—that is, in the "state of nature"—all people may be said to own their bodies. It was upon this seemingly obvious premise that Locke rested his defense. If one admits that one has the right to own one's body, it follows that one owns the actions of that body, or in other words, one's own labor, and that one is free to do what one pleases with one's body, one's abilities, and one's labor. Finally, one may also be said to own, and to have a right to own, the things that one mixes with one's labor. For example, if in the state of nature a person picks fruit from wild bushes, that person may be said to own the fruit. If we grant that property may be freely traded, given, and accumulated, we have the beginning of the basis for justification of vast ownership of capital and land. In sharp contrast to Locke's seemingly benign defense of private property, Marx argued that it is actually an institution that perpetuates the class struggle. He believed that it is likely that no such state of nature as Locke described ever existed, and he tried to give an accurate historical account of the evolution of the institution of property. He attempted to show how at every stage in the struggle for private property, one class succeeds in exploiting and alienating another. He argued that the institution of private property in a capitalistic economic system is nothing more than the means by which the privileged class—the capitalists—exploits the class of the less privileged—the workers.

We should remind ourselves that the immediate question confronting most people in the western world is probably not whether to adopt a purely communistic or a purely free-market economy. Moreover, one should be reminded that Marx's ideal was a communal society, not the more totalitarian socialist systems that the former Soviet Union and other communistic nations developed in his name.

The Impact of Technology on Traditional Views of Property

Technological advances of the past decade have triggered subtle changes in, and disagreements about, our traditional notions of private property. For example, do HIV-positive citizens of the Third World have a right to HIV/AIDS drugs at prices they can afford? Or is the medicinal technology the property of the drug manufacturer who is free to sell it under whatever terms and conditions it views as appropriate? Can a life-saving medication be deemed "private" property? If so, should there be any limits on this property type? The "Plasma International" case study deals with a similar issue.

The age of the Internet has triggered numerous controversies over property rights. The legal battle between on-line file-sharing services and the music industry highlights how new technology threatens traditional notions of "intellectual" property rights. Technology such as "cookies" enables firms to track an Internet user's cyberspace activities, including websites visited, purchasing behavior, and even requests for information. This presents a current thorny issue. Who "owns" the property of a person's Internet visits: the individual or the company collecting and analyzing the data? Most democratic societies believe that people have the freedom to move about without surveillance; this fundamental notion is coming under attack given new technology. Consider the new wireless systems capable of tracking people: Scientists have discovered a chip that can be inserted beneath the skin, so that a person's location can be pinpointed anywhere. While there may be many useful applications of this technology (e.g., monitoring the location of an Alzheimer's patient), it raises concerns about the privacy rights and ownership of one's physical body.

In our technology-dominant age, questions about *intellectual* property rights are among the most vexing. The case study "W.R. Grace and the Neemix Patent (A)" involves a question of intellectual property rights in a context of developing vs. developed countries. W.R. Grace, the world's largest manufacturer of specialty chemicals, secured a U.S. patent for a completely natural, environmentally friendly pesticide. The active ingredient in this chemical is derived from the seeds of the neem tree. The neem tree is native to numerous countries with subtropical climates. Particularly prevalent in India, neem seeds have been used by Indians for pesticides and other medicinal purposes for thousands of years; indeed the tree has played an active role in Indian culture.

Revenues at W.R. Grace from its neem pesticide product were growing rapidly. In September 1995, however, the Foundation for Economic Trends filed a protest (supported by more than 200 other organizations) with the U.S. Patent Office, claiming that the patent should not have been issued given preexisting knowledge of the tree's characteristics and that the patent system could not fairly compensate the indigenous people who have relied on the tree for thousands of years. One scientist claimed that Grace's patent was "the first case of genetic colonialism."

Noted management scholar Lester Thurow argues that technological advances and globalization have made the U.S. approach to intellectual property inefficient and ineffective in his article "Needed: A New System of Intellectual Property Rights." He argues that fundamental change in this system is necessary—minor adjustments will not work. Thurow also raises some interesting questions about what should be patentable. A tension exists between the dual goals of providing a financial incentive for innovation and the social desire for the wide dissemination of knowledge. Thurow argues for differentiating various intellectual property types and creating a unique system for each type.

Deborah Johnson extends Thurow's theme that technology demands a new approach to intellectual property. In her article, "Privacy," she argues that computer technology creates possibilities for behavior and activities that were impossible before. Can personal information sometimes count as a form of personal property? How about Internet snoops who dig up a detailed picture of our personal lives? Or data-mining activities that allow zip codes to be matched to bad credit risks? Johnson suggests that our quality of life and sense of personal freedom can be diminished in a world in which each step creates a digital record that may end up in someone's database.

Justice

The subject of social justice, both for traditional and modern philosophers, is directly connected to economics and ethical theory. One important subcategory of justice dealt with in this section—namely, distributive justice—concerns the issue of how, and according to what principles, society's goods should be distributed. When thinking about justice, it is important to remember that the concept of justice cannot include all ethical and political values. Thus, no matter how desirable it may be to have justice established in society, we must acknowledge other ideals such as benevolence and charity. Justice refers to a minimal condition that should exist in a good society, a condition that traditionally has been interpreted as "giving each individual his or her due."

The notion of distributive justice, i.e., what constitutes justice in distributing goods to persons, is an evasive concept, as is illustrated by the following story: Once a group of soldiers found themselves defending a fort against an enemy. The soldiers were in desperate need of water, and the only source was 200 yards from the fort in enemy territory. Courageously, a small group sneaked outside the fort, filled their canteens with water, and returned safely. After showing the water to their fellow soldiers, the successful adventurers proposed that the water should be distributed in accordance with the principles of justice. Since justice requires distribution on the basis of merit, they said, they themselves should get the water because they risked their lives in obtaining it. There was considerable disagreement. Although agreeing that justice requires distribution on the basis of deserving characteristics, a different group of soldiers, who had been longest without water, claimed they deserved it more because they needed it more than the others. After all, they were the thirstiest. And still a different group, agreeing with the same general principle of justice, argued that everyone deserved equal amounts of water because all human beings, considered generally, have equal worth. The moral, obviously, is that interpretations of justice have difficulty specifying a particular characteristic or set of characteristics which, when possessed by human beings, will serve as the basis for "giving each person his or her due."

Although the subject of distributive justice is a popular topic among modern philosophers, some thinkers, such as Robert Nozick, claim that the idea is prejudicial and controversial. If society's goods are to be distributed, this implies the existence of a distributing agency such as the government to enforce certain principles of distribution, thus taking away from those who have acquired holdings through voluntary exchanges and desert and giving to those who have and deserve less. In attacking any principles of distribution, Nozick is arguing that the very existence of such a process violates basic principles of individual liberty, because it denies individuals the opportunity to do as they please without interference and thus to engage freely in exchanges of goods and property. In this way, Nozick maintains, distributive and redistributive practices necessitate the violation of basic liberties, and therefore no willful distribution can itself be just.

Another modern writer presented in this section, John Rawls, also considers questions of justice and the social order. Rawls believes that the idea of distributive justice can be coordinated with principles of individual rights and liberties. He argues that a just society is one in which agreements are freely made, in which no one is left out, and in which deserving people are not shortchanged. Rawls argues that a just society is based on two principles: (1) "... each person engaged in an institution or affected by it has an equal right to the most extensive liberty compatible with a like liberty for all. ..." and (2) "... inequalities as defined by the institutional structure ... are arbitrary unless it is reasonable to expect that they will work out to everyone's advantage and provided that the positions and offices to which they attach or from which they may be gained are open to all." Thus, Rawls is not arguing that in a just society things would be structured so as to give all people an equal number of goods—for example, money, education, or status— and he allows that some people may have a great deal more than others. However, he believes, for a society to be just, such inequalities are only acceptable if their existence is to the advantage of the least fortunate as well as to everybody else. Rawls further specifies that no form of distribution in any society is just unless it satisfies the first condition of justice: freedom. Rawls's article, "Distributive Justice," excerpts of which are presented in this section, first appeared in 1967 and is a precursor of his influential book *A*

Theory of Justice (Harvard University Press, 1971) in which he more fully develops the views presented here. . . .

. . . With this philosophical background, one can turn to issues of justice that arise not only in large social systems, but also in corporate organizations. We take for granted a considerable amount of inequality in the modern workplace: inequality in salaries, working conditions, and status. But which inequalities should be tolerated, which should not, and why? If medical quality and availability of medical treatment are significantly different for managers than for ordinary workers, is the result unfair? To what extent should modern managers concerned about justice be attempting to "level" perks and advantages for all working in the corporation? In the case study, "The Oil Rig," we encounter dramatic disparities between expatriates and hired Angolan workers on an oil rig. The Angolans have dramatically lower salaries, fewer privileges, different clothing, limited access to medical treatment, and smaller quarters. Does justice require that the Tool Pusher (the boss of the oil rig) eliminate or substantially reduce inequalities?

Chapter 4

Traditional Theories of Property and Profit

Case Study

New Protocol: How Drug's Rebirth as Treatment for Cancer Fueled Price Rises

GEETA ANAND

WARREN, N.J. — When Celgene Corp. got its first drug approved, it priced a 50-milligram capsule at $6. Today, it sells the same white capsule for nearly five times the original price, or $29.

Little has changed to affect the cost of making the drug since it was first sold in 1998 as a treatment for leprosy and severe weight loss, or wasting, caused by AIDS. But today, it is primarily prescribed for **cancer,** a disease whose patients and advocacy groups have shown little interest in fighting for lower U.S. prices.

"When we launched it, it was going to be an AIDS-wasting drug," says Celgene's chief executive, John Jackson. "We couldn't charge more or there would have been demonstrations outside the company."

Celgene's drug is thalidomide, which earned world-wide notoriety in the 1960s for causing birth defects. The story of its reincarnation as an AIDS and cancer treatment shows how the political environment and drug companies' perception of what the market will bear drive decisions on drug prices in the U.S. For some serious diseases such as cancer, the sky is virtually the limit — although it may not stay that way.

The ability to price medicines ever higher has helped fund the pharmaceutical industry's research and development programs, which bring new medicines to patients. It also fills the coffers of some companies and their executives. Meanwhile employers, insurers, and sometimes patients must pay the tab.

What the market will bear

"For patients, the side effect of taking this drug is penury," says Raymond Comenzo, a hematologist at Memorial Sloan-Kettering Cancer Center in New York City.

Thalidomide is inexpensive to make. Fundacao Ezequiel Dias, a government laboratory in Brazil, sells 100-milligram capsules to the Brazilian government health system for seven cents. The pills are given to leprosy and cancer patients free of charge. A Netherlands pharmacy sells the same dose for about $2.60.

Celgene began as the biotechnology department inside a big chemical firm, Celanese Corp., in the late 1970s. In 1987, after Celanese merged with another company, it decided to spin off the biotechnology division. The new company, named Celgene, at first focused on using biological processes to make industrial chemicals. But in the early 1990s it decided to move into pharmaceuticals because the old focus was "a lousy business," says Sol J. Barer, a founder of Celgene who is now chief operating officer. "Chemicals are priced on the cost of ingredients," he says, while pharmaceuticals are "priced on value."

In the 1990s, Dr. Barer, a chemist, was wandering the halls of Rockefeller University in Manhattan in search of products when he bumped into a scientist who was studying why thalidomide helped treat leprosy. She theorized that the drug acted to inhibit a protein associated with inflammatory diseases from asthma to rheumatoid arthritis.

Dr. Barer grew excited about thalidomide's potential but was wary of its history. In the early 1960s, the drug was found to cause horrific birth defects in the babies of mothers who had taken the drug for morning sickness. Most of the babies were born in Europe because the drug was never approved by the U.S. Food and Drug Administration. Some babies had no arms or legs, while others had deformed limbs.

Thalidomide was still being used in poorer countries because it was cheap and effective in treating leprosy and wasting in tuberculosis patients. U.S. AIDS patients were importing thalidomide illegally to treat wasting. Dr. Barer concluded that Celgene could get the FDA to approve thalidomide, despite its notoriety, if the company sought to sell the drug for AIDS.

Celgene began clinical trials to show thalidomide could reduce wasting in AIDS patients but unexpectedly found the amount of AIDS virus in patients' blood seemed to rise temporarily on thalidomide. That meant more testing would be needed. Dr. Barer says he decided on a quicker route: getting the drug approved for treating leprosy, for which substantial data existed in public health databases around the world. Once the drug was on the market for leprosy, doctors could prescribe it for AIDS or any other disease, a practice known as "off label" prescribing.

The company devised a system for dispensing the drug that requires, among other things, regular pregnancy tests for patients of childbearing age. Since thalidomide had been around for decades and the composition couldn't be patented, Celgene would eventually patent this system of controlling distribution.

The FDA faced pressure from AIDS activists who wanted access to thalidomide. In July 1998, the FDA granted Celgene approval to market thalidomide for leprosy under the brand name Thalomid, giving the green light to those who wanted to prescribe the drug off-label for AIDS wasting.

The next challenge was setting the price. Mr. Jackson, a lanky former Marine who had held executive positions at Merck & Co. and American Cyanamid, took over as Celgene's chief executive in 1996. Mr. Jackson and Dr. Barer wanted to avoid antagonizing AIDS activists. "Our pricing people said if you charge more than $3,000 [per year], they'll show up at the door," Mr. Jackson says.

Only after the price had been set at $6 for each 50-milligram capsule did the two men fully realize thalidomide's potential to treat cancer. In 1997, Bart Barlogie, a cancer specialist in Little Rock, Ark., tried thalidomide on an elderly man with multiple myeloma, a cancer of the plasma cells in bone marrow that afflicts 50,000 Americans. Dr. Barlogie was acting on the suggestion of Judah Folkman, a researcher at Children's Hospital Boston who studied substances that can deprive cancer cells of new blood vessels for growth. Dr. Barlogie's patient had a nearly complete remission.

On Dec. 6, 1999, Dr. Barlogie reported the results of a clinical trial: About 30% of 169 patients who had relapsed after other treatments saw levels of a protein associated with myeloma decrease by 50% or more after taking thalidomide.

Thalidomide was reborn as a cancer medicine just as the drug was eclipsed by new AIDS medicines that made wasting virtually a thing of the past in the U.S. Again it was being prescribed off-label since Celgene hadn't received FDA approval to sell the drug for cancer.

Celgene, like many small biotech companies, had lost money every year since its founding. In 1998, it reported a loss of $32 million on revenue of $3.8 million. Now it could begin to tackle those losses. Mr. Jackson says he knew he could charge a lot more for thalidomide as a cancer drug. The question, he says, was whether to double or triple the price immediately or make more gradual increases. He decided on the latter. In 1999, he raised the price by 21% to $7.23 from $6 for the 50 milligram thalidomide capsule. The cost for consumers at pharmacies is typically between 20% and 25% higher than what Celgene charges to drug distributors.

Celgene's revenue soared to $38 million in 1999 and $85 million in 2000. It became a star on the stock market, even though it continued to post losses. In February 2000, Mr. Jackson did a secondary offering, raising $298 million at $101 a share. Mr. Jackson and Dr. Barer, who had dreamed of turning Celgene into a major pharmaceutical company, acquired a San Diego cancer research firm in June 2000 for $200 million in stock.

As the use of thalidomide spread, some cancer doctors noticed that they could get the same results with a lower dose. That was significant because thalidomide can cause a nerve disorder and sleepiness, especially at higher doses. At the end of 2000, the company says it found the average daily dose per patient had fallen by about 25% to 225 milligrams, from 300 milligrams a day per patient at the start of the year. That meant the average patient was spending less per day on thalidomide — $35.70 compared with $43.38 at the start of 1999. Mr. Jackson believed Celgene could raise the price.

Over 2001 and 2002, he did so several times. The medicine remained cheaper than many cancer drugs and Mr. Jackson says he received few, if any, complaints. By the end of 2002, Celgene was selling the 50-milligram capsule for $11.03. "By bringing it up every year, it was heading toward where it should be as a cancer drug," says Mr. Jackson.

It was a time in which "companies just raised the price and somebody paid the bill and nobody objected," says Margaret Tempero, a cancer specialist who is the immediate past president of the American Society of Clinical Oncology.

In December 2002, Mr. Jackson made another acquisition, a New Jersey company that harvested stem cells from human placentas after pregnancy, for $45 million in stock. At the end of 2002, Celgene reported a loss of $100 million on revenue of $136 million, as it continued to significantly boost its research and development spending.

The next year brought another reason for raising the price. A biotechnology firm in Cambridge, Mass., Millennium Pharmaceuticals Inc., brought the drug Velcade to market in May 2003 for multiple myeloma, priced about twice as high as thalidomide. Velcade, delivered in an infusion in the hospital, cost about $4,400 per month for the average patient, compared with around $1,800 per month for a typical thalidomide user.

In June, one month after Velcade came to market, Mr. Jackson raised thalidomide's price by 10% to $15.76 from $14.33. "We felt certainly from a competitive perspective that would be justifiable," he says. By the end of 2003, the 50-milligram capsule of thalidomide cost $22.32. In 2003, thalidomide sales nearly doubled to $244 million. Celgene declared its first profit, of $13.5 million.

Mr. Jackson says the price increase wasn't as rapid as it seems because in 2003 Celgene also introduced 100-milligram and 200-milligram doses of thalidomide and didn't raise the prices of those higher doses as frequently. More than 60% of patients take 200 milligrams per day or more of the drug, according to Celgene. Previously they had to take four 50-milligram pills; now they could take a single 200-milligram pill and save some money.

Each year, as thalidomide revenue grew, Mr. Jackson plowed more money into research and development of new medicines. By 2003, the R&D budget at Celgene had reached $123 million, which amounted to nearly half of the company's revenue of $271 million. Part of the research budget funded three clinical trials of Revlimid, a drug the company believes could be more effective than thalidomide in certain cancers without the potential to cause birth defects.

As revenue grew, the company raised pay for top officers. In 2003, Mr. Jackson earned $1.8 million in salary and bonus, compared with $365,000 in 1998. He says he took a pay cut to take the job in 1996 because of the potential upside, particularly the stock options. By the end of 2003, he held 1.5 million stock options valued at $31 million, according to the company's proxy statement. Other senior executives also received big increases in their salaries, bonuses and options.

Also last year, Celgene raised $400 million in a convertible debt offering. The money helped it buy a Welsh manufacturer of thalidomide for $110 million this year. The company still sits on about $800 million in cash and marketable securities. Celgene's shares, which have split twice since 2000, stood at $30.41 in 4 p.m. Nasdaq Stock Market trading Friday, giving the company a market capitalization of about $5 billion.

In theory a generic-drug company could sell thalidomide in the U.S., since the patent on the drug's composition expired long ago. However, it would need to get the FDA's approval for a distribution system to keep the drug out of the hands of pregnant women. Such a system would be difficult to devise without violating Celgene's five patents on its own system. And the FDA might hesitate to approve an alternative system because Celgene's system has worked well to prevent birth defects from thalidomide. Celgene says no other company has attempted to bring thalidomide to market in the U.S.

Celgene is seeking FDA approval to market thalidomide for multiple myeloma; currently, since the drug is only approved for leprosy, Celgene sales representatives aren't allowed to directly promote it for other uses.

This year, Mr. Jackson has raised the price of the 50-milligram capsule twice, by a total of 32%, to take it to $29.44 from $22.32. The current price of the 200-milligram capsule is $75.60, or about 36% cheaper than the 50-milligram capsule on a per-milligram basis. Patients who take 200 milligrams a day are now paying about three times as much as they did in 1998, while those with a 50-milligram daily dose are paying nearly five times as much.

Still, Mr. Jackson says a month of thalidomide for a typical patient costs only about 60% as much as a month of Velcade, meaning there's room for more price increases. He says if he brought his drug to market today he'd sell it for the same price as Velcade. In fact, he told investors during a recent presentation at an industry conference to expect Celgene's next product, Revlimid, to be priced at twice the cost of thalidomide "unless the political environment changes."

Some on Wall Street believe such a change is looming. Oncologists have begun to complain that prices are out of hand. And the Centers for Medicare and Medicaid Services, the federal agency that covers health-care costs for seniors and the indigent, has proposed cutting federal reimbursements for the infused biotechnology medicines covered at present. Analyst Eric Schmidt at SG Cowen & Co. says he expects the federal agency to exert more pressure on drug prices when it begins covering most prescription medicines for seniors in January 2006.

Mr. Jackson argues the high prices don't hurt patients. "Either people are wealthy enough to pay or health insurance pays or our company gives the medicine away for free," he says. Don Baylor, the New York Mets' hitting coach last season, takes thalidomide to treat his multiple myeloma and says in an interview the cost of the drug is covered under Major League Baseball's health-insurance plan.

But other patients bear much of the cost themselves. Mary Lou Wright, a retired insurance agent in Harrisonburg, Va., says she has paid a portion of the cost of thalidomide under her insurance plan, although she has enough income to make the expense manageable. Until Ms. Wright went off the drug recently, she paid $289 a month for her prescription of 50 milligrams a day. "The price of the drug is outrageous," says Dr. Comenzo, the Sloan-Kettering oncologist who treats Ms. Wright and Mr. Baylor.

Celgene's free drug program, generous by industry standards, helps patients who earn less than $38,000 a year and also have assets of less than $10,000. It doesn't apply to people whose insurance is paying part of the bill. Dr. Comenzo's nurse, Alice Ford, says she sees many patients who struggle to pay for thalidomide and don't qualify for Celgene's free drug program. For that reason, she says, "I discourage the doctor from putting people on it." Velcade, though more expensive, has been covered by Medicare.

The two biggest advocacy groups for multiple myeloma haven't made lower drug prices a priority. "I try to focus on the positive rather than coming after them on price," says Kathy Giusti, president of the Multiple Myeloma Research Foundation.

Susie Novis, president of the International Myeloma Foundation, says taking on drug companies over pricing is a losing battle. "They won't even discuss it. They say, 'It is what it is,'" she says.

Dr. Comenzo, while praising the advocacy groups' work, accuses them of shying away from the pricing issue because they receive substantial donations from Celgene and Millennium, among other drug companies. Ms. Giusti says drug-company donations don't influence her views on pricing. Ms. Novis says she surveyed her group and found only a minority of U.S. members worried about price. But she may take up the price issue in Europe, where patient groups and doctors have raised an outcry.

Celgene licensed the right to market thalidomide in Europe to Pharmion Corp. of Boulder, Colo. Pharmion sells the drug under a program for making lifesaving medicines available before they've been officially approved by regulators. A patient in Europe on a daily dose of 100 milligrams would pay about $30 a day to get thalidomide from Pharmion.

Pieter Sonneveld, a hematologist at the University of Rotterdam in the Netherlands, says his patients complained so much about Pharmion's price that he helped set up a pharmacy to make thalidomide and sell it at cost in the Netherlands through hospital pharmacies. It costs about $2.60 for 100 milligrams, he says. However, if Pharmion gets marketing approval from European regulators it would have exclusive rights to sell the drug for multiple myeloma, making it more difficult for low-cost alternatives such as Dr. Sonneveld's to survive.

Case Study

Plasma International

T. W. ZIMMERER ● P. L. PRESTON

The Sunday headline in the Tampa, Florida, newspaper read:

Blood Sales Result in Exorbitant Profits for Local Firm

The story went on to relate how the Plasma International Company, headquartered in Tampa, Florida, purchased blood in underdeveloped countries for as little a 90 cents a pint[i] and resold the blood to hospitals in the United States and South America. A recent disaster in Nicaragua produced

"Plasma International," case prepared by T. W. Zimmerer and P. L. Preston, reprinted from *Business and Society: Cases and Text*, ed. by Robert D. Hay, Edmund R. Gray, and James E. Gates (Cincinnati: South-Western Publishing Co., 1976). Reprinted with permission of the authors.

scores of injured persons and the need for fresh blood. Plasma International had 10,000 pints of blood flown to Nicaragua from West Africa and charged hospitals $150 per pint, netting the firm nearly 1.5 million dollars. As a result of the newspaper story, a group of irate citizens, led by prominent civic leaders, demanded that the City of Tampa, and the State of Florida, revoke Plasma International's licenses to practice business. Others protested to their congressmen to seek enactment of legislation designed to halt the sale of blood for profit. The spokesperson was reported as saying, "What kind of people are these—selling life and death? These men prey on the needs of dying people, buying blood from poor, ignorant Africans for 90 cents worth of beads and junk, and selling it to injured people for $150 a pint. Well, this company will soon find out that the people of our community won't stand for their kind around here."

"I just don't understand it. We run a business just like any other business; we pay taxes and we try to make an honest profit," said Jack Smith as he responded to reporters at the Tampa International Airport. He had just returned home from testifying before the House Subcommittee on Medical Standards. The recent publicity surrounding his firm's activities during the recent earthquakes had once again fanned the flames of public opinion.

Smith was a successful stockbroker when he founded Plasma International. Recognizing the world's need for safe, uncontaminated, and reasonably priced whole blood and blood plasma, Smith and several of his colleagues pooled their resources and went into this business. Initially most of the blood and plasma they sold was purchased through store-front operations in the United States. Most of the donors were, unfortunately, men and women who used the money obtained from the sale of their blood for wine and drugs. While sales of the blood and plasma grew dramatically several cases of hepatitis were reported in recipients. So the company began a search for new sources.

The company recruited a highly qualified team of medical consultants. This team, after extensive testing and a worldwide search, recommended that the blood profiles and donor characteristics of several rural West African tribes made them ideal prospective donors. After negotiating with the State Department and the government of Burami, the company was able to sign an agreement with several of the Burami tribal chieftains.

As Smith reviewed these facts, and the many costs involved in the sale of a commodity as fragile as blood, he concluded that the publicity was grossly unfair. His thoughts were interrupted by the reporter's question: "Mr. Smith, is it necessary to sell a vitally needed medical supply, like blood, at such high prices especially to poor people in such a critical situation?" "Our prices are determined on the basis of a lot of costs that we incur that the public isn't even aware of," Smith responded. However, when reporters pressed him for details of these "relevant" costs, Smith refused any further comment. He noted that such information was proprietary in nature and not for public consumption.

Note

i. Prices have been adjusted in this article to allow for inflation occurring since the article was written (ed.). Names of the CEO and the West African country are fictional. The case is not.

The Justification of Private Property

JOHN LOCKE

...God, who hath given the world to men in common, hath also given them reason to make use of it to the best advantage of life and convenience. The earth and all that is therein is given to men for the support and comfort of their being. And though all the fruits it naturally produces, and beasts it feeds, belong to mankind in common, as they are produced by the spontaneous hand of nature; and nobody has originally a private dominion exclusive of the rest of mankind in any of them as they are thus in their natural state; yet being given for the use of men, there must of necessity be a means to appropriate them some way or other before they can be of any use at all beneficial to any particular man. The fruit or venison which nourishes the wild Indian, who knows no enclosure, and is still a tenant in common, must be his, and so his, i.e., a part of him, that another can no longer have any right to it, before it can do any good for the support of his life.

Though the earth and all inferior creatures be common to all men, yet every man has a property in his own person; this nobody has any right to but himself. The labor of his body and the work of his hands we may say are properly his. Whatsoever, then, he removes out of the state that nature hath provided and left it in, he hath mixed his labor with, and joined to it something that is his own, and thereby makes it his property. It being by him removed from the common state nature placed it in, it hath by this labor something annexed to it that excludes the common right of other men. For this labor being the unquestionable property of the laborer, no man but he can have a right to what this is once joined to, at least where there is enough, and as good left in common for others.

He that is nourished by the acorns he picked up under an oak, or the apples he gathered from the trees in the wood, has certainly appropriated them to himself. Nobody can deny but the nourishment is his. I ask, then, When did they begin to be his—when he digested, or when he ate, or when he boiled, or when he brought them home, or when he picked them up? And 'tis plain if the first gathering made them not his, nothing else could. That labor put a distinction between them and common; that added something to them more than nature, the common mother of all, had done, and so they became his private right. And will anyone say he had no right to those acorns or apples he thus appropriated, because he had not the consent of all mankind to make them his? Was it robbery thus to assume to himself what belonged to all in common? If such a consent as that was necessary, man had starved, notwithstanding the plenty God had given him. We see in common which remains so by compact that 'tis the taking any part of what is common and removing it out of the state nature leaves it in, which begins the property; without which the common is of no use. And the taking of this or that does not depend on the express consent of all the commoners. Thus the grass my horse has bit, the turfs my servant has cut, the ore I have dug in any place where I have a right to them in common with others, become my property without the assignation or consent of anybody. The labor that

From John Locke, *The Second Treatise of Government* (1764; rpt. New York: Macmillan, 1956).

LABOR made Property

was mine removing them out of that common state they were in, hath fixed my property in them. . . . ✳

It will perhaps be objected to this, that if gathering the acorns, or other fruits of the earth, etc., makes a right to them, then anyone may engross as much as he will. To which I answer, Not so. The same law of nature that does by this means give us property, does also bound that property too. "God has given us all things richly" (1 Tim. vi. 17), is the voice of reason confirmed by inspiration. But how far has He given it us? To enjoy. As much as anyone can make use of any advantage of life before it spoils, so much he may by his labor fix a property in; whatever is beyond this, is more than his share, and belongs to others. Nothing was made by God for man to spoil or destroy. And thus considering the plenty of natural provisions there was a long time in the world, and the few spenders, and to how small a part of that provision the industry of one man could extend itself, and engross it to the prejudice of others—especially keeping within the bounds, set by reason, of what might serve for his use—there could be then little room for quarrels or contentions about property so established.

LABOR sets Limits

But the chief matter of property being now not the fruits of the earth, and the beasts that subsist on it, but the earth itself, as that which takes in and carries with it all the rest, I think it is plain that property in that, too, is acquired as the former. As much land as a man tills, plants, improves, cultivates, and can use the product of, so much is his property. He by his labor does as it were enclose it from the common. Nor will it invalidate his right to say, everybody else has an equal title to it; and therefore he cannot appropriate, he cannot enclose, without the consent of all his fellow-commoners, all mankind. God, when He gave the world in common to all mankind, commanded man also to labor, and the penury of his condition required it of him. God and his reason commanded him to subdue the earth, i.e., improve it for the benefit of life, and therein lay out something upon it that was his own, his labor. He that, in obedience to this command of God, subdued, tilled, and sowed any part of it, thereby annexed to it something that was his property, which another had no title to, nor could without injury take from him.

Nor was this appropriation of any parcel of land, by improving it, any prejudice to any other man, since there was still enough and as good left; and more than the yet unprovided could use. So that in effect, there was never the less left for others because of his enclosure for himself. For he that leaves as much as another can make use of, does as good as take nothing at all. Nobody could think himself injured by the drinking of another man, though he took a good draught, who had a whole river of the same water left him to quench his thirst; and the case of land and water, where there is enough of both, is perfectly the same.

God gave the world to men in common; but since He gave it them for their benefit, and the greatest conveniences of life they were capable to draw from it, it cannot be supposed He meant it should always remain common and uncultivated. He gave it to the use of the industrious and rational (and labor was to be his title to it), not to the fancy or coveteousness of the quarrelsome and contentious. He that had as good left for his improvement as was already taken up, needed not complain, ought not to meddle with what was already improved by another's labor; if he did, it is plain he desired the benefit of another's pains, which he had no right to, and not the ground

which God had given him in common with others to labor on, and whereof
there was as good left as that already possessed, and more than he knew
what to do with, or his industry could reach to.

It is true, in land that is common in England, or any other country
where there is plenty of people under Government, who have money and
commerce, no one can enclose or appropriate any part without the consent
of all his fellow-commoners: because this is left common by compact, i.e., by
the law of the land, which is not to be violated. And though it be common
in respect of some men, it is not so to all mankind; but is the joint property
of this country, or this parish. Besides, the remainder, after such enclosure,
would not be as good to the rest of the commoners as the whole was, when
they could all make use of the whole, whereas in the beginning and first
peopling of the great common of the world it was quite otherwise. The law
man was under was rather for appropriating. God commanded, and his
wants forced him, to labor. That was his property, which could not be taken
from him wherever he had fixed it. And hence subduing or cultivating the
earth, and having dominion, we see are joined together. The one gave title
to the other. So that God, by commanding to subdue, gave authority so far
to appropriate. And the condition of human life, which requires labor and
materials to work on, necessarily introduces private possessions. The measure
of property nature has well set by the extent of men's labor and the conveniency of life. No man's labor could subdue or appropriate all, nor could
his enjoyment consume more than a small part; so that it was impossible for
any man, this way, to entrench upon the right of another or acquire to himself a property to the prejudice of his neighbor, who would still have room
for as good and as large a possession (after the other had taken out his) as
before it was appropriated. Which measure did confine every man's possession to a very moderate proportion, and such as he might appropriate to
himself without injury to anybody in the first ages of the world, when men
were more in danger to be lost, by wandering from their company, in the
then vast wilderness of the earth than to be straitened for want of room to
plant in....

And thus, without supposing any private dominion and property in
Adam over all the world, exclusive of all other men, which can no way be
proved, nor any one's property be made out from it, but supposing the
world, given as it was to the children of men in common, we see how labor
could make men distinct titles to several parcels of it for their private uses,
wherein there could be no doubt of right, no room for quarrel.

Nor is it so strange, as perhaps before consideration it may appear, that
the property of labor should be able to overbalance the community of land.
For it is labor indeed that puts the difference of value on everything; and
let anyone consider what the difference is between an acre of land planted
with tobacco or sugar, sown with wheat or barley, and an acre of the same
land lying in common without any husbandry upon it, and he will find that
the improvement of labor makes the far greater part of the value. I think it
will be but a very modest computation to say that of the products of the
earth useful to the life of man nine-tenths are the effects of labor; nay, if we
will rightly estimate things as they come to our use, and cast up the several
expenses about them—what in them is purely owing to nature, and what to
labor—we shall find that in most of them ninety-nine hundredths are wholly
to be put on the account of labor....

From all which it is evident that, though the things of nature are given in common, yet man, by being master of himself and proprietor of his own person and the actions or labor of it, had still in himself the great foundation of property; and that which made up the great part of what he applied to the support or comfort of his being, when invention and arts had improved the conveniences of life, was perfectly his own, and did not belong in common to others.

Thus labor, in the beginning, gave a right of property, wherever anyone was pleased to employ it upon what was common, which remained a long while the far greater part, and is yet more than mankind makes use of. Men at first, for the most part, contented themselves with what unassisted nature offered to their necessities; and though afterwards, in some parts of the world (where the increase of people and stock, with the use of money, had made land scarce, and so of some value), the several communities settled the bounds of their distinct territories, and by laws within themselves, regulated the properties of the private men of their society, and so, by compact and agreement, settled the property which labor and industry began—and the leagues that have been made between several states and kingdoms, either expressly or tacitly disowning all claim and right to the land in the other's possession, have, by common consent, given up their pretenses to their natural common right, which originally they had to those countries; and so have, by positive agreement, settled a property amongst themselves in distant parts of the world—yet there are still great tracts of ground to be found which, the inhabitants thereof not having joined with the rest of mankind in the consent of the use of their common money, lie waste, and more than the people who dwell on it do or can make use of, and so still lie in common; though this can scarce happen amongst that part of mankind that have consented to the use of money.

The greatest part of things really useful to the life of man, and such as the necessity of subsisting made the first commoners of the world look after, as it doth the Americans now, are generally things of short duration, such as, if they are not consumed by use, will decay and perish of themselves: gold, silver, and diamonds are things that fancy or agreement have put the value on more than real use and the necessary support of life. Now of those good things which nature hath provided in common, everyone hath a right, as hath been said, to as much as he could use, and had a property in all he could effect with his labor—all that his industry could extend to, to alter from the state nature had put it in, was his. He that gathered a hundred bushels of acorns or apples had thereby a property in them; they were his goods as soon as gathered. He was only to look that he used them before they spoiled, else he took more than his share, and robbed others; and, indeed, it was a foolish thing, as well as dishonest, to hoard up more than he could make use of. If he gave away a part to anybody else, so that it perished not uselessly in his possession, these he also made use of; and if he also bartered away plums that would have rotted in a week, for nuts that would last good for his eating a whole year, he did no injury; he wasted not the common stock, destroyed no part of the portion of goods that belonged to others, so long as nothing perished uselessly in his hands. Again, if he would give his nuts for a piece of metal, pleased with its color, or exchange his sheep for shells, or wool for a sparkling pebble or a diamond, and keep those by him all his life, he invaded not the right of others; he might heap up as much as these durable things as he pleased, the exceeding of the bounds of his just property not lying in the largeness of his possessions, but the perishing of anything uselessly in it.

And thus came in the use of money—some lasting thing that men might keep without spoiling, and that, by mutual consent, men would take in exchange for the truly useful but perishable supports of life.

And as different degrees of industry were apt to give men possessions in different proportions, so this invention of money gave them the opportunity to continue and enlarge them; for supposing an island, separate from all possible commerce with the rest of the world, wherein there were but a hundred families—but there were sheep, horses, and cows, with other useful animals, wholesome fruits, and land enough for corn for a hundred thousand times as many, but nothing in the island, either because of its commonness or perishableness, fit to supply the place of money—what reason could anyone have there to enlarge his possessions beyond the use of his family and a plentiful supply to its consumption, either in what their own industry produced, or they could barter for like perishable useful commodities with others? Where there is not something both lasting and scarce, and so valuable to be hoarded up, there men will not be apt to enlarge their possessions of land, were it never so rich, never so free for them to take; for I ask, what would a man value ten thousand or a hundred thousand acres of excellent land, ready cultivated, and well stocked too with cattle, in the middle of the inland parts of America, where he had no hopes of commerce with other parts of the world, to draw money to him by the sale of the product? It would not be worth the enclosing, and we should see him give up again to the wild common of nature whatever was more than would supply the conveniences of life to be had there for him and his family.

Thus in the beginning all the world was America, and more so than that is now, for no such thing as money was anywhere known. Find out something that hath the use and value of money amongst his neighbors, you shall see the same man will begin presently to enlarge his possessions.

But since gold and silver, being little useful to the life of man in proportion to food, raiment, and carriage, has its value only from the consent of men, whereof labor yet makes, in great part, the measure, it is plain that the consent of men have agreed to a disproportionate and unequal possession of the earth—I mean out of the bounds of society and compact; for in governments the laws regulate it; they having, by consent, found out and agreed in a way how a man may rightfully and without injury possess more than he himself can make use of by receiving gold and silver, which may continue long in a man's possession, without decaying for the overplus, and agreeing those metals should have a value.

And thus, I think, it is very easy to conceive without any difficulty how labor could at first begin a title of property in the common things of nature, and how the spending it upon our uses bounded it; so that there could then be no reason of quarrelling about title, nor any doubt about the largeness of possession it gave. Right and conveniency went together; for as a man had a right to all he could employ his labor upon, so he had no temptation to labor for more than he could make use of. This left no room for controversy about the title, nor for encroachment on the right of others; what portion a man carved to himself was easily seen, and it was useless, as well as dishonest, to carve himself too much, or take more than he needed.

Benefits of the Profit Motive

ADAM SMITH

BOOK I

Of the causes of improvement in the productive powers of labor and of the order according to which its produce is naturally distributed among the different ranks of the people

Chapter I Of the Division of Labor

The greatest improvement in the productive powers of labor, and the greater part of the skill, dexterity, and judgment with which it is anywhere directed, or applied, seem to have been the effects of the division of labor....

To take an example, therefore, from a very trifling manufacture; but one in which the division of labor has been very often taken notice of, the trade of the pin-maker; a workman not educated to this business (which the division of labor has rendered a distinct trade), nor acquainted with the use of the machinery employed in it (to the invention of which the same division of labor has probably given occasion), could scarce, perhaps, with his utmost industry, make one pin in a day, and certainly could not make twenty. But in the way in which this business is now carried on, not only the whole work is a peculiar trade, but it is divided into a number of branches, of which the greater part are likewise peculiar trades. One man draws out the wire, another straights it, a third cuts it, a fourth points it, a fifth grinds it at the top for receiving the head; to make the head requires two or three distinct operations; to put it on is a peculiar business, to whiten the pins is another; it is even a trade by itself to put them into the paper; and the important business of making a pin is, in this manner, divided into about eighteen distinct operations, which in some manufactories, are all performed by distinct hands, though in others the same man will sometimes perform two or three of them. I have seen a small manufactory of this kind where ten men only were employed, and where some of them consequently performed two or three distinct operations. But though they were very poor, and therefore but indifferently accommodated with the necessary machinery, they could, when they exerted themselves, make among them about twelve pounds of pins a day. There are in a pound upwards of four thousand pins of a middling size. Those ten persons, therefore, could make among them upwards of forty-eight thousand pins in a day. Each person, therefore, making a tenth part of forty-eight thousand pins, might be considered as making four thousand eight hundred pins in a day. But if they had all wrought separately and independently, and without any of them having been educated to this peculiar business, they certainly could not each of them have made twenty, perhaps not one pin in a day; that is, certainly, not the two hundred and fortieth,

From Adam Smith, *The Wealth of Nations*, Books I dn IV (1776; rpt. Chicago: University of Chicago Press, 1976).

perhaps not the four thousand eight hundredth part, of what they are at present capable of performing in consequence of a proper division and combination of their different operations.

In every other art and manufacture, the effects of the division of labor are similar to what they are in this very trifling one; though in many of them, the labor can neither be so much subdivided, nor reduced to so great a simplicity of operation. The division of labor, however, so far as it can be introduced, occasions, in every art, a proportionate increase of the productive powers of labor. . . .

This great increase of the quantity of work, which in consequence of the division of labor, the same number of people are capable of performing, is owing to three different circumstances: first, to the increase of dexterity in every particular workman; secondly, to the saving of the time which is commonly lost in passing from one species of work to another; and lastly, to the invention of a great number of machines which facilitate and abridge labor, and enable one man to do the work of many.

First, the improvement of the dexterity of the workman necessarily increases the quantity of the work he can perform; and the division of labor, by reducing every man's business to some one simple operation and by making this operation the sole employment of his life, necessarily increases very much the dexterity of the workman. A common smith, who, though accustomed to handle the hammer, has never been used to make nails, if upon some particular occasion he is obliged to attempt it, will scarce, I am assured, be able to make about two or three hundred nails in a day, and those too very bad ones. A smith who has been accustomed to make nails, but whose sole or principal business has not been that of a nailer, can seldom with his utmost diligence make more than eight hundred or a thousand nails in a day. I have seen several boys under twenty years of age who had never exercised any other trade but that of making nails, and who, when they exerted themselves, could make, each of them, upwards of two thousand three hundred nails in a day. The making of a nail, however, is by no means one of the simplest operations. The same person blows the bellows, stirs or mends the fire as there is occasion, heats the iron, and forges every part of the nail: In forging the head too he is obliged to change his tools. The different operations into which the making of a pin or of a metal button is subdivided, are all of them much more simple; and the dexterity of the person, of whose life it has been the sole business to perform them, is usually much greater. The rapidity with which some of the operations of those manufacturers are performed exceeds what the human hand could, by those who had never seen them, be supposed capable of acquiring.

Secondly, the advantage which is gained by saving the time commonly lost in passing from one sort of work to another is much greater than we should at first view be apt to imagine it. It is impossible to pass very quickly from one kind of work to another, that is carried on in a different place, and with quite different tools. A country weaver who cultivates a small farm must lose a good deal of time in passing from his loom to the field, and from the field to his loom. When the two trades can be carried on in the same workhouse, the loss of time is no doubt much less. It is even in this case, however, very considerable. . . .

Thirdly, and lastly, every body must be sensible how much labor is facilitated and abridged by the application of proper machinery. . . .

. . . A great part of the machines made use of in those manufactures in which labor is most subdivided were originally the inventions of common workmen, who, being each of them employed in some very simple operation, naturally turned their thoughts toward finding out easier and readier methods of performing it. Whoever has been much accustomed to visit such manufacturers must frequently have been shown very pretty machines which were inventions of such workmen in order to facilitate and quicken their own particular part of the work. In the first fire-engines, a boy was constantly employed to open and shut alternately the communication between the boiler and the cylinder, according as the piston either ascended or descended. One of those boys, who loved to play with his companions, observed that, by tying a string from the handle of the valve which opened this communication to another part of the machine, the valve would open and shut without his assistance, and leave him at liberty to divert himself with his play-fellows. One of the greatest improvements that has been made upon this machine, since it was first invented, was in this manner the discovery of a boy who wanted to save his own labor. . . .

It is the great multiplication of the productions of all the different arts, in consequence of the division of labor, which occasions, in a well-governed society, that universal opulence which extends itself to the lowest ranks of the people. Every workman has a great quantity of his own work to dispose of beyond what he himself has occasion for; and every other workman being exactly in the same situation, he is enabled to exchange a great quantity of his own goods for a great quantity, or, what comes to the same thing, for the price of a great quantity of theirs. He supplies them abundantly with what they have occasion for, and they accommodate him as amply with what he has occasion for, and a general plenty diffuses itself through all the different ranks of the society. . . .

Chapter II Of the Principle Which Gives Occasion to the Division of Labor

This division of labor, from which so many advantages are derived, is not originally the effect of any human wisdom which forsees and intends that general opulence to which it gives occasion. It is the necessary, though very slow and gradual, consequence of a certain propensity in human nature which has in view no such extensive utility: the propensity to truck, barter, and exchange one thing for another.

. . . In almost every other race of animals each individual, when it is grown up to maturity, is entirely independent, and in its natural state has occasion for the assistance of no other living creature. But man has almost constant occasion for the help of his brethren, and it is in vain for him to expect it from their benevolence only. He will be more likely to prevail if he can interest their self-love in his favor, and show them that it is for their own advantage to do for him what he requires of them. Whoever offers to another a bargain of any kind, proposes to do this. Give me that which I want, and you shall have this which you want, is the meaning of every such offer; and it is in the manner that we obtain from one another the far greater part

of those good offices which we stand in need of. It is not from the benevolence
of the butcher, the brewer, or the baker, that we expect our dinner, but from
their regard to their own interest. We address ourselves, not to their humanity
but to their self-love, and never talk to them of our own necessities but of their
advantages. Nobody but a beggar chooses to depend chiefly upon the benevolence of his fellow-citizens. Even a beggar does not depend upon it entirely.
The charity of well-disposed people, indeed, supplies him with the whole
fund of his subsistence. But though this principle ultimately provides him
with all the necessaries of life which he has occasion for, it neither does nor
can provide him with them as he has occasion for them. The greater part
of his occasional wants are supplied in the same manner as those of other
people, by treaty, by barter, and by purchase. With the money which one
man gives him he purchases food. The old clothes which another bestows
upon him he exchanges for other old clothes which suit him better, or for
lodging, or for food, or for money, with which he can buy either food,
clothes, or lodging, as he has occasion.

As it is by treaty, by barter, and by purchase that we obtain from one
another the greater part of those mutual good offices which we stand in
need of, so it is this same trucking disposition which originally gives occasion to the division of labor. In a tribe of hunters or shepherds a particular
person makes bows and arrows, for example, with more readiness and dexterity than any other. He frequently exchanges them for cattle or for venison with his companions; and he finds at last that he can in this manner get
more cattle and venison than if he himself went to the field to catch them.
From a regard to his own interest, therefore, the making of bows and arrows
grows to be his chief business, and he becomes a sort of armorer. Another
excels in making the frames and covers of their little huts or moveable
houses. He is accustomed to be of use in this way to his neighbors, who reward him in the same manner with cattle and with venison till at last he
finds it his interest to dedicate himself entirely to this employment, and to
become a sort of house carpenter. In the same manner a third becomes a
smith or a brazier; a fourth a tanner or dresser of hides or skins, the principal part of the clothing of savages. And thus the certainty of being able to
exchange all that surplus part of the produce of his own labor, which is over
and above his own consumption, for such parts of the produce of other
men's labor as he may have occasion for, encourages every man to apply
himself to a particular occupation, and to cultivate and bring to perfection
whatever talent or genius he may possess for that particular species of business.

The difference of natural talents in different men is, in reality, much
less than we are aware of; and the very different genius which appears to distinguish men of different professions, when grown up to maturity, is not
upon many occasions so much the cause as the effect of the division of
labor. The difference between the most dissimilar characters, between a
philosopher and a common street porter, for example, seems to arise not so
much from nature as from habit, custom, and education. When they came
into the world, and for the first six or eight years of their existence, they
were, perhaps, very much alike, and neither their parents nor play-fellows
could perceive any remarkable difference. About that age, or soon after, they
come to be employed in very different occupations. The difference of talents comes then to be taken notice of, and widens by degrees, till at last the
vanity of the philosopher is willing to acknowledge scarce any resemblance.

But without the disposition to truck, barter, and exchange, every man must have procured to himself every necessary and conveniency of life which he wanted. All must have had the same duties to perform, and the same work to do, and there could have been no such difference of employment as could alone give occasion to any great difference of talents. . . .

BOOK IV

Chapter II

Every individual is continually exerting himself to find out the most advantageous employment for whatever capital he can command. It is his own advantage, indeed, and not that of the society, which he has in view. But the study of his own advantage, naturally, or rather necessarily, leads him to prefer that employment which is most advantageous to the society. . . .

As every individual, therefore, endeavours as much as he can both to employ his capital in the support of domestic industry, and so to direct that industry that its produce may be of the greatest value, every individual necessarily labors to render the annual revenue of the society as great as he can. He generally, indeed, neither intends to promote the public interest, nor knows how much he is promoting it. By preferring the support of domestic to that of foreign industry, he intends only his own security: and by directing that industry in such a manner as its produce may be of the greatest value, he intends only his own gain, and he is in this, as in many other cases, led by an invisible hand to promote an end which was no part of his intention. Nor is it always the worse for society that it was no part of it. By pursuing his own interest he frequently promotes that of the society more effectually than when he really intends to promote it. I have never known much good done by those who affected to trade for the public good. It is an affectation, indeed, not very common among merchants, and very few words need be employed in dissuading them from it.

Alienated Labour

KARL MARX

We shall begin from a *contemporary* economic fact. The worker becomes poorer the more wealth he produces and the more his production increases in power and extent. The worker becomes an ever cheaper commodity the more goods he creates. The *devaluation* of the human world increases in direct relation with the *increase in value* of the world of things. Labour does not only create goods; it also produces itself and the worker as a commodity, and indeed in the same proportion as it produces goods. . . .

From *Karl Marx: Early Writings. The Economic and Philosophic Manuscripts of 1844*, trans. T. B. Bottomore, Copyright © 1963 by McGraw-Hill Book Company. Used with permission of the McGraw-Hill Companies.

All these consequences follow from the fact that the worker is related to the *product of his labour* as to an *alien* object. For it is clear on this presupposition that the more the worker expends himself in work the more powerful becomes the world of objects which he creates in face of himself, the poorer he becomes in his inner life, and the less he belongs to himself. It is just the same as in religion. The more of himself man attributes to God the less he has left in himself. The worker puts his life into the object, and his life then belongs no longer to himself but to the object. The greater his activity, therefore, the less he possesses. What is embodied in the product of his labour is no longer his own. The greater this product is, therefore, the more he is diminished. The *alienation* of the worker in his product means not only that his labour becomes an object, assumes an external existence, but that it exists independently, *outside himself*, and alien to him, and that it stands opposed to him as an autonomous power. The life which he has given to the object sets itself against him as an alien and hostile force.

...The worker becomes a slave of the object; first, in that he receives an *object of work*, i.e., receives *work*, and secondly, in that he receives *means of subsistence*. Thus the object enables him to exist, first as a *worker* and secondly as a *physical subject*. The culmination of this enslavement is that he can only maintain himself as a physical subject so far as he is a worker, and that it is only as a physical subject that he is a worker. ...

What constitutes the alienation of labour? First, that the work is external to the worker, and that it is not part of his nature; and that, consequently, he does not fulfill himself in his work but denies himself, has a feeling of misery rather than well-being, does not develop freely his mental and physical energies but is physically exhausted and mentally debased. The worker, therefore, feels himself at home only during his leisure time, whereas at work he feels homeless. His work is not voluntary but imposed, *forced labour*. It is not the satisfaction of a need, but only a *means* for satisfying other needs. Its alien character is clearly shown by the fact that as soon as there is no physical or other compulsion it is avoided like the plague. External labour, labour in which man alienates himself, is a labour of self-sacrifice, of mortification. Finally, the external character of work for the worker is shown by the fact that it is not his own work but work for someone else, that in work he does not belong to himself but to another person. ...

We arrive at the result that man (the worker) feels himself to be freely active only in his animal functions—eating, drinking, and procreating, or at most also in his dwelling and in personal adornment—while in his human functions he is reduced to an animal. The animal becomes human and the human becomes animal.

Eating, drinking, and procreating are of course also genuine human functions. But abstractly considered, apart from the environment of human activities, and turned into final and sole ends, they are animal functions.

We have now considered the act of alienation of practical human activity, labour, from two aspects: (1) the relationship of the worker to the *product of labour* as an alien object which dominates him. This relationship is at the same time the relationship to the sensuous external world, to natural objects, as an alien and hostile world; (2) the relationship of labour to the *act of production* within *labour*. This is the relationship of the worker to his own activity as something alien and not belonging to him, activity as suffering (passivity), strength as powerlessness, creation as emasculation, the personal physical and mental energy of the worker, his personal life (for what is life but activity?), as an activity which is directed against himself, independent of him and not belonging to him. This is self-alienation as against the above-mentioned alienation of the *thing*.

We have now to infer a third characteristic of *alienated labour* from the two we have considered.

Man is a species-being not only in the sense that he makes the community (his own as well as those of other things) his object both practically and theoretically, but also (and this is simply another expression for the same thing) in the sense that he treats himself as the present, living species, as a *universal* and consequently free being.[1]

Species-life, for man as for animals, has its physical basis in the fact that man (like animals) lives from inorganic nature, and since man is more universal than an animal so the range of inorganic nature from which he lives is more universal. ... The universality of man appears in practice in the universality which makes the whole of nature into his inorganic body: (1) as a direct means of life; and equally (2) as the material object and instrument of his life activity. Nature is the inorganic body of man; that is to say nature, excluding the human body itself. To say that man *lives* from nature means that nature is his *body* with which he must remain in a continuous interchange in order not to die. The statement that the physical and mental life of man, and nature, are interdependent means simply that nature is interdependent with itself, for man is a part of nature.

Since alienated labour (1) alienates nature from man; and (2) alienates man from himself, from his own active function, his life activity; so it alienates him from the species. It makes *species-life* into a means of individual life. In the first place it alienates species-life and individual life, and secondly, it turns the latter, as an abstraction, into the purpose of the former, also in its abstract and alienated form.

For labour, *life activity, productive life*, now appear to man only as means for the satisfaction of a need, the need to maintain his physical existence. Productive life is, however, species-life. It is life creating life. In the type of life activity resides the whole character of a species, its species-character; and free, conscious activity is the species-character of human beings. Life itself appears only as a *means of life*.

The animal is one with its life activity. It does not distinguish the activity from itself. It is *its activity*. But man makes his life activity itself an object of his will and consciousness. He has a conscious life activity. It is not a determination with which he is completely identified. Conscious life activity distinguishes man from the life activity of animals. Only for this reason is he a species-being. Or rather, he is only a self-conscious being, i.e., for his own life is an object for him, because he is a species-being. Only for this reason is his activity free activity. Alienated labour reverses the relationship, in that man because he is a self-conscious being makes his life activity, his being, only a means for his *existence*.

The practical construction of an *objective* world, the *manipulation* of inorganic nature, is the confirmation of man as a conscious species-being, i.e., a being who treats the species as his own being or himself as a species-being. ...

It is just in his work upon the objective world that man really proves himself as a *species-being*. This production is his active species-life. By means of it nature appears as his work and his reality. The object of labour is, therefore, the *objectification of man's species-life:* for he no longer reproduces himself merely intellectually, as in consciousness, but actively and in a real sense, and he sees his own reflection in a world which he has constructed. While, therefore, alienated labour takes away the object of production from man, it also takes away his *species-life,* his real objectivity as a species-being, and changes his advantage over animals into a disadvantage in so far as his inorganic body, nature, is taken from him. Just as alienated labour transforms free and self-directed activity into a means, so it transforms the species-life of man into a means of physical existence.

Consciousness, which man has from his species, is transformed through alienation so that species-life becomes only a means for him. (3) Thus alienated labour turns the *species-life of man,* and also nature as his mental species-property, into an *alien* being and into a means for his *individual existence.* It alienates from man his own body, external nature, his mental life and his *human* life. (4) A direct consequence of the alienation of man from the product of his labour, from his life activity and from his species-life, is that *man is alienated* from other *men.* When man confronts himself he also confronts other men. What is true of man's relationship to his work, to the product of his work and to himself, is also true of his relationship to other men, to their labour and to the objects of their labour.

In general, the statement that man is alienated from his species-life means that each man is alienated from others, and that each of the others is likewise alienated from human life.

Human alienation, and above all the relation of man to himself, is first realized and expressed in the relationship between each man and other men. Thus in the relationship of alienated labour every man regards other men according to the standards and relationships in which he finds himself placed as a worker.

We began with an economic fact, the alienation of the worker and his production. Wb have expressed this fact in conceptual terms as *alienated labour,* and in analysing the concept we have merely analysed an economic fact. . . .

The *alien* being to whom labour and the product of labour belong, to whose service labour is devoted, and to whose enjoyment the product of labour goes, can only be *man* himself. If the product of labour does not belong to the worker, but confronts him as an alien power, this can only be because it belongs to *a man other than the worker.* . . .

Thus, through alienated labour the worker creates the relation of another man, who does not work and is outside the work process, to this labour. The relation of the workers to work also produces the relation of the capitalist (or whatever one likes to call the lord of labour) to work. *Private property* is, therefore, the product, the necessary result, of *alienated labour,* of the external relation of the worker to nature and to himself.

Private property is thus derived from the analysis of the concept of *alienated labor;* that is, alienated man, alienated labour, alienated life, and estranged man.

We have, of course, derived the concept of *alienated labour* (*alienated life*) from political economy, from the analysis of the *movement of private property.*

But the analysis of this concept shows that although private property appears to be the basis and cause of alienated labour, it is rather a consequence of the latter, just as the gods are *fundamentally* not the cause but the product of confusion of human reason. At a later stage, however, there is a reciprocal influence.

Only in the final state of the development of private property is its secret revealed, namely, that it is on one hand the product of alienated labour, and on the other hand the means by which labour is alienated, *the realization of this alienation.* . . .

Just as *private property* is only the sensuous expression of the fact that man is at the same time an *objective* fact for himself and becomes an alien and non-human object for himself; just as his manifestation of life is also his alienation of life and his self-realization a loss of reality, the emergence of an *alien* reality; so the positive supersession of private property, i.e., the *sensuous* appropriation of the human essence and of human life, of objective man and of human *creations*, by and for man, should not be taken only in the sense of *immediate*, exclusive *enjoyment*, or only in the sense of *possession* or *having*. Man appropriates his manifold being in an all-inclusive way, and thus as a whole man. All his *human* relations to the world—seeing, hearing, smelling, tasting, touching, thinking, observing, feeling, desiring, acting, loving—in short, all the organs of his individuality, like the organs which are directly communal in form, are in their objective action (their *action in relation to the object*) the appropriation of this object, the appropriation of human reality. The way in which they react to the object is the confirmation of *human reality*. It is human effectiveness and human *suffering*, for suffering humanly considered is an enjoyment of the self for man.

Private property has made us so stupid and partial that an object is only *ours* when we have it, when it exists for us as capital or when it is directly eaten, drunk, worn, inhabited, etc., in short, *utilized* in some way. But private property itself only conceives these various forms of possession as *means of life*, and the life for which they serve as means is the life of *private property*—labour and creation of capital.

The supersession of private property is, therefore, the complete emancipation of all the human qualities and senses. It is such an emancipation because these qualities and senses have become *human*, from the subjective as well as the objective point of view. The eye has become a *human* eye when its *object* has become a *human*, social object, created by man and destined for him. The senses have, therefore, become directly theoreticians in practice. They relate themselves to the thing for the sake of the thing, but the thing itself is an *objective human* relation to itself and to man, and vice versa. Need and enjoyment have thus lost their *egoistic* character and nature has lost its mere utility by the fact that its utilization has become *human* utilization. . . .

Note

1. In this passage Marx reproduces Feuerbach's argument in *Das Wesen des Christentums*.

Wealth

ANDREW CARNEGIE

This article is one of the clearest attempts to justify social Darwinism. Written in 1889, it defends the pursuit of wealth by arguing that society is strengthened and improved through the struggle for survival in the market-place. Interestingly, it was written by one of the world's wealthiest men, Andrew Carnegie, who came to the United States as a poor immigrant boy and quickly rose to enormous power. He began his career as a minor employee in a telegraph company, but emerged in a few years as a superintendent of the Pennsylvania Railroad. After the Civil War he entered the iron and steel business, and by 1889 he controlled eight companies, which he eventually consolidated into the Carnegie Steel Corporation. Shortly before he died, he merged the Carnegie Steel Corporation with the United States Steel Company. Carnegie took seriously the task of managing his vast fortune, and he made use of many of the ideas that are presented in the following article. He gave generously to many causes, including public libraries, public education, and the development of international peace.

The problem of our age is the proper administration of wealth, so that the ties of brotherhood may still bind together the rich and poor in harmonious relationship. The conditions of human life have not only been changed, but revolutionized, within the past few hundred years. In former days there was little difference between the dwelling, dress, food, and environment of the chief and those of his retainers. The Indians are today where civilized man then was. When visiting the Sioux, I was led to the wigwam of the chief. It was just like the others in external appearance, and even within the difference was trifling between it and those of the poorest of his braves. The contrast between the palace of the millionaire and the cottage of the laborer with us today measures the change which has come into civilization.

This change, however, is not to be deplored, but welcomed as highly beneficial. It is well, nay essential, for the progress of the race, that the houses of some should be homes for all that is highest and best in literature and art, and for all the refinements of civilization, rather than that none should be so. Much better this great irregularity than universal squalor. Without wealth there can be no Maecenases. When these apprentices rose to be masters, there was little or no change in their mode of life, and they, in turn, educated in the same routine succeeding apprentices. There was, substantially, social equality, and even political equality, for those engaged in industrial pursuits had then little or no political voice in the State.

But the inevitable result of such a mode of manufacture was crude articles at high prices. Today the world obtains commodities of excellent quality at prices which even the generation preceding this would have deemed incredible. In the commercial world similar causes have produced similar results, and the race is benefited thereby. The poor enjoy what the rich could not before afford. What were the luxuries have become the

First published in the *North American Review*, June, 1889.

necessaries of life. The laborer has now more comforts than the farmer had a few generations ago. The farmer has more luxuries than the landlord had, and is more richly clad and better housed. The landlord has books and pictures rarer, and appointments more artistic, than the King could then obtain.

The price we pay for this salutary change is, no doubt, great. We assemble thousands of operatives in the factory, in the mine, and in the counting-house, of whom the employer can know little or nothing, and to whom the employer is little better than a myth. All intercourse between them is at an end. Rigid Castes are formed, and, as usual, mutual ignorance breeds mutual distrust. Each Caste is without sympathy for the other, and ready to credit anything disparaging in regard to it. Under the law of competition, the employer of thousands is forced into the strictest economies, among which the rates paid to labor figure prominently, and often there is friction between the employer and the employed, between capital and labor, between rich and poor. Human society loses homogeneity.

The price which society pays for the law of competition, like the price it pays for cheap comforts and luxuries, is also great; but the advantages of this law are greater still, for it is to this law that we owe our wonderful material development, which brings improved conditions in its train. But, whether the law be benign or not, we must say of it, as we say of the change in the conditions of men to which we have referred: It is here; we cannot evade it; no substitutes for it have been found; and while the law may be sometimes hard for the individual, it is best for the race, because it insures the survival of the fittest in every department. We accept and welcome, therefore, as conditions to which we must accommodate ourselves, great inequality of environment, the concentration of business, industrial and commercial, in the hands of a few, and the law of competition between these, as being not only beneficial, but essential for the future progress of the race. Having accepted these, it follows that there must be great scope for the exercise of special ability in the merchant and in the manufacturer who has to conduct affairs upon a great scale. That this talent for organization and management is rare among men is proved by the fact that it invariably secures for its possessor enormous rewards, no matter where or under what laws or conditions. The experienced in affairs always rate the man whose services can be obtained as a partner as not only the first consideration, but such as to render the question of his capital scarcely worth considering, for such men soon create capital; while, without the special talent required, capital soon takes wings. Such men become interested in firms or corporations using millions; and estimating only simple interest to be made upon the capital invested, it is inevitable that their income must exceed their expenditures, and that they must accumulate wealth. Nor is there any middle ground which such men can occupy, because the great manufacturing or commercial concern which does not earn at least interest upon its capital soon becomes bankrupt. It must either go forward or fall behind: to stand still is impossible. It is a condition essential for its successful operation that it should be thus far profitable, and even that, in addition to interest on capital, it should make a profit. It is a law, as certain as any of the others named, that men possessed of this peculiar talent for affairs, under the free play of economic forces, must, of necessity, soon be in receipt of more revenue than can be judiciously expended upon themselves, and this law is as beneficial for the race as the others.

Objections to the foundations upon which society is based are not in order, because the condition of the race is better with these than it has been with any others which have been tried. Of the effect of any new substitutes proposed we cannot be sure. The Socialist or Anarchist who seeks to overturn present conditions is to be regarded as attacking the foundation upon which civilization itself rests, for civilization took its start from the day that the capable, industrious workman said to his incompetent and lazy fellow, "If thou dost not sow, thou shalt not reap," and thus ended primitive Communism by separating the drones from the bees. One who studies this subject will soon be brought face to face with the conclusion that upon the sacredness of property civilization itself depends—the right of the laborer to his hundred dollars in the savings bank, and equally the legal right of the millionaire to his millions. To those who propose to substitute Communism for this intense Individualism the answer, therefore, is: The race has tried that. All progress from that barbarous day to the present time has resulted from its displacement. Not evil, but good, has come to the race from the accumulation of wealth by those who have the ability and energy that produce it. But even if we admit for a moment that it might be better for the race to discard its present foundations, Individualism—that it is a nobler ideal that man should labor, not for himself alone, but in and for a brotherhood of his fellows, and share with them all in common, realizing Swedenborg's idea of Heaven, where, as he says, the angels derive their happiness, not from laboring for self, but for each other—even admit all this, and a sufficient answer is, This is not evolution, but revolution. It necessitates the changing of human nature itself—a work of aeons, even if it were good to change it, which we cannot know. It is not practicable in our day or in our age. Even if desirable theoretically, it belongs to another and long-succeeding sociological stratum. Our duty is with what is practicable now; with the next step possible in our day and generation. It is criminal to waste our energies in endeavoring to uproot, when all we can profitably or possibly accomplish is to bend the universal tree of humanity a little in the direction most favorable to the production of good fruit under existing circumstances. We might as well urge the destruction of the highest existing type of man because he failed to reach our ideal as to favor the destruction of Individualism, Private Property, the Law of Accumulation of Wealth, and the Law of Competition; for these are the highest results of human experience, the soil in which society so far has produced the best fruit. Unequally or unjustly, perhaps, as these laws sometimes operate, and imperfect as they appear to the Idealist, they are nevertheless, like the highest type of man, the best and most valuable of all that humanity has yet accomplished.

We start, then, with a condition of affairs under which the best interests of the race are promoted, but which inevitably gives wealth to the few. Thus far, accepting conditions as they exist, the situation can be surveyed and pronounced good. The question then arises—and, if the foregoing be correct, it is the only question with which we have to deal—What is the proper mode of administering wealth after the laws upon which civilization is founded have thrown it into the hands of the few? And it is of this great question that I believe I offer the true solution. It will be understood that fortunes are here spoken of, not moderate sums saved by many years of effort, the returns from which are required for the comfortable maintenance and education of families. This is not *wealth*, but only *competence*, which it should be the aim of all to acquire.

... Indeed, it is difficult to set bounds to the share of a rich man's estate which should go at his death to the public through the agency of the state, and by all means such taxes should be graduated, beginning at nothing upon moderate sums to dependents, and increasing rapidly as the amounts swell, until of the millionaire's hoard, as of Shylock's at least

> "_____The other half

> Comes to the privy coffer of the state."

This policy would work powerfully to induce the rich man to attend to the administration of wealth during his life, which is the end that society should always have in view, as being that by far most fruitful for the people. Nor need it be feared that this policy would sap the root of enterprise and render men less anxious to accumulate, for to the class whose ambition it is to leave great fortunes and be talked about after their death, it will attract more attention, and, indeed, be a somewhat nobler ambition to have enormous sums paid over to the state from their fortunes.

There remains, then, only one mode of using great fortunes; but in this we have the true antidote for the temporary unequal distribution of wealth, the reconciliation of the rich and the poor—a reign of harmony—another ideal, differing, indeed, from that of the Communist in requiring only the further evolution of existing conditions, not the total overthrow of our civilization. It is founded upon the present most intense individualism, and the race is prepared to put it in practice by degrees whenever it pleases. Under its sway we shall have an ideal state, in which the surplus wealth of the few will become, in the best sense, the property of the many, because administered for the common good, and this wealth, passing through the hands of the few, can be made a much more potent force for the elevation of our race than if it had been distributed in small sums to the people themselves. Even the poorest can be made to see this, and to agree that great sums gathered by some of their fellow-citizens and spent for public purposes, from which the masses reap the principal benefit, are more valuable to them than if scattered among them through the course of many years in trifling amounts.

The best uses to which surplus wealth can be put have already been indicated. Those who would administer wisely must, indeed, be wise, for one of the serious obstacles to the improvement of our race is indiscriminate charity. It were better for mankind that the millions of the rich were thrown into the sea than so spent as to encourage the slothful, the drunken, the unworthy. Of every thousand dollars spent in so-called charity today, it is probable that $950 is unwisely spent; so spent, indeed, as to produce the very evils which it proposes to mitigate or cure. A well-known writer of philosophic books admitted the other day that he had given a quarter of a dollar to a man who approached him as he was coming to visit the house of his friend. He knew nothing of the habits of this beggar; knew not the use that would be made of this money, although he had every reason to suspect that it would be spent improperly. This man professed to be a disciple of Herbert Spencer; yet the quarter-dollar given that night will probably work more injury than all the money which its thoughtless donor will ever be able to give in true charity will do good. He only gratified his own feelings, saved himself from annoyance—and this was probably one of the most selfish and very worst actions of his life, for in all respects he is most worthy.

In bestowing charity, the main consideration should be to help those who will help themselves; to provide part of the means by which those who desire to improve may do so; to give those who desire to rise the aids by which they may rise; to assist, but rarely or never to do all. Neither the individual nor the race is improved by alms-giving. Those worthy of assistance, except in rare cases, seldom require assistance. The really valuable men of the race never do, except in cases of accident or sudden change. Everyone has, of course, cases of individuals brought to his own knowledge where temporary assistance can do genuine good, and these he will not overlook. But the amount which can be wisely given by the individual for individuals is necessarily limited by his lack of knowledge of the circumstance connected with each. He is the only true reformer who is as careful and as anxious not to aid the unworthy as he is to aid the worthy, and perhaps, even more so, for in alms-giving more injury is probably done by rewarding vice than by relieving virtue.

Thus is the problem of Rich and Poor to be solved. The laws of accumulation will be left free; the laws of distribution free. Individualism will continue, but the millionaire will be but a trustee for the poor, entrusted for a season with a great part of the increased wealth of the community, but administrating it for the community far better than it could or would have done for itself. The best minds will thus have reached a stage in the development of the race in which it is clearly seen that there is no mode of disposing of surplus wealth creditable to thoughtful and earnest men into whose hands it flows save by using it year by year for the general good. This day already dawns. But a little while, and although, without incurring the pity of their fellows, men may die sharers in great business enterprises from which their capital cannot be or has not been withdrawn, and is left chiefly at death for public uses, yet the man who dies leaving behind him millions of available wealth, which was his to administer during life, will pass away "unwept, unhonored, and unsung," no matter to what uses he leaves the dross which he cannot take with him. Of such as these the public verdict will then be: "The man who dies thus rich dies disgraced."

Such, in my opinion, is the true Gospel concerning Wealth, obedience to which is destined some day to solve the problems of the Rich and the Poor, and to bring "Peace on earth, among men Good-Will."

Chapter 5

Contemporary Challenges
to Property Rights

Case Study

W.R. Grace & Co.
and the Neemix Patent (A)

KRISTI SEVERANCE ● LISA SHAPIRO ● PATRICIA H. WERHANE

"[Neem] seems to be one of the most promising of all plants and may eventually benefit every person on the planet."
—National Research Council Report on Neem, 1992

Derived from the seeds of the Indian neem tree and touted as a safe, natural biopesticide, Neemix seemed to be a benevolent product that promised W.R. Grace & Company (WRG) profits and farmers a sustainable means of fighting pests. Three years earlier, Grace researchers had been granted a patent on the pesticide, and since that time Neemix had become far more than just another product in the company's line. Grace, the world's largest manufacturer of specialty chemicals, had never expected Neemix to be a major source of income for the company, but steady sales since its introduction to market supported the prediction that consumers were interested in purchasing completely natural, environmentally friendly pesticides, rather than chemical ones. The active ingredient in Neemix, azadirachtin, is a compound that occurs naturally in neem seeds and possesses the ideal characteristic of being fatally harmful to more than 200 species of insect pests, while remaining non-toxic to other plants and beneficial animals. By early 1995, sales of Neemix brought in about $60 million annually out of Grace's total of $5 billion in annual sales, and references in the press to the effectiveness of Neemix were becoming frequent.[1]

This case was prepared by Kristi Severance and revised by Lisa Spiro under the supervision of Patricia H. Werhane, Ruffin Professor of Business Ethics. Copyright 1997 by the University of Virginia Darden School Foundation, Charlottesville, VA. All rights reserved.

By late summer of 1995, however, the product's success became clouded by a growing controversy over the patent held to protect it. Protests against Grace had been gaining momentum in India in the preceding months. Farmers in India had been using neem "teas," the emulsion resulting from crushing neem seeds and soaking them in water, as pesticides for thousands of years, and for that reason many Indians believed that Grace had no right to a patent on a neem-based pesticide. There were voices of protest in the United States as well, most notably that of the Foundation on Economic Trends (FET), a biotechnology industry watchdog agency. On September 14, 1995, the FET, together with more than 200 supporting organizations from the United States, India, and other countries, filed a petition with the U.S. Patent and Trademark Office to reexamine the Neemix patent in hopes of having it revoked. They charged Grace with committing what they called "biopiracy," saying that the company had appropriated and profited from knowledge of natural resources that rightfully belonged to the indigenous peoples in India.

W.R. GRACE—COMPANY BACKGROUND

From its inception Grace was a company defined by its interests in natural resource products.[2] In 1854 William Russell Grace traveled from Ireland to Callao, Peru, hoping to rebuild the family fortune, which had been depleted by the potato famine. He first became a clerk and later a partner in a trading firm that specialized in shipping guano (bird dung) and nitrate of soda (sodium nitrate), both used as fertilizers. Under William's direction, the company grew to be the largest of its kind in the country. In 1865, William moved to New York City, where he established W.R. Grace & Company (WRG). The company established three-way shipping routes from South America to North America and to Europe for trading fertilizer, agricultural products, and U.S.-manufactured goods, and remained connected with the Peruvian government as its agent for the sale of nitrate of soda. After William died in 1904, his brother Michael took control of the company and was succeeded in 1909 by William's son Joseph. With Joseph at the helm, the company underwent a period of rapid growth. He purchased cotton mills, sugar plantations, sugar refineries in Peru, and nitrate production facilities in Chile. During this time the company expanded its shipping interests, and in 1914 Grace Lines sent the first ship through the Panama Canal. Grace also moved into the banking industry with the establishment of Grace National Bank. Another new area of interest for Grace was aviation, and together with Pan American Airways, they established Panagra Airlines, which offered the first international air service down the west coast of South America.

In 1945, after his father's retirement, Joseph R. Grace's son, J. Peter Grace, was elected president of the company at age 32. At the time, W.R. Grace had $93 million in assets and J. Peter wanted to both protect and increase them. The company's primary interests were in Grace Lines, Grace National Bank, Panagra, and agricultural products. Concerned with political and economic instability in South America, J. Peter began to look for ways to make the future of Grace more secure. He was impressed with the success of chemical companies in the United States, and under his direction the company began its foray into the chemical industry. He initiated a plan to reduce South American investments from 100 percent to 5 percent, by expanding into the U.S. chemical industry, and, in order to raise the money to do so, the company went public in 1953. In 1952, Grace purchased its first U.S. chemical manufacturing plant in Memphis, Tennessee. In 1954 it purchased Davison Chemical and then Dewey and Almy Chemical, which provided the foundation from which Grace grew to be the world's largest specialty chemical company. The transfer to primarily chemical interests became more pronounced in the mid- to late-1960s, when Grace sold Grace National Bank, Panagra, and the Grace Line. During the next 11 years, Grace acquired 23 additional chemical companies for 4 million shares of stock.

In the 1960s and 1970s Grace expanded into the food and sporting goods industries, a diversification that lasted only until the mid-1980s. Later Grace expanded into the water treatment, food-service packaging, and health-care products industries. By 1988, Grace was prepared to begin research and development of a natural pesticide. Although soft pesticides would probably not knock synthetic insecticides out of the market, Grace nonetheless realized that a neem-based pesticide had the potential to provide the company with some of the profits from a natural pesticide market that was, according to a National Research Council survey, expected to increase from $450 million in 1993 to $813 million annually in 1998.[3] After investigating several avenues, Grace joined a growing number of Western scientists and companies who saw neem as the source with the most potential.

NEEM

The neem tree (*Azadirachta indica*) is a member of the mahogony family and is native to numerous countries with subtropical climates. It is particularly prevalent in India, where an estimated 18 million trees flourish.[4] Resembling an oak in stature, it is tall, with wide spreading branches bearing masses of white honey-scented flowers and bitter fruit similar in appearance to olives. The neem is a rapidly growing tree that only loses its leaves in cases of extreme drought and in general thrives in hot, arid conditions. Its extensive root system allows it to extract nutrients from even the poorest soils. The combination of these characteristics makes it ideal for growing in the areas most in need of its benefits. In many villages in the hottest parts of India, the only available relief from the heat is the substantial shade that the neem tree provides. Pilgrims to the holy Islamic site of the Plains of Arafat in Saudi Arabia are protected from the sun by 50 thousand neem trees planted by a Saudi philanthropist.[5] In Ghana and several other African countries where a need for fuel has led to problems with deforestation, a campaign to introduce the neem, which requires little maintenance and is non-invasive, helped counter the effects of massive soil erosion. The neem tree has provided a double benefit in these countries: in addition to stabilizing the soil, the tree provided an invaluable, renewable source of timber because it could mature in only 5–7 years.

NEEM'S ROLE IN INDIA

Neem has played an integral role in Indian culture for thousands of years. In a culture where the alliance between human beings and the natural environment is of great importance, the tree is one of the five "essentials" traditionally prescribed for planting in Indian gardens, and its properties are a focal point of daily Indian medicinal and agriculture life.[6]

Revered by Hindus, neem has always been an important part of annual New Year celebrations, when its leaves are eaten to ensure good health through the year. Accounts of its usefulness for medical purposes date back thousands of years. Ayurvedic doctors, who practice medicine based on the idea of harmony between humans and their environment, have continued to prescribe neem cures, and neem has been among the most frequently found items in Indian apothecary shops. In fact, neem has been so widely used throughout India to prevent and treat a variety of illnesses that it is commonly referred to as "the village pharmacy." Despite being too poor to afford either toothbrushes or toothpaste, millions of Indians have had good dental health because they chewed daily on neem twigs, fraying the ends and using them to clean teeth and gums. Compounds within the twigs have an antiseptic effect and appear to prevent tooth and gum disease. As a result, neem can now be found in numerous commercially available dentifrices. Neem is also used to treat skin ailments. Ground neem leaves are made into creams and poultices for application to skin disorders from acne to leprosy, and neem oil is a common ingredient in soaps valued for their antiseptic qualities. Neem has traditionally been believed to be effective against viruses like chicken pox.

Various neem components have been used as contraceptives, and tests have indicated that the oil is a strong spermicide. It has been considered a promising avenue for development of new birth-control methods, and researchers in several countries have been working to develop this aspect of neem. In New Delhi scientists at the Defense Institute of Physiology and Allied Sciences isolated a substance from neem oil that kills sperm on contact. They were particularly optimistic about the possibility of a viable neem contraceptive because neem's status as an important part of India's folklore may make it a more socially acceptable form of contraception than commercial birth-control methods.[7] Some scientists both in the United States and India have also cited neem as a potential weapon against the human immunodeficiency virus (HIV).

In addition to its medicinal uses, neem is one of the primary means of controlling insect pests in India. Planting neem trees in village centers is common practice because they help ward off biting insects. Neem leaves scattered in closets and food and grain bins keep pests away for up to several months. Farmers soak neem seeds overnight in water and apply the resulting emulsion to crops to keep pests away, and neem cake, the residue left once the oil has been removed from the seeds, is used to combat soil-borne pests. Neem cake also assists plants with nitrogen take-up. Use of neem products is not restricted to only those farmers too poor to have access to commercially produced insecticides: many wealthy growers of cardamon, an Indian spice and valuable export, use neem cake to protect their crops against invasion by pests in the soil. It was these numerous pesticidal qualities of neem that first attracted the attention of the West.

NEEM DEVELOPMENT

In addition to the substantial body of traditional knowledge, formal scientific study of neem's pesticidal properties began in India in the 1920s. At that time two Indian scientists conducted tests and found that a dilute suspension of ground neem seeds in water repelled the desert locust when it was applied to plants. Neem continued to be a topic of scientific study in India, but formal recognition of this work was scarce, despite important findings that emerged from it. In 1962, N. Pradhan conducted field tests in New Delhi that demonstrated the effectiveness of spraying a neem seed and water suspension on several crops to prevent insects from feeding on them and in 1965 a chemist at the National Chemical Laboratory in Pune identified the structure of nimbin, a compound in neem with anti-viral properties.[8]

Despite the results of research conducted in India, neem's attributes remained largely unrecognized in the West until German entomologist Heinrich Schmutterer observed its natural pesticidal properties in the Sudan in 1959. During a locust invasion, Schmutterer noticed that the entire landscape was defoliated except for the neem trees. Although the insects landed on the neem trees, they quickly flew off without feeding on them. Curious, he began to study neem in an attempt to understand how it worked as a pesticide. His interest in the tree subsequently became the focal point of his career and initiated an era of neem research in the West.

In the years since Schmutterer first observed the neem phenomenon, studies in labs in numerous Western countries confirmed that neem was a tree with vast potential. In 1992, the first comprehensive report on neem available for the lay person in the United States was published by an ad hoc panel of the Board on Science and Technology for International Development, a division of the National Research Council. In an effort to promote neem's potential, the publication was designed not for specialists in the field, but for government officials, voluntary organizations, entrepreneurs, and others who could play a role in developing or promoting the tree's myriad uses. Authors said they hoped the reports would help overcome ignorance of the tree in the West. Noel Vietmeyer, director of the study, said that the biggest obstacle to neem's acceptance in the West was that Western scientists were simply unfamiliar with the tree and were skeptical of extravagant claims about its potential. The report's claims for the neem tree were substantial and confirmed, according to Eugene Schulz, chair of the study.[9] According to the report,

> Probably no other plant yields as many strange and varied products or has as many exploitable by-products as the neem.... This plant may usher in a new era in pest control, provide millions with inexpensive medicines, cut down the rate of human population growth, and perhaps even reduce erosion, deforestation, and the excessive temperature of an overheated globe.[10]

Current neem research confirmed that the NRC report's optimistic claims were not exaggerated. Neem is currently the only viable candidate for development of a method to combat Chagas disease, an incapacitating disease caused by a parasite and affecting millions in Latin America. Chagas is transmitted by an insect known as the kissing bug, which acts as a host for the developing parasite. Research teams in Brazil determined that blood treated with neem and fed to parasite-infested kissing bugs caused the parasites to disappear 20 days later. A researcher at the U.S. Department of Agriculture has studied neem as a means of combating the fungus, *Aspergillus favus*, which grows on foods and produces highly carcinogenic chemicals called aflatoxins. Aflatoxins pose a serious health hazard, particularly in areas where grain and food storage is difficult due to weather conditions.

But while neem's many potential uses are compelling, it is its effectiveness as a pesticide that continues to motivate much of Western research on the tree. The NRC report concluded that in field tests neem proved as effective as pesticides such as malathion, with one notable advantage. Unlike chemical pesticides that could be harsh on the environment, neem's method of operation was compatible with the increasingly popular concept of integrated pest management (IPM). Integrated pest management emphasizes working within the environment to combat pests rather than relying on highly toxic chemical pesticides to control them. In IPM, every pest problem is monitored and then linked with the least toxic method possible to control it. Within the context of an idea like IPM, using neem as a pesticide is a natural and efficient way to deal with the problem: "To employ neem in pest control is to take advantage of the plant kingdom's 400 million years of experience at trying to frustrate the animal kingdom."[11]

IPM has attracted interest primarily because of concerns about two major problems facing the agriculture industry: synthetic pesticide toxicity to other animals, including humans, and insects' capability to develop resistance to synthetic insecticides. The World Health Organization rates the former problem a serious one, estimating that synthetic pesticides fatally poison 20,000 people per year.[12] Most chemical pesticides attack insects' central nervous systems, killing them outright. Neem's compounds work against them indirectly, but ultimately provide the same result. Neem contains several compounds that have both behavioral and physiological effects on pest insects. Instead of killing pest insects on contact, neem either deters them from feeding on plants they would normally eat or disrupts their maturation process so that they eventually die. This capability allows neem to both destroy pests and leave non-pests unharmed.

The compound within neem primarily responsible for these ideal effects is azadirachtin, one of the most potent substances found in neem. It is the most active of a class of chemical compounds found in neem that are both anti-feedants and growth regulators. Many leaf-chewing pests that would normally defoliate plants will starve to death rather than eat a plant that has been treated with an azadirachtin solution. Derived from the oil that is extracted from neem seeds, azadirachtin is structurally similar to insect hormones that control the process of metamorphosis. Azadirachtin replicates the work of ecdysones in insects, but imperfectly, so that the process of metamorphosis is disrupted. It blocks the insect's production and release of hormones vital to metamorphosis, thus preventing it from molting and ultimately killing it.

Pest insects seem unable to develop resistance to neem-based pesticides because of the complex workings of compounds like azadirachtin. It is for this reason that neem is one of the few pesticides currently available with any effect on the "superbug"—the so-called pest—which has devastated crops in California and proven resistant to standard synthetic pesticides.

The azadirachtin molecule, however, has one drawback. It is inherently unstable, breaking down easily in sunlight and heat, and it can degrade in a solution within days. For farmers in India who produced only enough solution to apply to their corps at any given time, this instability was not a major obstacle, but for individuals or companies trying to produce sufficient amounts to sell, the problem was significant. Several scientists, including some from India, have asserted that the instability of the azadirachtin molecule has been the biggest obstacle to widespread neem use.

NEEM DEVELOPMENT AT GRACE

James Walter, one of Grace's primary researchers and a member of the NRC report panel, described development of neem-based pesticides at Grace as "a relatively short story, owing to the great amount of work already accomplished by researchers throughout the world."[13] In 1988 Grace Horticultural Products, a unit of Grace Specialty Chemicals (USA), acquired the rights to a neem pesticide, Margosan-O, through a purchase agreement with Vikwood Botanicals of Sheboygan, WI. Robert Larson of Vikwood, a timber-importing firm, had been interested in neem's numerous beneficial properties since he had first heard about them on a trip to India in 1973. He began importing neem seeds and testing them. But while he was able to develop a neem-based pesticide, have it patented, and gain EPA registration, he ultimately faced the major stumbling block of azadirachtin's instability.

In order to produce commercial quantities of a neem pesticide he needed a much more stable solution than he was able to produce in his own laboratories. After a failed attempt to contract out the production to another firm, Larson began to look elsewhere. He approached Grace, which he knew to be looking for a viable pesticide that was not harmful to the environment. Grace purchased the rights to the formulation and process for producing Margosan-O and then also began work on a neem pesticide that would be even more storage-stable, a process that ultimately led to the development of Neemix. In March 1994, the EPA registered Neemix as the first neem product cleared in the United States for use on food crops.[14] Walter described the development of neem-based pesticides as an important step to dealing with the problem of pesticide toxicity: "This is a real significant advance in insecticides... with all the characteristics you want and none you don't want. I don't see a down side to it."

THE PATENT

Finally, the Neemix researchers were ready to apply for a patent. According to United States patent laws, an invention has to meet three criteria in order to be patented: it has to be novel with respect to "prior art," a legal term referring to previous knowledge about a particular subject matter; it has to be non-obvious from the "prior art" to someone possessing ordinary skill in the art at the time the invention was made; and it has to be useful. The second constraint narrows the first one. Even if the subject matter of a sought patent is different from what is known from prior art, a patent can be denied if the differences are not significant enough to prevent them from being obvious to someone having an ordinary level of knowledge in that subject area. U.S. patent regulations further specify that in order to qualify for a patent, an invention cannot have been known or used in the United States, or patented or described in a printed publication in the United States or elsewhere prior to its invention; nor can the invention have been described in print in the United States or elsewhere more than a year prior to the application of a patent for the invention. The law also mandates that a patent cannot be granted on a naturally occurring substance unless it has been modified in some way: "Patent law requires something more than just the discovery of a naturally occurring product: a legally significant amount of human innovation must have been involved."[15]

Grace submitted an application to patent its process for making a neem pesticide with a shelf-life of up to 2 years. The patent application stated that the purpose of the invention was "to provide a non-toxic, natural pesticide formulation based on an extract from neem seeds with improved storage ability." The application was filed on October 31, 1990, and on June 23, 1992, the patent was granted. At that point Grace became one of 22 companies, including three in India, to hold approximately 40 patents on neem-based products.

THE PROTEST

On September 14, 1995, the Foundation on Economic Trends (FET), led by its president, Jeremy Rifkin, filed its request for reexamination of the Neemix patent with the U.S. Patent and Trademark Office (PTO). More than 200 organizations from 35 countries joined the FET as petitioners, primary among them, The Research Foundation for Science, Technology, and Natural Resource Policy in Dehra Dun, India, headed by Dr. Vandana Shiva, a scientist and outspoken advocate for indigenous peoples in India, and an Indian farmers organization. In lodging the protest, the FET and its allies challenged the Neemix patent on two levels: they took issue with the granting of the patent within the confines of U.S. patent law and also raised the question of whether the existing patent system could fairly compensate indigenous people.

The coalition challenged the patent on grounds (1) that two of the three criteria necessary for patent granting, novelty with respect to prior art, and obviousness, were absent in the Neemix patient application and (2) that the patent should therefore never have been granted. The groups included in the protest claimed that the patent was invalid because the body of traditional knowledge about neem, including its use as a pesticide, qualified as prior art and therefore should have negated Grace's application with respect to novelty. "Whatever little incremental change W.R. Grace put on this is small compared to the native knowledge that has been accumulated generation after generation on the use of this tree," Rifkin said.[16] More specifically, the protest documents asserted that the patent should be overturned because "the company's method of extracting stable compounds has been widely used prior to the patent's issuance and because the extraction methods have been previously described in printed publication."

The protest claimed that Indian researchers had published descriptions of neem seed effectiveness as a pesticide as early as 1928, and cited the studies of neem in India in the 1960s and research conducted at the Indian Agricultural Research Institute on neem's potential as an insecticide and insect repellant, saying they had all preceded Larson and Grace's efforts by a decade. The protesters also asserted that it was unfair to expect any other records of prior knowledge about neem to exist in print because "the accumulated knowledge is the result of many anonymous and individual efforts carried out over hundreds of years. By citing a lack of formal publications as proof of non-obviousness, the company holds the villagers to a standard that is clearly unobtainable."[17] In reference to the obviousness of Grace's formulation, Rifkin asserted that "any chemist worth his salt could have come up with it."[18]

The coalition also argued that the Indian farmers who had traditionally used neem could not have been expected to file for a patent themselves because of pragmatic and legal constraints against it: "The fact that Indian researchers failed to obtain patent protection on stabilization techniques is attributable to India's cultural and legal opposition to such patenting. Not only does Indian law prohibit the patenting of agricultural products, but many Indian citizens are ethically opposed to the patenting and ownership of nature. These feelings are especially strong in regard to the neem tree because the tree has played such an important role within Indian culture and religion."[19]

In addition to filing a formal petition with the PTO, the FET and its supporters claimed that, technicalities of patent law aside, patents like the one Grace held on Neemix should not be allowed to exist because they presented appropriation of indigenous knowledge without compensation to the people who generated it. "What many Americans have not realized is that the anger, frustration, and resentment in the developing countries against what they regard as piracy of their heritage is every bit as intense as the outrage that has been drummed up by the United States over the violation of our intellectual copyright in the developing world," Rifkin said. He called Grace's patent "the first case of genetic colonialism," and said the neem tree was symbolic of a large debate over how developing countries and indigenous peoples should be compensated when commercial products based on traditional knowledge were developed.

One of the FET's supporters, Vandana Shiva, a vocal critic of the development of resources indigenous to third-world countries by more technologically advanced nations, argued that the Grace patent presented a serious economic threat to Indian farmers who used neem. The Persian name for neem means "free tree of India," and Shiva argued that patents of any kind on any neem-based product would prevent the free tree from being just that—financially accessible to the Indian farmers who have used it for centuries. She claimed that Grace's demand for the seeds would drive the price up beyond the reach of poor farmers and would ultimately cause a general shortage of the seeds. She also expressed concern that under the requirements of the World Trade Organization, successor agreement to the General Agreement on Tariffs and Trade, India as a member nation would have to move to align its patent requirements with the West's, and indigenous users of neem would end up having to pay Grace for using it as a pesticide.

THE REBUTTAL

As soon as the FET announced its intention to file the petition for reexamination, Grace issued a statement calling the FET's accusations "incorrect and without merit." Grace's reaction to the petition was one of surprise. The patent had been held for three years when the FET decided to file its protest, and company officials described themselves as flabbergasted by the controversy now surrounding it. Many protesters claimed that Grace had taken out a patent on the neem tree. The company emphatically denied that their patent was in any sense a patent on neem itself, since patenting of naturally occurring substances without any human modification or improvement was against U.S. patent law. Grace acknowledged that there was "nothing Buck Rogers" about their stabilizing formulation, but noted that they had spent approximately $10 million assessing previous ineffective preservation processes and as a result had come up with a procedure that worked.

In response to accusations that the patent would prevent Indian farmers who relied on neem as a pesticide from getting access to it, Grace said that U.S. patent law did not restrict Indians from accessing neem seeds in any way and the company had no intention of seeking a patent in India. Further, Grace maintained that it did not apply for a patent on any extraction procedure and its patent was also restricted to the liquid form of the successful process. Grace pointed out that it purchased the neem seeds on the open market and that since the Neemix patent had been granted, they had purchased less than 3 percent of the harvested neem crop. The company works with an Indian company, J.P. Margo, near Bangalor, India, to process the neem seeds, and it said it believes that the company's efforts had contributed positively both to India's exports and to new employment there. "I think we deserve an award," a company spokesman said.

What had begun as an effort to provide a product for consumers interested in protecting both their crops and the environment had culminated in a struggle to defend that product against accusations that it was doing far more harm than good. It was clear that each side felt its own position to be more persuasive. Grace's strongest detractors saw the Neemix patent as representative of illegal, immoral corporate behavior. Even some who supported Grace's legal right to the patent wondered whether such patents could not be more fairly granted under another kind of system, proposing instead that regulation of intellectual property protection take place under the International Convention on Biological Diversity (CBD) rather than the WTO. Unlike the CBD, the WTO did not stipulate that the country of origin of a species or body of knowledge be acknowledged or that those contributing pertinent knowledge to a sought patent be compensated for their contribution. Highlighting both the promise and problems raised by the patenting of neem-based products, Eugene Schultz, the director of the NRC study, said: "You've got a classic case of an ethical dilemma.... You can certainly devise new uses that will benefit at least one segment of humankind: those who can afford it. But in the rush to exploit a new profit opportunity, the peasant is often the last person in the world to be considered."[20]

Notes

1. Ralph T. King, "Grace's Patent on a Pesticide Enrages Indians," *Wall Street Journal*, September 13, 1995, B1.
2. Information in this section taken from "Conglomerates: W.R. Grace & Company," in *International Directory of Company Histories*, Thomas Derdak, ed. (St. James Press, 1988), pp. 547–550, and from "W.R. Grace & Co." in *Hoovers Handbook*, Bloomberg, Austin, TX.
3. Richard Stone, "A Biopesticidal Tree Begins to Blossom," *Science*, vol. 255 (Feb. 28, 1992), 1071.
4. Sy Montgomery, "Scientists Shop in Living 'Drugstore,'" *The Boston Globe*, August 10, 1992, 31.
5. National Research Council, *Neem: A Tree for Solving Global Problems* (Washington, DC: National Academy Press, 1992), p. 1.
6. Vithal Nadkarni, "New Role for Old Neem," *The Times of India* (online version), 27 June 1993), 1.
7. National Research Council, op. cit., p. 68.
8. Ibid., p. 32.
9. "Pesticide Tea," *Discover, 13* (14 July 1992), 14.
10. National Research Council, op. cit., p. v
11. Ibid.
12. Montgomery, op. cit.
13. National Research Council, op. cit.
14. *Science*, vol. 269, Sept. 15, 1995.
15. Richard H. Kjeldgaard and David R. Marsh, "A Biotech Battle Brewing," *Legal Times* (December 11, 1995), 16.
16. Mara Bovsun, "FET Challenges U.S. Patent on India's Natural Pesticide," *Biotechnology Newswatch* (September 18, 1995), 1.
17. "More than 200 Organisations from 35 Nations Challenge U.S. Patent on Neem," *Third World Network* (online newsletter) www. twnside. org. sg
18. "Biodiversity: Groups to Sue to Invalidate Pesticide Patent," *Greenwire* (Sept. 13, 1995).
19. *Third World Network*, op. cit. 4.
20. "Legal Battle Takes Root Over 'Miracle Tree,'" *USA Today* (October 18, 1995), 8a.

Needed: A New System of Intellectual Property Rights

LESTER C. THUROW

Fundamental shifts in technology and in the economic landscape are rapidly making the current system of intellectual property rights unworkable and ineffective. Designed more than 100 years ago to meet the simpler needs of an industrial era, it is an undifferentiated, one-size-fits-all system. Although treating all advances in knowledge in the same way may have worked when most patents were granted for new mechanical devices, today's brainpower industries pose challenges that are far more complex.

Consider the case of the physician who noticed a relationship between an elevated level of a particular human hormone and a congenital birth defect. He was awarded a patent for his observation, although by itself his test had too many false positives to be useful. But later developments showed that if his test were used along with two others, they would accurately forecast whether a baby would be born with Down's Syndrome. Today the physician is suing to get a $9 fee from every laboratory that uses his part of the test. If he wins, the cost of testing will more than double.

Should the physician who first observed how the existing gene works get some intellectual property rights? Probably. But they should not be the same kind of rights as those granted to someone who invents a new gene to replace the defective one. Noticing what an existing gene does is simply not equivalent to inventing a new gene. Such distinctions are necessary, yet our patent system has no basis for making them. All patents are identical—you either get one or you don't.

The prevailing wisdom among those who earn their living within our system of intellectual property protection is that some minor tweaking here and there will fix the problem. Much of this wisdom flows from nothing more profound than the belief that to open up the system to fundamental change would be equivalent to opening Pandora's box. All can vividly see themselves as potential losers. Few consider the private and public gains that might accrue from a different system.

The prevailing wisdom is wrong. The time has come not for marginal changes but for wide-open thinking about designing a new system from the ground up.

WHY THE OLD SYSTEM DOESN'T WORK

Today it is both more important than ever to protect intellectual property rights—and more difficult to do so. To understand why, consider the following four shifts in the economic landscape:

The Centrality of Intellectual Property Rights

With the advent of the information revolution—or the third industrial revolution (call it what you will)—skills and knowledge have become the only source of sustainable long-term competitive advantage. Intellectual property lies at the center of the modern company's economic success or failure.

Raw materials can be bought and moved, and they are falling in price and decreasing in value as a share of U.S. gross domestic product. Capital is a commodity that can be borrowed in New York, Tokyo, or London. Unique pieces of equipment that cannot be obtained by—or are too expensive for—one's competitors simply don't exist. What used to be tertiary after raw materials and capital in determining economic success is now primary.

Major companies such as Microsoft own nothing of value except knowledge. Fighting to defend and extend the domain of their intellectual property is how they play the economic game. With this reality comes the need for more differentiated systems of determining who owns what, better protection for whatever is owned, and faster systems of dispute resolution.

Bill Gates is the perfect example of the new centrality of intellectual property. For more than a century, the world's wealthiest human being has been associated with oil—starting with John D. Rockefeller in the late nineteenth century and ending with the Sultan of Brunei in the late twentieth century. But today, for the first time in history, the world's wealthiest person is a knowledge worker.

In addition, the world's major growth industries—such as microelectronics, biotechnology, designer-made materials, and telecommunications—are brainpower industries. If their intellectual property can be copied easily, they will not be able to generate either wealth for their owners or high wages for their employees.

These knowledge-based industries are important in their own right, but they also enable other industries, in turn, to become knowledge based. Consider the oil industry. The story of the famous James Dean movie, *Giant*, typified the old means of success in the oil business: luck and brawn. But new technologies such as three-dimensional acoustical sounding, horizontal drilling, and deep offshore drilling have turned the oil business into a knowledge industry. Luck and brawn have disappeared. Supercomputers have taken their place. The oil industry now has a big interest in intellectual property rights.

The growth of electronic commerce is bringing a similar transformation to retailing. The source of an retailer's future success is apt to be buried in the software of its electronic information and logistics systems rather than in the art of its window displays. Fast knockoffs makes it difficult to sell anything that is truly unique.

More directly, the rising importance of intellectual property can be seen in the earnings gained from the licensing of technology. In the past, companies were willing to share their technology because it did not seem to be the source of their success and could not be sold for much anyway. But those days are gone. For example, Polaroid and Kodak settled a patent infringement case for almost $1 billion. And Texas Instruments, after shifting to an aggressive licensing program, earned more than $1.5 billion in fees; in some years its licensing fees have been bigger than its operating income. Having noticed these numbers, many other corporations are now ordering their technology-licensing officers to step up their efforts.

Increasingly, intellectual property is becoming central to strategic battle plans. Companies such as Intel have big legal budgets to defend what they think is their property, but they are also accused of aggressively attacking what others think is theirs in order to create uncertainties, time delays, and higher start-up costs for their competitors. For example, Digital Equipment Corporation, unsuccessful in the marketplace, filed a huge triple-damages patent suit against Intel for infringing on its Alpha chip technologies. Perhaps DEC will gain in the courts what it could not gain in the economic arena. If it wins, the damages awarded will be in the billions. Or perhaps DEC's strategy is to make Intel more cautious, and hence slower, in designing its next generation of microprocessors.

DEC's suit was triggered by a remark in a *Wall Street Journal* article in which a top-level executive on an Intel chip-research team was reported as saying, "There's nothing left to copy." Wherever the truth lies in this case, reverse engineering is a way of life in the corporate world. But where should the limits be? Surely the answer is not where a patent system more than a century old sets them. . . .

The Emergence of New Technologies

New technologies have created new potential forms of intellectual property rights (can pieces of a human being be patented?) and made old rights unenforceable (when books can be downloaded from an electronic library, what does a copyright mean?) We need to rethink fundamentally what should and should not be appropriable as private property. At the same time we need to generate new ideas and technologies to offer effective protection of intellectual property rights.

How should we think about what should be patentable? It is clear that the invention of a new gene for making human beings different or better cannot be handled in the same way as the invention of a new gearbox. And society isn't going to let someone have a monopoly on the cure for cancer. Nor will biologists be allowed to clone and own whole human beings.

But it is equally clear that companies engaging in biological research must be allowed to own pieces of human beings; otherwise, no one would invest the funds necessary to find genetic cures for diseases such as Alzheimer's. Since patents on genetic cures for diseases cannot be differentiated from patents on genetic materials that make humans taller, smarter, or more beautiful, the exact line between what is and is not allowed is going to be difficult to draw. But inventing a new piece of biology that alters the natural characteristics of plants, animals, or humans is not equivalent to discovering how an existing piece of biology works. What a patent means has to be different in those two areas.

We also need to differentiate between fundamental advances in knowledge and logical extensions of existing knowledge. Each deserves a different kind of patent. One of the objections to the "first to file" system used outside the United States is that it allows smart, knowledgeable people to guess where technology is going and to file patents on things that have not yet been invented. If they guess right one out of ten times, they more than cover their costs of filing multiple patents.

New technologies make enforcement of property rights much tougher. People can use high-quality scanning technologies with optical character recognition to build electronic libraries quickly and easily. Electronic publishers can in turn just as quickly and easily convert that material back into printed form. When anything can be rapidly, cheaply, and privately replicated in low volumes at high levels of quality and then distributed in whatever form the user wants, the choke points available to prevent reproduction of what used to be printed materials have essentially evaporated.

With that evaporation comes the end of the copyright system—not just for books but for all information and data systems. A system designed to allow people to browse and borrow books from physical libraries cannot provide the right framework for dealing with the issues raised by the possibility of downloading a book from an electronic library.

What initially may seem relevant only to authors and book companies isn't. If books can be freely downloaded, then those selling financial information will also find that their databases can be downloaded and resold by lower-cost competitors—whose costs are lower precisely because they did not have to incur the costs of creating the databases! Telephone companies are trying to stop that practice by putting some phony numbers in their telephone books in order to prove in court that competitors have not generated their own list of names and numbers.

Magnify what is now happening in the recorded music business and you can see the future in printed materials. Even though the equipment needed to record compact discs is too expensive to be found in every household, CD pirates may hold as much as 20% share of the market. In contrast, in personal electronic publishing the equipment is as cheap and available as a personal computer plus a scanner. The fully electronic library does not yet exist, but is soon will. One has to expect that pirated works will end up with an even bigger market share of what used to be conventionally printed materials than they now have of CDs and tapes. The legal system may be able to stop factories from copying and selling CDs or books in volume, but it cannot stop individuals from replicating the materials for themselves or selling small numbers to their friends.

And consider software piracy. When computer makers ship their products "naked"—that is, without an operating system—as they often do in Asia, the only reason they do so is to allow the use of pirated software. Effectively, these computer makers have the tacit approval of local governments to violate patents and copyrights. In Thailand, up to 97% of the software in use has been illegally copied, and even in the United States as much as 40% of the software in use may have been illegally copied. Estimates of pirated software in Europe range from a high of 80% in Spain to a low of 25% in the United Kingdom.

Computer software provides a good illustration of what happens when patent and copyright laws do not keep up with technology. Judges end up making decisions that they should not be making. One such decision ruled that the "look and feel" of a software program could not be patented—which means, effectively, that any successful program can be legally copied. The copiers need to write their own code, but they start knowing exactly what the program is supposed to do, how the internal programming components are structured, how the final program is supposed to look and feel, and that a viable market exists for the product. Knowing exactly what to create lowers costs; but more important, the copier faces much less market uncertainty and risk than the original writers of successful software programs.

When software programs cannot be protected effectively, it is not just the Apples that will lose. Retailers, for example, that develop software to sell their products over the Internet will find their software copied and freely used by their competitors.

The Globalization of the Economy

Increasingly, the acquisition of knowledge is central for both "catch-up states" and "keep-ahead states." Smart developing countries understand that reality. Operating as a monopsonist (a buyer that controls a market) and dangling access to its domestic market as the enticement, China demands the sharing of technology from companies such as Boeing and Reuters that sell in its markets. It doesn't need their capital—it saves 30% of its income and has accumulated $100 billion in international exchange reserves—but it demands their knowledge in return for the right to operate in China. Americans deplore China's demands but remember fondly from their high-school history classes the clever Yankee engineers who visited British textile mills in the early 1800s and then reconstructed them in New England. Initially, Americans were amused in the aftermath of World War II when Japanese businessmen with their cameras were ubiquitously touring U.S. factories. They are no longer amused. Few today will let Third World visitors into their plants.

Yet copying to catch up is the only way to catch up. Every country that has caught up has done it by copying. Third World countries know that unless they can acquire the necessary knowledge, they will never make it into the First World. They cannot afford to buy what they need—even if those who have the knowledge were willing to sell, and they are not. So they have to copy.

Recently I heard a talk given by the managing partner of a large U.S. consulting firm. The partner urged his fellow consultants to recommend re-location to India because Indians were very good at copying, had few laws making copying illegal, and often did not enforce the laws that did exist. He remarked that India recognized patents only on the processes for making drugs, not on the drugs themselves, but then went on to say that Indians were very good at developing alternative manufacturing processes. The fact that no one checks those processes very closely to see that they are really different was left unsaid. Nor did he need to say that what was made in India could be slipped quietly into the channels of world commerce without any-one having to pay for knowledge that would be considered proprietary elsewhere.

The issues are not just those of where a country stands in the invention cycle or where it stands on the economic development ladder. Different cultures and different parts of the world look at intellectual property rights quite differently. The idea that people should be paid to be creative is a point of view that stems from the Judeo-Christian and Muslim belief in a God who created humankind in His image. It has no analogue in Hindu, Buddhist, or Confucian societies. There are real differences in beliefs about what should be freely available in the public domain and what should be for sale in the private marketplace. Countries also differ enormously in their propensities to use their patent systems. Switzerland, for example, issues four and one-half times as many patents per capita as the United States. Does anyone believe that the Swiss are really that much more creative than Americans?

Yet despite these differences in economic positions, cultures, and practices, no system of protecting intellectual property rights can work unless most of the governments of the world agree to enforce it. A law that does not exist or is not enforced in country X is essentially a law that cannot be enforced in country Y. Production simply moves to country X. What different countries want, need, and should have in a system of intellectual property rights is very different, depending on their level of economic development. National systems, such as that of the United States, are not going to evolve into *de facto* world standards. The economic game of catch-up is not the game of keep ahead. Countries playing either game have the right to a world system that lets them succeed.

BUILDING A NEW SYSTEM: BASIC PRINCIPLES

As those who launched capitalism two centuries ago discovered, enforce-able property rights had to be defined and enforced for capitalism to work. The old Communist countries now trying to convert to market economies are discovering the same reality today. Closer to home, the failure to develop adequate property rights lies behind many U.S. problems with air and water pollution. Free usage—that is, no enforceable property rights—is sensible for each individual, but it ends up depriving the whole community of clean air and water. So, too, with intellectual property rights; free usage of knowledge ends up with societies that create too little new knowledge.

The Industrial Revolution began with an enclosure movement that abolished common land in England. The world now needs a socially managed enclosure movement for intellectual property rights or it will witness a scramble among the powerful to grab valuable pieces of intellectual property, just as the powerful grabbed the common lands of England three centuries ago. Three basic design principles are needed:

A New System Must Strike the Right Balance Between the Production and the Distribution of New Ideas

In thinking about protecting intellectual property rights, one starts with an inherent tension in the system. To develop new products and processes, individuals must have a financial incentive to undertake the costs, risks, and efforts of developing new knowledge. Not surprisingly, bigger incentives lead to the production of more knowledge than do smaller incentives. A recent change allowing patents on plants, for example, has led to an explosion of new developments.

As the government role in R&D fades, the need for stronger private incentives grows. The standard incentive is to give inventors a monopoly on the right to produce the products that can be created with their knowledge— a right that they can use or sell. Whether we like it or not, the corollary of fading government efforts is the need for stronger private monopoly rights.

At the same time, once any piece of knowledge exists, the social incentives are reversed 180 degrees. The wider the use and the faster the distribution of that new knowledge, the greater the benefit to society. Free usage leads to the widest and fastest distribution. For this reason, whenever anyone has a really important patent it is often suggested that antitrust laws should be used to take away the monopoly rights that have been bestowed by the patent laws.

Any system of intellectual property rights must make a trade-off between these two inherently conflicting objectives—more production versus faster distribution. There is no single right answer about how to make that trade-off. It is a judgment call. But it is a call that should not be made by a judge.

Judges do not think about what makes sense from the perspective of accelerating technological and economic progress. Their concern is with how new areas of technology can be inserted into the legal framework with the least disruption to existing interpretations. Such lazy law-writing practices do not make for good economics or sensible technology policies. The right approach would be to investigate the underlying economics of an industry in order to determine what incentives are necessary for its successful development. Those are socioeconomic decisions that should be made in our legislatures, not in our courts.

In our modern economies, private monopoly power should be less worrisome than it was when our patent system was originally set up. As alternative technologies proliferate, there are fewer and fewer products with inelastic demand curves that would allow companies to raise their prices arbitrarily and earn monopoly returns. Today customers have many alternatives—very few products are necessities that lack close substitutes. And small amounts of monopoly power, which translate into slightly higher prices, simply don't matter as much with today's higher incomes as they did in the past.

As monopoly power wanes and social interests in encouraging the development of new intellectual property grow, the balance in our system should shift toward encouraging the production of new knowledge and be less concerned about the free distribution of existing knowledge. Tighter or longer-term patents and copyrights would seem to be warranted.

Laws on Intellectual Property Rights Must Be Enforceable or They Should Not Be Laws

Although the need for the protection of intellectual property has never been greater, the same technologies and developments that have made intellectual property rights more central to economic success have also made enforcement of those rights much more difficult. Laws can be written, but they are meaningless—and should not be written—unless a technological choke point exists to make enforcement is possible. Laws that cannot or will not be enforced make for neither good law nor good technology policies. The honest end up being suckers who pay more precisely because they are honest. And a law that is widely violated leads to disrespect for the law and more violations. Put bluntly, if someone cannot think of how a legal right can be enforced, it should not be a legal right.

The System Must Be Able to Determine Rights and Resolve Disputes Quickly and Efficiently

Many of the problems with the patent system flow from the lack of consistent, predictable, rapid, low-cost determinations about intellectual property rights and a means of quick, cheap dispute resolution. The first problem is easily solved, at least in part. In the United States, people who file for patents pay user fees that exceed the costs incurred by the patent office. Those fees are put into the general budget, and Congress then appropriates funds—less than the amount collected in fees—to run the patent office.

One easy change is to establish a system in which the user fees directly finance what they are supposed to finance but are set high enough to ensure speedy decisions. Like an income tax, fees could be adjusted to reflect the income levels of the applicants and equalize the burdens on large corporations and on small, individual inventors. The relevant agencies should be taken out of the civil service system, and salaries should be set high enough to attract and keep the people who could run the system efficiently and speedily.

For inventors of technologies that have very short useful lives, making use of today's system of dispute resolution—with its delayed, lengthy, and expensive court trials—is equivalent to losing one's rights. In seeking an alternative approach, the U.S. system for settling water rights disputes in irrigated areas might serve as a model. Federal water masters are given the authority to allocate water in dry years and to settle disputes quickly because crops die quickly.

ONE SIZE DOESN'T FIT ALL

Although simplicity can be a powerful virtue, builders of a new system must reconcile a number of competing interests and allow for some critical distinctions.

Public Versus Private Knowledge

To accomplish society's interest in expanding knowledge as rapidly as possible, certain classes of knowledge ought to be in the public domain and freely available to everyone. One can argue that basic scientific knowledge should be public while those who develop products from that knowledge should receive private monopoly rights. But the line between scientific principles and the knowledge that is necessary to allow products to be built is, in practice, hard to draw. Here again, the issue is a judgment call.

There are other reasons for keeping knowledge in the public domain. A society may determine, for example, that its interests in educating the young justify placing some types of knowledge—educational technologies, for example—in the public domain. And egalitarian democracies may want, say, lifesaving technologies to be generally available to everyone, not just to the rich.

Such considerations mean that we need principles to determine when knowledge should be publicly available and when it should be kept private. This does not meant that patents or copyrights should be forbidden in areas where there is a social interest in allowing general access to knowledge at little or no cost. That would be unacceptable because no one would have the incentive to produce such generally useful knowledge. Inventors who happened upon such discoveries would have an enormous incentive to keep them secret. We must ensure that those who generate knowledge in the public domain get paid.

The solution to this problem is found not in the patent system itself but in the establishment of some public agency—perhaps a branch of the National Science Foundation. Armed with funds and the power of eminent domain, the agency could decide to buy knowledge for the public's use when it seemed warranted. If the seller would not agree to sell at a reasonable price, adjudication principles very similar to those used in eminent domain land-acquisition proceedings could be used.

Developed Versus Developing Countries

In a global economy, a global system of intellectual property rights is needed. This system must reflect the needs both of countries that are developing and of those that have developed. The problem is similar to the one concerning which types of knowledge should be in the public domain in the developed world. But the Third World's need to get low-cost pharmaceuticals is not equivalent to its need for low-cost CDs. Any system that treats such needs equally, as our current system does, is neither a good nor a viable system. Depending on the income level of the country and the importance of the technologies to basic human needs, different predetermined levels of fees might be internationally imposed on those who want to use what others have invented.

Different Industries, Types of Knowledge, Type of Inventors, and Types of Patents

The optimal patent system will not be the same for all industries, all types of knowledge, or all types of inventors. Consider, for example, the electronics industry and the pharmaceutical industry. The first wants speed and short-term protection because most of its money is earned soon after new knowledge is developed. The second wants long-term protection because most of its money is earned after a long period of testing to prove a drug's effectiveness and the absence of adverse side effects.

Different types of advances in knowledge should be distinguished from one another and alternative patents awarded on that basis. Again, fundamental advances are not equivalent to logical extensions of existing knowledge and should not be treated as if they were. And individual inventors should not be treated in the same way as large corporations. As noted above, filing fees could be linked to income in order to level the playing field for all inventors.

Finally, inventors should be able to choose from a selection of patents or copyrights. A differentiated system might offer different levels of monopoly rights to inventors. Costs, speed of issuance, and dispute-settlement parameters could vary. Let filers decide what type of patent they wish to have. In no other market do we decide that everyone wants—and must buy—exactly the same product.

The world's current one-dimensional system must be overhauled to create a more differentiated one. Trying to squeeze today's developments into yesterday's system of intellectual property rights simply won't work. One size does not fit all.

Privacy

DEBORAH G. JOHNSON

SCENARIO 5.1: FUNDRAISING AND POTENTIAL DONORS

Jan Perez began college as a computer science major. She loves computers and has always been very good at figuring out how to do things on the Internet and the Web. However, after a year and a half of college, Jan decides that as much as she likes computing, she doesn't want to major in it; she chooses, instead, a major that is more likely to lead to a career involving

Deborah G. Johnson is the Anne Shirley Carter Olsson Professor of Applied Ethics in the Department of Science, Technology, and Society in the School of Engineering and Applied Sciences of the University of Virginia. Professor Johnson received the John Barwise prize from the American Philosophical Association in 2004. This selection is reprinted from Chapter 5 of her book *Computer Ethics*, 3rd ed., pp. 109–136. Reprinted by permission of Pearson Education, Inc., Upper Saddle River, NJ.

contact and interaction with people. She also wants something that involves public service or promoting good causes.

After college Jan is delighted to find that the development office of a large, private university wants to hire her. She accepts the job enthusiastically, thinking she will do some good by raising money for a great university.

Jan's supervisor is extremely pleased to find out how much Jan knows about computers and the Internet. Within a few months of starting the job, Jan is asked to find out what she can about a Frank Doe. Mr. Doe has never been approached by the university; Jan's supervisor only recently heard from another donor that Mr. Doe has a very positive impression of the university and has the capacity to make a major contribution.

The fundraising unit needs to know how wealthy Mr. Doe is to determine what kind of contribution to ask for. They need to know about his life and interests to know which of their projects he might want to support. And, they need to know about him personally so they can approach him, put him at ease, and not offend him in any way. Jan is given some suggestions about where to look, but she is also told to find out whatever she can.

Using the Internet Jan does the following:

1. She searches a variety of public databases which give her information about his real estate holdings; his memberships on the boards of public corporations; a list of corporations for which he is a major stockholder.
2. She searches other databases to find out if he has made contributions to political parties or campaigns.
3. She searches archives of newspapers to see if Mr. Doe has ever been written about in the news.
4. She searches other databases to see if he has had any encounters with law enforcement agencies.
5. She searches other databases to find out what religious organizations he supports.
6. She contacts credit agencies and requests his credit history.
7. Jan wonders if Amazon.com would tell her what types of books, if any, Mr. Doe purchases.
8. Jan wonders which Internet service provider Mr. Doe uses; she contemplates what she could learn about Mr. Doe if his service provider would tell her about his online activities, for examples, he may keep portfolio of stock holdings in an his account.
9. Mr. Doe is a local resident. Jan's supervisor mentions in passing that Mr. Doe, she has been told, uses the university's medical complex for all his medical treatment. Jan decides to see whether she can access patient files at the university medical complex. Much to her surprise, she is able to access Mr. Doe's insurance records and this tells her that in the last several years, he has been receiving frequent treatment for a kidney ailment. She wonders if this will make him interested in contributing to the hospital or for kidney research.
10. At the end of several weeks of research, Jan has an enormous amount of information about Mr. Doe. She ponders that as she acquired each bit of information from a separate database, there didn't seem anything wrong with acquiring it; now, however, the cumulative effect of putting all of this information together makes Jan feel uncomfortable. She wonders if this is right. She feels a bit like a voyeur or stalker.

Has Jan done anything wrong?

SCENARIO 5.2: TAKING DATA HOME

Max Brown works in the Department of Alcoholism and Drug Abuse of a northeastern state. The agency administers programs for individuals with alcohol and drug problems, and maintains huge databases of information on the clients who use their services. Max has been asked to take a look at the track records of the treatment programs. He is to put together a report which contains information about such factors as number of clients seen in each program each month for the past five years, length of each client's treatment, number of clients who return after completion of a program, criminal histories of clients, and so on.

In order to put together this report, Max has been given access to all files in the agency's mainframe computer. It takes Max several weeks to find the information he needs because it is located in a variety of places in the system. As he finds information, he downloads it to the computer in his office; that is, he copies the information from the mainframe onto the hard disk of his office microcomputer.

Under pressure to get the report finished by the deadline, Max finds that he is continuously distracted at work. He decides that he will have to work at home over the weekend in order to finish on time. This will not be a problem. He copies the information (containing, among other things, personal information on clients) onto several disks and takes them home. He finishes the report over the weekend. To be safe, he leaves a copy of the report on his home computer as well as copying it onto a disk which he takes up to work.

Was Max wrong in moving personal information from the mainframe to his office computer? In moving the information from his office computer to a disk? To his home computer? In leaving the information on his computer at home? What could happen as a result of Max's treatment of the data? Should the agency for which Max works have a policy on use of personal information stored in its system? What might such a policy specify?

SCENARIO 5.3: WORKPLACE MONITORING

Estelle Cavello was recently hired to supervise a large unit of a medical insurance company. Estelle will be in charge of a unit responsible for processing insurance claims. When she was hired, the Vice President made it clear to Estelle that he expects her to significantly increase the efficiency of the unit. The company has targets for the number of claims that should be processed by each unit and Estelle's unit has never been able to meet its target.

One of the first things Estelle does when she starts this job is to install a software system that will allow her to monitor the work of each and every claims processor. The software allows Estelle to record the number of keystrokes made per minute on any terminal in the unit. It also allows her to bring the work of others up on her computer screen so that she can watch individual work as it is being done. As well, Estelle can access copies of each employee's work at the end of each day. She can find out how much time each worker spent with the terminal off; she can see what correspondence the person prepared; she can review e-mail that the worker sent or received; and so on.

Should Estelle use this software to monitor her employees?

SCENARIO 5.4: DATA MINING

Ravi Singh works for one of the major credit card companies in its data processing center. The company is continuously developing new products to offer to customers and add revenue to the corporation. He is an avid reader of computer magazines and recently has been reading about data mining tools that are now available for a reasonable cost. Ravi goes to his supervisor with the suggestion that their unit purchase one of these tools and use it to find out more about its customers. The information may be telling in terms of customer interest and capability.

The supervisor likes the idea. After exploring the systems that are available, the unit purchases one and Ravi is assigned to explore patterns in the database of information on the company's customers and their purchasing habits.

Ravi discovers that certain zip codes are highly correlated with loan defaults. These zip codes must be in low income areas for the mined and analyzed data indicate that the company could reduce its losses significantly by refusing to extend credit to anyone living in twenty-five zip codes, while at the same time not significantly reducing its revenues. In other words, on average losses due to default generated by individuals in those zip codes were greater than revenue generated.

Ravi continues with his data mining. Next he discoverers a correlation between those who use their credit cards to make contributions to Hindu charitable organizations and those who charge over $40,000 a year on their credit cards. This information seems important. If the company made a special effort to solicit Hindus as customers, it might be able to increase its revenues significantly.

Ravi goes to his supervisor with the suggestion that they adopt these strategies. Has Ravi done anything wrong? If his company adopts these strategies, has it done anything wrong?

These scenarios depict just a few of the ways that information can be created, gathered, moved, and used with computer technology. Of all the social and ethical concerns surrounding computer technology, the threat to personal privacy was probably the first to capture public attention. And this issue persists in drawing public concern and leading to action by policy makers. One hears about it frequently in the popular media; major studies continue to be undertaken; new books continue to be written; and new legislation continues to be passed to regulate electronic information. It will be helpful to begin by laying out just why and how computer technology facilitates information gathering and seems to threaten personal privacy.

IS THERE ANYTHING NEW HERE?

In Chapter 1, I suggested that computer technology, like other new technologies, creates new possibilities; it creates possibilities for behavior and activities that were not possible before the technology. Public concern about computers and privacy arises for precisely this reason. Computers make it possible (and in many cases, cheap and easy) to gather detailed information about individuals to an extent never possible before. Federal, state, and local government agencies now maintain extensive records of individual behavior including such things as any interactions with criminal justice agencies, income taxes, employment history for social security, use of human services agencies, motor vehicle registration, and so on. As well, private organizations maintain extensive databases of information on individual purchases, airline travel, credit worthiness, health records, telephone or cellular phone usage, employment, and so on.

We have the technological capacity for the kind of massive, continuous surveillance of individuals that was envisioned in such frightening early twentieth century science fiction works as George Orwell's *1984* and Zamyatin's *We*. The only differences between what is now possible and what was envisioned then, is that much of the surveillance of individuals that takes place now is done by private institutions (marketing firms, insurance companies, credit agencies), *and* much of the surveillance now is via electronic records instead of by direct human observation or through cameras.

Indeed, many authors now suggest that we are building a world that is, in effect, a "panopticon." *Panopticon* is the word Jeremy Bentham used in 1887 to describe his idea for the design of prisons. In the panopticon, prison cells would be arranged in a circle and the side of each cell facing the inside of the circle would be all glass. The guard tower is placed in the center of the circle, from which every cell is in full view. Everything going on in each cell can be observed. The effect is not two-way; that is, the prisoners cannot see the guard in the tower. The idea of the panopticon was later picked up by Michel Foucault (1975) and brought to wider public attention (Bozovic, 1995). Bentham and Foucault recognized the power of surveillance to affect the behavior of individuals. In the panopticon, a prison guard need not even be there at every moment; when prisoners believe they are being watched, they adjust their behavior. When individuals believe they are being watched, they are compelled to think of themselves as the observer might think of them. This shapes how individuals see themselves and leads them to behave differently than they might if they weren't being observed.

Many authors have expressed concern that the degree of information gathering that now takes place in our society is having or will have a similar effect. We are building a panopticon in which everything we do is observed and could come back to haunt us.

Of course, one can try to be skeptical about the similarities between the panopticon prison and our world today; one can try to be critical of the parallel. Indeed, you can ask whether there is anything fundamentally different about today as compared to fifty years ago or a century ago. Record-keeping is far from a new phenomenon. Government agencies and private corporations have been keeping records for thousands of years and using this information in variety of ways. So, is there anything different about the kind or degree of privacy that we have today as compared to fifty or a hundred years ago?

Computer technology has changed record keeping activities in a number of undeniable and powerful ways. First, the *scale of information gathering* has changed. Second, the *kind of information* that can be gathered has changed. And, third, the *scale of exchange* of information has changed enormously.

In the pre-computer, "paper-and-ink" world, the mere fact that records were paper and stored in file cabinets imposed some limitations on the amount of data gathered, who had access, how long records were retained, and so on. Electronic records do not have these limitations. One can collect, store, manipulate, exchange, and retain practically infinite quantities of data. The point is that technology no longer limits what can be done; now only time and money and, perhaps, human capabilities impose limits on the quantity of information which can be gathered and processed.

The kind of information that it is now possible to collect and use is also new. Think about the workplace monitoring scenario at the beginning of this chapter. Employers can keep records of every keystroke an employee makes. Before computers, finger movements of this kind would not have been thought to be important, let alone, the kind of thing that could be recorded. Employers can monitor their employees' uses of the Web, their participation in chat rooms, not to mention their email.

One particularly important new form of information is referred to as TGI (transaction generated information). TGI includes purchases made with a credit card, telephone calls, entry and exit from intelligent highways, and so on. As you move about in the world, your activities (transactions) are automatically recorded.

You might argue that TGI does not exactly create a panoptic world because there is no one guard tower at the center of it all. There is no single government or private organization accumulating all of the information. Transaction generated information gathering seems to be fragmented and, therefore, seems not to pose the threat of Big Brother.

Indeed, in the very early days of computing, especially in the 1960s and 1970s, many social commentators expressed concern about the information gathering potential of computer technology and these fears were articulated as fears of Big Brother—fears that all the information would be funneled to a highly centralized U.S. government. The fear was that electronic information gathering practices would give too much power to government. It would create a potentially totalitarian government, a surveillance society. Those fears waned in part because legislation was passed that restricted government information gathering.

Fear also weakened because computer technology changed. It became smaller and cheaper, and, consequently, became available much more widely. On the one hand, this diffused fear of Big Brother because it promised computer power in the hands of "many" rather than just big government. At the same time, however, smaller computers in the hands of many companies and individuals facilitated the exchange of information to an extent previously unimaginable. Typically information of one kind will be gathered and stored separately from information of another kind; for example, marketing firms will gather and store information on buying habits, one government agency will record income tax information, another government agency will record criminal justice activities, and so on.

With computer technology, however, it is technically possible to combine all this information. In the private sector this is done routinely. Think of the fundraising example at the beginning of this chapter. Within government this happens less frequently because the Privacy Act of 1974 restricted data matching. Nevertheless, it does happen. Matches have been made, for example: between federal employee records and records of the Aid to Families with Dependent Children program, to investigate fraud; and between IRS records of taxpayer addresses and lists of individuals born in 1963 (supplied by the Selective Service System), to locate violators of the draft registration law. Matching of records can produce a profile of an individual which, before computers, would only have been available to those who knew the individual intimately.

And, the restriction on matching mentioned in the Privacy Act of 1974 did not apply to private organization, just to the federal government. What was called "matching" in the 1970s is today called data mining is quite common in private organizations. Indeed, you can now purchase data mining tools, sometimes called knowledge discovery instruments (kdi) that help find patterns of behavior among groups of individuals. Their use is described in Scenario 5.4.

Add to these changes in the scale and kind of information gathered with computer technology a further element. Because computerized information is electronic, it is easy to copy and distribute. Before computers were connected by telephone lines, information could be fairly easily copied using tapes or disks. Now that computers are connected via telecommunication lines, information can go anywhere in the world where there are telephone lines. Hence, the extent to which information can be exchanged is now practically limitless. Once information about an individual is recorded in a machine or on a disk, it can be easily transferred to another machine or disk. It can be bought and sold, given away, traded, and even stolen. The information can spread instantaneously from one company to another, from one sector to another, and from one country to another.

The Max Brown case (Scenario 5.2) is illustrative here. He takes sensitive data home on a disk. From a technical point of view, he could have simply accessed the data from home. But in either case, the data moves around. Once it moves out of its source, it is very difficult to keep track of all the places it might exist, be it on disks or hard drives.

Movement of data happens when you subscribe to a magazine and your name and address are sold to a marketing firm. The marketing firm infers from the subscription that you have certain tastes and begins sending you a variety of opportunities to buy the things you like. Forester and Morrison (1990) report the case of a women who took her landlord to court after he refused to do anything about the pest problem in her apartment. He did not show up for court but evicted her shortly after the court date. When she went looking for another apartment, she found that she was repeatedly turned down by landlords. She would look at an apartment, notify the landlord that she wanted it, and within a few days hear back that the apartment was already rented to someone else. It turned out that a database of names of individuals who take landlords to court is maintained and the information is sold to landlords. Needless to say, landlords don't want to rent to individuals who may take them to court.

As far as the technology goes, the distribution of information can take place with or without the knowledge of the person whom the information is about, and it can take place intentionally as well as unintentionally. There is an unintentional distribution when records are provided that contain more information than is requested. As well, when information is stolen, the exchange is unintentional from the point of view of the agency that gathered or maintained the records. Think again of the Max Brown scenario; Brown's wife, children, or friends might (while using his home computer) inadvertently access the data on individuals in the state's treatment programs and see the names of clients in the state programs.

If all of this were not cause enough for concern, there is more. Information stored in a computer can be erroneous, and, at the same time, can be readily distributed. The effect of a small error can be magnified enormously. Information can be erroneous due to unintentional human error or because someone has intentionally altered it to harm a competitor or enhance his or her own records. It is important to remember that databases of information are not always as secure as we would like them to be. When computers are connected via telecommunications lines, the possibilities of data being tampered with or stolen are increased.

Suppose John A. Smith's file is inadvertently combined with John B. Smith's. John A. has *never* failed to pay his debts, has a good job, and has a sizable holding of stocks, while John B. has a low paying job, declared bankruptcy three years ago, and is once again deeply in debt. John A. is wronged when he is turned down for a loan. Moreover, suppose that after a series of inquires and complaints by John A., the error is identified, and corrected. (This is not always as easy as it sounds. Companies are often very slow in responding to complaints about errors in records.) John A. asks his bank to send for the updated report, and the bank changes its mind about the loan when it sees the accurate information. It would appear that the injury to John A. has been remedied. Not necessarily. The inaccurate information may have been given to other companies before it was corrected, and they, in turn, may have given it to others. As a result, it may be difficult, if not impossible, to track down all the databases in which the error is now stored. It may be impossible to completely expunge the erroneous information from John A.'s records.

When information is stored in a computer, there is little incentive to get rid of it; hence, information may stay with an individual for a long period of time. Information stored in a computer takes up very little space and is easy to maintain and transfer. Because of this, details can be carried in a record forever. Something insignificant that happened to an individual when he was 10 years old may easily follow him through life because the information has been recorded once and there is little motivation to delete it. In the past, the inconvenience of paper served to some degree as an inhibitor to keeping and exchanging apparently useless information.[1]

Because it is so easy to keep information, some fear that individuals will get categorized and stigmatized at early stages in their lives. One way to see this is to imagine what it would be like if elementary and secondary school records were put into a national database where prospective employers, government agencies, or insurance companies could get access. We might find decisions being made about us on the basis of testing done when we were in elementary school or on the basis of disciplinary incidents in our teenage years.

When decision makers are faced with making decisions about individuals, they want data. They want data both to ensure a good decision and to justify their decision to others. When they must choose between making a decision on the basis of little or no data, and making it on the basis of lots of data known to be unreliable, many prefer the latter. Hence, information tends to get used if it is available even though it may not be relevant or reliable.

In summary, while record-keeping is, by no means, a new activity, it appears that computer technology has changed record-keeping activities in the following ways: (1) it has made a *new scale* of information gathering possible; (2) it has made *new kinds* of information possible, especially transaction generated information; (3) it has made *a new scale of* information *distribution and exchange* possible; (4) the *effect* of erroneous information can be *magnified*; and (5) information about events in one's life may *endure* much longer than ever before. These five changes make the case for the claim that the world we live is more like a panopticon than ever before.

As an aside here, you may be tempted to say that computers are not really the problem or the cause of the problem. It is individuals and organizations that are creating, gathering, exchanging, and using information. Computers, according to this line of argument, are simply tools; if there is a problem, the problem is the people who use computers, not the computers themselves.

While there is some truth to this, it is important to remember that computer technology facilitates certain kinds of activities. Computer technology makes it possible for individuals to do things they could not do before. Individuals and organizations are more likely to engage in activities when they are possible (not to speak of easy and inexpensive). For example, in Scenario 5.4, Estelle would not have monitored employees to the extent she did or in quite the way that she did if computers and the monitoring software were not available. Individuals choose actions because they find themselves in a world which has certain possibilities; in a world with different possibilities, they would behave differently. Insofar as computer technology changes what it is possible for human beings to do, it can be a major factor affecting what people do and the kind of society in which we live.

UNDERSTANDING THE "COMPUTERS AND PRIVACY" ISSUE

Uses of Information

Information about individuals would not exist if organizations did not have an interest in using it. Information is created, collected, and exchanged because organizations can use it to further their interests and activities. Information about individuals is used to make decisions about those individuals, and often the decisions profoundly affect the lives of those individuals whom the information is about. Information about you, stored in a database, may be used to decide whether or not you will be hired by a company, whether or not you will be given a loan, whether or not you will be called to the police station for interrogation, arrested, prosecuted, whether or not you will receive education, housing, social security, unemployment compensation, and so on.

The computers and privacy issue is often framed as an issue that calls for a balancing of the needs of those who use information about individuals (typically government agencies and private institutions) *against* the needs or rights of those individuals whom the information is about. Later in this chapter, I will argue against this framing of the issue on grounds that it is biased in favor of information gathering, but for the moment it is important to understand why organizations want information.

In general those who want information about individuals want it because they believe that it will help them to make better decisions. Several examples quickly illustrate this point. Banks believe that the more information they have about an individual, the better they will be able to make judgments about that individual's ability to pay back a loan or about the size of the credit line the individual can handle. The FBI's National Crime Information Center (NCIC) provides criminal histories of individuals to all the states. Law enforcement agencies justify the existence of this database on grounds that the more information they have about individuals, the better they will be able to identify and capture criminals. We might also bring in examples from the insurance industry where decisions are made about which individuals to insure at what rate, or from the Department of Health and Human Services where decisions are made about who qualifies for various welfare and medical benefits. And, of course, don't forget the fundraising organization, data mining, and workplace monitoring scenarios at the beginning of this chapter. In theory, the more and better the information these organizations have, the better their decision making will be.

Companies also claim that they need information about their customers in order to serve them better. If a company like Amazon.com keeps track of the books that you buy, it can infer from this information what new books you are likely to be interested in. When they send you information on these new books, they claim they are providing a service to you (even if it is one that you didn't ask for and one that happens also to serve their interest in selling more books). If an advertising firm knows what I buy at the grocery store, it can use that information to send me coupons for items I am likely to buy. If television stations know what I watch on television and when I change the channel, they can use that information to develop programming more suited to my tastes. If marketing companies know about my income level and my tastes in clothes, food, sports, and music, they can send me catalogues or special offers for products and services that fit my precise tastes.

In the standard understanding of the computers and privacy issue we have, on the one side, public and private institutions that want information about individuals. They make a powerful case for how this information improves their decision making and helps them to do their job better and more efficiently. In theory, all of that means better serving us, as consumers and citizens. It means, for example, better law enforcement; more efficient government; better, more customized services; and so on.

Personal privacy is, then, generally put on the other side of the balancing scales. The issue is framed so that we have to balance all the good things that are achieved through information gathering and exchange *against* the desire or need for personal privacy. Some even claim that we have a right to personal privacy for if that were true, the scales would weigh heavily on the side of personal privacy. From a legal and constitutional point of view, however, we have, at most, a limited and complex right to privacy.

This framing of the issue seems to be skewed heavily in favor of information gathering and exchange. The only way to counter the powerful case made on behalf of information gathering and exchange is, it would seem, to make a more powerful case for protecting and ensuring privacy in the lives of individuals. Either we must show that there is a grave risk or danger to these information gathering activities—a danger so great that it counterbalances the benefits of the activity. Or we must show that there is a greater benefit to be gained from constraining these activities. To put this another way, once the benefits of information gathering and exchange are on the table, the burden of proof is on privacy advocates to show either that there is something harmful about information gathering and exchange or that there is some benefit to be gained from constraining information gathering. Either way, there is daunting hurdle to overcome.

Many of us feel uncomfortable about the amount of information that is gathered about us. We do not like not knowing who has what information about us and how it is being used. Why are we so uncomfortable? What do we fear? Part of the fear is, no doubt, related to our mistrust of large, faceless organizations, and part of it is related to mistrust of government. The challenge is to translate this discomfort and fear into an argument that counterbalances the benefits of information gathering.

Odd as it may seem, the case for protecting personal privacy has not been easy to make. From the point of view of public policy, arguments on behalf of personal privacy have not "won the date." I am going to discuss a number of ways that the case for individual privacy can be and has been made, but I am also going to argue for a somewhat different framing of the issue. At least part of problem, I believe, lies in framing the issue as a matter of balancing the interests of private and public institutions against the interests of individuals. We ought, instead, to recognize that privacy is both an individual and a social good, one that goes to the heart of the kind of beings we are and important to the realization of a democratic society.

Personal Privacy

Two big questions have dominated the philosophical literature on privacy: What is it and why is it valuable? Needless to say, the two questions are intertwined. Neither has been easy to answer. The term *privacy* seems to be used to refer to a wide range of social practices and domains, for example, what one does in the privacy of his or her own home, domains of life in which the government should not interfere, things about one's self that one tells only closest friends. Privacy seems, also, to overlap other concepts such as freedom or liberty, seclusion, autonomy, secrecy, controlling information about ourselves. So, privacy is a complex and, in many respects, elusive concept. A variety of arguments have been put forward to explain the value of personal privacy.

As we review several of these, it will be helpful to keep in mind a distinction between privacy as an instrumental good and privacy as an intrinsic good. When privacy is presented as being valuable because it leads to something else, then it is cast as an instrumental good. In such arguments privacy is presented as a means to an end. Its value lies in its connection to something else. On the other hand, when privacy is presented as good in itself, it is presented as of value in and of itself. As you might predict, the latter argument is harder to make for it requires showing that privacy has value even when it leads to nothing else or even when it may lead to negative consequences.

The most important arguments on behalf of privacy as an instrumental good have focused either on its being necessary for special relationships or on its being necessary for democracy. Charles Fried (1968), for example, argued that we have to have privacy in order to have relationships of intimacy and trust. In a society in which individuals were always being observed (as in the panopticon), he argued, friendship, intimacy, and trust could not develop. If we want such relationships, we must create domains of privacy. Others argue that privacy is necessary for democracy. Here the important idea is that if individuals are constantly being observed, they will not be able to exercise the kind of independent thinking that is essential for democracy to work.

The arguments on behalf of privacy as an instrumental good begin to cross over into privacy as an intrinsic good when they suggest a connection between privacy and autonomy. . . . Autonomy is not just one among many values; autonomy is fundamental to what it means to be human, to our value as human beings. If privacy is essential to autonomy, then the loss of privacy would be a threat to our most fundamental values. But the connection between privacy and autonomy is often presented not exactly as a means-ends relationship. Rather the suggestion is that autonomy is inconceivable without privacy.

It will take us too far afield to explore all of these arguments. In what follows, I am going to explore several of the most salient arguments on behalf of privacy, and I will move from a focus on privacy as an individual good to privacy as a *social good.*

Information Mediates Relationships

To begin with what seems most clear, information about an individual seems to be a fundamental pre-condition for establishing a relationship with that individual. Moreover, the information determines the character of the relationship. James Rachels (1975) has argued that people need to control information about themselves in order to maintain a diversity of relationships. His insight is that individuals maintain a variety of relationships, e.g., with parents, spouses, employers, friends, casual acquaintances, and so on, and each of these relationships is different because of the different information that each party has. Think, for example, about what your best friend knows about you as compared with what your teacher, your employer, or your dentist knows about you. These diverse relationships are a function of differing information.

Take your relationship with your dentist. Suppose she has been your dentist for five years but she knows relatively little about you, except, of course, for what she knows about your teeth. Now suppose you need extensive work done on your teeth, and you begin to go to her office regularly at a time of the day when she is not rushed. You strike up conversations about your various interests. Each time you talk to her, she learns more about you and you learn more about her. Suppose you discover you have several hobbies and sports interests in common. She suggests that if you schedule your appointment next week so you are her last appointment, you could go out and play tennis afterwards. The story can go on about how this relationship might develop from one of patient-professional, to good friends, perhaps to one of intimate friends. The changes in the relationship will in large measure be a function of the amount and kind of information you acquire about one another.

Rachels uses this insight to argue that privacy is important because it allows us to maintain a diversity of relationships. If everything were open to all (that is, if everyone knew the same things about you), then diversity would not be possible. You would have similar relationships with everyone.

Rachels seems right about the way information affects relationships. We control relationships by controlling the information that others have about us. When we lose control over information, we lose significant control over how others perceive and treat us. However, while Rachels seems right about this, his analysis does not quite get at what is worrisome about all the information gathering that is facilitated by computer technology. That is, the information gathering and exchange that goes on via computer technology does not seem, on the face of it, to threaten the diversity of personal relationships each of us has. For example, despite the fact that huge quantities of data now exist about my purchases, phone calls, medical condition, work history, etc., I am able to maintain a diversity of personal relationships. Rachels seems slightly off target in putting the emphasis on the diversity of relationships, rather than simply on the loss of control of relationships that comes with loss of control of information. Perhaps, this is not surprising given that Rachels focused on personal relationships rather than relationships between individuals and organizations.

What happens when you lose control of information is better thought of on the model of an everyday case in which gossip generates some (false) information about you and the information is spread from one person to another. You are interested in being viewed and treated in a certain way and you know the information (true or false) will affect the way people see you and treat you. Once the information begins to move from person to person, you have no way of knowing who has heard it. If it is false information, you have no way contacting everyone and correcting their repository of information about you. Even if the information is true, there may be individuals that will treat you unfairly on the basis of this information and yet since you don't know who has it, you can't protect yourself. So, loss of control of information reduces your ability to establish and influence the relationships you have and the character of those relationships.

Individual-Organization Relationships

In trying to understand the threat to privacy posed by the new type and scale of personal information gathering made possible by computer technology, the relationships most at issue are those between *individuals and formal organizations.*[2] In these relationships what is important to the individual is that the individual have some power or control in establishing or shaping the relationship (not that he or she has a diversity of such relationships). Information about us is what allows an organization such as a marketing firm, a credit card company, or a law enforcement agency to establish a relationship with us. And, information determines how we are treated in that relationship. One is sent an offer to sign up for a credit card when the credit card company gets your name and address and finds out how much you earn and/or own. How much credit is extended depends on the information. Similarly, a relationship between you and your local police force is created when the police force receives information about you; the nature of the relationship depends on the information received.

Currently, organizations may establish (or try to establish) a relationship with you without any action on your part. That is, you may subscribe to a magazine or open a bank account and establish a relationship with one organization, but when that organization sells information about you, another organization creates a file on you and begins to evaluate you for their purposes.

As an aside, let me point out that the twentieth century was a period of enormous growth in the size of public and private organizations (facilitated in part by the development of computer and information technology). This growth is likely to continue in the twenty-first century on a global scale. What this trend means is that instead of interacting with small, local, family-owned businesses wherein one might know or come to know the decision makers personally, most of us now (and in the future will) interact mostly with large national or international organizations operating with complex rules and regulations. Indeed, it is often a computer that makes the decision about our credit line or loan application. We may shop at grocery stores, department stores, or franchises that are local units of national companies. We may purchase items from catalogues or on the Internet and have no idea where the offices of the company are located. We may deal with banks that are national or international, go to large impersonal agencies for government services such as driver's licenses or building permits, attend colleges of 2,000 to 40,000 students, and so on. While our dealings with these organizations may have the most powerful effects on our lives, we may know little about these organizations and the people who own or manage them. Yet they will have (or have access to) an enormous amount of information about us—be it accurate or relevant. And unless we make an exerted effort, we are not likely to know what information they have about us and upon which they will make decisions.

Everything that I have said here was recognized in the 1977 report of the Privacy Protection Study Commission when computer technology was in its early stages of development (i.e., when record-keeping practices were relatively primitive as compared with today's practices). Contrasting face-to-face relationships with relationships to record-keeping organizations, the report explains:

> What two people divulge about themselves when they meet for the first time depends on how much personal revelation they believe the situation warrants and how much confidence each has that the other will not misinterpret or misuse what is said. If they meet again, and particularly if they develop a relationship, their self-revelation may expand both in scope and detail. All the while, however, each is in a position to correct any misrepresentation that may develop and to judge whether the other is likely to misuse the personal revelations or pass them on to others without asking permission. Should either suspect that the other has violated the trust on which the candor of their communication depends, he can sever the relationship altogether, or alter its terms, perhaps by refusing thereafter to discuss certain topics or to reveal certain details about himself. Face-to-face encounters of this type, and the human relationships that result from them, are the threads from which the fabric of society is woven. The situations in which they arise are inherently social, not private, in that the disclosure of information about oneself is expected.

> An individual's relationship with a record-keeping organization has some of the features of his face-to-face relationships with other individuals. It, too, arises in an inherently social context, depends on the individual's willingness to divulge information about himself or to allow others to do so, and often carries some expectation as to its practical consequences. Beyond that, however, the resemblance quickly fades.

By and large it is the organization's sole prerogative to decide what information the individual shall divulge for its records or allow others to divulge about him and the pace at which he must divulge it. If the record-keeping organization is a private-sector one, the individual theoretically can take his business elsewhere if he objects to the divulgences required of him. Yet in a society in which time is often at a premium, in which organizations performing similar functions tend to ask similar questions, and in which organizational record-keeping practices and the differences among them are poorly perceived or understood, the individual often has little real opportunity to pick and choose. Moreover, if the record-keeping organization is a public-sector one, the individual may have no alternative but to yield whatever information is demanded of him.

So, private and public organizations are powerful actors in the everyday lives of most individuals in our society, and yet it would seem that individuals have very little power in those relationships. One major factor making this possible is that these organizations can acquire, use, and exchange information about us, without our knowledge or consent.

To summarize: individuals control what relationships they have and the nature of those relationships by controlling the flow of information to those others; when individuals have no control over information that others have about them, there is a significant reduction in their autonomy.

Now, while this seems a powerful argument, as I mentioned earlier, it has not "won the day" in public policy debates. Part of the reason is historical and political. While I will not go into detail, it is worth noting that in the late 1970s when major privacy legislation was being contemplated, American lawmakers adopted an approach that (1) emphasized protection from government record-keeping, leaving private organizations to self regulate with an informal code of fair information practices, and (2) was piecemeal rather than comprehensive. That is, each domain of activity has its own legislation. At a critical point in legislative history, lawmakers let go of the idea of a privacy protection commission which would have monitored database creation and use. Instead, we have separate legislation protecting our credit records, our educational records, and so on for medical records, video rentals, employment records, and so on.

Privacy legislation will be discussed more later; for now, the important point is that the American approach has been piecemeal. Within each domain, when the issue is framed as a trade-off between a social good to be achieved information gathering versus a loss of control of information by individuals, the trade-off seems worth making. Better law enforcement seems to justify giving up some control of information about ourselves. A reduction in the number of loan defaults which may lead to lower costs of borrowing may seem worth giving more information to credit agencies. Less expensive government (reduced taxes) may seem to justify allowing the government to sell information from our drivers' licenses. And so on.

REFRAMING THE COMPUTERS AND PRIVACY ISSUE—PRIVACY AS A SOCIAL GOOD

A major part of the problem seems to come from the combination of taking a piecemeal approach and then framing the computers and privacy issue as one involving a trade-off between social goods, such as law enforcement and government efficiency, and the interests of individuals in controlling information about themselves. Instead thinking comprehensively about what record-keeping and exchange practices would be best for our society, the problem has been framed as one in which interests are pitted against one another and, oddly, business and government seem to be pitted against individuals. This is odd when one remembers that ultimately business and government are justified in terms of their service to individuals as consumers and citizens.

In her 1995 book, *Legislating Privacy*, Priscilla M. Regan examined three privacy policy debates that took place in the U.S. in recent years, information privacy, communications privacy, and psychological privacy. She concludes that when individual privacy is pitted against social goods such as law enforcement or government efficiency, personal privacy loses. Regan suggests that privacy should be seen not as an individual good but rather as a social good. As an important social good, privacy would be on par with other social goods such as law enforcement or government efficiency. Instead of a social good outweighing an individual good, it would be clear that we have two social goods at stake. In reframing the issue in this way, privacy would be more likely to be treated as equally important, if not more important, than other social goods.

How, then, can the case be made for privacy as a social good? Earlier I argued that loss of control of information about us significantly reduces our autonomy — our power in relationships with formal organizations. Now I want to push this line of thinking even further. Instead of emphasizing loss of control, however, I want to return to the idea of the panopticon. If most everything that we do is recorded, then it would seem that the world that we live in is fundamentally changed from the world that existed in the past. And with this change comes an extremely important loss of freedom. One is unable to go places or do things without a record being created. The act of making a phone call is now the act of making a phone call *and* creating a record. One no longer has the option of making a phone call and not creating a record. If I no longer have the choice to make a phone call without creating a record, I have lost a degree of freedom. The loss of this freedom might be justified if one were in prison after having been fairly prosecuted and found guilty. But it hardly seems justified if you have done nothing wrong.

Even more important are the changes that take place in individuals as a result of constant surveillance. When a person is being watched, he or she tends to take on the perspective of the observer. When you know that decisions will be made about you on the basis of your activities (e.g., your educational records, work records, political activities, criminal activities), you think about that fact before you act. You take on the view of the private and public institutions that will make decisions about you. This can have a powerful effect on both on how individuals behave and on how they see themselves. Individuals may come more and more to view themselves as they are viewed by those who watch them.

You may think this is a good thing insofar as it means more social control and perhaps fewer crimes, fewer loan defaults, people working harder, and so on. The consequences of this kind of social control are, however, insidious. For one thing, it means that formal organizations exert an enormous amount of social control that may or may not be justified. Individuals may be inhibited about what they buy at the grocery store when they learn that their purchases are being recorded and analyzed. Remember that freedom is one of the most fundamental aspects of democracy. Yet freedom is eroded (or at least threatened) when every move is recorded. The result may be individuals who are ill-equipped to live in a democracy.

Consider how Jeffrey Reiman (1995), drawing on other authors, describes the situation:

> To the extent that a person experiences himself as subject to public observation, he naturally experiences himself as subject to public review. As a consequence, he will tend to act in ways that are publicly acceptable. People who are shaped to act in ways that are publicly acceptable will tend to act in safe ways, to hold and express and manifest the most widely-accepted views, indeed, the lowest-common denominator of conventionality.... Trained by society to act conventionally at all times, people will come so to think and so to feel.... As the inner life that is subject to social convention grows, the still deeper inner life that is separate from social convention contracts and, given little opportunity to develop, remains primitive.... You lose both the practice of making your own sense out of the your deepest and most puzzling longings, and the potential for self-discovery and creativity that lurk within a rich inner life.... To say that people who suffer this loss will be easy to oppress doesn't say enough. They won't have to be oppressed, since there won't be anything in them that is tempted to drift from the beaten path (pp. 27–44).

The idea of democracy is the idea of citizens having the freedom to exercise their autonomy and in so doing to develop their capacities and to do things that have not been thought of and to be critical. All of this makes for a citizenship that is active and by their contributions pushing their world forward progressively. But if the consequences of trying something new, expressing a new idea, acting unconventionally are too negative, then there is no doubt that few citizens will take the risks. Democracy will diminish.

When the argument for privacy is framed in this way, privacy is shown to be something which is not just an individual good which can be diminished for the sake of a social good; rather it is shown to be a social good in its own right and more important than efficiency and better consumer services.

Possible Counterarguments

The case for privacy seems powerful and suggests that there are serious dangers with the amount and kind of data gathering that now goes on in the U.S. However, before we turn our attention to privacy legislation, some readers may still not be convinced that there is much of a problem. Let's consider what the skeptics might say to the analysis of privacy I just presented.

1. Someone might argue that the situation is not so bad, that individuals who have done nothing wrong, have nothing to fear. If you haven't broken the law, if you are doing a good job at work, if you are paying your bills, and so on, then you have nothing to worry about. This argument might even go as far as to say that privacy only protects people who have something to hide.

Unfortunately, this argument does not work on several grounds. First, erroneous information can dramatically affect your life. Suppose you are traveling away from your home and the police begin chasing your car. They point guns and rifles at you and force you to get out of your car. They frisk you. If you panic and respond suspiciously, you could be beaten or killed. The police officers believe you are driving a stolen vehicle and disregard your explanation and evidence that the car is *yours,* that it *had* been stolen, but was found last week and returned to you by the police in the city where you live. When you reported the car stolen, the information was put into a database available to patrol cars in several bordering states. Evidently, however, the information that the car was found never made its way into the database. It takes these police officers a day to confirm the error, while you are sitting in jail. Even though you have done nothing wrong, you have been harmed as a result of inaccurate information in a database. So, it is not true to say that as long as you have done nothing wrong, you have nothing to worry about.

Second, organizations, be they private or public, corporations, nonprofits or government, can use criteria in their decision making that are inappropriate and discriminatory. Imagine databases containing information about the race, religion, ethnic background, or political affiliations of individuals. Such databases could be sold to decision makers and used by them even though the information is irrelevant and often illegal for decision makers to use. As a result, you, who have done nothing wrong, could be turned down for insurance, for a job, not given a loan, and so on.

Finally, remember the subtle change in the behavior of individuals when they know they are being watched. Social pressure leads to conformity and when information on all your activities is being gathered, the pressure to conform is great. Remember also that some of the most important progressive changes that have shaped our society (from the American Revolution, to women's suffrage, to civil rights legislation), have been led by individuals who were willing to non-conform. The less privacy we have, the harder it will be to bring about social change.

So, the computers and personal privacy issue cannot be written off as only of concern to those who have something to hide. The way in which personal information is gathered, exchanged, and used in our society affects all of us.

2. A second possible counter to the account of personal privacy given above is to argue that individuals in our society do have some power to control their relationships with private and public organizations. Many individuals, it might be argued, have simply opted to give up their privacy. After all, each of us could refuse to give out information about ourselves.

This argument contains an ounce of truth, but hides a much more complicated situation. In particular it hides the fact that the price of privacy in our society has become extremely high. Yes, I can choose not to use credit cards (using only cash) so that there is no information gathered about my buying activities. I can choose not to subscribe to magazines so that no company ever identifies my interests and sells my name and address to a marketing firm. I can choose not to buy a home until I have saved enough to pay for it in cash (that way I don't have to ask a bank for a mortgage loan and tell them all the facts about my financial standing). I can choose to pay for all my medical care myself to afford records being created by a health insurance company. I can choose not to have an account with an Internet access provider or if I do have such an account, I could choose never to access information on the Web so that there would be no records of what I had viewed. These choices will reduce the amount of information that private organizations have about me. Notice, however, that I will have to give up a great deal; I have to pay a high price for my privacy.

When it comes to public organizations what I have to give up in order to get privacy is even more precious. Citizens are entitled to many benefits such as social security, medicare, driver's licenses, as well as having rights to due process, protection from law enforcement agencies, and so on. However, the moment I request these entitlements, information is created about me and stored in a computer. The information becomes a matter of public record. For example, in many localities when one purchases or sells property, the transaction becomes a matter of public record, and may subsequently be published in a local newspaper. Soon after I perform such a transaction I will begin to get an onslaught of telephone calls and mail offering me services appropriate to new homeowners. As well, the information may now be matched with other records on me in other government agencies. Remember also the case of the database of tenants who sued their landlords. In order to avoid my name being put into such a database, I would have to give up my right to take my landlord to court; in other words, I would have to give up participating in a process which protects my rights as a citizen.

So, while there are many things an individual can do to protect his or her personal privacy, the cost is extremely high and goes counter to the idea of living in a free society. It doesn't seem fair or accurate to argue that individuals have freely chosen to give up their privacy.

Finally, someone might still insist that we have nothing to worry about because we are protected by a wide array of legislation against abuses of information. Indeed, it may be argued that the government has decided to allow these information gathering and exchange practices to go on because it has deemed these to be in our best interests. Moreover, one could argue that we have voluntarily given up our privacy by supporting legislators who believe we prefer less privacy to better law enforcement and more efficient organizations.

This is a more complicated question because it raises the question of how information gathering practices have evolved to where they are today; and, it raises the question of whether the legislation we have today is enough. Let us now turn our attention to the legislative background of the current situation.

LEGISLATIVE BACKGROUND

How, you may ask, have we gotten here? Why is our personal privacy so poorly protected? Does it have to be this way? Is it this way in other countries? What can we do to change things? Answers to these questions are crucial to understanding what any of us should do (as citizens, consumers, or computer professionals) to bring about change. I will only be able to begin to answer these questions here.

I have already mentioned that the American approach to privacy protection has been piecemeal. We have a patchwork of legislation dealing separately with personal information in different domains or sectors. Federal laws that cover the collection and use of personal and consumer data include the Fair Credit Reporting Act (1992), the Electronic Communications Privacy

Act (1986), the Family and Educational Privacy Act (1974), the Privacy Act (1974), the Video Privacy Protection Act (1988), the Telephone Customer's Protection Act, and the Driver's Privacy Protection Act (1994) to mention a few. In addition to federal statutes, each state has its own array of laws protecting various aspects of privacy and various types of records. On the Web site of the Electronic Privacy Information Center (www. epic. org), you will find a checklist for each state indicating which type of records are protected by some for of state legislation. The list of possible privacy-related topics that a state law might address includes: arrest records, bank records, cable television, credit, criminal justice, government data banks, employment, insurance, mailing lists, medical records, polygraphing, school records, social security numbers, tax records, and more.

Up until the mid-1980s, most American statutes had been modeled after the Privacy Act of 1974 and it in turn had been modeled after the "Code of Fair Information Practices." The "Code of Fair Information Practices" was developed and recommended for implementation in the 1973 Report of the Secretary of Health, Education, and Welfare's Advisory Committee on Automated Personal Data Systems (titled "Records, Computers and the Rights of Citizens"). The Code was never made into law, but in the 1970s and early 1980s it was treated as a standard. In addition to being a model for legislation, businesses treated it as an informal standard to which they must adhere both to protect them for suits by individuals and to fend off government regulation. While the influence of the Code can still be seen in legislation, it no longer seems to be the standard.

The Code consists of five principles:

1. There must be no personal data recordkeeping system whose very existence is secret.
2. There must be a way for an individual to find out what information about him or her is in a record and how it is used.
3. There must be a way for an individual to prevent information about him or her that was obtained for one purpose from being used or made available for other purposes without his or her consent.
4. There must be a way for an individual to correct or amend a record of identifiable information about him or her.
5. Any organization creating, maintaining, using, or disseminating records of identifiable personal data must assure the reliability of the data for their intended use and must take precautions to prevent misuse of data.

As just mentioned, for the most part, these principles seem to continue to be recognized, but with several important exceptions. First, information collected for one purpose seems now routinely to be used for other purposes. Think of the fundraising scenario at the beginning of the chapter. Or think of information that is gathered on your web navigation activities. Or think of data mining. You may think of these activities as innocuous since your personal identity is not attached to this information. Still the point is that information is being gathered for purposes other than those for which it was gathered.

Another area of slippage in the intention of the Code is the right that it gives you to access to information about you in a database. While this right may exist in principle, how would an individual go about checking information about him or her? It would seem that it would be impossible to do this given the number of databases that now exist and given the extent to which information is now routinely exchanged.

GLOBAL PERSPECTIVE

In the twenty-first century information gathering and exchange is likely to take on a new scale because of the Internet. Oddly this expansion of information gathering has the potential to improve privacy protection, though it could also go the other way. Expanding use of the Internet means an powerful expansion in the scale of information gathering and exchange, but it also means that regulating and/or control of information gathering has to occur at the global level. Information about individuals will flow across national borders more and more, so that whatever approach an individual nation state takes to privacy, there will be pressure on it to harmonize its information policy with protection provided in other countries. Otherwise, individuals will have no guarantees once information is collected. So, for example, if you are a citizen of an European Union country, information about you gathered by one organization cannot be used by another. However, if the information is sent to the United States, there is no telling what will happen to it. Unless we have policies that recognize the laws of other countries or we have common policies, privacy protection is uncertain.

The European Union has developed a policy that applies to all the member-countries of the EU. It looks very much like the code of fair information practices. While it is a long document, consider the provisions in Chapter II, Section 1 entitled "Principles Relating to Data Quality."[3]

1. Member States shall provide that personal data must be:
   (a) processed fairly and lawfully;
   (b) collected for specified, explicit, and legitimate purposes and not further processed in a way incompatible with those purposes. Further processing of data for historical, statistical, or scientific purposes shall not be considered as incompatible provided that the Member States provide appropriate safeguards;
   (c) adequate, relevant, and not excessive in relation to the purposes for which they are collected and/or for which they are further processed;
   (d) accurate and, where necessary, kept up to date; every reasonable step must be taken to ensure that data which are inaccurate or incomplete, having regard to the purposes for which they were collected or for which they are further processed, are erased or rectified;
   (e) kept in a form which permits identification of data subjects for no longer than is necessary for the purposes of which the data were collected or for which they are further processed. Member States shall lay down appropriate safeguards of personal data stored for longer periods for historical, statistical or scientific use.

Privacy protection in the United States could be improved if the United States were compelled to harmonize its laws with those of the EU, but it is also possible that EU protection will give way to the U.S. model. Harmonization of privacy policies throughtout the world is a process you should watch closely in the coming years.

PROPOSALS FOR BETTER PRIVACY PROTECTION

In the remainder of this chapter, a variety of ways to bring about change will be briefly discussed. For a problem so deeply embedded in the fabric of our society, it would seem that a many-pronged approach will be necessary. Change will not be easy to bring about.

Broad Conceptual Changes and Legislative Initiatives

There are a number of broad conceptual changes that would have a powerful impact on public policy with regard to personal privacy. The first is to think of privacy as a social good at the heart of liberal democratic societies and hence to be given much more weight in the balancing of social goods. To make this shift is to move from seeing privacy as simply something individuals want for their personal protection, but not worth the cost in terms of inefficiency; to recognizing privacy's role in democracy and, hence, recognizing that it is worth what it may cost in terms of less efficient institutions.

As mentioned before, the U.S. has taken a piecemeal, ad hoc approach to information privacy with each sector being dealt with separately. Significant improvement could be had by taking a comprehensive approach and developing legislation that lays out the parameters for public and private information gathering. Such legislation should be made with an eye to global exchange of information.

Issues in the private sector are especially worrisome in the United States because they are not covered by the Constitutional tradition. Our legal notions of privacy can be traced back to two of the Amendments to the Constitution. The First Amendment addresses freedom of speech and the press, while the Fourth Amendment proscribes unreasonable search and seizure, and insures security in person, houses, papers and effects. These two amendments deal respectively with the relationship between the government and the press, and the government and the individual. Our American forefathers were concerned about protecting us from the power of government (as they should have been). They did not envision the enormous power that private organizations might have over the lives of individuals. Corporations are treated, in law, as persons in need of protection from government, rather than as powerful actors that need to be constrained in their dealings with individuals. We need to consider broad changes that would address this gap in our tradition.

We might be better served if we treated personal information as part of the infrastructure of our society. Infrastructure activities are those that facilitate commerce and affect so many aspects of our lives that they serve us better when managed outside the marketplace. We ought, at least, to explore whether we might be better served by a system in which personal information were *not* treated as a commodity to be bought and sold, but instead managed as part of a public utility. This way of thinking about information might lead us to adopt a system similar to those that have been adopted in some European countries. Sweden, for example, has a system in which a Data Inspection Board (DIB) has the responsibility for licensing all automated personal information systems in both the public and private sectors. The DIB has the authority to control the collection and dissemination of personal data and has the power to investigate complaints, to inspect information systems, and to require information from organizations. It is responsible for designing detailed rules for particular systems and users, including what information may be collected, and the uses and disclosures of this information (OTA 1986).

Computer Professionals

Computer professionals can play an important role, individually and collectively. First and foremost, individual professionals must not wash their hands of privacy issues. For example, a computer professional can point out privacy matters to clients or employers when building databases containing sensitive information. Whether or not computer professionals should refuse to build systems which they judge to be insecure is a tough question, but certainly one that ought to be considered an appropriate question for a "professional."

Individually and collectively computer professionals can inform the public and public policy makers about privacy/security issues, and they can take positions on privacy legislation as it pertains to electronic records. As mentioned in Chapter 3, computer professionals are often in the best position because of their technical expertise to evaluate the security of databases and the potential uses and abuses of information.

The original ACM Code of Professional Conduct (passed by the ACM Council in 1973) specified that: An ACM member, whenever dealing with data concerning individuals, shall always consider the principle of the individuals' privacy and seek the following:

- To minimize the data collected
- To limit authorized access to the data
- To provide proper security for the data
- To determine the required retention period of the data
- To ensure proper disposal of the data

These principles were not included in the 1992 ACM Code but they continue to be useful general guidelines for computer professionals.

One of the General Moral Imperatives of the 1992 ACM Code of Ethics and Professional Conduct is that an ACM member will "Respect the privacy of others." The Guidelines explain that: "It is the responsibility of professionals to maintain the privacy and integrity of data describing individuals. This includes taking precautions to ensure the accuracy of data, as well as protecting it from unauthorized access or accidental disclosure to inappropriate individuals."

Technology

Related to the contribution of computer professionals is the potential of technology to be developed to protect rather than erode privacy. Privacy enhancing technologies (sometimes referred to as PETs) are now being developed, though I think it is too soon to tell whether they will succeed. Computer scientists and engineers have been working on and have developed IT tools which allow one to navigate the Web with anonymity; to send email anonymously through anonymous remailers; or to detect the privacy level of Websites before one accesses them. More generally crytographic techniques are being developed with various schemes which would allow one to make various transactions such as banking, purchasing, etc. with confidentiality or to authenticate mail of various kinds.

Institutional Policies

Where no law applies or the law is unclear, private and public organizations can do a great deal to protect privacy by adopting internal policies with regard to the handling of personal information. Computer professionals working in such organizations can recommend and support such policies. For example, organizations such as banks, insurance companies, registrars' offices of universities, marketing agencies, and credit agencies should have rules for employees dealing with personal information. They ought to be impose sanctions against those who fail to comply. It is not uncommon now to hear of employees who casually reveal interesting information about individuals which they discovered while handling their records at work. Remember the case of Max Brown in the scenario at the very beginning of this chapter. Perhaps his agency should have had a policy prohibiting employees from moving personal information out of an agency computer without special authorization.

Personal Actions

As suggested above, it will not easy, and may be quite costly, for individuals to achieve a significant degree of personal privacy in our society. Gary Marx (1991) has provided a list of steps that individuals can take. His list includes the following: (1) Don't give out any more information than is necessary; (2) don't say things over a cellular or cordless phone that you would mind having overheard by strangers; (3) ask your bank to sign an agreement that it will not release information about your accounts to anyone lacking legal authorization and that in the event of legal authorization, it will contact you within two days; (4) obtain copies of your credit, health, and other records and check for accuracy and currency; (5) if you are refused credit, a job, a loan, or an apartment, ask why (there may be a file with inaccurate, incomplete, or irrelevant information); (6) remember that when you respond to telephone or door-to-door surveys, the information will go into a databank; (7) realize that when you purchase a product or service and file a warranty card or participate in a rebate program, your name may well be sold to a mailing-list company.

CONCLUSION

Privacy is, perhaps, the most important of the ethical issues surrounding information technology. I have tried to show this by making clear the importance of privacy to democratic society and the subtle ways in which our lives are changed when we are being watched. Individuals who walk through life knowing that each step creates a record which may or may not end up in a database somewhere are very different from individuals who walk through life feeling free, confident that they live in an open society in which the rules are known and fair.

Protecting personal privacy is not easy and is not likely to get easier. The most effective approach to privacy protection is a many-pronged approach. One thing is for sure, the use of electronic information on individuals is not going to diminish of its own accord. Information about individuals is extremely valuable both in the private and in the public sector. This issue is not going to go away until we do something about it.

References

Bozovic, Miran, *Jeremy Bentham: The Panopticon Writings* (London: Verso, 1995).
Forester, Tom, and Perry Morrison, *Computer Ethics: Cautionary Tales and Ethical Dilemmas in Computing* (Cambridge, MA: MIT Press, 1990).

Fried, Charles, "Privacy," *Yale Law Journal*, vol. 77 (1968), p. 477.

Marx, Gary, "Privacy and Technology," *Whole Earth Review* (winter 1991), pp. 91–95.

Rachels, James, "Why Privacy Is Important," *Philosophy and Public Affairs*, vol. 4 (summer, 1975), pp. 323–333.

Suggested Further Reading

Agre, Philip E., and Marc Rotenbert, *Technology and Privacy The New Landscape* (Cambridge, MA: MIT Press, 1997).

Bennett, Colin J., and Rebecca Grant, *Visions of Privacy, Policy Choices for the Digital Age* (Toronto, Ontario: University of Toronto Press, 1999).

De Cew, Judith Wagner, *In Pursuit of Privacy, Law, Ethics and the Rise of Technology* (Ithaca, New York: Cornell University Press, 1997).

Regan, Priscilla M., *Legislating Privacy, Technology, Social Values and Public Policy* (Chapel Hill: University of North Carolina Press, 1995).

Smith, Robert Ellis, "Compilation of State and Federal Privacy Laws," *Privacy Journal (2000)*.

Web Sites

For the Electronic Privacy Information Center, see: www. epic. org

For Privacy International, see: www. privacyinternational. org/

Notes

1. Ironically, it can work the other was as well. Sometimes, that is, changes in technology may result in data being forgotten. In other words, where paper records stored in boxes in an archive may be obtained (even with difficulty), data stored on an old computer may be much more difficult to access because the technology is obsolete.
2. Of course, information stored in databases could affect personal relationships and gossip can spread on the Internet, but most large-scale, massive databases are maintained by formal organizations who make powerful decisions about individuals.
3. For the full text of the directive, see www. privacy. org/pi/ intl_orgs/ec/ final_EU_Data_Protection.html

Chapter 6

Justice

Case Study

The Oil Rig

JOANNE B. CIULLA

This description focuses on one of the three exploratory rigs which have been drilling for several years along the coast of Angola, under contract to a major U.S. multinational oil company. All three rigs are owned and operated by a large U.S. drilling company.

The "Explorer IV" rig is a relatively small jack-up (i.e., with legs) with dimensions of approximately 200 ft. by 100 ft. which houses a crew of 150 men. The crew comprises laborers, roustabouts (unskilled laborers) and maintenance staff, and 30 expatriate workers who work as roughnecks, drillers or in administrative or technical positions. The top administrator on the Explorer IV is the "tool pusher," an American Expat, who wields almost absolute authority over matters pertaining to life on the rig.

The crew quarters on the Explorer IV were modified for operations in Angola. A second galley was installed on the lower level and cabins on the upper level were enlarged to permit a dormitory style arrangement of 16 persons per room. The lower level is the "Angolan section" of the rig, where the 120 local workers eat, sleep, and socialize during their 28-day "hitch."

The upper level houses the 30 Expats in an area equal in square footage to that of the Angolan section. The Expat section's quarters are semi-private with baths and this section boasts its own galley, game room and movie room. Although it is nowhere explicitly written, a tacit regulation exists prohibiting Angolan workers from entering the Expat section of the rig, except in emergencies. The only Angolans exempt from this regulation are those assigned to the highly valued positions of cleaning or galley staff in the Expat section. These few positions are highly valued because of the potential for receiving gifts or recovering discarded razors, etc., from the Expats.

The separation of Angolan workers from Expats is reinforced by several other rig policies. Angolan laborers travel to and from the rig by boat (an

From *Business Ethics Module*, 1990, pages 13–14, by Dr. Joanne B. Ciulla, University of Richmond. Reprinted with permission.

eighteen-hour trip) whereas the Expats are transported by helicopter. Also, medical attention is dispensed by the British R.N. throughout the day for Expats, but only during shift changes for the Angolans (except in emergencies). When there are serious injuries, the response is different for the two groups. If, for example, a finger is severed, Expats are rushed to Luanda for reconstructive surgery, whereas Angolan workers have the amputation operation performed on the rig by a medic.

Angolan workers are issued grey overalls and Expats receive red coveralls. Meals in the two galleys are vastly different; they are virtually gourmet in the Expat galley and somewhat more proletarian in the Angolan section. The caterers informed the author that the two galleys' budgets were nearly equal (despite the gross disparity in numbers served).

Communication between Expats and Angolans is notable by its absence on the Explorer IV. This is principally because none of the Expats speaks Portuguese and none of the Angolans speaks more than a few words of English. Only the chef of the Portuguese catering company speaks both English and Portuguese, and consequently, he is required to act as interpreter in all emergency situations. In the working environment, training and coordination of effort is accomplished via sign language or repetition of example.

From time to time an entourage of Angolan government officials visits the Explorer IV. These visits normally last only for an hour or so, but invariably, the officials dine with the Expats and take a brief tour of the equipment before returning to shore via helicopter. Never has an entourage expressed concern about the disparity in living conditions on the rig, nor have the officials bothered to speak with the Angolan workers. Observers comment that the officials seem disinterested in the situation of the Angolan workers, most of whom are from outside the capital city.

The rig's segregated environment is little affected by the presence of an American black. The American black is assigned to the Expat section and is, of course, permitted to partake of all Expat privileges. Nevertheless, it should be noted that there are few American blacks in the international drilling business and those few are frequently less than completely welcomed into the rig's social activities.

Distributive Justice

JOHN RAWLS

We may think of a human society as a more or less self-sufficient association regulated by a common conception of justice and aimed at advancing the good of its members.[1] As a co-operative venture for mutual advantage, it is characterized by a conflict as well as an identity of interests. There is an identity of interests since social co-operation makes possible a better life for all than any would have if everyone were to try to live by his own efforts; yet

From John Rawls, "Distributive Justice," *Philosophy, Politics and Society*, 3rd series, ed. by Peter Laslett and W.G. Runcimann (Blackwell Publishers, Oxford; Barnes & Noble Books, Div. Harper & Row, Publishers, New York, 1967). Reprinted by permission of the author.

at the same time men are not indifferent as to how the greater benefits produced by their joint labours are distributed, for in order to further their own aims each prefers a larger to a lesser share. A conception of justice is a set of principles for choosing between the social arrangements which determine this division and for underwriting a consensus as to the proper distributive shares.

Now at first sight the most rational conception of justice would seem to be utilitarian. For consider: each man in realizing his own good can certainly balance his own losses against his own gains. We can impose a sacrifice on ourselves now for the sake of a greater advantage later. A man quite properly acts, as long as others are not affected, to achieve his own greatest good, to advance his ends as far as possible. Now, why should not a society act on precisely the same principle? Why is not that which is rational in the case of one man right in the case of a group of men? Surely the simplest and most direct conception of the right, and so of justice, is that of maximizing the good. This assumes a prior understanding of what is good, but we can think of the good as already given by the interests of rational individuals. Thus just as the principle of individual choice is to achieve one's greatest good, to advance so far as possible one's own system of rational desires, so the principle of social choice is to realize the greatest good (similarly defined) summed over all the members of society. We arrive at the principle of utility in a natural way: by this principle a society is rightly ordered, and hence just, when its institutions are arranged so as to realize the greatest sum of satisfactions.

The striking feature of the principle of utility is that it does not matter, except indirectly, how this sum of satisfactions is distributed among individuals, any more than it matters, except indirectly, how one man distributes his satisfactions over time. Since certain ways of distributing things affect the total sum of satisfactions, this fact must be taken into account in arranging social institutions; but according to this principle the explanation of common-sense precepts of justice and their seemingly stringent character is that they are those rules which experience shows must be strictly respected and departed from only under exceptional circumstances if the sum of advantages is to be maximized. The precepts of justice are derivative from the one end of attaining the greatest net balance of satisfactions. There is no reason in principle why the greater gains of some should not compensate for the lesser losses of others; or why the violation of the liberty of a few might not be made right by a greater good shared by many. It simply happens, at least under most conditions, that the greatest sum of advantages is not generally achieved in this way. From the standpoint of utility the strictness of common-sense notions of justice has a certain usefulness, but as a philosophical doctrine it is irrational.

If, then, we believe that as a matter of principle each member of society has an inviolability founded on justice which even the welfare of everyone else cannot override, and that a loss of freedom for some is not made right by a greater sum of satisfactions enjoyed by many, we shall have to look for another account of the principles of justice. The principle of utility is incapable of explaining the fact that in a just society the liberties of equal citizenship are taken for granted, and the rights secured by justice are not subject to political bargaining nor to the calculus of social interests. Now, the most natural alternative to the principle of utility is its traditional rival, the theory of the social contract. The aim of the contract doctrine is precisely to account for the strictness of justice by supposing that its principles arise from an agreement among free and independent persons in an original position of equality and hence reflect the integrity and equal sovereignty of the rational persons who are the contractees. Instead of supposing that a conception of right, and so a conception of justice, is simply an extension of the principle of choice for one man to society as a whole, the contract doctrine assumes that the rational individuals who belong to society must choose together, in one joint act, what is to count among them as just and unjust. They are to decide among themselves once and for all what is to be their conception of justice. This decision is thought of as being made in a suitably defined initial situation one of the significant features of which is that no one knows his position in society, nor even his place in the distribution of natural talents and abilities. The principles of justice to which all are forever bound are chosen in the absence of this sort of specific information. A veil of ignorance prevents anyone from being advantaged or disadvantaged by the contingencies of social class and fortune; and hence the bargaining problems which arise in everyday life from the possession of this knowledge do not affect the choice of principles. On the contract doctrine, then, the theory of justice, and indeed ethics itself, is part of the general theory of rational choice, a fact perfectly clear in its Kantian formulation.

Once justice is thought of as arising from an original agreement of this kind, it is evident that the principle of utility is problematical. For why should rational individuals who have a system of ends they wish to advance agree to a violation of their liberty for the sake of a greater balance of satisfactions enjoyed by others? It seems more plausible to suppose that, when situated in an original position of equal right, they would insist upon institutions which returned compensating advantages for any sacrifices required. A rational man would not accept an institution merely because it maximized the sum of advantages irrespective of its effect on his own interests. It appears, then, that the principle of utility would be rejected as a principle of justice, although we shall not try to argue this important question here. Rather, our aim is to give a brief sketch of the conception of distributive shares implicit in the principles of justice which, it seems would be chosen in the original position. The philosophical appeal of utilitarianism is that it seems to offer a single principle on the basis of which a consistent and complete conception of right can be developed. The problem is to work out a contractarian alternative in such a way that it has comparable if not all the same virtues.

In our discussion we shall make no attempt to derive the two principles of justice which we shall examine; that is, we shall not try to show that they would be chosen in the original position.[2] It must suffice that it is plausible that they would be, at least in preference to the standard forms of traditional theories. Instead we shall be mainly concerned with three questions: first, how to interpret these principles so that they define a consistent and complete conception of justice; second, whether it is possible to arrange the institutions of a constitutional democracy so that these principles are satisfied, at least approximately; and third, whether the conception of distributive shares which they define is compatible with common-sense notions of justice. The significance of these principles is that they allow for the strictness

Theory distillation

The Caring Imperative

Cave as telos

of the claims of justice; and if they can be understood so as to yield a consistent and complete conception, the contractarian alternative would seem all the more attractive.

The two principles of justice which we shall discuss may be formulated as follows: first, each person engaged in an institution or affected by it has an equal right to the most extensive liberty compatible with a like liberty for all; and second, inequalities as defined by the institutional structure or fostered by it are arbitrary unless it is reasonable to expect that they will work out to everyone's advantage and provided that the positions and offices to which they attach or from which they may be gained are open to all. These principles regulate the distributive aspects of institutions by controlling the assignment of rights and duties throughout the whole social structure, beginning with the adoption of a political constitution in accordance with which they are then to be applied to legislation. It is upon a correct choice of a basic structure of society, its fundamental system of rights and duties, that the justice of distributive shares depends.

The two principles of justice apply in the first instance to this basic structure, that is, to the main institutions of the social system and their arrangement, how they are combined together. Thus, this structure includes the political constitution and the principal economic and social institutions which together define a person's liberties and rights and affect his life-prospects, what he may expect to be and how well he may expect to fare. The intuitive idea here is that those born into the social system at different positions, say in different social classes, have varying life-prospects determined, in part, by the system of political liberties and personal rights, and by the economic and social opportunities which are made available to these positions. In this way the basic structure of society favours certain men over others, and these are the basic inequalities, the ones which affect their whole life-prospects. It is inequalities of this kind, presumably inevitable in any society, with which the two principles of justice are primarily designed to deal.

Now the second principle holds that an inequality is allowed only if there is reason to believe that the institution with the inequality, or permitting it, will work out for the advantage of every person engaged in it. In the case of the basic structure this means that all inequalities which affect life-prospects, say the inequalities of income and wealth which exist between social classes, must be to the advantage of everyone. Since the principle applies to institutions, we interpret this to mean that inequalities must be to the advantage of the representative man for each relevant social position; they should improve each such man's expectation. Here we assume that it is possible to attach to each position an expectation, and that this expectation is a function of the whole institutional structure: it can be raised and lowered by reassigning rights and duties throughout the system. Thus the expectation of any position depends upon the expectations of the others, and these in turn depend upon the pattern of rights and duties established by the basic structure. But it is not clear what is meant by saying that inequalities must be to the advantage of every representative man.... [One] ... interpretation [of what is meant by saying that inequalities must be to the advantage of every representative man] ... is to choose some social position by reference to which the pattern of expectations as a whole is to be judged, and then to maximize with respect to the expectations of this representative man consistent with the demands of equal liberty and equality of opportunity. Now, the one obvious candidate is the representative man of those who are least favoured by the system of institutional inequalities. Thus we arrive at the following idea: the basic structure of the social system affects the life-prospects of typical individuals according to their initial places in society, say the various income classes into which they are born, or depending upon certain natural attributes, as when institutions make discriminations between men and women or allow certain advantages to be gained by those with greater natural abilities. The fundamental problem of distributive justice concerns the differences in life-prospects which come about in this way. We interpret the second principle to hold that these differences are just if and only if the greater expectations of the more advantaged, when playing a part in the working of the whole social system, improve the expectations of the least advantaged. The basic structure is just throughout when the advantages of the more fortunate promote the well-being of the least fortunate, that is, when a decrease in their advantages would make the least fortunate even worse off than they are. The basic structure is perfectly just when the prospects of the least fortunate are as great as they can be.

In interpreting the second principle (or rather the first part of it which we may, for obvious reasons, refer to as the difference principle), we assume that the first principle requires a basic equal liberty for all, and that the resulting political system, when circumstances permit, is that of a constitutional democracy in some form. There must be liberty of the person and political equality as well as liberty of conscience and freedom of thought. There is one class of equal citizens which defines a common status for all. We also assume that there is equality of opportunity and a fair competition for the available positions on the basis of reasonable qualifications. Now, given this background, the differences to be justified are the various economic and social inequalities in the basic structure which must inevitably arise in such a scheme. These are the inequalities in the distribution of income and wealth and the distinctions in social prestige and status which attach to the various positions and classes. The difference principle says that these inequalities are just if and only if they are part of a larger system in which they work out to the advantage of the most unfortunate representative man. The just distributive shares determined by the basic structure are those specified by this constrained maximum principle.

Thus, consider the chief problem of distributive justice, that concerning the distribution of wealth as it affects the life-prospects of those starting out in the various income groups. These income classes define the relevant representative men from which the social system is to be judged. Now, a son of a member of the entrepreneurial class (in a capitalist society) has a better prospect than that of the son of an unskilled labourer. This will be true, it seems, even when the social injustices which presently exist are removed and the two men are of equal talent and ability; the inequality cannot be done away with as long as something like the family is maintained. What, then, can justify this inequality in life-prospects? According to the second principle it is justified only if it is to the advantage of the representative man who is worse off, in this case the representative unskilled labourer. The inequality is permissible because lowering it would, let's suppose, make the working man even worse off than he is. Presumably, given the principle of open offices (the second part of the second principle), the greater expectations allowed to entrepreneurs has the effect in the longer run of raising the life-prospects of the labouring class. The inequality in expectation provides an incentive so that the economy is more efficient, industrial advance proceeds at a quicker pace, and so on, the end result of which is that greater material and other benefits are distributed throughout the system. Of course, all of this is familiar, and whether true or not in particular cases, it is the sort of thing which must be argued if the inequality in income and wealth is to be acceptable by the difference principle.

We should now verify that this interpretation of the second principle gives a natural sense in which everyone may be said to be made better off. Let us suppose that inequalities are chain-connected: that is, if an inequality raises the expectations of the lowest position, it raises the expectations of all positions in between. For example, if the greater expectations of the representative entrepreneur raises that of the unskilled labourer, it also raises that of the semi-skilled. Let us further assume that inequalities are close-knit: that is, it is impossible to raise (or lower) the expectation of any representative man without raising (or lowering) the expectations of every other representative man, and in particular, without affecting one way or the other that of the least fortunate. There is no loose-jointedness, so to speak, in the way in which expectations depend upon one another. Now with these assumptions, everyone does benefit from an inequality which satisfies the difference principle, and the second principle as we have formulated it reads correctly. For the representative man who is better off in any pair-wise comparison gains by being allowed to have his advantage, and the man who is worse off benefits from the contribution which all inequalities make to each position below. Of course, chain-connection and close-knitness may not obtain; but in this case those who are better off should not have a veto over the advantages available for the least advantaged. The stricter interpretation of the difference principle should be followed, and all inequalities should be arranged for the advantage of the most unfortunate even if some inequalities are not to the advantage of those in middle positions. Should these conditions fail, then, the second principle would have to be stated in another way.

It may be observed that the difference principle represents, in effect, an original agreement to share in the benefits of the distribution of natural talents and abilities, whatever this distribution turns out to be, in order to alleviate as far as possible the arbitrary handicaps resulting from our initial starting places in society. Those who have been favoured by nature, whoever they are, may gain from their good fortune only on terms that improve the well-being of those who have lost out. The naturally advantaged are not to gain simply because they are more gifted, but only to cover the costs of training and cultivating their endowments and for putting them to use in a way which improved the position of the less fortunate. We are led to the difference principle if we wish to arrange the basic social structure so that no one gains (or loses) from his luck in the natural lottery of talent and ability, or from his initial place in society, without giving (or receiving) compensating advantages in return. (The parties in the original position are not said to be attracted by this idea and so agree to it; rather, given the symmetries of their situation, and particularly their lack of knowledge, and so on, they will find it to their interest to agree to a principle which can be understood in this way.) And we should note also that when the difference principle is perfectly satisfied, the basic structure is optimal by the efficiency principle. There is no way to make anyone better off without making someone worse off, namely, the least fortunate representative man. Thus the two principles of justice define distributive shares in a way compatible with efficiency, at least as long as we move on this highly abstract level. If we want to say (as we do, although it cannot be argued here) that the demands of justice have an absolute weight with respect to efficiency, this claim may seem less paradoxical when it is kept in mind that perfectly just institutions are also efficient.

Our second question is whether it is possible to arrange the institutions of a constitutional democracy so that the two principles of justice are satisfied, at least approximately. We shall try to show that this can be done provided the government regulates a free economy in a certain way. More fully, if law and government act effectively to keep markets competitive, resources fully employed, property and wealth widely distributed over time, and to maintain the appropriate social minimum, then if there is equality of opportunity underwritten by education for all, the resulting distribution will be just. Of course, all of these arrangements and policies are familiar. The only novelty in the following remarks, if there is any novelty at all, is that this framework of institutions can be made to satisfy the difference principle. To argue this, we must sketch the relations of these institutions and how they work together.

First of all, we assume that the basic social structure is controlled by a just constitution which secures the various liberties of equal citizenship. Thus the legal order is administered in accordance with the principle of legality, and liberty of conscience and freedom of thought are taken for granted. The political process is conducted, so far as possible, as a just procedure for choosing between governments and for enacting just legislation. From the standpoint of distributive justice, it is also essential that there be equality of opportunity in several senses. Thus, we suppose that, in addition to maintaining the usual social overhead capital, government provides for equal educational opportunities for all either by subsidizing private schools or by operating a public school system. It also enforces and underwrites equality of opportunity in commercial ventures and in the free choice of occupation. This result is achieved by policing business behaviour and by preventing the establishment of barriers and restriction to the desirable positions and markets. Lastly, there is a guarantee of a social minimum which the government meets by family allowances and special payments in times of unemployment, or by a negative income tax.

In maintaining this system of institutions the government may be thought of as divided into four branches. Each branch is represented by various agencies (or activities thereof) charged with preserving certain social and economic conditions. These branches do not necessarily overlap with the usual organization of government, but should be understood as purely conceptual. Thus the allocation branch is to keep the economy feasibly competitive, that is, to prevent the formation of unreasonable market power. Markets are competitive in this sense when they cannot be made more so consistent with the requirements of efficiency and the acceptance of the facts of consumer preferences and geography. The allocation branch is also charged with identifying and correcting, say by suitable taxes and subsidies wherever possible, the more obvious departures from efficiency caused by the failure of prices to measure accurately social benefits and costs. The stabilization branch strives to maintain reasonably full employment so that there is no waste through failure to use resources and the free choice of occupation and the deployment of finance is supported by strong effective demand. These two branches together are to preserve the efficiency of the market economy generally. *transfer branch*

The social minimum is established through the operations of the transfer branch. Later on we shall consider at what level this minimum should be set, since this is a crucial matter; but for the moment, a few general remarks will suffice. The main idea is that the workings of the transfer branch take into account the precept of need and assign it an appropriate weight with respect to the other common-sense precepts of justice. A market economy ignores the claims of need altogether. Hence there is a division of labour between the parts of the social system as different institutions answer to different common-sense precepts. Competitive markets (properly supplemented by government operations) handle the problem of the efficient allocation of labour and resources and set a weight to the conventional precepts associated with wages and earnings (the precepts of each according to his work and experience, or responsibility and the hazards of the job, and so on), whereas the transfer branch guarantees a certain level of well-being and meets the claims of need. Thus it is obvious that the justice of distributive shares depends upon the whole social system and how it distributes total income, wages plus transfers. There is with reason strong objection to the competitive determination of total income, since this would leave out of account the claims of need and of a decent standard of life. From the standpoint of the original position it is clearly rational to insure oneself against these contingencies. But now, if the appropriate minimum is provided by transfers, it may be perfectly fair that the other part of total income is competitively determined. Moreover, this way of dealing with the claims of need is doubtless more efficient, at least from a theoretical point of view, than trying to regulate prices by minimum wage standards and so on. It is preferable to handle these claims by a separate branch which supports a social minimum. Henceforth, in considering whether the second principle of justice is satisfied, the answer turns on whether the total income of the least advantaged, that is, wages plus transfers, is such as to maximize their long-term expectations consistent with the demands of liberty.

Finally, the distribution branch is to preserve an approximately just distribution of income and wealth over time by affecting the background conditions of the market from period to period. Two aspects of this branch may be distinguished. First of all, it operates a system of inheritance and gift taxes. The aim of these levies is not to raise revenue, but gradually and continually to correct the distribution of wealth and to prevent the concentrations of power to the detriment of liberty and equality of opportunity. It is perfectly true, as some have said,[3] that unequal inheritance of wealth is no more inherently unjust than unequal inheritance of intelligence; as far as possible the inequalities founded on either should satisfy the difference principle. Thus, the inheritance of greater wealth is just as long as it is to the advantage of the worst off and consistent with liberty, including equality of opportunity. Now by the latter we do not mean, of course, the equality of expectations between classes, since differences in life-prospects arising from the basic structure are inevitable, and it is precisely the aim of the second principle to say when these differences are just. Indeed, equality of opportunity is a certain set of institutions which assures equally good education and chances of culture for all and which keeps open the competition for positions on the basis of qualities reasonably related to performance, and so on. It is these institutions which are put in jeopardy when inequalities and concentrations of wealth reach a certain limit; and the taxes imposed by the distribution branch are to prevent this limit from being exceeded. Naturally enough where this limit lies is a matter for political judgment guided by theory, practical experience, and plain hunch; on this question the theory of justice has nothing to say.

The second part of the distribution branch is a scheme of taxation for raising revenue to cover the costs of public goods, to make transfer payments, and the like. This scheme belongs to the distribution branch since the burden of taxation must be justly shared. Although we cannot examine the legal and economic complications involved, there are several points in favour of proportional expenditure taxes as part of an ideally just arrangement. For one thing, they are preferable to income taxes at the level of common-sense precepts of justice, since they impose a levy according to how much a man takes out of the common store of goods and not according to how much he contributes (assuming that income is fairly earned in return for productive efforts). On the other hand, proportional taxes treat everyone in a clearly defined uniform way (again assuming that income is fairly earned) and hence it is preferable to use progressive rates only when they are necessary to preserve the justice of the system as a whole, that is, to prevent large fortunes hazardous to liberty and equality of opportunity, and the like. If proportional expenditure taxes should also prove more efficient, say because they interfere less with incentives, or whatever, this would make the case for them decisive provided a feasible scheme could be worked out.[4] Yet these are questions of political judgment which are not our concern; and, in any case, a proportional expenditure tax is part of an idealized scheme which we are describing. It does not follow that even steeply progressive income taxes, given the injustice of existing systems, do not improve justice and efficiency all things considered. In practice we must usually choose between unjust arrangements and then it is a matter of finding the lesser injustice.

Whatever form the distribution branch assumes, the argument for it is to be based on justice: we must hold that once it is accepted the social system as a whole—the competitive economy surrounded by a just constitutional legal framework—can be made to satisfy the principles of justice with the smallest loss in efficiency. The long-term expectations of the least advantaged are raised to the highest level consistent with the demands of equal liberty. In discussing the choice of a distribution scheme we have made no reference to the traditional criteria of taxation according to ability to pay or benefits received; nor have we mentioned any of the variants of the sacrifice principle. These standards are subordinate to the two principles of justice; once the problem is seen as that of designing a whole social system, they assume the status of secondary precepts with no more independent force than the precepts of common sense in regard to wages. To suppose otherwise is not to take a sufficiently comprehensive point of view. In setting up a just distribution branch these precepts may or may not have a place depending upon the demands of the two principles of justice when applied to the entire system. ...

The sketch of the system of institutions satisfying the two principles of justice is now complete. ...

In order ... to establish just distributive shares a just total system of institutions must be set up and impartially administered. Given a just constitution and the smooth working of the four branches of government, and so on, there exists a procedure such that the actual distribution of wealth, whatever it turns out to be, is just. It will have come about as a consequence of a just system of institutions satisfying the principles to which everyone would agree and against which no one can complain. The situation is one of pure procedural justice, since there is no independent criterion by which the outcome can be judged. Nor can we say that a particular distribution of wealth is just because it is one which could have resulted from just institutions although it has not, as this would be to allow too much. Clearly there are many distributions which may be reached by just institutions, and this is true whether we count patterns of distributions among social classes or whether we count distributions of particular goods and services among particular individuals. There are definitely many outcomes and what makes one of these just is that it has been achieved by actually carrying out a just scheme of cooperation as it is publicly understood. It is the result which has arisen when everyone receives that to which he is entitled given his and others' actions guided by their legitimate expectations and their obligations to one another. We can no more arrive at a just distribution of wealth except by working together within the framework of a just system of institutions than we can win or lose fairly without actually betting.

This account of distributive shares is simply an elaboration of the familiar idea that economic rewards will be just once a perfectly competitive price system is organized as a fair game. But in order to do this we have to begin with the choice of a social system as a whole, for the basic structure of the entire arrangement must be just. The economy must be surrounded with the appropriate framework of institutions, since even a perfectly efficient price system has no tendency to determine just distributive shares when left to itself. Not only must economic activity be regulated by a just constitution and controlled by the four branches of government, but a just saving-function must be adopted to estimate the provision to be made for future generations. ...

Notes

1. In this essay I try to work out some of the implications of the two principles of justice discussed in "Justice as Fairness," which first appeared in *The Philosophical Review*, 1958, and which is reprinted in *Philosophy, Politics and Society*, Series II eds, Peter Laslett and W.G. Runciman, Oxford, Basil Blackwell, 1962. pp. 132–57.

2. This question is discussed very briefly in "Justice as Fairness," see pp. 138–41. The intuitive idea is as follows: Given the circumstances of the original position, it is rational for a

man to choose as if he were designing a society in which his enemy is to assign him his place. Thus, in particular, given the complete lack of knowledge (which makes the choice one uncertainty), the fact that the decision involves one's life-prospects as a whole and is constrained by obligations to third parties (e.g., one's descendants) and duties to certain values (e.g., to religious truth), it is rational to be conservative and so to choose in accordance with an analogue of the maximum principle. Viewing the situation in this way, the interpretation given to the principles of justice earlier is perhaps natural enough. Moreover, it seems clear how the principle of utility can be interpreted; it is the analogue of the Laplacean principle for choice uncertainty. (For a discussion of these choice criteria, see R. D. Luce and H. Raiffa, *Games and Decisions* New York: Wiley [1957], pp. 275–98.)

3. Example F. von Hayek, *The Constitution of Liberty* (1960), p. 90 Chicago; U. of Chicago Press.

4. See N. Kaldor, *An Expenditure Tax* (1955) London: Allen & Unwin.

The Entitlement Theory

Robert Nozick

The minimal state is the most extensive state that can be justified. Any state more extensive violates people's rights. Yet many persons have put forth reasons purporting to justify a more extensive state. It is impossible within the compass of this book to examine all the reasons that have been put forth. Therefore, I shall focus upon those generally acknowledged to be most weighty and influential, to see precisely wherein they fail. In this chapter we consider the claim that a more extensive state is justified, because necessary (or the best instrument) to achieve distributive justice; . . .

The term "distributive justice" is not a neutral one. Hearing the term "distribution," most people presume that some thing or mechanism uses some principle or criterion to give out a supply of things. Into this process of distributing shares some error may have crept. So it is an open question, at least, whether redistribution should take place; whether we should do again what has already been done once, though poorly. However, we are not in the position of children who have been given portions of pie by someone who now makes last-minute adjustments to rectify careless cutting. There is no central distribution, no person or group entitled to control all the resources, jointly deciding how they are to be doled out. What each person gets, he gets from others who give to him in exchange for something, or as a gift. In a free society, diverse persons control different resources, and new holdings arise out of the voluntary exchanges and actions of persons. There is no more a distributing or distribution of shares than there is a distributing of mates in a society in which persons choose whom they shall marry. The total result is the product of many individual decisions which the different individuals involved are entitled to make. Some uses of the term "distribution," it is true, do not imply a previous distributing appropriately judged by some criteron (for example, "probability distribution"); nevertheless, despite the title of this chapter, it would be best to use a terminology that clearly is neutral. We shall speak of people's holdings; a principle of justice in holdings describes (part of) what justice tells us (requires) about holdings. I shall state first what I take to be the correct view about justice in holdings, and then turn to the discussion of alternate views.

I

THE ENTITLEMENT THEORY

The subject of justice in holdings consists of three major topics. The first is the *original acquisition of holdings*, the appropriation of unheld things. This includes the issues of how unheld things may come to be held, the process, or processes, by which unheld things may come to be held, the things that may come to be held by these processes, the extent of what comes to be held by a particular process, and so on. We shall refer to the complicated truth about this topic, which we shall not formulate here, as the principle of justice in acquisition. The second topic concerns the *transfer of holdings* from one person to another. By what processes may a person transfer holdings to another? How may a person acquire a holding from another who holds it? Under this topic come general descriptions of voluntary exchange, and gift and (on the other hand) fraud, as well as reference to particular conventional details fixed upon in a given society. The complicated truth about this subject (with placeholders for conventional details) we shall call the principle of justice in transfer. (And we shall suppose it also includes principles governing how a person may divest himself of a holding, passing it into an unheld state.)

If the world were wholly just, the following inductive definition would exhaustively cover the subject of justice in holdings.

1. A person who acquires a holding in accordance with the principle of justice in acquisition is entitled to that holding.
2. A person who acquires a holding in accordance with the principle of justice in transfer, from someone else entitled to the holding, is entitled to the holding.
3. No one is entitled to a holding except by (repeated) applications of 1 and 2.

The complete principle of distributive justice would say simply that a distribution is just if everyone is entitled to the holdings they possess under the distribution.

A distribution is just if it arises from another just distribution by legitimate means. The legitimate means of moving from one distribution to another are specified by the principle of justice in transfer. The legitimate first "moves" are specified by the principle of justice in acquisition.[1] Whatever arises from a just situation by just steps is itself just. The means of change specified by the principle of justice in transfer preserve justice. As correct rules of inference are truth-preserving, and any conclusion deduced via repeated application of such rules from only true premises is itself true, so the means of transition from one situation to another specified by the principle of justice in transfer are justice-preserving, and any situation actually arising from repeated transitions in accordance with the principle from a just situation is itself just. The parallel between justice-preserving transformations and truth-preserving transformations illuminates where it fails as well as where it holds. That a conclusion could have been deduced by truth-preserving means from premises that are true suffices to show its truth. That from a just situation a situation could have arisen via justice-preserving means does not suffice to show its justice. The fact that a thief's victims voluntarily could have presented him with gifts does not entitle the thief to his ill-gotten gains. Justice in holdings is historical; it depends upon what actually has happened. We shall return to this point later.

Not all actual situations are generated in accordance with the two principles of justice in holdings: the principle of justice in acquisition and the principle of justice in transfer. Some people steal from others, or defraud them, or enslave them, seizing their product and preventing them from living as they choose, or forcibly exclude others from competing in exchanges. None of these are permissible modes of transition from one situation to another. And some persons acquire holdings by means not sanctioned by the principle of justice in acquisition. The existence of past injustice (previous violations of the first two principles of justice in holdings) raises the third major topic under justice in holdings: the rectification of injustice in holdings. If past injustice has shaped present holdings in various ways, some identifiable and some not, what now, if anything, ought to be done to rectify these injustices? What obligations do the performers of injustice have toward those whose position is worse than it would have been had the injustice not been done? Or, than it would have been had compensation been paid promptly? How, if at all, do things change if the beneficiaries and those made worse off are not the direct parties in the act of injustice, but, for example, their descendants? Is an injustice done to someone whose holding was itself based upon an unrectified injustice? How far back must one go in wiping clean the historical slate of injustices? What may victims of injustice permissibly do in order to rectify the injustices being done to them, including the many injustices done by persons acting through their government? I do not know of a thorough or theoretically sophisticated treatment of such issues. Idealizing greatly, let us suppose theoretical investigation will produce a principle of rectification. This principle uses historical information about previous situations and injustices done in them (as defined by the first two principles of justice and rights against interference), and information about the actual course of events that flowed from these injustices, until the present, and it yields a description (or descriptions) of holdings in the society. The principle of rectification presumably will make use of its best estimate of subjunctive information about what would have occurred (or a probability distribution over what might have occurred, using the expected value) if the injustice had not taken place. If the actual description of holdings turns out not to be one of the descriptions yielded by the principle, then one of the descriptions yielded must be realized.

The general outlines of the theory of justice in holdings are that the holdings of a person are just if he is entitled to them by the principles of justice in acquisition and transfer, or by the principle of rectification of injustice (as specified by the first two principles). If each person's holdings are just, then the total set (distribution) of holdings is just. To turn these general outlines into a specific theory we would have to specify the details of each of the three principles of justice in holdings: the principle of acquisition of holdings, the principle of transfer of holdings, and the principle of rectification of violations of the first two principles. I shall not attempt that task here....

HISTORICAL PRINCIPLES AND END-RESULT PRINCIPLES

The general outlines of the entitlement theory illuminate the nature and defects of other conceptions of distributive justice. The entitlement theory of justice in distribution is historical; whether a distribution is just depends upon how it came about. In contrast, current time-slice principles of justice hold that the justice of a distribution is determined by how things are distributed (who has what) as judged by some structural principle(s) of just distribution. A utilitarian who judges between any two distributions by seeing which has the greater sum of utility and, if the sums tie, applies some fixed equality criterion to choose the more equal distribution, would hold a current time-slice principle of justice. As would someone who had a fixed schedule of trade-offs between the sum of happiness and equality. According to a current time-slice principle, all that needs to be looked at, in judging the justice of a distribution, is who ends up with what; in comparing any two distributions one need look only at the matrix presenting the distributions. No further information need be fed into a principle of justice. It is a consequence of such principles of justice that any two structurally identical distributions are equally just. (Two distributions are structurally identical if they present the same profile, but perhaps have different persons occupying the particular slots. My having ten and your having five, and my having five and your having ten are structurally identical distributions.) Welfare economics is the theory of current time-slice principles of justice. The subject is conceived as operating on matrices representing only current information about distribution. This, as well as some of the usual conditions (for example, the choice of distribution is invariant under relabeling of columns), guarantees that welfare economics will be a current time-slice theory, with all of its inadequacies.

Most persons do not accept current time-slice principles as constituting the whole story about distributive shares. They think it relevant in assessing the justice of a situation to consider not only the distribution it embodies, but also how that distribution came about. If some persons are in prison for murder or war crimes, we do not say that to assess the justice of the distribution in the society we must look only at what this person has, and that person has, and that person has, ... at the current time. We think it relevant to ask whether someone did something so that he *deserved* to be punished, deserved to have a lower share. Most will agree to the relevance of further information with regard to punishments and penalties. Consider also desired things. One traditional socialist view is that workers are entitled to the product and full fruits of their labor; they have earned it; a distribution is unjust if it does not give the workers what they are entitled to. Such entitlements are based upon some past history. No socialist holding this view would find it comforting to be told that because the actual distribution A happens to coincide structurally with the one he desires D, A therefore is no less just than D; it differs only in that the "parasitic" owners of capital receive under A what the workers are entitled to under D, and the workers receive under A what the owners are entitled to under D, namely very little. This socialist rightly, in my view, holds onto the notions of earning, producing, entitlement, desert, and so forth, and he rejects current time-slice principles that look only to the structure of the resulting set of holdings. (The set of holdings resulting from what? Isn't it implausible that how holdings are produced and come to exist has no effect at all on who should hold what?) His mistake lies in his view of what entitlements arise out of what sorts of productive processes.

We construe the position we discuss too narrowly by speaking of current time-slice principles. Nothing is changed if structural principles operate upon a time sequence of current time-slice profiles and, for example, give someone more now to counterbalance the less he has had earlier. A utilitarian or an egalitarian or any mixture of the two over time will inherit the difficulties of his more myopic comrades. He is not helped by the fact that some of the information others consider relevant in assessing a distribution is reflected, unrecoverably, in past matrices. Henceforth, we shall refer to such unhistorical principles of distributive justice, including the current time-slice principles, as end-result principles or end-state principles.

In contrast to end-result principles of justice, historical principles of justice hold that past circumstances or actions of people can create differential entitlements or differential deserts to things. An injustice can be worked by moving from one distribution to another structurally identical one, for the second, in profile the same, may violate people's entitlements or deserts; it may not fit the actual history.

HOW LIBERTY UPSETS PATTERNS

It is not clear how those holding alternative conceptions of distributive justice can reject the entitlement conception of justice in holdings. For suppose a distribution favored by one of these nonentitlement conceptions is realized. Let us suppose it is your favorite one and let us call this distribution D_1; perhaps everyone has an equal share, perhaps shares vary in accordance with some dimension you treasure. Now suppose that Wilt Chamberlain is greatly in demand by basketball teams, being a great gate attraction. (Also suppose contracts run only for a year, with players being free agents.) He signs the following sort of contract with a team: In each home game, twenty-five cents from the price of each ticket of admission goes to him. (We ignore the question of whether he is "gouging" the owners, letting them look out for themselves.) The season starts, and people cheerfully attend his team's games; they buy their tickets, each time dropping a separate twenty-five cents of their admission price into a special box with Chamberlain's name on it. They are excited about seeing him play; it is worth the total admission price to them. Let us suppose that in one season one million persons attend his home games, and Wilt Chamberlain winds up with $250,000, a much larger sum than the average income and larger even than anyone else has. Is he entitled to this income? Is this new distribution D_2, unjust? If so, why? There is *no* question about whether each of the people was entitled to the control over the resources they held in D_1; because that was the distribution (your favorite) that (for the purposes of argument) we assumed was acceptable. Each of these persons chose to give twenty-five cents of their money to Chamberlain. They could have spent it on going to the movies, or on candy bars, or on copies of *Dissent* magazine, or of *Monthly Review*. But they all, at least one million of them, converged on giving it to Wilt Chamberlain in exchange for watching him play basketball. If D_1 was a just distribution, and people voluntarily moved from it to D_2, transferring parts of their shares they were given under D_1 (what was it for if not to do something with?), isn't D_2 also just? If the people were entitled to dispose of the resources to which they were entitled (under D_1), didn't this include their being entitled to give it to, or exchange it with, Wilt Chamberlain? Can anyone else complain on grounds of justice? Each other person already has his legitimate share under D_1. Under D_1, there is nothing that anyone has that anyone else has a claim of justice against. After someone transfers something to Wilt Chamberlain, third parties still have their legitimate shares; their shares are not changed. By what process could such a transfer among two persons give rise to a legitimate claim of distributive justice on a portion of what was transferred, by a third party who had no claim of justice on any holding of the others before the transfer? To cut off objections irrelevant here, we might imagine the exchanges occurring in a socialist society, after hours. After playing whatever basketball he does in his daily work, or doing whatever other daily work he does, Wilt Chamberlain decides to put in overtime to earn additional money. (First his work quota is set; he works time over that.) Or imagine it is a skilled juggler people like to see, who puts on shows after hours.

Why might someone work overtime in a society in which it is assumed their needs are satisfied? Perhaps because they care about things other than needs. I like to write in books that I read, and to have easy access to books for browsing at odd hours. It would be very pleasant and convenient to have the resources of Widener Library in my back yard. No society, I assume, will provide such resources close to each person who would like them as part of his regular allotment (under D_1). Thus, persons either must do without some extra things that they want, or be allowed to do something extra to get some of these things. On what basis could the inequalities that would eventuate be forbidden? Notice also that small factories would spring up in a socialist society, unless forbidden. I melt down some of my personal possessions (under D_1) and build a machine out of the material. I offer you, and others, a philosophy lecture once a week in exchange for your cranking the handle on my machine, whose products I exchange for yet other things, and so on. (The raw materials used by the machine are given to me by others who possess them under D_1, in exchange for hearing lectures.) Each person might participate to gain things over and above their allotment under D_1. Some persons even might want to leave their job in socialist industry and work full time in this private sector. I shall say something more about these issues in the next chapter. Here I wish merely to note how private property even in means of production would occur in a socialist society that did not forbid people to use as they wished some of the resources they are given under the socialist distribution D_1. The socialist society would have to forbid capitalist acts between consenting adults.

The general point illustrated by the Wilt Chamberlain example and the example of the entrepreneur in a socialist society is that no end-state principle or distributional patterned principle of justice can be continuously realized without continuous interference with people's lives. Any favored pattern would be transformed into one unfavored by the principle, by people choosing to act in various ways; for example, by people exchanging goods and services with other people, or giving things to other people, things the transferrers are entitled to under the favored distributional pattern. To maintain a pattern one must either continually interfere to stop people from transferring resources as they wish to, or continually (or periodically) interfere to take from some persons resources that others for some reason chose to transfer to them. (But if some time limit is to be set on how long people may keep resources others voluntarily transfer to them, why let them keep these resources for any period of time? Why not have immediate confiscation?) It might be objected that all persons voluntarily will choose to refrain from actions which would upset the pattern. This presupposes unrealistically (1) that all will most want to maintain the pattern (are those who don't, to be "reeducated" or forced to undergo "self-criticism"?), (2) that each can gather enough information about his own actions and the ongoing activities of others to discover which of his actions will upset the pattern, and (3) that diverse and far-flung persons can coordinate their actions to dove-tail into the pattern. Compare the manner in which the market is neutral among persons' desires, as it reflects and transmits widely scattered information via prices, and coordinates persons' activities.

It puts things perhaps a bit too strongly to say that every patterned (or end-state) principle is liable to be thwarted by the voluntary actions of the individual parties transferring some of their shares they receive under the principle. For perhaps some very weak patterns are not so thwarted. Any distributional pattern with any egalitarian component is overturnable by the voluntary actions of individual persons over time; as is every patterned condition with sufficient content so as actually to have been proposed as presenting the central core of distributive justice. Still, given the possibility that some weak conditions or patterns may not be unstable in this way, it would be better to formulate an explicit description of the kind of interesting and contentful patterns under discussion, and to prove a theorem about their instability. Since the weaker the patterning, the more likely it is that the entitlement system itself satisfies it, a plausible conjecture is that any patterning either is unstable or is satisfied by the entitlement system.

Note

1. Applications of the principle of justice in acquisition may also occur as part of the move from one distribution to another. You may find an unheld thing now and appropriate it. Acquisitions also are to be understood as included when, to simplify, I speak only of transitions by transfers.

Corporations, Persons, and Morality

INTRODUCTION

People eat, sleep, vote, love, hate, and suffer guilt. They also go to work for, and manage, corporations that do none of these. Yet corporations are considered "persons" under the law and have many of the same rights as humans: to sue, to own property, to conduct business and conclude contracts, and to enjoy freedom of speech, of the press, and from unreasonable searches and seizures. Corporations are legal citizens of the state in which they are chartered. They even possess two rights not held by humans: unlimited longevity and limited liability. Corporations in the United States have unlimited charters, they never "die" in the ordinary sense of the term, although some companies go bankrupt, but their shareholders are liable for corporate debts only up to the extent of their personal investments. Are corporations, then, morally responsible in the ways in which people are?

CHAPTER 7: THE ROLE OF ORGANIZATIONAL VALUES

One of the most stubborn ethical issues surrounding the corporation is not what it should do, but rather how it should be understood. What is a corporation? Is it a distinct individual in its own right or merely an aggregate of individuals—for example, its stockholders, managers, and employees? The answer to this question is crucial for the understanding of corporations and their activities. We already know that individual members of a corporation can be held morally responsible. For example, if a chemical engineer intentionally puts a dangerous chemical in a new cosmetic product, he or she is morally blameworthy. But can we hold the corporation, considered as something distinct from its individual members, morally blameworthy, too? This is the issue raised by Peter French in Part I.

The very concept of a corporation seems to involve more than the individual actions of specific persons. The corporation is understood to exist even after all its original members are deceased, it is said to hire or fire *employees* when only a handful of the corporate members are involved in the decision, and it is said to have obligations through its charter that override the desires of its individual members. Let us grant that the corporation is a distinct entity whose actions are not reducible, at least in a straightforward way, to the actions of individuals. Does it follow that the corporation has moral characteristics that are not reducible to the moral characteristics of its members? Philosophers have addressed this issue by asking whether the corporation is a moral agent. Rocks, trees, and machines are clearly not moral agents. People clearly are. What are we to say about corporations?

When discussing whether corporations are moral agents, a good place to begin is with corporate legal history, that is, with the series of legislative acts and court decisions that have defined the corporation's existence. From its beginning in the Middle Ages, the corporation has been subject to differing legal interpretations. In the Middle Ages, the law did not recognize any profit-making organizations as corporations; instead, it granted corporate status only to guilds, boroughs, and the church. In some instances, the law decreed that corporations follow strict guidelines; for example, in 1279 the French Statute of Mortmain declared that a corporation's property could not exceed a specified amount. Even hundreds of years after its beginning, the corporation remained subject to strict legal sanctions on the conditions of its charter. As late as the nineteenth century, some U.S. corporations were granted charters only on the condition that they restrict land purchases to a certain geographic location and to a maximum number of acres. Thus corporations were viewed merely as artificial beings, created by the state and owing their very existence to a decree by the government.

In the latter part of the nineteenth century and in the twentieth century, especially in the United States, this view changed dramatically. Instead of treating corporations as mere creations of the state, the courts began to see them as natural outcomes of the habits of businesspersons. They saw them as the predictable results of the actions of businesspersons who, exercising their inalienable right to associate freely with others, gathered together to conduct business and pursue a profit. As such, incorporation came to be seen less as a privilege granted by the state and more as a right to be protected by the state. Chartering a corporation became easier, and government restrictions were less severe. Even so, the traditional view of a corporation continues to influence the law. The most accepted legal definition of a corporation remains the one offered by Chief Justice John Marshall in 1819: "A corporation is an artificial being, invisible, intangible, and existing only in the contemplation of law. Being the mere creation of law, it possesses only those properties which the charter of its creation confers upon it. . . ."[1]

Throughout the evolution of corporation law, the problem of whether and how to ascribe responsibility to the corporation has persisted. In the sixteenth century, the large trading corporations were not held responsible when one ship collided with another; instead, the individual boat owners, who participated in the corporation only to secure special trading rights, were held individually responsible. By the seventeenth century, the notion of corporate responsibility was thoroughly established in the law, but some sticky issues remained. Could a corporation be criminally liable? What rights, if any, did corporations share with ordinary persons? In the early twentieth century and again in recent years, U.S. corporations have been charged with homicide. One such case involved the Ford Pinto's exploding gas tank. But in every instance so far, the court has stopped short of entering a verdict of homicide, although it has been willing to impose stiff fines.

In 1978 the U.S. Supreme Court delivered a landmark verdict in the case of *First National Bank of Boston v. Bellotti.* The fundamental issue was whether a corporation should be allowed the right to free speech even when it is exercising that right by spending corporate money to promote political causes not directly related to corporate profits. Should corporations have full-fledged First Amendment rights to free speech even when that means that they can use their vast financial reserves to support partisan political ends? In a split decision, the Supreme Court decided in favor of recognizing such a right, although the decision itself remains controversial.

Whatever the courts eventually decide about the legal status of a corporation, questions about its moral status will remain. While courts have upheld corporate rights to free speech, the federal government has tried to devise ways to hold corporations accountable for wrongdoing. As the article "The 'New' U.S. Sentencing Commission Guidelines" explains in a later section, in 1991 the United States Sentencing Commission instituted guidelines to encourage corporate compliance through the institution of ethics programs, establishing codes of conduct, the installation of ombudspeople, and activities within the corporation designed to elicit appropriate managerial behavior. The idea is to encourage good corporate citizenship through internal standards of compliance. The Sentencing Guidelines pressure companies to develop standards of conduct, and they also help to protect other stakeholders and the public from corporate wrongdoing by imposing stiff financial penalties for noncompliance. In the years to follow, their effectiveness will be tested, demonstrated, and challenged.

Regardless of whether a corporation is a moral agent, it must adhere to certain norms of behavior. For example, at a minimum, a corporation must not deliberately kill or systematically harm others. But beyond specifying a bare minimum, what can one say? How can one evaluate corporate behavior from a moral perspective?

The case study, "Merck & Co., Inc." illustrates this issue. Merck is a pharmaceutical company long recognized for its commitment to the health of the customer over profits, despite the fact that Merck has been enormously successful financially. During the course of research into an unrelated product stream, Merck scientists discovered a drug that had the potential of curing a disease known as "river blindness," which affects approximately 80 million people in highly remote areas around the globe. Symptoms include severe itching, and the disease ultimately progresses to cause blindness in its victims. With the potential to dramatically improve the lives of millions, the newly discovered drug showed promise. However, people inflicted with "river blindness" did not have the resources to pay for the treatment. Should Merck proceed with its development, even if it will lose money in the process?

How are we to understand the moral responsibility of a corporation? Does it extend to funding the development and distribution of a drug that can improve the quality of human life without a profit motive? Does it extend to fighting proposed laws that the corporation opposes? In this section, we find three articles that help answer such questions. Economics Nobel Laureate Amartya Sen's article, "Does Business Ethics Make Economic Sense?," refutes the notion that ethics has no role to play in an economic system. Arguing that the eighteenth-century "father" of economics, Adam Smith, has been far too narrowly interpreted with respect to the idea that self-interest is the only necessary motivator for economic exchange, Sen reminds the reader of the role that trust, humanity, concern for others, and justice play in Smith's works. Indeed, without trust and rules governing civil behavior, an efficient economic system would not be possible. Sen further argues that the success of firms is a "social good" that benefits all members of society. In addition, firms that build and maintain a reputation for being concerned with the welfare of others may lead to favorable business performance. These two concepts—one normative and the other instrumental—are inextricably linked. According to Sen, business ethics must relate to both. Many people believe that firms simply cannot afford to be ethical. Metaphors equating business to the jungle, war, and games serve to reinforce the idea that there is no room in business activities for other-directed motives.

In his article in this section, "Can Socially Responsible Firms Survive in a Competitive Environment?" economist Robert Frank describes ways in which socially responsible firms may sometimes make more money precisely because of their social responsibility. Socially responsible firms, for example, may solve "commitment" problems with employees, customers, and other firms in a way that promotes greater efficiency. For example, an ethically responsible law firm may be able to command a higher fee from its clients simply because the firm can be trusted not to overcharge. Or, an ethical company may have more productive employees because the employees believe that the company has made a commitment to them. The employees are willing to invest their time in developing firm-specific skills (rather than developing only skills they can sell on the open market), because they trust the company to treat them sympathetically and not to fire them at the first sign of an economic downturn. In his article, Robert Frank describes five specific ways in which a socially responsible firm might prosper in a competitive environment. Lynn Sharpe Paine's article, "Managing for Organizational Integrity," suggests a comprehensive strategy for dealing with ethics in organizations. Paine contrasts an approach that relies exclusively on rules and hierarchy with one that reflects the deeper values of the organization. The values approach, she argues, is far more persuasive and successful. An overemphasis on compliance and policing ethics diminishes ethical motivation and frustrates cooperative ethical solutions.

In retelling a dramatic true-to-life episode in which he played a role, Wall Street financier Bowen McCoy attempts to establish an analogy between personal and corporate ethics. When mountain climbing in the Himalayan Mountains, McCoy and his climbing party left a Sadhu, an Indian holy man, behind in the snow in order to achieve their goal of reaching the summit. What similarities, he asks, are there between this episode and decisions facing corporate managers? Equally important, what lessons from the behavior of McCoy's climbing party extend to the corporate organization and its obligations to its stakeholders?

CHAPTER 8: VALUES AND THE VIRTUOUS MANAGER

Despite the individual managerial locus of decision making in business, it is often this individual—the individual manager—and his or her values and character that are ignored in business ethics. In an age in which techno-logical systems and complex organizational structures dominate business ac-tivity, what role can the integrity of the individual manager play? Large conglomerates, transnational corporations, and worldwide trading systems appear to mask the importance of the single businessperson, even though he or she is the final focal point of all business activities.

Frederick B. Bird and James A. Waters report on an empirical investi-gation of the use of moral language among business managers in their arti-cle, "The Moral Muteness of Managers." They conclude that while individual managers are in fact concerned with ethical issues at work—and their be-havior often follows their normative beliefs—managers rarely speak about the ethical issues they encounter at work. Reasons for this "moral muteness" include concerns over threatening the harmony in the organization, dis-rupting efficiency, and being perceived as weak and ineffective. Bird and Waters discuss several detrimental consequences of failing to talk openly about ethical dilemmas: moral amnesia (i.e., failing to learn from past mis-takes), a narrowed conception of morality, increased moral stress on man-agers as a result of role conflict and ambiguity, and a neglect of moral standards.

Robert Jackall, who decries the hypocrisy of modern management cul-ture, illustrates the view of business and business managers as being morally "mute." Jackall's research suggests that the connection between excellence of work and reward has become more capricious. The moral virtues, if they ever existed or were extolled in business, have been replaced by bureau-cratic conventions in which loyalties and alliances, patronage, luck, and the ability to outrun one's mistakes contribute to managerial success. The prob-lem is serious, writes Jackall, in that many men and women no longer see success as necessarily connected to excellence. The Protestant work ethic, characterized by self-reliance and devotion to work, has been replaced by ad-ministrative hierarchies, standardized work procedures, regularized timeta-bles, uniform policies, office politics, and centralized control. It all adds up, believes Jackall, to office political games and the capriciousness of success. The result is what Jackall calls "the bureaucratic ethic," an "ethic" that be-lies what Robert Solomon believes to be the exemplification of the Aristotelian virtues of managerial excellence (see Solomon's article, "Corporate Roles, Per-sonal Virtues: An Artistotelean Approach," in Part 1). Solomon's challenge, then, is to reformulate managerial thinking in terms of managerial and cor-porate excellence, integrity, and civic virtue so that it will avoid what Jackall de-picts as downsides to modern management and the contemporary business enterprise.

The Enron case and the ultimate collapse of that company illustrates how managers can become morally mute, especially when a company is ap-parently doing well or when jobs are on the line. And perhaps the maze of financial instruments created by Enron and in particular, the CFO, Andrew Fastow, created a system almost impossible to understand. In that circum-stance, one can imagine going along with Fastow in order to get ahead, po-litically, particularly when so much mystery surrounded these financial creations. Unfortunately, one of the major gatekeepers, the public audit firm of Arthur Andersen, allegedly abetted these schemes, and there were law firms involved as well.

As a result of Enron and a number of other corporate scandals, including WorldCom, the case we presented in Part 1, the United States Congress passed the Sarbanes-Oxley Act, a set of restrictive compliance measures to reduce or prevent corporate misdeeds. John Coffee, an expert on corporate law, analyzes these and other recent corporate misdeeds. He blames their occurrence on a number of phemomena. The increase in executive salaries and stock options that inflated executive pay pushed CEOs to inflate, if not sometimes misrepresent, corporate earnings for their own benefit. But this could not have occurred without the collusion with lawyers, auditors, consultants, and securities analysts at the large investment management firms. Shareholders, even large institutional shareholders, were ignored, and many boards did not exercise their fiduciary oversight carefully. Thus external gatekeepers whose professional duties include duties to the public and the public interest neglected those obligations. The result, Sarbanes-Oxley, Coffee believes, while placing massive restrictions on auditors and increasing the fiduciary duties of boards, is not enough to prevent future misdeeds, particularly when executive compensation continues to rise disproportionately to the salaries of other employees and corporate earnings. Coffee concludes that lawyers, up to now virtually exempt from the mandates of Sarbanes-Oxley, must reinvigorate their professional obligations to balance their duties to their clients with their professional role as gatekeepers to public interest.

CHAPTER 9: ISSUES IN EMPLOYMENT

Citing financial difficulties and an underfunded pension plan, all of which resulted in going into Chapter 11 bankruptcy, United Airlines recently cancelled its employee pension plan, turning the plan over to the U.S. government's Pension Benefit Guarantee Corporation. But the PBGC guarantees pensions only up to about $45,000 for those who are 65 and older. Many United pilots and other employees had expected pensions of double that, and indeed those were promised as part of their contracts with the airline. It turns out that only about 20 percent of all workers in the private sector may have corporate-funded pensions, and that number is dwindling as other companies follow United's decision and cancel pension plans.

Barbara Ehrenreich's experiences as a low-wage employee at Wal-Mart tells another tale. As she relates this, it turns out that allegedly "unskilled" work is indeed very difficult to learn and working at places like Wal-Mart are demanding and require certain kinds of talents. At Wal-Mart she was not allowed to organize or bring in a union, and indeed, the Wal-Mart employees she met seems disinterested in unionizing, despite sometimes questionable employer practices.

The United Airlines pension bankruptcy case and Barbara Ehrenreich's experiences at Wal-Mart illustrate a pressing contemporary concern: the relationship between employers and employees, especially in the area of employee rights. Do employees have rights in the workplace despite having voluntarily entered into a formal employee-employer relationship? For example, does a worker have the right to a pension if this was promised at the outset as part of deferred compensation? Does an employee have a right to blow the whistle on a dangerous product without reprisal from management? Does he or she have a right to refuse a lie detector or polygraph test or have a urine test without being fired? Does he or she have the right to organize a union or participate in the management of the organization for which he or she works? And, what are the concomitant rights of employers vis-à-vis their employees? What might an employer justifiably and reasonably expect in terms of loyalty and trust from his or her employees? These questions are among those falling under the heading of "employee rights," and their discussion has become one of the most heated and controversial in the field of business ethics.

When talking about employee rights, a few philosophical distinctions about the concept of rights should be made. We take the concept of rights for granted, often forgetting that it was unknown only a few centuries ago. The first instance of the word in English appeared during the sixteenth century in the phrase "the rights of Englishmen." But these "rights" referred literally to Englishmen, not to Englishwomen, and included only those who owned property. History waited for the English philosopher John Locke to provide the word "right" with its present, far-reaching significance. In Locke's writings, the word came to refer to something that, by definition, is possessed unconditionally by all rational adult human beings. The talk of rights in our own Declaration of Independence and Constitution owes much to Locke's early doctrine of rights, a reading we included in Part 2.

Philosophers disagree about the precise definition of a right. Three of the most widely used definitions are (1) a right is a justified claim (for example, the right to freedom); (2) a right is an entitlement to something, held against someone else (for example, the right to equal protection is an entitlement that requires positive action on the part of others, including government); and (3) a right is a "trump" over a collective goal. The right to worship as one pleases, for example, overrides or trumps the collective goal of ideological unity within our society and thus overrides any claims by certain groups or by a government that certain religions must be suppressed for the sake of the common good.

Rights may be divided into legal rights and moral rights. The former are rights that are either specified formally by law or protected by it. In the United States, the right to sue, to have a jury trial, to own property, and to have a free public education are legal rights. Not all such rights were included in the founding documents of the U.S. government: The right to free publication, the right of women and African Americans to vote, and the right of workers to form unions were historical additions made in the nineteenth and twentieth centuries. Moral rights, on the other hand, are rights that are not necessarily protected and specified by the law. Moral rights are rights everyone has or should have; they are normative claims about what people are entitled to, but they may not be universally recognized or incorporated into law. They would include, for example, the right to be treated with equal respect, the right to equal freedom, and the right not to be systematically deceived or harmed. The law might stop short of preventing private clubs, for instance, from excluding Jews and African Americans, yet most of us would agree that these groups have a moral right in such situations not to be excluded. Similarly, for many years South African law perpetuated the apartheid system, yet few of us think that those laws were morally correct.

Turning to employee rights, although the Constitution and Bill of Rights protect the political rights of citizens, as late as 1946 the Supreme Court argued that the protection of the right to due process under the Fourteenth Amendment did not extend to private industry unless that particular business was performing a public function.[2] It is not that some rights are denied to employees in private industry, but rather that they are not always explicitly protected, nor are employers always restrained when rights are abrogated.

One of the most controversial issues in the area of employee rights, then, is whether, given that employees have some moral rights, those rights should remain only as moral rights or also be protected as legal rights. Until recently the lack of protection of employee rights has been rationalized by appealing to the common-law doctrine of the principle of Employment at Will (EAW). This principle states that, in the absence of law or a specific contract, an employer may hire, fire, demote, or promote an employee whenever the employer wishes, without having to give reasons or justify that action. In raising some issues about EAW in the article "Employment at Will, Employee Rights, and Future Directions for Employment," Tara Radin and Patricia Werhane assert that the three grounds upon which EAW is typically defended are also grounds on which it can be attacked. As Richard Epstein argues, in "In Defense of the Contract of Will," considerations of equal freedom, efficiency, and freedom of contract are often introduced in support of the prerogative of employers to fire "at will." But the grounds for defending EAW—inequality of freedom and power between employee and employer, inefficient outcomes, and violations of an employee's or employer's freedom of contract—are also grounds on which it can be attacked. The problem is not so much the doctrine of EAW, *per se,* but rather the way in which it is interpreted to imply that managers, when dealing with "at will" employees, can act without having to give reasons for their actions, a phenomenon that is inexcusable in the exercise of other managerial decision making. At a minimum, Radin and Werhane argue, the reasonable free exercise of management requires that employees be given reasons, publicly stated and verifiable, for firing decisions. Due process is a means to institutionalize that requirement while protecting the employer from not being able to fire someone for good reasons. Moreover, drawing on the work of a number of scholars, they argue that it is in the company's best interests to promote a fair working environment. However, Radin and Werhane conclude, this is not the whole answer. Employees too, have responsibilities—to take charge of their employment opportunities and their careers.

One of the most serious issues facing late-twentieth-century business is the question of job security. It has often been argued that long-time good employees and managers have rights to their jobs. In a number of European countries and in Japan, companies often grant these rights, whereas in the United States "at will" employment has been the norm. In an interesting short article, entitled "Employability Security," Rosabeth Moss Kanter, an early defender of employee rights, introduces a new and challenging concept: "employability." While she does not make the case for lifetime employment in any one corporation, she argues that companies have obligations to train and retrain employees and managers so that they are employable in the changing markets of this and the next century. Thus, while managers may move from company to company with skills enhancement, they become flexible and adaptable to changing work environments.

This section ends with an article by Jeffrey Pfeiffer, a long-time advocate for creating a positive work environment including good pay, delegation of responsibilities, and Kanter's demand for employability: training and retraining for skills enhance in a changing technological environment. Pfeiffer defends these employment practices not merely because they enhance the work environment for employees. He presents a great deal of data that shows that companies that focus on employee development are more profitable and sustainable than those that do not.

CHAPTER 10: DIVERSITY

One important moral right that directly concerns business is the right of every person to be treated as an equal in every respect, and in particular, in matters of hiring, pay, and promotion. For example, business organizations should be obliged to hire on the basis of applicant competence without being swayed by irrelevant factors such as gender, religion, race, or ethnic origin. Most business people today recognize this obligation, one that is enforced fully in the law. By the year 2040 less than 25 percent of all new hires will be white men. So how one integrates the workforce and treats an increasingly diverse population of employees is no longer merely a matter of philosophical or legal interest.

A more controversial issue is whether business has an obligation to go beyond the point of merely not discriminating to take more positive steps to create equal opportunities. This might be achieved through practices and policies of deliberately hiring and promoting equally qualified minorities and women when considering candidates for a position. Or employers might take the more controversial step of favoring qualified, but not necessarily equally qualified, minorities and women when hiring or promoting.

Perhaps the most common objection to the second type of practice is that such practices are inconsistent; that is, that they make the same mistakes they hope to remedy. If discrimination entails using a morally irrelevant characteristic, such as a person's skin color, as a factor in hiring, is deliberately hiring or promoting with those objectives (i.e., as in certain affirmative action programs) itself perpetuating unjust discrimination? In giving preference to, say, African Americans over Whites, are such programs using the same morally irrelevant characteristic previously used in discriminatory practices, thus themselves committing discrimination?

Defenders of the aim to create a more diverse workplace on all levels argue that these programs are, all things considered, fair and consistent with equal opportunity. They are not merely necessary to compensate past injustices in employment practices, injustices that clearly damaged the well-being and prospects of many members of society. Rather, they are also necessary to guarantee fairness in hiring and promotion for future generations. How will minority applicants ever seriously compete for positions in, say, medical school unless the educational and economic opportunities for minorities and non-minorities are equalized? And, how will educational and economic opportunities be equalized unless minorities are able to attain a fair share of society's highest level of jobs? The current legalized ban on affirmative action initiatives in states such as California and Texas presents new challenges to equal opportunity.

Equal opportunity in hiring has improved dramatically in the last 20 years. Where there has been less success is in organizational leadership positions. At the time of preparing this book, in 2006, there were only three African American CEOs in the Fortune 500 companies, none of which was a woman, and only eight women (all white). Board representation of women and minorities reflects this paucity of women and minorities in leadership positions—this, despite educational and hiring gains. Judy B. Rosener addresses the question of women leaders in her article, "Ways Women Lead." Studying women in high-profile positions, Rosener concludes that by and large women lead differently than men. Judy Rosener suggests that one of the distinctive and characteristic features of women in leadership positions is their ability to engage in interactive leadership relationships with their managers and employees and a preoccupation with empowering others. Rosener does not mean to imply that men do not do this, but suggests that empowerment is almost a mantra for women in leadership positions. As a result, she contends, women are usually not afraid of hiring or working with managers who are smarter or more capable than they are. Judy Rosener has labeled this style "nontraditional" or "transformational." Unlike leaders in hierarchically structured organizations, the women she studied do not view their authority as a matter of power. They do not think of themselves as persons in superior positions of formal authority. Their interactions with managers and employees are seldom transactional exchanges of rewards or demotions for superior or inferior performance. Instead, these women see themselves as working to coordinate and balance their interests and those of their employees, transforming these into shared corporate goals. This is usually translated into forms of interactive and participatory leadership that empowers employees while achieving corporate ends. This style of leadership is not merely aimed at transforming employees to adapt the values and goals of the company. Rather, leadership is thought of as a two-way interaction where both managers and employees are motivated and sometimes even changed.[3]

While extremely important, equal opportunity is only one of the issues at the center of the constellation of concerns involving race and sex, and discussions often tend to focus on a narrow range of equal opportunity, that of hiring and promotion. In a controversial article that sheds new light on affirmative action, "White Privilege and Male Privilege," Peggy McIntosh points out that equal opportunity proponents argue for the equalizing of disadvantages. Seldom, however, do we recognize how being white or male is an advantage. Being white gives one implicit privileges that are neither acknowledged nor taken into account when questioning affirmative action programs. Being white and male offers more such privileges, all of which are simply due to one's race or gender, none of which is earned or deserved. Privilege is often accompanied by power, thus creating inevitable advantages that are hard to dismantle. McIntosh argues that race and gender inequalities will persist even with affirmative action programs until or unless we recognize, acknowledge, and work at changing unearned privileges of being white or white and male. McIntosh's analysis of privilege can also explain how gays in our society are disadvantaged by the fact of sexual orientation.

The case, "Foreign Assignment," presents a set of difficult dilemmas. How should a company operate in a foreign setting, particularly if there is a perception that this country is less accepting of women in leadership positions? Should a female manager, who has been the beneficiary of this assignment, go along with this perceived attitude? What alternatives might be available to her and to her manager in a situation like this?

Notes

1. Chief Justice John Marshall, from *Trustees of Dartmouth College v. William Woodward, 17 U.S. 518,* Decided February 2, 1819.
2. *Marsh v. State of Alabama,* 66 S. Ct. 276 (1946).
3. Richard A. Couto, "The Transformation of Transforming Leadership," in J. Thomas Wren, *Leader's Companion* (New York: Free Press, 1994), 102–107.

Chapter 7

The Role of Organizational Values

Case Study

Merck & Co., Inc.

THE BUSINESS ENTERPRISE TRUST

In 1978, Dr. P. Roy Vagelos, then head of the Merck research labs, received a provocative memorandum from a senior researcher in parasitology, Dr. William C. Campbell. Dr. Campbell had made an intriguing observation while working with ivermectin, a new antiparasitic compound under investigation for use in animals.

Campbell thought that ivermectin might be the answer to a disease called river blindness that plagued millions in the Third World. But to find out if Campbell's hypothesis had merit, Merck would have to spend millions of dollars to develop the right formulation for human use and to conduct the field trials in the most remote parts of the world. Even if these efforts produced an effective and safe drug, virtually all of those afflicted with river blindness could not afford to buy it. Vagelos, originally a university researcher but by then a Merck executive, had to decide whether to invest in research for a drug that, even if successful, might never pay for itself.

RIVER BLINDNESS

River blindness, formally known as *onchocerciasis*, was a disease labeled by the World Health Organization (WHO) as a public health and socioeconomic problem of considerable magnitude in over 35 developing countries throughout the Third World. Some 85 million people in thousands of tiny settlements throughout Africa and parts of the Middle East and Latin America were thought to be at risk. The cause: a parasitic worm carried by a tiny black fly which bred along fast-moving rivers. When the flies bit humans—a single person could be bitten thousands of times a day—the larvae of a parasitic worm, *Onchocerca volvulus*, entered the body.

Yuck

These worms grew to more than two feet in length, causing grotesque but relatively innocuous nodules in the skin. The real harm began when the adult worms reproduced, releasing millions of microscopic offspring, known as microfilariae, which swarmed through body tissue. A terrible itching resulted, so bad that some victims committed suicide. After several years, the microfilariae caused lesions and depigmentation of the skin. Eventually they invaded the eyes, often causing blindness.

The World Health Organization estimated in 1978 that some 340,000 people were blind because of onchocerciasis, and that a million more suffered from varying degrees of visual impairment. At that time, 18 million or more people were infected with the parasite, though half did not yet have serious symptoms. In some villages close to fly-breeding sites, nearly all residents were infected and a majority of those over age 45 were blind. In such places, it was said, children believed that severe itching, skin infections and blindness were simply part of growing up.

In desperate efforts to escape the flies, entire villages abandoned fertile areas near rivers, and moved to poorer land. As a result, food shortages were frequent. Community life disintegrated as new burdens arose for already impoverished families.

The disease was first identified in 1893 by scientists and in 1926 was found to be related to the black flies. But by the 1970s, there was still no cure that could safely be used for community-wide treatment. Two drugs, diethylcarbamazine (DEC) & Suramin, were useful in killing the parasite, but both had severe side effects in infected individuals, needed close monitoring, and had even caused deaths. In 1974, the Onchocerciasis Control Program was created to be administered by the World Health Organization, in the hope that the flies could be killed through spraying of larvacides at breeding sites, but success was slow and uncertain. The flies in many areas developed resistance to the treatment, and were also known to disappear and then reinfest areas.

MERCK & CO., INC.

Merck & Co., Inc. was, in 1978, one of the largest producers of prescription drugs in the world. Headquartered in Rahway, New Jersey, Merck traced its origins to Germany in 1668 when Friedrich Jacob Merck purchased an apothecary in the city of Darmstadt. Over three hundred years later, Merck, having become an American firm, employed over 28,000 people and had operations all over the world.

In the late 1970s, Merck was coming off a 10-year drought in terms of new products. For nearly a decade, the company had relied on two prescription drugs for a significant percentage of its approximately $2 billion in annual sales: Indocin, a treatment for rheumatoid arthritis, and Aldomet, a treatment for high blood pressure. Henry W. Gadsden, Merck's chief executive from 1965 to 1976, along with his successor, John J. Horan, were concerned that the 17-year patent protection on Merck's two big moneymakers would soon expire, and began investing an enormous amount in research.

Merck management spent a great deal of money on research because it knew that its success ten and twenty years in the future critically depended upon present investments. The company deliberately fashioned a corporate culture to nurture the most creative, fruitful research. Merck scientists were among the best-paid in the industry, and were given great latitude to pursue intriguing leads. Moreover, they were inspired to think of their work as a quest to alleviate human disease and suffering world-wide. Within certain proprietary constraints, researchers were encouraged to publish in academic journals and to share ideas with their scientific peers. Nearly a billion dollars was spent between 1975 and 1978, and the investment paid off. In that period, under the direction of head of research, Dr. P. Roy Vagelos, Merck introduced Clinoril, a painkiller for arthritis; a general antibiotic called Mefoxin; a drug for glaucoma named Timoptic; and Ivomec (ivermectin, MSD), an antiparasitic for cattle.

In 1978, Merck had sales of $1.98 billion and net income of $307 million. Sales had risen steadily between 1969 and 1978 from $691 million to almost $2 billion. Income during the same period rose from $106 million to over $300 million. (See Exhibit 7.1 for a 10-year summary of performance.)

At that time, Merck employed 28,700 people, up from 22,200 ten years earlier. Human and animal health products constituted 84% of the company's sales, with environmental health products and services representing an additional 14% of sales. Merck's foreign sales had grown more rapidly during the 1970s than had domestic sales, and in 1978 represented 47% of total sales. Much of the company's research operations were organized separately as the Merck Sharp & Dohme Research Laboratories, headed by Vagelos. Other Merck operations included the Merck Sharp & Dohme Division, the Merck Sharp & Dohme International Division, Kelco Division, Merck Chemical Manufacturing Division, Merck Animal Health Division, Calgon Corporation, Baltimore Aircoil Company, and Hubbard Farms.

The company had 24 plants in the United States, including one in Puerto Rico, and 44 in other countries. Six research laboratories were located in the United States and four abroad.

While Merck executives sometimes squirmed when they quoted the "unbusinesslike" language of George W. Merck, son of the company's founder and its former chairman, there could be no doubt that Merck employees found the words inspirational. "We try never to forget that medicine is for the people," Merck said. "It is not for the profits. The profits follow, and if we have remembered that, they have never failed to appear. The better we have remembered it, the larger they have been." These words formed the basis of Merck's overall corporate philosophy.

THE DRUG INVESTMENT DECISION

Merck invested hundreds of millions of dollars each year in research. Allocating those funds amongst various projects, however, was a rather involved and inexact process. At a company as large as Merck, there was never a single method by which projects were approved or money distributed.

Studies showed that, on the average, it took 12 years and $200 million to bring a new drug to market. Thousands of scientists were continually working on new ideas and following new leads. Drug development was always a matter of trial and error; with each new iteration, scientists would

EXHIBIT 7.1. 10-Year Summary of Financial Performance

Merck & Co., Inc. and Subsidiaries (Dollar amounts in thousands except per-share figures)

Results for Year:	1978	1977	1976	1975	1974	1973	1972	1971	1970	1969
Sales	$1,981,440	$1,724,410	$1,561,117	$1,401,979	$1,260,416	$1,104,035	$942,631	$832,416	$761,109	$691,453
Materials and production costs	744,249	662,703	586,963	525,853	458,837	383,879	314,804	286,646	258,340	232,878
Marketing/administrative expenses	542,186	437,579	396,975	354,525	330,292	304,807	268,856	219,005	201,543	178,593
Research/development expenses	161,350	144,898	133,826	121,933	100,952	89,155	79,692	71,619	69,707	61,100
Interest expense	25,743	25,743	26,914	21,319	8,445	6,703	4,533	3,085	2,964	1,598
Income before taxes	507,912	453,487	416,439	378,349	361,890	319,491	274,746	252,061	228,555	217,284
Taxes on income	198,100	173,300	159,100	147,700	149,300	134,048	121,044	118,703	108,827	109,269
Net income**	307,534	277,525	255,482	228,778	210,492	182,681	151,180	131,381	117,878	106,645
Per common share**	$4.07	$3.67	$3.38	$3.03	$2.79	$2.43	$2.01	$1.75	$1.57	$1.43
Dividends declared on common stock	132,257	117,101	107,584	105,564	106,341	93,852	84,103	82,206	76,458	75,528
Per common share	$1.75	$1.55	$1.42-½	$1.40	$1.40	$1.23-½	$1.12	$1.10	$1.02-½	$1.02-½
Gross plant additions	155,853	177,167	153,894	249,015	159,148	90,194	69,477	67,343	71,540	48,715
Depreciation	75,477	66,785	58,198	52,091	46,057	40,617	36,283	32,104	27,819	23,973
Year-End Position:										
Working Capital	666,817	629,515	549,840	502,262	359,591	342,434	296,378	260,350	226,084	228,296
Property, plant, and equipment (net)	924,179	846,784	747,107	652,804	459,245	352,145	305,416	274,240	239,638	197,220
Total assets	2,251,358	1,993,389	1,759,371	1,538,999	1,243,287	988,985	834,847	736,503	664,294	601,484
Stockholders' equity	1,455,135	1,277,753	1,102,154	949,991	822,782	709,614	621,792	542,978	493,214	451,030
Year-End Statistics:										
Average number of common shares outstanding(in thousands)	75,573	75,546	75,493	75,420	75,300	75,193	75,011	74,850	74,850	74,547
Number of stockholders	62,900	63,900	63,500	65,500	61,400	60,000	58,000	54,300	54,600	53,100
Number of employees	28,700	28,100	26,800	26,300	26,500	25,100	24,100	23,200	23,000	22,200

*The above data are as previously reported, restated for poolings-of-interests and stock splits.

**Net income for 1977 and related per-share amounts exclude gain on disposal of businesses of $13,225 and 18¢, respectively.

close some doors and open others. When a Merck researcher came across an apparent breakthrough—either in an unexpected direction, or as a derivative of the original lead—he or she would conduct preliminary research. If the idea proved promising, it was brought to the attention of the department heads.

Every year, Merck's research division held a large review meeting at which all research programs were examined. Projects were coordinated and consolidated, established programs were reviewed and new possibilities were considered. Final approval on research was not made, however, until the head of research met later with a committee of scientific advisors. Each potential program was extensively reviewed, analyzed on the basis of the likelihood of success, the existing market, competition, potential safety problems, manufacturing feasibility and patent status before the decision was made whether to allocate funds for continued experimentation.

THE PROBLEM OF RARE DISEASES AND POOR CUSTOMERS

Many potential drugs offered little chance of financial return. Some diseases were so rare that treatments developed could never be priced high enough to recoup the investment in research, while other diseases afflicted only the poor in rural and remote areas of the Third World. These victims had limited ability to pay even a small amount for drugs or treatment.

In the United States, Congress sought to encourage drug companies to conduct research on rare diseases. In 1978 legislation had been proposed which would grant drug companies tax benefits and seven-year exclusive marketing rights if they would manufacture drugs for diseases afflicting fewer than 200,000 Americans. It was expected that this "orphan drug" program would eventually be passed into law.

There was, however, no U.S. or international program that would create incentives for companies to develop drugs for diseases like river blindness which afflicted millions of the poor in the Third World. The only hope was that some Third World government, foundation, or international organization might step in and partially fund the distribution of a drug that had already been developed.

THE DISCOVERY OF IVERMECTIN

The process of investigating promising drug compounds was always long, laborious and fraught with failure. For every pharmaceutical compound that became a "product candidate," thousands of others failed to meet the most rudimentary pre-clinical tests for safety and efficacy. With so much room for failure, it became especially important for drug companies to have sophisticated research managers who could identify the most productive research strategies.

Merck had long been a pioneer in developing major new antibiotic compounds, beginning with penicillin and streptomycin in the 1940s. In the 1970s, Merck Sharp & Dohme Research Laboratories were continuing this tradition. To help investigate for new microbial agents of potential therapeutic value, Merck researchers obtained 54 soil samples from the Kitasato Institute of Japan in 1974. These samples seemed novel and the researchers hoped they might disclose some naturally occurring antibiotics. As Merck researchers methodically put the soil through hundreds of tests, Merck scientists were pleasantly surprised to detect strong antiparasitic activity in Sample No. OS3153, a scoop of soil dug up at a golf course near Ito, Japan. The Merck labs quickly brought together an interdisciplinary team to try to isolate a pure active ingredient from the microbial culture. The compound eventually isolated—ivermectin—proved to have an astonishing potency and effectiveness against a wide range of parasites in cattle, swine, horses and other animals. Within a year, the Merck team also began to suspect that a group of related compounds discovered in the same soil sample could be effective against many other intestinal worms, mites, ticks and insects.

After toxicological tests suggested that ivermectin would be safer than related compounds, Merck decided to develop the substance for the animal health market. In 1978 the first ivermectin-based animal drug, Ivomec, was nearing approval by the U.S. Department of Agriculture and foreign regulatory bodies. Many variations would likely follow: drugs for sheep and pigs, horses, dogs, and others. Ivomec had the potential to become a major advance in animal health treatment.

As clinical testing of ivermectin progressed in the late 1970s, Dr. William Campbell's ongoing research brought him face-to-face with an intriguing hypothesis. Ivermectin, when tested in horses, was effective against the microfilariae of an exotic, fairly unimportant gastrointestinal parasite, *Onchocerca cervicalis*. This particular worm, while harmless in horses, had characteristics similar to the insidious human parasite that causes river blindness, *Onchocerca volvulus*.

Dr. Campbell wondered: Could ivermectin be formulated to work against the human parasite? Could a safe, effective drug suitable for community-wide treatment of river blindness be developed? Both Campbell and Vagelos knew that it was very much a gamble that it would succeed. Furthermore, both knew that even if success were attained, the economic viability of such a project would be nil. On the other hand, because such a significant amount of money had already been invested in the development of the animal drug, the cost of developing a human formulation would be much less than that for developing a new compound. It was also widely believed at this point that ivermectin, though still in its final development stages, was likely to be very successful.

A decision to proceed would not be without risks. If a new derivative proved to have any adverse health effects when used on humans, its reputation as a veterinary drug could be tainted and sales negatively affected, no matter how irrelevant the experience with humans. In early tests, ivermectin had had some negative side effects on some specific species of mammals. Dr. Brian Duke of the Armed Forces Institute of Pathology in Washington, D.C., said the cross-species effectiveness of antiparasitic drugs are unpredictable, and there is "always a worry that some race or subsection of the human population" might be adversely affected. Isolated instances of harm to humans or improper use in Third World settings might also raise some unsettling questions: Could drug residues turn up in meat eaten by humans? Would any human version of ivermectin distributed to the Third World be diverted into the black market, undercutting sales of the veterinary drug? Could the drug harm certain animals in unknown ways?

Despite these risks, Vagelos wondered what the impact might be of turning down Campbell's proposal. Merck had built a research team dedicated to alleviating human suffering. What would a refusal to pursue a possible treatment for river blindness do to morale?

Ultimately, it was Dr. Vagelos who had to make the decision whether to fund research toward a treatment for river blindness.

Does Business Ethics Make Economic Sense?

AMARTYA SEN

I. INTRODUCTION

I begin not with the need for business ethics, but at the other end—the idea that many people have that there is no need for such ethics. That conviction is quite widespread among practitioners of economics, though it is more often taken for granted implicitly rather than asserted explicitly. We have to understand better what the conviction rests on, to be able to see its inadequacies. Here, as in many other areas of knowledge, the importance of a claim depends to a great extent on what it denies.

How did this idea of the redundancy of ethics get launched in economics? The early authors on economic matters, from Aristotle and Kautilya (in ancient Greece and ancient India respectively—the two were contemporaries, as it happens) to medieval practitioners (including Aquinas, Ockham, Maimonides, and others), to the economists of the early modern age (William Petty, Gregory King, François Quesnay, and others) were all much concerned, in varying degrees, with ethical analysis. In one way or another, they saw economics as a branch of "practical reason," in which concepts of the good, the right and the obligatory were quite central.

What happened then? As the "official" story goes, all this changed with Adam Smith, who can certainly be described—rightly—as the father of modern economics. He made, so it is said, economics scientific and hard-headed, and the new economics that emerged in the nineteenth and twentieth centuries was all ready to do business, with no ethics to keep it tied to "morals and moralizing." That view of what happened—with Smith

Lamont University Professor, and Professor of Economics and Philosophy, at Harvard University. A paper presented at the International Conference on the Ethics of Business in a Global Economy, held in Columbus, Ohio, in March 1992. Reprinted by permission of the author, Amartya Sen, University of Cambridge, and *Business Ethics Quarterly*, January 1993, vol. 5, Issue 1.

doing the decisive shooting of business and economic ethics—is not only reflected in volumes of professional economic writings, but has even reached the status of getting into the English literature via a limerick by Stephen Leacock, who was both a literary writer and an economist:

Adam, Adam, Adam Smith
Listen what I charge you with!
Didn't you say
In a class one day
That selfishness was bound to pay?
Of all doctrines that was the Pith.
Wasn't it, wasn't it, wasn't it, Smith?[1]

The interest in going over this bit of history—or alleged history—does not lie, at least for this conference, in scholastic curiosity. I believe it is important to see how that ethics-less view of economics and business emerged in order to understand what it is that is being missed out. As it happens, that bit of potted history of "who killed business ethics" is altogether wrong, and it is particularly instructive to understand how that erroneous identification has come about.

II. EXCHANGE, PRODUCTION AND DISTRIBUTION

I get back, then, to Adam Smith. Indeed, he did try to make economics scientific, and to a great extent was successful in this task, within the limits of what was possible then. While that part of the alleged history is right (Smith certainly did much to enhance the scientific status of economics), what is altogether mistaken is the idea that Smith demonstrated—or believed that he had demonstrated—the redundancy of ethics in economic and business affairs. Indeed, quite the contrary. The Professor of Moral Philosophy at the University of Glasgow—for that is what Smith was—was as interested in the importance of ethics in behavior as anyone could have been. It is instructive to see how the odd reading of Smith—as a "no-nonsense" skeptic of economic and business ethics—has come about.

Perhaps the most widely quoted remark of Adam Smith is the one about the butcher, the brewer and the baker in The Wealth of Nations: "It is not from the benevolence of the butcher, the brewer, or the baker that we expect our dinner, but from their regard to their own interest. We address ourselves, not to their humanity but to their self-love. . . ."[2] The butcher, the brewer and the baker want our money, and we want their products, and the exchange benefits us all. There would seem to be no need for any ethics—business or otherwise—in bringing about this betterment of all the parties involved. All that is needed is regard for our own respective interests, and the market is meant to do the rest in bringing about the mutually gainful exchanges.

In modern economics this Smithian tribute to self-interest is cited again and again—indeed with such exclusivity that one is inclined to wonder whether this is the only passage of Smith that is read these days. What did Smith really suggest? Smith did argue in this passage that the pursuit of self-interest would do fine to motivate the exchange of commodities. But that is a very limited claim, even though it is full of wonderful insights in explaining why it is that we seek exchange and how come exchange can be such a beneficial thing for all. But to understand the limits of what is being claimed here, we have to ask, first: Did Smith think that economic operations and business activities consist only of exchanges of this kind? Second, even in the context of exchange, we have to question: Did Smith think that the result would be just as good if the businesses involved, driven by self-interest, were to try to defraud the consumers, or the consumers in question were to attempt to swindle the sellers?

The answers to both these questions are clearly in the negative. The butcher-brewer-baker simplicity does not carry over to problems of production and distribution (and Smith never said that it did), nor to the problem as to how a system of exchange can flourish institutionally. This is exactly where we begin to see why Smith could have been right in his claim about the motivation for exchange without establishing or trying to establish the redundancy of business or ethics in general (or even in exchange). . . .

The importance of self-interest pursuit is a helpful part of understanding many practical problems, for example, the supply problems in the Soviet Union and East Europe. But it is quite unhelpful in explaining the success of, say, Japanese economic performance vis-à-vis West Europe or North America (since behavior modes in Japan are often deeply influenced by other conventions and pressures). Elsewhere in *The Wealth of Nations*, Adam Smith considers other problems which call for a more complex motivational structure. And in his The Theory of Moral Sentiments, Smith goes extensively into the need to go beyond profit maximization, arguing that "humanity, justice, generosity, and public spirit, are the qualities most useful to others."[3] Adam Smith was very far from trying to deny the importance of ethics in behavior in general and business behavior in particular.[4]

Overlooking everything else that Smith said in his wide-ranging writings and concentrating only on this one butcher-brewer-baker passage, the father of modern economics is too often made to look like an ideologue. He is transformed into a partisan exponent of an ethics-free view of life which would have horrified Smith. To adapt a Shakespearian aphorism, while some men are born small and some achieve smallness, the unfortunate Adam Smith has had much smallness thrust upon him.

It is important to see how Smith's whole tribute to self-interest as a motivation for exchange (best illustrated in the butcher-brewer-baker passage) can co-exist peacefully with Smith's advocacy of ethical behavior elsewhere. Smith's concern with ethics was, of course, extremely extensive and by no means confined to economic and business matters. But since this is not the occasion to review Smith's ethical beliefs, but only to get insights from his combination of economic and ethical expertise to understand better the exact role of business ethics, we have to point our inquiries in that particular direction.

The butcher-brewer-baker discussion is all about motivation for exchange, but Smith was—as any good economist should be—deeply concerned also with production as well as distribution. And to understand how exchange might itself actually work in practice, it is not adequate to concentrate only on the motivation that makes people seek exchange. It is necessary to look at the behavior patterns that could sustain a flourishing system of mutually profitable exchanges. The positive role of intelligent self-seeking in motivating exchange has to be supplemented by the motivational demands of production and distribution, and the systemic demands on the organization of the economy.

These issues are taken up now, linking the general discussion with practical problems faced in the contemporary world. In the next three sections I discuss in turn (1) the problem of organization (especially that of exchange), (2) the arrangement and performance of production, and (3) the challenge of distribution.

III. ORGANIZATION AND EXCHANGE: RULES AND TRUST

I come back to the butcher-brewer-baker example. The concern of the different parties with their own interests certainly can adequately motivate all of them to take part in the exchange from which each benefits. But whether the exchange would operate well would depend also on organizational conditions. This requires institutional development which can take quite some time to work—a lesson that is currently being learned rather painfully in East Europe and the former Soviet Union. That point is now being recognized, even though it was comprehensively ignored in the first flush of enthusiasm in seeking the magic of allegedly automatic market processes.

But what must also be considered now is the extent to which the economic institutions operate on the basis of common behavior patterns, shared trusts, and a mutual confidence in the ethics of the different parties. When Adam Smith pointed to the motivational importance of "regard to their own interest," he did not suggest that this motivation is all that is needed to have a flourishing system of exchange. If he cannot trust the householder, the baker may have difficulty in proceeding to produce bread to meet orders, or in delivering bread without prepayment. And the householder may not be certain whether he would be sensible in relying on the delivery of the ordered bread if the baker is not always altogether reliable. These problems of mutual confidence—discussed in a very simple form here—can be incomparably more complex and more critical in extended and multifarious business arrangements.

Mutual confidence in certain rules of behavior is typically implicit rather than explicit—indeed so implicit that its importance can be easily overlooked in situations in which confidence is unproblematic. But in the context of economic development across the Third World, and also of institutional reform now sweeping across what used to be the Second World, these issues of behavioral norms and ethics can be altogether central.

In the Third World there is often also a deep-rooted skepticism of the reliability and moral quality of business behavior. This can be directed both at local businessmen and the commercial people from abroad. The latter may sometimes be particularly galling to well-established business firms including well-known multinationals. But the record of some multinationals and their unequal power in dealing with the more vulnerable countries have left grounds for much suspicion, even though such suspicion may be quite misplaced in many cases. Establishing high standards of business ethics is certainly one way of tackling this problem.

I have been discussing problems of organization in exchange, and it would seem to be right to conclude this particular discussion by noting that the need for business ethics is quite strong even in the field of exchange (despite the near-universal presence of the butcher-brewer-baker motivation of "regard to their own interest"). If we now move on from exchange to production and distribution, the need for business ethics becomes even more forceful and perspicuous. The issue of trust is central to all economic operations. But we now have to consider other problems of interrelation in the process of production and distribution.

IV. ORGANIZATION OF PRODUCTION: FIRMS AND PUBLIC GOODS

Capitalism has been successful enough in generating output and raising productivity. But the experiences of different countries are quite diverse. The recent experiences of Eastern Asian economies—most notably Japan—raise deep questions about the modeling of capitalism on traditional economic theory. Japan is often seen—rightly in a particular sense—as a great example of successful capitalism, but it is clear that the motivation patterns that dominate Japanese business have much more content than would be provided by pure profit maximization.

Different commentators have emphasized distinct aspects of Japanese motivational features. Michio Morishima has outlined the special characteristics of "Japanese ethos" as emerging from its particular history of rule-based behavior pattern.[5] Ronald Dore has seen the influence of "Confucian ethics."[6] Recently, Eiko Ikegami has pointed to the importance of the traditional concern with "honor"—a kind of generalization of the Samurai code—as a crucial modifier of business and economic motivation.[7]

Indeed, there is some truth, oddly enough, even in the puzzlingly witty claim made by The Wall Street Journal that Japan is "the only communist nation that works" (30 January 1989, p. 1). It is, as one would expect, mainly a remark about the non-profit motivations underlying many economic and business activities in Japan. We have to understand and interpret the peculiar fact that the most successful capitalist nation in the world flourishes economically with a motivation structure that departs firmly—and often explicitly—from the pursuit of self-interest, which is meant to be the bedrock of capitalism.

In fact, Japan does not, by any means, provide the only example of a powerful role of business ethics in promoting capitalist success. The productive merits of selfless work and devotion to enterprise have been given much credit for economic achievements in many countries in the world. Indeed, the need of capitalism for a motivational structure more complex than pure profit maximization has been acknowledged in various forms, over a long time, by various social scientists (though typically not by any "mainstream" economists): I have in mind Marx, Weber, Tawney, and others.[8] The basic point about the observed success of non-profit motives is neither unusual nor new, even though that wealth of historical and conceptual insights is often thoroughly ignored in professional economics today.

It is useful to try to bring the discussion in line with Adam Smith's concerns, and also with the general analytical approaches successfully developed in modern microeconomic theory. In order to understand how motives other than self-seeking can have an important role, we have to see the limited reach of the butcher-brewer-baker argument, especially in dealing with what modern economists call "public good." This becomes particularly relevant because the overall success of a modern enterprise is, in a very real sense, a public good.

But what is a public good? That idea can be best understood by contrasting it with a "private good," such as a toothbrush or a shirt or an apple, which either you can use or I, but not both. Our respective uses would compete and be exclusive. This is not so with public goods, such as a livable environment or the absence of epidemics. All of us may benefit from breathing fresh air, living in an epidemic-free environment, and so on. When uses of commodities are non-competitive, as in the case of public goods, the rationale of the self-interest-based market mechanism comes under severe strain. The market system works by putting a price on a commodity and the allocation between consumers is done by the intensities of the respective willingness to buy it at the prevailing price. When "equilibrium prices" emerge, they balance demand with supply for each commodity. In contrast, in the case of public goods, the uses are—largely or entirely—non-competitive, and the system of giving a good to the highest bidder does not have much merit, since one person's consumption does not exclude that of another. Instead, optimum resource allocation would require that the combined benefits be compared with the costs of production, and here the market mechanism, based on profit maximization, functions badly.[9]

A related problem concerns the allocation of private goods involving strong "externalities," with interpersonal interdependencies working outside the markets. If the smoke from a factory makes a neighbor's home dirty and unpleasant, without the neighbor being able to charge the factory owner for the loss she suffers, then that is an "external" relation. The market does not help in this case, since it is not there to allocate the effects—good or bad— that work outside the market.[10] Public goods and externalities are related phenomena, and they are both quite common in such fields as public health care, basic education, environmental protection, and so on.

There are two important issues to be addressed in this context, in analysing the organization and performance of production. First, there would tend to be some failure in resource allocation when the commodities produced are public goods or involve strong externalities. This can be taken either (1) as an argument for having publicly owned enterprises, which would be governed by principles other than profit maximization, or (2) as a case for public regulations governing private enterprise, or (3) as establishing a need for the use of non-profit values—particularly of social concern— in private decisions (perhaps because of the goodwill that it might generate). Since public enterprises have not exactly covered themselves with glory in the recent years, and public regulations—while useful—are sometimes quite hard to implement, the third option has become more important in public discussions. It is difficult, in this context, to escape the argument for encouraging business ethics, going well beyond the traditional values of honesty and reliability, and taking on social responsibility as well (for example, in matters of environmental degradation and pollution).

The second issue is more complex and less recognized in the literature, but also more interesting. Even in the production of private commodities, there can be an important "public good" aspect in the production process itself. This is because production itself is typically a joint activity, supervisions are costly and often unfeasible, and each participant contributes to the over-all success of the firm in a way that cannot be fully reflected in the private rewards that he or she gets.

The over-all success of the firm, thus, is really a public good, from which all benefit, to which all contribute, and which is not parcelled out in little boxes of person-specific rewards strictly linked with each person's re-spective contribution. And this is precisely where the motives other than narrow self-seeking become productively important. Even though I do not have the opportunity to pursue the point further here, I do believe that the successes of "Japanese ethos," "Confucian ethics," "Samurai codes of honor," etc., can be fruitfully linked to this aspect of the organization of production.

V. THE CHALLENGE OF DISTRIBUTION: VALUES AND INCENTIVES

I turn now to distribution. It is not hard to see that non-self-seeking motiva-tions can be extremely important for distributional problems in general. In dividing a cake, one person's gain is another's loss. At a very obvious level, the contributions that can be made by ethics—business ethics and others—include the amelioration of misery through policies explicitly aimed at such a result. There is an extensive literature on donations, charity, and philan-thropy in general, and also on the willingness to join in communal activities geared to social improvement. The connection with ethics is obvious enough in these cases.

What is perhaps more interesting to discuss is the fact that distribu-tional and productional problems very often come mixed together, so that how the cake is divided influences the size of the cake itself. The so-called "incentive problem" is a part of this relationship. This too is a much discussed problem, but it is important to clarify in the present con-text that the extent of the conflict between size and distribution depends crucially on the motivational and behavioral assumptions. The incentive problem is not an immutable feature of production technology. For ex-ample, the more narrowly profit-oriented an enterprise is, the more it would, in general, tend to resist looking after the interests of others—workers, associates, consumers. This is an area in which ethics can make a big difference.

The relevance of all this to the question we have been asked to address ("Does business ethics make economic sense?") does, of course, depend on how "economic sense" is defined. If economic sense includes the achieve-ment of a good society in which one lives, then the distributional improve-ments can be counted in as parts of sensible outcomes even for business. Visionary industrialists and businesspersons have tended to encourage this line of reasoning.

On the other hand, if "economic sense" is interpreted to mean noth-ing other than achievement of profits and business rewards, then the concerns for others and for distributional equity have to be judged entirely instrumentally—in terms of how they indirectly help to promote profits. That connection is not to be scoffed at, since firms that treat their workers well are often very richly rewarded for it. For one thing, the workers are then more reluctant to lose their jobs, since more would be sacrificed if dismissed from this (more lucrative) employment, compared with alternative opportunities. The contribution of goodwill to team spirit and thus to productivity can also be quite plentiful.

We have then an important contrast between two different ways in which good business behavior could make economic sense. One way is to see the improvement of the society in which one lives as a reward in itself; this works directly. The other is to use ultimately a business criterion for improvement, but to take note of the extent to which good business behavior could in its turn lead to favorable business performance; this enlightened self-interest involves an indirect reasoning.

It is often hard to disentangle the two features, but in understanding whether or how business ethics make economic sense, we have to take note of each feature. If, for example, a business firm pays inadequate attention to the safety of its workers, and this results accidentally in a disastrous tragedy, like the one that happened in Bhopal in India some years ago (though I am not commenting at present on the extent to which Union Carbide was in fact negligent there), that event would be harmful both for the firm's profits and for the general objectives of social well-being in which the firm may be expected to take an interest. The two effects are distinct and separable and should act cumulatively in an overall consequential analysis. Business ethics has to relate to both.

Notes

1. Stephen Leacock, *Hellements of Hickonomics* (New York: Dodd, Mead & Co., 1936), p. 75.
2. Adam Smith, *An Inquiry into the Nature and Causes of the Wealth of Nations* (1776; republished, London: Dent, 1910), vol. I, p. 13.
3. Adam Smith, *The Theory of Moral Sentiments* (revised edition, 1790; reprinted, Oxford: Clarendon Press, 1976), p. 189.
4. On this and related manners, see my *On Ethics and Economics* (Oxford: Blackwell, 1987); Patricia H. Werhane, *Adam Smith and His Legacy for Modern Capitalism* (New York: Oxford University Press, 1991); Emma Rothschild, "Adam Smith and Conservative Economics," *Economic History Review* 45 (1992).
5. Michio Morishima, *Why Has Japan 'Succeeded'? Western Technology and Japanese Ethos* (Cambridge, UK: Cambridge University Press, 1982).
6. Ronald Dore, "Goodwill and the Spirit of Market Capitalism," *British Journal of Sociology* 34 (1983), and *Taking Japan Seriously: A Confucian Perspective on Leading Economic Issues* (Stanford, CA: Stanford University Press, 1987).
7. Eiko Ikegami, "The Logic of Cultural Change: Honor, State-Making, and the Samurai," mimeographed, Department of Sociology, Yale University, 1991.
8. Karl Marx (with F. Engels), *The German Ideology* (1845–46, English translation, New York: International Publishers, 1947); Richard Henry Tawney, *Religion and the Rise of Capitalism* (London: Murray, 1926); Max Weber, *The Protestant Ethic and the Spirit of Capitalism* (London: Allen & Unwin, 1930).
9. The classic treatment of public goods was provided by Paul A. Samuelson, "The Pure Theory of Public Expenditure," *Review of Economics and Statistics* 35 (1954).

10. For a classic treatment of external effects, see A. C. Pigou, *The Economics of Welfare* (London: Macmillan, 1920). There are many different ways of defining "externalities," with rather disparate bearings on policy issues; on this see the wide-ranging critical work of Andreas Papandreou (*Jr.*, I should add to avoid an ambiguity, though I do not believe he uses that clarification), *Ideas of Externality*, to be published by Clarendon Press, Oxford, and Oxford University Press, New York.

Can Socially Responsible Firms Survive in a Competitive Environment?

Robert H. Frank

In his celebrated 1970 article, Milton Friedman wrote that "there is one and only one social responsibility of business—to use its resources and engage in activities designed to increase its profits so long as it stays within the rules of the game, which is to say, engages in open and free competition without deception or fraud" (p. 126). In Friedman's view, managers who pursue broader social goals—say, by adopting more stringent emissions standards than required by law, or by donating corporate funds to charitable organizations—are simply spending other people's money. Firms run by these managers will have higher costs than those run by managers whose goal is to maximize shareholder wealth. According to the standard theory of competitive markets, the latter firms will attract more capital and eventually drive the former firms out of business.

Of course, as Friedman himself clearly recognized, there are many circumstances in which the firm's narrow interests coincide with those of the broader community. He noted, for example, that "it may well be in the long-run interest of a corporation that is a major employer in a small community to devote resources to providing amenities to that community or to improving its government. That may make it easier to attract desirable employees, it may reduce the wage bill or lessen losses from pilferage and sabotage or have other worthwhile effects" (p. 124).

Friedman argued against using the term *social responsibility* to characterize those activities of a firm that, while serving the broader community, also augment the firm's profits. He believes that this language has great potential to mislead politicians and voters about the proper role of the corporation in society and will foster excessive regulation.

In the years since Friedman wrote this article, the development of the theory of repeated games has given us ever more sophisticated accounts of the forces that often align self-interest with the interests of others. For example, Robert Axelrod (1984) suggests that firms pay their suppliers not because they feel a moral obligation to do so but because they require future shipments from them.

From David Messick and Ann Tenbrunsel, *Codes of Conduct: Behavioral Research into Business Ethics*, © 1996 Russell Sage Foundation, New York, New York, pp. 86–103.

Clearly, repeated interactions often do give rise to behaviors that smack of social responsibility. Yet as Friedman suggested, it is erroneous—or at least misleading—to call these behaviors morally praiseworthy. After all, even a firm whose owners and managers had no concern about the welfare of the broader community would have ample motive to engage in them. When material incentives favor cooperation, it is more descriptive to call the cooperating parties prudent than socially responsible.

It is also an error to assume that repeated interactions always provide ready solutions to social dilemmas and other collective action problems. Even among parties who deal with one another repeatedly, one-shot dilemmas—opportunities for cheating and other opportunistic behavior—often arise. Even a longstanding client of a law firm, for example, has no way to verify that the firm has billed only the number of hours actually worked.

In many cases, the knowledge that opportunities to cheat will arise may preclude otherwise profitable business ventures. Consider a person whose mutual fund has just been taken over by new management. She wants advice about whether to stay with the fund under its new management or switch to a different fund. She considers seeking a consultation, for a fee, from a knowledgeable stockbroker—a mutually beneficial exchange. Yet the investor also knows that a broker's interests may differ from her own. Perhaps, for example, the broker will receive a large commission or finder's fee if the client switches to a new fund. Fearing the consequences of opportunistic behavior, the investor may refrain from seeking advice, in the process depriving both herself and an informed broker of the gains from trade.

When parties to a business transaction confront a one-shot dilemma, their profits will be higher if they defect—that is, if they cheat—than if they cooperate. Yet when each party defects, profits for each are lower than if both had cooperated. In this paper, I will refer to firms that cooperate in one-shot dilemmas as socially responsible firms.

The question I pose is whether such firms can survive in competitive environments. At first glance, it would appear that the answer must be no, for if defecting were indeed a dominant strategy, then socially responsible firms would always have lower returns than pure profit maximizers. Evolutionary models pertaining to individuals have recently shown, however, that conditions often exist in which cooperation in one-shot dilemmas is sustainable in competitive environments. I will review some of this work and suggest that many of its conclusions carry over to populations of competitive firms.

EVOLUTIONARY MODELS OF ONE-SHOT COOPERATION

One of the enduring questions in evolutionary biology is whether altruistic individuals can survive. In this framework, the design criterion for each component of human motivation is the same as for an arm or a leg or an eye: To what extent does it assist the individual in the struggle to acquire the resources required for survival and reproduction? If it works better than the available alternatives, selection pressure will favor it. Otherwise, selection pressure will work against it (see Dawkins 1976, especially chapter 3).

At first glance, this theoretical structure appears to throw its weight squarely behind the self-interest conception of human motivation. Indeed, if natural selection favors the traits and behaviors that maximize individual reproductive fitness, and if we define behaviors that enhance personal fitness as selfish, then self-interest becomes the only viable human motive by definition. This tautology was a central message of much of the sociobiological literature of the 1970s and 1980s.

On closer look, however, the issues are not so simple. There are many situations in which individuals whose only goal is self-interest are likely to be especially bad at acquiring and holding resources. Thomas Schelling (1960) provided a vivid illustration with his account of a kidnapper who gets cold feet and wants to set his victim free but fears that if he does so, the victim will go to the police. The victim promises to remain silent. The problem, however, is that both he and the kidnapper know that it will not be in the victim's narrow self-interest to keep this promise once he is free. And so the kidnapper reluctantly concludes that he must kill his victim.

Suppose, however, that the victim were not a narrowly self-interested person but rather a person of honor. If this fact could somehow be communicated to the kidnapper, their problem would be solved. The kidnapper could set the victim free, secure in the knowledge that even though it would then be in the victim's interests to go to the police, he would not want to do so.

Schelling's kidnapper and victim face a commitment problem, a situation in which they have an incentive to commit themselves to behave in a way that will later seem contrary to self-interest. Such problems are a common feature of social life. Consider, for example, the farmer who is trying to deter a transient thief from stealing his ox. Suppose this farmer is known to be a narrowly self-interested rational person. If the thief knows that the farmer's cost of pursuing him exceeds the value of the ox, he can then steal the ox with impunity. But suppose that the farmer cares also about not being victimized, quite independently of the effect of victimization on his wealth. If he holds this goal with sufficient force, and if the potential thief knows of the farmer's commitment, the ox will no longer be such an inviting target.

In the one-shot prisoner's dilemma, if the two players cooperate, each does better than if both defect, and yet each individual gets a higher payoff by defecting no matter which strategy the other player chooses. Both players thus have a clear incentive to commit themselves to cooperate. Yet a mere promise issued by a narrowly self-interested person clearly will not suffice, for his partner knows he will have no incentive to keep this promise. If both players know one another to be honest, however, both could reap the gains of cooperation.

In both these examples, note that merely having the relevant motivations or goals is by itself insufficient to solve the problem. It is also necessary that the presence of these goals be discernible by others. Someone with a predisposition to cooperate in the one-shot prisoner's dilemma, for instance, is in fact at a disadvantage unless others can identify that predisposition in him and he can identify similar predispositions in others.

Can the moral sentiments and other psychological forces that often drive people to ignore narrow self-interest be reliably discerned by outsiders? A recent study (Frank, Gilovich, and Regan 1993) found that subjects were surprisingly accurate at predicting who would cooperate and who would defect in one-shot prisoner's dilemmas played with near strangers.

In our study, the base rate of cooperation was 73.7 percent, the base rate of defection only 26.3 percent. A random prediction of cooperation would thus have been accurate 73.7 percent of the time, a random prediction of defection accurate only 26.3 percent of the time. The actual accuracy rates for these two kinds of prediction were 80.7 percent and 56.8 percent, respectively. The likelihood of such high accuracy rates occurring by chance is less than one in one thousand.

Subjects in this experiment were strangers at the outset and were able to interact with one another for only thirty minutes before making their predictions.[1] It is plausible to suppose that predictions would be considerably more accurate for people we have known for a long time. For example, consider a thought experiment based on the following scenario:

> An individual has a gallon jug of unwanted pesticide. To protect the environment, the law requires that unused pesticide be turned in to a government disposal facility located thirty minutes' drive from her home. She knows, however, that she could simply pour the pesticide down her basement drain with no chance of being caught and punished. She also knows that her one gallon of pesticide, by itself, will cause only negligible harm if disposed of in this fashion.

Now the thought experiment: Can you think of anyone who you feel certain would dispose of the pesticide properly? Most people respond affirmatively, and usually they have in mind someone they have known for a long time. If you answer yes, then you, too, accept the central premise of the commitment model—namely, that it is possible to identify non-self-interested motives in at least some other people.

The presence of such motives, coupled with the ability of others to discern them, makes it possible to solve commitment problems of the sort that have been presented. Knowing that others could discern her motives, even a rational, self-interested individual would have every reason to choose preferences that were not narrowly self-interested. Of course, people do not choose their preferences in any literal sense. The point is that if moral sentiments can be reliably discerned by others, the complex interaction of genes and culture that yields human preferences can sustain preferences that lead people to subordinate narrow self-interest in the pursuit of other goals.

AN EQUILIBRIUM MIX OF MOTIVES

It might seem that if moral sentiments help solve important commitment problems, then evolutionary forces would assure that everyone have a full measure of these sentiments. But a closer look at the interplay between selfish and other-regarding motives suggests that this is unlikely (see Frank 1988, Chapter 3, for an extended discussion of this point). Imagine, for example, an environment populated by two types of people, cooperators and defectors. And suppose that people earn their livelihood by interacting in pairs, where the commitment problem they confront is the one-shot prisoner's dilemma.

If cooperators and defectors were perfectly indistinguishable, interactions would occur on a random basis and the average payoffs would always be larger for the defectors (owing to the dominance of defection in all prisoner's dilemmas). In evolutionary models, the rule governing population dynamics is that each type reproduces in proportion to its material payoff relative to other types. This implies that if the two types were indistinguishable, the eventual result would be extinction for the cooperators. In highly simplified form, this is the Darwinian story that inclines many social scientists to believe that self-interest is the only important human motive.

But now suppose that cooperators were distinguishable at a glance from defectors. Then interaction would no longer take place on a random basis. Rather, the cooperators would pair off systematically with one another to reap the benefits of mutual cooperation. Defectors would be left to interact with one another, and would receive the lower payoff associated with these pairings. The eventual result this time is that the defectors would be driven to extinction.

Neither of these two polar cases seems descriptive of actual populations, which typically contain a mix of cooperators and defectors. Such a mixed population is precisely the result we get if we make one small modification to the original story. Again suppose that cooperators are observably different from defectors, but that some effort is required to make the distinction. If the population initially consisted almost entirely of cooperators, it would not pay to expand this effort because one would be overwhelmingly likely to achieve a high payoff merely by interacting at random with another person. In such an environment, cooperators would cease to be vigilant in their choice of trading partners. Defectors would then find a ready pool of victims, and their resulting higher payoffs would cause their share of the total population to grow.

As defectors became more numerous, however, it would begin to pay cooperators to exercise greater vigilance in their choice of partners. With sufficient defectors in the population, cooperators would be vigilant in the extreme, and we would again see pairings among like types only. That, in turn, would cause the prevalence of cooperators to grow. At some point, a stable balance would be struck in which cooperators were just vigilant enough to prevent further encroachment by defectors. The average payoff to the two types would be the same, and their population shares would remain constant. There would be, in other words, a stable niche for each type.

FIVE WAYS A SOCIALLY RESPONSIBLE FIRM MIGHT PROSPER

The commitment model just described shows how it is possible for cooperative individuals to survive in competitive environments. What does this model have to say about the possibilities for survival of socially responsible firms? Recall that the socially responsible firm's problem is that by cooperating in one-shot dilemmas, it receives a lower payoff than do firms that defect. In the sections that follow, I will describe five possible areas in which the socially responsible firm might compensate for that disadvantage. The first three involve the recognition of potential commitment problems that arise within firms and between firms and the outside world.

The last two involve the fact that people value socially responsible action and are willing to pay for it in the marketplace, even when they do not benefit from it directly in a material sense.

By Solving Commitment Problems with Employees

Just as commitment problems arise between independent individuals, so too do they arise among owners, managers, and employees. Many of these problems, like those among independent individuals, hinge on perceptions of trustworthiness and fairness. Some examples:

Shirking and Opportunism. The owner of a business perceives an opportunity to open a branch in a distant city. He knows that if he can hire an honest manager, the branch will be highly profitable. He cannot monitor the manager, however, and if the manager cheats, the branch will be unprofitable. By cheating, the manager can earn three times as much as he could by being honest. This situation defines a commitment problem. If the owner lacks the ability to identify an honest manager, the venture cannot go forward, but if he has that ability, he can pay the manager well and still earn an attractive return.

Piece Rates. In cases where individual productivity can be measured with reasonable accuracy, economic theory identifies piece-rate pay schemes as a simple and attractive way to elicit effort from workers. Workers, however, are notoriously suspicious of piece rates. They fear that if they work as hard as they can and do well under an existing piece rate, management will step in and reduce the rate. There is indeed a large literature that describes the elaborate subterfuges employed by workers to prevent this from happening and numerous cases in which piece rates were abandoned although they had led to significant increases in productivity. If piece-rate decisions were placed in the hands of someone who had earned the workers' trust, both owners and workers would gain.

Career Lock-In. Many of the skills one acquires on the job are firm-specific. By accepting long-term employment with a single firm, a worker can anticipate that the day will come when her particular mix of skills, although still of value to her employer, will be of relatively little value in the market at large. And with her outside opportunities diminished, she will find herself at her employer's mercy. Firms have a narrow self-interest, of course, in establishing a reputation for treating workers fairly under these circumstances, for a good reputation will aid them in their recruiting efforts.

But many workers will find that the firm's self-interest alone may not provide adequate security. A firm may determine, for example, that its employment base will shift overseas during the coming years, and therefore that diminished recruiting ability in the domestic market is not a serious problem. Any firm believed to be motivated only by economic self-interest would thus have been at a recruiting disadvantage from the very beginning. By contrast, a firm whose management can persuade workers that fair treatment of workers is a goal valued for its own sake will have its pick of the most able and attractive workers.

Rising Wage Profiles. It is a common pattern in industrial pay schemes for pay to rise more rapidly than productivity. A worker's pay is less than the value of his productivity early in his career, and it rises until it is more than the value of his productivity later in his career. Various reasons are offered for this pattern. One is that it discourages shirking, for the worker knows that if he is caught shirking, he may not survive to enjoy the premium pay of the out years. A second rationale is that workers simply like upward-sloping wage profiles. Given a choice between two jobs with the same present value of lifetime income, one with a flat wage profile and the other with a rising profile, most people opt for the second. Whatever the reason for upward-sloping wage profiles, they create an incentive for opportunistic behavior on the part of employers, who stand to gain by firing workers once their pay begins to exceed their productivity. Given the advantages of upward-sloping wage profiles, a firm whose management can be trusted not to renege on its implicit contract stands at a clear advantage.

Other Implicit Contracts. A firm with a skilled legal department might be able to devise some formal contractual arrangement whereby it could commit itself not to fire older workers. But such a contract would entail a potentially costly loss of flexibility. No firm can be certain of the future demand for its product, and the time may come when its survival may depend on its ability to reduce its work force. Both the firm and its workers would pay a price if this flexibility were sacrificed.

There are a host of other contingencies that might seriously affect the terms of the bargain between employers and workers. Many of these contingencies are impossible to foresee and hence impossible to resolve in advance by formal contractual arrangements. Any firm whose management can persuade workers that these contingencies will be dealt with in an equitable manner will have a clear advantage in attracting the most able workers.

By Solving Commitment Problems with Customers

A variety of commitment problems arise between firms and their customers, and at least some of these are amenable to solution along lines similar to those just discussed. Quality assurance is a clear example.

George Akerlof's celebrated paper on lemons (1970) describes a commitment problem in which sellers and buyers alike would benefit if the seller could somehow commit to providing a product or service of high quality. A variety of means have been suggested for solving this problem through reliance on material incentives. Firms can guarantee their products, for example, or they can develop public reputations for supplying high quality (see Klein and Leffler 1981).

Many forms of the quality assurance problem, however, cannot be resolved by manipulating material incentives. Consider a law firm that could provide the legal services a client wants at a price the client would be willing to pay. But suppose that the client has no way to evaluate the quality of his lawyer's services. The outcome of his case by itself is not diagnostic. He might win despite having received shoddy legal help, or he might lose despite having received the best possible help. In such situations, clients are willing to pay premium fees to a firm run by someone they feel they can trust.

By Solving Commitment Problems with Other Firms

Commitment problems also arise in the context of business transactions between firms, and here too solutions that rely on character assessment often play a role.

The Subcontractor Holdup Problem. Consider the familiar example of the subcontractor that does most of its business with a single buyer. To serve this buyer at the lowest possible price, much of the subcontractor's human and physical capital has to be tailored to the buyer's specific needs. Having made those investments, however, the subcontractor is vulnerable to the holdup problem; because the buyer knows that the subcontractor's customized assets cost more than they would bring in the open market, it can pay its subcontractor a price that is above the subcontractor's marginal cost but lower than its average cost. Anticipating this problem, subcontractors will be willing to invest in the capital that best serves their customers' needs only if they believe their partners can be trusted not to exploit them.

In a recent study, Edward Lorenz (1988) spelled out why material incentives are inadequate to solve the commitment problems that arise between small French manufacturing firms and their subcontractors. He described in detail how parties shop for trustworthy partners. For example, all the respondents in his sample emphasized the heavy weight they placed on personal relationships in this process.

Quality Assurance. The problem of quality assurance arises not just between firms and consumers but also between one firm and another. Consider, for example, the relationship between a parent company and its franchisees. When a franchise owner provides high-quality service to the public he enhances not just his own reputation with local consumers but also the reputations of other outlets. The parent firm would like him to take both these benefits into account in setting his service levels, but his private incentives are to focus only on how good service affects his own customers. Accordingly, it is common for franchise agreements to call on franchisees to provide higher quality service than would otherwise be in their interests to provide. Franchisers incur costs in the attempt to enforce these agreements, but their ability to monitor service at the local level is highly imperfect. The franchiser thus has a strong incentive to recruit franchisees who assign intrinsic value to living up to their service agreements. And prospective franchisees so identified are at a competitive advantage over those motivated by self-interest alone.

Maintaining Confidentiality. Many consulting firms provide services that require access to competitively sensitive information. Clearly no firm could succeed in this line of work if it acquired a reputation for making such information available to rivals. When employees leave these firms, however, their material incentives to maintain confidentiality fall considerably. In some cases, material incentives to maintain confidentiality are weakened by the fact that a number of people have had access to the sensitive information, so that it is much harder to trace the source of a leak. With these possibilities in mind, a client would be much more willing to deal with a consulting firm that is able to identify and attract employees who assign intrinsic value to honoring confidentiality agreements.

In the examples just discussed, firms compensate for the higher costs of socially responsible behavior by their ability to solve commitment problems. In addition, socially responsible firms benefit from a match with the moral values of socially responsible consumers and recruits.

By Reflecting Consumers' Moral Values

The standard free-rider model suggests that buyers will not be willing to pay a premium for products produced by socially responsible firms. For example, consumers may not like the fact that Acme Tire Corporation pollutes the air, but they are said to realize that their own purchase of Acme tires will have a virtually unmeasurable effect on air quality. Accordingly, the theory predicts, if Acme tires sell for even a little less than those produced by a rival with a cleaner technology, consumers will buy from Acme.

The commitment model challenges this account by showing that many people have come to develop a taste for socially responsible behavior. People with such a taste will prefer dealing with socially responsible firms even when they realize that their own purchases are too small to affect the outcomes they care about. Conventional free-rider theory predicted that Star Kist Tuna's sales and profits would fall when it raised its prices to cover the added cost of purchasing tuna only from suppliers who used dolphin-safe nets. Star Kist's sales and profits went up, however, not down. Any consumer who stopped to ponder the matter would know that a single household's tuna purchase would have no discernible impact on the fate of dolphins. Even so, it appears that many consumers were willing to pay higher prices in the name of a cause they cared about. There is also evidence that Ben & Jerry's sells more ice cream because of its preservation efforts on behalf of Amazon rain forests, that The Body Shop sells more cosmetics because of its environmentally friendly packaging, and that McDonald's sells more hamburgers because of its support for the parents of seriously ill children.

Experimental evidence from the "dictator game" provides additional evidence of consumers' willingness to incur costs on behalf of moral values. The dictator game is played by two players. The first is given a sum of money—say, $20—and is then asked to choose one of two ways of dividing it with the second player: either $10 each or $18 for the first player and $2 for the second. One study (Kahneman, Knetsch, and Thaler 1986) found that more than three-quarters of subjects chose the $10–$10 split. The researchers then described this experiment to a separate group of subjects, to whom they then gave a choice between splitting $10 with one of the subjects who had chosen the $10–$10 split or splitting $12 with one of the subjects who had chosen the $18–$2 split. More than 80 percent of these subjects chose the first option, which the authors of the study interpreted as a willingness to spend $1 to punish an anonymous stranger who had behaved unfairly in the earlier experiment.

Taken together, the market data and experimental evidence appears to shift the burden of proof to proponents of the free-rider hypothesis.

By Reflecting Prospective Employees' Moral Values

A fifth and final benefit that accrues to socially responsible firms is the relative advantage they enjoy in recruiting. Jobs differ in countless dimensions, one of which is the degree to which the worker contributes to the well-being of others. Consider two jobs identical along all dimensions except this one. (For example, one job might involve writing advertising copy for a product known to cause serious health problems, while the other involves writing advertising copy for the United Way.) If people derive satisfaction from engaging in altruistic behavior, it follows that if the wages in these two jobs were the same, there would be an excess supply of applicants to the second job, a shortage of applicants to the first. In equilibrium, we would therefore expect a compensating wage premium for the less altruistic job. A job applicant who wants to occupy the moral high ground can do so only by accepting lower wages. And these lower wages, in turn, help balance the higher costs of socially responsible operations.

CONCLUSIONS

When a business confronts an ethical dilemma, it must incur higher costs if it takes the high road. For example, in the process of refusing to supply master automobile keys to mail-order customers he believes to be car thieves, a locksmith sustains a penalty on the bottom line. Indeed, if the morally preferred action involved no such penalty, there would be no moral dilemmas.

In this chapter, I have described five advantages that help a socially responsible firm to compensate for the higher direct costs of its actions. Three of these involve the ability to avoid commitment problems and other one-shot dilemmas. The socially responsible firm is better able than its opportunistic rivals to solve commitment problems that might arise with employees, with customers, and with other firms. A fourth advantage is that buyers are often willing to pay more for the products of socially responsible firms. And finally, the socially responsible firm often enjoys an advantage when recruiting against its less responsible rivals. Taken together, these advantages often appear to be sufficient to offset the higher costs of socially responsible action.

This claim may invite the complaint that what I am calling socially responsible behavior is really just selfishness by another name. Consider this trenchant commentary by Albert Carr, an economic advisor to Harry Truman:

> The illusion that business can afford to be guided by ethics as conceived in private life is often fostered by speeches and articles containing such phrases as "It pays to be ethical," or, "Sound ethics is good business." Actually this is not an ethical question at all; it is a self-serving calculation in disguise. The speaker is really saying that in the long run a company can make more money if it does not antagonize competitors, suppliers, employees, and customers by squeezing them too hard. He is saying that oversharp policies reduce ultimate gains. That is true, but it has nothing to do with ethics (Carr 1968, 148).

This line of reasoning implies that any business behavior consistent with survival is selfish by definition. Such a definition, however, is completely at odds with our everyday understanding of the concept. Cooperation in one-shot dilemmas is costly in both the short run and the long run, and for that reason it is properly called unselfish. I have argued that because traits of character are discernible by others, the kinds of people who cooperate in one-shot dilemmas enjoy advantages in other spheres, and these advantages may help them survive in competition with less scrupulous rivals. It simply invites confusion to call the cooperative behaviors themselves self-serving.

Note

1. In the version of the experiment reported here, subjects were permitted to discuss the PD game itself, and, if they chose, to make promises concerning their strategy choices.

References

Akerlof, G. 1970. "The Market for Lemons," *Quarterly Journal of Economics* 84: 488–500.

Axelrod, R. 1984. *The Evolution of Cooperation.* New York: Basic Books.

Carr, A. 1968. "Is Business Bluffing Ethical?" In *Ethical Issues in Business*, 4th ed., Thomas Donaldson and Patricia Werhane (eds.). (Englewood Cliffs, NJ.: Prentice Hall).

Dawkins, R. 1976. *The Selfish Gene.* (New York: Oxford University Press).

Frank, R.H., T. Gilovich, and D. Regan. 1993. "The Evolution of One-Shot Cooperation," *Ethology and Sociobiology* 14 (July): 247–56.

Frank, R.H. 1988. "Passions Within Reason: The Strategic Role of the Emotions." (New York: Norton).

Friedman, M. 1970. "The Social Responsibility of Business Is to Increase Its Profits." *New York Times Magazine* 33 (September 13): 116–29.

Kahneman, D., J. Knetsch, and R. Thaler. 1986. "Perceptions of Unfairness: Constraints on Wealth Seeking," *American Economic Review* 76: 728–41.

Klein, B., and K. Leffler. 1981. "The Role of Market Forces in Assuring Contractual Performance." *Journal of Political Economy* 89: 615–41.

Lorenz, E. 1988. "Neither Friends Nor Strangers: Informal Networks of Subcontracting in French Industry." In *Trust: The Making and Breaking of Cooperative Relations*, Diego Gambetta (ed.). (New York: Basil Blackwell).

Schelling, T.C. 1960. *Strategy and Conflict* (Cambridge: Harvard University Press).

[handwritten: Can an Organization have integrity?]

Managing for Organizational Integrity

LYNN SHARP PAINE

Many managers think of ethics as a question of personal scruples, a confidential matter between individuals and their consciences. These executives are quick to describe any wrongdoing as an isolated incident, the work of a rogue employee. The thought that the company could bear any responsibility for an individual's misdeeds never enters their minds. Ethics, after all, has nothing to do with management.

ENRON?

In fact, ethics has everything to do with management. Rarely do the character flaws of a lone actor fully explain corporate misconduct. More typically, unethical business practice involves the tacit, if not explicit, cooperation of others and reflects the values, attitudes, beliefs, language, and behavioral patterns that define an organization's operating culture. Ethics, then, is as much an organizational as a personal issue. Managers who fail to provide proper leadership and to institute systems that facilitate ethical conduct share responsibility with those who conceive, execute, and knowingly benefit from corporate misdeeds.

Managers must acknowledge their role in shaping organizational ethics and seize this opportunity to create a climate that can strengthen the relationships and reputations on which their companies' success depends. Executives who ignore ethics run the risk of personal and corporate liability in today's increasingly tough legal environment. In addition, they deprive their organizations of the benefits available under new federal guidelines for sentencing organizations convicted of wrongdoing. These sentencing guidelines recognize for the first time the organizational and managerial roots of unlawful conduct and base fines partly on the extent to which companies have taken steps to prevent that misconduct.

Prompted by the prospect of leniency, many companies are rushing to implement compliance-based ethics programs. Designed by corporate counsel, the goal of these programs is to prevent, detect, and punish legal violations. But organizational ethics means more than avoiding illegal practice; and providing employees with a rule book will do little to address the problems underlying unlawful conduct. To foster a climate that encourages exemplary behavior, corporations need a comprehensive approach that goes beyond the often punitive legal compliance stance.

An integrity-based approach to ethics management combines a concern for the law with an emphasis on managerial responsibility for ethical behavior. Though integrity strategies may vary in design and scope, all strive to define companies' guiding values, aspirations, and patterns of thought and conduct. When integrated into the day-to-day operations of an organization, such strategies can help prevent damaging ethical lapses while tapping into powerful human impulses for moral thought and action. Then an ethical framework becomes no longer a burdensome constraint within which companies must operate, but the governing ethos of an organization.

HOW ORGANIZATIONS SHAPE INDIVIDUALS' BEHAVIOR

The once familiar picture of ethics as individualistic, unchanging, and impervious to organizational influences has not stood up to scrutiny in recent years. Sears Auto Centers' and Beech-Nut Nutrition Corporation's experiences illustrate the role organizations play in shaping individuals' behavior—and how even sound moral fiber can fray when stretched too thin.

In 1992, Sears, Roebuck & Company was inundated with complaints about its automotive service business. Consumers and attorneys general in more than 40 states had accused the company of misleading customers and selling them unnecessary parts and services, from brake jobs to front-end alignments. It would be a mistake, however, to see this situation exclusively in terms of any one individual's moral failings. Nor did management set out to defraud Sears customers. Instead, a number of organizational factors contributed to the problematic sales practices.

In the face of declining revenues, shrinking market share, and an increasingly competitive market for undercar services, Sears management attempted to spur the performance of its auto centers by introducing new goals and incentives for employees. The company increased minimum work quotas and introduced productivity incentives for mechanics. The automotive service advisers were given product-specific sales quotas—sell so many springs, shock absorbers, alignments, or brake jobs per shift—and paid a commission based on sales. According to advisers, failure to meet quotas could lead to a transfer or a reduction in work hours. Some employees spoke of the "pressure, pressure, pressure" to bring in sales.

Under this new set of organizational pressures and incentives, with few options for meeting their sales goals legitimately, some employees' judgment understandably suffered. Management's failure to clarify the line between unnecessary service and legitimate preventive maintenance, coupled with consumer ignorance, left employees to chart their own courses through a vast gray area, subject to a wide range of interpretations. Without active management support for ethical practice and mechanisms to detect and check questionable sales methods and poor work, it is not surprising that some employees may have reacted to contextual forces by resorting to exaggeration, carelessness, or even misrepresentation.

Shortly after the allegations against Sears became public, CEO Edward Brennan acknowledged management's responsibility for putting in place compensation and goal-setting systems that "created an environment in which mistakes did occur." Although the company denied any intent to deceive consumers, senior executives eliminated commissions for service advisers and discontinued sales quotas for specific parts. They also instituted a system of unannounced shopping audits and made plans to expand the internal monitoring of service. In settling the pending lawsuits, Sears offered coupons to customers who had bought certain auto services between 1990 and 1992. The total cost of the settlement, including potential customer refunds, was an estimated $60 million.

Contextual forces can also influence the behavior of top management, as a former CEO of Beech-Nut Nutrition Corporation discovered. In the early 1980s, only two years after joining the company, the CEO found evidence suggesting that the apple juice concentrate, supplied by the company's vendors for use in Beech-Nut's "100% pure" apple juice, contained nothing more than sugar water and chemicals. The CEO could have destroyed the bogus inventory and withdrawn the juice from grocers' shelves, but he was under extraordinary pressure to turn the ailing company around. Eliminating the inventory would have killed any hope of turning even the meager $700,000 profit promised to Beech-Nut's then parent, Nestlé.

A number of people in the corporation, it turned out, had doubted the purity of the juice for several years before the CEO arrived. But the 25% price advantage offered by the supplier of the bogus concentrate allowed the operations head to meet cost-control goals. Furthermore, the company lacked an effective quality control system, and a conclusive lab test for juice purity did not yet exist. When a member of the research department voiced concerns about the juice to operating management, he was accused of not being a team player and of acting like "Chicken Little." His judgment, his supervisor wrote in an annual performance review, was "colored by naïveté and impractical ideals." No one else seemed to have considered the company's obligations to its customers or to have thought about the potential harm of disclosure. No one considered the fact that the sale of adulterated or misbranded juice is a legal offense, putting the company and its top management at risk of criminal liability.

An FDA investigation taught Beech-Nut the hard way. In 1987, the company pleaded guilty to selling adulterated and misbranded juice. Two years and two criminal trials later, the CEO pleaded guilty to ten counts of mislabeling. The total cost to the company—including fines, legal expenses, and lost sales—was an estimated $25 million.

Such errors of judgment rarely reflect an organizational culture and management philosophy that sets out to harm or deceive. More often, they reveal a culture that is insensitive or indifferent to ethical considerations or one that lacks effective organizational systems. By the same token, exemplary conduct usually reflects an organizational culture and philosophy that is infused with a sense of responsibility.

For example, Johnson & Johnson's handling of the Tylenol crisis is sometimes attributed to the singular personality of then-CEO James Burke. However, the decision to do a nationwide recall of Tylenol capsules in order to avoid further loss of life from product tampering was in reality not one decision but thousands of decisions made by individuals at all levels of the organization. The "Tylenol decision," then, is best understood not as an isolated incident, the achievement of a lone individual, but as the reflection of an organization's culture. Without a shared set of values and guiding principles deeply ingrained throughout the organization, it is doubtful that Johnson & Johnson's response would have been as rapid, cohesive, and ethically sound.

Many people resist acknowledging the influence of organizational factors on individual behavior—especially on misconduct—for fear of diluting people's sense of personal moral responsibility. But this fear is based on a false dichotomy between holding individual transgressors accountable and holding "the system" accountable. Acknowledging the importance of organizational context need not imply exculpating individual wrongdoers. To understand all is not to forgive all.

THE LIMITS OF A LEGAL COMPLIANCE PROGRAM

The consequences of an ethical lapse can be serious and far-reaching. Organizations can quickly become entangled in an all-consuming web of legal proceedings. The risk of litigation and liability has increased in the past decade as lawmakers have legislated new civil and criminal offenses, stepped up penalties, and improved support for law enforcement. Equally—if not more—important is the damage an ethical lapse can do to an organization's reputation and relationships. Both Sears and Beech-Nut, for instance, struggled to regain consumer trust and market share long after legal proceedings had ended.

As more managers have become alerted to the importance of organizational ethics, many have asked their lawyers to develop corporate ethics programs to detect and prevent violations of the law. The 1991 Federal Sentencing

Guidelines offer a compelling rationale. Sanctions such as fines and probation for organizations convicted of wrongdoing can vary dramatically depending both on the degree of management cooperation in reporting and investigating corporate misdeeds and on whether or not the company has implemented a legal compliance program.

Such programs tend to emphasize the prevention of unlawful conduct, primarily by increasing surveillance and control and by imposing penalties for wrongdoers. While plans vary, the basic framework is outlined in the sentencing guidelines. Managers must establish compliance standards and procedures; designate high-level personnel to oversee compliance; avoid delegating discretionary authority to those likely to act unlawfully; effectively communicate the company's standards and procedures through training or publications; take reasonable steps to achieve compliance through audits, monitoring processes, and a system for employees to report criminal misconduct without fear of retribution; consistently enforce standards through appropriate disciplinary measures; respond appropriately when offenses are detected; and, finally, take reasonable steps to prevent the occurrence of similar offenses in the future.

 There is no question of the necessity of a sound, well-articulated strategy for legal compliance in an organization. After all, employees can be frustrated and frightened by the complexity of today's legal environment. And even managers who claim to use the law as a guide to ethical behavior often lack more than a rudimentary understanding of complex legal issues.

Managers would be mistaken, however, to regard legal compliance as an adequate means for addressing the full range of ethical issues that arise every day. "If it's legal, it's ethical," is a frequently heard slogan. But conduct that is lawful may be highly problematic from an ethical point of view. Consider the sale in some countries of hazardous products without appropriate warnings or the purchase of goods from suppliers who operate inhumane sweatshops in developing countries. Companies engaged in international business often discover that conduct that infringes on recognized standards of human rights and decency is legally permissible in some jurisdictions.

Legal clearance does not certify the absence of ethical problems in the United States either, as a 1991 case at Salomon Brothers illustrates. Four top-level executives failed to take appropriate action when learning of unlawful activities on the government trading desk. Company lawyers found no law obligating the executives to disclose the improprieties. Nevertheless, the executives' delay in disclosing and failure to reveal their prior knowledge prompted a serious crisis of confidence among employees, creditors, shareholders, and customers. The executives were forced to resign, having lost the moral authority to lead. Their ethical lapse compounded the trading desk's legal offenses, and the company ended up suffering losses—including legal costs, increased funding costs, and lost business—estimated at nearly $1 billion.

A compliance approach to ethics also overemphasizes the threat of detection and punishment in order to channel behavior in lawful directions. The underlying model for this approach is deterrence theory, which envisions people as rational maximizers of self-interest, responsive to the personal costs and benefits of their choices, yet indifferent to the moral legitimacy of those choices. But a recent study reported in *Why People Obey the Law* by Tom R. Tyler (New Haven: Yale University Press) shows that obedience to the law is strongly influenced by a belief in its legitimacy and its moral correctness. People generally feel that they have a strong obligation to obey the law. Education about the legal standards and a supportive environment may be all that's required to ensure compliance.

Discipline is, of course, a necessary part of any ethical system. Justified penalties for the infringement of legitimate norms are fair and appropriate. Some people do need the threat of sanctions. However, an overemphasis on potential sanctions can be superfluous and even counterproductive. Employees may rebel against programs that stress penalties, particularly if they are designed and imposed without employee involvement or if the standards are vague or unrealistic. Management may talk of mutual trust when unveiling a compliance plan, but employees often receive the message as a warning from on high. Indeed, the most skeptical among them may view compliance programs as nothing more than liability insurance for senior management. This is not an unreasonable conclusion, considering that compliance programs rarely address the root causes of misconduct.

Even in the best cases, legal compliance is unlikely to unleash much moral imagination or commitment. The law does not generally seek to inspire human excellence or distinction. It is no guide for exemplary behavior—or even good practice. Those managers who define ethics as legal compliance are implicitly endorsing a code of moral mediocrity for their organizations. As Richard Breeden, former chairman of the Securities and Exchange Commission, noted, "It is not an adequate ethical standard to aspire to get through the day without being indicted."

INTEGRITY AS A GOVERNING ETHIC

A strategy based on integrity holds organizations to a more robust standard. While compliance is rooted in avoiding legal sanctions, organizational integrity is based on the concept of self-governance in accordance with a set of guiding principles. From the perspective of integrity, the task of ethics management is to define and give life to an organization's guiding values, to create an environment that supports ethically sound behavior, and to instill a sense of shared accountability among employees. The need to obey the law is viewed as a positive aspect of organizational life, rather than an unwelcome constraint imposed by external authorities.

An integrity strategy is characterized by a conception of ethics as a driving force of an enterprise. Ethical values shape the search for opportunities, the design of organizational systems, and the decision-making process used by individuals and groups. They provide a common frame of reference and serve as a unifying force across different functions, lines of business, and employee groups. Organizational ethics helps define what a company is and what it stands for.

Many integrity initiatives have structural features common to compliance-based initiatives: a code of conduct, training in relevant areas of law, mechanisms for reporting and investigating potential misconduct, and audits and controls to insure that laws and company standards are being met. In addition, if suitably designed, an integrity-based initiative can establish a foundation for seeking the legal benefits that are available under the sentencing guidelines should criminal wrongdoing occur. (See the exhibit "The Hallmarks of an Effective Integrity Strategy.")

EXHIBIT. The Hallmarks of an Effective Integrity Strategy

There is no one right integrity strategy. Factors such as management personality, company history, culture, lines of business, and industry regulations must be taken into account when shaping an appropriate set of values and designing an implementation program. Still, several features are common to efforts that have achieved some success:

- *The guiding values and commitments make sense and are clearly communicated.* They reflect important organizational obligations and widely shared aspirations that appeal to the organization's members. Employees at all levels take them seriously, feel comfortable discussing them, and have a concrete understanding of their practical importance. This does not signal the absence of ambiguity and conflict but a willingness to seek solutions compatible with the framework of values.
- *Company leaders are personally committed, credible, and willing to take action on the values they espouse.* They are not mere mouthpieces. They are willing to scrutinize their own decisions. Consistency on the part of leadership is key. Waffling on values will lead to employee cynicism and a rejection of the program. At the same time, managers must assume responsibility for making tough calls when ethical obligations conflict.
- *The espoused values are integrated into the normal channels of management decision making and are reflected in the organization's critical activities:* the development of plans, the setting of goals, the search for opportunities, the allocation of resources, the gathering and communication of information, the measurement of performance, and the promotion and advancement of personnel.
- *The company's systems and structures support and reinforce its values.* Information systems, for example, are designed to provide timely and accurate information. Reporting relationships are structured to build in checks and balances to promote objective judgment. Performance appraisal is sensitive to means as well as ends.
- *Managers throughout the company have the decision-making skills, knowledge, and competencies needed to make ethically sound decisions on a day-to-day basis.* Ethical thinking and awareness must be part of every manager's mental equipment. Ethics education is usually part of the process.

Success in creating a climate for responsible and ethically sound behavior requires continuing effort and a considerable investment of time and resources. A glossy code of conduct, a high-ranking ethics officer, a training program, an annual ethics audit—these trappings of an ethics program do not necessarily add up to a responsible, law-abiding organization whose espoused values match its actions. A formal ethics program can serve as a catalyst and a support system, but organizational integrity depends on the integration of the company's values into its driving systems.

But an integrity strategy is broader, deeper, and more demanding than a legal compliance initiative. Broader in that it seeks to enable responsible conduct. Deeper in that it cuts to the ethos and operating systems of the organization and its members, their guiding values and patterns of thought and action. And more demanding in that it requires an active effort to define the responsibilities and aspirations that constitute an organization's ethical compass. Above all, organizational ethics is seen as the work of management. Corporate counsel may play a role in the design and implementation of integrity strategies, but managers at all levels and across all functions are involved in the process. (See the chart, "Strategies for Ethics Management.")

Strategies for Ethics Management

Characteristics of Compliance Strategy

Ethos	conformity with externally imposed standards
Objective	prevent criminal misconduct
Leadership	lawyer driven
Methods	education, reduced discretion, auditing and controls, penalties
Behavioral Assumptions	autonomous beings guided by material self-interest

Characteristics of Integrity Strategy

Tougher

Ethos	self-governance according to chosen standards
Objective	enable responsible conduct
Leadership	management driven with aid of lawyers, HR, others
Methods	education, leadership, accountability, organizational systems and decision processes, auditing and controls, penalties
Behavioral Assumptions	social beings guided by material self-interest, values, ideals, peers

Implementation of Compliance Strategy

Standards	criminal and regulatory law
Staffing	lawyers
Activities	develop compliance standards
	train and communicate
	handle reports of misconduct
	conduct investigations
	oversee compliance audits
	enforce standards
Education	compliance standards and system

Implementation of Integrity Strategy

Standards	company values and aspirations, social obligations, including law
Staffing	executives and managers with lawyers, others
Activities	lead development of company values and standards
	train and communicate
	integrate into company systems
	provide guidance and consultation
	assess values performance
	identify and resolve problems
	oversee compliance activities
Education	decision making and values
	compliance standards and system

During the past decade, a number of companies have undertaken integrity initiatives. They vary according to the ethical values focused on and the implementation approaches used. Some companies focus on the core values of integrity that reflect basic social obligations, such as respect for the rights of others, honesty, fair dealing, and obedience to the law. Other companies emphasize aspirations—values that are ethically desirable but not necessarily morally obligatory—such as good service to customers, a commitment to diversity, and involvement in the community.

When it comes to implementation, some companies begin with behavior. Following Aristotle's view that one becomes courageous by acting as a courageous person, such companies develop codes of conduct specifying appropriate behavior, along with a system of incentives, audits, and controls. Other companies focus less on specific actions and more on developing attitudes, decision-making processes, and ways of thinking that reflect their values. The assumption is that personal commitment and appropriate decision processes will lead to right action.

Martin Marietta, NovaCare, and Wetherill Associates have implemented and lived with quite different integrity strategies. In each case, management has found that the initiative has made important and often unexpected contributions to competitiveness, work environment, and key relationships on which the company depends.

Martin Marietta: Emphasizing Core Values

Martin Marietta Corporation, the U.S. aerospace and defense contractor, opted for an integrity-based ethics program in 1985. At the time, the defense industry was under attack for fraud and mismanagement, and Martin Marietta was under investigation for improper travel billings. Managers knew they needed a better form of self-governance but were skeptical that an ethics program could influence behavior. "Back then people asked, 'Do you really need an ethics program to be ethical?'" recalls current President Thomas Young. "Ethics was something personal. Either you had it, or you didn't."

The corporate general counsel played a pivotal role in promoting the program, and legal compliance was a critical objective. But it was conceived of and implemented from the start as a companywide management initiative aimed at creating and maintaining a "do-it-right" climate. In its original conception, the program emphasized core values, such as honesty and fair play. Over time, it expanded to encompass quality and environmental responsibility as well.

Today the initiative consists of a code of conduct, an ethics training program, and procedures for reporting and investigating ethical concerns within the company. It also includes a system for disclosing violations of federal procurement law to the government. A corporate ethics office manages the program, and ethics representatives are stationed at major facilities. An ethics steering committee, made up of Martin Marietta's president, senior executives, and two rotating members selected from field operations, oversees the ethics office. The audit and ethics committee of the board of directors oversees the steering committee.

The ethics office is responsible for responding to questions and concerns from the company's employees. Its network of representatives serves as a sounding board, a source of guidance, and a channel for raising a range of issues, from allegations of wrongdoing to complaints about poor management, unfair supervision, and company policies and practices. Martin

Marietta's ethics network, which accepts anonymous complaints, logged over 9,000 calls in 1991, when the company had about 60,000 employees. In 1992, it investigated 684 cases. The ethics office also works closely with the human resources, legal, audit, communications, and security functions to respond to employee concerns.

Shortly after establishing the program, the company began its first round of ethics training for the entire workforce, starting with the CEO and senior executives. Now in its third round, training for senior executives focuses on decision making, the challenges of balancing multiple responsibilities, and compliance with laws and regulations critical to the company. The incentive compensation plan for executives makes responsibility for promoting ethical conduct an explicit requirement for reward eligibility and requires that business and personal goals be achieved in accordance with the company's policy on ethics. Ethical conduct and support for the ethics program are also criteria in regular performance reviews.

Today top-level managers say the ethics program has helped the company avoid serious problems and become more responsive to its more than 90,000 employees. The ethics network, which tracks the number and types of cases and complaints, has served as an early warning system for poor management, quality and safety defects, racial and gender discrimination, environmental concerns, inaccurate and false records, and personnel grievances regarding salaries, promotions, and layoffs. By providing an alternative channel for raising such concerns, Martin Marietta is able to take corrective action more quickly and with a lot less pain. In many cases, potentially embarrassing problems have been identified and dealt with before becoming a management crisis, a lawsuit, or a criminal investigation. Among employees who brought complaints in 1993, 75% were satisfied with the results.

Company executives are also convinced that the program has helped reduce the incidence of misconduct. When allegations of misconduct do surface, the company says it deals with them more openly. On several occasions, for instance, Martin Marietta has voluntarily disclosed and made restitution to the government for misconduct involving potential violations of federal procurement laws. In addition, when an employee alleged that the company had retaliated against him for voicing safety concerns about his plant on CBS news, top management commissioned an investigation by an outside law firm. Although failing to support the allegations, the investigation found that employees at the plant feared retaliation when raising health, safety, or environmental complaints. The company redoubled its efforts to identify and discipline those employees taking retaliatory action and stressed the desirability of an open work environment in its ethics training and company communications.

Although the ethics program helps Martin Marietta avoid certain types of litigation, it has occasionally led to other kinds of legal action. In a few cases, employees dismissed for violating the code of ethics sued Martin Marietta, arguing that the company had violated its own code by imposing unfair and excessive discipline.

Still, the company believes that its attention to ethics has been worth it. The ethics program has led to better relationships with the government, as well as to new business opportunities. Along with prices and technology, Martin Marietta's record of integrity, quality, and reliability of estimates plays a role in the awarding of defense contracts, which account for some 75% of the company's revenues. Executives believe that the reputation they've earned through their ethics program has helped them build trust with government auditors, as well. By opening up communications, the company has reduced the time spent on redundant audits.

The program has also helped change employees' perceptions and priorities. Some managers compare their new ways of thinking about ethics to the way they understand quality. They consider more carefully how situations will be perceived by others, the possible long-term consequences of short-term thinking, and the need for continuous improvement. CEO Norman Augustine notes, "Ten years ago, people would have said that there were no ethical issues in business. Today employees think their number-one objective is to be thought of as decent people doing quality work."

NovaCare: Building Shared Aspirations

NovaCare Inc., one of the largest providers of rehabilitation services to nursing homes and hospitals in the United States, has oriented its ethics effort toward building a common core of shared aspirations. But in 1988, when the company was called InSpeech, the only sentiment shared was mutual mistrust.

Senior executives built the company from a series of aggressive acquisitions over a brief period of time to take advantage of the expanding market for therapeutic services. However, in 1988, the viability of the company was in question. Turnover among its frontline employees—the clinicians and therapists who care for patients in nursing homes and hospitals—escalated to 57% per year. The company's inability to retain therapists caused customers to defect and the stock price to languish in an extended slump.

After months of soul-searching, InSpeech executives realized that the turnover rate was a symptom of a more basic problem: the lack of a common set of values and aspirations. There was, as one executive put it, a "huge disconnect" between the values of the therapists and clinicians and those of the managers who ran the company. The therapists and clinicians evaluated the company's success in terms of its delivery and high-quality health care. InSpeech management, led by executives with financial services and venture capital backgrounds, measured the company's worth exclusively in terms of financial success. Management's single-minded emphasis on increasing hours of reimbursable care turned clinicians off. They took management's performance orientation for indifference to patient care and left the company in droves.

CEO John Foster recognized the need for a common frame of reference and a common language to unify the diverse groups. So he brought in consultants to conduct interviews and focus groups with the company's health care professionals, managers, and customers. Based on the results, an employee task force drafted a proposed vision statement for the company, and another 250 employees suggested revisions. Then Foster and several senior managers developed a succinct statement of the company's guiding purpose and fundamental beliefs that could be used as a framework for making decisions and setting goals, policies, and practices.

Unlike a code of conduct, which articulates specific behavioral standards, the statement of vision, purposes, and beliefs lays out in very simple terms the company's central purpose and core values. The purpose—meeting the rehabilitation needs of patients through clinical leadership—is supported by four key beliefs: respect for the individual, service to the customer, pursuit of excellence, and commitment to personal integrity. Each value is discussed with examples of how it is manifested in the day-to-day activities and policies of the company, such as how to measure the quality of care.

To support the newly defined values, the company changed its name to NovaCare and introduced a number of structural and operational changes. Field managers and clinicians were given greater decision-making authority; clinicians were provided with additional resources to assist in the delivery of effective therapy; and a new management structure integrated the various therapies offered by the company. The hiring of new corporate personnel with health care backgrounds reinforced the company's new clinical focus.

The introduction of the vision, purpose, and beliefs met with varied reactions from employees, ranging from cool skepticism to open enthusiasm. One employee remembered thinking the talk about values "much ado about nothing." Another recalled, "It was really wonderful. It gave us a goal that everyone aspired to, no matter what their place in the company." At first, some were baffled about how the vision, purpose, and beliefs were to be used. But, over time, managers became more adept at explaining and using them as a guide. When a customer tried to hire away a valued employee, for example, managers considered raiding the customer's company for employees. After reviewing the beliefs, the managers abandoned the idea.

NovaCare managers acknowledge and company surveys indicate that there is plenty of room for improvement. While the values are used as a firm reference point for decision making and evaluation in some areas of the company, they are still viewed with reservation in others. Some managers do not "walk the talk," employees complain. And recently acquired companies have yet to be fully integrated into the program. Nevertheless, many NovaCare employees say the values initiative played a critical role in the company's 1990 turnaround.

The values reorientation also helped the company deal with its most serious problem: turnover among health care providers. In 1990, the turnover rate stood at 32%, still above target but a significant improvement over the 1988 rate of 57%. By 1993, turnover had dropped to 27%. Moreover, recruiting new clinicians became easier. Barely able to hire 25 new clinicians each month in 1988, the company added 776 in 1990 and 2,546 in 1993. Indeed, one employee who left during the 1988 turmoil said that her decision to return in 1990 hinged on the company's adoption of the vision, purpose, and beliefs.

Wetherill Associates: Defining Right Action

Wetherill Associates, Inc.—a small, privately held supplier of electrical parts to the automotive market—has neither a conventional code of conduct nor a statement of values. Instead, WAI has a Quality Assurance Manual—a combination of philosophy text, conduct guide, technical manual, and company profile—that describes the company's commitment to honesty and its guiding principle of right action.

WAI doesn't have a corporate ethics officer who reports to top management, because at WAI, the company's corporate ethics officer is top management. Marie Bothe, WAI's chief executive officer, sees her main function as keeping the 350-employee company on the path of right action and looking for opportunities to help the community. She delegates the "technical" aspects of the business—marketing, finance, personnel, operations—to other members of the organization.

Right action, the basis for all of WAI's decisions, is a well-developed approach that challenges most conventional management thinking. The company explicitly rejects the usual conceptual boundaries that separate morality and self-interest. Instead, they define right behavior as logically, expediently, and morally right. Managers teach employees to look at the needs of the customers, suppliers, and the community—in addition to those of the company and its employees—when making decisions.

WAI also has a unique approach to competition. One employee explains, "We are not 'in competition' with anybody. We just do what we have to do to serve the customer." Indeed, when occasionally unable to fill orders, WAI salespeople refer customers to competitors. Artificial incentives, such as sales contests, are never used to spur individual performance. Nor are sales results used in determining compensation. Instead, the focus is on teamwork and customer service. Managers tell all new recruits that absolute honesty, mutual courtesy, and respect are standard operating procedure.

Newcomers generally react positively to company philosophy, but not all are prepared for such a radical departure from the practices they have known elsewhere. Recalling her initial interview, one recruit described her response to being told that lying was not allowed, "What do you mean? No lying? I'm a buyer. I lie for a living!" Today she is persuaded that the policy makes sound business sense. WAI is known for informing suppliers of overshipments as well as undershipments and for scrupulous honesty in the sale of parts, even when deception cannot be readily detected.

Since its entry into the distribution business 13 years ago, WAI has seen its revenues climb steadily from just under $1 million to nearly $98 million in 1993, and this in an industry with little growth. Once seen as an upstart beset by naysayers and industry skeptics, WAI is now credited with entering and professionalizing an industry in which kickbacks, bribes, and "gratuities" were commonplace. Employees—equal numbers of men and women ranging in age from 17 to 92—praise the work environment as both productive and supportive.

WAI's approach could be difficult to introduce in a larger, more traditional organization. WAI is a small company founded by 34 people who shared a belief in right action; its ethical values were naturally built into the organization from the start. Those values are so deeply ingrained in the company's culture and operating systems that they have been largely self-sustaining. Still, the company has developed its own training program and takes special care to hire people willing to support right action. Ethics and job skills are considered equally important in determining an individual's competence and suitability for employment. For WAI, the challenge will be to sustain its vision as the company grows and taps into markets overseas.

At WAI, as at Martin Marietta and NovaCare, a management-led commitment to ethical values has contributed to competitiveness, positive workforce morale, as well as solid sustainable relationships with the company's key constituencies. In the end, creating a climate that encourages exemplary conduct may be the best way to discourage damaging misconduct. Only in such an environment do rogues really act alone.

The Parable of the Sadhu

BOWEN H. MCCOY

It was early in the morning before the sun rose, which gave them time to climb the treacherous slope to the pass at 18,000 feet before the ice steps melted. They were also concerned about their stamina and altitude sickness, and felt the need to press on. Into the chance collection of climbers on that Himalayan slope an ethical dilemma arose in the guise of an unconscious, almost naked sadhu, an Indian holy man. Each climber gave the sadhu help but none made sure he would be safe. Should somebody have stopped to help the sadhu to safety? Would it have done any good? Was the group responsible? Since leaving the sadhu on the mountain slope, the author, who was one of the climbers, has pondered these issues. He sees many parallels for business people as they face ethical decisions at work.

Last year, as the first participant in the new six-month sabbatical program that Morgan Stanley has adopted, I enjoyed a rare opportunity to collect my thoughts as well as do some traveling. I spent the first three months in Nepal, walking 600 miles through 200 villages in the Himalayas and climbing some 120,000 vertical feet. On the trip my sole Western companion was an anthropologist who shed light on the cultural patterns of the villages we passed through.

During the Nepal hike, something occurred that has had a powerful impact on my thinking about corporate ethics. Although some might argue that the experience has no relevance to business, it was a situation in which a basic ethical dilemma suddenly intruded into the lives of a group of individuals. How the group responded I think holds a lesson for all organizations no matter how defined.

THE SADHU

The Nepal experience was more rugged and adventuresome than I had anticipated. Most commercial treks last two or three weeks and cover a quarter of the distance we traveled.

My friend Stephen, the anthropologist, and I were halfway through the 60-day Himalayan part of the trip when we reached the high point, an 18,000-foot pass over a crest that we'd have to traverse to reach the village of Muklinath, an ancient holy place for pilgrims.

Six years earlier I had suffered pulmonary edema, an acute form of altitude sickness, at 16,500 feet in the vicinity of Everest base camp, so we were understandably concerned about what would happen at 18,000 feet. Moreover, the Himalayas were having their wettest spring in 20 years; hip-deep powder and ice had already driven us off one ridge. If we failed to cross the pass, I feared that the last half of our "once in a lifetime" trip would be ruined.

The night before we would try the pass, we camped at a hut at 14,500 feet. In the photos taken at that camp, my face appears wan. The last village we'd passed through was a sturdy two-day walk below us, and I was tired.

During the late afternoon, four backpackers from New Zealand joined us, and we spent most of the night awake, anticipating the climb. Below we could see the fires of two other parties, which turned out to be two Swiss couples and a Japanese hiking club.

To get over the steep part of the climb before the sun melted the steps cut in the ice, we departed at 3:30 A.M. The New Zealanders left first, followed by Stephen and myself, our porters and Sherpas, and then the Swiss. The Japanese lingered in their camp. The sky was clear, and we were confident that no spring storm would erupt that day to close the pass.

At 15,500 feet, it looked to me as if Stephen were shuffling and staggering a bit, which are symptoms of altitude sickness. (The initial stage of altitude sickness brings a headache and nausea. As the condition worsens, a climber may encounter difficult breathing, disorientation, aphasia, and paralysis.) I felt strong, my adrenaline was flowing, but I was very concerned about my ultimate ability to get across. A couple of our porters were also suffering from the height, and Pasang, our Sherpa sirdar (leader), was worried.

Just after daybreak, while we rested at 15,500 feet, one of the New Zealanders, who had gone ahead, came staggering down toward us with a body slung across his shoulders. He dumped the almost naked, barefoot body of an Indian holy man—a sadhu—at my feet. He had found the pilgrim lying on the ice, shivering and suffering from hypothermia. I cradled the sadhu's head and laid him out on the rocks. The New Zealander was angry. He wanted to get across the pass before the bright sun melted the snow. He said, "Look, I've done what I can. You have porters and Sherpa guides. You care for him. We're going on!" He turned and went back up the mountain to join his friends.

I took a carotid pulse and found that the sadhu was still alive. We figured he had probably visited the holy shrines at Muklinath and was on his way home. It was fruitless to question why he had chosen this desperately high route instead of the safe, heavily traveled caravan route through the

Kali Gandaki gorge. Or why he was almost naked and with no shoes, or how long he had been lying in the pass. The answers weren't going to solve our problem.

Stephen and the four Swiss began stripping off outer clothing and opening their packs. The sadhu was soon clothed from head to foot. He was not able to walk, but he was very much alive. I looked down the mountain and spotted below the Japanese climbers marching up with a horse.

Without a great deal of thought, I told Stephen and Pasang that I was concerned about withstanding the heights to come and wanted to get over the pass. I took off after several of our porters who had gone ahead.

On the steep part of the ascent where, if the ice steps had given way, I would have slid down about 3,000 feet, I felt vertigo. I stopped for a breather, allowing the Swiss to catch up with me. I inquired about the sadhu and Stephen. They said that the sadhu was fine and that Stephen was just behind. I set off again for the summit.

Stephen arrived at the summit an hour after I did. Still exhilarated by victory, I ran down the snow slope to congratulate him. He was suffering from altitude sickness, walking 15 steps, then stopping, walking 15 steps, then stopping. Pasang accompanied him all the way up. When I reached them, Stephen glared at me and said: "How do you feel about contributing to the death of a fellow man?"

I did not fully comprehend what he meant.

"Is the sadhu dead?" I inquired.

"No," replied Stephen, "but he surely will be!"

After I had gone, and the Swiss had departed not long after, Stephen had remained with the sadhu. When the Japanese had arrived, Stephen had asked to use their horse to transport the sadhu down to the hut. They had refused. He had then asked Pasang to have a group of our porters carry the sadhu. Pasang had resisted the idea, saying that the porters would have to exert all their energy to get themselves over the pass. He had thought they could not carry a man down 1,000 feet to the hut, reclimb the slope, and get across safely before the snow melted. Pasang had pressed Stephen not to delay any longer.

The Sherpas had carried the sadhu down to a rock in the sun at about 15,000 feet and had pointed out the hut another 500 feet below. The Japanese had given him food and drink. When they had last seen him he was listlessly throwing rocks at the Japanese party's dog, which had frightened him.

We do not know if the sadhu lived or died.

For many of the following days and evenings Stephen and I discussed and debated our behavior toward the sadhu. Stephen is a committed Quaker with deep moral vision. He said, "I feel that what happened with the sadhu is a good example of the breakdown between the individual ethic and the corporate ethic. No one person was willing to assume ultimate responsibility for the sadhu. Each was willing to do his bit just so long as it was not too inconvenient. When it got to be a bother, everyone just passed the buck to someone else and took off. Jesus was relevant to a more individualistic stage of society, but how do we interpret his teaching today in a world filled with large, impersonal organizations and groups?"

I defended the larger group, saying, "Look, we all cared. We all stopped and gave aid and comfort. Everyone did his bit. The New Zealander carried him down below the snow line. I took his pulse and suggested we treat him for hypothermia. You and the Swiss gave him clothing and got him warmed up. The Japanese gave him food and water. The Sherpas carried him down to the sun and pointed out the easy trail toward the hut. He was well enough to throw rocks at a dog. What more could we do?"

"You have just described the typical affluent Westerner's response to a problem. Throwing money—in this case food and sweaters—at it, but not solving the fundamentals!" Stephen retorted.

"What would satisfy you?" I said. "Here we are, a group of New Zealanders, Swiss, Americans, and Japanese who have never met before and who are at the apex of one of the most powerful experiences of our lives. Some years the pass is so bad no one gets over it. What right does an almost naked pilgrim who chooses the wrong trail have to disrupt our lives? Even the Sherpas had no interest in risking the trip to help him beyond a certain point."

Stephen calmly rebutted, "I wonder what the Sherpas would have done if the sadhu had been a well-dressed Nepali, or what the Japanese would have done if the sadhu had been a well-dressed Asian, or what you would have done, Buzz, if the sadhu had been a well-dressed Western woman?"

"Where, in your opinion," I asked instead, "is the limit of our responsibility in a situation like this? We had our own well-being to worry about. Our Sherpa guides were unwilling to jeopardize us or the porters for the sadhu. No one else on the mountain was willing to commit himself beyond certain self-imposed limits."

Stephen said, "As individual Christians or people with a Western ethical tradition, we can fulfill our obligations in such a situation only if (1) the sadhu dies in our care, (2) the sadhu demonstrates to us that he could undertake the two-day walk down to the village, or (3) we carry the sadhu for two days down to the village and convince someone there to care for him."

"Leaving the sadhu in the sun with food and clothing, while he demonstrated hand-eye coordination by throwing a rock at a dog, comes close to fulfilling items one and two," I answered. "And it wouldn't have made sense to take him to the village where the people appeared to be far less caring than the Sherpas, so the third condition is impractical. Are you really saying that, no matter what the implications, we should, at the drop of a hat, have changed our entire plan?"

THE INDIVIDUAL VS. THE GROUP ETHIC

Despite my arguments, I felt and continue to feel guilt about the sadhu. I had literally walked through a classic moral dilemma without fully thinking through the consequences. My excuses for my actions include a high adrenaline flow, a superordinate goal, and a once-in-a-lifetime opportunity—factors in the usual corporate situation, especially when one is under stress.

Real moral dilemmas are ambiguous, and many of us hike right through them, unaware that they exist. When, usually after the fact, someone makes an issue of them, we tend to resent his or her bringing it up. Often, when the full import of what we have done (or not done) falls on us, we dig into a defensive position from which it is very difficult to emerge. In rare circumstances we may contemplate what we have done from inside a prison.

Had we mountaineers been free of physical and mental stress caused by the effort and the high altitude, we might have treated the sadhu differently. Yet isn't stress the real test of personal and corporate values? The instant decisions executives make under pressure reveal the most about personal and corporate character.

Among the many questions that occur to me when pondering my experience are: What are the practical limits of moral imagination and vision? Is there a collective or institutional ethic beyond the ethics of the individual? At what level of effort or commitment can one discharge one's ethical responsibilities? Not every ethical dilemma has a right solution. Reasonable people often disagree; otherwise there would be no dilemma. In a business context, however, it is essential that managers agree on a process for dealing with dilemmas.

The sadhu experience offers an interesting parallel to business situations. An immediate response was mandatory. Failure to act was a decision in itself. Up on the mountain we could not resign and submit our résumés to a headhunter. In contrast to philosophy, business involves action and implementation—getting things done. Managers must come up with answers to problems based on what they see and what they allow to influence their decision-making processes. On the mountain, none of us but Stephen realized the true dimensions of the situation we were facing.

One of our problems was that as a group we had no process for developing a consensus. We had no sense of purpose or plan. The difficulties of dealing with the sadhu were so complex that no one person could handle it. Because it did not have a set of preconditions that could guide its action to an acceptable resolution, the group reacted instinctively as individuals. The cross-cultural nature of the group added a further layer of complexity. We had no leader with whom we could all identify and in whose purpose we believed. Only Stephen was willing to take charge, but he could not gain adequate support to care for the sadhu.

Some organizations do have a value system that transcends the personal values of the managers. Such values, which go beyond profitability, are usually revealed when the organization is under stress. People throughout the organization generally accept its values, which, because they are not presented as a rigid list of commandments, may be somewhat ambiguous. The stories people tell, rather than printed materials, transmit these conceptions of what is proper behavior.

For 20 years I have been exposed at senior levels to a variety of corporations and organizations. It is amazing how quickly an outsider can sense the tone and style of an organization and the degree of tolerated openness and freedom to challenge management.

Organizations that do not have a heritage of mutually accepted, shared values tend to become unhinged during stress, with each individual bailing out for himself. In the great takeover battles we have witnessed during past years, companies that had strong cultures drew the wagons around them and fought it out, while other companies saw executives, supported by their golden parachutes, bail out of the struggles.

Because corporations and their members are interdependent, for the corporation to be strong the members need to share a preconceived notion of what is correct behavior, a "business ethic," and think of it as a positive force, not a constraint.

As an investment banker I am continually warned by well-meaning lawyers, clients, and associates to be wary of conflicts of interest. Yet if I were to run away from every difficult situation, I wouldn't be an effective investment banker. I have to feel my way through conflicts. An effective manager can't run from risk either; he or she has to confront and deal with risk. To feel "safe" in doing this, managers need the guidelines of an agreed-on process and set of values within the organization.

After my three months in Nepal, I spent three months as an executive-in-residence at both Stanford Business School and the Center for Ethics and Social Policy at the Graduate Theological Union at Berkeley. These six months away from my job gave me time to assimilate 20 years of business experience. My thoughts turned often to the meaning of the leadership role in any large organization. Students at the seminary thought of themselves as antibusiness. But when I questioned them they agreed that they distrusted all large organizations, including the church. They perceived all large organizations as impersonal and opposed to individual values and needs. Yet we all know of organizations where peoples' values and beliefs are respected and their expressions encouraged. What makes the difference? Can we identify the difference and, as a result, manage more effectively?

The word "ethics" turns off many and confuses more. Yet the notions of shared values and an agreed-on process for dealing with adversity and change—what many people mean when they talk about corporate culture—seem to be at the heart of the ethical issue. People who are in touch with their own core beliefs and the beliefs of others and are sustained by them can be more comfortable living on the cutting edge. At times, taking a tough line or a decisive stand in a muddle of ambiguity is the only ethical thing to do. If a manager is indecisive and spends time trying to figure out the "good" thing to do, the enterprise may be lost.

Business ethics, then, has to do with the authenticity and integrity of the enterprise. To be ethical is to follow the business as well as the cultural goals of the corporation, its owners, its employees, and its customers. Those who cannot serve the corporate vision are not authentic business people and, therefore, are not ethical in the business sense.

At this stage of my own business experience I have a strong interest in organizational behavior. Sociologists are keenly studying what they call corporate stories, legends, and heroes as a way organizations have of transmitting the value system. Corporations such as Arco have even hired consultants to perform an audit of their corporate culture. In a company, the leader is the person who understands, interprets, and manages the corporate value system. Effective managers are then action-oriented people who resolve conflict, are tolerant of ambiguity, stress, and change, and have a strong sense of purpose for themselves and their organizations.

If all this is true, I wonder about the role of the professional manager who moves from company to company. How can he or she quickly absorb the values and culture of different organizations? Or is there, indeed, an art of management that is totally transportable? Assuming such fungible managers do exist, is it proper for them to manipulate the values of others?

What would have happened had Stephen and I carried the sadhu for two days back to the village and become involved with the villagers in his care? In four trips to Nepal my most interesting experiences occurred in

1975 when I lived in a Sherpa home in the Khumbu for five days recovering from altitude sickness. The high point of Stephen's trip was an invitation to participate in a family funeral ceremony in Manang. Neither experience had to do with climbing the high passes of the Himalayas. Why were we so reluctant to try the lower path, the ambiguous trail? Perhaps because we did not have a leader who could reveal the greater purpose of the trip to us.

Why didn't Stephen with his moral vision opt to take the sadhu under his personal care? The answer is because, in part, Stephen was hard-stressed physically himself, and because, in part, without some support system that involved our involuntary and episodic community on the mountain, it was beyond his individual capacity to do so.

I see the current interest in corporate culture and corporate value systems as a positive response to Stephen's pessimism about the decline of the role of the individual in large organizations. Individuals who operate from a thoughtful set of personal values provide the foundation for a corporate culture. A corporate tradition that encourages freedom of inquiry, supports personal values, and reinforces a focused sense of direction can fulfill the need for individuality along with the prosperity and success of the group. Without such corporate support, the individual is lost.

That is the lesson of the sadhu. In a complex corporate situation, the individual requires and deserves the support of the group. If people cannot find such support from their organization, they don't know how to act. If such support is forthcoming, a person has a stake in the success of the group, and can add much to the process of establishing and maintaining a corporate culture. It is management's challenge to be sensitive to individual needs, to shape them, and to direct and focus them for the benefit of the group as a whole.

For each of us the sadhu lives. Should we stop what we are doing and comfort him; or should we keep trudging up toward the high pass? Should I pause to help the derelict I pass on the street each night as I walk by the Yale Club en route to Grand Central Station? Am I his brother? What is the nature of our responsibility if we consider ourselves to be ethical persons? Perhaps it is to change the values of the group so that it can, with all its resources, take the other road.

Chapter 8

Values and the Virtuous Manager

Case Study

The Enron Collapse

STEWART HAMILTON

When Enron filed for bankruptcy protection on December 2, 2001, the financial world was shocked. How could this high profile leader in the world of energy trading have failed? The employees, many of whom had a large part of their retirement and other savings tied up in Enron shares, were devastated. Not only were they likely to be out of a job but they also faced financial ruin.

Enron was the seventh largest company by revenues in the United States. It employed 25,000 people worldwide. The readers of *Fortune* magazine had voted it as one of the most admired companies in the United States. Its performance had been lauded in the media, and business school cases had been written holding it up as a glowing example of the transformation of a conservative, domestic energy company into a global player. In fact, other, more traditional, energy companies had been criticised for not producing the performance that Enron had apparently achieved.

Indeed, the consulting firm McKinsey had frequently cited Enron in its *Quarterly* as an example of how innovative companies can outperform their more traditional rivals.

As more and more facts emerged, it became clear that Enron had many elements of a "Ponzi" scheme.[1] The drive to maintain reported earnings growth, and thus the share price, led to the extensive use of "aggressive" accounting policies to accelerate earnings. In particular, the "Special Purpose Entities" (SPEs) Enron used to move assets and liabilities off the balance sheet attracted the most attention. The financial involvement of Enron officers and employees in the SPEs increased that interest.

BACKGROUND: FOUNDING OF ENRON AND GROWTH OF THE TRADITIONAL BUSINESS

The advent of energy deregulation in the late 1970s in the United States, which started with allowing open market prices for new natural gas discoveries, was to fundamentally change the way that energy was produced and traded.

Kenneth Lay, who at one point in his career had been an energy economist at the U.S. Interior Department, rising to the rank of Under Secretary, was a convinced "free marketer." After his stint in Washington, he first joined an energy company in Florida and ultimately ended up as CEO of Houston Natural Gas. After he engineered the merger with InterNorth, a larger traditional gas pipeline company, to form Enron in 1985, he became chairman and CEO of the new entity.

This combination created the largest company-owned natural gas pipeline system in the United States of some 37,000 miles stretching from the border of Canada to Mexico and from the Arizona–California border to Florida. It also had significant oil and gas exploration and production interests, which later would be spun off as a separately quoted company.

Lay, with the help of Richard Kinder as chief operating officer (COO), set about building up Enron through a series of new ventures and acquisitions. Many of these were financed by debt, including some deals underwritten by the "Junk Bond King," Michael Milken of Drexel Burnham Lambert. In the meantime, Enron had to buy off a potential hostile bidder, a hangover from the merger, which cost the company some $350 million. By the end of 1987, Enron's debt was 75% of its market capitalisation. Thereafter, managing the debt burden was to be one of Enron's constant preoccupations.

Kinder, a lawyer by training, was a traditional oil and gas man who insisted on rigorous controls and who had a reputation for being a fair but tough manager. He was considered the perfect foil to Lay.

Lay knew that, as energy deregulation progressed, the process would create commercial opportunities for the more farsighted energy companies, and would open the way to energy trading. Anxious to take advantage of the new environment, in 1985, Enron had opened an office in Valhalla, New York to trade oil and petroleum products. However, unauthorised dealing by two employees led to substantial losses and the office was closed in 1987. Enron took a charge of $85 million, and one of the employees concerned was jailed for fraud.

In 1989, Lay hired Jeffrey Skilling, a Harvard MBA and the partner in charge of McKinsey's energy practice in Houston, to be head of Enron Finance. Skilling had advised Lay on how to take advantage of gas deregulation. In particular, he had been responsible for Enron's establishing a "gas bank," a mechanism to provide funding for smaller gas producers to enable them to invest more in exploration and development and, at the same time, provide Enron with reliable sources of natural gas to feed its pipeline system. The following year Enron Gas Services was formed as a trading and marketing arm

At the end of the 1980s, the vast proportion of electricity generated in the United States came from coal fired or nuclear power stations. Gas fired plants were not favoured because of concerns about the reliability of supply and the stability of the price of gas. Enron, in order to grow its market, had to find new industrial customers for its gas.

The big breakthrough came in January 1992, with a 20-year deal with Sithe Energies to supply all the natural gas for a 1,000-megawatt electricity generating plant that Sithe was constructing in New York. This was a huge deal involving an estimated $3.5 billion over the lifetime of the contract. The price was fixed for the first five years and thereafter would fluctuate with the market. The terms were sufficiently good to persuade Sithe to use gas instead of coal to power the plant. Other similar deals soon followed. The advantage for the power producer was that knowing the price of gas for the early part of any project eliminated a major uncertainty and made it easier to raise the necessary finance.

THE OVERSEAS EXPANSION OF ENRON'S TRADITIONAL ENERGY BUSINESS (1990–2000)

In the early 1990s, Enron substantially increased its foreign activities, driven by Rebecca Mark who had joined Enron in 1985 and was responsible for international power and pipeline development. Enron later sponsored her to obtain a Harvard MBA. In 1992, Enron signed the contract for the Dabhol power project in Maharashtra State in India,[2] which, at around $3 billion, was the largest direct foreign investment ever in that country.

In its drive to become a global player, Enron bought energy plants in Brazil and Bolivia and an interest in a 4,000-mile Argentinian pipeline system that delivered two-thirds of that country's gas. In 1993, Enron built a gas turbine power plant on Teesside in England, its first foray into the European energy markets. It was granted permission to do so by Lord Wakeham, a UK energy minister, and an English chartered accountant (CA), who subsequently joined Enron's board. By 1994, Enron was operating power and pipeline projects in 15 countries and developing a similar number in several others.

In July 1998, as part of its strategy to build a worldwide water utility company, Enron purchased, for $2.2 billion, Wessex Water in the UK and formed a new company, Azurix. The intention was to develop and operate water and wastewater assets including distribution systems and treatment facilities and related infrastructures. Azurix pursued such projects in Europe, Asia and Latin America.

THE TRADING OPERATIONS (1985–1995)

The piecemeal process of deregulation, which had started in 1985, continued over a number of years, and during this time, while it was expanding its traditional business with heavy overseas expansion, Enron increased its trading activities. Recognising that this required new skills, in 1989 the company entered into a joint venture with Bankers Trust to set up a financial trading desk. This arrangement was short-lived, ending in 1991, but helped establish Enron as a major player. Thereafter, Enron hired its own traders from the investment banking and brokerage industries and, increasingly, newly graduated MBAs from high-ranking business schools.

In 1990, Skilling hired Andrew Fastow from Continental Illinois Bank to help run Enron Capital and Trading. Fastow's background was in asset securitisation and structured finance. His role would be to develop the company's funding business and to obtain and manage the debt and equity capital to fund its third-party finance business.

One major innovation was the development of "Volumetric Production Payments" (VPPs) in 1990. To get round the problem in the gas industry of the large number of small producers who lacked access to capital to improve their facilities and to search for new reserves, Enron provided liquidity by prepaying for long-term fixed-price gas supplies, with the payment secured on the gas itself and not on the assets of the producer. This reduced the risk of default to Enron who had first call on a proportion (usually half) of the gas from the field. In effect, Enron was being repaid in gas rather than cash. This arrangement also meant that Enron had secure long-term natural gas supplies. To finance these up-front payments, Enron sold the rights to future cash flows from each deal to investors in a series of off balance sheet vehicles (usually limited partnerships).

The first VPP deal was with Forest Oil, where Enron paid $44 million for the right to receive 32 billion cubic feet of gas over the next five years. Many similar deals followed.

Enron's first trading activities were straightforward, but this would soon change.

Initially confined to contracts for physical delivery, the trading extended to gas and, after deregulation, electricity futures. The industry, led by Enron, lobbied hard for exemption from the normal regulatory oversight of derivatives trading in order to avoid restrictions on margin trading and other potential limitations. In early 1993 Wendy Gramm, as outgoing chairman of the US Commodities and Futures Trading Commission (and the wife of the senior US senator for Texas), granted that exemption. Sometime afterwards, she joined Enron's board as a non-executive director.

The development of trading was greatly assisted by the decision, in 1990, of the New York Mercantile Exchange (NYMEX) to trade futures on the delivery of gas to the Henry Hub, a major gas depot in Louisiana where 14 inter- and intra-state pipelines converged. This would mean the availability of transparent prices. This added to Enron's existing information advantage about pricing that came from being a major supplier in the gas market.

After obtaining exemption from regulation as a utility company in 1994, Enron began buying and selling electricity.

Prior to deregulation, the industry was vertically integrated, from the generation of electricity to its transportation, distribution and sale in to a captive market. While low risk, it was capital intensive and heavily regulated. Success came through technical expertise and economies of scale and the whole industry was characterised by slow trends requiring a long-term view. Deregulation effectively "unbundled" the industry value chain so that companies were free to choose in which parts to operate. In other words, it was not necessary to be a generator or a transporter in order to market and sell power to the end customer. One could source the electricity from generators and rent transmission capacity or indeed trade it like any other commodity. Enron's strategy was to focus on the high value added activities such as trading and retail sales, and optimise them independently of one another.

INTERNAL CONFLICTS

Within Enron, almost from the day in 1990 that Jeff Skilling had joined the company, there had been conflict over the strategic direction to be followed. On the one hand, Rebecca Mark favoured investment in traditional power generating assets, both in the United States and overseas, and on the other, Skilling favoured an "asset light" strategy. He believed that Enron would make more money by trading in energy rather than generating and supplying it.

Richard Kinder is credited with containing the dispute, but matters came to a head with his unexpected departure in 1996. Many insiders believed that, had Senator Bob Dole won the presidential election in November 1996, Ken Lay would have been offered a cabinet-level post in Washington. Instead, with Clinton safely back in the White House, Lay signed on for a further five years as CEO. Unwilling to remain as number two for that length of time, Richard Kinder resigned to form his own company. As a result, Skilling became president and chief operating officer (COO) of the company, and was thus free to pursue his "asset light" vision. As an Enron employee, a traditional Texan Republican, trying to explain the collapse said, "It was all Bill Clinton's fault."

Skilling quickly promoted Fastow to chief financial officer (CFO). Although not a certified public accountant (CPA), Fastow would, in 1999, be voted by *CFO magazine* the "most creative financial officer of the year" in the US.

The consequence of the dispute between Mark and Skilling, both of whom were pretenders to Kenneth Lay's mantle as CEO,[3] was that Enron continued to pursue dual strategies of investing heavily in physical assets and simultaneously expanding its trading activities. Both strategies required significant investment and placed considerable strain on the company's balance sheet and, therefore, on its investment ratings.

ENRON TRADING (1996–2000)

By the time Skilling took over from Kinder in 1996, the US energy market was essentially fully open and Enron was able to exploit the expanded opportunities. Enron's aggressive electricity trading was to cause considerable controversy in California, where Enron was accused (with others) of seeking to manipulate supplies and thus prices during the power crisis in the summer of 2000.

On the trading front, Enron had started off with oil and gas futures, and long-term supply contracts and hedges. Later, the portfolio extended to more exotic items including weather derivatives. The rationale for these was that an energy supplier concerned that the weather was going to be too warm, and that its customers would consequently consume less energy, would want to find a way of hedging this income shortfall. As markets for existing products matured and competition eroded margins, Enron had to find new and more innovative instruments to trade. These would include things as diverse as wood pulp futures and oil tanker freight rates. Ultimately there were over 1,200 separate trading "books"[4] including broadband capacity, which would give rise to some special problems.

In late 1999, EnronOnline was launched, creating an electronic trading floor for oil and gas in the United States and Canada, and quickly expanded to other products and countries. Although it was developed at the relatively low cost of $15 million, it required a large amount of working capital to fund the "book." Enron used the short-term commercial paper market for this, a market that was to dry up in the immediate aftermath of September 11, 2001, which would pose major liquidity problems.

"MARK-TO-MARKET" ACCOUNTING

The Volumetric Production Payments (VPPs) Enron introduced in 1990 opened the way for the use of "mark-to-market" accounting[5] for contracts. The Enron board agreed to adopt this policy for the 1991 annual report. The VPPs were in effect contracts that had a predictable future cash flow and could be treated as "merchant assets."[6] Following this logic, Enron applied to the Securities and Exchange Commission (SEC) to be allowed to mark these assets to market. This permission was granted for 1991 on an exceptional basis and thus Enron became the first company outside the financial sector to adopt this method.

Although the permission was supposed to be temporary, the SEC seems to have forgotten to revisit it, thus paving the way for Enron to make increasing use of this accounting treatment in the ensuing years. The result was to allow Enron to take up front most, if not all, of the anticipated profits on such contracts, and of course the requirement to write them down if their value diminished.

The basic methodology was simple. To create a merchant asset or "monetize" a deal, the trader would forecast the future price curve for the underlying product, calculate the future cash flows and apply a discount rate to compute the net present value which could either be sold to an SPE created for that purpose or kept on Enron's books as a merchant asset. For some products, e.g. gas futures, market prices could be obtained from NYMEX but usually for a limited time horizon, say four years. Enron extended the mark-to-market principle to much longer contracts, for which it had to derive its own price curves, and as one trader put it, for some products where Enron was the only supplier, it was more a case of "marking to Enron."

Enron had a large risk assessment and control group, headed by the chief risk officer (CRO), Rick Buy, who had been with Bankers Trust. The group was split into four departments: credit, underwriting, investment & valuation and trading. This last was supposed to ensure that the traders' pricing was appropriate for the risks being assumed. However, sometimes the level of activity was such that it had time to do little more than check the arithmetic rather than to question the underlying assumptions.

ENRON'S REPORTED FINANCIAL PERFORMANCE

In the five years from 1996 to 2000, Enron reported consolidated net income rising from $580 million to $970 million, with a blip in 1997 (*refer to Exhibits 8.1, 8.2 and 8.3 for last published accounts*). This was in marked contrast with the tax losses of $3 billion declared to the Internal Revenue Service (IRS) for the four years to 1999.

EXHIBIT 8.1. Enron and Subsidiaries Consolidated Income Statement

	Year ended December 31		
(In $ millions, except per share amounts)	*2000*	*1999*	*1998*
REVENUES			
Natural gas and other products	50,500	19,536	13,276
Electricity	15,238	13,939	33,823
Metals	9,234	—	—
Other	7,232	5,338	4,045
Total revenues	100,789	40,112	31,260
COSTS AND EXPENSES			
Cost of gas, electricity, metals and other products	94,517	34,761	26,381
Operating expenses	3,184	3,045	2,473
Depreciation, depletion and amortization	855	870	827
Taxes, other than income taxes	280	193	201
Impairment of long-lived assets	—	41	—
Total costs and expenses	98,836	39,310	29,882
Operating Income	**1,953**	**802**	**1,378**
OTHER INCOME AND DEDUCTIONS			
Equity in earnings of unconsolidated equity affiliates	87	309	97
Gains on sales of non-merchant assets	146	541	56
Gains on the issuance of stock by TNPC, Inc.	121	—	—
Interest income	212	162	88
Other income, net	(37)	181	(37)
Income Before Interest, Minority Interests and			
Income Taxes	**2,482**	**1,995**	**1,582**
Interest and related charges, net	838	656	550
Dividends on company-obligated preferred securities			
of subsidiaries	77	76	77
Minority interests	154	135	77
Income tax expense	434	104	175
Net income before cumulative effect of accounting			
changes	979	1,024	703
Cumulative effect of accounting changes, net of tax	—	(131)	—
Net Income	**979**	**893**	**703**
Preferred stock dividends	83	66	17
Earnings on Common Stock	**896**	**827**	**686**
Earnings Per Share of Common Stock			
BASIC			
Before cumulative effect of accounting changes	1.22	1.36	1.07
Cumulative effect of accounting changes	—	(0.19)	—
Basic earnings per share	1.22	1.17	1.07
Diluted			
Before Cumulative effect of accounting charges	1.12	1.27	1.01
Cumulative effect of accounting changes	—	(0.17)	—
Diluted earnings per share	1.12	1.10	1.01
AVERAGE NUMBER OF COMMON SHARES USED IN COMPUTATION			
Basic	736	705	642
Diluted	814	769	695

Source: Company annual report

EXHIBIT 8.2.   Enron and Subsidiaries Consolidated Balance Sheet

	Year ended December 31	
(In $ millions, except per share amounts)	*2000*	*1999*

ASSETS

Current Assets

Cash and cash equivalents	1,374	288
Trade receivables (net of allowance for doubtful accounts of 133 and 40, respectively)	10,396	3,030
Other receivables	1,874	518
Assets from price risk management activities	12,018	2,205
Inventories	953	598
Deposits	2,433	81
Other	1,333	535
Total current assets	30,381	7,255

Investments and Other Assets

Investments in and advance to unconsolidated	5,294	5,036
Assets from price risk management activities	8,988	2,929
Goodwill	3,638	2,799
Other	5,459	4,681
Total investments and other assets	23,379	15,445

Property, Plant and Equipment, at cost

Natural gas transmission	6,916	6,948
Electric generation and distribution	4,766	3,552
Fiber-optic network and equipment	839	379
Construction in progress	682	1,120
Other	2,256	1,913
Total	**15,459**	**13,912**
Less accumulated depreciation, depletion and amortization	3,716	3,231
Property, plant and equipment, net	11,743	10,681
Total Assets	**65,603**	**33,381**

LIABILITIES AND SHAREHOLDERS' EQUITY

Current liabilities

Accounts payable	9,777	2,154
Liabilities from price risk management activities	10,495	1,836
Short-term debt	1,679	1,001
Customers' deposits	4,277	44
Other	2,178	1,724
Total current liabilities	28,406	6,759
Long-Term Debt	**8,550**	**7,151**

Deferred Credits and Other Liabilities

Deferred income taxes	1,644	1,894
Liabilities from price risk management activities	9,423	2,990
Other	2,414	1,587
Total deferred credits and other liabilities	13,759	6,471
Commitments and Contingencies Minority Interests	**2,414**	**2,430**
Company-Obligated Preferred Securities of Subsidiaries	**904**	**1,000**

(continued)

EXHIBIT 8.2. *(continued)*

Shareholders' Equity

Second preferred stock, cumulative, no par-value, 1,370,000 shares authorized, 1,240,933 shares and 1,296,184 shares issued, respectively	124	130
Mandatorily Convertible Junior Preferred Stock, Series B, no par value, 250,000 shares issued	1,000	1,000
Common stock, no par value, 1,200,000,000 shares authorized, 752,205,112 shares and 716,865,081 shares issued, respectively	8,348	6,637
Retained earnings	3,226	2,698
Accumulated other comprehensive income	(1,048)	(741)
Common stock held in treasury, 577,066 shares and 1,337,714 shares, respectively	(32)	(49)
Restricted stock and other	(148)	(105)
Total shareholders' equity	11,470	9,570
Total Liabilities and Shareholders' Equity	**65,503**	**33,381**

Source: Company annual report

Over the four years to December 2000, while revenues from the traditional physical asset energy-generating business grew relatively slowly, reported revenues from trading grew exponentially to become 80% of Enron's turnover, which leapt from $40 billion in 1999 to $100 billion in 2000.

THE ROLE OF ANDERSEN

This is not the familiar story that "recessions uncover what the auditors do not."

Arthur Andersen had been Enron's auditors[7] since the company's formation in 1985. In the years leading up to the collapse, David Duncan had been the client engagement partner based in Andersen's Houston office, and within the firm, was known to be a "client advocate" with a reputation for "aggressive accounting."

Enron was one of Andersen's largest clients, generating audit fees of $25 million and additional consulting fees of $26 million in 2000. A large team of Andersen staffers was based in Enron's offices and Enron had many employees who had joined from the audit firm. Skilling was on record as saying that one of Andersen's most useful services was to provide a pool of accounting talent that Enron could tap.

Within Andersen, Enron was known as difficult and demanding and was included in its "high risk" category of client. Internal Andersen memos reveal concerns being expressed by technical partners as early as 1999, and one of them, Carl Bass, was removed from the engagement after Enron complained that he was being deliberately obstructive. There were particular doubts about the accounting treatment of some of Enron's off balance sheet activities. The memos (and e-mails), released by the U.S. House Committee on Energy and Commerce in April 2002, show that the local engagement partner and his team were able to override the advice of the specialists even though David Duncan was aware that "these . . . policies . . . push limits and have a high risk profile . . . others could have a different view."

EXHIBIT 8.3. Enron and Subsidiaries Consolidated Statement of Cash Flows

	Year ended December 31		
(In $ millions)	*2000*	*1999*	*1998*
CASH FLOWS FROM OPERATING ACTIVITIES			
Net income	979	893	703
Cumulative effect of accounting changes	—	131	—
Depreciation, depletion and amortization	855	870	827
Impairment of long-lived assets (including equity investments)	326	441	—
Deferred income taxes	207	21	87
Gains on sales of non-merchant assets	(146)	(541)	(82)
Changes in components of working capital	1,769	(1,000)	(233)
Net assets from price risk management activities	(763)	(395)	350
Merchant assets and investments:			
Realized gains on sales	(104)	(756)	(628)
Proceeds from sales	1,838	2,217	1,434
Additions and unrealised gains	(1,295)	(827)	(721)
Other operating activities	1,113	174	(97)
Net Cash Provided by Operating Activities	**4,779**	**1,228**	**1,640**
Cash Flows From Investing Activities			
Capital expenditures	(2,381)	(2,363)	(1,905)
Equity investments	(933)	(722)	(1,659)
Proceeds from sales of non-merchant assets	494	294	239
Acquisition of subsidiary stock	(485)	—	(180)
Business acquisitions, net of cash acquired	(777)	(311)	(104)
Other investing activities	(182)	(405)	(356)
Net Cash Used in Investing Activities	**(4,264)**	**(3,507)**	**(3,965)**
Cash Flows From Financing Activities			
Insurance of long-term debt	3,994	1,776	1,903
Repayment of long-term debt	(2,337)	(1,837)	(870)
Net increase (decrease) in short-term borrowings	(1,595)	1,565	(158)
Net issuance (redemption) of company-obligated preferred securities of subsidiaries	(96)	—	8
Issuance of common stock	307	852	867
Issuance of subsidiary equity	500	568	828
Dividends paid	(523)	(467)	(414)
Net disposition of treasury stock	327	139	13
Other financing activities	(6)	(140)	89
Net Cash Provided by Financing Activities	**571**	**2,456**	**2,266**
Increase (Decrease) in Cash and Cash Equivalents	**1,086**	**177**	**(59)**
Cash and Cash Equivalents, Beginning of Year	**288**	**111**	**170**
Cash and Cash Equivalents, End of Year	**1,374**	**288**	**111**
CHANGES IN COMPONENTS OF WORKING CAPITAL			
Receivables	(8,203)	(662)	(1,055)
Inventories	1,336	(133)	(372)
Payables	7,167	(246)	433
Other	1,469	41	761
Total	**1,769**	**(1,000)**	**(233)**

Source: Company annual report

The accounting policies Enron adopted, and which Andersen sanctioned, were unusual for a non-financial company. As one employee recounted:

> The issue, which was unnerving, was their focus on immediate earnings (accounting not cash). Whenever a transaction or business plan was presented, the focus was on how much earnings the deal would bring rather than if it made business sense or made cash. Another example is the way they conducted their trading business: Enron would create forward price curves on commodities, based in many cases on rather sketchy data or pricing points. Using these curves, Enron would enter into long-term transactions with counter parties (10 years was usual in illiquid markets like bandwidth). For Enron, it didn't matter if they lost money in years 1–5 of a deal (i.e. sold below current market values), as long as they recovered the investment and made a "profit" on years 6-10. The reason was because Enron used "mark-to-market" accounting and would take the NPV of the ten-year deal on day one, using the sketchy curves I mentioned before as price points for discounting and, therefore, making a "profit." The fact that the company was bleeding cash in years 1-5 in exchange for potential gains in years 6-10 was usually not considered in these transactions. The only thing that mattered was "earnings." (Anonymous)

THE ENRON CULTURE

The occupants of 1400 Smith Street, Houston, regarded themselves as elite. Enron had largely left behind the Texan "good ol' boy" culture—and certainly the culture of the regulated utility—and had embraced Lay's free market vision. Encouraged by Skilling, a highly paid army of financially literate MBAs sought innovative ways to "translate any deal into a mathematical formula" that could then be traded or sold on, often to SPEs set up for that purpose. By the end, Enron had in excess of 3,000 subsidiaries and unconsolidated associates, including more than 400 registered in the Cayman Islands.

Although the SPEs set up by Enron, often with Andersen's advice, have attracted much comment and criticism, there is nothing inherently wrong with such vehicles. In fact, almost all major companies use various forms of SPEs to manage, for example, joint ventures in foreign countries, or investments in hostile environments. What was unusual in this case was the sheer number of SPEs involved.

Skilling had introduced a rigorous employee performance assessment process that became known as "rank or yank." Under this system the bottom 10% in performance were shown the door. There was heavy pressure to meet targets and remuneration was linked to the deals done and profits booked in the previous quarter. This pressure was particularly acute at the quarter-end and gave rise to the expression "Friday night specials." These were deals put together at the last moment, often inadequately documented, despite the efforts of the 200 or so in-house lawyers that Enron employed. The emphasis was on doing deals and not necessarily worrying about how they were to be managed in the future. Even internally it was recognised that project management was not a core competence.

Enron's accounting policies led to deals being struck that would be cash negative in the early years. In one example, Enron entered into a 12-year, fixed-price gas supply deal in the Far East at a price below the current "spot," and as Enron did not have its own supply it had to go into the market to purchase at the higher price. Nevertheless, the forecast price curve was such that it showed a positive net present value and a profit was booked to reflect that. The manager who had done the deal was subsequently approached by his boss towards the end of the quarter, and told that, as they were not going to meet their budget, he should revisit the deal and "tweak the numbers" to squeeze out a bit more. This he did (an action of which he is now somewhat ashamed). This process was so common, he said, that it was known as "marking up the curve."

Those who worked in Enron were reluctant to challenge such deals. One former employee described his experience:

> From a cultural perspective, what shocked me was that no one could explain to me what the fundamentals of the business were. As a new person I have always been used to asking questions—many might seem dumb, but it is part of the learning process. In Enron, questions were not encouraged and saying things like "This doesn't make sense" was unofficially sanctioned. Further, I got the impression that many people did not understand what was going on, so asking questions would show this lack of knowledge. (Anonymous)

Despite, or perhaps because of, all the pressure, Enron's senior employees were loyal and well rewarded. In 2000, the top 200 employees shared remuneration packages of salaries, bonuses, stock options and restricted stock totaling $1.4 billion, up from $193 million in 1998 (refer to Exhibit 8.4). The board also enjoyed handsome benefits well in excess of the normal levels of remuneration paid to non-executive directors of public companies in the United States.

The belief that they were changing the world ran deep even after the problems emerged. Following Skilling's resignation as CEO in August 2001, there were some lay-offs in the trading and risk management areas, and in at least one case an individual used a substantial proportion of his severance package to buy more Enron stock in the market. Another, after hearing expressions of sympathy for the redundant employees, said:

> I would disagree on your view of the "poor employees," however. When I was there it was pretty obvious that most employees knew what was going on and the fact that many people had an overly large exposure to Enron shares was based on greed and share price growth which had taken a disproportionate part of personal assets. As an example, I clearly remember discussing the sale of shares by Skilling and other executives while they were being simultaneously talked up. This was a company-wide known fact. Of course, some of the technical and lower level employees did not understand what was going on, but I fume when I see some of the VPs on U.S. television complaining about their egregious treatment. (Anonymous)

EXHIBIT 8.4. Compensation Paid to the Top-Paid 200 Employees for 1998–2000

Year	Bonus	Stock Options	Restricted Stock	Wages	Total
1998	$41,193,000	$61,978,000	$23,966,000	$66,143,000	$193,281,000
1999	$51,195,000	$244,579,000	$21,943,000	$84,145,000	$401,863,000
2000	$56,606,000	$1,063,537,000	$131,701,000	$172,597,000	$1,424,442,000

Extracted from: "Written Testimony of the Staff of the Joint Committee on Taxation on the Report of Investigation of Enron Corporation and Related Entities Regarding Federal Tax and Compensation Issues, and Policy Recommendations." US Senate Committee on Finance Hearing, February 13, 2003.

THE BROADBAND STORY

Enron's venture into broadband was more opportunistic than planned. In 1997, it had acquired Portland General Electric, an Oregon electricity generator and distributor that had laid some 1,500 miles of fibre-optic cable along its transmission rights of way. Ken Rice, a long-time Enron employee and by all accounts a born salesman and rather bored with his current role, decided that this could be the great new thing. Enron, through its new subsidiary Enron Broadband Services (EBS), making use of its own substantial rights of way, started to build its own network, adding 4,000 miles in 1998 and a further 7,000 the following year. The intention was to sell capacity to heavy data users, such as Internet providers and telecom companies, on long-term contracts which could then be "marked to market," and to trade bandwidth in a manner similar to gas or electricity. Such was the speed with which this business developed that no fundamental supply and demand analysis was carried out and indeed Enron was competing with the likes of WorldCom and Global Crossing for customers in a market which had huge overcapacity. Even more worrying was that technological improvements were exponentially increasing the amount of data that could be carried by existing cable. Getting the dark fibre lit[8] considerably increased overheads, and in 2000 EBS lost $60 million on revenues of $415 million. The anticipated volumes of traffic did not materialise, which caused great problems as the only way to generate profits from cable is to get data flowing through it.

In an attempt to generate traffic, EBS announced, in July 2000, that it had entered into a memorandum of understanding with Blockbuster Video to provide "video on demand," whereby the former would provide the means of delivery and the latter the content. Small trials in four parts of the US proved that the technology worked and the service was rolled out with much fanfare in Seattle, Portland and Salt Lake City just before Christmas. However, it proved impossible to attract enough subscribers to make it pay. Fearful of the cannibalising effect of the project on its existing business if it were to work, Blockbuster walked away from the deal after a few months, leaving EBS to go it alone. This did not preclude Enron from booking a "mark-to-market" profit based on its predictions of the project's future cash flows.

However, despite this setback, by the end of that year broadband was seen as a major part of the company's future and was being promoted as such to the financial markets.

After the collapse, a former employee posted his thoughts on his MBA class website:

> OK, now that it's bust, I can tell you a little bit of what was going on—at least where I was. Imagine that you make a spreadsheet model of a business plan (in this case it was taking over the world). You discount it with Montecarlo simulations (more like Atlantic City, really), sensitise it to all possible shocks, but still make sure you obtain a huge NPV. Then you sell this "idea" to a company that does not consolidate and which finances the purchase with debt guaranteed by Enron's liquid stock (remember no consolidation). You book all the NPV (or profit) UPFRONT.

MARKET AND OTHER PRESSURES

Enron's shares, in the late 1990s, had significantly outperformed the market (refer to Exhibit 8.5) and at their highest price the market capitalisation of the company reached $60 billion. At this level, the share price implied a price-earnings multiple of around 60, or nearly three times the sector average. Although the "irrational exuberance" of the time may have contributed, Enron was not a simple "dot-com" story. When the Nasdaq index was falling through the floor, Enron shares continued to outperform the market.

Performing well on the stock market brings its own problems by raising market expectations. Consequently, there was tremendous pressure on Enron to maintain earnings-per-share (EPS) growth, which in turn led to the need to find new sources of revenue and new sources of capital. Large investments in major power projects needed cash. Such investments were not expected to generate earnings or positive cash flow in the short term, placing immediate pressure on the balance sheet. The much expanded trading book added to this pressure, especially after the creation of EnronOnline. Enron was already highly leveraged, and funding new investments with debt was unattractive as they would not generate sufficient cash flow to service that debt and would put pressure on credit ratings.

Enron had never been a "triple A" company, but its debt had to stay within investment grade. If it did not, this would affect the company's ability to issue further debt and would trigger bank covenants and influence the perceptions of, and its credibility with, counterparties. One answer might have been to issue new equity, but this was resisted as it would dilute EPS and in turn affect the share price.

EXHIBIT 8.5. Enron Share Price Movements

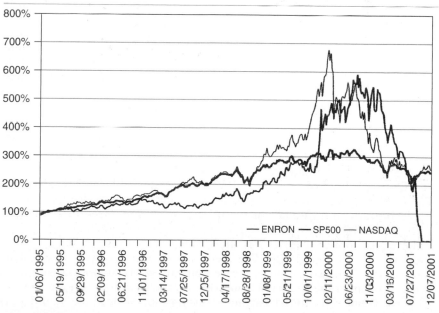

Source: Datastream.

THE ENRON SOLUTION

The chosen solution was to get some of the assets and related debt off the balance sheet. This required finding outside investors willing to take some of the risk through equity participation in separate entities, which, in turn, could borrow from third parties (outside lenders). This would only work if these special purpose entities (SPEs), which are also known as special purpose vehicles, did not have to be consolidated in Enron's results, otherwise it would defeat the objective of such financial engineering.

Under U.S. Generally Accepted Accounting Principles (US GAAP), to avoid consolidation of an SPE there must be an independent owner that would take a "substantive" capital investment in the SPE. That investment must have substantive risks and rewards throughout the period of ownership. The Financial Accounting Standards Board (FASB) had determined 3%[9] of total capital to be the minimum acceptable level of equity (raised to 10% post Enron). The independent owner must exercise control of the SPE. Investments are not considered at risk if supported by a letter of credit or other form of guarantee, or if there is a guaranteed return. Finding truly independent investors proved difficult so Enron turned to related parties.

THE "OFF BALANCE SHEET" TRANSACTIONS

The first controversial deal involving an Enron employee and using an SPE was Chewco. This Limited Liability Partnership (LLP)[10] was formed in 1997 with the purpose of acquiring the California Public Employees Retirement Scheme's (CalPERS) interest in an earlier joint venture with Enron called the Joint Energy Development Investment (JEDI), where CalPERS' initial investment of $250 million in 1993 had been valued at $383 million. Chewco was to borrow a like amount on an unsecured basis. In a rather complicated deal (*refer to* Exhibits 8.6a *and* 8.6b), the loan would be guaranteed by Enron.

The debt was provided by BZW, a subsidiary of Barclays Bank in the UK. Enron charged Chewco a fee of $40 million for providing the guarantee and booked that sum as part of its profit for the quarter. The general partners in the SPE were Enron employees or associates, in particular Fastow's assistant, Michael Kopper, and his partner, William Dodson. Fastow had wanted to do this deal himself but the Enron board would not allow that to happen, so Kopper, a graduate of the London School of Economics, who had joined Enron in 1994 from Toronto Dominion Bank and had become close to Fastow both professionally and privately, took his place. Kopper would later plead guilty to a number of criminal charges and agree to co-operate with the authorities in order to reduce his 15-year jail sentence.

The next significant event was the formation of LJM1 in June 1999, a Cayman Islands registered SPE. The name was derived from the first initials of Fastow's wife and two children. Aware that Enron was anxious to get more debt off its balance sheet, Fastow had taken to the board a proposal to raise $15 million from two limited partners, through an SPE, which would purchase from Enron certain assets and associated liabilities that the company wished to remove from its balance sheet. Although the Enron code of ethics

EXHIBIT 8.6a. Chewco Deal (simplified)

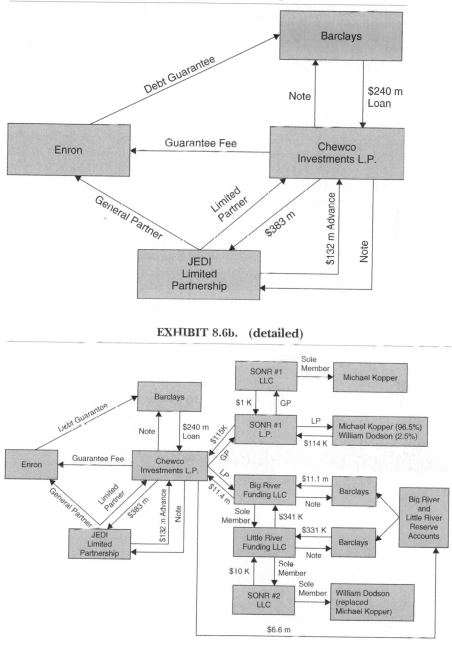

EXHIBIT 8.6b. (detailed)

Source: Powers committee report.

prohibited Enron from having any dealings with an officer of the company because of the potential for conflicts of interests, the board gave special permission for this to proceed subject to certain checks being put in place to protect the company's interests.

The ultimate structure was a little complex and designed to ensure that Fastow was shielded from any possible personal liability. Fastow was the sole and managing member of LJM Partners LLC,[11] which in turn was the general partner of LJM Partners LP.[12] This then became the general partner of LJM1. LJM1 then entered into a number of transactions with Enron.

In one, it hedged Enron's position in Rhythms NetConnections stock (a dot-com company that Enron had bought into at $1.85 a share and which had an initial public offering (IPO) at $21, subsequently rising to $69 by the close of the trading day). In May 1999, Enron wished to protect the profit of $300 million, which, under "mark-to-market" accounting, it had already recognised. As there was a lock-up agreement that prevented Enron from selling the holding until the end of 1999, it needed to find some other way to do so. LJM1 provided such a mechanism, by granting Enron a "put option" to require an LJM subsidiary to buy the Rhythms shares at a price which would crystallise the profit. (*Refer to* Exhibit 8.7 *for a diagram of the* deal.)

The two parties that put up the debt finance were subsidiaries of Credit Suisse First Boston (CSFB) and NatWest (now part of the Royal Bank of Scotland group), whose loans were secured by options on Enron's shares. These options, once exercised, would cover them for any reduction in the lenders' collateral.

A few months later, Fastow put a more ambitious proposal to the board that he would raise $200 million of institutional private equity in order to purchase assets that Enron wanted to syndicate. At that level, the leverage potential was huge. The board agreed that he could go ahead, and so LJM2 was formed in October 1999 as a Delaware limited partnership. Merrill Lynch prepared a private placement memorandum for a co-partnership with

EXHIBIT 8.7. LJM1 Deal.

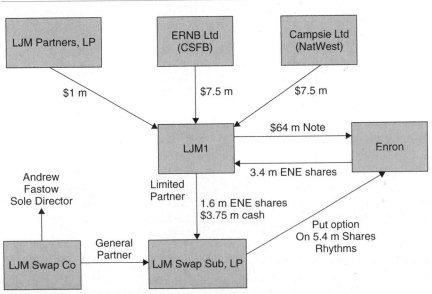

Source: Powers committee report.

LJM2, which ultimately had some 50 limited partners, which included well-known financial institutions such as GE Capital, Citigroup, Deutsche Bank and JP Morgan. Enron was a significant purchaser of investment banking services, and Fastow was the gatekeeper.

The memorandum clearly identified Andrew Fastow, together with Kopper and Ben Glisan, as the managers and, in an unusual twist, highlighted their use of inside information:

> . . . their access to Enron's information pertaining to potential investments will contribute to superior returns.

Glisan had joined Enron three years earlier from Andersen and was described as being responsible for the deal structuring of the company's "highly complex non-recourse or limited recourse joint venture and asset-based financings."

Enron's own disclosure was less frank. In a note to the 2000 Annual Report, on page 48, it simply said, "In 2000 and 1999, Enron entered into transactions with limited partnerships (the Related Party) whose general partner's managing member is a senior officer of Enron." The note then went on to outline some of the transactions.

THE IMPACT OF THESE DEALS

At the end of Quarter 3 and Quarter 4 of 1999, Enron sold interests in seven assets to LJM1 and LJM2. Enron bought back five of the seven assets shortly after the close of the respective financial reporting periods. While the LJM partnerships made a profit on every transaction, the transactions generated Enron "earnings" of $229 million in the second half of 1999 (out of $570 million).

In June 2000, Enron sold $100 million of dark fibre optical cables to LJM, on which it booked a profit of $67 million. LJM sold on cable for $40 million to "industry participants" and the remainder to another Enron-related partnership for $113 million in December. Between June and December, these deals suggested that the value of fibre had increased by 53% while the open market value had fallen 67% in the same period.

Fastow is reported to have profited to the extent of $45 million from these deals.

THE RAPTOR VEHICLES

In addition to the LJM transactions, Enron entered into a series of deals with the so-called Raptors, the purpose of which seems to have been the hedging of Enron's own investments. (*Refer to* Exhibit 8.8 *for an example of the complexity of the structures.*) The deals were complicated and the nature and extent of the inter-company liabilities, undertakings and commitments were difficult to grasp. Most appear to be predicated on Enron's share price being maintained as Enron shares had been used to fund the vehicles. Although the existence of these entities had been disclosed in Enron's accounts and SEC filings, the financial exposure had not been made clear (*refer to* Exhibit 8.9, *Inadequate disclosure*). The company had been renowned for being less

EXHIBIT 8.8. Raptor Transactions.

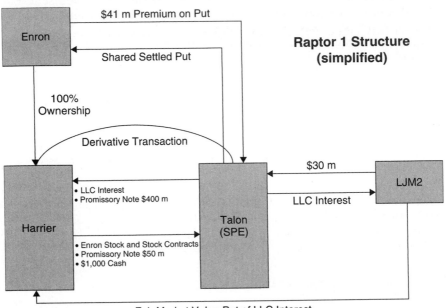

Source: Powers committee report

than open with the analysts and financial press as to exactly what their business was, and they were notoriously reluctant to give information. An example of this was Lay's comment in October 2000:

> We are an energy and broadband company that also does a lot of other stuff.

STORM CLOUDS GATHER

In February 2001, Lay, while remaining as chairman, handed over the role of CEO to Jeff Skilling. Meanwhile, Enron's investment in the broadband business, and its continuing overseas operations, were placing a strain on its liquidity position.

In the course of 2000, a number of problems had emerged. The power project in India had run into political difficulties and the local state government was refusing to honour its obligations under the contract. In fact, the plant was shut down in 2001. In Brazil, the issue had arisen of impaired asset values, compounded by the devaluation of the local currency. The Azurix venture had already resulted in write-downs of $326 million relating to assets in Argentina, and the Wessex Water business in England was experiencing both financial and operational difficulties.

Both inside and outside Enron, Rebecca Mark was widely regarded as being responsible for the difficulties and she had resigned in August 2000.

EXHIBIT 8.9.   Excerpts from the Powers Committee Report

THE BOARD OF DIRECTORS

"With respect to the issues that are the subject of this investigation, the Board of Directors failed, in our judgment, in its oversight duties."
Op. cit., p. 22.

POOR CONTROLS

"These controls as designed were not rigorous enough, and their implementation and oversight was inadequate at both Management and Board levels."
Op. cit., p. 10.

AND THE CEO'S ROLE . . .

"Skilling, . . . , bears substantial responsibility for the failure of the system of internal controls to mitigate the risk inherent in the relationship between Enron and the LJM partnerships."
Op. cit., p. 21.

THE AUDITOR'S ROLE . . .

". . . , Andersen also failed to bring to the attention of Enron's Audit and Compliance Committee serious reservations Andersen partners voiced internally about the related party transactions."
Op. cit., p. 25.

CREATIVE ACCOUNTING

". . . accounting judgments that, . . . , went well beyond the aggressive . . . , the fact that these judgments were, in most if not all cases, made with the concurrence of Andersen is a significant, . . . , fact."
Op. cit. p. 27.

INADEQUATE DISCLOSURE

". . . However these disclosures were obtuse, did not communicate the essence of the transactions completely or clearly, and *failed to convey the substance of what was going on between Enron and the partnerships.*"
Op. cit. p. 1.

AND A LACK OF UNDERSTANDING . . .

"It appears that many of [the board] members did not understand those transactions—the economic rationale, the consequences, and the risks."
Op. cit., p. 23.

Source: Enron Special Committee report, February 1, 2002 (the Powers Report)

Furthermore, the broadband venture was losing money, with no short-term likelihood of generating profits, while continuing to suck up capital expenditure. To make matters worse, the fall in the value of Enron's share price was likely to trigger its guarantee obligations in relation to many of the SPEs.

To compound these problems, some hedge funds had become short sellers of Enron Stock. On March 5, 2001, *Fortune* published an article by Bethany McLean in which she questioned the current stock market value of Enron. Her main arguments were that it was very difficult to ascertain how the company was making its profits, that these profits did not seem to be generating a commensurate amount of cash, and that there was a lack of transparency in Enron's reporting and its handling of media questions. In the meantime, Enron's share price continued to slide.

A real blow came on August 14, 2001, when Skilling resigned after only six months as CEO citing "personal reasons." Lay resumed the role of CEO. Subsequently, in an interview with *Business Week*, Lay said, "There's no other shoe to fall," and went on to add "There are absolutely no problems [. . . .]. There are no accounting issues, no trading issues, no reserve issues, no previously unknown problem issues. The company is probably in the strongest and best shape that it has ever been in"[13] Enron watchers, fearing there was more to the story, were not convinced and the share slide continued.

At the same time as seeking to reassure investors, Lay was cashing in his share options, netting himself in the process more than $100 million. As a rather jaundiced employee put it after the crash:

> If the business works, super, if it doesn't then you have to take a hit. Fun, hey? Meanwhile, as CEO, you take all your compensation in equity. You find out that as long as you keep making this paper money, the shares go up. Woohooo! But, oh shit! Something's going on—maybe the world is pretty hard to take over. "I think I'll sell my shares," says he. Of course, he keeps talking the stock up, while the guy is selling his shirt as fast as possible.

THE DOWNFALL

On August 15, the day after Skilling quit, an Enron employee, Sharon Watkins, herself an Andersen alum who was working in the Fastow team, had sent a memo to Ken Lay expressing fears over the company's accounting practices, particularly with regard to the Raptor transactions and asked whether Enron had become a "risky place to work." She expressed the view that "Skilling's abrupt departure will raise suspicions of accounting improprieties and valuation issues."

Lay, who briefly met with Watkins a few days later, passed her memo to Enron's principal legal advisors, Vinson & Elkins. This well-respected Houston legal firm, which had advised on some of the transactions being questioned, concluded that there was no need to get a second opinion on the accounting policies.

Watkins also called someone she knew at Andersen and voiced her concerns. Andersen had been uncomfortable for some time with Enron's accounting practices that it had previously accepted. Revisiting some of the SPEs, particularly in relation to the 3% rule, it decided that, at least in the case of Chewco, there had been a breach and that Chewco would have to be consolidated. It also looked again at the Raptor transactions and came to the same conclusion. Accordingly, it advised Enron that the accounts would need to be restated.

On October 16, in a conference call with analysts, Lay disclosed a $1.2 billion write down of shareholders' equity, focusing attention on the SPEs. Fastow was fired on October 24th and the SEC announced an investigation into Enron's accounting practices and related party transactions.

Little over a week later, on October 26th Enron's board announced the establishment of a Special Investigation Committee chaired by the newly and specially appointed William Powers Jr., Dean of the University of Texas School of Law, with existing board members Raymond S. Troubh and Herbert S. Winoker. The committee was given a very limited remit, which was "to address transactions between Enron and investment partnerships created and managed by Andrew Fastow, Enron's former Executive Vice President and Chief Financial Officer, and by other Enron employees who worked with Fastow."[14]

Against this background, Enron's management were in frantic discussions with their many bankers—trying to win some breathing space—and with the rating agencies—trying to persuade them not to downgrade Enron's stock. And all the while they were trying to find a "White Knight" to bail them out.

In the meantime, Enron implemented a bonus plan for some 60 key traders and about 500 other employees whose retention was thought critical to enable the company to continue to operate in the future. In order to qualify, an employee had to agree to repay the bonus plus 25% if he left within 90 days. The plan cost the company $105 million.

Enron's great local Houston rival, the much smaller Dynergy Inc., announced a bid to acquire Enron but withdrew it on November 28th having done some due diligence. Moody's, the rating agency, downgraded Enron's debt to "Junk," (Ca), on November 29th with the inevitable result of forcing Enron to seek protection from its creditors a few days later.

The speed of the collapse surprised many. After all, the rating agencies had been slow to indicate a credit risk problem and most financial analysts following the stock were still rating it a "buy" or "hold." Indeed, in June, David Fleischer, an analyst with Goldman Sachs, had described Enron as "a world-class company" and as "the clear leader in the energy industry." While acknowledging that Enron's "transparency" was "pretty low" and that "[the company] had been indifferent to cash flow as it sought to build businesses," his view was that "an investment in Enron shares right now represents one of the best risk/reward opportunities in the marketplace." This was not untypical.

THE POST-MORTEMS

Working with commendable speed, the Powers committee team interviewed a number of the main Enron employees involved (although not all were willing to co-operate) and examined numerous documents. The committee claimed that they were denied access to Andersen personnel and papers (an allegation strongly refuted by Andersen), which limited their enquiries. Their report[15] was published on February 1, 2002 and posted on the Internet. Contrary to many expectations, although restricted in scope and without access to some information that may have assisted, Powers and his colleagues produced a report that contained some damning criticisms of many involved, including the board themselves. (*Refer to* Exhibit 8.9 on p. 313 *for excerpts from the report.*)

Their principal conclusion was that "many of the most significant transactions apparently were designed to accomplish favourable financial statement results, not to achieve bone fide economic objectives or to transfer risk." They went on to say "[. . . .], the LJM partnerships functioned as a vehicle to accommodate Enron in the management of its reported financial results."[16]

In their summary they said:

> The tragic consequences of the related-party transactions and accounting errors were the result of failures at many levels and by many people: A flawed idea, self-enrichment by employees, inadequately-designed controls, poor implementation, inattentive oversight, simple (and not-so-simple) accounting mistakes, and over-reaching in a culture that appears to have encouraged pushing the limits.[17]

THE ENRON BOARD

The 15 members of Enron's board were heavily criticised for their oversight failure, both by the Powers committee and, later, in a US Senate Committee Report.[18]

The main accusations were that they knew of and authorised high risk accounting policies in the face of warnings from Andersen; they allowed excessive remuneration; they did not follow their own code of ethics by allowing Fastow to transact with the company and they failed to ensure that sufficient controls were in place to safeguard Enron's interests in the deals with the special purpose vehicles. This was despite the presence on the Audit committee of Dr Robert Jaedicke, a distinguished academic accountant and former Dean of Stanford Business School, and Lord Wakeham.

AFTERMATH

Following the collapse, there was an immediate media frenzy, much of it highly speculative, and acres of newsprint were covered. The politicians were also quick to get in on the act with numerous House and Senate investigations set up and televised hearings organised. Lay and Fastow pled the Fifth Amendment,[19] as did many others. Skilling did not, but used the phrase "I don't recall" many times.

It may yet be years before the full picture emerges but that will be too late for Andersen, which imploded after being found guilty, in July 2002, of obstructing justice.

POSTSCRIPT

The Enron story continues to evolve. This case has been written to provide a background to the events leading to the then biggest bankruptcy in U.S. history. I have drawn upon information in the public domain and on interviews with a number of former Enron employees, together with internal documentation made available to me. Against the background of pending civil litigation and further criminal proceedings, those with whom I have spoken wish, at this stage, to remain anonymous.

Notes

1. A swindle, also known as a pyramid scheme, that involves "borrowing from Peter to pay Paul." It is named after Charles Ponzi, who, in the 1920s, conned tens of thousands of

people in Boston into investing in international postal reply coupons by offering to pay vast amounts of interest, which he paid using the investments.

2. This was a joint venture with GE and Bechtel, the international construction giant.

3. Skilling would succeed Lay as CEO in February 2001.

4. The "book" is the portfolio of contracts to buy or sell the futures, options, or other derivatives that are being traded.

5. An accounting method that adjusts the valuation of a security or other asset to reflect current market values, with the paper gain or loss taken through the income statement.

6. "Merchant assets" were those assets (including options and futures contracts) held on Enron's books that could be traded at any time if they received a suitable offer.

7. Anderson performed not only external but also internal auditing for Enron.

8. Dark fibre is fibre that has been installed but is not yet activated; once it is activated it is referred to as being "lit."

9. The other 97% could be borrowed.

10. In the US, a Limited Liability Partnership is one in which, except for the "general partner(s)," the partners' or investors' liability is limited to the amount they have invested. A partner is not liable for professional malpractice that does not involve that partner.

11. Limited Liability Company.

12. Limited [Liability] Partnership.

13. *Business Week online* August 24, 2001.

14. Enron Special Committee Report, February 1, 2002 (the Powers Report).

15. Op. cit., p. 4.

16. Op. cit., p. 4.

17. Op. cit., p. 1.

18. Report of the Permanent Subcommittee on the Investigations of the Committee of Governmental Affairs, United States Senate, July 8, 2002.

19. The constitutional right of a U.S. citizen to remain silent to avoid self-incrimination.

Moral Mazes: Bureaucracy and Managerial Work

ROBERT JACKALL

Corporate leaders often tell their charges that hard work will lead to success. Indeed, this theory of reward being commensurate with effort has been an enduring belief in our society, one central to our self-image as a people where the "main chance" is available to anyone of ability who has the gumption and the persistence to seize it. Hard work, it is also frequently asserted, builds character. This notion carries less conviction because businessmen, and our society as a whole, have little patience with those who make a habit of finishing out of the money. In the end, it is success that matters, that legitimate striving, and that makes work worthwhile.

What if, however, men and women in the big corporation no longer see success as necessarily connected to hard work? What becomes of the social morality of the corporation—I mean the everyday rules in use that people play by—when there is thought to be no "objective" standard of excellence to explain how and why winners are separated from also-rans, how and why some people succeed and others fail?

This is the puzzle that confronted me while doing a great many extensive interviews with managers and executives in several large corporations, particularly in a large chemical company and a large textile firm. I went into these corporations to study how bureaucracy—the prevailing organizational form of our society and economy—shapes moral consciousness. I came to see that managers' rules for success are at the heart of what may be called the bureaucratic ethic.

This article suggests no changes and offers no programs for reform. It is, rather, simply an interpretive sociological analysis of the moral dimensions of managers' work. Some readers may find the essay sharp-edged, others familiar. For both groups, it is important to note at the outset that my materials are managers' own descriptions of their experiences.[1] In listening to managers, I have had the decided advantages of being unencumbered with business responsibilities and also of being free from the taken-for-granted views and vocabularies of the business world. As it happens, my own research in a variety of other settings suggests that managers' experiences are by no means unique; indeed they have a deep resonance with those of other occupational groups.

WHAT HAPPENED TO THE PROTESTANT ETHIC?

To grasp managers' experiences and the more general implications they contain, one must see them against the background of the great historical transformations, both social and cultural, that produced managers as an occupational group. Since the concern here is with the moral significance of work in business, it is important to begin with an understanding of the original Protestant Ethic, the world view of the rising bourgeois class that spearheaded the emergence of capitalism.

The Protestant Ethic was a set of beliefs that counseled "secular asceticism"—the methodical, rational subjection of human impulse and desire to God's will through "restless, continuous, systematic work in a worldly calling."[2] This ethic of ceaseless work and ceaseless renunciation of the fruits of one's toil provided both the economic and the moral foundations for modern capitalism.

On one hand, secular asceticism was a ready-made prescription for building economic capital; on the other, it became for the upward-moving bourgeois class—self-made industrialists, farmers, and enterprising artisans—the ideology that justified their attention to this world, their accumulation of wealth, and indeed the social inequities that inevitably followed such accumulation. This bourgeois ethic, with its imperatives for self-reliance, hard work, frugality, and rational planning, and its clear definition of success and failure, came to dominate a whole historical epoch in the West.

But the ethic came under assault from two directions. First, the very accumulation of wealth that the old Protestant Ethic made possible gradually stripped away the religious basis of the ethic, especially among the rising middle class that benefited from it. There were, of course, periodic reassertions of the religious context of the ethic, as in the case of John D. Rockefeller and his turn toward Baptism. But on the whole, by the late 1800s the religious roots of the ethic survived principally among the independent farmers and proprietors of small businesses in rural areas and towns across America.

In the mainstream of an emerging urban America, the ethic had become secularized into the "work ethic," "rugged individualism," and especially the "success ethic." By the beginning of this century, among most of the economically successful, frugality had become an aberration, conspicuous consumption the norm. And with the shaping of the mass consumer society later in this century, the sanctification of consumption became widespread, indeed crucial to the maintenance of the economic order.

Affluence and the emergence of the consumer society were responsible, however, for the demise of only aspects of the old ethic—namely, the imperatives for saving and investment. The core of the ethic, even in its later, secularized form—self-reliance, unremitting devotion to work, and a morality that postulated just rewards for work well done—was undermined by the complete transformation of the organizational form of work itself. The hallmarks of the emerging modern production and distribution systems were administrative hierarchies, standardized work procedures, regularized timetables, uniform policies, and centralized control—in a word, the bureaucratization of the economy.

This bureaucratization was heralded at first by a very small class of salaried managers, who were later joined by legions of clerks and still later by technicians and professionals of every stripe. In this century, the process spilled over from the private to the public sector and government bureaucracies came to rival those of industry. This great transformation produced the decline of the old middle class of entrepreneurs, free professionals, independent farmers, and small independent businessmen—the traditional carriers of the old Protestant Ethic—and the ascendance of a new middle class of salaried employees whose chief common characteristic was and is their dependence on the big organization.

Any understanding of what happened to the original Protestant Ethic and to the old morality and social character it embodied—and therefore any understanding of the moral significance of work today—is inextricably tied to an analysis of bureaucracy. More specifically, it is, in my view, tied to an analysis of the work and occupational cultures of managerial groups within bureaucracies. Managers are the quintessential bureaucratic work group; they not only fashion bureaucratic rules, but they are also bound by them. Typically, they are not just in the organization; they are of the organization. As such, managers represent the prototype of the white-collar salaried employee. By analyzing the kind of ethic bureaucracy produces in managers, one can begin to understand how bureaucracy shapes morality in our society as a whole.

PYRAMIDAL POLITICS

American businesses typically both centralize and decentralize authority. Power is concentrated at the top in the person of the chief executive officer and is simultaneously decentralized; that is, responsibility for decisions and profits is pushed as far down the organizational line as possible. For example, the chemical company that I studied—and its structure is typical of other organizations I examined—is one of several operating companies of a large and growing conglomerate. Like the other operating companies, the chemical concern has its own president, executive vice presidents, vice presidents, other executive officers, business area managers, entire staff divisions, and operating plants. Each company is, in effect, a self-sufficient organization, though they are all coordinated by the corporation, and each president reports directly to the corporate CEO.

Now, the key interlocking mechanism of this structure is its reporting system. Each manager gathers up the profit targets or other objectives of his or her subordinates, and with these formulates his commitments to his boss; this boss takes these commitments, and those of his subordinates, and in turn makes a commitment to his boss. (Note: henceforth only "he" or "his" will be used to allow for easier reading.) At the top of the line, the president of each company makes his commitment to the CEO of the corporation, based on the stated objectives given to him by his vice presidents. There is always pressure from the top to set higher goals.

This management-by-objectives system, as it is usually called, creates a chain of commitments from the CEO down to the lowliest product manager. In practice, it also shapes a patrimonial authority arrangement which is crucial to defining both the immediate experiences and the long-run career chances of individual managers. In this world, a subordinate owes fealty principally to his immediate boss. A subordinate must not overcommit his boss; he must keep the boss from making mistakes, particularly public ones; he must not circumvent the boss. On a social level, even though an easy, breezy informality is the prevalent style of American business, the subordinate must extend to the boss a certain ritual deference: for instance, he must follow the boss's lead in conversation, must not speak out of turn at meetings, and must laugh at the boss's jokes while not making jokes of his own.

In short, the subordinate must not exhibit any behavior which symbolizes parity. In return, he can hope to be elevated when and if the boss is elevated, although other important criteria also intervene here. He can also expect protection for mistakes made up to a point. However, that point is never exactly defined and always depends on the complicated politics of each situation.

WHO GETS CREDIT?

It is characteristic of this authority system that details are pushed down and credit is pushed up. Superiors do not like to give detailed instructions to subordinates. The official reason for this is to maximize subordinates' autonomy; the underlying reason seems to be to get rid of tedious details and to protect the privilege of authority to declare that a mistake has been made.

It is not at all uncommon for very bold and extremely general edicts to emerge from on high. For example, "Sell the plant in St. Louis. Let me know when you've struck a deal." This pushing down of details has important consequences:

1. Because they are unfamiliar with entangling details, corporate higher echelons tend to expect highly successful results without complications. This is central to top executives' well-known aversion to bad news and to the resulting tendency to "kill the messenger" who bears that news.
2. The pushing down of detail creates great pressure on middle managers not only to transmit good news but to protect their corporations, their bosses, and themselves in the process. They become the "point men" of a given strategy and the potential "fall guys" when things go wrong.

Credit flows up in this structure and usually is appropriated by the highest ranking officer involved in a decision. This person redistributes credit as he chooses, bound essentially by a sensitivity to public perceptions of his fairness. At the middle level, credit for a particular success is always a type of refracted social honor; one cannot claim credit even if it is earned. Credit has to be given, and acceptance of the gift implicitly involves a reaffirmation and strengthening of fealty. A superior may share some credit with subordinates in order to deepen fealty relationships and induce greater future efforts on his behalf. Of course, a different system is involved in the allocation of blame, a point I shall discuss later.

FEALTY TO THE "KING"

Because of the interlocking character of the commitment system, a CEO carries enormous influence in his corporation. If, for a moment, one thinks of the presidents of individual operating companies as barons, then the CEO of the parent company is the king. His word is law; even the CEO's wishes and whims are taken as commands by close subordinates on the corporate staff, who zealously turn them into policies and directives.

A typical example occurred in the textile company last year when the CEO, new at the time, expressed mild concern about the rising operating costs of the company's fleet of rented cars. The following day, a stringent system for monitoring mileage replaced the previous casual practice.

Great efforts are made to please the CEO. For example, when the CEO of the large conglomerate that includes the chemical company visits a plant, the most important order of business for local management is a fresh paint job, even when, as in several cases last year the cost of paint alone exceeds $100,000. I am told that similar anecdotes from other organizations have been in circulation since 1910; this suggests a certain historical continuity of behavior toward top bosses.

The second order of business for the plant management is to produce a complete book describing the plant and its operations, replete with photographs and illustrations, for presentation to the CEO; such a book costs about $10,000 for the single copy. By any standards of budgetary stringency, such expenditures are irrational. But by the social standards of the corporation, they make perfect sense. It is far more important to please the king today than to worry about the future economic state of one's fief, since if one does not please the king, there may not be a fief to worry about or indeed any vassals to do the worrying.

By the same token, all of this leads to an intense interest in everything the CEO does and says. In both the chemical and the textile companies, the most common topic of conversation among managers up and down the line is speculation about their respective CEOs' plans, intentions, strategies, actions, styles, and public images.

Such speculation is more than idle gossip. Because he stands at the apex of the corporation's bureaucratic and patrimonial structures and locks the intricate system of commitments between bosses and subordinates into place, it is the CEO who ultimately decides whether those commitments have been satisfactorily met. Moreover, the CEO and his trusted associates determine the fate of whole business areas of a corporation.

SHAKE-UPS AND CONTINGENCY

One must appreciate the simultaneously monocratic and patrimonial character of business bureaucracies in order to grasp what we might call their contingency. One has only to read the *Wall Street Journal* or the *New York Times* to realize that, despite their carefully constructed "eternal" public image, corporations are quite unstable organizations. Mergers, buy-outs, divestitures, and especially "organizational restructuring" are commonplace aspects of business life. I shall discuss only organizational shake-ups here.

Usually, shake-ups occur because of the appointment of a new CEO and/or division president, or because of some failure that is adjudged to demand retribution; sometimes these occurrences work together. The first action of most new CEOs is some form of organizational change. On the one hand, this prevents the inheritance of blame for past mistakes; on the other, it projects an image of bareknuckled aggressiveness much appreciated on Wall Street. Perhaps most important, a shake-up rearranges the fealty structure of the corporation, placing in power those barons whose style and public image mesh closely with that of the new CEO.

A shake-up has reverberations throughout an organization. Shortly after the new CEO of the conglomerate was named, he reorganized the whole business and selected new presidents to head each of the five newly formed companies of the corporation. He mandated that the presidents carry out a thorough reorganization of their separate companies complete with extensive "census reduction"—that is, firing as many people as possible.

The new president of the chemical company, one of these five, had risen from a small but important specialty chemicals division in the former company. Upon promotion to president, he reached back into his former division, indeed back to his own past work in a particular product line, and systematically elevated many of his former colleagues, friends, and allies. Powerful managers in other divisions, particularly in a rival process chemicals division, were: (1) forced to take big demotions in the new power structure; (2) put on "special assignment"—the corporate euphemism for Siberia (the saying is: "No one ever comes back from special assignment"); (3) fired; or (4) given "early retirement," a graceful way of doing the same thing.

Up and down the chemical company, former associates of the president now hold virtually every important position. Managers in the company view all of this as an inevitable fact of life. In their view, the whole reorganization could easily have gone in a completely different direction had another CEO been named or had the one selected picked a different president for the chemical company, or had the president come from a different work group in the old organization. Similarly, there is the abiding feeling that another significant change in top management could trigger yet another sweeping reorganization.

Fealty is the mortar of the corporate hierarchy, but the removal of one well-placed stone loosens the mortar throughout the pyramid and can cause things to fall apart. And no one is ever quite sure, until after the fact, just how the pyramid will be put back together.

SUCCESS AND FAILURE

It is within this complicated and ambiguous authority structure, always subject to upheaval, that success and failure are meted out to those in the middle and upper middle managerial ranks. Managers rarely spoke to me of objective criteria for achieving success because once certain crucial points in one's career are passed, success and failure seem to have little to do with one's accomplishments. Rather, success is socially defined and distributed. Corporations do demand, of course, a basic competence and sometimes specified training and experience; hiring patterns usually ensure these. A weeding-out process takes place, however, among the lower ranks of managers during the first several years of their experience. By the time a manager reaches a certain numbered grade in the ordered hierarchy—in the chemical company this is Grade 13 out of 25, defining the top $8\frac{1}{2}\%$ of management in the company—managerial competence as such is taken for granted and assumed not to differ greatly from one manager to the next. The focus then switches to social factors, which are determined by authority and political alignments—the fealty structure—and by the ethos and style of the corporation.

MOVING TO THE TOP

In the chemical and textile companies as well as the other concerns I studied, five criteria seem to control a person's ability to rise in middle and upper middle management. In ascending order they are:

1. **Appearance and dress.** This criterion is so familiar that I shall mention it only briefly. Managers have to look the part, and it is sufficient to say that corporations are filled with attractive, well-groomed, and conventionally well-dressed men and women.

2. **Self-control.** Managers stress the need to exercise iron self-control and to have the ability to mask all emotion and intention behind bland, smiling, and agreeable public faces. They believe it is a fatal weakness to lose control of oneself, in any way, in a public forum. Similarly, to betray valuable secret knowledge (for instance, a confidential reorganization plan) or intentions through some relaxation of self-control—for example, an indiscreet comment or a lack of adroitness in turning aside a query—can not only jeopardize a manager's immediate position but can undermine others' trust in him.

3. **Perception as a team player.** While being a team player has many meanings, one of the most important is to appear to be interchangeable with other managers near one's level. Corporations discourage narrow specialization more strongly as one goes higher. They also discourage the expression of moral or political qualms. One might object, for example, to working with chemicals used in nuclear power, and most corporations today would honor that objection. The public statement of such objections, however, would end any realistic aspirations for higher posts because one's usefulness to the organization depends on versatility. As one manager in the chemical company commented: "Well, we'd go along with his request but we'd always wonder about the guy. And in the back of our minds, we'd be thinking that he'll soon object to working in the soda ash division because he doesn't like glass."

Another important meaning of team play is putting in long hours at the office. This requires a certain amount of sheer physical energy, even though a great deal of this time is spent not in actual work but in social rituals—like reading and discussing newspaper articles, taking coffee breaks, or having informal conversations. These rituals, readily observable in every corporation that I studied, forge the social bonds that make real managerial work—that is, group work of various sorts—possible. One must participate in the rituals to be considered effective in the work.

4. **Style.** Managers emphasize the importance of "being fast on your feet"; always being well organized; giving slick presentations complete with color slides; giving the appearance of knowledge even in its absence; and possessing a subtle, almost indefinable sophistication, marked especially by an urbane, witty, graceful, engaging, and friendly demeanor.

I want to pause for a moment to note that some observers have interpreted such conformity, team playing, affability, and urbanity as evidence of the decline of the individualism of the old Protestant Ethic.[3] To the extent that commentators take the public images that managers project at face value, I think they miss the main point. Managers up and down the corporate ladder adopt the public faces that they wear quite consciously; they are, in fact, the masks behind which the real struggles and moral issues of the corporation can be found.

Karl Mannheim's conception of self-rationalization or self-streamlining is useful in understanding what is one of the central social psychological processes of organizational life.[4] In a world where appearances—in the broadest sense—mean everything, the wise and ambitious person learns to cultivate assiduously the proper, prescribed modes of appearing. He dispassionately takes stock of himself, treating himself as an object. He analyzes his strengths and weaknesses, and decides what he needs to change in order to survive and flourish in his organization. And then he systematically undertakes a program to reconstruct his image. Self-rationalization curiously parallels the methodical subjection of self to God's will that the old Protestant Ethic counseled; the difference, of course, is that one acquires not moral virtues but a masterful ability to manipulate personae.

5. **Patron power.** To advance, a manager must have a patron, also called a mentor, a sponsor, a rabbi, or a godfather. Without a powerful patron in the higher echelons of management, one's prospects are poor in most corporations. The patron might be the manager's immediate boss or someone several levels higher in the chain of command. In either case the manager is still bound by the immediate, formal authority and fealty patterns of his position; the new—although more ambiguous—fealty relationships with the patron are added.

A patron provides his "client" with opportunities to get visibility, to showcase his abilities, to make connections with those of high status. A patron cues his client to crucial political developments in the corporation, helps arrange lateral moves if the client's upward progress is thwarted by a particular job or a particular boss, applauds his presentations or suggestions at meetings, and promotes the client during an organizational shake-up. One must, of course, be lucky in one's patron. If the patron gets caught in a political crossfire, the arrows are likely to find his clients as well.

SOCIAL DEFINITIONS OF PERFORMANCE

Surely, one might argue, there must be more to success in the corporation than style, personality, team play, chameleonic adaptability, and fortunate connections. What about the bottom line—profits, performance?

Unquestionably, "hitting your numbers"—that is, meeting the profit commitments already discussed—is important, but only within the social context I have described. There are several rules here. First, no one in a line position—that is, with responsibility for profit and loss—who regularly "misses his numbers" will survive, let alone rise. Second, a person who always hits his numbers but who lacks some or all of the required social skills will not rise. Third, a person who sometimes misses his numbers but who has all the desirable social traits will rise.

Performance is thus always subject to a myriad of interpretations. Profits matter, but it is much more important in the long run to be perceived as "promotable" by belonging to central political networks. Patrons protect those already selected as rising stars from the negative judgments of others; and only the foolhardy point out even egregious errors of those in power or those destined for it.

Failure is also socially defined. The most damaging failure is, as one middle manager in the chemical company puts it, "when your boss or someone who has the power to determine your fate says: 'You failed.'" Such a godlike pronouncement means, of course, out-and-out personal ruin; one must, at any cost, arrange matters to prevent such an occurrence.

As it happens, things rarely come to such a dramatic point even in the midst of an organizational crisis. The same judgment may be made but it is usually called "nonpromotability." The difference is that those who are publicly labeled as failures normally have no choice but to leave the organization; those adjudged nonpromotable can remain, provided they are willing to accept being shelved or, more colorfully, "mushroomed"—that is, kept in a dark place, fed manure, and left to do nothing but grow fat. Usually, seniors do not tell juniors they are nonpromotable (though the verdict may be common knowledge among senior peer groups). Rather, subordinates are expected to get the message after they have been repeatedly overlooked for promotions. In fact, middle managers interpret staying in the same job for more than two or three years as evidence of a negative judgment. This leads to a mobility panic at the middle levels which, in turn, has crucial consequences for pinpointing responsibility in the organization.

CAPRICIOUSNESS OF SUCCESS

Finally, managers think that there is a tremendous amount of plain luck involved in advancement. It is striking how often managers who pride themselves on being hardheaded rationalists explain their own career patterns and those of others in terms of luck. Various uncertainties shape this perception. One is the sense of organizational contingency. One change at the top can create profound upheaval throughout the entire corporate structure, producing startling reversals of fortune, good or bad, depending on one's connections. Another is the uncertainty of the markets that often makes managerial planning simply elaborate guesswork, causing real economic outcome to depend on factors totally beyond organizational and personal control.

It is interesting to note in this context that a line manager's credibility suffers just as much from missing his numbers on the up side (that is, achieving profits higher than predicted) as from missing them on the down side. Both outcomes undercut the ideology of managerial planning and control, perhaps the only bulwark managers have against market irrationality.

Even managers in staff positions, often quite removed from the market, face uncertainty. Occupational safety specialists, for instance, know that the bad publicity from one serious accident in the workplace can jeopardize years of work and scores of safety awards. As one high-ranking executive in the chemical company says, "In the corporate world, 1,000 'Attaboys!' are wiped away by one 'Oh, shit!'"

Because of such uncertainties, managers in all the companies I studied speak continually of the great importance of being in the right place at the right time and of the catastrophe of being in the wrong place at the wrong time. My interview materials are filled with stories of people who were transferred immediately before a big shake-up and, as a result, found themselves riding the crest of a wave to power; of people in a promising business area who were terminated because top management suddenly decided that the area no longer fit the corporate image desired; of others caught in an unpredictable and fatal political battle among their patrons; of a product manager whose plant accidentally produced an odd color batch of chemicals, who sold them as a premium version of the old product, and who is now thought to be a marketing genius.

The point is that managers have a sharply defined sense of the *capriciousness* of organizational life. Luck seems as good an explanation as any of why, after a certain point, some people succeed and others fail. The upshot is that many managers decide that they can do little to influence external events in their favor. One can, however, shamelessly streamline oneself, learn to wear all the right masks, and get to know all the right people. And then sit tight and wait for things to happen.

"GUT DECISIONS"

Authority and advancement patterns come together in the decision-making process. The core of the managerial mystique is decision-making prowess, and the real test of such prowess is what managers call "gut decisions," that is, important decisions involving big money, public exposure, or significant effect on the organization. At all but the highest levels of the chemical and textile companies, the rules for making gut decisions are, in the words of one upper middle manager: "(1) Avoid making any decisions if at all possible; and (2) if a decision has to be made, involve as many people as you can so that, if things go south, you're able to point in as many directions as possible."

Consider the case of a large coking plant of the chemical company. Coke making requires a gigantic battery to cook the coke slowly and evenly for long periods; the battery is the most important piece of capital equipment in a coking plant. In 1975, the plant's battery showed signs of weakening and certain managers at corporate headquarters had to decide whether to invest $6 million to restore the battery to top form. Clearly, because of the amount of money involved, this was a gut decision.

No decision was made. The CEO had sent the word out to defer all unnecessary capital expenditures to give the corporation cash reserves for other investments. So the managers allocated small amounts of money to patch the battery up until 1979, when it collapsed entirely. This brought the company into a breach of contract with a steel producer and into violation of various Environmental Protection Agency pollution regulations. The total bill, including lawsuits and now federally mandated repairs to the battery, exceeded $10 million. I have heard figures as high as $150 million, but because of "creative accounting," no one is sure of the exact amount.

This simple but very typical example gets to the heart of how decision making is intertwined with a company's authority structure and advancement patterns. As the chemical company managers see it, the decisions facing them in 1975 and 1979 were crucially different. Had they acted decisively in 1975—in hindsight, the only rational course—they would have salvaged the battery and saved their corporation millions of dollars in the long run.

In the short run, however, since even seemingly rational decisions are subject to widely varying interpretations, particularly decisions which run counter to a CEO's stated objectives, they would have been taking a serious risk in restoring the battery. What is more, their political networks might have unraveled, leaving them vulnerable to attack. They chose short-term safety over long-term gain because they felt they were judged, both by higher authority and by their peers, on their short-term performances. Managers feel that if they do not survive the short run, the long run hardly matters. Even correct decisions can shorten promising careers.

By contrast, in 1979 the decision was simple and posed little risk. The corporation had to meet its legal obligations; also it had to either repair the battery the way the EPA demanded or shut down the plant and lose several hundred million dollars. Since there were no real choices, everyone could agree on a course of action because everyone could appeal to inevitability. Diffusion of responsibility, in this case by procrastinating until total crisis, is intrinsic to organizational life because the real issue in most gut decisions is: Who is going to get blamed if things go wrong?

"BLAME TIME"

There is no more feared hour in the corporate world than "blame time." Blame is quite different from responsibility. There is a cartoon of Richard Nixon declaring: "I accept all of the responsibility, but none of the blame." To blame someone is to injure him verbally in public; in large organizations, where one's image is crucial, this poses the most serious sort of threat. For managers, blame—like failure—has nothing to do with the merits of a case; it is a matter of social definition. As a general rule, it is those who are or who become politically vulnerable or expendable who get "set up" and become blamable. The most feared situation of all is to end up inadvertently in the wrong place at the wrong time and get blamed.

Yet this is exactly what often happens in a structure that systematically diffuses responsibility. It is because managers fear blame time that they diffuse responsibility; however, such diffusion inevitably means that someone, somewhere is going to become a scapegoat when things go wrong. Big corporations encourage this process by their complete lack of any tracking system. Whoever is currently in charge of an area is responsible—that is, potentially blamable—for whatever goes wrong in the area, even if he has inherited others' mistakes. An example from the chemical company illustrates this process.

When the CEO of the large conglomerate took office, he wanted to rid his capital accounts of all serious financial drags. The corporation had been operating a storage depot for natural gas which it bought, stored, and then resold. Some years before the energy crisis, the company had entered into a long-term contract to supply gas to a buyer—call him Jones. At the time, this was a sound deal because it provided a steady market for a stably priced commodity.

When gas prices soared, the corporation was still bound to deliver gas to Jones at 20¢ per unit instead of the going market price of $2. The CEO ordered one of his subordinates to get rid of this albatross as expeditiously as possible. This was done by selling the operation to another party—call him Brown—with the agreement that Brown would continue to meet the contractual obligations to Jones. In return for Brown's assumption of these costly contracts, the corporation agreed to buy gas from Brown at grossly inflated prices to meet some of its own energy needs.

In effect, the CEO transferred the drag on his capital accounts to the company's operating expenses. This enabled him to project an aggressive, asset-reducing image to Wall Street. Several levels down the ladder, however, a new vice president for a particular business found himself saddled with exorbitant operating costs when, during a reorganization, those plants purchasing gas from Brown at inflated prices came under his purview. The high costs helped to undercut the vice president's division earnings and thus to erode his position in the hierarchy. The origin of the situation did not matter. All that counted was that the vice president's division was steadily losing big money. In the end, he resigned to "pursue new opportunities."

One might ask why top management does not institute codes or systems for tracking responsibility. This example provides the clue. An explicit system of accountability for subordinates would probably have to apply to top executives as well and would restrict their freedom. Bureaucracy expands the freedom of those on top by giving them the power to restrict the freedom of those beneath.

ON THE FAST TRACK

Managers see what happened to the vice president as completely capricious, but completely understandable. They take for granted the absence of any tracking of responsibility. If anything, they blame the vice president for not recognizing soon enough the dangers of the situation into which he was being drawn and for not preparing a defense—even perhaps finding a substitute scapegoat. At the same time, they realize that this sort of thing could easily happen to them. They see few defenses against being caught in the wrong place at the wrong time except constant wariness, the diffusion of responsibility, and perhaps being shrewd enough to declare the ineptitude of one's predecessor on first taking a job.

What about avoiding the consequences of their own errors? Here they enjoy more control. They can "outrun" their mistakes so that when blame time arrives, the burden will fall on someone else. The ideal situation, of course, is to be in a position to fire one's successors for one's own previous mistakes.

Some managers, in fact, argue that outrunning mistakes is the real key to managerial success. One way to do this is by manipulating the numbers. Both the chemical and the textile companies place a great premium on a division's or a subsidiary's return on assets. A good way for business managers to increase their ROA is to reduce their assets while maintaining sales. Usually they will do everything they can to hold down expenditures in order to decrease the asset base, particularly at the end of the fiscal year. The most common way of doing this is by deferring capital expenditures, from maintenance to innovative investments, as long as possible. Done for a short time, this is called "starving" a plant; done over a longer period, it is called "milking" a plant.

Some managers become very adept at milking businesses and showing a consistent record of high returns. They move from one job to another in a company, always upward, rarely staying more than two years in any post. They may leave behind them deteriorating plants and unsafe working conditions, but they know that if they move quickly enough, the blame will fall on others. In this sense, bureaucracies may be thought of as vast systems of organized irresponsibility.

FLEXIBLITY AND DEXTERITY WITH SYMBOLS

The intense competition among managers takes place not only behind the agreeable public faces I have described but within an extraordinarily indirect and ambiguous linguistic framework. Except at blame time, managers do not publicly criticize or disagree with one another or with company policy. The sanction against such criticism or disagreement is so strong that it constitutes, in managers' view, a suppression of professional debate. The sanction seems to be rooted principally in their acute sense of organizational contingency; the person one criticizes or argues with today could be one's boss tomorrow.

This leads to the use of an elaborate linguistic code marked by emotional neutrality, especially in group settings. The code communicates the meaning one might wish to convey to other managers, but since it is devoid of any significant emotional sentiment, it can be reinterpreted should social relationships or attitudes change. Here, for example, are some typical phrases describing performance appraisals followed by their probable intended meanings:

Stock Phrase	Probable Intended Meaning
Exceptionally well qualified	Has commited no major blunders to date
Tactful in dealing with superiors	Knows when to keep his mouth shut
Quick thinking	Offers plausible excuses for errors
Meticulous attention to detail	A nitpicker
Slightly below average	Stupid
Unusually loyal	Wanted by no one else

For the most part, such neutered language is not used with the intent to deceive; rather, its purpose is to communicate certain meanings within specific contexts with the implicit understanding that, should the context change, a new, more appropriate meaning can be attached to the language already used. In effect, the corporation is a setting where people are not held to their word because it is generally understood that their word is always provisional.

The higher one gets in the corporate world, the more this seems to be the case; in fact, advancement beyond the upper middle level depends greatly on one's ability to manipulate a variety of symbols without becoming tied to or identified with any of them. For example, an amazing variety of organizational improvement programs marks practically every corporation. I am referring here to the myriad ideas generated by corporate staff, business consultants, academics, and a host of others to improve corporate structure; sharpen decision making; raise morale; create a more humanistic workplace; adopt Theory X, Theory Y, or, more recently, Theory Z of management; and so on. These programs become important when they are pushed from the top.

The watchword in the large conglomerate at the moment is productivity and, since this is a pet project of the CEO himself, it is said that no one goes into his presence without wearing a blue Productivity! button and talking about "quality circles" and "feedback sessions." The president of another company pushes a series of managerial seminars that endlessly repeats the basic functions of management: (1) planning, (2) organizing, (3) motivating, and (4) controlling. Aspiring young managers attend these sessions and with a seemingly dutiful eagerness learn to repeat the formulas under the watchful eyes of senior officials.

Privately, managers characterize such programs as the "CEO's incantations over the assembled multitude," as "elaborate rituals with no practical effect," or as "waving a magic wand to make things wonderful again." Publicly, of course, managers on the way up adopt the programs with great enthusiasm, participate in or run them very effectively, and then quietly drop them when the time is right.

PLAYING THE GAME

Such flexibility, as it is called, can be confusing even to those in the inner circles. I was told the following by a highly placed staff member whose work requires him to interact daily with the top figures of his company:

> I get faked out all the time and I'm part of the system. I come from a very different culture. Where I come from, if you give someone your word, no one ever questions it. It's the old hard-work-will-lead-to-success ideology. Small community, Protestant, agrarian, small business, merchant-type values. I'm disadvantaged in a system like this.

He goes on to characterize the system more fully and what it takes to succeed within it:

> It's the ability to play this system that determines whether you will rise. . . . And part of the adeptness [required] is determined by how much it bothers people. One thing you have to be able to do is to play the game, but you can't be disturbed by the game. What's the game? It's bringing troops home from Vietnam and declaring peace with honor. It's saying one thing and meaning another.
>
> It's characterizing the reality of a situation with any description that is necessary to make that situation more palatable to some group that matters. It means that you have to come up with a culturally accepted verbalization to explain why you are not doing what you are doing. . . . [Or] you say that we had to do what we did because it was inevitable; or because the guys at the [regulatory] agencies were dumb; [you] say we won when we really lost; [you] say we saved money when we squandered it; [you] say something's safe when it's potentially or actually dangerous. . . . Everyone knows that it's bullshit, but it's accepted. This is the game.

In addition, then, to the other characteristics that I have described, it seems that a prerequisite for big success in the corporation is a certain adeptness at inconsistency. This premium on inconsistency is particularly evident in the many areas of public controversy that face top-ranking managers. Two things come together to produce this situation. The first is managers' sense of beleaguerment from a wide array of adversaries who, it is thought, want to disrupt or impede management's attempts to further the economic interests of their companies. In every company that I studied, managers see themselves and their traditional prerogatives as being under siege, and they respond with a set of caricatures of their perceived principal adversaries.

For example, government regulators are brash, young, unkempt hippies in blue jeans who know nothing about the business for which they make rules; environmental activists—the bird and bunny people—are softheaded idealists who want everybody to live in tents, burn candles, ride horses, and eat berries; workers' compensation lawyers are out-and-out crooks who prey on corporations to appropriate exorbitant fees from unwary clients; labor activists are radical troublemakers who want to disrupt harmonious industrial communities; and the news media consist of rabble-rousers who propagate sensational antibusiness stories to sell papers or advertising time on shows like *60 Minutes*.

Second, within this context of perceived harassment, managers must address a multiplicity of audiences, some of whom are considered adversaries.

These audiences are the internal corporate hierarchy with its intricate and shifting power and status cliques, key regulators, key local and federal legislators, special publics that vary according to the issues, and the public at large, whose goodwill and favorable opinion are considered essential for a company's free operation.

Managerial adeptness at inconsistency becomes evident in the widely discrepant perspectives, reasons for action, and presentations of fact that explain, excuse, or justify corporate behavior to these diverse audiences.

ADEPTNESS AT INCONSISTENCY

The cotton dust issue in the textile industry provides a fine illustration of what I mean. Prolonged exposure to cotton dust produces in many textile workers a chronic and eventually disabling pulmonary disease called byssinosis or, colloquially, brown lung. In the early 1970s, the Occupational Safety and Health Administration proposed a ruling to cut workers' exposure to cotton dust sharply by requiring textile companies to invest large amounts of money in cleaning up their plants. The industry fought the regulation fiercely but a final OSHA ruling was made in 1978 requiring full compliance by 1984.

The industry took the case to court. Despite an attempt by Reagan appointees in OSHA to have the case removed from judicial consideration and remanded to the agency they controlled for further cost/benefit analysis, the Supreme Court ruled in 1981 that the 1978 OSHA ruling was fully within the agency's mandate, namely, to protect workers' health and safety as the primary benefit exceeding all cost considerations.

During these proceedings, the textile company was engaged on a variety of fronts and was pursuing a number of actions. For instance, it intensively lobbied regulators and legislators and it prepared court materials for the industry's defense, arguing that the proposed standard would crush the industry and that the problem, if it existed, should be met by increasing workers' use of respirators.

The company also aimed a public relations barrage at special-interest groups as well as at the general public. It argued that there is probably no such thing as byssinosis; workers suffering from pulmonary problems are all heavy smokers and the real culprit is the government-subsidized tobacco industry. How can cotton cause brown lung when cotton is white? Further, if there is a problem, only some workers are afflicted, and therefore the solution is more careful screening of the work force to detect susceptible people and prevent them from ever reaching the workplace. Finally, the company claimed that if the regulation were imposed, most of the textile industry would move overseas where regulations are less harsh.[5]

In the meantime, the company was actually addressing the problem but in a characteristically indirect way. It invested $20 million in a few plants where it knew such an investment would make money; this investment automated the early stages of handling cotton, traditionally a very slow procedure, and greatly increased productivity. The investment had the side benefit of reducing cotton dust levels to the new standard in precisely those areas of the work process where the dust problem is greatest. Publicly, of course, the company claims that the money was spent entirely to eliminate dust, evidence of its corporate good citizenship. (Privately, executives admit that, without the productive return, they would not have spent the money and they have not done so in several other plants.)

Indeed, the productive return is the only rationale that carries weight within the corporate hierarchy. Executives also admit, somewhat ruefully and only when their office doors are closed, that OSHA's regulation on cotton dust has been the main factor in forcing technological innovation in a centuries-old and somewhat stagnant industry.

Such adeptness at inconsistency, without moral uneasiness, is essential for executive success. It means being able to say, as a very high-ranking official of the textile company said to me without batting an eye, that the industry has never caused the slightest problem in any worker's breathing capacity. It means, in the chemical company, propagating an elaborate hazard/benefit calculus for appraisal of dangerous chemicals while internally conceptualizing "hazards" as business risks. It means publicly extolling the carefulness of testing procedures on toxic chemicals while privately ridiculing animal tests as inapplicable to humans.

It means lobbying intensively in the present to shape government regulations to one's immediate advantage and, ten years later, in the event of a catastrophe, arguing that the company acted strictly in accordance with the standards of the time. It means claiming that the real problem of our society is its unwillingness to take risks, while in the thickets of one's bureaucracy avoiding risks at every turn; it means as well making every effort to socialize the risks of industrial activity while privatizing the benefits.

THE BUREAUCRATIC ETHIC

The bureaucratic ethic contrasts sharply with the original Protestant Ethic. The Protestant Ethic was the ideology of a self-confident and independent propertied social class. It was an ideology that extolled the virtues of accumulating wealth in a society organized around property and that accepted the stewardship responsibilities entailed by property. It was an ideology where a person's word was his bond and where the integrity of the handshake was seen as crucial to the maintenance of good business relationships. Perhaps most important, it was connected to a predictable economy of salvation—that is, hard work will lead to success, which is a sign of one's election by God—a notion also containing its own theodicy to explain the misery of those who do not make it in this world.

Bureaucracy, however, breaks apart substance from appearances, action from responsibility, and language from meaning. Most important, it breaks apart the older connection between the meaning of work and salvation. In the bureaucratic world, one's success, one's sign of election, no longer depends on one's own efforts and on an inscrutable God but on the capriciousness of one's superiors and the market; and one achieves economic salvation to the extent that one pleases and submits to one's employer and meets the exigencies of an impersonal market.

In this way, because moral choices are inextricably tied to personal fates, bureaucracy erodes internal and even external standards of morality, not only in matters of individual success and failure but also in all the issues that managers face in their daily work. Bureaucracy makes its own internal rules and social context the principal moral gauges for action. Men and women in bureaucracies turn to each other for moral cues for behavior and come to fashion specific situational moralities for specific significant people in their worlds.

As it happens, the guidance they receive from each other is profoundly ambiguous because what matters in the bureaucratic world is not what a person is but how closely his many personae mesh with the organizational ideal; not his willingness to stand by his actions but his agility in avoiding blame; not what he believes or says but how well he has mastered the ideologies that serve his corporation; not what he stands for but whom he stands with in the labyrinths of his organization.

In short, bureaucracy structures for managers is an intricate series of moral mazes. Even the inviting paths out of the puzzle often turn out to be invitations to jeopardy.

Author's Note

I presented an earlier version of this paper in the Faculty Lecture Series at Williams College on March 18, 1982. The intensive field work done during 1980 and 1981 was made possible by a Fellowship for Independent Research from the National Endowment for the Humanities and by a Junior Faculty Leave and small research grant from Williams College.

Notes

1. There is a long sociological tradition of work on managers and I am, of course, indebted to that literature. I am particularly indebted to the work, both joint and separate, of Joseph Bensman and Arthur J. Vidich, two of the keenest observers of the new middle class. See especially their *The New American Society: The Revolution of the Middle Class* (Chicago: Quadrangle Books, 1971).
2. See Max Weber, *The Protestant Ethic and the Spirit of Capitalism*, translated by Talcott Parsons (New York: Charles Scribner's Sons, 1958), p. 172.
3. See William H. Whyte, *The Organization Man* (New York: Simon & Schuster, 1956), and David Riesman, in collaboration with Reuel Denney and Nathan Glazer, *The Lonely Crowd: A Study of the Changing American Character* (New Haven: Yale University Press, 1950).
4. Karl Mannheim, *Man and Society in an Age of Reconstruction* [London: Paul (Kegan), Trench, Trubner Ltd. 1940], p. 55.
5. On February 9, 1982, the Occupational Safety and Health Administration issued a notice that it was once again reviewing its 1978 standard on cotton dust for "cost-effectiveness." See *Federal Register*, vol. 47, p. 5906. As of this writing (May 1983), this review has still not been officially completed.

The Moral Muteness of Managers

FREDERICK B. BIRD • JAMES A. WATERS

Many managers exhibit a reluctance to describe their actions in moral terms even when they are acting for moral reasons. They talk as if their actions were guided exclusively by organizational interests, practicality, and economic good sense even when in practice they honor morally defined standards codified in law, professional conventions, and social mores. They characteristically defend morally defined objectives such as service to customers, effective cooperation among personnel, and utilization of their own skills and resources in terms of the long-run economic objectives of their organizations. Ostensibly moral standards regarding colleagues, customers, and suppliers are passed off as "street smarts" and "ways to succeed."[1]

Many observers have called attention to this reluctance of managers to use moral expressions publicly to identify and guide their decision making even when they are acting morally. A century and a half ago, de Tocqueville noted the disinclination of American business people to admit they acted altruistically even when they did.[2] More recently, McCoy has observed that managers are constantly making value choices, privately invoking moral standards, which they in turn defend in terms of business interests. Silk and Vogel note that many managers simply take for granted that business and ethics have little relation except negatively with respect to obvious cases of illegal activities, like bribery or price-fixing. Solomon and Hanson observe that, although managers are often aware of moral issues, the public discussion of these issues in ethical terms is ordinarily neglected.[3]

Current research based on interviews with managers about how they experience ethical questions in their work reveals that managers seldom discuss with their colleagues the ethical problems they routinely encounter.[4] In a very real sense, "Morality is a live topic for individual managers but it is close to a non-topic among groups of managers."[5]

This article explores this phenomenon of moral muteness and suggests ways that managers and organizations can deal openly with moral questions.

ACTIONS, SPEECH, AND NORMATIVE EXPECTATIONS

To frame the exploration of moral muteness, it is useful to consider in general terms the relationships among managers' actions, their communicative exchanges, and relevant normative expectations. Normative expectations are standards for behavior that are sufficiently compelling and authoritative that people feel they must either comply with them, make a show of complying with them, or offer good reasons why not.

While normative expectations influence conduct in many areas of life from styles of dress to standards of fair treatment, in most societies certain types of activities are considered to be morally neutral. Choices of how to act with respect to morally neutral activities are considered to be matters of personal preference, practical feasibility, or strategic interest.[6]

Although managers often disagree regarding the extent to which business activities are morally neutral, their interactions in contemporary industrial societies are influenced by a number of normative expectations. These expectations are communicated by legal rulings, regulatory agencies' decrees, professional codes, organizational policies, and social mores.[7] Considerable consensus exists with respect to a number of general ethical principles bearing upon management regarding honest communication, fair treatment, fair competition, social responsibility, and provision of safe and worthwhile services and products.[8]

Through verbal exchanges people identify, evoke, and establish normative expectations as compelling cultural realities. Moral expressions are articulated to persuade others, to reinforce personal convictions, to criticize, and to justify decisions. Moral expressions are also invoked to praise and to blame, to evaluate and to rationalize. Moral discourse plays a lively role communicating normative expectations, seeking cooperation of others, and rendering judgments.

For those decisions and actions for which moral expectations are clearly relevant, it is possible to conceive of four different kinds of relationship between managers' actions and their verbal exchanges. These are depicted in Figure 8-1. One pattern (Quadrant I) identifies those situations in which speaking and acting correspond with each other in keeping with moral expectations. A second congruent pattern (Quadrant III) is the mirror image of the first: no discrepancy exists between speech and action, but neither is guided by moral expectations.

The other two patterns represent incongruence between speech and action. In Quadrant II, actual conduct falls short of what is expected. Verbal exchanges indicate a deference for moral standards that is not evident in actual conduct. Discrepancy here represents hypocrisy, when people intentionally act contrary to their verbalized commitments.[9] Discrepancy may also

FIGURE 8-1   **Relations Between Moral Action and Speech**

	Actions Follow Normative Conduct	Actions Do Not Follow Normative Expectations
	I	II
Moral Terms Used in Speech	Congruent Moral Conduct	Hypocrisy, Moral Weakness
	IV	III
Moral Terms Not Used in Speech	Moral Muteness	Congruent Immoral or Amoral Conduct

assume the form of moral backsliding or moral weakness. In this case, the failure to comply with verbalized commitments occurs because of moral fatigue, the inability to honor conflicting standards, or excusable exceptions.[10] Because they are intuitively understandable, none of these three patterns are our concern in this article.

Rather, our focus is on the more perplexing fourth pattern (Quadrant IV) which corresponds with situations of moral muteness: managers avoid moral expressions in their communicative exchanges but would be expected to use them either because their actual conduct reveals deference to moral standards, because they expect others to honor such standards, or because they privately acknowledge that those standards influence their decisions and actions. In other words, with respect to those instances where the managers involved feel that how they and others act ought to be and is guided by moral expectations, why do they avoid moral references in their work-related communications?

For example, a given manager may argue that the only ethic of business is making money, but then describe at length the non-remunerative ways she fosters organizational commitment from her co-workers by seeking their identification with the organization as a community characterized by common human objectives and styles of operation. In another example, managers may enter into formal and informal agreements among themselves. In the process they necessarily make promises and undertake obligations. Implicitly, they must use moral terms to enter and confirm such understandings even though explicitly no such expressions are voiced. This discrepancy occurs most pervasively in relation to countless existing normative standards regarding business practices that are passed off as common sense or good management—e.g., taking care of regular customers in times of shortage even though there is opportunity to capture new customers, respecting the bidding process in purchasing even though lower prices could be forced on dependent suppliers, and ensuring equitable pricing among customers even though higher prices could be charged to less-knowledgeable or less-aggressive customers.

CAUSES OF MORAL MUTENESS

Interviews with managers about the ethical questions they face in their work indicate that they avoid moral talk for diverse reasons.[11] In the particular pattern of moral muteness, we observe that in general they experience moral talk as dysfunctional. More specifically, managers are concerned that moral talk will threaten organizational harmony, organizational efficiency, and their own reputation for power and effectiveness.

Threat to Harmony

Moral talk may, on occasion, require some degree of interpersonal confrontation. In extreme cases, this may take the form of blowing the whistle on powerful persons in the organization who are involved in illegal or unethical practices and may involve significant personal risk for the whistleblower.[12] Even in less-extreme cases, moral talk may involve raising questions about or disagreeing with practices or decisions of superiors, colleagues, or subordinates. Managers typically avoid any such confrontation, experiencing it as difficult and costly—as witnessed, for example, by the frequent avoidance of candid performance appraisals. Faced with a situation where a subordinate or colleague is involved in an unethical practice, managers may "finesse" a public discussion or confrontation by publishing a general policy statement or drawing general attention to an existing policy.

In the case of moral questions, managers find confrontations particularly difficult because they experience them as judgmental and likely to initiate cycles of mutual finger-pointing and recrimination. They are aware of the small and not-so-small deceits which are pervasive in organizations, e.g., juggling budget lines to cover expenditures, minor abuses of organizational perks, favoritism, nepotism, and fear that if they "cast the first stone" an avalanche may ensue.[13]

Many managers conclude that it is disruptive to bring up moral issues at work because their organizations do not want public discussion of such issues. We interviewed or examined the interviews of sixty managers who in turn talked about nearly 300 cases in which they had faced moral issues in their work. In only twelve percent of these cases had public discussion of moral issues taken place and more than half of these special cases were cited by a single executive. Give-and-take discussions of moral issues typically took place in private conversations or not at all.

Threat to Efficiency

Many managers avoid or make little use of moral expressions because moral talk is associated with several kinds of exchanges that obstruct or distract from responsible problem-solving. In these instances, moral talk is viewed as being self-serving and obfuscating. Thus, for example, while moral talk may be legitimately used to praise and blame people for their conduct, praising and blaming do not facilitate the identification, analysis, and resolution of difficult moral conundrums. Similarly, while moral talk in the form of ideological exhortations may function to defend structures of authority and to rally support for political goals, it does not facilitate problem solving among people with varied ideological commitments.[14]

Because of the prevalence of such usages, many managers are loath to use moral talk in their work. Blaming, praising, and idcological posturing do not help to clarify issues. Moreover, such moral talk frequently seems to be narrowly self-serving. Those who praise, blame, or express ideological convictions usually do so in order to protect and advance their own interests.

In addition, managers shun moral talk because such talk often seems to result in burdening business decisions with considerations that are not only extraneous, but at times antagonistic to responsible management. Moral talk may distract by seeking simplistic solutions to complicated problems. For example, discussions of justice in business often divert attention to theoretical formulas for distributing rewards and responsibilities without first considering how resources as a whole might be expanded and how existing contractual relations might already have built-in standards of fair transactions and allocations.

Moral talk may also be experienced as a threat to managerial flexibility. In order to perform effectively, managers must be able to adapt to changes in their organizations and environments. They are correspondingly wary of contractual relations that seem to be too binding, that too narrowly circumscribe discretionary responses. They therefore seek out working agreements, when they legally can, that are informal, flexible, and can be amended easily. They assume that if the stipulations are formally articulated in terms of explicit promises, obligations, and rights, then flexibility is likely to be reduced. In order to preserve flexibility in all their relations, managers frequently seek verbal, handshake agreements that make minimal use of explicit moral stipulations.[15]

Many managers also associate moral talk with rigid rules and intrusive regulations. Too often, public talk about moral issues in business is felt to precede the imposition of new government regulations that are experienced as arbitrary, inefficient, and meddlesome. Complaints about particular immoral practices too often seem to lead to government harassment through procedures and rules that make little economic sense. Managers may therefore avoid using moral expressions in their exchanges so that they do not invite moralistic criticisms and rigid restrictions.[16]

Threat to Image of Power and Effectiveness

Ambitious managers seek to present themselves as powerful and effective. They avoid moral talk at times because moral arguments appear to be too idealistic and utopian. Without effective power, the uses of moral expressions are like empty gestures. Many managers experience futility after they attempt unsuccessfully to change corporate policies which they feel are morally questionable. They privately voice their objections but feel neither able to mount organized protests within their organization nor willing to quit in public outcry. De facto they express a loyalty they do not wholeheartedly feel.[17]

This sense of futility may even be occasioned by management seminars on ethics. Within these workshops managers are encouraged to discuss hypothetical cases and to explore potential action alternatives. Many find these workshops instructive and stimulating. However, when managers begin to consider problems that they actually face in their organizations, then the character of these discussions often changes. Moral expressions recede and are replaced by discussions of organizational politics, technical qualifications, competitive advantages, as well as costs and benefits measured solely in economic terms. In the midst of these kinds of practical considerations, moral terms are abandoned because they seem to lack robustness. They suggest ideals and special pleadings without too much organizational weight.

Managers also shun moral talk in order to not expose their own ethical illiteracy. Most managers neither know nor feel comfortable with the language and logic of moral philosophy. At best they received instruction in juvenile versions of ethics as children and young adults in schools and religious associations. They have little or no experience using ethical concepts to analyze issues. They may more readily and less self-consciously use some ethical terms to identify and condemn obvious wrongdoings, but do not know how to use ethical terms and theories with intellectual rigor and sophistication to identify and resolve moral issues.

Finally, the "value of autonomy places great weight on lower managers' ability to solve creatively all their own problems they regularly face."[18] They observe how this valuing of autonomy actually decreases the likelihood that managers will discuss with their superiors the ethical questions they experience. Figure 8-2 summarizes these three causes of moral muteness.

CONSEQUENCES OF MORAL MUTENESS

The short-term benefits of moral muteness as perceived by managers (i.e., preservation of harmony, efficiency, and image of self-sufficiency) produce significant long-term costs for organizations. These costly consequences include:

- creation of moral amnesia;
- inappropriate narrowness in conceptions of morality;
- moral stress for individual managers;
- neglect of moral abuses; and
- decreased authority of moral standards.

Moral Amnesia

The avoidance of moral talk creates and reinforces a caricature of management as an amoral activity, a condition we describe as moral amnesia. Many business people and critics of business seem to be unable to recognize the degree to which business activities are in fact regulated by moral expectations. Critics and defenders of current business practices often debate about the legitimacy of bringing moral considerations to bear as if most business decisions were determined exclusively by considerations of profit and personal and organizational self-interest. In the process they ignore the degree to which actual business interactions are already guided by moral expectations communicated by law, professional codes, organizational conventions, and social mores.

FIGURE 8-2 Causes of Moral Muteness

Moral talk is viewed as creating these negative effects . . .	. . . because of these assumed attributes of moral talk.
• Threat to Harmony	• Moral talk is intrusive and confrontational and invites cycles of mutual recrimination.
• Threat to Efficiency	• Moral talk assumes distracting moralistic forms (praising, blaming, ideological) and is simplistic, inflexible, soft and inexact.
• Threat to Image of Power and Effectiveness	• Moral talk is too esoteric and idealistic, and lacks rigor and force.

When particular business practices seem not to honor particular standards, then it may be wrongly assumed that such actions are guided by no normative expectations whatsoever. Actually, specific business practices which are not, for example, guided primarily by particular standards such as social welfare and justice may in fact be determined in a large part by other moral expectations such as respect for fair contractual relations, the efficient and not wasteful use of human and natural resources, and responsiveness to consumer choices and satisfactions. Often, when businesses act in ways that are judged to be immoral, such as the unannounced closure of a local plant, they may well be acting in keeping with other normative standards, regarding, for example, organizational responsibility. To assume that conduct judged to be unethical because it is counter to particular standards necessarily springs solely from amoral consideration is to fail to grasp the extent to which such conduct may well be guided and legitimated by other, conflicting norms.

The moral amnesia regarding business practices is illustrated by the debate occasioned by an article by Friedman entitled "The Social Responsibility of Business Is to Increase Its Profit."[19] To many, Friedman seemed to conclude that business people had no moral responsibility other than to use any legal means to increase the returns on the investments of stockholders. He did argue that business people were ill-equipped to become social reformers and that such moral crusading might well lead them to do harm both to those they sought to help and to their own organizations. Both defenders and critics assumed that Friedman was defending an amoral position. However, although cloaked in the language of economic self-interest, Friedman's article alluded in passing to eight different normative standards relevant for business practices: namely, businesses should operate without fraud, without deception in interpersonal communications, in keeping with conventions regarding fair competition, in line with existing laws, with respect to existing contractual agreements, recognizing the given rights of employees and investors, seeking to maximize consumer satisfactions, and always in ways that allow for the free choices of the individual involved. It can be argued that Friedman invited misunderstanding by polarizing issues of profit and social responsibility. It cannot be argued that according to his position profits can be pursued without any other moral criteria than legality.

It is characteristic of this moral amnesia that business people often feel themselves moved by moral obligations and ideals and find no way to refer explicitly to these pushes and pulls except indirectly by invoking personal preferences, common sense, and long-term benefits. They remain inarticulate and unself-conscious of their convictions.

Narrowed Conception of Morality

In order to avoid getting bogged down in moral talk which threatens efficiency, managers who are convinced they are acting morally may argue that their actions are a morally neutral matter. They "stonewall" moral questions by arguing that the issues involved are ones of feasibility, practicality, and the impersonal balancing of costs and benefits, and that decisions on these matters are appropriately made by relevant managers and directors without public discussion.

We interviewed a number of managers who made these kinds of claims with respect to issues that others might consider contentious. A utilities executive argued, for example, that studies had exaggerated the impact of steam plants on water supplies. He also contended that no moral issues were relevant to the decisions regarding the domestic use of nuclear power. A pharmaceutical company manager criticized those who attempted to make a moral issue out of a leak in a rinse water pipe. An accountant criticized a colleague for arguing that the procedure recently used with a customer involved moral improprieties. These managers attempted to treat issues that had been questioned as if they were not publicly debatable.

Insofar as it is thought that moral issues are posed only by deviance from acceptable standards of behavior, then managers have a legitimate case to shun moral discussions of their actions which are neither illegal nor deviant. However, while appropriately claiming that their actions are not morally improper, managers stonewall whenever they insist, in addition, that their actions are constituted not only by deviance, but also by dilemmas (when two or more normative standards conflict) and by shortfalls (from the pursuit of high ideals). In the examples cited above, the managers were correct in asserting that no illegal nor blatantly deviant actions were involved. However, they were incorrect to argue that these actions were morally neutral.

Moral muteness in the form of stonewalling thus perpetuates a narrow conception of morality, i.e., as only concerned with blatant deviance from moral standards. Most importantly, moral muteness in this case prevents creative exploration of action alternatives that might enable the organization to balance better conflicting demands or to approximate better the highest ideals.

Moral Stress

Managers experience moral stress as a result of role conflict and role ambiguity in connection with moral expectations.[20] They treat their responsibility to their organizations as a moral standard and, when confronted with an ethical question, they frequently have difficulty deciding what kinds of costs will be acceptable in dealing with the question (e.g., it costs money to upgrade toilet facilities and improve working conditions). Moreover, moral expectations (for example, honesty in communications) are often very general and the manager is frequently faced with a decision on what is morally appropriate behavior in a specific instance. He or she may have to decide, for example, when legitimate entertainment becomes bribery or when legitimate bluffing or concealment of basic positions in negotiations with a customer or supplier becomes dishonesty in communication.

A certain degree of such moral stress is unavoidable in management life. However, it can be exacerbated beyond reasonable levels by the absence of moral talk. If managers are unable to discuss with others their problems and questions, they absorb the uncertainty and stress that would more appropriately be shared by colleagues and superiors. In the absence of moral talk, managers may cope with intolerable levels of moral stress by denying the relevance or importance of particular normative expectations. This may take the form of inappropriate idealism in which the legitimacy of the organization's economic objectives is given inadequate attention. Conversely, and perhaps more frequently, managers may cope with excessive moral stress by treating decisions as morally neutral, responding only to economic concerns and organizational systems of reward and censure. In either case, moral muteness eliminates any opportunity that might exist for creative, collaborative problem solving that would be best for the manager, as well as for the organization and its stakeholders.

Neglect of Abuses

The avoidance of moral talk by managers also means that many moral issues are simply not organizationally recognized and addressed. Consequently, many moral abuses are ignored, many moral ideals are not pursued, and many moral dilemmas remain unresolved. Managers we interviewed readily cited moral lapses of colleagues and competitors.[21] The popular press continually cites examples of immoral managerial conduct, often failing in the process to credit the extent to which managers actually adhere to moral standards.

Just as norms of confrontation contribute to moral muteness, in circular fashion that muteness reinforces those norms and leads to a culture of neglect. Organizational silence on moral issues makes it more difficult for members to raise questions and debate issues. What could and should be ordinary practice—i.e., questioning of the propriety of specific decisions and actions—tends to require an act of heroism and thus is less likely to occur.

Decreased Authority of Moral Standards

Moral arguments possess compelling authority only if the discourse in which these arguments are stated is socially rooted. It is an idealistic misconception to suppose that moral reasons by virtue of their logic alone inspire the feelings of obligation and desire that make people willingly adhere to moral standards. Blake and Davis refer to this assumption as the "fallacy of normative determinism."[22] The pushes and pulls which lead people to honor normative standards arise as much, if not more, from social relationships as from verbal communication of moral ideas. The articulations of moral ideas gain compelling authority to the degree that these expressions call to mind existing feelings of social attachments and obligations, build upon tacit as well as explicit agreements and promises, seem to be related to realistic rewards and punishments, and connect feelings of self-worth to moral compliance.[23] That is, moral expressions become authoritative, and therefore genuinely normative, to the degree that they both arouse such feelings and reveal such agreements, and also connect these feelings and recollections with moral action.

Moral ideas communicated without being socially rooted simply lack compelling authority. Such expressions are like inflated currency: because they possess little real authority, there is a tendency to use more and more of them in order to create hoped-for effects. Such language, unless it has become socially rooted, is experienced as disruptive, distracting, inflexible, and overblown. Simply attempting to talk more about moral issues in business is not likely to make these conversations more weighty and authoritative. What is needed is to find ways of realistically connecting this language with the experiences and expectations of people involved in business.

Indeed, in an even more general effect, the resolution of organizational problems through cooperation becomes more difficult to the extent that managers shun moral talk. Cooperation may be gained in several ways. For example, it may be inspired by charismatic leadership or achieved by forceful commands. Charisma and command are, however, limited temporary devices for gaining cooperation. Many managers do not have the gift for charismatic leadership. In any case, such leadership is best exercised in relation to crises and not ordinary operations. Commands may achieve compliance, but a compliance that is half-hearted, foot-dragging, and resentful. Cooperation is realized more enduringly and more fully by fostering commitments to shared moral values. Shared values provide a common vocabulary for identifying and resolving problems. Shared values constitute common cultures which provide the guidelines for action and the justifications for decisions.[24]

It is impossible to foster a sense of ongoing community without invoking moral images and normative expectations. Moral terms provide the symbols of attachment and guidelines for interactions within communities.[25] In the absence of such images and norms, individuals are prone to defend their own interests more aggressively and with fewer compromises. Longer range and wider conceptions of self-interest are likely to be abandoned. Without moral appeals to industry, organizational well-being, team work, craftsmanship, and service, it is much more difficult to cultivate voluntary rather than regimented cooperation.[26]

THE NATURE OF CHANGE INTERVENTIONS

Several factors must be taken into account by those who wish to reduce this avoidance of moral talk by managers. Those who wish to "institutionalize ethics" in business, "manage values in organizations," or gain "the ethical edge"[27] must take into account the factors which give rise to this avoidance. It is impossible to foster greater moral responsibility by business people and organizations without also facilitating more open and direct conversations about these issues by managers.

First, business people will continue to shun open discussions of actual moral issues unless means are provided to allow for legitimate dissent by managers who will not be personally blamed, criticized, ostracized, or punished for their views. From the perspective of the managers we interviewed, their organizations seemed to expect from them unquestioning loyalty and deference. Although many had privately spoken of their moral objections to the practices of other managers and their own firms, few had publicly voiced these concerns within their own organizations. Full discussions of moral issues are not likely to take place unless managers and workers feel they can openly voice arguments regarding policies and practices that will not be held against them when alternatives are adopted.

Business organizations often do not tolerate full, open debate of moral issues because they perceive dissent as assuming the form either of carping assaults or of factional divisiveness. Carping is a way of airing personal grievances and frustrations, often using moral expressions in order to find fault.[28] Ideally, managers ought to be able openly to voice dissent and then, once decisions have been made contrary to their views, either respectfully support such choices or formally protest. However, business organizations that stifle open discussions of moral concerns invite the carping they seek to avoid by limiting debate in the first place. Managers are most likely to complain, to express resentment, and to find personal fault in others if they feel they have no real opportunities to voice justifiable dissents.

Legitimate expressions of dissent may be articulated in ways that do not aggravate and reinforce factional divisiveness. Before considering recommendations for organizational change (about which various managers and workers are likely to have vested interests), it is useful to set aside time for all those involved to recognize the degree to which they both hold similar long-run objectives and value common ethical principles.[29] These exercises are valuable because they help to make shared commitments seem basic and the factional differences temporary and relative. In addition, factional differences are less likely to become contentious if these factions are accorded partial legitimacy as recognized functional sub-groups within larger organizations. Finally, legitimate dissent is less likely to aggravate factional divisiveness if ground rules for debate and dissent include mutual consultations with all those immediately involved. These rules can help reduce the chances of discussions turning into empty posturing and/or irresolute harangues.

Second, if business people are going to overcome the avoidance of moral talk, then they must learn how to incorporate moral expressions and arguments into their exchanges. Learning how to talk ethics is neither as simple nor as difficult as it seems to be to many managers. Initially, managers must learn to avoid as much as possible the ordinary abuses of moral talk. In particular, efforts must be made to limit the degree to which moral talk is used for publicly extolling the virtues or excoriating the vices of other managers. Evaluations of personal moral worth ought to remain as private as possible. Furthermore, the use of moral expressions to rationalize and to express personal frustrations ought to be censored. In addition, the use of moral expression to take ideological postures ought to be minimized. Moral talk ought to be used primarily to identify problems, to consider issues, to advocate and criticize policies, and to justify and explain decisions.

Managers should recognize and learn to use several of the typical forms in which moral arguments are stated. An elementary knowledge of moral logics as applied to business matters is a useful skill not only for defending one's own argument, but also for identifying the weaknesses and strengths in the arguments of others. It is important, however, to recognize that verbal skill at talking ethics is primarily a rhetorical and discursive skill and not a matter of philosophical knowledge. Like the skill of elocution, learning how to talk ethics involves learning how to state and criticize moral arguments persuasively. What is critical is that managers are able to use moral reasoning to deal with issues they actually face in their lives and to influence others to consider carefully their positions.

Managers must regularly and routinely engage with each other in reflection and dialogue about their own experiences with moral issues. The attempt to overcome the avoidance of moral talk by managers by introducing them to formal philosophical languages and logics not rooted in their social experiences is likely to fail. Philosophical ethics is indeed an instructive and critical tool that can be used to analyze moral arguments of business people and to propose creative solutions to perceived dilemmas. It is improbable, however, that many managers are likely to adopt philosophical discourse on a day-to-day basis to talk about moral issues. At best, this language might serve as a technical instrument, much like the specialized languages of corporate law and advanced accounting used by specialized experts in consultation with executives. Such technical use does not overcome the moral amnesia that infects ordinary communications among managers. To be compelling, moral discourse must be connected with, express, foster, and strengthen managers' feelings of attachment, obligation, promises, and agreements.

Moral ideas rarely possess compelling authority unless some group or groups of people so closely identify with these ideas as to become their articulate champions. Moral ideas are likely to gain widespread following by business people as smaller groups of managers and workers so closely identify with these ideas—which in turn express their own attachments, obligations, and desires—that they champion them. This identification is most likely to occur where business people with existing feelings of community, due to professional, craft, or organizational loyalties, begin to articulate their moral convictions and to discuss moral issues. It is precisely in these sorts of subgroups of people who have to work with each other as colleagues that managers will be willing to risk speaking candidly and see the benefits of such candor in fuller cooperation.

The role of senior managers in fostering such "good conversation" among managers in an organization cannot be overemphasized.[30] If they seek to provide moral leadership to an organization, senior managers must not only signal the importance they place on such conversations, but also demand that they take place. They need also to build such conversations into the fabric of organizational life through management mechanisms such as requiring that managers include in their annual plans a statement of the steps they will take to ensure that questionable practices are reviewed, or that new business proposals include an assessment of the ethical climate of any new business area into which entry is proposed.[31]

Finally, interventions require patience. Open conversations of the kind we have been describing will, in the short-run, be slow and time-consuming and thus reduce organizational efficiency. They will, in the short-run, be awkward and fumbling and appear futile, and thus they will be quite uncomfortable for managers used to smooth control of managerial discussions. Patience will be required to persevere until these short-run problems are overcome, until new norms emerge which encourage debate without carping and acrimony, until managers develop the skills necessary for efficient and reflective problem solving with respect to moral issues, until moral voices and commitments are heard clearly and strongly throughout their organizations.

Note

The research on which this article is based was made possible in part by a grant from the Social Science and Humanities Research Council of Canada. The Center for Ethics and Social Policy in Berkeley, California, aided this research by helping to arrange for interviews with executives. The authors wish to thank William R. Torbert and Richard P. Nielsen for their helpful comments on an earlier draft of this article.

Notes

1. Chester Barnard, *The Functions of the Executive* (Cambridge, MA: Harvard University Press, 1938), p. 154; George E. Breen, "Middle Management Morale in the 80's," *An AMA Survey Report* (New York: The American Management Association, 1983); Mark H. McCormick, *What They Don't Teach You at Harvard Business School* (Toronto: Bantam Books, 1984), Chapter 2.

2. Alexis deTocqueville, *Democracy in America,* Vol. 2., translated by Henry Reeve, revised by Francis Bowen (New York: Mentor Books, 1945), pp. 129–132.

3. Charles McCoy, *Management of Values: The Ethical Differences in Corporate Policy and Performance* (Boston: Pitman, 1985), pp. 8, 9, 16, 98; Leonard Silk and David Vogel, *Ethics and Profits: The Crisis of Confidence in American Business* (New York: Simon and Schuster, 1976), chapter 8; Robert C. Solomon and Kristine R. Hanson, *It's Good Business* (New York: Atheneum, 1985), p. xiv; see also, Mark Pastin, *The Hard Problems of Management: Gaining the Ethics Edge* (San Francisco: Jossey-Bass, 1986), Introduction, Part One.

4. James A. Waters, Frederick Bird, and Peter D. Chant, "Everyday Moral Issues Experienced by Managers," *Journal of Business Ethics* (Fall 1986), pp. 373–384; Barbara Ley Toffler, *Tough Choices: Managers Talk Ethics* (New York: John Wiley and Sons, 1986); Kathy E. Kram, Peter C. Yaeger, and Gary Reed, "Ethical Dilemmas in Corporate Context," paper presented at Academy of Management, August 1988; Robin Derry, "Managerial Perceptions of Ethical Conflicts and Conceptions of Morality: A Qualitative Interview Study," paper presented at Academy of Management, August 1988.

5. James A. Waters and Frederick B. Bird, "The Moral Dimension of Organizational Culture," *Journal of Business Ethics,* 6/1 (1987): 18.

6. Jurgen Habermas, *The Theory of Communicative Action,* Vol. I, translated by Thomas McCarthy (Boston: The Beacon Press, 1984), Part I, Chapter 3.

7. Mark L. Taylor, *A Study of Corporate Ethical Policy Statements* (Dallas, TX: The Foundation of the Southwestern Graduate School of Banking, 1980).

8. Frederick Bird and James A. Waters, "The Nature of Managerial Moral Standards," *Journal of Business Ethics,* 6 (1987): 1–13.

9. George Wilhelm Frederick Hegel, *Philosophy of Right,* translated by T. M. Knox (London: Oxford University Press, 1952, 1967), pp. 93–103.

10. Aristotle, *The Nichomachean Ethics,* translated by J. A. R. Rhomson (Middlesex, UK: Penguin Books, 1953), Book VII; Peter Winch, *Ethics and Action* (London: Routledge and Kegan Paul, 1972), Chapters 4, 8.

11. Waters, Bird, and Chant, op. cit.; Frederick Bird, Frances Westley, and James A. Waters, "The Uses of Moral Talk: Why Do Managers Talk Ethics?" *Journal of Business Ethics* (1989).

12. Ralph Nader, Peter Petkas, and Kate Blackwell, eds., *Whistle Blowing* (New York: Grossman, 1972); Richard P. Nielsen, "What Can Managers Do About Unethical Management?" *Journal of Business Ethics* 6/4 (1987).

13. Kerr, "Integrity in Effective Leadership," in Suresh Srivastra and Associates, eds., *Executive Integrity* (San Francisco: Jossey-Bass, 1988).

14. Clifford Geertz, *The Interpretation of Cultures* (New York: Basic Books, 1973), Chapter 9.

15. Oliver E. Williamson, "Transactional Cost Economics: The Governance of Contractual Relations," *Journal of Law and Economics* (1980), pp. 233–261.

16. Pastin, op. cit., Chapter 3; Silk and Vogel, op. cit., Chapter 2; Solomon and Hanson, op. cit., p. 5; Kerr, op. cit., p. 138.

17. Albert Hirschman, *Exit, Voice and Loyalty: Responses to Decline in Firms and States* (Cambridge, MA: Harvard University Press, 1970), Chapter 7.

18. Kram, Yaeger, and Read, op. cit., p. 28.

19. Milton Friedman, "The Social Responsibility of Business Is to Increase its Profit," *New York Times Magazine,* September 13, 1970.

20. Waters and Bird, op. cit., pp. 16–18.

21. Waters, Bird, and Chant, op. cit.

22. Judith Blake and Kingsley Davis, "Norms, Values and Sanctions," in Dennis Wrong and Harry L. Gracey, *Readings in Introductory Sociology* (New York: Macmillan Co., 1967).

23. Emile Durkheim, *Suicide*, translated by John A. Spaulding and George Simpson (New York: The Free Press, 1974), Chapter 2; Frederick Bird, "Morality and Society: An Introduction to Comparative Sociological Study of Moralities," unpublished manuscript, 1988, Chapter 4.

24. Karl E. Weick, "Organizational Culture as a Source of High Reliability," *California Management Review*, 29/2 (Winter 1987): 112–127.

25. Basil Bernstein, *Class Codes, and Control* (St. Albans, NY: Palladin, 1973).

26. Frances Westley and Frederick Bird, "The Social Psychology of Organizational Commitment," unpublished paper, 1989.

27. Kirk Hanson, "Ethics and Business: A Progress Report," in Charles McCoy, ed., *Management of Values* (Boston: Pitman, 1985), pp. 280–88; Fred Twining and Charles McCoy, "How to Manage Values in Organizations," unpublished manuscript, 1987; Pastin, op. cit.

28. Bird, Westley, and Waters, op. cit.

29. Twining and McCoy, op. cit.

30. James A. Waters, "Integrity Management: Learning and Implementing Ethical Principles in the Workplace," in S. Srivastva, ed., *Executive Integrity* (San Francisco: Jossey-Bass, 1988).

31. James A. Waters and Peter D. Chant, "Internal Control of Management Integrity: Beyond Accounting Systems," *California Management Review*, 24/3 (Spring 1982): 60–66.

Legislative Summary of the Sarbanes-Oxley Act of 2002

On July 25, 2002, Congress passed the "Sarbanes-Oxley Act of 2002" by a vote of 423–3 in the House, and 99–0 in the Senate.

It is important to note that many elements of the Act are not effective immediately.

Under the Act, a new accounting oversight Board must be established within 270 days after enactment. Once the Board is established, accounting firms will have 180 days in which to register with the Board. It appears that it is only at that time—up to 450 days (15 months) from now—that the new requirements in Titles I and II of the Act, which establish the new Board and impose new auditor independence procedures, will take effect. For many provisions, the SEC is required to issue interpretive rules within 180 days after enactment. Certain other elements of the Act, such as new corporate "certification" requirements and heightened criminal penalties for corporate officials, will take effect sooner because they are not tied to the establishment of the Board or SEC rulemaking.

The following is an outline of the major requirements of the Act, broken into four sections: (1) consequences for issuers; (2) audit committee requirements; (3) board and corporate officer requirements; and (4) accounting firm requirements.

I ISSUERS

The Act will have the following consequences for issuers:

1. **Issuers Will Be Subject to the Act:** The Act defines "issuer" as any company whose securities are registered, whether the issuer is domiciled in the United

States or elsewhere, and any company required to file reports under § 15(d) of the Exchange Act. (§ 2)

2. **Issuers Must Establish Audit Committees:** The Act effectively requires all listed companies, whether US or non-US, to have fully independent audit committees. (Title II generally)

3. **The Board Can Compel Testimony and Audit Work Papers Related to an Issuer:** The Board may require testimony or the production of documents or information in the possession of any registered public accounting firm or "associated person" of the firm relevant to an investigation. The Board may also "request" documents and testimony from other persons, including issuers. If necessary, the Board may request that the SEC issue a subpoena to assist the Board in its investigation. (§ 105)

4. **Issuers Will Be Held Responsible for Associating with Suspended or Barred Auditors:** The Act prohibits an issuer from employing a person who has been suspended or barred from associating with any accounting firm. (§ 105)

5. **Issuers Will Fund the Board's and FASB's Operations:** The Act authorizes the Board to fund itself by requiring issuers to pay an "annual accounting support fee." Issuers will also be responsible for funding FASB. (§ 108, § 109)

6. **An Issuer May Not Engage Its Auditor for Nine Specifically-Listed Categories of Non-Audit Services:** The Act statutorily prohibits specifically-listed categories of non-audit services from being offered by accounting firms to their public audit clients, most of which are already proscribed under SEC rules. (§ 201)

7. **An Issuer's Audit Committee Must Pre-Approve All Audit and Non-Audit Services:** Before an auditor can provide audit services or any non-audit service to a public audit client, the audit committee of the client must approve. (§ 202)

8. **Issuers Must Disclose Approvals of Non-Audit Services:** Audit committee approvals of non-audit services are to be disclosed in SEC periodic reports. (§ 202)

9. **Issuers Must Wait One Year Before Hiring an Audit Engagement Team Member to Be CEO, CFO, CAO or Equivalent:** The Act provides that an accounting firm may not provide audit services for a public company if that company's chief executive officer, controller, chief financial officer, chief accounting officer, or other individual serving in an equivalent position, was employed by the accounting firm and worked on the company's audit during the one year before the start of the audit services. (§ 206)

10. **Issuers Must Provide Audit Committees with Adequate Funding:** Issuers must provide appropriate funding, as determined by the audit committee, for payment of compensation to the auditor and any advisers employed by the audit committee. (§ 301)

11. **Issuers Must Disclose Off-Balance Sheet Transactions:** The SEC must issue rules requiring that annual and quarterly financial reports disclose all material off-balance sheet transactions, arrangements, obligations, and other relationships of the issuer that may have a material current or future effect on the financial condition of the issuer. (§ 401)

12. **Issuers Must Reconcile Pro Forma Information with GAAP and Not Omit Information That Makes Financial Disclosures Misleading:** The SEC must issue rules providing that pro forma financial information disclosures must reconcile with GAAP and not be misleading. (§ 401)

13. **Issuers May Not Extend Loans to Directors or Corporate Officers:** The Act makes it unlawful for an issuer to extend a loan to any director or executive officer that is not made in the ordinary course of business of the issuer, and is not of a type generally made available to the public and on market terms. (§ 402)

14. **Issuers Must Disclose Transactions Involving Management and Principal Stockholders:** Section 16 of the Securities Exchange Act of 1934 is amended to require that changes in equity ownership by directors, officers, and 10% stockholders must be reported within two business days after the day of the transaction. Within one year of enactment of the Act, such "Section 16 filings" will have to be filed electronically and posted on the company's web site. (§ 403)

15. **Issuers Must Make Annual Internal Control Reports:** Issuers must (1) state the responsibility of management for establishing and maintaining an adequate internal control structure and procedures for financial reporting, and (2) contain an assessment as of the end of the most recent fiscal year of the effectiveness of the internal control structure procedures of the issuer for financial reporting. The auditor must attest to, and report on, management's assertion. (§ 404)

16. **Issuers Must Disclose Whether They Have Adopted Codes of Ethics for Their Senior Officers:** The SEC must issue rules requiring companies to disclose whether they have adopted codes of ethics for senior officers. If not, issuers must explain their rationale for failing to do so. (§ 406)

17. **Issuers Must Disclose the Existence of a "Financial Expert" on the Audit Committee:** The SEC must issue rules requiring issuers to disclose whether or not (and if not, reasons therefore) the audit committee has at least one member who is a "financial expert," a term to be defined by the SEC, considering whether a person has through education or experience "an understanding of generally accepting accounting principles and financial statements;" "experience in the preparation or auditing of financial statements of generally comparable issuers;" "the application of such principles in connection with the accounting for estimate, accruals, and reserves;" "experience with internal accounting controls;" and an understanding of audit committee functions." (§ 407)

18. **Issuers Must Disclose Information about "Material Changes" on a Real Time Basis:** Public companies must disclose in plain English and "on a rapid and current basis" such information regarding material changes in their financial conditions or operations, including trend and qualitative information and graphic presentations, as the SEC may mandate. (§ 408)

19. **The Act Creates New Criminal Penalties for Obstruction of Justice by Destruction of Documents:** The Act creates new criminal penalties for obstruction of federal agency or other official proceedings by destruction of records. The Act provides for up to 20 years in jail for knowingly destroying or creating evidence with intent to obstruct a federal investigation or matter in bankruptcy. (§ 802, § 1102)

20. **The Act Changes Bankruptcy Law Regarding Obligations Incurred in Violation of Securities Laws:** The Act amends the federal bankruptcy code so that obligations arising from securities law violations cannot be discharged in bankruptcy. (§ 803)

21. **The Act Creates Longer Statutes of Limitations for Securities Fraud Cases:** The Act lengthens the statute of limitations for private federal securities fraud lawsuits from one year after the date of discovery of the facts constituting the violation and three years after the fraud to two years from discovery and five years after the fraud. (§ 804)

22. **The Act Creates New "Whistleblower" Protections for Employees of Issuers:** The Act provides whistleblower protection to employees of publicly traded companies when they disclose information or assist in detecting and stopping fraud. (§ 806, § 1107)

23. **The Act Creates New Criminal Penalties for Defrauding Shareholders of Publicly Traded Companies:** The Act provides that anyone who "knowingly" defrauds shareholders of publicly traded companies may be subject to fines and imprisonment of up to 25 years. (§ 807)

24. **The Act Enhances Penalties for White Collar Crime:** The Act increases jail time for conspiracy, mail and wire fraud, violations of ERISA, Exchange Act violations, and retaliation against informants. (§ 902, § 903, § 904, § 1106, § 1107)

II AUDIT COMMITTEES

The Act requires that audit committees:

25. **Pre-Approve All Audit and Non-Audit Services:** The Act provides that both auditing and non-audit services must be pre-approved by the audit committee. The Act makes it "unlawful" for accounting firms to perform nine specifically listed categories of non-audit services for their public audit clients. The services in this list are essentially the same as those that were contained in the final SEC independence rule, adopted in December 2000, with three exceptions: the Act prohibits internal audit outsourcing services, "financial information systems" work, and "expert" services. The Act specifically indicates that the performance of any *other* non-audit service by an accounting firm for a public audit client is not prohibited, provided such services are "pre-approved" by the client's audit committee. (§ 201, § 202)

26. **Have the Ability to Delegate Pre-Approval Authority:** The pre-approval of non-audit services may be delegated to a member of the audit committee. The decisions of any audit committee member to whom pre-approval authority is delegated must be presented to the full audit committee at its next scheduled meeting. (§ 202)

27. **Receive Regular Reports From the Auditor on Accounting Treatments:** An auditor must report to the audit committee on the critical accounting policies and practices to be used, all alternative treatments of financial information within GAAP that have been discussed with management, including the ramifications of the use of such alternative treatments, and the treatment preferred by the auditor; any accounting disagreements between the auditor and management; and other material written communications between the auditor and management (such as any management letter and schedule of unadjusted differences). (§ 204)

28. **Be Responsible for Oversight of the Auditor:** The Act provides that auditors shall report to and be overseen by the audit committee of a client, not management. The audit committee "shall be directly responsible for the appointment, compensation, and oversight" of the auditor's work. (§ 301)

29. **Be Independent of the Issuer:** Audit committee members must be independent. In order to be considered "independent," an audit committee member may not accept any consulting, advisory, or other compensatory fees from the issuer or be an "affiliated person" of the issuer or a subsidiary thereof. (§ 301)

30. **Establish Complaint Procedures:** Audit committees must establish procedures for receiving and treating complaints regarding accounting and auditing matters, including complaints from those who wish to remain anonymous. (§ 301)

31. **Be Given Authority to Engage Advisers:** Audit committees must "have the authority to engage independent counsel and other advisers, as it determines necessary to carry out its duties." (§ 301)

32. **Receive Corporate Attorneys' Reports of Evidence of a Material Violation of Securities Laws or Breaches of Fiduciary Duty:** The SEC must establish rules for attorneys appearing before the Commission requiring them to report evidence of a material violation of securities laws or breach of fiduciary duty or similar violation by the company to the Chief Legal Counsel or the CEO. If management does not appropriately respond to the evidence, the attorney must report the evidence to the audit committee. (§ 307)

III BOARDS OF DIRECTORS / CORPORATE OFFICERS

The Act imposes the following requirements on boards of directors and corporate officers:

33. **The Board Must Either Form an Audit Committee or Take on Such Responsibilities:** The Act requires Boards of Directors to either form an audit committee or otherwise take on the responsibilities of one. (§ 2)

34. **CEO and CFO Must Certify Financial Reports:** An issuer's CEO and CFO must certify that periodic reports filed with the SEC are materially correct; that financial statements and disclosures "fairly present" the company's operations and financial condition in all material respects; and that they are responsible for evaluating and maintaining internal controls, have designed such controls to ensure that material information related to the issuer and its consolidated subsidiaries is made known to such officials and others within such entities, have evaluated the effectiveness as of a date within 90 days prior to the report, and have presented in their report their conclusions about the effectiveness of their internal controls. Further, they shall certify that they have disclosed to the auditor and audit committee all "significant deficiencies" in the design or operation of internal controls, including any material weaknesses, and any fraud, whether or not material, that involved management or other employees who have a significant role in the issuer's internal controls. (§ 302)

   A separate criminal provision requires the signing officer to certify that each periodic report containing financial statements complies with securities laws and that the information in such report fairly presents, in all material respects, the financial condition and results of operations of the company. Failure to do so is a criminal felony, punishable by up to ten years in jail. A willful violation is punishable by a fine up to $5 million and/or imprisonment of up to 20 years. (§ 906)

35. **Officers, Directors, and Others Are Prohibited From Fraudulently Misleading Their Auditors:** The Act prohibits "any officer or director of an issuer" and persons "acting under the direction thereof" from taking any action to fraudulently influence, coerce, manipulate, or mislead any accountant engaged in preparing an audit report, for the purpose of rendering the audit report misleading. (§ 303)

36. **CEO/CFO Must Disgorge Bonuses and Profits After Restatements Due to Misconduct:** CEOs and CFOs must forfeit bonuses, incentive-based compensation, and profits on stock sales if the issuer is required to issue a restatement due to misconduct. (§ 304)

37. **The SEC Can Bar "Unfit" Officers and Directors:** The Act gives the SEC authority to bring administrative proceedings to bar persons who are found to be "unfit" from serving as officers or directors of publicly traded companies. (Note: Under current law, the SEC must go to court to obtain such a bar, and the standard is "substantial unfitness.") (§ 305, § 1105)

38. **Officers and Directors Are Prohibited from Trading During Pension "Blackout" Periods:** The Act prohibits corporate officers and directors from trading company securities during a pension fund "blackout" period. (§ 306)

39. **The CEO and Chief Legal Counsel Must Receive Corporate Attorneys' Reports of Evidence of a Material Violation of Securities Laws or Breaches of Fiduciary Duty:** The SEC must establish rules for attorneys appearing before the Commission requiring them to report evidence of a material violation of securities laws or breach of fiduciary duty or similar violation by the company to the Chief Legal Counsel or the CEO. If management does not appropriately respond to the evidence, the attorney must report the evidence to the audit committee. (§ 307)

40. **The Act Gives the SEC Authority to Temporarily Freeze the Pay of Corporate Officers:** The Act gives the SEC authority to temporarily freeze the pay of corporate officers pending an investigation of securities fraud. (§ 1103)

IV ACCOUNTING FIRMS

The Act's new regulatory board provisions will require accounting firms to:

41. **Be Subject to Oversight by a New Accounting Oversight Board:** The Act establishes a Public Company Accounting Oversight Board, which will have broad powers over the profession. The Board will have five full-time members, appointed for staggered five-year terms. Two (and no more than two) of the members must be or have been CPAs. The SEC will appoint Board members (after consultation with other agencies). (§ 101)

42. **Register with the Board:** Accounting firms that perform audits of public companies must register with the Board. The registration form requires firms to disclose: the names of audit clients; annual fees received from each issuer for "audit services, other accounting services, and non audit services;" other financial information that the Board may request; a statement of the firm's quality control policies; a list of all the firm's auditors, and licensing information; information relating to criminal, civil, or administrative actions or disciplinary proceedings pending against the firm or associated persons in connection with any audit report; copies of any SEC reports disclosing accounting disagreements between the firm and an issuer in connection with an audit report; any additional information the Board specifies as necessary or appropriate in the public interest or for the protection of investors; consent to cooperate in and comply with any testimony or document production request made by the Board; and an agreement to secure and enforce similar consents from "associated persons" of the firm. (§ 102)

43. **Submit Periodic Reports:** Accounting firms must submit annual updates of their registration to the Board (more frequently if the Board determines it necessary). (§ 102)

44. **Pay Fees to the Board:** Accounting firms must pay registration fees and annual fees to the Board to cover the costs of processing applications and annual reports. (§ 102)

45. **Comply with Auditing and Other Professional Standards:** The Act requires the Board to establish, or adopt by rule, "auditing and related attestation standards," as well as "ethics standards" to be used by accounting firms in the preparation and issuance of audit reports. The Act indicates that the Board may adopt standards proposed by "professional groups of accountants." (§ 103)

46. **Comply with Quality Control Standards:** The Act requires the Board to issue standards for accounting firms' quality controls, including: monitoring of ethics and independence, internal and external consulting on audit issues, audit supervision, hiring, development and advancement of audit personnel, client acceptance and continuance, and internal inspections. (§ 103)

47. **Submit to Quality Control Inspections:** The Board will regularly inspect accounting firms' audit operations (annually for large firms) to assess the degree of compliance by those firms with the Act, the rules of the Board, the firm's own quality control policies, and professional standards relating to audits of public companies. (§ 104)

48. **Subject Foreign Firms to Board Regulation:** Foreign accounting firms that "prepare or furnish" an audit report with respect to US registrants must register with the Board and are treated the same as US accounting firms for purposes of the Act. (§ 106)

49. **Secure the Consent of Foreign Firms to Board Requests for Documents if a Domestic Firm Relies on Its Opinion:** A domestic accounting firm that relies upon the opinion of a foreign accounting firm must "secure" the foreign firm's agreement to supply audit work papers to the Board. (§ 106)

The Act's new legal and disciplinary provisions will have the following consequences for accounting firms:

50. **Investigations and Disciplinary Actions:** The Board will investigate potential violations of the Act, the Board's rules, related provisions of the securities laws (and the Commission's rules), and professional accounting and conduct standards. (§ 105)

51. **Testimony and Documents Production Requests:** The Board may require testimony or the production of documents or information in the possession of any accounting firm, "associated person," or any other person (including any client of an accounting firm) if relevant to an investigation. (§ 105)

52. **Board Sanctions, Including Suspension:** The Board may impose sanctions for non-cooperation or violations, including revocation or suspension of an accounting firm's registration, suspension from auditing public companies, and imposition of civil penalties. (§ 105)

53. **State and Federal Prosecution after Referral from the Board:** The Board may refer investigations to the SEC, or with the SEC's approval to the Department of Justice, state attorneys general, or state boards of accountancy, if such disclosure is "necessary to accomplish the purposes of the Act or to protect investors." (§ 105)

54. **Sanctions for Failure to Supervise:** The Board may also impose sanctions upon an accounting firm or its supervisory personnel for failure reasonably to supervise a partner or employee. (§ 105)

55. **Members of the Audit Engagement Team Must Wait One Year before Accepting Employment as an Audit Client's CEO, CFO, CAO or Equivalent:** The Act provides that an accounting firm may not provide audit services for a public company if that company's chief executive officer, controller, chief financial officer, chief accounting officer, or other individual serving in an equivalent position, was employed by the accounting firm and worked on the company's audit during the one year before the start of the audit services. (§ 206)

56. **Criminal Penalties for Destruction of Corporate Audit Records:** The Act creates a new 5-year felony for the willful failure to maintain "all audit or review work papers" for five years. The Act further instructs the SEC to promulgate a rule

on the retention of other audit records (paper and electronic) in addition to actual work papers. (§ 802)

57. **Longer Statutes of Limitations for Securities Fraud Cases:** The Act lengthens the statute of limitations for securities fraud from one year after the date of discovery of the facts constituting the violation and three years after the fraud to two years from discovery and five years after the fraud. (§ 804)

The Act's internal procedure provisions require accounting firms to:

58. **Retain Documents:** The Act requires the Board to issue standards compelling accounting firms to maintain for seven years "audit work papers, and other information related to an audit report, in sufficient detail to support the conclusions reached in such a report." (§ 103)

59. **Submit Audits to Second Partner Reviews:** The Act requires the Board to issue standards requiring accounting firms to have second partner review and approval of each public company audit report. (§ 103)

60. **Rotate Audit Partners Every Five Years:** An accounting firm must rotate its lead partner and its review partner on audits so that neither role is performed by the same accountant for more than five consecutive years. (§ 203)

With respect to their public clients, the Act requires accounting firms to:

61. **Comply with Board-Issued Internal Controls Testing Standards:** The Act requires the Board to issue standards requiring an auditor's report on its "findings" with respect to the audit client's internal control structure and the auditor's "evaluation" of whether the internal control structure and procedures "include a maintenance of records that in reasonable detail accurately and fairly reflect the transactions and dispositions of the assets of the issuer; provide reasonable assurance that transactions are recorded as necessary to permit preparation of financial statements in accordance with [GAAP], and that receipts and expenditures of the issuer are being made only in accordance with authorizations of management and directors of the issuers." (§ 103)

62. **Attest to Management's Representations on Internal Controls:** The Act requires management to assess and make representations regarding the quality of internal controls and requires accounting firms to attest to and report on management's assessment. (§ 404)

63. **Cease Offering Certain Non-Audit Services to Public Audit Clients:** The Act statutorily prohibits a number of non-audit services from being offered to public audit clients, most of which are already proscribed under SEC rules. (§ 201)

64. **Obtain Audit Committee Pre-approval for Services:** Before an accounting firm can provide audit or non-audit services to a public audit client, the audit committee of the client must approve. (§ 202)

65. **Regularly Report to Audit Committees on Accounting Treatments:** Accounting firms must report to the audit committee on the critical accounting policies and practices to be used, all alternative treatments of financial information within GAAP that have been discussed with management officials, the ramifications of the use of such alternative treatments, and the treatment preferred by the auditor; any accounting disagreements between the accounting firm and management and other material written communications between the accounting firm and management. (§ 204)

66. **Be Responsible to the Audit Committee, Not Management:** The Act provides that accounting firms shall report to and be overseen by the audit committee of a client, not management. (§ 301)

Limited Options

The authors of the Sarbanes-Oxley Act had the right diagnosis for the corporate scandals of the 1990s. But that doesn't mean they had the cure.

JOHN C. COFFEE JR.

Every big financial scandal has had its rogues, but generally their colorful misdeeds do not explain what caused the deeper mess. In the 1980s, Charles Keating became synonymous with the savings-and-loan debacle, and Ivan Boesky epitomized insider trading scandals. But their notoriety taught us little about the underlying causes of these affairs. Today it is recognized that the promoters who acquired S&Ls had a rational, but perverse, incentive to gamble with their depositors' money, because, so long as the promoters enjoyed limited liability and the government guaranteed their depositors, the promoters could leverage their firms to the eyeballs at little cost to themselves. Hence, they could rationally take long-shot gambles with other people's money; predictably, financial disaster followed. Similarly, while Boesky symbolized the corruption in investment banking in the late 1980s, the new factor that truly destabilized the old corporate equilibrium of the prior era was the appearance of junk bonds. With their advent, virtually any company could be taken over, the mergers and acquisitions business went into hyperdrive, and relatively riskless opportunities for insider trading proliferated.

The corporate scandals of 2002—Enron, WorldCom, Tyco, and others—will populate an entire hall of shame by themselves, but it is more debatable whether these scandals' relatively colorless defendants have individual stories that reveal much about what caused the scandals. It is not just that a Ken Lay or an Andrew Fastow at Enron pales in comparison to the larger-than-life Robert Vesco, Ivan Boesky, and Michael Milken, but that the 2002 scandals typically involved fraud by committee, not by financial buccaneers of the old school. The accounting irregularities that were their common denominator involved a bureaucratic process that linked multiple corporate officials with outside professionals.

But this only deepens the mystery: Why did professionals acquiesce so systematically in irregularities and thereby produce a sudden concentration of scandals? What destabilized the old equilibrium this time? Finally, once the underlying causes are identified, the critical policy question becomes: How adequately have these causes been addressed by either the Sarbanes-Oxley Act of 2002 or other recent reforms?

John C. Coffee Jr. is the Adolf A. Berle Professor of Law and director of the Center on Corporate Governance at Columbia University Law School. First published in *Legal Affairs*, November–December 2003. Reprinted by permission of *Legal Affairs Magazine*, www.legalaffairs.org.

Apologists who wish to minimize the 2002 scandals tend to present them as the work of a "few bad apples" who in due course will be sent to the slammer. In reality, however, the 2002 scandals share some basic characteristics with the savings-and-loan debacle: They were pervasive, involved a material percentage of the industry, and developed an exponential momentum, as firms learned from each other.

The modus operandi of the 2002 frauds was the use of highly aggressive accounting principles that inflated earnings, deferred costs, and buried liabilities—until things got so out of hand that the firm was required to go back and restate its previously certified earnings. According to a 2002 study by the Government Accounting Office, between January 1997 and June 2002—the peak of the bubble years—approximately 10 percent of all companies in the United States listed on stock exchanges announced at least one financial restatement. These restatements were not merely technical accounting adjustments: On average each firm's restatement was followed by an immediate market-adjusted decline of almost 10 percent in its stock price, revealing that the market both cared about and was surprised by this news.

Because financial restatements provide a yardstick by which we can measure the development of the scandals that crested in 2002, it is interesting to look at the accelerating pace at which restatements increased during the 1990s. From 1990 to 1995, the annual number of restatements stayed relatively flat and low at around 50 per year; then they climbed rapidly through 2002.

Not all companies that engage in aggressive earnings management are compelled to restate earnings. The 10 percent of all listed companies that did restate earnings probably amount only to the proverbial tip of the iceberg, signaling a far larger concentration of companies that manipulated their earnings and got away with it. What drove this sudden spike in restatements?

And why did the incentive to manipulate earnings increase suddenly and significantly in the 1990s? Part of the answer is that deterrence failed. As the 1990s wore on, the principal gatekeepers of corporate governance—auditors, securities analysts, and debt-rating agencies, who collectively certify and assess corporations' performance and prospects—saw the risks from acquiescing in managerial fraud decreasing just as the expected benefits from such conduct suddenly soared.

In 1994, in *Central Bank of Denver v. First Interstate Bank of Denver,* a closely divided Supreme Court ruled that secondary participants (such as auditors and investment bankers) could not be held liable by investors for "aiding and abetting" securities fraud, thereby reversing the prior law in every circuit. In 1995, over President Clinton's veto, Congress passed the Private Securities Litigation Reform Act, which chilled private securities litigation and especially protected the auditing firms that had lobbied hardest for its passage. By 1996, an SEC report to Congress on the impact of the law found that securities litigation against secondary participants (and auditors and attorneys in particular) had declined dramatically over the space of just a few years.

As the expected legal costs went down, the expected benefits from gatekeeper acquiescence in accounting irregularities correspondingly rose. During the late 1990s, the major auditing firms began to earn as much or more in consulting income from their audit clients as for their auditing services.

This was a marked change because, prior to the mid-1990s, the Big Five audit firms had not aggressively marketed non-taxconsulting services to their audit clients. But by the end of the decade, auditing began to look more like a loss leader, which diversified accounting firms could best use not as a profit center, but instead as a portal of entry into major corporations through which they could pursue more lucrative consulting contracts.

Still, this deterrence-failure explanation cannot alone adequately account for the spike in financial restatements during the 1990s. At best, it explains the behavior of the counselors, not that of the companies and executives they advised. Why did corporate managers become obsessed with earnings management in the mid- to late 1990s—so much so that they apparently began to seduce auditors with lucrative consulting contracts?

Now we get to the heart of the matter. Something did change dramatically during the 1990s. It was executive compensation. The executive compensation package of the typical chief executive officer went from being 92 percent cash (and 8 percent equity) in 1990 to 34 percent cash (and 66 percent equity) in 2001. Not only did the composition of the compensation package change, but the size of the package soared—by 150 percent between 1992 and 1998 for the median S&P 500 chief executive—with option-based compensation accounting for most of this increase.

With this transition from cash-based to equity-based compensation also came a basic change in managerial incentives. A cash-compensated CEO has a natural incentive to grow the firm at the possible expense of profitability (because cash compensation correlates closely with firm size). Thus, under a primarily cash-based system of compensation, managers tended to maximize firm size, not return to shareholders, with the consequence that firms grew into the bloated, inefficient conglomerates of the 1980s. (Remember Gulf & Western?) Institutional investors were appalled and pressured for a shift to equity compensation.

In hindsight, they should have been more careful in their wishes. Although an equity-compensated CEO is rewarded principally for maximizing the firm's stock price, which seems efficient, a corollary of an equity compensation system is that the CEO's time horizon may rationally shift from the long-run to the short-run. That is, an equity-compensated manager has a rational preoccupation with the day-to-day stock price. Unlike the other shareholders, such a manager can profit from a short-term price spike by bailing out well before any adverse news reaches the market. Thus, with the shift to equity compensation, an incentive arises to manipulate the accounting numbers and inflate the stock market price, even if this short-term price spike could not be sustained, because the manager alone can sell at the top of the market.

As a result, as the 1990s progressed, the interests of senior corporate managers became increasingly misaligned with those of the corporation's shareholders, because these senior officers could create and profit from short-term price spikes, while the ordinary shareholder could not. The senior corporate managers of the late 1990s had "excessive liquidity"—the ability to exploit short-term market windows and bail out. At companies such as Enron, WorldCom, and Global Crossing, it is possible to identify senior executives who bailed early and often.

The GAO study of earnings restatements provides evidence to support this diagnosis. It finds that nearly 40 percent of all financial restatements in the 1997–2002 period were the product of revenue recognition errors; this was by far the largest category. Such "errors" arise when managers try to recognize income prematurely—in effect, stealing from next year's earnings to maximize this year's. Eventually, this process of stealing from the future must come to an end, but just before it does, the executive who sees the end in sight can sell.

Ironically, the SEC compounded these problems in the early 1990s by deregulating stock options. Previously, a senior corporate officer who exercised a stock option had to hold the stock so acquired for at least six months before the officer could sell it (or all profit on such a stock sale would revert to the corporation). The SEC effectively eliminated this holding period requirement in 1991 (for reasons that made sense at the time), but that ultimately compounded the excessive liquidity problem.

Let's redefine the problem: During the 1990s, managers facing overwhelming incentives to inflate earnings tacitly "bribed" their corporation's gatekeepers—auditors, attorneys, and securities analysts—to acquiesce in dubious accounting policies and presentations. In the case of auditors, managers used consulting services, and in the case of analysts, who depend on a subsidy from investment banking, they used both a carrot and a stick. Because underwriting revenues subsidized analysts' salaries, stock issuers and their investment banks could handsomely reward loyal analysts, while disloyal analysts (i.e., those who put out "sell" or "neutral" ratings) were simply cut off from the free flow of nonpublic material information that firms selectively leaked to favored analysts.

If these conflicts of interest are the underlying problem, what is the answer? The Sarbanes-Oxley Act and related SEC reforms have prohibited a broad range of conflicts in both the case of the auditor and the analyst. Both are today more independent, although in each case their level of independence may still fall well short of optimal. Selective disclosure has also been prohibited by the SEC. What remains is the problem of executive compensation and excessive liquidity.

Only a Luddite would want to return to the prior system of cash compensation, which produced its own inefficiencies. Expensing stock options may marginally reduce their attractiveness, but it does not directly respond to the bailout problem. Rather, the more focused issue is how to reduce the "excess liquidity" of the senior corporate manager, so that the manager's goal is to maximize long-term shareholder value. A number of recognized techniques to this end exist, all of which are coming into greater use. Boards can adopt retention ratios under which they condition the grant of stock options on a requirement that the recipient officer will continue to hold some defined percentage of the stock during the officer's period of employment with the company; alternatively, they can issue "restricted stock," instead of granting options. But boards are moving slowly, in part because most directors are themselves corporate officers somewhere else (and they are thus reluctant to restrict options or their own liquidity).

What should regulators do? The short answer is that there is no one optimal compensation policy for all corporations. More than in any other area of corporate law, one size does not fit all. Thus, the SEC cannot mandate any uniform executive compensation policy; nor is it needed. Most institutional investors have clear ideas about what they would like to do in specific cases. The problem is they cannot get boards to listen. Even when institutions make formal shareholder proposals on executive compensation issues and obtain a majority shareholder vote (as has repeatedly happened over the last year), boards can ignore that vote, treating it as legally only a plea rather than an order. As a result, shareholder activism has been stalemated in this arena, and institutional shareholders want a new weapon. Specifically, they want a low-cost mechanism by which they can nominate one or two watchdog directors to the corporate board. Their intent is to use this procedure not to threaten a corporate control contest (the last thing that most institutions want is to possess control themselves), but to respond to the board's rejection of a shareholder proposal for which they have secured a majority vote.

Increasingly, it appears that the SEC may give institutions some of what they want. This summer, the SEC indicated that it will act to increase shareholder access to the proxy statement, and it is considering proposals for shareholder-nominated candidates to run on the same proxy statement alongside the board's own nominees. Still, a bruising battle is in store. Any SEC effort to force boards to share control over the nomination process will be resisted by many managements as an intrusion upon their ultimate authority. Yet tilting, at least modestly, the balance of power between shareholders and the board in the former's direction seems a natural and logical response to the 2002 scandals. Procedural self-help remedies make the greatest sense in this context when regulators cannot begin to define the optimal compensation policy they want to achieve.

Did Enron, WorldCom, and the related scandals reveal anything new that had not been seen in prior financial scandals? Breakdowns in corporate governance and accounting transparency are far from unprecedented in the United States. One can review the major financial scandals of recent decades, dating back at least to Penn Central's bankruptcy in 1970, and find similar overreaching of the accountants. In each case, it can be debated whether the accountants were deceived or whether they knowingly played along. Still, the 2002 scandals were distinctive to the extent that they were contagious. Firms copied each other's financial manipulations, in part because they felt compelled to do so. Enron may have led the way in the exploitation of "special-purpose entities" to keep liabilities off their balance sheet, but Dynegy, El Paso, Williams Co., and the rest of the energy industry did not lag very far behind. Why? If Enron could show greater returns on its equity than its competitors, it would be in a position to outcompete them and emerge dominant in a consolidating industry. Similar industry-specific accounting irregularities also characterized the telecommunications industry, where WorldCom led, but Qwest, Global Crossing and others strived to copy every ploy that WorldCom initiated. The net result was a race to the bottom among competitors who could not afford to let a rival show a significantly higher rate of return.

Facilitating this perverse competition was the other new aspect of the 2002 scandals: the degree to which the corporate wrongdoers were educated in accounting manipulation by their own gatekeepers. Enron was, after all, originally a provincial gas pipeline company, which had operated in a quiet backwater. How did it learn to manipulate earnings in new state-of-the-art ways? It was taught to—by accountants, investment bankers, law firms, and banks who, having taught one firm in an industry, could then advise its competitors that they had better catch up. Thus, we return again to the role of the gatekeepers. They possessed unique technical expertise, and because they operated on a nationwide scale, ideas could diffuse through them that might have otherwise have stayed locked within a single firm. Their capacity to teach the techniques of evasion, coupled with the competitive need to do so, probably best explains the contagion-like spread of the technology of accounting manipulation during the late 1990s.

If a common denominator to the recent scandals was the failure of the gatekeepers, where should this lead us on the policy level? Accountants, analysts, and attorneys all belong to self-regulating professions. Much like medieval guilds, professions regulate themselves protectively, weeding out the occasional egregious crook but guarding their profession's autonomy jealously and expending very little on enforcement. Scandals can, however, force changes on professions, including the substitution of a public regulator for the former private one. This first happened during the 1930s, when Congress, dissatisfied with the brokerage industry after the 1929 crash, imposed a public regulator—the National Association of Securities Dealers—upon the brokerage industry and instructed the NASD to adopt "fair and equitable principles of trade" to govern the industry. Correspondingly, the Sarbanes-Oxley Act has done much the same thing to accountants who audit public companies. The new Public Company Accounting Oversight Board will largely supersede the American Institute of Certified Public Accountants and is instructed to set ethical standards and monitor their enforcement.

Analysts were already subject to the NASD and the SEC, both of which have been prodded by New York attorney general Eliot Spitzer and have in response adopted new rules to protect the independence of analysts. Time will tell how well these rules will work and whether professional independence is even a realistic goal for the "sell-side" analyst, but by 2002 little attempt was made even by the securities industry to defend continued reliance on private self-regulation in the case of analysts.

This brings us to lawyers, long the profession that has most closely guarded its autonomy. The Sarbanes-Oxley Act authorizes the SEC to adopt "minimum standards of professional conduct" for attorneys "appearing or practicing" before the SEC. Pursuant to this authority, the SEC has already adopted an "up-the-ladder" reporting rule that will require some attorneys, under some circumstances, to report serious fraud or other law violations that they discover in representing a public company, first to the corporation's general counsel and, if necessary, up to the corporation's audit committee. While this reform—i.e., internal reporting within the client—has been largely accepted by the bar, a firestorm has greeted another proposed SEC rule that would require the attorney to make a "noisy withdrawal" (i.e., to resign and inform the SEC of the reason for this resignation) if the corporation does not act to terminate a serious ongoing fraud or illegal act. In part to head off the SEC, the American Bar Association adopted a far milder rule this summer that permits, but does not require, the attorney to notify regulators and injured victims of the fraud. In effect, the profession will permit ethically motivated actions by the attorney, but not mandate them.

The position of the legal profession is thus anomalous and possibly transitional. Unlike the other professions that serve investors, it has escaped direct public regulation. But the same forces that brought accountants, analysts, and brokers under the oversight of a public regulatory body with authority to prescribe their professional norms have begun to circumscribe the legal profession's autonomy as well. How far the tide of reform will carry before it ebbs is uncertain. Lawyers may well be able to successfully resist such regulation—until the next major scandal. Eventually, however, even the legal profession seems likely to be dragged, kicking and screaming, to the recognition that it too plays a gatekeeping role and that lawyers must balance their duties to clients with new duties to the public and the market. The government of the profession by the profession and for the profession will likely be the final and inevitable casualty of the Enron scandals.

Chapter 9

Issues in Employment

Case Study

United wins approval to dump pension plans

MARK SKERTIC

A bankruptcy judge in Chicago ruled Tuesday that a federal agency can take over United Airlines' pension plans, allowing the carrier to walk away from nearly $10 billion in unfunded liabilities, the largest pension default in U.S. history.

It helps United clear one of the biggest financial hurdles in its 29-month effort to exit bankruptcy protection. The airline's pension funds are short $9.8 billion, but the Pension Benefit Guaranty Corp. will pick up only $6.6 billion of that, meaning current and former employees will lose more than $3 billion in retirement benefits.

The decision was "the least bad among a number of unfortunate choices," said U.S. Bankruptcy Judge Eugene Wedoff, who had the proceedings piped into a second courtroom when his proved too small to handle the overflow crowd.

Speaking after an emotional daylong hearing, Wedoff said allowing the pension agency to take over United's retirement plans would not violate labor agreements, a warning to unions that have said contract changes could open the door to a strike.

The agency's assumption of United's pension obligations "keeps the airline functioning, keeps people employed" and allows those owed money by the carrier to receive some compensation, Wedoff said.

Efforts by United to avoid its pension liabilities are being closely watched in an industry that's losing billions of dollars a year. Some analysts have said that operating without pension liabilities would give United a financial advantage.

Some employees in the audience wiped away tears as it became clear Wedoff would allow United to dump the plans. Because of pension agency limits on benefits, many will see their retirement income reduced.

Dianne Tamuk of New York, a United flight attendant for the past 27 years, was among many who flew in for the hearing.

"We've agreed to rounds of concessions in order to save our pension plan, and now this happens," said Tamuk, 49.

She had expected to receive $1,700 a month when she retires at age 55, but under pension agency rules, her benefit will drop to about $800, she said.

On Wednesday United will be back before Wedoff to ask him to approve plans to throw out the contracts of two of its largest unions. The airline claims the pay and benefit levels in the agreements are too expensive and could hurt efforts to emerge from bankruptcy protection.

Cutting the bottom line was the reason United reached a deal with the pension agency, which is funded through payments made by companies with pension plans that guarantee a set income upon retirement.

United agreed to pay the government agency as much as $1.5 billion in securities when it emerges from bankruptcy. By casting off its pension obligations, United estimates it would save about $645 million a year.

Even without a deal, the pension agency could have taken over the plans if it believed United would default on them, said James Sprayregen, United's lead bankruptcy attorney. With an agreement in place, it benefits both the carrier and the agency, he said.

Some members of United's management team looked nearly as somber as their workers after Wedoff's ruling.

"This is not in any way a joyous day," Chief Financial Officer Jake Brace said after the hearing. "This is not a good outcome. Unfortunately, it's a necessary outcome."

United still faces significant labor challenges. It is seeking to throw out the contracts of the International Association of Machinists and Aerospace Workers and the Aircraft Mechanics Fraternal Association. It is also in arbitration on wage and benefit terms with the Association of Flight Attendants.

The flight attendants union has been the most vocal opponent of the carrier's moves. Strikes that could shut down an airport, specific routes or the entire airline remain a possibility, said spokeswoman Sara Dela Cruz, but the union won't make any decisions until meeting with leadership.

"We've got to consider our options," she said. "We've got 15,000 flight attendants who just lost half their retirement benefits."

For many employees, their pensions have been the single benefit they refused to give ground on. Many complained bitterly after the hearing about Chief Executive Glenn Tilton's $4.5 million retirement plan.

The Elk Grove Township-based airline will have to rebuild relationships with many workers, Brace conceded, but he said it had no alternative. United has said it plans to replace the pensions with a less expensive retirement program.

"We fought for 18 months," he said of efforts to cut costs without touching pensions. "That proved undoable."

Several unions, retired pilots and others had challenged United's agreement with the pension agency, arguing it was unfair and limited their rights.

United did not involve unions in talks with the pension agency, said Sharon Levine, an attorney for the machinists union.

"Nobody called me or anybody else at the IAM to tell me, 'We've got a back-room negotiation to terminate the pension plans, why don't you come to the table?'" she said. "They kept us at the kids' table."

But Sprayregen said the problem has been the union's refusal to budge on demands to end their pensions. A deal "can't be done when the parameter is there's no change to the present situation," he said.

Case Study

Unkept promises hit retirees

Federal rules that allow huge funding gaps in defined-benefit pension plans leave unsuspecting former workers and taxpayers holding the bag when companies bail out on their obligations

BARBARA ROSE

Ken Bradley, a United Airlines pilot for 35 years, never doubted his pension was secure when he retired four years ago.

Despite United's financial troubles, the pilots' retirement trust had more than enough money to meet all its future obligations, according to U.S. Labor Department filings.

Yet the airline's reports to investors told a different story. Using generally accepted accounting rules, United's retirement trusts were headed for trouble, sliding in 2002 to half of the assets needed to cover the carrier's pension promises.

Despite the shortfall, federal rules allowed United to skip making cash contributions.

"How the trusts could go to 50 percent funded while United was allowed to stop contributing is beyond comprehension," Bradley said.

United illustrates why pension reform has become a front-burner issue. Thirty-four million Americans are covered by private pensions governed by federal rules that encourage cash-strapped companies to cut back their contributions, even while promising workers benefits they can't afford.

"You can have a hugely underfunded pension plan and yet give little or no notice to employees," said Kevin Smith, a spokesman for U.S. Rep. John Boehner (R-Ohio), chairman of a House committee that oversees private pensions.

United observed all the pension rules, yet its trusts sickened, while employees labored under the impression their retirements were secure.

Bradley stands to lose nearly 70 percent of his six-figure pension income if United persuades a bankruptcy judge that it can't survive without jettisoning its retiree obligations.

The employee trusts would be taken over by a federal insurer, the Pension Benefit Guaranty Corp. But the agency limits payouts to highly compensated pensioners such as pilots.

Pilots hardly would be the only losers. Taxpayers may have to share the pain.

The pension agency is struggling with billions of dollars in obligations dumped by bankrupt companies, mainly in the steel and airline industries. Without some kind of fix, the agency will run out of cash around 2020, according to the non-partisan Center on Federal Financial Institutions.

"Unless the PBCG gets an infusion, or we substantially change the rules so future losses are lower, I can see almost nothing in the markets that could keep us from running out of money" within 15 to 20 years, said Douglas Elliott, the center's president.

The center estimates it would cost $78 billion to put the agency on sound footing, a tab that would grow to $100 billion if all the major airlines terminate their pensions. It would be the government's second-costliest bailout, after the 1980s rescue of the savings and loan industry.

Despite the size of the problem, the vast majority of plans are healthy, experts say.

"There are a couple of industries that have created a crisis for the PBGC, and this has put the entire system under a cloud," said Mark Beilke, who heads the pension accounting committee of the American Academy of Actuaries.

Yet few, including Beilke, dispute the need for reform. The Bush administration has proposed hiking the premiums employers pay to the pension agency, while tightening funding rules and improving disclosure.

Business, labor and consumer groups warn that the measures, if not crafted carefully, could push more employers to drop pensions in favor of plans such as 401(k) savings accounts, which entail far less risk for sponsors but provide less secure retirements for employees.

"Pension plans are the best hope of providing employees with adequate retirement income," said Karen Friedman, policy director at the Pension Rights Center, a consumer group.

Fewer than 20 percent of private sector workers are covered by traditional pensions, down from 35 percent in 1980. And the number is dwindling.

"We need to focus not only on what can be done to shore up the integrity of the PBGC, but the defined-benefit system itself," said James Klein, president of the American Benefits Council, which represents employers and plan service providers.

Defined-benefit plans promise a guaranteed stream of payments to retirees, while 401(k) plans offer a defined contribution from an employer and shift investment risk to employees.

The rules governing pensions were established by the Employee Retirement Income Security Act of 1974, which also created the pension agency. Every decade since, new rules were created, often with conflicting aims.

"There was at one point a concern that employers were contributing too much, then the next decade that the plans were getting underfunded," said Beilke, director of benefits research at Milliman Inc.

"Now, in situations where you would have expected employers to pony up, they didn't," he said. "It's a mess, it really is a mess."

United is a case in point. The airline's pension funds deteriorated after the stock market bubble burst in 2000, but the Elk Grove Township-based carrier made no cash contributions to its employee retirement trusts in 2001 and 2002, according to Securities and Exchange Commission filings.

Instead, the airline relied on credits carried over from profitable years when United contributed more than the minimum.

With no new money coming in to offset stock market and interest rate declines, funding levels fell to 50 cents for every $1 of obligations at the end of 2002, down from 92 cents per $1 at the end of 2000, according to SEC filings.

Yet United's trusts tripped none of the government triggers that would have required the airline to notify employees of a funding problem or boost premiums to the pension agency.

Using government accounting rules, the pilot's plan had $1.02 for every $1 of long-term liabilities in 2002, according to U.S. Labor Department filings.

But the pension agency bases its accounting on the cost of terminating a plan and buying an annuity to cover obligations. By those rules, the pilot's plan was 49 percent funded in December, with a $2.9 billion shortfall.

The agency expects to be liable for $1.4 billion, which would be the third-largest claim in the insurance program's history.

The rest of the shortfall would be borne by pilots who were promised six-figure pensions. The pension agency's maximum annual payment for workers who retire at age 60, the mandatory age for pilots, is $29,649.

For Bradley, 64, of Williamsburg, Va., the plans' takeover would mean a drastic change in lifestyle. He had dreamed of cruising the intercoastal waterway with his family. Now, his 43-foot Bayliner is up for sale.

Roger Hall, 66, president of the United Retired Pilots Benefit Protection Association, said some retirees would be forced to sell their homes or file for bankruptcy.

"Financial advisers tell everyone to plan ahead, to make sure you've got your retirement put aside, and we did that through our contract negotiations," Hall said. "This was part of our deferred compensation, and now all of a sudden the company is saying they're not going to pay it.

"The laws that allow this to happen need to be fixed."

Pension snapshot

$1.8 trillion	U.S. private pension assets
$450 billion	Estimated funding shortfall
Up to $100 billion	Cost to bail out federal pension insurance system

What went wrong?

- Stock market decline hurt pension fund investment returns.
- Falling interest rates increased funding costs.
- Taking over plans of bankrupt companies swamped insurance system.
- Funding of pension plans at Fortune 100 companies hit low of 78 percent in 2002.

Sources: Pension Benefit Guaranty Corp.; Center on Federal Financial Institutions; Towers Perrin HR Services

Case Study

"Working at Walmart"

BARBARA EHRENREICH

It's Saturday and the time has come to leave my free lodgings and neurotic avian roommate. A few hours before my hosts are scheduled to return, I pack up and head down to Twin Lakes, where—no big surprise—I find out that all the second-story rooms have been taken. The particular room I'd requested, which looks out on a backyard instead of a parking lot, is now occupied by a woman with a child, the owner tells me, and he is good enough to feel uncomfortable about asking them to move to a smaller one. So I decide that this is my out and call another weekly rental place on my list, the Clearview Inn (not its real name) which has two big advantages: it's about a twenty-minute drive from my Wal-Mart as opposed to at least forty-five in the case of Twin Lakes, and the weekly rate is $245, compared to $295. This is still scandalously high, higher in fact than my aftertax weekly pay will amount to. But in our latest conversation Hildy has promised to rent me a room with a kitchenette by the end of next week, and I am confident I can get a weekend job at the supermarket I applied to, in bakery if I am lucky.

To say that some place is the worst motel in the country is, of course, to set oneself up for considerable challenge.[1] I have encountered plenty of contenders in my own travels—the one in Cleveland that turned into a brothel at night, the one in Butte where the window looked out into another room. Still, the Clearview Inn leaves the competition in the dust. I slide $255 in cash (the extra $10 is for telephone service) under the glass window that separates me from the young East Indian owner—East Indians seem to have a lock on the midwestern motel business—and am taken by his wife to a room memorable only for its overwhelming stench of mold. I don't have enough Claritin-D for this situation, a point I have to make by holding my nose, since her English does not extend to the concept of allergy. Air freshener? she suggests when she catches my meaning. Incense? There is a better room, her husband says when we return to the office, but—and here he fixes me with a narrow-eyed stare—I'd better not "trash" it. I attempt a reassuring chuckle, but the warning rankles me for days: have I been fooling myself all these years, thinking I look like a mature and sober person when in fact anyone can see I'm a vandal?

Room 133 contains a bed, a chair, a chest of drawers, and a TV fastened to the wall. I plead for and get a lamp to supplement the single overhead bulb. Instead of the mold smell, I now breathe a mixture of fresh paint and what I eventually identify as mouse droppings. But the real problems arc all window- and door-related: the single small window has no screen, and the room has no AC or fan. The curtain is transparently thin; the door has no bolt. Without a screen, the window should be sensibly closed at night, meaning no air, unless I'm willing to take my chances with the bugs and the neighbors. Who are the neighbors? The motel forms a toilet-seat shape around the parking lot, and I can see an inexplicable collection. A woman with a baby in her arms leans in the doorway of one room. Two bunches of teenagers, one group black and the other white, seem to share adjoining rooms. There are several unencumbered men of various ages, including an older white man in work clothes whose bumper sticker says "Don't steal, the government hates competition"—as if the income tax were the only thing keeping him from living at the Embassy Suites right now. When it gets dark I go outside and look through my curtain, and yes, you can see pretty much everything, at least in silhouette. I eat the deli food I've brought with me from a Minneapolis supermarket and go to bed with my clothes on, but not to sleep.

I am not a congenitally fearful person, for which you can blame or credit my mother, who never got around to alerting me to any special vulnerabilities that went with being a girl. Only when I got to college did I begin to grasp what rape involves and discover that my custom of exploring strange cities alone, on foot, day or night, looked more reckless to others than eccentric. I had no misgivings about the trailer park in Key West or the motel in Maine, but the trailer's door had a bolt, and both had effective shades and screens. Here, only the stuffiness of the air with window shut reminds me that I'm really indoors; otherwise I'm pretty much open to anyone's view or to anything that might drift in from the highway, and I wouldn't want to depend on my hosts for help. I think of wearing earplugs to block out the TV sounds from the next room and my sleep mask to cut the light from the Dr Pepper sign on the pop machine in the parking lot. Then I decide it's smarter to keep all senses on ready alert. I sleep and wake up, sleep and wake up again, listen to the cars coming and going watch the silhouettes move past my window.

Sometime around four in the morning it dawns on me that it's not just that I'm a wimp. Poor women—perhaps especially single ones and even those who are just temporarily living among the poor for whatever reason—really do have more to fear than women who have houses with double locks and alarm systems and husbands or dogs. I must have know this theoretically or at least heard it stated, but now for the first time the lesson takes hold.

So this is the home from which I go forth on Monday to begin my life as a Wal-Martian. After the rigors of orientation, I am expecting a highly structured welcome, perhaps a ceremonial donning of my bright blue Wal-Mart vest and a forty-five-minute training on the operation of the vending machines in the break room. But when I arrive in the morning for the ten-to-six shift, no one seems to be expecting me. I'm in "soft-lines," which has a wonderful, sinuous sound to it, but I have no idea what it means. Someone in personnel tells me I'm in ladies wear (a division of softlines, I learn) and sends me to the counter next to the fitting rooms, where I am passed around from one person to the next—finally ending up with Ellie, whose lack of a vest signals that she is management. She sets me to work "zoning" the Bobbie Brooks knit summer dresses, a task that could serve as an IQ test for the severely cognitively challenged. First the dresses must be grouped by color—olive, peach, or lavender, in this case—then by decorative pattern—the leafy design on the bodice, the single flower, or the grouped flowers—and within each pattern by size. When I am finished, though hardly exhausted by the effort, I meet Melissa, who is, with only a couple of weeks on the job, pretty much my equivalent. She asks me to help her consolidate the Kathie Lee knit dresses so the Kathie Lee silky ones can take their place at the "image," the high-traffic corner area. I learn, in a couple of hours of scattered exchanges, that Melissa was a waitress before this job, that her husband works in construction and her children are grown. There have been some disorganized patches in her life—an out of wedlock child, a problem with alcohol and drugs—but that's all over now that she has given her life to Christ.

Our job, it emerges in fragments throughout the day, is to keep ladies' wear "shoppable." Sure, we help customers (who are increasingly called "guests" here as well), if they want any help. At first I go around practicing the "aggressive hospitality" demanded by our training videos: as soon as anyone comes within ten feet of a sales associate, that associate is supposed to smile warmly and offer assistance. But I never see a more experienced associate doing this—first, because the customers are often annoyed to have their shopping dazes interrupted and, second, because we have far more pressing things to do. In ladies' wear, the big task, which has no real equivalent in, say, housewares or lawn and garden, is to put away the "returns"—clothes that have been tried on and rejected or, more rarely, purchased and then returned to the store. There are also the many items that have been scattered by customers, dropped on the floor, removed from their hangers and strewn over the racks, or secreted in locations far from their natural homes. Each of these items, too, must be returned to the precise place, matched by color, pattern, price and size. Any leftover time is to be devoted to zoning. When I relate this to Caroline on the phone, she commiserates, "Ugh, a no-brainer."

But no job is as easy as it looks to the uninitiated. I have to put clothes away—the question is, Where? Much of my first few days is devoted to trying to memorize the layout of ladies' wear, one thousand (two thousand?) square feet of space bordered by men's wear, children's wear, greeting cards, and underwear. Standing at the fitting rooms and facing toward the main store entrance, we are looking directly at the tentlike, utilitarian plus sizes, also known as "woman" sizes. These are flanked on the left by our dressiest and costliest line (going up to $29 and change), the all-polyester Kathie Lee collection, suitable for dates and subprofessional levels of office work. Moving clockwise, we encounter the determinedly sexless Russ and Bobbie Brooks lines, seemingly aimed at pudgy fourth-grade teachers with important barbecues to attend. Then, after the sturdy White Stag, come the breezy, revealing Faded Glory, No Boundaries, and Jordache collections, designed for the younger and thinner crowd. Tucked throughout are nests of the lesser brands, such as Athletic Works, Basic Equipment, and the whimsical Looney Tunes, Pooh, and Mickey lines, generally decorated with images of the eponymous characters. Within each brand-name area, there are of course dozens of items, even dozens of each *kind* of item. This summer, for example, pants may be capri, classic, clam-digger, boot, or flood, depending on their length and cut, and I'm probably leaving a few categories out. So my characteristic stance is one of rotating slowly on one foot, eyes wide, garment in hand, asking myself, "Where have I seen the $9.96 Athletic Works knit overalls?" or similar query. Inevitably there are mystery items requiring extra time and inquiry: clothes that have wandered over from girls' or men's, clearanced items whose tags haven't been changed to reflect their new prices, the occasional one-of-a-kind.

Then, when I have the layout memorized, it suddenly changes. On my third morning I find, after a few futile searches, that the Russ shirt-and-short combinations have edged Kathie Lee out of her image. When I groaningly accuse Ellie of trying to trick me into thinking I'm getting Alzheimer's, she's genuinely apologetic, explaining that the average customer shops the store three times a week, so you need to have the element of surprise. Besides, the layout is about the only thing she *can* control, since the clothes and at least the starting prices are all determined by the home office in Arkansas. So as fast as I can memorize, she furiously rearranges.

My first response to the work is disappointment and a kind of sexist contempt. I could have been in plumbing, mastering the vocabulary of valves, dangling tools from my belt, joshing around with Steve and Walt, and instead the mission of the moment is to return a pink bikini top to its place on the Bermuda swimwear rack. Nothing is heavy or, as far as I can see, very urgent. No one will go hungry or die or be hurt if I screw up; in fact, how would anyone ever know if I screwed up, given the customers' constant depredations? I feel oppressed, too, by the mandatory gentility of Wal-Mart culture. This is ladies' and we are all "ladies" here, forbidden, by storewide rule, to raise our voice or cuss. Give me a few weeks of this and I'll femme out entirely, my stride will be reduced to a mince, I'll start tucking my head down to one side.

My job is not, however, as genteel as it first appears, thanks to the sheer volume of clothing in motion. At Wal-Mart, as opposed to say Lord & Taylor, customers shop with the supermarket-style shopping carts, which they can fill to the brim before proceeding to the fitting room. There the rejected items, which are about 90 percent of try-ons, are folded and put on hangers by whoever is staffing the fitting room, then placed in fresh shopping carts for Melissa and me. So this is how we measure our workload—in carts. When I get in, Melissa, whose shift begins earlier than mine, will tell me how things have been going—"Can you believe, eight carts this morning!"— and how many carts are awaiting me. At first a cart takes me an average of forty-five minutes and there may still be three or four mystery items left at the bottom. I get this down to half an hour, and still the carts keep coming.

Most of the time, the work requires minimal human interaction, of either the collegial or the supervisory sort, largely because it is so self-defining. I arrive at the start of a shift or the end of a break, assess the damage wrought by the guests in my absence, count the full carts that await me, and plunge in. I could be a deaf mute as far as most of this goes, and despite all the orientation directives to smile and exude personal warmth, autism might be a definite advantage. Sometimes, if things are slow, Melissa and I will invent a task we can do together—zoning swimsuits, for example, a nightmarish tangle of straps—and giggle, she in her Christian way, me from a more feminist perspective, about the useless little see-through wraps meant to accompany the more revealing among them. Or sometimes Ellie will give me something special to do, like putting all the Basic Equipment T-shirts on hangers, because things on hangers sell faster, and then arranging them neatly on racks. I like Ellie. Gray-faced and fiftyish, she must be the apotheosis of "servant leadership" or, in more secular terms, the vaunted "feminine" style of management. She says "please" and "thank you"; she doesn't order, she asks. Not so, though, with young Howard—*assistant manager* Howard, as he is uniformly called—who rules over all of softlines, including infant's, children's, men's accessories, and underwear. On my first day, I am called off the floor to an associates' meeting, where he spends ten minutes taking attendance, fixing each of us with his unnerving Tom Cruise-style smile, in which the brows come together as the corners of the mouth turn up, then reveals (where have I heard this before?) his "pet peeve": associates standing around talking to one another, which is, of course, a prime example of time theft.

A few days into my career at Wal-Mart, I return home to the Clearview to find the door to my room open and the motel owner waiting outside. There's been a "problem"—the sewage has backed up and is all over the floor, though fortunately my suitcase is OK. I am to move into room 127, which will be better because it has a screen. But the screen turns out to be in tatters, not even fastened at the bottom, just clapping uselessly in the breeze. I ask for a real screen, and he tells me he doesn't have any that fit. I ask for a fan and he doesn't have any that work. I ask why—I mean, this is supposedly a working motel—and he rolls his eyes, apparently indicating my fellow residents: "I could tell you stories . . ."

So I lug my possessions down to 127 and start trying to reconstruct my little domestic life. Since I don't have a kitchen, I have what I call my food bag, a supermarket bag containing my tea bags, a few pieces of fruit, various condiment packets salvaged from fast-food places, and a half dozen string cheeses, which their labels say are supposed to be refrigerated but I figure are safe in their plastic wraps. I have my laptop computer, the essential link to my normal profession, and it has become a matter of increasing concern. I figure it's the costliest portable item in the entire Clearview Inn, so I hesitate to leave it in my room for the nine or so hours while I'm away at work. During the first couple of days at Wal-Mart, the weather was cool and I kept it in the trunk of my car. But now, with the temperature rising to the nineties at midday, I worry that it'll cook in the trunk. More to the point at the moment is the state of my clothing, most of which is now residing in the other brown paper bag, the one that serves as a hamper. My khakis have a day or two left in them and two clean T-shirts remain until the next trip to a Laundromat, but a question has been raised about the T-shirts. That afternoon Alyssa, one of my co-orientees, now in sporting goods, had come by ladies' to inquire about a polo shirt that had been clearanced at $7. Was there any chance it might fall still further? Of course I had no idea—Ellie decides about clearancing—but why was Alyssa so fixated on this particular shirt? Because one of the rules is that our shirts have to have collars, so they had to be polos, not tees. Somehow I'd missed this during orientation, and now I'm wondering how long I have before my stark-naked neck catches Howard's attention. At $7 an hour, a $7 shirt is just not going to make it to my shopping list.

Now it's after seven and time to resume my daily routine at the evening food-gathering phase. The town of Clearview presents only two low-priced options (there are no high-priced options) to its kitchenless residents—a Chinese all-you-can-eat buffet or Kentucky Fried Chicken—each with its own entertainment possibilities. If I eat out at the buffet I can watch the large Mexican families or the even larger, in total body mass terms, families of Minnesota Anglos. If I eat KFC in my room, I can watch TV on one of the half dozen available channels. The latter option seems somehow less lonely, especially if I can find one of my favorite programs—*Titus* or *Third Rock from the Sun.* Eating is tricky without a table. I put the food on the chest of drawers and place a plastic supermarket bag over my lap, since spills are hard to avoid when you eat on a slant and spills mean time and money at the Laundromat. Tonight I find the new sensation, *Survivor,* on CBS where "real people" are struggling to light a fire on their desert island. Who are these nutcases who would volunteer for an artificially daunting situation in order to entertain millions of strangers with their half-assed efforts to survive? Then I remember who I am and why I am here.

Dinner over, I put the remains in the plastic bag that served as a tablecloth and tie it up tightly to discourage the flies that have free access to my essentially screenless abode. I do my evening things—writing in my journal and reading a novel—then turn out the lights and sit for a while by the open door for some air. The two African American men who live in the room next door have theirs open too, and since it's sometimes open in the daytime as well, I've noticed that their room, like mine, has only one bed. This is no gay tryst, though, because they seem to take turns in the bed, one sleeping in the room and the other one napping in their van outside. I shut the door, put the window down, and undress in the dark so I can't be seen through the window. I still haven't found out much about my fellow Clearview dwellers—it's bad enough being a woman alone, especially a woman rich enough to have a bed of her own, without being nosy on top of that. As far as I can tell, the place isn't a nest of drug dealers and prostitutes; these are just working people who don't have the capital to rent a normal apartment. Even the teenagers who worried me at first seem to have mother figures attached to them, probably single mothers I hadn't seen before because they were at work.

Finally I lie down and breathe against the weight of unmoving air on my chest. I wake up a few hours later to hear a sound not generated by anyone's TV: a woman's clear alto singing two lines of the world's saddest song, lyrics undecipherable, to the accompaniment of trucks on the highway.

Morning begins with a trip, by car, to the Holiday gas station's convenience store, where I buy a pop container full of ice and a packet of two hard-boiled eggs. The ice, a commodity unavailable at the motel, is for iced tea, which I brew by letting tea bags soak in a plastic cup of water overnight. After breakfast I tidy up my room, make the bed, wiping the sink with a wad of toilet paper, and taking the garbage out to the Dumpster. True, the owner's wife (or maybe she's the co-owner) goes around from room to room every morning with a cleaning cart, but her efforts show signs of deep depression or perhaps attention deficit disorder. Usually she remembers to replace the thin little towels, which, even when clean, contain embedded hairs and smell like cooking grease, but there's nothing else, except maybe an abandoned rag or bottle of air freshener, to suggest that she's been through on her rounds. I picture an ad for a "traditional-minded, hard-working wife," a wedding in her natal village, then—plop—she's in Clearview, Minnesota, with an Indian American husband who may not even speak her language, thousands of miles from family, a temple, a sari shop.[2] So I clean up myself, then do my hair with enough bobby pins to last though the shift, and head off for work. The idea is to make myself look like someone who spent the night in a regular home with kitchen and washer and dryer, not like someone who's borderline homeless.

The other point of my domestic rituals and arrangements is to get through the time when I can't be at work, when it would look weird to be hanging around in the Wal-Mart parking lot or break room. Because home life is more stressful than I consciously acknowledged, and I would be dreading my upcoming day off if I weren't confident of spending it on the move to better quarters at the Hopkins Park Plaza. Little nervous symptoms have arisen. Sometimes I get a tummy ache after breakfast, which makes lunch dicey, and there's no way to get through the shift without at least one major refueling. More disturbing is the new habit of plucking away at my shirt or my khakis with whichever hand can be freed up for the task. I have to stop this. My maternal grandmother, who still lives on, in a fashion, at the age of a hundred and one, was a perfect model of stoicism, but she used to pick at her face and her wrist, creating dark red circular sores, and claimed not to know she was doing it. Maybe it's an inherited twitch and I will soon be moving on from fabric to flesh.

I arrive at work full of bounce, pausing at the fitting room to jolly up the lady on duty—usually the bossy, self-satisfied Rhoda—because the fitting room lady bears the same kind of relation to me as a cook to a server: she can screw me up if she wants, giving me carts contaminated with foreign, nonladies' items and items not properly folded or hangered. "Here I am," I announce grandiosely, spreading out my arms. "The day can begin!" For this I get a wrinkled nose from Rhoda and a one-sided grin from Lynne, the gaunt blonde who's working bras. I search out Ellie, whom I find shooting out new labels from the pricing gun, and ask if there's anything special I need to be doing. No, just whatever needs to be done. Next I find Melissa to get a report on the cartage so far. Today she seems embarrassed when she sees me: "I probably shouldn't have done this and you're going to think it's really silly . . . " but she'd brought me a sandwich for lunch. This is because I'd told her I was living in a motel almost entirely on fast-food, and she felt sorry for me. Now *I'm* embarrassed, and beyond that overwhelmed to discover a covert stream of generosity running counter to the dominant corporate miserliness. Melissa probably wouldn't think of herself as poor, but I know she calculates in very small units of currency, twice reminding me, for example, that you can get sixty-eight cents off the specials at the Radio Grill every Tuesday, so a sandwich is something to consider. I set off with my cart, muttering contentedly, "Bobbie Brooks turquoise elastic-waist shorts" and "Faded Glory V-neck red tank top."

Then, in my second week, two things change. My shift changes from 10:00–6:00 to 2:00–11:00, the so-called closing shift, although the store remains open 24/7. No one tells me this; I find it out by studying the schedules that are posted, under glass, on the wall outside the break room. Now I have nine hours instead of eight, I have a net half an hour a day more on my feet. My two fifteen-minute breaks, which seemed almost superfluous on the 10:00–6:00 shift, now become a matter of urgent calculation. Do I take both before dinner, which is usually around 7:30, leaving an unbroken two-and-a-half hour stretch when I'm weariest, between 8:30 and 11:00? Or do I try to go two and a half hours without a break in the afternoon, followed by a nearly three-hour marathon before I can get away for dinner? Then there's the question of how to make the best use of a fifteen-minute break when you have three or more urgent, simultaneous needs—to pee, to drink something, to get outside the neon and into the natural light, and most of all, to sit down. I save about a minute by engaging in a little time theft and stopping at the rest room before I punch out of the break (and, yes, we do have to punch out even for breaks, so there's no padding them with a few stolen minutes). From the time clock it's a seventy-five second walk to the store exit; if I stop at the Radio Grill, I could end up wasting a full four minutes waiting in line, not to mention the fifty nine cents for a small-sized iced tea. So if I treat myself to an outing in the tiny fenced-off area beside the store, the only place where employees are allowed to smoke, and get about nine minutes off my feet.

The other thing that happens is that the post-Memorial Day weekend lull definitely comes to an end. Now there are always a dozen or more shoppers rooting around in ladies', reinforced in the evening by a wave of multi-generational gangs—Grandma, Mom, a baby in the shopping cart, and a gaggle of sullen children in tow. New tasks arise, such as bunching up the carts left behind by customers and steering them to their place in the front of the store every half hour or so. Now I am picking up not only dropped clothes but all the odd items customers carry off from foreign departments and decide to leave with us in ladies'—pillows, upholstery hooks, Pokémon cards, earrings, sunglasses, stuffed animals, even a package of cinnamon buns. And always there are the returns, augmented now by the huge volume of items that have been tossed on the floor or carried fecklessly to inappropriate sites. Sometimes I am lucky to achieve a steady state between replacing the returns and picking up items strewn on the racks and the floor. If I pick up misplaced items as quickly as I replace the returns, my cart never empties and things back up dangerously at the fitting room, where Rhoda or her nighttime replacement is likely to hiss: "You've got three cars waiting, Barb. What's the *problem?*" Think Sisyphus here or the sorcerer's apprentice.

Still, for the first half of my shift, I am the very picture of good-natured helpfulness, fascinated by the multiethnic array of our shoppers—Middle Eastern, Asian, African American, Russian, former Yugoslavian, old-fashioned Minnnesota white—and calmly accepting of the second law of thermodynamics, the one that says that entropy always wins. Amazingly, I get praised by Isabelle, the thin little seventyish lady who seems to be Ellie's adjutant: I am doing "wonderfully," she tells me, and—even better—am "great to work with." I prance from rack to rack, I preen. But then, somewhere around 6:00 or 7:00, when the desire to sit down becomes a serious craving, a Dr. Jekyll/Mr. Hyde transformation sets in. I cannot ignore the fact that it's the customers' sloppiness and idle whims that make me bend and crouch and run. They are the shoppers, I am the antishopper, whose goal is to make it look as if they'd never been in the store. At this point, "aggressive hospitality" gives way to aggressive hostility. Their carts bang into mine, their children run amok. Once I stand and watch helplessly while some rug rat pulls everything he can reach off the racks, and the thought that abortion is wasted on the unborn must show on my face, because his mother finally tells him to stop.

I even start hating the customers for extraneous reasons, such as, in the case of the native Caucasians, their size. I don't mean just bellies and butts, but huge bulges in completely exotic locations, like the backs of their neck and the knees. This summer, Wendy's, where I often buy lunch, has introduced the verb *biggiesize*, as in "Would you like to biggiesize that combo?" meaning double the fries and pop, and something like biggiesizing seems to have happened to the female guest population. All right, everyone knows that midwesterners, and especially those in the lower middle class, are tragically burdened by the residues of decades of potato chips and French toast sticks, and I probably shouldn't even bring this up. In my early-shift, Dr. Jekyll form, I feel sorry for the obese, who must choose from among our hideous woman-size offerings, our drawstring shorts, and huge horizontally striped tees, which are obviously designed to mock them. But compassion fades as the shift wears on. Those of us who work in ladies' are for obvious reason a pretty lean lot—probably, by Minnesota standards, candidates for emergency IV nutritional supplementation—and we live with the fear of being crushed by some wide-body as she hurtles through the narrow passage from Faded Glory to woman size, lost in fantasies involving svelte Kathie Lee sheaths.

It's the clothes I relate to, though, not the customers. And now a funny thing happens to me here on my new shift: I start thinking they're mine, not mine to take home and wear, because I have no such designs on them, just mine to organize and rule over. Same with ladies' wear as a whole. After 6:00, when Melissa and Ellie go home, and especially after 9:00, when Isabelle leaves, I start to *own* the place. Out of the way, Sam, this is Bar-Mart now. I patrol the perimeter with my cart, darting in to pick up misplaced and fallen items, making everything look spiffy from the outside. I don't fondle the clothes, the way customers do; I slap them into place, commanding them to hang straight, at attention, or lie subdued on the shelves in perfect order. In this frame of mind, the last thing I want to see is a customer riffling around, disturbing the place. In fact, I hate the idea of things being sold—uprooted from their natural homes, whisked off to some closet that's in God-knows-what state of disorder. I want ladies' wear sealed off in a plastic bubble and trucked away to some place of safety, some museum of retail history.

One night I come back bone-tired from my last break and am distressed to find a new person, an Asian American or possibly Hispanic woman who can't be more than four and a half feet tall, folding T-shirts in the White Stag area, *my* White Stag area. It's already been a vexing evening. Earlier, when I'd returned from dinner, the evening fitting room lady upbraided me for being late—which I actually wasn't—and said that if Howard knew, he probably wouldn't yell at me this time because I'm still pretty new, but if it happened again. . . . And I'd snapped back that I could care less if Howard yelled at me, which is a difficult sentiment to fully convey without access to the forbidden four-letter words. So I'm a little wary with this intruder in White Stag and, sure enough, after our minimal introductions, she turns on me.

"Did you put anything away here today?" she demands.

"Well, yes, sure." In fact I've put something away everwhere today, as I do on every other day.

"Because this is not in the right place. See the fabric—it's different," and she thrusts the errant item up toward my chest.

True, I can see that this olive green shirt is slightly ribbed while the others are smooth. "You've *got* to put them in their right places," she continues. "Are you checking the UPC numbers?"

Of course I am not checking the ten or more digit UPC numbers, which lied just under the bar codes—nobody does. What does she think this is, the National Academy of Sciences? I'm not sure what kind of deference, if any, is due here: Is she my supervisor now? Or are we involved in some kind of test to see who will dominate the 9:00–11:00 time period? But I don't care, she's pissing me off, messing with my stuff. So I say, only without the numerals or the forbidden curse word that (1) plenty of other people work here during the day, not to mention all the customers coming through, so why is she blaming me? (2) it's after 10:00 and I've got another cart full of returns to go, and wouldn't it make more sense if we both worked on the carts, instead of zoning the goddamn T-shirts?

To which she responds huffily, "I don't *do* returns. My job is to *fold*."

A few minutes later I see why she doesn't do returns—she can't reach the racks. In fact, she has to use a ladder to get to the higher shelves. And you know what I feel when I see the poor little mite pushing that ladder around? A surge of evil mirth. I peer around from where I am working in Jordache, hoping to see her go splat.

I leave that night shaken by my response to the intruder. If she's a supervisor, I could be written up for what I said, but even worse is what I thought. Am I turning mean here, and is that a normal response to the end of a nine-hour shift? There was another outbreak of mental wickedness that night. I'd gone back to the counter by the fitting room to pick up the next cart full of returns and found the guy who answers the phone at the counter at night, a pensive young fellow in a wheelchair, staring into space, looking even sadder than usual. And my uncensored thought was, At least you get to sit down.

This is not me, at least not any version of me I'd like to spend much time with, just as my tiny coworker is probably not usually a bitch. She's someone who works all night and naps during the day when her baby does, I find out later, along with the information that she's not anyone's supervisor and is in fact subject to constant criticism by Isabelle when the two overlap. What I have to face is that "Barb," the name on my ID tag, is not exactly the same person as Barbara. "Barb" is what I was called as a child, and still am by my siblings, and I sense that at some level I'm regressing. Take away the career and the higher education, and maybe what you're left with is this original Barb, the one who might have ended up working at Wal-Mart for real if her father hadn't managed to climb out of the mines. So it's interesting, and more than a little disturbing, to see how Barb turned out—that she's meaner and slyer than I am, more cherishing of grudges, and not quite as smart as I'd hoped.

Notes

1. I may have to withdraw my claim. Until it was closed for fire code violations in 1997, the Parkway Motel in southern Maryland boasted exposed electrical wires, holes in room doors, and raw sewage on bathroom floors. But if price is entered into the competition, the Clearview Inn may still win, since the Parkway was charging only $20 a day at the time (Todd Shields, "Charles Cracks Down on Dilapidated Motels," *Washington Post*, April 20, 1997).
2. I thank Sona Pai, an Indian American graduate student in literary nonfiction at the University of Oregon, for giving me a glimpse into the Indian American motel-operating community and the lives of immigrant wives.

Employment at Will, Employee Rights, and Future Directions for Employment

Tara J. Radin • Patricia H. Werhane

Private employment in the United States has traditionally been governed by "employment at will" (EAW), which provides for minimal regulation of employment practices. It allows either the employer or the employee to terminate their employment relationship at any time for virtually any reason or for no reason at all. At least 55% of all employees and managers in the private sector of the workforce in the United States today are "at will" employees.

During the past several years, the principle and practice of employment at will have been under attack. While progress has been made in eroding the practice, the principle still governs the philosophical assumption underlying employment practices in the United States, and, indeed, EAW has been promulgated as one of the ways to address economic ills in other countries. In what follows, we will briefly review the major critiques of EAW. Given the failure of these arguments to erode the underpinnings of EAW, we shall suggest new avenues for approaching employment issues.

CRITIQUES OF EAW

Rights Talk

The first set of arguments critiquing the principle of EAW are grounded on a commonly held theory of moral rights, that is, the claim that human beings have moral claims to a set of basic rights vis-à-vis their being human. This set of arguments makes three points. First, principles governing employment practices that interfere with commonly guaranteed political rights, such as free speech (including legitimate whistle blowing), privacy,

Reprinted by permission of the authors, Tara J. Radin and Patricia H. Werhane, and *Business Ethics Quarterly* 13, 2003.

due process, and democratic participation, would therefore appear to be questionable principles and practices from a rights perspective. Moreover, if employers and managers have certain rights, say, to respect, free speech, and choice, employees also should have equal claims to those rights. Third, if property rights are constitutionally guaranteed, it would appear to follow that employees should have some rights to their work contributions, just as managers, as representatives of companies, have rights to exercise property claims (Werhane, 1985).

There are at least three countervailing arguments against these conclusions, however. In the United States, constitutional guarantees apply to interactions between persons or institutions and the state, but they do not extend to the private sector or to the home, except in cases of egregious acts. Claims to employee rights are not, therefore, guaranteed by the Constitution. Second, employment agreements are contractual agreements between consenting adults. Unless a person is forced to work or to perform a particular task, EAW thus protects liberty rights in allowing a person freely to enter into and leave contracts of his or her own choosing. Third, accepting that there are property rights protects companies and their property, and companies and their managers should be free to hire and fire as they see fit (Epstein, 1984; Maitland, 1990). Indeed, Christopher McMahon, a defender of employee rights, argues that, as property owners or agents for companies, employers and managers have rights to hire and fire "at will," although they do not have any moral justification not to respect other employee rights claims (McMahon, 1995), including, for example, rights to participation in corporate decision-making.

Fairness

A second set of arguments against EAW stems from fairness concerns, regarding the fairness of employment at will agreements and practices. EAW has, on numerous occasions, seemingly translated into a license for employers and employees to treat one another *amorally, if not immorally.* "'Why are you firing me, Mr. Ford?' asked Lee Iacocca, president of Ford Motor Company. Henry, looking at Iacocca, said: 'I just don't like you!'" (Abodaher, 1982: 202). While EAW demands ostensibly equal treatment of both employers and employees, the result is often not inherently *fair* to either.

Except under conditions of very low unemployment, employers ordinarily stand in a position of power relative to prospective employees, and most employees, at any level, are replaceable. At a minimum, though, employees deserve good reasons for employment decisions that involve them. We have thus concluded that due process procedures should be instituted as mandatory procedures in every workplace (Radin and Werhane, 1996).

On the other side, employers suffer when employees simply walk off jobs without notice. In a much earlier work, Werhane therefore has argued that employees *and* employers have equal rights, rights that would entail reciprocal obligations to inform each other about firing or quitting and to give reasons for these actions (Werhane, 1985).

Even if it is possible to defend EAW on the basis of freedom of contracts, in practice, EAW supports inconsistent, and even irrational, management behavior by permitting arbitrary treatment of employees—behavior that is not tolerated as best management practice (Werhane, 1999). Since arbitrary accounting, marketing, and investment practices are not tolerated, arbitrary human resource practices are equally questionable management practices.

Interestingly, to safeguard against arbitrary treatment, due process procedures have become mandatory guarantees for employees in the public sectors of the economy, on the federal, state, and local levels, but not in the private sector. Again, on the basis of the fairness of equal treatment for all workers, this appears to be unfair. Nevertheless, the inapplicability of constitutional guarantees in the private sector of the economy prevails in employment.

EROSION OF EAW: LAW AND PUBLIC POLICY

Despite these and other arguments, the principle, if not the practice, of EAW is alive and well. Rather than attacking the principle directly, legislatures and courts have created ways to reduce the impact of the practice, and Congress has chosen to control the scope of EAW through limited legislation. A recent wave of federal legislation that has had a significant impact on private employment began with the passing of Title VII of the Civil Rights Act of 1964, which prohibits the discrimination of employees on the basis of "race, color, religion, sex, or national origin."[1] It has been followed by the Age Discrimination in Employment Act,[2] the Pregnancy Discrimination Act,[3] and the employment provisions of the Americans with Disabilities Act.[4] Together, such legislation demonstrates Congress' recognition that there are limits to EAW, and that the default rule cannot, and should not, be used as a license to disregard fundamental rights.

The real limited power lies in the hands of state and local legislatures. Many have sidestepped EAW to recognize employee rights, such as in the area of privacy, by passing statutes on issues ranging from workplace discrimination to drug-testing. A few states, such as Colorado, North Dakota, and Nevada, have enacted statutes barring employers from firing employees for legal off-work activity. In 1987, Montana became the first state to pass a comprehensive statute rejecting EAW in favor of "just cause" terminations.[5] Contrary to EAW, the "just cause" standard requires that the reasons offered in termination decisions be defensible.[6] Montana currently stands alone in demanding "just cause" dismissals. Although it is too early to know whether one state's move in this direction signals a trend toward the increasing state challenges to EAW, there is currently no evidence that this is the case.

Courts have also begun to step in and carve out exceptions to EAW as a default rule. Many employers and employees have opted to alter the employment relationship through contractual agreements. Since evidence of such agreements is not always lodged in an explicit arrangement, courts often find it necessary to delve further in order to determine the reasonable assurances and expectations of employers and employees. For example, the court has held that an employment contract exists, even where it exists only as a result of assumed behavior, through a so-called "implied-in-fact" contract. In *Pugh v. See's Candies, Inc.*, an employee was fired after 32 years of service without explanation.[7] Although no contract existed that specified the duration of employment, the court determined that the implied corporate policy was not to discharge employees without good reasons. The court in *Pugh* determined: "[T]here were facts in evidence from which the jury could determine the existence of such an implied promise: the duration of appellant's employment, the commendations and promotions he received, the apparent lack of any direct criticism of his work, the assurances he was given, and the employer's acknowledged policies."[8] Where an employer's behavior and/or policies encourage an employee's reliance upon employment, the employer cannot dismiss that employee without a good reason.

In some states, it can be considered a breach of contract to fire a long-term employee without sufficient cause, under normal economic conditions, even when the implied contract is only a verbal one. In California, for example, the majority of recent implied contract cases have been decided in favor of the employee (Bastress, 1988: 319–51). Reliance upon employee manuals has also been determined to give rise to reasonable employment expectations. In *Woolley v. Hoffmann-La Roche, Inc.*, the court held that companies are contractually bound by the statements in their employment manuals.[9] In *Woolley*, the employment manual implicitly provided that employees would not be terminated without good cause: "It is the policy of Hoffmann-La Roche to retain to the extent consistent with company requirements, the services of all employees who perform their duties efficiently and effectively."[10] The court thus held that an employee at Hoffmann-La Roche could not be dismissed without good cause and due process. *Woolley* is but one of many decisions that demonstrate that employers are accountable to employees for what is contained in employment manuals, as if the manual is part of an implicit employment contract.

Courts also have been known to override EAW in order to respond to or deter tortuous behavior. Out of this has arisen the "public policy" exception to EAW. The court has carved out the "public policy" exception to handle situations where employers attempt to prevent their employees from exercising fundamental liberties, such as the rights to vote, to serve on a jury,[11] and to receive state minimum wages.[12] In *Frampton v. Central Indiana Gas Company*, the court found in favor of an employee who was discharged for attempting to collect worker compensation:

> If employers are permitted to penalize employees for filing workmen's compensation claims, a most important public policy will be undermined. The fear of discharge would have a deleterious effect on the exercise of a statutory right. Employees will not file claims for justly deserved compensation . . . [and] the employer is effectively relieved of his obligation . . . Since the Act embraces such a fundamental . . . policy, strict employer adherence is required.[13]

Such decisions clearly demonstrate the court's unwillingness to stand by without doing anything as employers attempt to interfere with fundamental liberties.

The public policy exception is also used so as to discourage fraudulent or wrongful behavior on the part of employers, such as in situations where employees are asked to break a law or to violate state public policies. In *Petermann v. International Brotherhood of Teamsters*, the court confronted a situation where an employee refused to perjure himself to keep his job. The court held that compelling an employee to commit perjury "would encourage criminal conduct . . . and . . . serve to contaminate the honest administration of public affairs."[14] Then, in *Palmateer v. International Harvester Corporation*, the court reinstated an employee who was fired for reporting theft at his plant on the grounds that criminal conduct requires such reporting.[15]

Whistleblower protection is also provided as a result of tort theory. Nevertheless in *Pierce v. Ortho Pharmaceutical Corporation*, the court did not reinstate a physician who was fired from a company for refusing to seek approval to test a certain drug on human subjects. The court held that safety clearly lies in the interest of public welfare, but employees may be fired for refusing to conduct research because of personal beliefs.[16]

Similarly, in *Bowman v. State Bank of Keysville*, a Virginia court asserted its refusal to condone retaliatory discharges.[17] In *Bowman*, a couple of employee-shareholders of a bank voted for a merger at the request of the bank's officers. After the vote was counted, the employee-shareholders subsequently retracted their votes and contended that their vote had been coerced. They alleged that the bank officers had warned them that they would lose their jobs if they did not vote in favor of the merger. They were then fired. The court in *Bowman* found in favor of the employee-shareholders. According to the *Bowman* court, "Virginia has not deviated from the common law doctrine of employment-at-will. . . . And we do not alter the traditional rule today. Nonetheless, the rule is not absolute."[18] In this way, the *Bowman* court demonstrated that EAW is subject to limitations and exceptions. Even where the EAW doctrine still appears to "thrive," it does so within definite restrictive legal and policy constraints.

NEW MINDSETS FOR EMPLOYMENT: EMPLOYEES AS ECONOMIC VALUE ADDED

Without attacking or circumventing EAW, there are new signs of a changing mindset about employment, a mindset that values the competitive advantage of the contributions of good employees and managers. The extensive work of scholars such as Jeffrey Pfeffer illustrates this change. Pfeffer, a management professor at Stanford, has argued in a series of books and articles that a "people first" strategy can serve as an economic advantage for companies. To provide evidence for his point, Pfeffer has studied a number of North American and international companies and amassed a great deal of data that demonstrates that economic success is linked to fair labor practices when employees and managers are considered critical stakeholders for the long-term viability of their companies. According to Pfeffer, the most successful companies—those that have sustained long-term economic profitability and growth—work carefully to engage in employment practices that include selective hiring, employment security, high compensation, decentralization, empowerment and selfmanaged teams, training, open information, and fair treatment of all of their employees (Pfeffer, 1998, especially 64–98).

Rosabeth Moss Kanter further argues that it is both desirable and obligatory for companies to give their employees what she calls "employability security": abilities and skills that are transferable to other jobs and other situations in that company or elsewhere so that employees are adaptable in a world of technological and economic change (Kanter, 1993). Today, while some companies engage in layoffs to change employee skills, many managers and companies are training and retraining old workers, giving them new skills. Kanter would argue, with Pfeffer, that it is valuable, in terms of both economics and respect for workers, to have a workforce that is comprised of a collection of highly skilled and employable people who would be desirable assets in a number of employment settings, both within a particular company and among industries (Kanter, 1993).

Linking Pfeffer's and Kanter's findings with a notion of employee rights, if we could reenvision the mindset of employment to consider each job applicant, employee, manager, or CEO as a unique individual—as a potential corporate citizen with rights—we might then begin to rethink employment, not in terms of generalized numbers, but in terms of particulars—*particular individuals.* If a company's core values were to drive the assumption that each employee is a corporate citizen analogous to a national citizen with similar rights, then the way we would think about employment would change. This process would take into account productivity and performance, and it would also require rethinking the hiring in terms of long-time employment. This does not entail keeping every employee hired, or even guaranteeing lifetime employment, but, at a minimum, it does require due process for all employment changes, protection of fundamental rights such as free speech and privacy, and the provision of adequate information to employees about their future and the future of the company. If Pfeffer's data is correct, such measures add value to shareholders as well.

EAW IN 2000 AND BEYOND

Despite inroads in eroding EAW with law and public policy, changing mindsets regarding the value of employment and employment practices, and the work of Pfeffer, Kanter, and others demonstrating the worth of good employment practices for long-term profitability and success, the principle of EAW continues to underlie North American management practice, and the language of rights, or employee rights, still evades popular management thinking about employment, at least in the private sectors of the economy. That this is the case is most clearly demonstrated by three sets of phenomena. First, there has been a consistent demise of unions and unionism in this country. Since the 1950s, union membership has dropped from about 33% of all workers to barely 10% today. This demise not only reflects the philosophy of corporations, but it is also the result of a series of public policy initiatives. In addition, it reflects interests of workers, even low-wage workers who work under strenuous or dangerous conditions, who find no incentive to unionize.[19]

Second, despite the enlightened focus on employability and despite an almost full employment economy, layoffs still dominate the ways in which corporations think about employment when making changes in their strategic direction. In 1999 alone, there were more than a million people laid off.[20] Admittedly, given low unemployment, most of these folks found new jobs, but this often requires relocation and, sometimes, even in this economy, taking less desirable jobs for lower wages. This is particularly true for unskilled workers.

Third, one of the criticisms of Northern Europe's high unemployment and Japan's recent economic difficulties are that these countries have massive restrictions on the ability of their companies to engage in flexible employment practices. We are thus exporting our EAW mindset, sometimes as a panacea for economic difficulties that are not always traceable to overemployment. It is important for us to think carefully about the practices we export, particularly considering their questionable success here.

RETHINKING EMPLOYMENT RELATIONSHIPS: A PROFESSIONAL MODEL

Given these seemingly contradictory conclusions, namely, the persistence of the principle of EAW, the argument that employees and managers have moral responsibilities to each other, and the economic value-added of employees to firms, we are challenged to try to reformulate the notion of employment. Employment is a phenomenon embedded in a complex set of interrelationships, between employees and managers or employers, between workers, worker organizations such as unions, and between employment and public policy. It involves customer relationships, human resource policies, and, given pension plans, often employee/owner relationships with management. Employees are just one of many stakeholders who affect and are affected by the companies in which they work. Moreover, companies and, indeed, industries, and the system of commerce are embedded within a complex structure of laws, regulations and regulatory agencies, public policy, media interaction and public opinion, and this system is part of a global economy of exchange, ownership, and trade (see Mitroff and Linstone, 1993).

Employees, as "players" in these overlapping sets of systems, are at the same time individuals, part of a company, and embroiled in a system of commerce. Their interests are important, but they are not the only interests that must be taken into account. Like the phenomenon of employment, employee rights and responsibilities are embedded in a complex social system of rights and responsibilities. Employee rights claims are thus not merely individual manifesto claims to certain privileges, but they also entail reciprocal respect for others' rights and responsibilities.

If employment relationships are embedded in a set of systems or subsystems, then it is important—strategically important—for managers and employees to attack employment issues systemically from a fact-finding perspective, from an organizational or social perspective, and from the perspective of the individuals involved, in this case, employees and managers. Conceptualizing employment systemically may help to reconsider their importance in the underlying system of which they are a contributing part. This sort of analysis will neither eliminate nor replace the principle of EAW, but it is a step in the process of reconceptualizing the notion of employment.

Pfeffer's conclusion that employees are critical to corporate success is grounded in such a systems approach that views employees, as well as products, services, and customers, as part of the strategic advantage of the company. Using a method of fact-finding, he shows that, without good employees, a company will fail, just as it will fail without customers, and fail if it does not think strategically about its products and services.

From an organizational perspective, contrary to some points of view, it is a mistake to sort out employees, customers, products, services, shareholders, and so on, as if each is an autonomous set of phenomena. For example, a firm cannot do business without people, products, finance and accounting, markets, and a strategy. So, in times of economic exigency, a merger, or corporate change, it may not be to the advantage of a company merely to lop off employees (even if they are the "low hanging [most easily disposable] fruit") without thinking carefully about their employees as people and their contributions to the long-term survival and success of the company. In certain times no company would simply quit doing accounting, it would be to its peril to quit marketing its products and services, and similarly, to get rid of too many employees cannot serve its long-term viability very well either.

A third point of view focuses on individuals. We have been preoccupied with manager/employer responsibilities to employees. Part of a more systematic approach requires that we deal also with accountabilities of employees to themselves, and the responsibilities of the work force to look after itself, to take working and career choices seriously as personal responsibilities, instead of leaving such concerns to the fate of a particular employer. As part of the workforce, each of us has claims to certain rights, such as free choice, free speech, rights to strike, property rights to contributions, rights to information, and rights to safe workplace. As a result, every other worker, employee, or manager, in every sector of the economy, has responsibilities as well—responsibilities not merely to employers, but to him- or herself and his or her future, and to manage that future as he or she is able and sees fit. Thinking about employment systemically and thinking about personal responsibilities as well as responsibilities to others within that system may help employees to take charge of their own working lives, professions, and careers.

The popular literature is filled with laments that the "good old days" of alleged employee-employer lifetime employment contracts, company paternalism, and lifetime benefits, are under threat of extinction (Werhane, 1999). So, too, are the expectations of loyalty, total commitment, company-first sacrifices, and perhaps, even, obedience and trust. But this may be good news, for it should prompt employees and managers to rethink who they are—to manage their own careers within the free enterprise system, and to rejoice in the demise of paternalism such that they no longer even imagine that a person is dependent upon, or co-dependent upon, a particular employer, training program, or authority. It is necessary to change what we have called elsewhere the "boss" mental model, so aptly exploited by Dilbert, and to alter our vision of ourselves from that of "just an employee" to that of an independent worker or manager with commitments to self-development (see Hirsch, 1987). Unskilled workers, like many managers today, would have to rethink of themselves as independent contractors with trained or trainable skills that are transferable to a number of job settings, rather than as mere wage earners. By taking their work and productivity contributions seriously, workers with these sorts of mindsets would create economic value-added—for firms and a sense of self-worth.

While all of this might seem farfetched, particularly for unskilled and uneducated workers, this sort of thinking dates back at least two centuries. As Adam Smith and later Karl Marx argued, the Industrial Revolution provided the opportunity for workers to become independent of landholder serfdom and free from those to whom they had been previously apprenticed. This occurred because, by providing workers opportunities to choose and change jobs and to be paid for their productivity, people were able to trade their labor without chatteling themselves. This sense of economic independence was never fully realized, because, in fact, circumstances often prevent most of us from achieving Smith's ideal "where every man was perfectly free both to chuse what occupation he thought proper, and to change it as often as he thought proper" (Smith, 1776; 1976, I.x.a.l).

During and after the Industrial Revolution, one of the great debates about labor was the status of "free labor" verses "wage labor." Free labor was "labor carried out under conditions likely to cultivate the qualities of character that suits citizens to self-government" (Sandel, 1996, 169). These conditions included being economically independent, and indeed Thomas Jefferson, and later, the authors of *Rerum Novarum* (1892), the first Papal social encyclical, associated free labor with property ownership and farming. Wage earning was thought by some to be equivalent to slavery since it "denied [workers] economic and political independence essential to republican citizenship" (Sandel, 1996, 172).

But how, in the twenty-first century, is a person to develop this sort of independence and independent thinking about her work, when the vast majority work for others? A new model of employment is required, and this model requires developing different mindsets about work and working that draw from Smith's and Jefferson's ideas, and, at the same time, take into account the fact that most of us are, and will be, employees. It is a model that has developed in the high tech and dot.com industries, and it is one that should be emulated elsewhere. The model is that of the professional. A professional is a person who has trained skills in certain areas so that person is employable in his or her area of expertise. The professional has a commitment to his or her professional work, and to the ability to be versatile. This is not a model of the "loyal servant," but rather of a person who manages him- or herself with employable skills that he or she markets, even as he or she is simultaneously managed by others. This is a person who commits to excellence in whatever employment situations he or she encounters, but is not wedded to one employer or one particular job.

If employment is part of a set of complex systems of commerce, the model of the worker, the employee, the manager, and the executive as a professional, offers a paradigm for thinking about him- or herself as both independent and part of a political economy. With the end of implied job security in every sector of the economy, with global demands on management skills, and with the loss of union representation, this is a model for the future—a model that would circumvent EAW and take us fittingly into a new millennium of global capitalism.

References

Abodaher, D., 1982. *Iacocca: A Biography* (New York: Harper Collins).

Bastress, R. M., 1988. "A Synthesis and a Proposal for Reform of the Employment at Will Doctrine." *West Virginia Law Review*, 90: 319–351.

Epstein, Richard, 1984. "In Defense of the Contract at Will." *University of Chicago Law Review*, 34. Reprinted in this volume.

Goodman, Peter. 1999. "Eating Chicken Dust," *Washington Post*, November 28. A 23–25.

Hirsch, Paul, 1987. *Pack Your Own Parachute* (Reading, MA: Addison-Wesley Publishing).

Kanter, Rosabeth Moss, 1993. "Employability Security," *Business and Society Review*, 11–14. Reprinted in this volume.

Maitland, Ian, 1990. "Rights in the Workplace: A Nozickian Argument." *Taking Sides*, ed. Lisa Newton and Maureen Ford (Guilford, CT: Dushkin Publishing Group).

McMahon, Christopher, 1995. *Authority and Democracy* (Princeton, NJ: Princeton University Press).

Mitroff, Ian I. and Linstone, Harold, 1993. *The Unbounded Mind* (New York: Oxford University Press).

Pfeffer, Jeffrey, 1998. *The Human Equation* (Boston: Harvard Business School Press).

Pope Leo XIII, 1892. *Rerum Novarum.*

Radin, T. J., and Werhane, P. H., 1996. "The Public/Private Distinction and the Political Status of Employment," *American Business Law Journal*, 34, 2: 245–260.

Sandel, Michael J., 1996. *Democracy's Discontent* (Cambridge, MA: Harvard University Press).

Smith, Adam, 1776; 1976. *The Wealth of Nations*, ed. R. H. Campbell and A. S. Skinner. (Oxford: Oxford University Press).

Werhane, P. H., 1999. "Justice and Trust." *Journal of Business Ethics*, 21: 237–249.

Werhane, P. H., 1985. *Persons, Rights, and Corporations* (Englewood Cliffs, NJ: Prentice-Hall).

Notes

1. Title VII of the Civil Rights Act of 1964, 42 U.S.C. 2000e-2(a).
2. Age Discrimination in Employment Act, 29 U.S.C. 621–634 (1994).
3. Pregnancy Discrimination Act, 42 U.S.C. 2000E(k) (1994).
4. Americans with Disabilities Act, 42 U.S.C. 12112 (1994).
5. In 1991, the Commissioners on Uniform State Laws passed the Model Employment Termination Act, which offers a framework for "just-cause" regimes. State legislatures have looked toward this Act as a model, but no state has yet adopted it.
6. "Just cause" advocates differ as to whether or not they define the standard as demanding merely "fair and honest" reasons or "good" reasons.
7. *Pugh v. See's Candies, Inc.*, 171 Cal. Rptr. 917 (1981).
8. *Pugh v. See's Candies, Inc.*, 171 Cal. Rptr. 917 (1981).
9. *Woolley v. Hoffmann-La Roche, Inc.*, 491 A.2d 1257, modified, 499 A.2d 515 (1985).
10. *Woolley v. Hoffmann-La Roche, Inc.*, 491 A.2d 1257, modified, 499 A.2d 515 (1985).
11. *Nees v. Hocks*, 272 Ore. 210 (1975).
12. *Jackson v. Minidoka Irrigation Dist.*, 98 Idaho 330 (1977).
13. *Frampton v. Central Indiana Gas Company*, 260 Ind. 249 (1973).
14. *Petermann v. International Brotherhood of Teamsters*, 174 Cal. App. 2d 184 (Cal. D.C. App. 1959).
15. *Palmateer v. International Harvester Corporation*, 85 Ill. App. 2d 124 (1981).
16. *Pierce v. Ortho Pharmaceutical Corporation*, A-S1, Supreme Court of New Jersey, 84 N.J. 58. (1980).
17. *Bowman v. State Bank of Keysville* (1985).
18. *Bowman v. State Bank of Keysville* (1985).
19. For example, less than 40% of all chicken catchers are unionized, despite the fact that they are exposed to pecking and chicken feather dust all day and work under very dangerous and stressful conditions (Goodman, A23).
20. According to "Extended Mass Layoffs in the Second Quarter of 2000," USDL 00-266, released September 20, 2000, http://stats. bls. gov/newsrels. htm, 1,099,267 people were separated from their jobs for more than 30 days in 1999, and 971,619 people filed initial claims for unemployment insurance during a consecutive 5-week period. During the second quarter of 2000, there were 227,114 separations, and 162,726 initial claimants.

In Defense of the Contract at Will

RICHARD A. EPSTEIN

The persistent tension between private ordering and government regulation exists in virtually every area known to the law, and in none has that tension been more pronounced than in the law of employer and employee relations. During the last fifty years, the balance of power has shifted heavily in favor of direct public regulation, which has been thought strictly necessary to redress the perceived imbalance between the individual and the firm. In particular the employment relationship has been the subject of at least two major statutory revolutions. The first, which culminated in the passage of the National Labor Relations Act in 1935, set the basic structure for collective bargaining that persists to the current time. The second, which is embodied in Title VII of the Civil Rights Act of 1964, offers extensive protection to all individuals against discrimination on the basis of race, sex, religion, or national origin. The effect of these two statutes is so pervasive that it is easy to forget that, even after their passage, large portions of the employment relation remain subject to the traditional common law rules, which when all was said and done set their face in support of freedom of contract and the system of voluntary exchange. One manifestation of that position was the prominent place that the common law, especially as it developed in the nineteenth century, gave to the contract at will. The basic position was set out in an oft-quoted passage from *Payne v. Western & Atlantic Railroad*:

> [M]en must be left, without interference to buy and sell where they please, and to discharge or retain employees at will for good cause or for no cause, or even for bad cause without thereby being guilty of an unlawful act per se. It is a right which an employee may exercise in the same way, to the same extent, for the same cause or want of cause as the employer.[1]

In the remainder of this paper, I examine the arguments that can be made for and against the contract at will. I hope to show that it is adopted not because it allows the employer to exploit the employee, but rather because over a very broad range of circumstances it works to the mutual benefit of both parties, where the benefits are measured, as ever, at the time of the contract's formation and not at the time of dispute. To justify this result, I examine the contract in light of the three dominant standards that have emerged as the test of the soundness of any legal doctrine: intrinsic fairness, effects upon utility or wealth, and distributional consequences. I conclude that the first two tests point strongly to the maintenance of the at-will rule, while the third, if it offers any guidance at all, points in the same direction.

From "In Defense of the Contract at Will" by Richard A. Epstein, *University of Chicago Law Review* 34 (1984). Reprinted by permission of the University of Chicago Law Review.

I. THE FAIRNESS OF THE CONTRACT AT WILL

The first way to argue for the contract at will is to insist upon the importance of freedom of contract as an end in itself. Freedom of contract is an aspect of individual liberty, every bit as much as freedom of speech, or freedom in the selection of marriage partners or in the adoption of religious beliefs or affiliations. Just as it is regarded as prima facie unjust to abridge these liberties, so too is it presumptively unjust to abridge the economic liberties of individuals. The desire to make one's own choices about employment may be as strong as it is with respect to marriage or participation in religious activities, and it is doubtless more pervasive than the desire to participate in political activity. Indeed for most people, their own health and comfort, and that of their families, depend critically upon their ability to earn a living by entering the employment market. If government regulation is inappropriate for personal, religious, or political activities, then what makes it intrinsically desirable for employment relations?

It is one thing to set aside the occasional transaction that reflects only the momentary aberrations of particular parties who are overwhelmed by major personal and social dislocations. It is quite another to announce that a rule to which vast numbers of individuals adhere is so fundamentally corrupt that it does not deserve the minimum respect of the law. With employment contracts we are not dealing with the widow who has sold her inheritance for a song to a man with a thin mustache. Instead we are dealing with the routine stuff of ordinary life; people who are competent enough to marry, vote, and pray are not unable to protect themselves in their day-to-day business transactions.

Courts and legislatures have intervened so often in private contractual relations that it may seem almost quixotic to insist that they bear a heavy burden of justification every time they wish to substitute their own judgment for that of the immediate parties to the transactions. Yet it is hardly likely that remote public bodies have better information about individual preferences than the parties who hold them. This basic principle of autonomy, moreover, is not limited to some areas of individual conduct and wholly inapplicable to others. It covers all these activities as a piece and admits no ad hoc exceptions, but only principled limitations.

This general proposition applies to the particular contract term in question. Any attack on the contract at will in the name of individual freedom is fundamentally misguided. As the Tennessee Supreme Court rightly stressed in *Payne*, the contract at will is sought by both persons.[2] Any limitation upon the freedom to enter into such contracts limits the power of workers as well as employers and must therefore be justified before it can be accepted. In this context the appeal is often to an image of employer coercion. To be sure, freedom of contract is not an absolute in the employment context, any more than it is elsewhere. Thus the principle must be understood against a backdrop that prohibits the use of private contracts to trench upon third-party rights, including uses that interfere with some clear mandate of public policy, as in cases of contracts to commit murder or perjury.

In addition, the principle of freedom of contract also rules out the use of force or fraud in obtaining advantages during contractual negotiations; and it limits taking advantage of the young, the feeble-minded, and the insane. But the recent wrongful discharge cases do not purport to deal with the delicate situations where contracts have been formed by improper means or where individual defects of capacity or will are involved. Fraud is not a frequent occurrence in employment contracts, especially where workers and employers engage in repeat transactions. Nor is there any reason to believe that such contracts are marred by misapprehensions, since employers and employees know the footing on which they have contracted: the phrase "at will" is two words long and has the convenient virtue of meaning just what it says, no more and no less.

An employee who knows that he can quit at will understands what it means to be fired at will, even though he may not like it after the fact. So long as it is accepted that the employer is the full owner of his capital and the employee is the full owner of his labor, the two are free to exchange on whatever terms and conditions they see fit, within the limited constraints just noted. If the arrangement turns out to be disastrous to one side, that is his problem; and once cautioned, he probably will not make the same mistake a second time. More to the point, employers and employees are unlikely to make the same mistake once. It is hardly plausible that contracts at will could be so pervasive in all businesses and at all levels if they did not serve the interests of employees as well as employers. The argument from fairness then is very simple, but not for that reason unpersuasive.

II. THE UTILITY OF THE CONTRACT AT WILL

The strong fairness argument in favor of freedom of contract makes short work of the various for-cause and good-faith restrictions upon private contracts. Yet the argument is incomplete in several respects. In particular, it does not explain why the presumption in the case of silence should be in favor of the contract at will. Nor does it give a descriptive account of why the contract at will is commonly found in all trades and professions. Nor does the argument meet on their own terms the concerns voiced most frequently by the critics of the contract at will. Thus, the commonplace belief today (at least outside the actual world of business) is that the contract at will is so unfair and one-sided that it cannot be the outcome of a rational set of bargaining processes any more than, to take the extreme case, a contract for total slavery. While we may not, the criticism continues, be able to observe them, defects in capacity at contract formation nonetheless must be present: the ban upon the contract at will is an effective way to reach abuses that are pervasive but difficult to detect, so that modest government interference only strengthens the operation of market forces.

In order to rebut this charge, it is necessary to do more than insist that individuals as a general matter know how to govern their own lives. It is also necessary to display the structural strengths of the contract at will that explain why rational people would enter into such a contract, if not all the time, then at least most of it. The implicit assumption in this argument is that contracts are typically for the mutual benefit of both parties. Yet it is hard to see what other assumption makes any sense in analyzing institutional arrangements (arguably in contradistinction to idiosyncratic, nonrepetitive transactions). To be sure, there are occasional cases of regret after the fact, especially after an infrequent, but costly, contingency comes to pass. There will be cases in which parties are naive, befuddled, or worse. Yet in framing either a rule of policy or a rule of construction, the focus cannot be on that biased set of cases in which the contract aborts and litigation ensues. Instead, attention must be directed to standard repetitive transactions, where the centralizing tendency powerfully promotes expected mutual gain. It is simply incredible to postulate that either employers or employees, motivated as they are by self-interest, would enter routinely into a transaction that leaves them worse off than they were before, or even worse off than their next best alternative.

From this perspective, then, the task is to explain how and why the at-will contracting arrangement (in sharp contrast to slavery) typically works to the mutual advantage of the parties. Here, as is common in economic matters, it does not matter that the parties themselves often cannot articulate the reasons that render their judgment sound and breathe life into legal arrangements that are fragile in form but durable in practice. The inquiry into mutual benefit in turn requires an examination of the full range of costs and benefits that arise from collaborative ventures. It is just at this point that the nineteenth-century view is superior to the emerging modern conception. The modern view tends to lay heavy emphasis on the need to control employer abuse. Yet, as the passage from *Payne* indicates, the rights under the contract at will are fully bilateral, so that the employee can use the contract as a means to control the firm, just as the firm uses it to control the worker.

The issue for the parties, properly framed, is not how to minimize employer abuse, but rather how to maximize the gain from the relationship, which in part depends upon minimizing the sum of employer and employee abuse. Viewed in this way the private-contracting problem is far more complex. How does each party create incentives for the proper behavior of the other? How does each side insure against certain risks? How do both sides minimize the administrative costs of their contracting practices? . . .

1. Monitoring Behavior. The shift in the internal structure of the firm from a partnership to an employment relation eliminates neither bilateral opportunism nor the conflicts of interest between employer and employee. Begin for the moment with the fears of the firm, for it is the firm's right to maintain at will power that is now being called into question. In all too many cases, the firm must contend with the recurrent problem of employee theft and with the related problems of unauthorized use of firm equipment and employee kickback arrangement. . . . [The] proper concerns of the firm are not limited to obvious forms of criminal misconduct. The employee on a fixed wage can, at the margin, capture only a portion of the gain from his labor, and therefore has a tendency to reduce output. The employee who receives a commission equal to half the firm's profit attributable to his labor may work hard, but probably not quite as hard as he would if he received the entire profit from the completed sale, an arrangement that would solve the agency-cost problem only by undoing the firm. . . .

The problem of management then is to identify the forms of social control that are best able to minimize these agency costs. . . . One obvious form of control is the force of law. The state can be brought in to punish cases of embezzlement or fraud. But this mode of control requires extensive cooperation with public officials and may well be frustrated by the need to prove the criminal offense (including *mens rea*) beyond a reasonable doubt, so that vast amounts of abuse will go unchecked. Private litigation instituted by the firm may well be used in cases of major grievances, either to recover the property that has been misappropriated or to prevent the individual employee from further diverting firm business to his own account. But private litigation, like public prosecution, is too blunt an instrument to counter employee shirking or the minor but persistent use of firm assets for private business. . . .

Internal auditors may help control some forms of abuse, and simple observation by coworkers may well monitor employee activities. (There are some very subtle tradeoffs to be considered when the firm decides whether to use partitions or separate offices for its employees.) Promotions, bonuses, and wages are also critical in shaping the level of employee performance. But the carrot cannot be used to the exclusion of the stick. In order to maintain internal discipline, the firm may have to resort to sanctions against individual employees. It is far easier to use those powers that can be unilaterally exercised: to fire, to demote, to withhold wages, or to reprimand. These devices can visit very powerful losses upon individual employees without the need to resort to legal action, and they permit the firm to monitor employee performance continually in order to identify both strong and weak workers and to compensate them accordingly. The principles here are constant, whether we speak of senior officials or lowly subordinates, and it is for just this reason that the contract at will is found at all levels in private markets. . . .

In addition, within the employment context firing does not require a disruption of firm operations, much less an expensive division of its assets. It is instead a clean break with consequences that are immediately clear to both sides. The lower cost of both firing and quitting, therefore, helps account for the very widespread popularity of employment-at-will contracts. There is no need to resort to any theory of economic domination or inequality of bargaining power to explain at-will contracting, which appears with the same tenacity in relations between economic equals and subordinates and is found in many complex commercial arrangements, including franchise agreements, except where limited by statutes.

Thus far, the analysis generally has focused on the position of the employer. Yet for the contract at will to be adopted ex ante, it must work for the benefit of workers as well. And indeed it does, for the contract at will also contains powerful limitations on employers' abuses of power. To see the importance of the contract at will to the employee, it is useful to distinguish between two cases. In the first, the employer pays a fixed sum of money to the worker and is then free to demand of the employee whatever services he wants for some fixed period of time. In the second case, there is no fixed period of employment. The employer is free to demand whatever he wants of the employee, who in turn is free to withdraw for good reason, bad reason, or no reason at all.

The first arrangement invites abuse by the employer, who can now make enormous demands upon the worker without having to take into account either the worker's disutility during the period of service or the value of the worker's labor at contract termination. A fixed-period contract that leaves the worker's obligations unspecified thereby creates a sharp tension between the parties, since the employer receives all the marginal benefits and the employee bears all the marginal costs.

Matters are very different where the employer makes increased demands under a contract at will. Now the worker can quit whenever the net value of the employment contract turns negative. As with the employer's power to fire or demote, the threat to quit (or at a lower level to come late or leave early) is one that can be exercised without resort to litigation. Furthermore, that threat turns out to be most effective when the employer's opportunistic behavior is the greatest because the situation is one in which the worker has least to lose. To be sure, the worker will not necessarily make a threat whenever the employer insists that the worker accept a less favorable set of contractual terms, for sometimes the changes may be accepted as an uneventful adjustment in the total compensation level attributable to a change in the market price of labor. This point counts, however, only as an additional strength of the contract at will, which allows for small adjustments in both directions in ongoing contractual arrangements with a minimum of bother and confusion. . . .

2. Reputational Losses. Another reason why employees are often willing to enter into at-will employment contracts stems from the asymmetry of reputational losses. Any party who cheats may well obtain a bad reputation that will induce others to avoid dealing with him. The size of these losses tends to differ systematically between employers and employees—to the advantage of the employee. Thus in the usual situation there are many workers and a single employer. The disparity in number is apt to be greatest in large industrial concerns, where the at-will contract is commonly, if mistakenly, thought to be most unsatisfactory because of the supposed inequality of bargaining power. The employer who decides to act for bad reason or no reason at all may not face any legal liability under the classical common law rule. But he faces very powerful adverse economic consequences. If coworkers perceive the dismissal as arbitrary, they will take fresh stock of their own prospects, for they can no longer be certain that their faithful performance will ensure their security and advancement. The uncertain prospects created by arbitrary employer behavior is functionally indistinguishable from a reduction in wages unilaterally imposed by the employer. At the margin some workers will look elsewhere, and typically the best workers will have the greatest opportunities. By the same token the large employer has more to gain if he dismisses undesirable employees, for this ordinarily acts as an implicit increase in wages to the other employees, who are no longer burdened with uncooperative or obtuse coworkers.

The existence of both positive and negative reputational effects is thus brought back to bear on the employer. The law may tolerate arbitrary behavior, but private pressures effectively limit its scope. Inferior employers will be at a perpetual competitive disadvantage with enlightened ones and will continue to lose in market share and hence in relative social importance. The lack of legal protection to the employees is therefore in part explained by the increased informal protections that they obtain by working in large concerns.

3. Risk Diversification and Imperfect Information. The contract at will also helps workers deal with the problem of risk diversification. . . . Ordinarily, employees cannot work more than one, or perhaps two, jobs at the same time.

Thereafter the level of performance falls dramatically, so that diversification brings in its wake a low return on labor. The contract at will is designed in part to offset the concentration of individual investment in a single job by allowing diversification among employers over time. The employee is not locked into an unfortunate contract if he finds better opportunities elsewhere or if he detects some weakness in the internal structure of the firm. A similar analysis applies on the employer's side where he is a sole proprietor, though ordinary diversification is possible when ownership of the firm is widely held in publicly traded shares.

The contract at will is also a sensible private adaptation to the problem of imperfect information over time. In sharp contrast to the purchase of standard goods, an inspection of the job before acceptance is far less likely to guarantee its quality thereafter. The future is not clearly known. More important, employees, like employers, know what they do not know. They are not faced with a bolt from the blue, with an "unknown unknown." Rather they face a known unknown for which they can plan. The at-will contract is an essential part of that planning because it allows both sides to take a wait-and-see attitude to their relationship so that new and more accurate choices can be made on the strength of improved information. ("You can start Tuesday and we'll see how the job works out" is a highly intelligent response to uncertainty.) To be sure, employment relationships are more personal and hence often stormier than those that exists in financial markets, but that is no warrant for replacing the contract at will with a for-cause contract provision. The proper question is: will the shift in methods of control work a change for the benefit of both parties, or will it only make a difficult situation worse?

4. *Administrative Costs.* There is one last way in which the contract at will has an enormous advantage over its rivals. It is very cheap to administer. Any effort to use a for-cause rule will in principle allow all, or at least a substantial fraction of, dismissals to generate litigation. Because motive will be a critical element in these cases, the chances of either side obtaining summary judgment will be negligible. Similarly, the broad modern rules of discovery will allow exploration into every aspect of the employment relation. Indeed, a little imagination will allow the plaintiff's lawyer to delve into the general employment policies of the firm, the treatment of similar cases, and a review of the individual file. The employer for his part will be able to examine every aspect of the employee's performance and personal life in order to bolster the case for dismissal. . . .

III. DISTRIBUTIONAL CONCERNS

Enough has been said to show that there is no principled reason of fairness or utility to disturb the common law's longstanding presumption in favor of the contract at will. It remains to be asked whether there are some hitherto unmentioned distributional consequences sufficient to throw that conclusion into doubt. . . .

The proposed reforms in the at-will doctrine cannot hope to transfer wealth systematically from rich to poor on the mode of comprehensive systems of taxation or welfare benefits. Indeed it is very difficult to identify in advance any deserving group of recipients that stands to gain unambiguously from the universal abrogation of the at-will contract. The proposed rules cover the whole range from senior executives to manual labor. At every wage level, there is presumably some differential in workers' output. Those who tend to slack off seem on balance to be most vulnerable to dismissal under the at-will rule; yet it is very hard to imagine why some special concession should be made in their favor at the expense of their more diligent fellow workers.

The distributional issues, moreover, become further clouded once it is recognized that any individual employee will have interests on both sides of the employment relation. Individual workers participate heavily in pension plans, where the value of the holdings depends in part upon the efficiency of the legal rules that govern the companies in which they own shares. If the regulation of the contract at will diminishes the overall level of wealth, the losses are apt to be spread far and wide, which makes it doubtful that there are any gains to the worst off in society that justify somewhat greater losses to those who are better off. The usual concern with maldistribution gives us situations in which one person has one hundred while each of one hundred has one and asks us to compare that distribution with an even distribution of, say, two per person. But the stark form of the numerical example does not explain how the skewed distribution is tied to the concrete choice between different rules governing employment relations. Set in this concrete context, the choices about the proposed new regulation of the employment contract do not set the one against the many but set the many against each other, all in the context of a shrinking overall pie. The possible gains from redistribution, even on the most favorable of assumptions about the diminishing marginal utility of money, are simply not present.

If this is the case, one puzzle still remains: who should be in favor of the proposed legislation? One possibility is that support for the change in common law rules rests largely on ideological and political grounds, so that the legislation has the public support of persons who may well be hurt by it in their private capacities. Another possible explanation could identify the hand of interest-group politics in some subtle form. For example, the lawyers and government officials called upon to administer the new legislation may expect to obtain increased income and power, although this explanation seems insufficient to account for the current pressure. A more uncertain line of inquiry could ask whether labor unions stand to benefit from the creation of a cause of action for wrongful discharge. Unions, after all, have some skill in working with for-cause contracts under the labor statutes that prohibit firing for union activities, and they might be able to promote their own growth by selling their services to the presently nonunionized sector. In addition, the for-cause rule might give employers one less reason to resist unionization, since they would be unable to retain the absolute power to hire and fire in any event. Yet, by the same token, it is possible that workers would be less inclined to pay the costs of union membership if they received some purported benefit by the force of law without unionization. The ultimate weight of these considerations is an empirical question to which no easy answers appear. What is clear, however, is that even if one could show that the shift in the rule either benefits or hurts unions and their members, the answer would not justify the rule, for it would not explain why the legal system should try to skew the balance one way or the other.

The bottom line therefore remains unchanged. The case for a legal requirement that renders employment contracts terminable only for cause is as weak after distributional considerations are taken into account as before. . . .

CONCLUSION

The recent trend toward expanding the legal remedies for wrongful discharge has been greeted with wide approval in judicial, academic, and popular circles. In this paper, I have argued that the modern trend rests in large measure upon a misunderstanding of the contractual processes and the ends served by the contract at will. No system of regulation can hope to match the benefits that the contract at will affords in employment relations. The flexibility afforded by the contract at will permits the ceaseless marginal adjustments that are necessary in any ongoing productive activity conducted, as all activities are, in conditions of technological and business change. The strength of the contract at will should not be judged by the occasional cases in which it is said to produce unfortunate results, but rather by the vast run of cases where it provides a sensible private response to the many and varied problems in labor contracting. All too often the case for a wrongful discharge doctrine rests upon the identification of possible employer abuses, as if they were all that mattered. But the proper goal is to find the set of comprehensive arrangements that will minimize the frequency and severity of abuses by employers and employees alike. Any effort to drive employer abuses to zero can only increase the difficulties inherent in the employment relation. Here, a full analysis of the relevant costs and benefits shows why the constant minor imperfections of the market, far from being a reason to oust private agreements, offer the most powerful reason for respecting them. The doctrine of wrongful discharge is the problem and not the solution. This is one of the many situations in which courts and legislatures should leave well enough alone.

Notes

1. *Payne v. Western & Atl. R.R.*, 81 Tenn. 507, 518–19 (1884), *overruled on other grounds, Hutton v. Watters*, 132 Tenn. 527, 544, 179 S.W. 134, 138 (1915). . . .
2. *Payne v. Western & Atl. R.R.*, 81 Tenn. 507, 518–19 (1884). . . .

Employability Security

ROSABETH MOSS KANTER

For many people in the twentieth century, careers were constituted by institutions. Large employers were expected to provide—and guarantee—jobs, benefits, and upward mobility. Long-term employment has long been considered a central component of high-commitment, high-productivity work systems. And corporate entitlements, from health benefits to pensions, were based on an assumption of longevity, especially as U.S. employers were expected to offer benefits guaranteed by governments in other countries.

Now recessionary pressures and sweeping industrial transformations are forcing large companies to downsize—a euphemism that masks the human turmoil involved. Even in Japan, the bastion of life-time employment in big businesses where nearly three quarters of the country's 60 million workers stayed with one employer throughout their working life, cutbacks and lay-offs beginning in 1992 have been shaking the social contract.

The job-tenure ideal of the past is colliding with the job-insecurity reality of the present. Institutionally dependent careers are declining; self-reliant careers as professionals and entrepreneurs are proliferating, increasing the burdens on people. And women are joining men as peers in nearly every corner of the labor market, bringing new issues—inclusion, empowerment, accommodation to family needs—at a time when companies are struggling to stay afloat.

CHURN AND DISPLACEMENT

The United States has been fortunate in not depending solely on large enterprises. America has a vibrant entrepreneurial economy, a small business sector that creates a higher proportion of jobs than are similarly created in European nations. But employment in smaller organizations is inherently less secure, especially given the high failure rate of new small businesses, and such jobs often come without the benefits and safeguards mandated for companies with more than fifty employees. Some Americans count on entrepreneurs to pull the country out of the economic doldrums as large companies sputter and downsize. But an entrepreneurial economy is full of churn and displacement—and the fate of small companies is often linked to the fate of big ones which they supply and service.

New policies must reflect new forms of security while embracing the emerging realities of flexibility, mobility, and change.

"We promise to increase opportunity and power for our entire, diverse work force. We will:

Look at these

- Recruit for the potential to increase in competence, not simply for narrow skills to fill today's slots.
- Offer ample learning opportunities, from formal training to lunchtime seminars—the equivalent of three weeks a year.
- Provide challenging jobs and rotating assignments that allow growth in skills even without promotion to higher jobs.
- Measure performance beyond accounting numbers and share the data to allow learning by doing and continuous improvement—turning everyone into self-guided professionals.
- Retrain employees as soon as jobs become obsolete.
- Emphasize team building, to help our diverse work force appreciate and utilize fully each other's skills.
- Recognize and reward individual and team achievements, thereby building external reputations and offering tangible indicators of value.
- Provide three-month educational sabbaticals, external internships, or personal time-out every five years.

- Find growth opportunities in our network of suppliers, customers, and venture partners.
- Ensure that pensions and benefits are portable, so that people have safety nets for the future even if they seek employment elsewhere.
- Help people be productive while carrying family responsibilities, through flex-time, provision for sick children, and renewal breaks between major assignments.
- Measure the building of human capital and the capabilities of our people as thoroughly and frequently as we measure the building and use of financial capital.
- Encourage entrepreneurship—new ventures within our company or outside that help our people start businesses and create alternative sources of employment.
- Tap our people's ideas to develop innovations that lower costs, serve customers, and create new markets—the best foundation for business growth and continuing employment, and the source of funds to reinvest in continuous learning."

Policies like these could renew loyalty, commitment, and productivity for all men and women, of corporations both large and small, as they struggle to create jobs, wealth, and well-being in the global economy.

People, Profits, and Perspective

Jeffrey Pfeffer

The key to managing people in ways that lead to profits, productivity, innovation, and real organizational learning ultimately lies in how you think about your organization and its people. It lies in mind set and perspective. When you look at your people, do you see costs to be reduced? Do you see recalcitrant employees prone to opportunism, shirking, and free riding who can't be trusted and who need to be closely controlled through monitoring, rewards, and sanctions? Do you see people performing activities that can and should be contracted out to save on labor costs? Or, when you look at your people, do you see intelligent, motivated trustworthy individuals—the most critical and valuable strategic assets your organization can have? When you look at your people, do you see them as the fundamental resources on which your success rests and the primary means of differentiating yourself from the competition? Perhaps even more importantly, would someone observing how your organization manages its people recognize your point of view in what you do as opposed to what you talk about doing?

With the right perspective and mind set, leaders can determine how to implement high performance management practices. With the wrong perspective, change efforts and new programs become gimmicks, and no army of consultants, seminars, and slogans can provide very much help.

WHAT DOES IT MEAN TO PUT PEOPLE FIRST?

What does it mean to put people first, recognizing and acting on the fact that in today's world (and probably yesterday's, as well) almost every other source of organizational success—technology, financial structure, competitive strategy—can be imitated in an amazingly short period of time?

It means, first of all, publicly and repeatedly stating the primacy and importance of people to organizational success. Richard Branson, the enormously successful entrepreneur who founded Virgin Records, Virgin Atlantic Airways, and many other enterprises, has stated in numerous speeches that at Virgin Atlantic, the people come first, the customers second, and the shareholders third.[1]

The rationale for this ranking is sound, its logic firmly based on the connection between how firms manage people and the profits they achieve. In a speech in London to the Institute of Directors in 1993, Branson stated the relation this way:

> We know that the customer satisfaction which generates all important . . . recommendations and fosters a repeat purchase depends on high standards of service from our people. And we know that high standards of service depend upon having staff who are proud of the company. This is why the interests of our people come first. . . . In the end the long-term interests of shareholders are actually damaged by giving them superficial short-term priority.[2]

Another organization that has taken a similar view is Wal-Mart, the discount retailer with sales in excess of $100 billion. Over the twenty year period from 1972 to 1992, Wal-Mart was second only to Southwest Airlines among all firms traded in the United States in the return earned by its shareholders, providing stockholders with a return of more than 19,000 percent over this time. Sam Walton's philosophy and perspective on Wal-Mart's people, called associates, emphasized their importance to business success:

> The more you share profits with your associates—whether it's in salaries or incentives or bonuses or stock discounts—the more profit will accrue to the company. Why? *Because the way management treats the associates is exactly how the associates will treat the customers.* And if the associates treat the customers well, the customers will return again and again, and *that* is where the real profit . . . lies, not in trying to drag strangers into your stores for one-time purchases based on splashy sales or expensive advertising.[3]

The company's 1989 annual report stated that "We believe Wal-Mart's dynamic range in retailing continues to be written in direct proportion and as a result of our associates' involvement and contribution."[4] All the [F]irms mentioned in this book, such as Norwest, Men's Wearhouse, ServiceMaster, Southwest Airlines, and many others, publicly and emphatically state the importance of their people to their basic strategy and to their success. Norwest, both in its annual reports and elsewhere, proclaims that people are the firm's real competitive advantage. The Men's Wearhouse states that "our success is attributable to a highly productive workforce. Our store personnel comprise one of the retail industry's finest selling organizations."5 George Zimmer, founder and CEO, has stated that there are a number of stakeholders the firm must satisfy, but the most important are its people. Customers come second, vendors third, the community fourth, and shareholders are last—and this from the leader of an organization that has produced outstanding growth and shareholder returns.

Such public statements, by themselves, are obviously not sufficient. Many firms proclaim the importance of their people but do not manage in ways consistent with this claim. Talk, as they say, is cheap. But without the organization's affirmation through its senior leadership of the importance of people, little else will happen. It may not be a sufficient condition, but it is probably a necessary one.

Second, putting people first means fixing the firm's language to ensure consistent use of terminology that does not convey disrespect or disdain of its people. Not by accident that Branson refers to Virgin's *people*, Sam Walton to his company's *associates*, or everyone at Whole Foods to everyone else, from the CEO on down, as a *team member*. The term "worker" or even "employee" conveys someone who is in a subordinate role, and conveys less respect and concern than do these alternative terms. Dennis Bakke of AES disdains the term "human resources" because by making people sound like assets, it relegates them to the same status as machines, and, moreover, views them in mostly instrumental terms. Again, fixing the technology is not likely, by itself, to be sufficient to guarantee the implementation of high performance management practices. But because language does influence how we see things, the right language is clearly useful in helping everyone to see people as important.

Third, leaders and organizations who believe that putting their people first is important actually act on that belief in numerous ways. One of the simplest but also most important is providing everyone access to the organization's leaders. At Southwest Airlines, every person has the home phone number of every company officer. At Virgin Atlantic, every person who works for the company has Richard Branson's home phone number. In a dramatic gesture, CEO Jack Watts of Portola Packaging, a $180 million designer and packager of bottle caps and package closures, dealt with diminishing quality and customer focus, a result of mergers and expansion, by writing in the company's newsletter, "We can best improve our operations by having each member of the team taking action. . . . If we aren't solving problems effectively, contact me and I will make sure the problem is dealt with."6 He included his home phone number, fax number, and e-mail address.

This action symbolically tells people that all of them are important and are taken seriously in the firm. More importantly, people actually call. As Richard Branson has stated, he would much rather hear about problems from his people before he hears about them from his customers. Jack Watts learned about customer service and people issues that, before he signaled his interest in hearing from everyone and made it easy for them to reach him, had been hidden from him. Knowing what is going on in the organization is critical to leaders of large, geographically dispersed firms. Making oneself available to all kinds of information permits the leader to learn and also conveys an important message to the organization: Information is more important than the chain of command, and everyone is important to the organization's success.

Another way organizations signal their commitment to their people is through training expenditures. In many organizations, training is viewed as a discretionary expense, something that can be readily cut or even eliminated in times of economic distress or poor profits. But other companies take a different view, because they have a different perspective on their people and on the role of training in building organizational capability as well as signaling to people that they are truly valued by and valuable to the firm. Singapore Airlines, for instance, spends about $80 million per year on training, in a company with revenues of about $4 billion. It provides an average of eleven days of training per person per year, and its core programs are "mandatory and sequentially planned—courses which staff have to attend during the various stages of their career with the company."[7] The training not only imparts skills essential to an organization that is constantly seeking productivity and service improvements, the training also reinforces the company culture and helps to build a community within the company as people get to know each other. This commitment to training is maintained virtually regardless of economic conditions.

Another such organization is USAA, a mutual insurance company begun about sixty years ago to offer insurance to military officers. USAA has since expanded its scope and now offers mutual funds to the general public, has a bank, and offers a broad range of insurance products. USAA has two unique aspects. First, it is frequently mentioned in books about excellent companies because it has continued to thrive even as its primary target population, the military, has substantially shrunk following the end of the Cold War and the subsequent cuts in the U.S. defense budget. The company has prospered by achieving an incredibly high level of customer retention by delivering high value and exceptional service and by selling additional products and services to its current customer base.

A second unique aspect of USAA is its emphasis on training. When I visited the company in 1995, I learned that it had approximately one person in its training department for every sixty-three people. The training department is separate from human resources and reports independently to the same level in the organization. And yes, you read those numbers correctly. USAA, a company with about 16,000 people, has almost 300 people in its training department. USAA is willing to devote this level of effort to training because the firm sees training and the productivity and customer service benefits training provides as a key competitive advantage. Thus it does not outsource its training activity and it doesn't cut training when profitability diminishes. Maintaining training signals a commitment to an organization's people in a tangible way; it says, we value you enough to continue to invest in you, even when times aren't the best. Men's Wearhouse and Singapore Airlines do the same. These organizations see training not as a cost but as a key strategic weapon, and behave accordingly.

Fourth, putting people first means gathering measurements so the organization can assess how well it is doing and being willing to act on those measurements. At Hewlett-Packard, part of managers' performance evaluation depends on how well they are living up to the H-P Way, assessed through a survey of the people who work for them. One is unlikely to do well at Hewlett-Packard if the people one manages are dissatisfied with their work environment. At AES and Whole Foods Markets, surveys of attitudes and beliefs about how well the organization is living up to its values and aspirations are important enough to draw attention in the annual report. At General Electric, the company evaluates managers both by their financial performance and by assessments provided by their people. Getting outstanding results in the right way—by treating people well, developing and retaining them, and managing in a way consistent with the company's values—is the mark of success. Getting good financial numbers at the cost of people is not only not rewarded but not tolerated for very long, reflecting the company's belief that in the long run, the numbers will decline if people are not being treated properly. Citibank uses a balanced scorecard, the category people comes first, a signal that effective teamwork and people management is important to the organization.

Fifth, and perhaps most importantly, putting people first entails ensuring that those in leadership positions have people-oriented values and manage in ways consistent with building high performance work environments. Probably no company exemplifies this practice better than ServiceMaster, a company that over a twenty-five year period, 1970 to 1995, achieved a return to shareholders of 25 percent compounded annually, more than double the return achieved by the stock market as a whole over the same period.[8] The company has been willing to invest in leadership training and courses to help people develop their communication skills and self-confidence for individuals at all levels in the organization. Developing management talent and instilling in those leaders the organization's core values is critical to the success of the firm.

ServceMaster has grown, in part, through acquisitions, and one of the first companies it acquired was Terminix, a company in the business of eliminating termites from buildings. Carlos Cantu, now the president and chief executive of ServiceMaster, was the CEO of Terminix at the time of its acquisition. His story of his meeting with William Pollard, now the chairman of ServiceMaster and at the time its CEO, is revealing.

> When I first met Bill Pollard, I was . . . presenting the company to potential buyers. . . . I was surprised when much of our conversation focused on people, leadership, and responsibility to associates in the work place. Bill was sharing his experience in a unique business environment which champions the principle that customers, associates, and shareholders should be treated with dignity and respect.[9]

How many acquisition meetings have you been in that entailed, before getting down to discussions of merger terms and finances, a general discussion of philosophy, including the company's philosophy about leadership and people? I suspect the answer is not too many.

ServiceMaster has recognized that its basic core competence, and the key to is outstanding business success in an industry with essentially no barriers to entry, is its ability to train and develop people. Having recognized this fact, the company has chosen for its leadership positions individuals who exemplify its values and who truly put people first. William Pollard has written a book, *The Soul of the Firm*, and excerpts from that book, published in the company's 1995 annual report, provide compelling evidence of both his values and the fact that those values are precisely what one would want in a leader in a company that succeeds by putting people first.

> At ServiceMaster, the task before us is to train and motivate people to serve so that they will do a more effective job, be more productive in their work, and, yes, even be better people. . . . It is more than a job, a means to earn a living. It is, in fact, our mission. . . . [I]f we focused exclusively on profit, we would be a firm that had failed to nurture its soul. Eventually . . . firms that do this experience a loss in the direction and purpose of their people, a loss in customers, and then a loss in profits. Both people and profit are part of our mission. . . . You can't run a business without people. . . . Only people—not machines—can respond to the unexpected and surprise the customer with extraordinary performance. Only people can serve. Only people can lead, only people can innovate and create.[10]

This perspective on people and organizations is, in many ways, counter to that found in conventional economic perspectives with their emphasis on individual financial incentives and requirements for hierarchy, surveillance, and control. It is all too rare a perspective in the world of contemporary organizations, but essential to making the connection between people and profits. Pollard explicitly recognized the critical difference between Service-Master's values and philosophy and much of modern management theory.

> [B]usiness is not just a game of manipulation that accomplished a series of tasks for a profit with the gain going to a few and with the atrophy of the soul of the person producing the results. People are not just economic animals or non-personal production units. . . . [W]hen you view the person only as a production unit or something that can be defined solely in economic terms, motivational or even incentive schemes have a tendency to be mechanical and manipulative . . . . [T]he soulless, adversarial, or work rights environment should not be the model of the future.[11]

Finally, putting people first entails recognizing the importance of people—all of a company's people in all organizations—to organizational success. . . . In 1997 and going forward, successful organizations will be those that recognize that *all work is knowledge work.* Is cleaning a hospital knowledge work? It is to ServiceMaster, which has profited in part by providing its front-line people both with high technical skills and with sales skills, permitting better customer retention and therefore enhanced profitability. It is to the Men's Wearhouse, which, through its training programs, not only generates more sales revenue from people better equipped to sell but also a more committed and motivated work force with reduced turnover and inventory shrinkage, in part due to the enhanced self-esteem that comes from being taken very seriously. Is automobile assembly work knowledge work? It is to Toyota and similar companies that have both recognized and capitalized on the skills and knowledge of those people who do the work and have the best knowledge of it. The list could go on. Putting people first means, in the end, taking all of them seriously and, most importantly, recognizing the opportunities to leverage knowledge and build capability and skill in all jobs, in all organizations.

Putting people first means having articulated values and goals, organizational language and terminology, measurements, role models in senior leadership positions, and specific practices that make real the noble sentiments so often honored in the breach. It entails doing things that both reinforce the importance of people to organizational success and simultaneously make it more likely that the organization will have an advantage in attracting and retaining the best people and realizing their full potential. ServiceMaster, for the most part, treats its people, many of whom have only high school educations and who are doing relatively unskilled work, with more dignity and respect than many professional service firms I have seen—firms that rely on a more educated and more expensive work force that is also the key to their success. The Men's Wearhouse, operating in an industry, retailing, that has typically treated its people badly, calls its store salespeople "wardrobe consultants" and instills in them the belief that they can truly be "artists" in the realm of providing customer service and selling clothing that will make their customers look better. Lessons for all organizations can be found in these few that have achieved outstanding success by how they manage their people.

WHAT A PEOPLE-CENTERED STRATEGY DOES

We have talked about what putting people first entails. What does it do? Figure 9-1 diagrams what a people-focused strategy can accomplish. . . . Basic people management practices—I have identified seven—constitute the fundamental building blocks of high performance management systems. Those practices provide competitive advantage for two interrelated reasons.

First, they are difficult to imitate. They are difficult to imitate because implementation entails changing basic views about people, organizations, and sources of success—and changing basic assumptions is always harder than altering a few superficial organizational arrangements. They are difficult to imitate because many of them defy conventional wisdom and common practice. . . . How do we know these practices are difficult to imitate? Because we have seen ample evidence that even when organizations know what to do to achieve higher levels of quality, productivity, and customer service, even when, as in the case of the apparel industry, a recipe exists for changing the basic dynamics to ways that favor them, all too frequently implementation is slow and backsliding frequent. We also know these practices are difficult to imitate because the organizations that followed them have, for the most part, enjoyed outstanding competitive success not just for a quarter or two, but many years and even for decades. This suggests that, unlike technology or other strategies, the outstanding economic returns produced are less likely to be reduced through the imitation of these strategies by competitors—at least in the short run.

The second reason these practices provide economic advantage is because they are positively related to organizational learning and skill development, innovation, customer service, labor productivity, costs—including not only labor costs, but also material costs such as scrap and materials handling and costs of turnover—and organizational flexibility to adapt to new competitive conditions and threats. How do we know these high performance management practices have these effects? . . . I have reviewed literally scores of systematic quantitative studies as well as numerous case examples that provide evidence for the business case for managing people right. We have seen evidence from studies of specific industries; from studies that span industries; from studies of manufacturing companies, service companies, and

FIGURE 9-1   What a People-Based Strategy Does

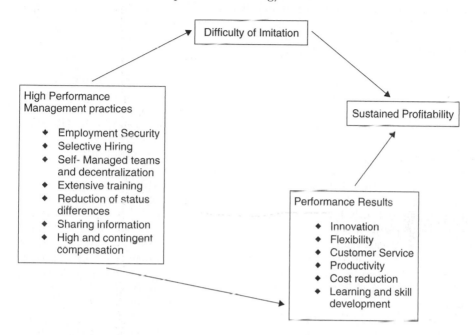

even financial service firms such as banks. We have seen evidence from research that has examined the implications of high performance management practices for learning, innovation, and customer service—not just cost and productivity.

As Figure 9-1 suggests, if a set of management practices are at once difficult to imitate and positively related to numerous sources of competitive success, the result is outstanding levels of profitability, achieved over a long time. Such a management approach produces profitability and success that is robust in that it can succeed:

1. across changes in leadership (ServiceMaster is now fifty years old and has gone through several generations of leaders);
2. across changes in the political environment (Southwest has faced airline deregulation and Northwest has confronted vast changes in financial regulation);
3. across changes in technology (Hewlett-Packard has gone from being primarily an instruments company to being a computer and printer company);
4. across changes in economic circumstances (Wal-Mart has prospered even when, in the late 1980s and early 1990s, much of the retailing industry was in bankruptcy);
5. across different cultures (AES, Virgin Atlantic, and Singapore Airlines operate globally); and
6. across changes in the competitive environment (Whole Foods' higher margins have attracted entry even from more conventional store chains, but these new entrants have not had much success, so far).

It is the robustness of people as a source of competitive success—the ability of organizations than manage this way to survive and prosper in many different circumstances and to respond to numerous types of change—that has so much to recommend putting people first as a basic organizational approach.

ORGANIZATIONAL LEVERAGE

A people-centered strategy can provide organizational leverage that, in turn, can produce opportunities for profit. Let me explain. Consider an organization that has invested a great deal in capital resources. Many organizations operate in capital intensive businesses, such as airlines, hotels, oil refineries, pulp and paper mills, steel mills, semiconductor fabrication plants, electric power plants, and so forth. In each of these businesses, much if not most of the cost is in the fixed capital investment, and those costs continue whether or not the airlines and hotels are occupied and whether or not the manufacturing facilities are operating. Thus, the people who work in these organizations are highly leveraged, with considerable capital per person. If the people are motivated, trained, and committed, results are outstanding; if they aren't, results can be disastrous.

Here is the opportunity to profit. Find an organization that is mismanaging its people. Buy the business or facility based on what it is earning, or even at a premium. Then, implement high commitment management practices. The returns can be enormous. A former student told me about a diaper factory in Latin America. Although the owners had installed the most modern machinery, they had terrible policies regarding their people. They paid them poorly, gave them little training, and exercised autocratic if not despotic management. Safety in the plant was terrible, machine breakdowns were frequent, and the equipment operated less than 50% of the time. Then Procter & Gamble came along and offered to buy the plant. The firm was even willing to pay a premium, in the sense of being willing to pay more than would be justified on the basis of the plant's production operating at 50% uptime. P & G completed the acquisition and installed its typical management approach. This company has pioneered in implementing self-managing teams, emphasizing decentralization, and focusing on the safety and training of its people. Within months, the plant was operating about 95 percent of the time. The difference in productivity was all profit to P & G, as it required relatively few incremental costs to make the management in the facility more effective.

As another example, consider Whole Foods Markets. Whole Foods has grown by acquisition. A Whole Foods market, at six to seven years of age, earns about 10 percent on sales before taking out corporate overhead (which generally runs about 3 to 4 percent). Most grocery stores earn one to two percent. The profitability of a Whole Foods store is, after two years, indistinguishable between its internally developed and acquired stores. Indeed, one of the company's core competencies is its ability to absorb acquisitions. Whole Foods has been able to buy companies such as Fresh Fields, a large, basically unprofitable competitor, purchasing the stores and sales at a discounted price because of their poor economic results. Then, by installing its people-centered management practices, the company turns the store around and profits handsomely as a consequence. I have seen the Men's Wearhouse do similar things with its acquisitions.

Changing management practices in ways that build commitment and competence can transform poorly performing assets. By so doing, companies and entrepreneurs can profit handsomely—as can investors who understand this process and its dynamics.

THE COURAGE TO PUT PEOPLE FIRST

We have seen through both case studies and systematic evidence a compelling case for the connection between how organizations manage people and their profits. Many of the practices associated with high performance or high commitment management have been known and understood for a long time and have been subject to extensive study and discussion. Nevertheless, adoption of these ideas has proceeded slowly and sporadically. Although many of the ideas—things such as providing some sense of security for people you want to commit to the organization—are commonsensical, in their actual application they run up against a number of versions of conventional wisdom that appear to be contradictory.

In the end, doing things differently and going against conventional wisdom is difficult. Achieving profits through people thus often comes down to courage. I have been fortunate to know a number of leaders who have had the wisdom, insight, and courage to manage people effectively in spite of what their organizations or conventional wisdom has said was the right thing to do. The following is just one example.

Some years ago I met a man named Dave Spence who had joined Boise Cascade as plant manager in the company's DeRidder, Louisiana, papermaking plant. At the time he joined the company, it was involved in a contentious strike with the employees and their Louisiana union—a strike that included violence, threats and intimidation. In the years Spence managed the plant, he worked with the people there and with the union in a different way, listening to and caring about them, while at the same time increasing production some 40 percent, an increase equivalent to the purchase of an additional $500 million in capital equipment. When I met Spence he was the head of manufacturing for the paper division. He has since been promoted to senior vice president and general manager in charge of all aspects of the paper division at Boise Cascade. He was continuing to implement his philosophy of management, nicely summarized on the first overhead he used in a presentation to my class at Stanford: "Capital and Machinery Make It Possible—People Make It Happen."

It was clear to me through my own dealings with the company that Spence's philosophy at the time he was making changes in DeRidder was not really shared by all of the senior management, despite the talk of total quality and team work. Over dinner together in Boise when I was there to do some executive education, I noted that although I thought he was on the right track, his approach seemed to be at odds with what had been the dominant management orientation and culture. Without a moment's hesitation he replied, "I took the position that I've worked at other places before, and I may have to again. I've always believed you have to do your job like you are independently wealthy; then you can do the right things all the time."

Spence's career at Boise Cascade has thrived as he and his working partners have helped turn an adversarial relationship with the union around and have harnessed the ideas and energy of more and more of the paper division's people. But executives who manage in a way not consistent with the dominant corporate ideology have no guarantees that they will prosper, regardless of the results achieved by their methods. Many, therefore, won't translate their knowledge of what needs to be done about managing people into actions that actually implement that knowledge. But for the organizations that have leaders possessing both insight and courage, the evidence demonstrates that the economic returns can be enormous.

Notes

1. Tim Jackson, *Richard Branson: Virgin King* (Rocklin, CA: Prima Publishing, 1996), 5.
2. INSEAD, *Branson's Virgin: The Coming of Age of a Counter-Cultural Enterprise. Case Supplement: Extracts from Richard Branson's Speech to the Institute of Directors, 1993* (Fontainbleau, France: INSEAD, 1995), 1.
3. Sam Walton with John Huey, *Made in America* (New York: Bantam, 1992), 163–164.
4. Wal-Mart, *1989 Annual Report,* Bentonville, AR, 3.
5. Men's Wearhouse, *1995 Annual Report,* Fremont, CA, 3.
6. "Message from Jack Watts, Chairman and CEO," *Portola Planet,* Winter/Spring 1997, 1.
7. Ling Sing Chee, "Singapore Airlines: Strategic Human Resource Initiatives," in *International Human Resource Management: Think Globally, Act Locally,* ed. Derek Torrington (New York: Prentice-Hall, 1994), 157.
8. ServiceMaster, *1995 Annual Report,* Downers Grove, IL, 2.
9. Ibid., 18.
10. Ibid.
11. Ibid.

Chapter 10

Diversity

Case Study

Foreign Assignment

Thomas Dunfee ● Diana Robertson

Sara Strong graduated with an MBA from UCLA four years ago. She immediately took a job in the correspondent bank section of the Security Bank of the American Continent. Sara was assigned to work on issues pertaining to relationships with correspondent banks in Latin America. She rose rapidly in the section and received three good promotions in three years. She consistently got high ratings from her superiors, and she received particularly high marks for her professional demeanor.

In her initial position with the bank, Sara was required to travel to Mexico on several occasions. She was always accompanied by a male colleague even though she generally handled similar business by herself on trips within the United States. During her trips to Mexico she observed that Mexican bankers seemed more aware of her being a woman and were personally solicitous to her, but she didn't discern any major problems. The final decisions on the work that she did were handled by male representatives of the bank stationed in Mexico.

A successful foreign assignment was an important step for those on the "fast track" at the bank. Sara applied for a position in Central or South America and was delighted when she was assigned to the bank's office in Mexico City. The office had about twenty bank employees and was headed by Willam Vitam. The Mexico City office was seen as a preferred assignment by young executives at the bank.

Thomas Dunfee is the Joseph Kolodny Professor of Social Responsibility in Business, Professor of Legal Studies and Business Ethics, and Chairperson of the Legal Studies and Business Ethics Department of The Wharton School at the University of Pennsylvania. Diana Robertson is a Professor of Organization and Management at the Goizueta Business School of Emory University. This piece was developed by Professors Dunfee and Robertson for in-class use at The Wharton School, where they served as colleagues in the 1980s and is distilled from actual experiences reported from students in their classes. Reprinted by permission of the authors.

After a month, Sara began to encounter problems. She found it difficult to be effective in dealing with Mexican bankers—the clients. They appeared reluctant to accept her authority and they would often bypass her in important matters. The problem was exacerbated by Vitam's compliance in her being bypassed. When she asked that the clients be referred back to her, Vitam replied, "Of course that isn't really practical." Vitam made matters worse by patronizing her in front of clients and by referring to her as "my cute assistant" and "our lady banker." Vitam never did this when only Americans were present, and in fact treated her professionally and with respect in internal situations.

Sara finally complained to Vitam that he was undermining her authority and effectiveness; she asked him in as positive a manner as possible to help her. Vitam listened carefully to Sara's complaints, then replied: "I'm glad you brought this up, because I've been meaning to sit down and talk to you about my little game-playing in front of the clients. Let me be frank with you. Our clients think you're great, but they just don't understand a woman in authority, and you and I aren't going to be able to change their attitudes overnight. As long as the clients see you as my assistant and deferring to me, they can do business with you. I'm willing to give you as much responsibility as they can handle your having. I *know* you can handle it. But we just have to tread carefully. You and I know that my remarks in front of clients don't mean anything. They're just a way of playing the game Latin style. I know it's frustrating for you, but I really need you to support me on this. It's not going to affect your promotions, and for the most part you really will have responsibility for these clients' accounts. You just have to act like it's my responsibility." Sara replied that she would try to cooperate, but that basically she found her role demeaning.

As time went on, Sara found that the patronizing actions in front of clients bothered her more and more. She spoke to Vitam again, but he was firm in his position, and urged her to try to be a little more flexible, even a little more "feminine."

Sara also had a problem with Vitam over policy. The Mexico City office had five younger women who worked as receptionists and secretaries. They were all situated at work stations at the entrance to the office. They were required to wear standard uniforms that were colorful and slightly sexy. Sara protested the requirement that uniforms be worn because (1) they were inconsistent to the image of the banking business and (2) they were demeaning to the women who had to wear them. Vitam just curtly replied that he had a lot of favorable comments about the uniforms from clients of the bank.

Several months later, Sara had what she thought would be a good opportunity to deal with the problem. Tome Fried, an executive vice president who had been a mentor for her since she arrived at the bank, was coming to Mexico City; she arranged a private conference with him. She described her problems and explained that she was not able to be effective in this environment and that she worried that it would have a negative effect on her chance of promotion within the bank. Fried was very careful in his response. He spoke of certain "realities" that the bank had to respect and he urged her to "see it through" even though he could understand how she would feel that things weren't fair.

Sara found herself becoming more aggressive and defensive in her meetings with Vitam and her clients. Several clients asked that other bank personnel handle their transactions. Sara has just received an Average rating, which noted "the beginnings of a negative attitude about the bank and its policies."

Ways Women Lead

JUDY B. ROSENER

The command-and-control leadership style associated with men is not the only way to succeed.

Women managers who have broken the glass ceiling in medium-sized, non-traditional organizations have proven that effective leaders don't come from one mold. They have demonstrated that using the command-and-control style of managing others, a style generally associated with men in large, traditional organizations, is not the only way to succeed.

The first female executives, because they were breaking new ground, adhered to many of the "rules of conduct" that spelled success for men. Now a second wave of women is making its way into top management, not by adopting the style and habits that have proved successful for men but by drawing on the skills and attitudes they developed from their shared experience as women. These second-generation managerial women are drawing on what is unique to their socialization as women and creating a different path to the top. They are seeking and finding opportunities in fast-changing and growing organizations to show that they can achieve results—in a different way. They are succeeding because of—not in spite of—certain characteristics generally considered to be "feminine" and inappropriate in leaders.

The women's success shows that a non-traditional leadership style is well suited to the conditions of some work environments and can increase an organization's chances of surviving in an uncertain world. It supports the belief that there is strength in a diversity of leadership styles.

In a recent survey sponsored by the International Women's Forum, I found a number of unexpected similarities between men and women leaders along with some important differences. Among these similarities are characteristics related to money and children. I found that the men and women respondents earned the same amount of money [and the household income of the women is twice that of the men]. This finding

Dr. Judy B. Rosener is Professor Emerita at the Paul Merage School of Business at the University of California, Irvine. Professor Rosener teaches and does research in the areas of men and women at work, cultural diversity, and business and government. Reprinted by permission of the *Harvard Business Review*. "Ways Women Lead" by Judy B. Rosener, Nov./Dec. 1968. Copyright © 1968 by the Harvard Business School Publishing Corporation.

is contrary to most studies, which find a considerable wage gap between men and women, even at the executive level. I also found that just as many men as women experience work-family conflicts [although when there are children at home, the women experience slightly more conflict than men].

But the similarities end when men and women describe their leadership performance and how they usually influence those with whom they work. The men are more likely than the women to describe themselves in ways that characterize what some management experts call "transactional" leadership.[i] That is, they view job performance as a series of transactions with subordinates—exchanging rewards for services rendered or punishment for inadequate performance. The men are also more likely to use power that comes from the organizational position and formal authority.

The women respondents, on the other hand, described themselves in ways that characterize "transformational" leadership—getting subordinates to transform their own self-interest into the interest of the group through concern for a broader goal. Moreover, they ascribe their power to personal characteristics like charisma, interpersonal skills, hard work, or personal contacts rather than to organizational stature.

Intrigued by these differences, I interviewed some of the women respondents who described themselves as transformational. These discussions gave me a better picture of how these women view themselves as leaders and a greater understanding of the important ways in which their leadership style differs from the traditional command-and-control style. I call their leadership style "interactive leadership" because these women actively work to make their interactions with subordinates positive for everyone involved. More specifically, the women encourage participation, share power and information, enhance other people's self-worth, and get others excited about their work. All these things reflect their belief that allowing employees to contribute and to feel powerful and important is a win-win situation—good for the employees and for the organization.

INTERACTIVE LEADERSHIP

From my discussions with the women interviewees, several patterns emerged. The women leaders made frequent reference to their efforts to encourage participation and share power and information—two things that are often associated with participative management. But their self-description went beyond the usual definitions of participation. Much of what they described were attempts to energize followers. In general, these leaders believe that people perform best when they feel good about themselves and their work, and they try to create situations that contribute to that feeling.

Encourage Participation

Inclusion is at the core of interactive leadership. In describing nearly every aspect of management, the women interviewees made reference to trying to make people feel part of the organization. They try to instill this group identity in a variety of ways, including encouraging others to have a say in almost every aspect of work, from setting performance goals to determining strategy. To facilitate inclusion, they create mechanisms that get people to participate and they use a conversational style that sends signals inviting people to get involved. One example of the kinds of mechanisms that encourage participation is the "bridge club" that one interviewee, a group executive at a large East Coast financial firm, created. The club is an informal gathering of people who have information she needs but over whom she has no direct control. The word *bridge* describes the effort to bring together these "members" from different functions. The word *club* captures the relaxed atmosphere. Despite the fact that attendance at club meetings is voluntary and over and above the usual work demands, the interviewee said that those whose help she needs make the time to come. "They know their contributions are valued, and they appreciate the chance to exchange information across functional boundaries in an informal setting that's fun." She finds participation in the club more effective than memos.

Whether or not the women create special forums for people to interact, they try to make people feel included as a matter of course, often by trying to draw them into conversation or soliciting their opinions. Frieda Caplan, founder and CEO of Frieda's Finest, a California-based marketer and distributor of unusual fruits and vegetables, described an approach she uses typical of the other women interviewed: "When I face a tough decision, I always ask my employees, 'What would you do if you were me?' This approach generates good ideas and introduces my employees to the complexity of management decisions."

Of course, saying that you include others doesn't mean others necessarily feel included. The women acknowledge the possibility that their efforts to draw people in may be seen as symbolic, so they try to avoid that perception by acting on the input they receive. They ask for suggestions before they reach their own conclusions, and they test—and sometimes change—particular decisions before they implement them. These women use participation to clarify their own views by thinking things through out loud and to ensure that they haven't overlooked an important consideration.

The fact that many of the interviewees described their participatory style as coming "naturally" suggests that these leaders do not consciously adopt it for its business value. Yet they realize that encouraging participation has benefits. For one thing, making it easy for people to express their ideas helps ensure that decisions reflect as much information as possible. To some of the women, this point is just common sense. Susan S. Elliott, president and founder of Systems Service Enterprises, a St. Louis computer consulting company, expressed this view: "I can't come up with a plan and then ask those who manage the accounts to give me their reactions. They're the ones who really know the accounts. They have information I don't have. Without their input, I'd be operating in an ivory tower."

Participation also increases support for decisions ultimately reached and reduces the risk that ideas will be undermined by unexpected opposition. Claire Rothman, general manager of Great Western Forum, a large sports and entertainment arena in Los Angeles, spoke about the value of open disagreement. "When I know ahead of time that someone disagrees with a decision, I can work especially closely with that person to try to get his or her support."

Getting people involved also reduces the risk associated with having only one person handle a client, project, or investment. For Patricia M. Cloherty, senior vice president and general partner of Alan Patricof Associates, a New York venture capital firm, including people in decision making and planning gives investments longevity. If something happens to one person, others will be familiar enough with the situation to "adopt" the investment. That way, there are no orphans in the portfolio, and a knowledgeable second opinion is always available.

Like most who are familiar with participatory management, these women are aware that being inclusive also has its disadvantages. Soliciting ideas and information from others takes time, often requires giving up some control, opens the door to criticism, and exposes personal and turf conflicts. In addition, asking for ideas and information can be interpreted as not having answers.

Further, it cannot be assumed that everyone wants to participate. Some people prefer being told what to do. When Mary Jane Rynd was a partner in a Big Eight accounting firm in Arizona (she recently left to start her own company—Rynd, Carneal & Associates), she encountered such a person: "We hired this person from an out-of-state CPA firm because he was experienced and smart—and because it's always fun to hire someone away from another firm. But he was just too cynical to participate. He was suspicious of everybody. I tried everything to get him involved—including him in discussions and giving him pep talks about how we all work together. Nothing worked. He just didn't want to participate."

Like all those who responded to the survey, these women are comfortable using a variety of leadership styles. So when participation doesn't work, they act unilaterally. "I prefer participation," said Elliott, "but there are situations where time is short and I have to take the bull by the horns."

Share Power and Information

Soliciting input from other people suggests a flow of information from employees to the "boss." But part of making people feel included is knowing that open communication flows in two directions. These women say they willingly share power and information rather than guard it and they make apparent their reasoning behind decisions. While many leaders see information as power and power as a limited commodity to be coveted, the interviewees seem to be comfortable letting power and information change hands. As Adrienne Hall, vice chairman of Eisaman, Johns & Laws, a large West Coast advertising firm, said: "I know territories shift, so I'm not preoccupied with turf."

One example of power and information sharing is the open strategy sessions held by Debi Coleman, vice president of information systems and technology at Apple Computer. Rather than closeting a small group of key executives in her office to develop a strategy based on her own agenda, she holds a series of meetings over several days and allows a larger group to develop and help choose alternatives.

The interviewees believe that sharing power and information accomplishes several things. It creates loyalty by signaling to coworkers and subordinates that they are trusted and their ideas respected. It also sets an example for other people and therefore can enhance the general communication flow. And it increases the odds that leaders will hear about problems before they explode. Sharing power and information also gives employees and coworkers the wherewithal to reach conclusions, solve problems, and see the justification for decisions.

On a more pragmatic level, many employees have come to expect their bosses to be open and frank. They no longer accept being dictated to but want to be treated as individuals with minds of their own. As Elliott said, "I work with lots of people who are bright and intelligent, so I have to deal with them at an intellectual level. They're very logical, and they want to know the reasons for things. They'll buy in only if it makes sense."

In some cases, sharing information means simply being candid about work-related issues. In early 1990, when Elliott hired as employees many of the people she had been using as independent contractors, she knew the transition would be difficult for everyone. The number of employees nearly doubled overnight, and the nature of working relationships changed. "I warned everyone that we were in for some rough times and reminded them that we would be experiencing them together. I admitted that it would also be hard for me, and I made it clear that I wanted them to feel free to talk to me. I was completely candid and encouraged them to be honest with me. I lost some employees who didn't like the new relationships, but I'm convinced that being open helped me understand my employees better, and it gave them a feeling of support."

Like encouraging participation, sharing power and information has its risks. It allows for the possibility that people will reject, criticize, or otherwise challenge what the leader as to say or, more broadly, her authority. Also, employees get frustrated when leaders listen to—but ultimately reject—their ideas. Because information is a source of power, leaders who share it can be seen as naïve or needing to be liked. The interviewees have experienced some of these downsides but find the positives overwhelming.

Enhance the Self-Worth of Others

One of the by-products of sharing information and encouraging participation is that employees feel important. During the interviews, the women leaders discussed other ways they build a feeling of self-worth in coworkers and subordinates. They talked about giving others credit and praise and sending small signals of recognition. Most important, they expressed how they refrain from asserting their own superiority, which asserts the inferiority of others. All those I interviewed expressed clear aversion to behavior that sets them apart from others in the company—reserved parking places, separate dining facilities, pulling rank.

Examples of sharing and giving credit to others abound. Caplan, who has been the subject of scores of media reports hailing her innovation in the labeling of vegetables so consumers know what they are and how to cook them, originally got the idea from a farmer. She said that whenever someone raises the subject, she credits the farmer and downplays her role. Rothman is among the many note-writers; she writes them a personal note to tell them she noticed. Like many of the women I interviewed, she said she also makes a point of acknowledging good work by talking about it in front of others.

Bolstering coworkers and subordinates is especially important in businesses and jobs that tend to be hard on a person's ego. Investment banking is one example because of the long hours, high pressures, intense competition, and inevitability that some deals will fail. One interviewee in investment banking hosts dinners for her division, gives out gag gifts as party favors, passes out M&Ms at meetings, and throws parties "to celebrate ourselves." These things, she said, balance the anxiety that permeates the environment.

Rynd compensates for the negativity inherent in preparing tax returns: "In my business we have something called a query sheet, where the person who reviews the tax return writes down everything that needs to be corrected. Criticism is built into the system. But at the end of every review, I always include a positive comment—your work paper technique looks good, I appreciate the fact that you got this done on time, or something like that. It seems trivial, but it's one way to remind people that I recognize their good work and not just their shortcomings.

Energize Others

The women leaders spoke of their enthusiasm for work and how they spread their enthusiasm around to make work a challenge that is exhilarating and fun. The women leaders talked about it in those terms and claimed to use their enthusiasm to get others excited. As Rothman said, "There is rarely a person I can't motivate."

Enthusiasm was a dominant theme throughout the interviews. In computer consulting: "Because this business is on the forefront of technology, I'm sort of evangelistic about it, and I want other people to be as excited as I am." In venture capital: "You have to have a head of steam." In executive search: "Getting people excited is an important way to influence those you have no control over." Or in managing sports arenas: "My enthusiasm gets others excited. I infuse them with energy and make them see that even boring jobs contribute to the fun of working in a celebrity business."

Enthusiasm can sometimes be misunderstood. In conservative professions like investment banking, such an upbeat leadership style can be interpreted as cheerleading and can undermine credibility. In many cases, the women said they won and preserved their credibility by achieving results that could be measured easily. One of the women acknowledged that her colleagues don't understand or like her leadership style and have called it cheerleading, "But," she added, "in this business you get credibility from what you produce, and they love the profits I generate." While energy and enthusiasm can inspire some, it doesn't work for everyone. Even Rothman conceded, "Not everyone has a flame that can be lit."

PATHS OF LEAST RESISTANCE

Many of the women I interviewed said the behaviors and beliefs that underlie their leadership style come naturally to them. I attribute this to two things: their socialization and the career paths they have chosen. Although socialization patterns and career paths are changing, the average

age of the men and women who responded to the survey is 51—old enough to have had experiences that differed *because* of gender.

Until the 1960s, men and women received different signals about what was expected of them. To summarize a subject that many experts have explored in depth, women have been expected to be wives, mothers, community volunteers, teachers, and nurses. In all these roles, they are supposed to be cooperative, supportive, understanding, gentle, and to provide service to others. They are to derive satisfaction and a sense of self-esteem from helping others, including their spouses. While men have had to appear to be competitive, strong, tough, decisive, and in control, women have been allowed to be cooperative, emotional, supportive, and vulnerable. This may explain why women today are more likely than men to be interactive leaders.

Men and women have also had different career opportunities. Women were not expected to have careers, or at least not the same kinds of careers as men, so they either pursued different jobs or were simply denied opportunities men had. Women's career tracks have usually not included long series of organizational positions with formal authority and control of resources. Many women had their first work experience outside the home as volunteers. While some of the challenges they faced as managers in volunteer organizations are the same as those in any business, in many ways, leading volunteers is different because of the absence of concrete rewards like pay and promotion.

As women entered the business world, they tended to find themselves in positions consistent with the roles they played at home: in staff positions rather than in line positions, supporting the work of others, and in functions like communications or human resources where they had relatively small budgets and few people reporting directly to them.

The fact that most women have lacked formal authority over others and control over resources means that by default they have had to find other ways to accomplish their work. As it turns out, the behaviors that were natural and/or socially acceptable for them have been highly successful in at least some managerial settings.

What came easily to women turned out to be a survival tactic. Although leaders often begin their careers doing what comes naturally and what fits within the constraints of the job, they also develop their skills and styles over time. The women's use of interactive leadership has its roots in socialization, and the women interviewees firmly believe that it benefits their organizations. Through the course of their careers, they have gained conviction that their style is effective. In fact, for some, it was their own success that caused them to formulate their philosophies about what motivates people, how to make good decisions, and what it takes to maximize business performance.

They now have formal authority and control over vast resources, but still they see sharing power and information as an asset rather than a liability. They believe that although pay and promotion are necessary tools of management, what people really want is to feel that they are contributing to a higher purpose and that they have the opportunity as individuals to learn and grow. The women believe that employees and peers perform better when they feel they are part of an organization and can share it is success. Allowing them to get involved and to work to their potential is a way of maximizing their contributions and using human resources more efficiently.

ANOTHER KIND OF DIVERSITY

The IWF survey shows that a non-traditional leadership style can be effective in organizations that accept it. This lesson comes especially hard to those who think of the corporate world as a game of the fittest, where the fittest is always the strongest, toughest, most decisive, and powerful. Such a workplace seems to favor leaders who control people by controlling resources, and by controlling people, gain control of more resources. Asking for information and sharing decision-making power can be seen as having serious disadvantages, but what is a disadvantage under one set of circumstances can be an advantage under another. The "best" leadership style depends on the organizational context.

Only one of the women interviewees is in a traditional, large-scale company. More typically, the women's organizations are medium-sized and tend to have experienced fast growth and fast change. They demand performance and/or have a high proportion of professional workers. These organizations seem to create opportunities for women and are hospitable to those who use a nontraditional management style.

The degree of growth or change in an organization is an important factor in creating opportunities for women. When change is rampant, everything is up for grabs, and crises are frequent. Crises are generally not desirable, but they do create opportunities for people to prove themselves. Many of the women interviewees said they got their first break because their organizations were in turmoil.

Fast-changing environments also play havoc with tradition. Coming up through the ranks and being part of an established network is no longer important. What is important is how you perform. Also, managers in such environments are open to new solutions, new structures, and new ways of leading.

The fact that many of the women respondents are in organizations that have clear performance standards suggests that they have gained credibility and legitimacy by achieving results. In investment banking, venture capital, accounting, and executive placement, for instance, individual performance is easy to measure.

A high proportion of young professional workers—increasingly typical of organizations—is also a factor in some women's success. Young, educated professionals impose special requirements on their organizations. They demand to participate and contribute. In some cases, they have knowledge or talents their bosses don't have. If they are good performers, they have many employment options. It is easy to imagine that these professionals will respond to leaders who are inclusive and open, who enhance the self-worth of others, and who create a fun work environment. Interactive leaders are likely to win the cooperation needed to achieve their goals.

Interactive leadership has proved to be effective, perhaps even advantageous, in organizations in which the women I interviewed have succeeded. As the work force increasingly demands participation and the economic environment increasingly requires rapid change, interactive leadership may emerge as the management style of choice for many organizations. For interactive leadership to take root more broadly, however, organizations must be willing to question the notion that the traditional command-and-control leadership style that has brought success in earlier decades is the only way to get results. This may be hard in some organizations, especially those with long histories of male-oriented, command-and-control leadership. Changing these organizations will not be easy. The fact that women are more likely than men to be interactive leaders raises the risk that these companies will perceive interactive leadership as "feminine" and automatically resist it.

Linking interactive leadership directly to being female is a mistake. We know that women are capable of making their way through corporations by adhering to the traditional corporate model and that they can wield power in way similar to men. Indeed, some women may prefer that style. We also know from the survey findings that some men use the transformational leadership style.

Large, established organizations should expand their definition of effective leadership. If they were to do that, several things might happen, including the disappearance of the glass ceiling and the creation of a wider path for all sorts of executives—men and women—to attain positions of leadership. Widening the path will free potential leaders to lead in ways that play to their individual strengths. Then the newly recognized interactive leadership style can be valued and rewarded as highly as the command-and-control style has been for decades. By valuing a diversity of leadership styles, organizations will find the strength and flexibility to survive in a highly competitive, increasingly diverse economic environment.

Note

i. Transactional and transformational leadership were first conceptualized by James McGregor Burns in *Leadership* (New York: Harper & Row, 1978) and later by Bernard Bass in *Leadership and Performance Beyond Expectations* (New York: Free Press, 1985).

White Privilege and Male Privilege: A Personal Account of Coming to See Correspondences Through Work in Women's Studies

PEGGY MCINTOSH   *Privilege*

Through work to bring materials and perspectives from Women's Studies into the rest of the curriculum, I have often noticed men's unwillingness to grant that they are over-privileged in the curriculum, even though they may grant that women are disadvantaged. Denials which amount to taboos surround the subject of advantages which men gain from women's disadvantages. These denials protect male privilege from being fully recognized, acknowledged, lessened, or ended.

Thinking through unacknowledged male privilege as a phenomenon with a life of its own, I realized that since hierarchies in our society are interlocking, there was most likely a phenomenon of white privilege which was similarly denied and protected but alive and real in its effects. As a white person, I realized I had been taught about racism as something which puts others at a disadvantage, but had been taught not to see one of its corollary aspects, white privilege, which puts me at an advantage.

I think whites are carefully taught not to recognize white privilege, as males are taught not to recognize male privilege. So I have begun in an untutored way to ask what it is like to have white privilege. This paper is a partial record of my personal observations, and not a scholarly analysis. It is based on my daily experiences within my particular circumstances.

I have come to see white privilege as an invisible package of unearned assets which I can count on cashing in each day, but about which I was "meant" to remain oblivious. White privilege is like an invisible weightless knapsack of special provisions, assurances, tools, maps, guides, codebooks, passports, visas, clothes, compass, emergency gear, and blank checks.

Since I have had trouble facing white privilege and describing its results in my life, I saw parallels here with men's reluctance to acknowledge male privilege. Only rarely will a man go beyond acknowledging that women are disadvantaged to acknowledging that men have unearned advantage, or that unearned privilege has not been good for men's development as human beings, or for society's development, or that privilege systems might ever be challenged and changed.

I will review here several types or layers of denial which I see at work protecting, and preventing awareness about, entrenched male privilege. Then I will draw parallels, from my own experience, with the denials which veil the facts of white privilege. Finally, I will list 46 ordinary and daily ways in which I experience white privilege within my life and its particular social and political frameworks.

Writing this paper has been difficult, despite warm receptions for the talks on which it is based.[1] For describing white privilege makes one newly accountable. As we in Women's Studies work to reveal male privilege and ask men to give up some of their power, so one who writes about having white privilege must ask, "Having described it, what will I do to lessen or end it?"

The denial of men's overprivileged status takes many forms in discussions of curriculum change work. Some claim that men must be central in the curriculum because they have done most of what is important or distinctive in life or in civilization. Some recognize sexism in the curriculum but deny that it makes male students seem unduly important in life. Others agree that certain individual thinkers are blindly male-oriented but deny that there is any systemic tendency in disciplinary frameworks or epistemology to overempower men as a group. Those men who do grant that male privilege takes institutionalized and embedded forms are still likely to deny that male hegemony has opened doors for them personally. Virtually all men deny that male overreward alone can explain men's centrality in all the inner sanctums of our most powerful institutions. Moreover, those few who will acknowledge that male privilege systems have overempowered them usually end up doubting that these privilege systems could ever be dismantled. They may say they will work to improve women's status in society or in the university, but they can't or won't support the idea of lessening men's. In curricular terms, this is the point at which men say that they regret they cannot use any of the interesting new scholarship on women because the syllabus is full. When the talk turns to giving men less cultural room, even the most thoughtful and fair-minded of the men I know well tend to reflect or fall back on conservative assumptions about the inevitability of present gender relations and distributions of power, calling on precedent or sociobiology and psychobiology to demonstrate that male domination is natural and follows inevitably from evolutionary pressures. Others resort to arguments from "experience," religion, social responsibility or wishing and dreaming.

After I realized, through faculty development work in Women's Studies, the extent to which men work from a base of unacknowledged privilege, I understood that much of their oppressiveness was unconscious. Then I remembered the frequent charges from women of color that white women whom they encounter are oppressive. I began to understand why we are justly seen as oppressive, even when we don't see ourselves that way. At the very least, obliviousness of one's privileged state can make a person or group irritating to be with. I began to count the ways in which I enjoy unearned skin privilege and have been conditioned into oblivion about its existence, unable to see that it put me "ahead" in any way, or put my people ahead, overrewarding us and yet also paradoxically damaging us, or that it could or should be changed.

My schooling gave me no training in seeing myself as an oppressor, as an unfairly advantaged person, or as a participant in a damaged culture. I was taught to see myself as an individual whose moral state depended on her individual moral will. At school, we were not taught about slavery in any depth; we were not taught to see slaveholders as damaged people. Slaves were seen as the only group at risk of being dehumanized. My schooling followed the pattern which Elizabeth Minnich has pointed out: whites are taught to think of their lives as morally neutral, normative, and average, and also ideal, so that when we work to benefit others, this is seen as work which will allow "them" to be more like "us." I think many of us know how obnoxious this attitude can be in men.

After frustration with men who would not recognize male privilege, I decided to try to work on myself at least by identifying some of the daily effects of white privilege in my life. It is crude work, at this stage, but I will give here a list of special circumstances and conditions I experience which I did not earn but which I have been made to feel are mine by birth, by citizenship, and by virtue of being a conscientious law-abiding "normal" person of good will. I have chosen those conditions which I think in my case attach somewhat more to skin-color privilege than to class, religion, ethnic status, or geographical location, though of course all these other factors are intricately intertwined. As far as I can see, my African-American co-workers, friends, and acquaintances with whom I come into daily or frequent contact in this particular time, place, and line of work cannot count on most of these conditions.

1. I can if I wish arrange to be in the company of people of my race most of the time.
2. I can avoid spending time with people whom I was trained to mistrust and who have learned to mistrust my kind or me.
3. If I should need to move, I can be pretty sure of renting or purchasing housing in an area which I can afford and in which I would want to live.
4. I can be pretty sure that my neighbors in such a location will be neutral or pleasant to me.
5. I can go shopping alone most of the time, pretty well assured that I will not be followed or harassed.
6. I can turn on the television or open to the front page of the newspaper and see people of my race widely represented.
7. When I am told about our national heritage or about "civilization," I am shown that people of my color made it what it is.
8. I can be sure that my children will be given curricular materials that testify to the existence of their race.
9. If I want to, I can be pretty sure of finding a publisher for this piece on white privilege.
10. I can be pretty sure of having my voice heard in a group in which I am the only member of my race.
11. I can be casual about whether or not to listen to another woman's voice in a group in which she is the only member of her race.
12. I can go into a music shop and count on finding the music of my race represented, into a supermarket and find the staple foods which fit with my cultural traditions, or into a hairdresser's shop and find someone who can cut my hair.
13. Whether I use checks, credit cards, or cash, I can count on my skin color not to work against the appearance of financial reliability.
14. I can arrange to protect my children most of the time from people who might not like them.
15. I do not have to educate my children to be aware of systemic racism for their own daily physical protection.
16. I can be pretty sure that my children's teachers and employers will tolerate them if they fit school and workplace norms; my chief worries about them do not concern others' attitudes toward their race.
17. I can talk with my mouth full and not have people put this down to my color.
18. I can swear, dress in second-hand clothes, or not answer letters without having people attribute these choices to the bad morals, poverty, or the illiteracy of my race.
19. I can speak in public to a powerful male group without putting my race on trial.
20. I can do well in a challenging situation without being called a credit to my race.
21. I am never asked to speak for all the people of my racial group.
22. I can remain oblivious of the language and customs of persons of color who constitute the world's majority without feeling in my culture any penalty for such oblivion.
23. I can criticize our government and talk about how much I fear its policies and behavior without being seen as a cultural outsider.
24. I can be pretty sure that if I ask to talk to "the person in charge," I will be facing a person of my race.
25. If a traffic cop pulls me over or if the IRS audits my tax return, I can be sure I haven't been singled out because of my race.
26. I can easily buy posters, post-cards, picture books, greeting cards, dolls, toys, and children's magazines featuring people of my race.

27. I can go home from most meetings of organizations I belong to feeling somewhat tied in, rather than isolated, out-of-place, outnumbered, unheard, held at a distance, or feared.

28. I can be pretty sure that an argument with a colleague of another race is more likely to jeopardize her chances for advancement than to jeopardize mine.

29. I can be pretty sure that if I argue for the promotion of a person of another race, or a program centering on race, this is not likely to cost me heavily within my present setting, even if my colleagues disagree with me.

30. If I declare there is a racial issue at hand, or there isn't a racial issue at hand, my race will lend me more credibility for either position than a person of color will have.

31. I can choose to ignore developments in minority writing and minority activist programs, or disparage them, or learn from them, but in any case, I can find ways to be more or less protected from negative consequences of any of these choices.

32. My culture gives me little fear about ignoring the perspectives and powers of peoples of other races.

33. I am not made acutely aware that my shape, bearing, or body odor will be taken as a reflection on my race.

34. I can worry about racism without being seen as self-interested or self-seeking.

35. I can take a job with an affirmative action employer without having my co-workers on the job suspect that I got it because of my race.

36. If my day, week, or year is going badly, I need not ask of each negative episode or situation whether it has racial overtones.

37. I can be pretty sure of finding people who would be willing to talk with me and advise me about my next steps, professionally.

38. I can think over many options, social, political, imaginative, or professional, without asking whether a person of my race would be accepted or allowed to do what I want to do.

39. I can be late to a meeting without having the lateness reflect on my race.

40. I can choose public accommodation without fearing that people of my race cannot get in or will be mistreated in the places I have chosen.

41. I can be sure that if I need legal or medical help, my race will not work against me.

42. I can arrange my activities so that I will never have to experience feelings of rejection owing to my race.

43. If I have low credibility as a leader, I can be sure that my race is not the problem.

44. I can easily find academic courses and institutions which give attention only to people of my race.

45. I can expect figurative language and imagery in all of the arts to testify to experiences of my race.

46. I can choose blemish cover or bandages in "flesh" color and have them more or less match my skin.

I repeatedly forgot each of the realizations on this list until I wrote it down. For me, white privilege has turned out to be an elusive and fugitive subject. The pressure to avoid it is great, for in facing it I must give up the myth of meritocracy. If these things are true, this is not such a free country; one's life is not what one makes it; many doors open for certain people through no virtues of their own. These perceptions mean also that my moral condition is not what I had been led to believe. The appearance of being a good citizen rather than a troublemaker comes in large part from having all sorts of doors open automatically because of my color.

A further paralysis of nerve comes from literary silence protecting privilege. My clearest memories of finding such analysis are in Lillian Smith's unparalleled *Killers of the Dream* and Margaret Andersen's review of Karen and Mamie Fields' *Lemon Swamp*. Smith, for example, wrote about walking toward black children on the street and knowing they would step into the gutter; Andersen contrasted the pleasure which she, as a white child, took on summer driving trips to the south with Karen Fields' memories of driving in a closed car stocked with all necessities lest, in stopping, her black family should suffer "insult, or worse." Adrienne Rich also recognizes and writes about daily experiences of privilege, but in my observation, white women's writing in this area is far more often on systemic racism than on our daily lives as light-skinned women.[2]

In unpacking this invisible knapsack of white privilege, I have listed conditions of daily experience which I once took for granted as neutral, normal, and universally available to everybody, just as I once thought of a male-focused curriculum as the neutral or accurate account which can speak for all. Nor did I think of any of these perquisites as bad for the holder. I now think that we need a more finely differentiated taxonomy of privilege, for some of these varieties are only what one would want for everyone in a just society, and others give license to be ignorant, oblivious, arrogant and destructive. Before proposing some more finely tuned categorization, I will make some observations about the general effects of these conditions on my life and expectations.

In this potpourri of examples, some privileges make me feel at home in the world. Others allow me to escape penalties or dangers which others suffer. Through some, I escape fear, anxiety, or a sense of not being welcome or not being real. Some keep me from having to hide, to be in disguise, to feel sick or crazy, to negotiate each transaction from the position of being an outsider or, within my group, a person who is suspected of having too close links with a dominant culture. Most keep me from having to be angry.

I see a pattern running through the matrix of white privilege, a pattern of assumptions which were passed on to me as a white person. There was one main piece of cultural turf; it was my own turf, and I was among those who could control the turf. I could measure up to the cultural standards and take advantage of the many options I saw around me to make what the culture would call a success of my life. My skin color was an asset for any move I was educated to want to make. I could think of myself as "belonging" in major ways, and of making social systems work for me. I could freely disparage, fear, neglect, or be oblivious to anything outside of the dominant cultural forms. Being of the main culture, I could also criticize it fairly freely. My life was reflected back to me frequently enough so that I felt, with regard to my race, if not to my sex, like one of the real people.

Whether through the curriculum or in the newspaper, the television, the economic system, or the general look of people in the streets, we received daily signals and indications that my people counted, and that others either didn't exist or must be trying, not very successfully, to be like people of my race. We were given cultural permission not to hear voices of people of other races, or a tepid cultural tolerance for hearing or acting on such voices. I was also raised not to suffer seriously from anything which darker-skinned people might say about my group, "protected," though perhaps I should more accurately say prohibited, through the habits of my economic class and social group, from living in racially mixed groups or being reflective about interactions between people of differing races.

In proportion as my racial group was being made confident, comfortable, and oblivious, other groups were likely being made inconfident, uncomfortable, and alienated. Whiteness protected me from many kinds of hostility, distress, and violence, which I was being subtly trained to visit in turn upon people of color.

For this reason, the word "privilege" now seems to me misleading. Its connotations are too positive to fit the conditions and behaviors which "privilege systems" produce. We usually think of privilege as being a favored state, whether earned or conferred by birth or luck. School graduates are reminded that they are privileged and urged to use their (enviable) assets well. The word "privilege" carries the connotation of being something everyone must want. Yet some of the conditions I have described here work to systemically overempower certain groups. Such privilege simply confers dominance, gives permission to control, because of one's race or sex. The kind of privilege which gives license to some people to be, at best, thoughtless and, at worst, murderous should not continue to be referred to as a desirable attribute. Such "privilege" may be widely desired without being in any way beneficial to the whole society.

Moreover, though "privilege" may confer power, it does not confer moral strength. Those who do not depend on conferred dominance have traits and qualities which may never develop in those who do. Just as Women's Studies courses indicate that women survive their political circumstances to lead lives which hold the human race together, so "underprivileged" people of color who are the world's majority have survived their oppression and lived survivors' lives from which the white global minority can and must learn. In some groups, those dominated have actually become strong through not having all of these unearned advantages, and this gives them a great deal to teach the others. Members of so-called privileged groups can seem foolish, ridiculous, infantile or dangerous by contrast.

I want, then, to distinguish between earned strength and unearned power conferred systemically. Power from unearned privilege can look like strength when it is in fact permission to escape or to dominate. But not all of the privileges on my list are inevitably damaging. Some, like the expectation that neighbors will be decent to you, or that your race will not count against you in court, should be the norm in a just society and should be considered as the entitlement of everyone. Others, like the privilege not to listen to less powerful people, distort the humanity of the holders as well as the ignored groups. Still others, like finding one's staple foods everywhere, may be a function of being a member of a numerical majority in the population. Others have to do with not having to labor under pervasive negative stereotyping and mythology.

We might at least start by distinguishing between positive advantages which we can work to spread, to the point where they are not advantages at all but simply part of the normal civic and social fabric, and negative types of advantage which unless rejected will always reinforce our present hierarchies. For example, the positive "privilege" of belonging, the feeling that one belongs within the human circle, as Native Americans say, fosters development and should not be seen as privilege for a few. It is, let us say, an entitlement which none of us should have to earn; ideally it is an un-earned entitlement. At present, since only a few have it, it is an unearned advantage for them. The negative "privilege" which gave me cultural per-mission not to take darker-skinned Others seriously can be seen as arbi-trarily conferred dominance and should not be desirable for anyone. This paper results from a process of coming to see that some of the power which I originally saw as attendant on being a human being in the U.S. consisted in unearned advantage and conferred dominance, as well as other kinds of special circumstances not universally taken for granted.

In writing this paper I have also realized that white identity and status (as well as class identity and status) give me considerable power to choose whether to broach this subject and its trouble. I can pretty well decide whether to disappear and avoid and not listen and escape the dislike I may engender in other people through this essay, or interrupt, take over, domi-nate, preach, direct, criticize, or control to some extent what goes on in re-action to it. Being white, I am given considerable power to escape many kinds of danger or penalty as well as to choose which risks I want to take.

There is an analogy here, once again, with Women's Studies. Our male colleagues do not have a great deal to lose in supporting Women's Studies, but they do not have a great deal to lose if they oppose it either. They sim-ply have the power to decide whether to commit themselves to more equi-table distributions of power. They will probably feel few penalties whatever the choice they make; they do not seem, in any obvious short-term sense, the ones at risk, though they and we are all at risk because of the behaviors which have been rewarded in them.

Through Women's Studies work I have met very few men who are truly distressed about systemic, unearned male advantage and conferred domi-nance. And so one question for me and others like me is whether we will be like them, or whether we will get truly distressed, even outraged, about unearned race advantage and conferred dominance and if so, what we will do to lessen them. In any case, we need to do more work in identifying how they actually affect our daily lives. We need more down-to-earth writing by people about these taboo subjects. We need more understanding of the ways in which white "privilege" damages white people, for these are not the same ways in which it damages the victimized. Skewed white psyches are an in-separable part of the picture, though I do not want to confuse the kinds of damage done to the holders of special assets and to those who suffer the deficits. Many, perhaps most, of our white students in the U.S. think that racism doesn't affect them because they are not people of color; they do not see "whiteness" as a racial identity. Many men likewise do not see themselves as having gendered identities. Insisting on the universal effects of "privilege" systems, then, becomes one of our chief tasks, and being more explicit about the particular effects in particular contexts is another. Men need to join us in this work.

In addition, since race and sex are not the only advantaging systems at work, we need to similarly examine the daily experience of having age ad-vantage, or ethnic advantage, or physical ability, or advantage related to na-tionality, religion, or sexual orientation. Professor Marnie Evans suggested to me that in many ways the list I made also applies directly to heterosexual privilege. This is a still more taboo subject than race privilege: the daily ways in which heterosexual privilege makes married persons comfortable or powerful, providing supports, assets, approvals, and rewards to those who live or expect to live in heterosexual pairs. Unpacking that content is still more difficult, owing to the deeper imbeddedness of heterosexual advantage and dominance, and stricter taboos surrounding these.

But to start such an analysis I would put this observation from my own experience: The fact that I live under the same roof with a man triggers all kinds of societal assumptions about my worth, politics, life, and values, and triggers a host of unearned advantages and powers. After recasting many elements from the original list I would add further observations like these:

1. My children do not have to answer questions about why I live with my partner (my husband).
2. I have no difficulty finding neighborhoods where people approve of our household.
3. My children are given texts and classes which implicitly support our kind of family unit and do not turn them against my choice of domestic partnership.
4. I can travel alone or with my husband without expecting embarrassment or hostility in those who deal with us.
5. Most people I meet will see my marital arrangements as an asset to my life or as a favorable comment on my likability, my competence, or my mental health.
6. I can talk about the social events of a weekend without fearing most listeners' reactions.
7. I will feel welcomed and "normal" in the usual walks of public life, institutional, and social.
8. In many contexts, I am seen as "all right" in daily work on women because I do not live chiefly with women.

Difficulties and dangers surrounding the task of finding parallels are many. Since racism, sexism, and heterosexism are not the same, the advantaging associated with them should not be seen as the same. In addition, it is hard to disentangle aspects of unearned advantage which rest more on social class, economic class, race, religion, sex and ethnic identity than on other factors. Still, all of the oppressions are interlocking, as the Combahee River Collective statement of 1977 continues to remind us eloquently.[3]

One factor seems clear about all of these interlocking oppressions. They take both active forms which we can see and embedded forms which as a member of the dominant group one is taught not to see.[4] In my class and place, I did not see myself as racist because I was taught to recognize racism only in individual acts of meanness by members of my group, never in invisible systems conferring unsought racial dominance on my group from birth. Likewise, we are taught to think that sexism or heterosexism is carried on only through individual acts of discrimination, meanness, or cruelty toward women, gays, and lesbians, rather than in invisible systems conferring unsought dominance on certain groups. Disapproving of the systems won't be enough to change them. I was taught to think that racism could end if white individuals changed their attitudes; many men think sexism can be ended by individual changes in daily behavior toward women. But a man's sex provides advantage for him whether or not he approves of the way in which dominance has been conferred on his group. A "white" skin in the

United States opens many doors for whites whether or not we approve of the way dominance has been conferred on us. Individual acts can palliate, but cannot end, these problems. To redesign social systems we need first to acknowledge their colossal unseen dimensions. The silences and denials surrounding privilege are the key political tool here. They keep the thinking about equality or equity incomplete, protecting unearned advantage and conferred dominance by making these taboo subjects. Most talk by whites about equal opportunity seems to me now to be about equal opportunity to try to get into a position of dominance while denying that systems of dominance exist.

It seems to me that obliviousness about white advantage, like obliviousness about male advantage, is kept strongly inculturated in the United States so as to maintain the myth of meritocracy, the myth that democratic choice is equally available to all. Keeping most people unaware that freedom of confident action is there for just a small number of people props up those in power and serves to keep power in the hands of the same groups that have most of it already. Though systemic change takes many decades, there are pressing questions for me and I imagine for some others like me if we raise our daily consciousness on the perquisites of being light-skinned. What will we do with such knowledge? As we know from watching men, it is an open question whether we will choose to use unearned advantage to weaken hidden systems of advantage, and whether we will use any of our arbitrarily awarded power to try to reconstruct power systems on a broader base.

Notes

1. This paper was funded by the Anna Wilder Phelps Fund through the generosity of Anna Emery Hanson. I have appreciated commentary on this paper from the Working Papers Committee of the Wellesley College Center for Research on Women, from members of the Dodge seminar, and from many individuals, including Margaret Andersen, Sorel Berman, Joanne Braxton, Johnella Butler, Sandra Dickerson, Marnie Evans, Beverly Guy-Sheftall, Sandra Harding, Eleanor Hinton Hoytt, Pauline Houston, Paul Lauter, Joyce Miller, Mary Norris, Gloria Oden, Beverly Smith, and John Walter.

2. This paper was presented at the Virginia Women's Studies Association conference in Richmond in April, 1986, and the American Educational Research Association conference in Boston in October, 1986, and discussed with two groups of participants in the Dodge Seminars for Secondary School Teachers in New York and Boston in the spring of 1987.

3. Margaret Andersen, "Race and the Social Science Curriculum: A Teaching and Learning Discussion." *Radical Teacher*, November, 1984, pp. 17–20. Lillian Smith, *Killers of the Dream*, New York, 1949.

4. "A Black Feminist Statement," The Combahee River Collective, pp. 13–22. In G. Hull, P. Scott, B. Smith, eds., *All the Women Are White, All the Blacks Are Men, But Some of Us Are Brave: Black Women's Studies*. Old Westbury, N.Y.: The Feminist Press, 1982.

PART 4

International Business

INTRODUCTION

CHAPTER 11: ETHICAL RELATIVISM

Ethical relativism is the belief that there are deeply irresolvable value differences, because there are no ultimate, universal, or absolute ethical principles that apply to everyone and to every situation. As James Rachels notes in "The Challenge of Cultural Relativism," the ethical relativist is someone who believes that what is really right or wrong is what the culture says is right or wrong. Since there are no universal standards, one can neither judge the moral principles of another culture nor adjudicate between two clashing principles.

Ethical relativism frequently uses evidence provided by a closely related point of view known as *cultural relativism.* Cultural relativism emphasizes how people reason differently about morality in different cultures because of different customs, religious traditions, methods of education, or beliefs about the world. But it requires an additional step to argue from a description of cultural relativism to a position of ethical cultural relativism. After noting the fact of cultural relativism and moral diversity, ethical cultural relativism holds that no ethical assertion or set of assertions has any greater claim to objectivity or universality than any other. From the obvious empirical differences between cultures, an ethical relativist may go further to argue that all values, and thus all value judgments, are relative to particular contexts. Therefore, the truth of ethical statements such as "bribery is wrong" is determined solely by the beliefs of the culture espousing or denying those claims. The case study "What Price Safety?" brings up the question of how to enforce what seem to be basically universal, morally minimal standards of worker safety in a culture where local customs and value differences appear to question that standard. If values are merely relative, there is no satisfactory cross-cultural resolution to this issue.

Questions of ethical relativism challenge managers on an almost daily basis. The end of the cold war has seen a massive growth of international business. Almost every corporation of any size conducts business transnationally. As managers increasingly work in international settings they face a multitude of questions of value differences. The "Facing Face" case study illustrates the difficulties managers face in deciding between home and host-country practices. It is a case about truth-telling and integrity, about whether the context— that is, a particular Asian country called "Chikorpan"—makes it something less than a lie when terminating a substandard employee. Is it a lie in Chikorpan to make vague reference to the possibility of re-employment—even though the employee himself will not believe it? Is it ethically wrong when the underlying aim of a "white lie" is to help the employee "save face" in his home village, especially when in that country saving face is far more important than in the United States?

The development of transnational corporations that function globally without a "home country" of origin further complicates the job of managers. If there is no home country whose values and mores serve as a basis for ethical judgments, the difficulty of sorting out practices and values of any particular country and between countries in transnational exchanges becomes exacerbated.

The relativity of value judgments can be an issue within a culture, as well. One can argue that values are not merely relative to particular cultures but also relative to particular spheres of activity. For example, although tackling in football is part of that game, it is not an accepted practice in other social interactions. If business itself is a game, as Albert Carr argues in Part 1, then that sphere of activity has certain conventions and values that might not be acceptable in other spheres. According to this line of reasoning, the values of the medical community might differ from, say, those of certain religious groups, or the values espoused by corporations might differ from, and even conflict with, ideals espoused by nonprofit organizations. One could extend this argument to each of us. My religious values, for example, might clash with my work ethics. The standards of behavior I adhered to as a teenager might be different from those I hold today.

One of the ways to challenge relativism, then, is to show that if all moral judgments are relative, this leads ultimately to the dead end of subjectivism. If all values are subject to change and challenge, even my own, then there is no basis for moral judgments except what one feels in a particular instance, a feeling that has no objective basis. Another and more obvious way to challenge ethical relativism is to argue that there are some values that are universal, that is, that apply in every case without exception. But while philosophers such as James Rachels and Richard De George find relativism implausible, they do recognize the difficulty of isolating universal truths. What those universal truths or standards are has been subject to philosophical debate since the beginning of human thinking, because the fallibility of human nature and diversity of human cultures preclude a final determination of absolute moral standards.

How can this issue of differing cultural traditions be adjudicated? The process of moral reasoning involves making judgments that set or appeal to standards that cross individual, institutional, and even cultural boundaries. When one asserts that slavery is wrong, one ordinarily means that it was always wrong, and will always be wrong, no matter the circumstances. We appeal to notions of autonomy, community, freedom, and human rights in making such judgments, even though we have no final absolute knowledge of their universal validity. What we are doing is offering these values as candidates for universal moral standards, ones that we continue to challenge and refine. The United Nations Declaration of Human Rights sets out a list of basic rights as standards, as candidates for universal truths to be tested and perhaps even restated as we appeal to this set in making cross-cultural moral judgments and trying to resolve value differences in universal settings.

Thomas Donaldson and Thomas Dunfee's article, "A Social Contracts Approach to Business Ethics," seeks to facilitate the moral reasoning of global business managers. The authors argue that one way to resolve ethical conflicts between cultures is to understand the implicit understandings or "contracts" that govern the moral relationships among industries, companies, and economic systems. While recognizing that certain social contracts that arise from specific cultural or geographic traditions have legitimacy, Donaldson and Dunfee place a limit on the moral authority of these "micro" contracts. All such contracts are subordinated to "hypernorms," developed in a hypothetical "macro" social contract. As long as a micro contract does not conflict with the hypernorms, that micro contract may be viewed as morally legitimate. When conflicts in these two contracts arise, however, the hypernorms prevail—no matter how completely the local community believes in the micro contract values.

An example of a potential hypernorm is reflected in the challenge of bribery. As a result of incidents involving sensitive payments, in 1977 the U.S. Congress passed the Foreign Corrupt Practices Act (FCPA). The FCPA is an attempt to legislate standards of conduct for multinational corporations by making it a crime for United States-based multinationals to offer or to acquiesce to sensitive payments to officials of foreign governments. The Act implies that what U.S. citizens in this country think is morally right should apply to their dealings in other countries. Since 1977 more than twenty of the world's most developed nations adopted the OECD Convention Against Bribery that mirrors the FCPA legislation in the United States. Ethical relativists would criticize both the FCPA and the OECD Convention, since according to them, value differences between cultures preclude the justification of exporting the laws or moral principles of one country to another.

CHAPTER 12: BUSINESS VALUES AWAY FROM HOME

In the case study, "Gift Giving and the African Elder," business executives from the United States confront an issue of bribery. They visit a senior cabinet minister in order to help to expand their business in a rapidly liberalizing sub-Saharan African economy, but learn in the process that it is an established custom there for visitors to give gifts to senior African elders. The case forces you to ask what you would do if you were in a similar situation. Would you follow the custom of giving a gift to the African elder?

Background social and political institutions often confound cross-cultural ethical pronouncements. As Richard De George argues, in "International Business Ethics and Incipient Capitalism," these background conditions often provide practical difficulties in specifying particular ethical principles that apply universally. "Some actions," he writes, "are wrong no matter which system of background institutions are in place." Still, ethical issues in business are always embedded in a socioeconomic and political background that helps to form and constrain moral decision making. Present circumstances in countries such as Russia and China suggest that some policies or actions will appropriately be judged unethical when viewed from the assumption that socialist or communist background conditions are operative. The same policies or actions might appropriately be viewed as ethically justifiable when viewed from the assumption that free market conditions are operative. China's one-child-per-family policy might be one such example.

The case study "Alchemist's Dream Come True" illustrates another conundrum of clashing international norms, this time involving health and safety. It describes how when the Great Lakes Chemical Corporation bought control of the world's biggest maker of lead additives for gasoline, it remained legal in many developing countries to make and sell leaded gasoline—despite the fact that lead exposure has been shown to have extremely harmful health effects. Under what conditions, if any, should legal products that are being phased out of the developed world be sold to poorer nations? Does it make any difference that the product the company sells is enormously profitable? And that if the company refuses to sell it, other companies will rush in to take its place? Which ethical frameworks or ideas might apply to this case?

In his article, "Values in Tension: Ethics Away from Home," Thomas Donaldson examines a very similar issue. He looks at the range of problems that arise when moral and legal standards vary between countries, especially between a multinational corporation's home and host countries. How, he asks, should highly placed multinational managers, typically schooled in home-country moral traditions, reconcile conflicts between their values and the practices of the host country? If host-country standards appear lower than home-country ones, should the multinational manager always take the "high road" and implement home-country standards? Or, does the "high road" sometimes signal a failure to respect cultural diversity and national integrity? The answer may be fairly obvious in the instance of South Africa (where acquiescing to racism and discrimination would surely be immoral), but would the answer be so obvious in other instances involving differences in wage rates, pollution standards, or "sensitive payments"?

To deal with these complex issues, Donaldson appeals to what he calls an ethical threshold, or a set of core values that cross cultural and country boundaries and are shared by most religious traditions. Respect for human dignity whether in a community or as individuals, respect for basic rights, and good citizenship are three values that set basic standards for developing corporate guidelines for conduct in international settings as well as "at home." These core values are not maximal absolutes. Rather, they set the moral minimums for integrity and business practice. At the same time, Donaldson recognizes that there are cultural differences and conflicts of traditions that cannot be adjudicated. Thus there is a "moral free space" within countries that allows for differences of business practice without challenging core values. Are core values at stake in the Great Lake Company's decision? Or are there merely less critical cultural differences between the United States and developing countries that allow a moral free space in which the company may operate?

Chapter 11

Ethical Relativism

Case Study

What Price Safety?

This case takes place in 1995 in Nambu, an Asian nation with a centuries-old philosophical and ethical tradition emphasizing duty and harmony in all human relationships. In 1969 Motorola formed a joint venture (JV) partnership with a Nambunese multinational company to produce microelectronic products at a new facility in the city of Anzen, Nambu. Motorola's ownership share was 60 percent; the local partner company's, 40 percent. Many of the Anzen facility's key managerial personnel were Motorolans, while the lower-level associates were Nambunese citizens and employees of the partner company.

From its very beginning, the Anzen facility developed a strong tradition of safety consciousness. Even the most casual visitor to the Anzen plant would notice numerous signs and displays, in both Nambunese and English, urging associates to "Think and Act Safely," "Wear Protective Eyeglasses," "Report Dangerous Situations," etc.

Motorola also had other operations in Nambu. In charge of Human Resources for all these operations, including the Anzen joint venture, was Canadian Stan Stark, 47. Stan was based at Motorola headquarters, 300 kilometers north of Anzen. Since first assuming his position five years ago, Stan had made safety one of his top priorities. He took pride in the fact that during this period he had further reduced the Anzen facility's already-low rate of accidents and lost workdays.

Sharing in his pride was a Motorolan of Dutch nationality, Henk Van Dyke, 38. Henk had been at Anzen for three years, assigned by Motorola to serve as the Human Resources manager for the entire JV facility. He enjoyed working in Nambu, but was somewhat handicapped because he did not speak Nambunese. Henk reported to Stan.

From R.S. Moorthy, Richard T. De George, Thomas Donaldson, William S. J. Ellos, Robert Solomon, Robert B. Textor, eds., *Uncompromising Integrity: Motorola's Challenge: 24 Global Case Studies with Commentaries.* Copyright © 1998 Motorola, Inc. Used with permission of Motorola University Press, USA.

One of the operations at the Anzen facility was "Final Test Assembly," carried out by three eight-person teams on each daily shift. These team members were all Nambunese employees of the partner company.

The employee relations manager for the Anzen facility was Willard Wa. Willard, an employee of the partner company, was born 54 years ago in a small village in northern Nambu, and had been assigned to the JV partnership since its very first day of operation. Willard reported to Henk.

The manufacturing manager for the Final Test Assembly operation was a Nambunese Motorolan named Victor Min, 49, whom Motorola had assigned to the JV partnership for this purpose. To all who knew him, Victor personified a deep dedication to traditional Nambunese cultural values of duty and obedience.

One of the most respected of the Final Test Assembly teams was Team Three, nicknamed the "Morning Glory" team. Members of this team were intensely proud of their performance in both productivity and safety, which was among the best in the entire facility. Morning Glory team members viewed this performance as the result not only of exceptional skill, but equally important, of an unusual degree of harmony and cooperation within their team.

When Victor took over management of the Final Test Assembly operation in 1994, he made an effort to get acquainted with everyone under his supervision. He soon felt comfortable with all the Morning Glory team members except one, namely Tommy Tang, 31. Tommy had been hired by the partner company only two years earlier, after having spent several years as a mountaineering guide. Compared with most Nambunese, Tommy's values leaned a bit more toward freedom and a bit less toward duty. He hated to wear the protective eyeglasses that all Final Test Assembly associates were required to wear on duty. When his teammates would urge him to put on his safety glasses, he would give a variety of reasons why he couldn't.

On several occasions Victor spotted Tommy in the Final Test Assembly Area without his protective eyeglasses. Each time he would counsel Tommy on the need to wear them. The last time he shouted, "Tommy, this is the last time I will see you here without your safety glasses. From now on, you will either wear them or else!"

Then, four weeks later, a terrible event occurred. Victor entered the Final Test Assembly Area and noticed Tommy working closely with his Morning Glory teammates. All of them were wearing their protective eyeglasses except Tommy. Suddenly Victor lost control of his temper. He jumped at Tommy and slapped him several times on both sides of the head, screaming, "This will teach you!" Tommy doubled over in pain, holding his ears. Then, despite his pain, he apologized over and over to Victor for not having complied with safety regulations. After two or three minutes of apology, Tommy went to see the facility's nurse.

The other seven Morning Glory members stood in shocked silence. Nothing like this had ever happened before at Anzen. None of them reported the incident. Nonetheless, rumors about it, both accurate and otherwise, spread instantly throughout the entire facility.

That night Victor had trouble sleeping. The following morning he went directly to see Tommy in the Final Test Assembly Area. He noted that Tommy was wearing the required eyeglasses. In the presence of several Morning Glory team members, Victor apologized and presented Tommy with a red envelope inside of which he had placed a substantial amount of his own money. Tommy accepted the envelope and the apology. The two men then shook hands and parted amicably.

Then, a few days later came some shocking news from the facility's doctor: Tommy had suffered permanent partial loss of his hearing as a result of the slaps he received from Victor. As a matter of standard procedure, the doctor reported this finding to both Stan Stark and Henk Van Dyke.

Stan was stunned. He sat silently for a moment. Then he placed a conference call to Henk and Willard, and questioned them about the incident and the doctor's report. Then Stan decided: "Both of you know that no Motorolan is ever allowed to physically assault a fellow associate. Could each of you please investigate this incident, and give me your recommendations within 48 hours?"

Willard proceeded immediately to conduct the most thorough investigation he could. The first thing he discovered was that neither Tommy nor any of his teammates wanted to discuss the matter at all. They all felt that their team's harmony would be best served by treating the entire matter as if it had never happened. After all, Victor had apologized; Tommy had accepted the apology; and Tommy was now complying with all safety regulations. So, the only really important thing was to get on with the team's heavy workload. But Willard persisted. Finally he got some solid facts:

- Several Morning Glory members stated categorically that Victor had never before struck a subordinate or threatened to.
- These team members believed that Victor's outburst of temper was unique, and they considered any repetition unlikely. "Victor has learned his lesson," said one, "and from now on he will handle his stress better. We will help him."
- Victor's personnel file revealed nothing to suggest he was prone to losing his temper or "acting out" violently.
- Tommy, despite his impaired hearing, could still function effectively with his Morning Glory teammates.

Two days later Willard phoned Stan with his recommendations. "Frankly," said Willard, "I think the solution is pretty simple. I recommend that the JV partnership cover all of Tommy's medical costs and then quietly, without any ceremony, make a reasonable indemnification payment to him with our apologies. Beyond that, I recommend that we do nothing—except, of course, to keep monitoring the situation carefully. In my opinion as a former manufacturing associate, this would be the best solution, because it is now clear to me that the Morning Glory team is functioning well, and continuing to accept Victor's leadership."

A few minutes later, Stan got a call from Henk. "Well," said Henk, "I recommend that we terminate Victor right away. Victor is a Motorolan, and knows very well that he is not supposed to strike an associate. That would be a violation of the basic dignity to which every Motorolan is entitled, and to which I believe all JV partnership employees are also entitled. We cannot allow a Motorolan to enforce regulations for our associates' safety by violating that safety! That just doesn't make any sense at all. And while we are at it, we should pay Tommy's medical bills and terminate him, too."

Next Stan walked down the hall to consult Cuthbert Kim, senior counsel in the Motorola Law Department for Nambu. Stan carefully explained the facts of the case and then asked, "Cuthbert, what's the procedure if I decide to terminate Victor and Tommy?"

"Well, I'm afraid there is no such procedure," replied Cuthbert. "While it is true that under Nambunese law striking a subordinate is grounds for termination, it is also true that once an apology has been offered and accepted, the law determines that life can and should go on again, and that termination is not legally justified. So, you can't terminate him. And you can't terminate Tommy, either. But of course you could separate them from the company, provided you could manage to negotiate buy-out agreements that they would accept."

Stan found this hard to believe, but when he checked with an external Nambunese consulting attorney, he received essentially the same answer.

The next day, Stan asked Cuthbert to do some research and find out how much it would cost to buy the two associates out. Soon Cuthbert came back with the answer: "Since Victor still has about 11 years before he is due to retire from Motorola, he could probably bargain hard. My estimate is that the JV partnership would probably have to pay him about five years' worth of salary plus benefits and fringes. For Tommy, it might be three years' worth, because he is a relatively new employee."

"That's a huge amount of money," gasped Stan. "On the other hand, the behavior that both Victor and Tommy have modeled is certainly not the kind of behavior I want at Anzen. I'll think about it and then let you know my decision."

Case Study

Facing Face

This case takes place in the recent past in Chikorpan, an East Asian nation with a culture deeply influenced by the Confucian tradition. Motorola's business has been booming in Chikorpan, outpacing the corporation's ability to find and train qualified Chikorpanese Motorolans to handle the rapidly growing management workload. Consequently, it has been necessary to assign a large number of transpatriate Motorolans to Chikorpan. These transpatriates are enormously expensive, and partly for this reason corporate leadership is sponsoring numerous "localizing" initiatives to recruit, train, and upgrade high-potential Chikorpanese Motorolans, and to induct them as quickly as possible into the corporate culture.

Among these initiatives are several by Motorola University. For example, MU has sent Frank Blunt to Chikorpan to offer training to the Human Resources (HR) staff. Frank's assignment was to serve as moderator and primary resource person for a two-week seminar in Fusan.

Frank is from the American Midwest. In his 35 years with Motorola he has built an enviable reputation as an HR specialist, both in the United States and also, for briefer periods, in Europe.

A keystone of Frank's working philosophy of HR is honesty and openness in performance evaluation. For some years he has passionately advocated putting an end to the practice in which a supervisor gives a marginal employee a high performance evaluation in order to get rid of him/her by arranging his/her transfer to another, unsuspecting, department. "Such fraudulent evaluations betray trust and are a danger to Motorola and a favor to no one, including the employee," Frank has said.

Frank feels pretty much the same way about terminations. "If the employee isn't cutting it, he should be terminated, and told why," he told the Fusan Seminar participants. "Integrity necessitates nothing less."

Among the participants at the Fusan Seminar were Siew Chee-Wah and Ingrid Marklund. Chee-Wah, 43, known informally among his Westerner friends as "Chuck," was former chief of HR at the corporation's Mei An Facility. His performance was good, and the need for qualified Chikorpanese HR specialists was urgent, so that after only two years at Mei An, Chuck was promoted and transferred to a top job in Fusan. There was at the time no Chikorpanese Motorolan available to replace him at Mei An, so his job went to a Swedish transpatriate, Ingrid Marklund, 29. Chuck thought highly of Ingrid, who, among all his foreign colleagues, seemed to be the one with the deepest understanding of "the Chikorpanese culture."

During the Fusan Seminar, Chuck politely and indirectly asked Frank whether it would be OK to terminate a substandard Chikorpanese employee

From R.S. Moorthy, Richard T. De George, Thomas Donaldson, William S. J. Ellos, Robert Solomon, Robert B. Textor, eds., *Uncompromising Integrity: Motorola's Challenge: 24 Global Case Studies with Commentaries.* Copyright © 1998 Motorola, Inc. Used with permission of Motorola University Press, USA.

by both gently pointing out the employee's shortcomings and making some vague reference to the possibility of re-employment at some future time— "if and when demand for the product requires upsizing the force."

Frank replied with apparent incredulity, "Well, Chuck, let's see, that would be lying to the employee, wouldn't it?" Chuck immediately sensed that he had gone too far, and made a vague reply of polite demurral.

At this point the normally cool Ingrid spoke up heatedly: "But if I send a man of 30 or 40 back to his family and village without giving him some means of saving face, he and his family will lose the respect of people who have been part of their lives for decades, even generations. Why can't I just give him some kind of a—what you Americans call—a 'fig leaf'? My study of Chikorpanese culture tells me that even if he himself doesn't really believe the fig leaf story, as long as it has a surface plausibility back in the village, he can use it and everybody will feel better that way."

Frank was obviously taken aback by Ingrid's apparent support of Chuck's apparent disagreement. But Frank held his ground: "What I say is, integrity is integrity. Here's the real test: If Chuck can look at himself in the mirror in the morning and feel good about lying to an employee he is about to terminate, maybe that is OK. But I could not. Could you, Ingrid?"

Ingrid paused. Was she about to commit an enormous political mistake? But she decided to be gutsy: "Well," she said, "I think termination must be handled sensitively, and if the culture requires certain cosmetics, I am prepared to use them, provided that there is no legal risk in doing so, and that in doing so I do not sacrifice the essence of my own true integrity."

Frank was getting excited: "But Ingrid, that is precisely the question: Just what is true integrity? If you did that, Ingrid, would you be showing true integrity to yourself? If not, then I would advise against it."

The Challenge of Cultural Relativism

JAMES RACHELS

Morality differs in every society, and is a convenient term for socially approved habits.

RUTH BENEDICT, *PATTERNS OF CULTURE* (1934)

HOW DIFFERENT CULTURES HAVE DIFFERENT MORAL CODES

Darius, a king of ancient Persia, was intrigued by the variety of cultures he encountered in his travels. He had found, for example, that the Callatians (a tribe of Indians) customarily ate the bodies of their dead fathers. The Greeks, of course, did not do that—the Greeks practiced cremation and regarded the funeral pyre as the natural and fitting way to dispose of the dead. Darius thought that a sophisticated understanding of the world must include an appreciation of such differences between cultures. One day, to teach this lesson, he summoned some Greeks who happened to be present at his court and asked them what they would take to eat the bodies of their dead fathers. They were shocked, as Darius knew they would be, and replied that no amount of money could persuade them to do such a thing. Then Darius called in some Callatians, and while the Greeks listened asked them what they would take to burn their dead father's bodies. The Callatians were horrified and told Darius not even to mention such a dreadful thing.

This story, recounted by Herodotus in his *History*, illustrates a recurring theme in the literature of social science: different cultures have different moral codes. What is thought right within one group may be utterly abhorrent to the members of another group, and vice versa. Should we eat the bodies of the dead or burn them? If you were a Greek, one answer would seem obviously correct; but if you were a Callatian, the opposite would seem equally certain.

It is easy to give additional examples of the same kind. Consider the Eskimos. They are a remote and inaccessible people. Numbering only about 25,000, they live in small, isolated settlements scattered mostly along the northern fringes of North America and Greenland. Until the beginning of [the 20th] century, the outside world knew little about them. Then explorers began to bring back strange tales.

Eskimo customs turned out to be very different from our own. The men often had more than one wife, and they would share their wives with guests, lending them for the night as a sign of hospitality. Moreover, within a community, a dominant male might demand—and get—regular sexual access to other men's wives. The women, however, were free to break these arrangements simply by leaving their husbands and taking up with new partners—free, that is, so long as their former husbands chose not to make trouble. All in all, the Eskimo practice was a volatile scheme that bore little resemblance to what we call marriage.

But it was not only their marriage and sexual practices that were different. The Eskimos also seemed to have less regard for human life. Infanticide, for example, was common. Knud Rasmussen, one of the most famous early explorers, reported that he met one woman who had borne twenty children but had killed ten of them at birth. Female babies, he found, were especially liable to be destroyed, and this was permitted simply at the parents' discretion, with no social stigma attached to it. Old people also, when they became too feeble to contribute to the family, were left out in the snow to die. So there seemed to be, in this society, remarkably little respect for life.

To the general public, these were disturbing revelations. Our own way of living seems so natural and right that for many of us it is hard to conceive of others living so differently. And when we do hear of such things, we tend immediately to categorize those other peoples as "backward" or "primitive." But to anthropologists and sociologists, there was nothing particularly surprising about the Eskimos. Since the time of Herodotus, enlightened observers have been accustomed to the idea that conceptions of right and wrong differ from culture to culture. If we assume that our ideas of right and wrong will be shared by all peoples at all times, we are merely naive.

Descriptive vs. Prescriptive

CULTURAL RELATIVISM

To many thinkers, this observation—"Different cultures have different moral codes"—has seemed to be the key to understanding morality. The idea of universal truth in ethics, they say, is a myth. The customs of different societies are all that exist. These customs cannot be said to be "correct" or "incorrect," for that implies we have an independent standard of right and wrong by which they may be judged. But there is no such independent standard; every standard is culture-bound. The great pioneering sociologist William Graham Sumner, writing in 1906, put the point like this:

> The "right" way is the way which the ancestors used and which has been handed down. The tradition is its own warrant. It is not held subject to verification by experience. The notion of right is in the folkways. It is not outside of them, of independent origin, and brought to test them. In the folkways, whatever is, is right. This is because they are traditional, and therefore contain in themselves the authority of the ancestral ghosts. When we come to the folkways we are at the end of our analysis.

This line of thought has probably persuaded more people to be skeptical about ethics than any other single thing. Cultural Relativism, as it has been called, challenges our ordinary belief in the objectivity and universality of moral truth. It says, in effect, that there is no such thing as universal truth in ethics; there are only the various cultural codes, and nothing more. Moreover, our own code has no special status; it is merely one among many.

As we shall see, this basic idea is really a compound of several different thoughts. It is important to separate the various elements of the theory because, on analysis, some parts of the theory turn out to be correct, whereas others seem to be mistaken. As a beginning, we may distinguish the following claims, all of which have been made by cultural relativists:

1. Different societies have different moral codes.
2. There is no objective standard that can be used to judge one societal code better than another.
3. The moral code of our own society has no special status; it is merely one among many.
4. There is no "universal truth" in ethics—that is, there are no moral truths that hold for all peoples at all times.
5. The moral code of a society determines what is right within that society; that is, if the moral code of a society says that a certain action is right, then that action is right, at least within that society.
6. It is mere arrogance for us to try to judge the conduct of other peoples. We should adopt an attitude of tolerance toward the practices of other cultures.

Although it may seem that these six propositions go naturally together, they are independent of one another, in the sense that some of them might be true even if others are false. In what follows, we will try to identify what is correct in Cultural Relativism, but we will also be concerned to expose what is mistaken about it.

THE CULTURAL DIFFERENCES ARGUMENT

Cultural Relativism is a theory about the nature of morality. At first blush it seems quite plausible. However, like all such theories, it may be evaluated by subjecting it to rational analysis; and when we analyze Cultural Relativism we find that it is not so plausible as it first appears to be.

The first thing we need to notice is that at the heart of Cultural Relativism there is a certain *form of argument*. The strategy used by cultural relativists is to argue from facts about the differences between cultural outlooks to a conclusion about the status of morality. Thus we are invited to accept this reasoning:

1. The Greeks believed it was wrong to eat the dead, whereas the Callatians believed it was right to eat the dead.
2. Therefore, eating the dead is neither objectively right nor objectively wrong. It is merely a matter of opinion, which varies from culture to culture.

Or, alternatively:

1. The Eskimos see nothing wrong with infanticide, whereas Americans believe infanticide is immoral.
2. Therefore, infanticide is neither objectively right nor objectively wrong. It is merely a matter of opinion, which varies from culture to culture.

Clearly, these arguments are variations of one fundamental idea. They are both special cases of a more general argument, which says:

1. Different cultures have different moral codes.
2. Therefore, there is no objective "truth" in morality. Right and wrong are only matters of opinion, and opinions vary from culture to culture.

We may call this the *Cultural Differences Argument*. To many people, it is very persuasive. But from a logical point of view, is it a sound argument?

It is not sound. The trouble is that the conclusion does not really follow from the premise—that is, even if the premise is true, the conclusion still might be false. The premise concerns what people believe: in some societies, people believe one thing; in other societies, people believe differently. The conclusion, however, concerns *what really is the case*. The trouble is that this sort of conclusion does not follow logically from this sort of premise.

Consider again the example of the Greeks and Callatians. The Greeks believed it was wrong to eat the dead; the Callatians believed it was right. Does it follow, *from the mere fact that they disagreed*, that there is no objective truth in the matter? No, it does not follow; for it *could* be that the practice was objectively right (or wrong) and that one or the other of them was simply mistaken.

To make the point clearer, consider a very different matter. In some societies, people believe the earth is flat. In other societies, such as our own, people believe the earth is (roughly) spherical. Does it follow, *from the mere fact that they disagree*, that there is no "objective truth" in geography? Of course not; we would never draw such a conclusion because we realize that, in their beliefs about the world, the members of some societies might simply be wrong. There is no reason to think if the world is round everyone must know it. Similarly, there is no reason to think that if there is moral truth everyone must know it. The fundamental mistake in the Cultural Differences Argument is that it attempts to derive a substantive conclusion about a subject (morality) from the mere fact that people disagree about it.

It is important to understand the nature of the point that is being made here. We are not saying (not yet, anyway) that the conclusion of the argument is false. Insofar as anything being said here is concerned, it is still an open question whether the conclusion is true. We are making a purely logical point and saying that the conclusion does not follow from the premise. This is important, because in order to determine whether the conclusion is true, we need arguments in its support. Cultural Relativism proposes this argument, but unfortunately the argument turns out to be fallacious. So it proves nothing.

THE CONSEQUENCES OF TAKING CULTURAL RELATIVISM SERIOUSLY

Even if the Cultural Differences Argument is invalid, Cultural Relativism might still be true. What would it be like if it were true?

In the passage quoted above, William Graham Sumner summarizes the essence of Cultural Relativism. He says that there is no measure of right and wrong other than the standards of one's society: "The notion of right is in the folkways. It is not outside of them, of independent origin and brought to test them. In the folkways, whatever is, is right."

Suppose we took this seriously. What would be some of the consequences?

1. *We could no longer say that the customs of other societies are morally inferior to our own.* This, of course, is one of the main points stressed by Cultural Relativism. We would have to stop condemning other societies merely because they are "different." So long as we concentrate on certain examples, such as the funerary practices of the Greeks and Callatians, this may seem to be a sophisticated, enlightened attitude.

However, we would also be stopped from criticizing other, less benign practices. Suppose a society waged war on its neighbors for the purpose of taking slaves. Or suppose a society was violently anti-Semitic and its leaders set out to destroy the Jews. Cultural Relativism would preclude us from saying that either of these practices was wrong. We would not even be able to say that a society tolerant of Jews is *better* than the anti-Semitic society, for that would imply some sort of transcultural standard of comparison. The failure to condemn *these* practices does not seem "enlightened"; on the contrary, slavery and anti-Semitism seem wrong *wherever* they occur. Nevertheless, if we took Cultural Relativism seriously, we would have to admit that these social practices also are immune from criticism.

2. *We could decide whether actions are right or wrong just by consulting the standards of our society.* Cultural Relativism suggests a simple test for determining what is right and what is wrong: all one has to do is ask whether the action is in accordance with the code of one's society. Suppose a resident of South Africa is wondering whether his country's [previous] policy of *apartheid*—rigid racial segregation—is morally correct. All he has to do is ask whether this

policy conforms to his society's moral code. If it does, there is nothing to worry about, at least from a moral point of view.

This implication of Cultural Relativism is disturbing because few of us think that our society's code is perfect—we think of ways it might be improved. Yet Cultural Relativism would not only forbid us from criticizing the codes of *other* societies; it would stop us from criticizing our *own*. After all, if right and wrong are relative to culture, this must be true for our own culture just as much as for others.

3. *The idea of moral progress is called into doubt.*   Usually, we think that at least some changes in our society have been for the better. (Some, of course, may have been changes for the worse.) Consider this example: Throughout most of Western history the place of women in society was very narrowly circumscribed. They could not own property; they could not vote or hold political office; with a few exceptions, they were not permitted to have paying jobs; and generally they were under the almost absolute control of their husbands. Recently much of this has changed, and most people think of it as progress.

If Cultural Relativism is correct, can we legitimately think of this as progress? Progress means replacing a way of doing things with a better way. But by what standard do we judge the new ways as better? If the old ways were in accordance with the social standards of their time, then Cultural Relativism would say it is a mistake to judge them by the standards of a different time. Eighteenth-century society was, in effect, a different society from the one we have now. To say that we have made progress implies a judgment that present-day society is better, and that is just the sort of transcultural judgment that, according to Cultural Relativism, is impermissible.

Our idea of social *reform* will also have to be reconsidered. A reformer such as Martin Luther King, Jr., seeks to change his society for the better. Within the constraints imposed by Cultural Relativism, there is one way this might be done. If a society is not living up to its own ideals, the reformer may be regarded as acting for the best: the ideals of the society are the standard by which we judge his or her proposals as worthwhile. But the "reformer" may not challenge the ideals themselves, for those ideals are by definition correct. According to Cultural Relativism, then, the idea of social reform makes sense only in this very limited way.

These three consequences of Cultural Relativism have led many thinkers to reject it as implausible on its face. It does make sense, they say, to condemn some practices, such as slavery and anti-Semitism, wherever they occur. It makes sense to think that our own society has made some moral progress, while admitting that it is still imperfect and in need of reform. Because Cultural Relativism says that these judgments make no sense, the arguments goes, it cannot be right.

WHY THERE IS LESS DISAGREEMENT THAN IT SEEMS

The original impetus for Cultural Relativism comes from the observation that cultures differ dramatically in their views of right and wrong. But just how much do they differ? It is true that there are differences. However, it is easy to overestimate the extent of those differences. Often, when we examine what seems to be a dramatic difference we find that the cultures do not differ nearly as much as it appears.

Consider a culture in which people believe it is wrong to eat cows. This may even be a poor culture, in which there is not enough food; still, the cows are not to be touched. Such a society would *appear* to have values very different from our own. But does it? We have not yet asked why these people will not eat cows. Suppose it is because they believe that after death the souls of humans inhabit the bodies of animals, especially cows, so that a cow may be someone's grandmother. Now do we want to say that their values are different from ours? No; the difference lies elsewhere. The difference is in our belief systems, not in our values. We agree that we shouldn't eat Grandma; we simply disagree about whether the cow *is* (or could be) Grandma.

The general point is this. Many factors work together to produce the customs of a society. The society's values are only one of them. Other matters, such as the religious and factual beliefs held by its members and the physical circumstances in which they must live, are also important. We cannot conclude, then, merely because customs differ, that there is a disagreement about values. The difference in customs may be attributable to some other aspect of social life. Thus there may be less disagreement about values than there appears to be.

Consider the Eskimos again. They often kill perfectly normal infants, especially girls. We do not approve of this at all; a parent who did this in our society would be locked up. Thus there appears to be a great difference in the values of our two cultures. But suppose we ask *why* the Eskimos do this. The explanation is not that they have less affection for their children or less respect for human life. An Eskimo family will always protect its babies if conditions permit. But they live in a harsh environment, where food is often in short supply. A fundamental postulate of Eskimo thought is: "Life is hard, and the margin of safety small." A family may want to nourish its babies but be unable to do so.

As in many "primitive" societies, Eskimo mothers will nurse their infants over a much longer period of time than mothers in our culture. The child will take nourishment from its mother's breast for four years, perhaps even longer. So even in the best of times there are limits to the number of infants that one mother can sustain. Moreover, the Eskimos are a nomadic people—unable to farm, they must move about in search of food. Infants must be carried, and a mother can carry only one baby in her parka as she travels and goes about her outdoor work. Other family members can help, but this is not always possible.

Infant girls are more readily disposed of because, first, in this society the males are the primary food providers—they are the hunters according to the traditional division of labor—and it is obviously important to maintain a sufficient number of food gatherers. But there is an important second reason as well. Because the hunters suffer a high casualty rate, the adult men who die prematurely far outnumber the women who die early. Thus if male and female infants survived in equal numbers, the female adult population would greatly outnumber the male adult population. Examining the available statistics, one writer concluded that "were it not for female infanticide . . . there would be approximately one-and-a-half times as many females in the average Eskimo local group as there are food-producing males."

So among the Eskimos, infanticide does not signal a fundamentally different attitude toward children. Instead it is a recognition that drastic measures are sometimes needed to ensure the family's survival. Even then, however, killing the baby is not the first option considered. Adoption is common; childless couples are especially happy to take a more fertile couple's "surplus." Killing is only the last resort. I emphasize this in order to show that the raw data of the anthropologists can be misleading; it can make the differences in values between cultures appear greater than they are. The Eskimos' values are not all that different from our values. It is only that life forces upon them choices that we do not have to make.

HOW ALL CULTURES HAVE SOME VALUES IN COMMON

It should not be surprising that, despite appearances, the Eskimos are protective of their children. How could it be otherwise? How could a group survive that did not value its young? This suggests a certain argument, one which shows that all cultural groups must be protective of their infants:

1. Human infants are helpless and cannot survive if they are not given extensive care for a period of years.
2. Therefore, if a group did not care for its young, the young would not survive, and the older members of the group would not be replaced. After a while the group would die out.
3. Therefore, any cultural group that continues to exist must care for its young. Infants that are not cared for must be the exception rather than the rule.

Similar reasoning shows that other values must be more or less universal. Imagine what it would be like for a society to place no value at all on truth telling. When one person spoke to another, there would be no presumption at all that he was telling the truth—for he could just as easily be speaking falsely. Within that society, there would be no reason to pay attention to what anyone says. (I ask you what time it is, and you say "Four o'clock." But there is no presumption that you are speaking truly; you could just as easily have said the first thing that came into your head. So I have no reason to pay attention to your answer—in fact, there was no point in my asking you in the first place!) Communication would then be extremely difficult, if not impossible. And because complex societies cannot exist without regular communication among their members, society would become impossible. It follows that in any complex society there *must* be a presumption in favor of truthfulness. There may of course be exceptions to this rule: there may be situations in which it is thought to be permissible to lie. Nevertheless, these will be exceptions to a rule that *is* in force in the society.

Let me give one further example of the same type. Could a society exist in which there was no prohibition on murder? What would this be like? Suppose people were free to kill other people at will, and no one thought there was anything wrong with it. In such a "society," no one could feel secure. Everyone would have to be constantly on guard. People who wanted to survive would have to avoid other people as much as possible. This would inevitably result in individuals trying to become as self-sufficient as possible—after all, associating with others would be dangerous. Society on any large scale would collapse. Of course, people might band together in smaller groups with others that they *could* trust not to harm them. But notice what this means: they would be forming smaller societies that *did* acknowledge a rule against murder. The prohibition of murder, then, is a necessary feature of all societies.

There is a general theoretical point here, namely, that *there are some moral rules that all societies will have in common, because those rules are necessary for society to exist.* The rules against lying and murder are two examples. And in fact, we do find these rules in force in all viable cultures. Cultures may differ in what they regard as legitimate exceptions to the rules, but this disagreement exists against a background of agreement on the larger issues. Therefore, it is a mistake to overestimate the amount of difference between cultures. Not *every* moral rule can vary from society to society.

WHAT CAN BE LEARNED FROM CULTURAL RELATIVISM

At the outset, I said that we were going to identify both what is right and what is wrong in Cultural Relativism. Thus far I have mentioned only its mistakes: I have said that it rests on an invalid argument, that it has consequences that make it implausible on its face, and that the extent of the cultural disagreement is far less than it implies. This all adds up to a pretty thorough repudiation of the theory. Nevertheless, it is still a very appealing idea, and the reader may have the feeling that all this is a little unfair. The theory must have something going for it, or else why has it been so influential? In fact, I think there *is* something right about Cultural Relativism, and now I want to say what that is. There are two lessons we should learn from the theory, even if we ultimately reject it.

1. Cultural Relativism warns us, quite rightly, about the danger of assuming that all our preferences are based on some absolute rational standard. They are not. Many (but not all) of our practices are merely peculiar to our society, and it is easy to lose sight of that fact. In reminding us of it, the theory does a service.

Funerary practices are one example. The Callatians, according to Herodotus, were "men who eat their fathers"—a shocking idea, to us at least. But eating the flesh of the dead could be understood as a sign of respect. It could be taken as a symbolic act that says: We wish this person's spirit to dwell within us. Perhaps this was the understanding of the Callatians. On such a way of thinking, burying the dead could be seen as an act of rejection, and burning the corpse as positively scornful. If this is hard to imagine, then we may need to have our imaginations stretched. Of course we may feel a visceral repugnance at the idea of eating human flesh in any circumstances. But what of it? This repugnance may be, as the relativists say, only a matter of what is customary in our particular society.

There are many other matters that we tend to think of in terms of objective right and wrong, but that are really nothing more than social conventions. Should women cover their breasts? A publicly exposed breast is scandalous in our society, whereas in other cultures it is unremarkable. Objectively speaking, it is neither right nor wrong—there is no objective reason why either custom is better. Cultural Relativism begins with the valuable insight that many of our practices are like this—they are only cultural products. Then it goes wrong by concluding that, because *some* practices are like this, *all* must be.

2. The second lesson has to do with keeping an open mind. In the course of growing up, each of us has acquired some strong feelings: we have learned to think of some types of conduct as acceptable, and others we have learned to regard as simply unacceptable. Occasionally, we may find those feelings challenged. We may encounter someone who claims that our feelings are mistaken. For example, we may have been taught that homosexuality is immoral, and we may feel quite uncomfortable around gay people and see them as alien and "different." Now someone suggests that this may be a mere prejudice; that there is nothing evil about homosexuality; that gay people are just people, like anyone else, who happen, through no choice of their own, to be attracted to others of the same sex. But because we feel so strongly about the matter, we may find it hard to take this seriously. Even after we listen to the arguments, we may still have the unshakable feeling that homosexuals *must,* somehow, be an unsavory lot.

Cultural Relativism, by stressing that our moral views can reflect the prejudices of our society, provides an antidote for this kind of dogmatism. When he tells the story of the Greeks and Callatians, Herodotus adds:

> For if anyone, no matter who, were given the opportunity of choosing from amongst all the nations of the world the set of beliefs which he thought best, he would inevitably, after careful consideration of their relative merits, choose that of his own country. Everyone without exception believes his own native customs, and the religion he was brought up in, to be the best.

Realizing this can result in our having more open minds. We can come to understand that our feelings are not necessarily perceptions of the truth—they may be nothing more than the result of cultural conditioning. Thus when we hear it suggested that some element of our social code is *not* really the best and we find ourselves instinctively resisting the suggestion, we might stop and remember this. Then we may be more open to discovering the truth, whatever that might be.

We can understand the appeal of Cultural Relativism, then, even though the theory has serious shortcomings. It is an attractive theory because it is based on a genuine insight—that many of the practices and attitudes we think so natural are really only cultural products. Moreover, keeping this insight firmly in view is important if we want to avoid arrogance and have open minds. These are important points, not to be taken lightly. But we can accept these points without going on to accept the whole theory.

Notes

1. The story of the Greeks and the Callatians is from Herodotus, *The Histories,* translated by Aubrey de Selincourt, revised by A. R. Burn (Harmondsworth, Middlesex: Penguin Books, 1972), pp. 219–220. The quotation from Herodotus toward the end of the chapter is from the same source.
2. Information about the Eskimos was taken from Peter Freuchen, *Book of the Eskimos* (New York: Fawcett, 1961); and E. Adamson Hoebel, *The Law of Primitive Man* (Cambridge: Harvard University Press, 1954), Chapter 5. The estimate of how female infanticide affects the male/female ratio in the adult Eskimo population is from Hoebel's work.
3. The William Graham Sumner quotation is from his *Folkways* (Boston: Ginn and Company, 1906), p. 28.

A Social Contracts Approach to Business Ethics

THOMAS DONALDSON • THOMAS W. DUNFEE

We wrote the book, *Ties that Bind* ("TIES"), out of our conviction that answering today's questions requires a new approach to business ethics, an approach that exposes the implicit understandings or "contracts" that bind industries, companies, and economic systems into moral communities. It is in these economic communities, and in the often unspoken understandings that provide their ethical glue, that we believe many of the answers to business ethics quandaries lie. Further, we think that answering such questions requires the use of a yet deeper, and universal "contract" superseding even individual ones. The theory that combines both these deeper and thinner kinds of contracts we label "Integrative Social Contracts Theory," or "ISCT" for short.

ISCT does not overturn popular wisdom. While it asserts that the social contracts that arise from specific cultural and geographic contexts have legitimacy, it acknowledges a *limit* to that legitimacy. It recognizes the moral authority of key transcultural truths, for example, the idea that human beings everywhere are deserving of respect. The social contract approach we detail holds that any social contract terms existing outside these boundaries must be deemed illegitimate, no matter how completely subscribed to within a given economic community. In this sense, all particular or "micro" social contracts, whether they exist at the national, industry, or corporate level, must conform to a hypothetical "macro" social contract that lays down moral boundaries for any social contracting. ISCT thus lies midway on the spectrum of moral belief separating relativism from absolutism. It allows substantial "moral free space" for nations and other economic communities to shape their distinctive concepts of economic fairness, but it draws the line at flagrant neglect of core human values.

Our approach takes "moral free space" seriously. It insists that morality can be "conditional" or "situational" at least in the sense that two conflicting conceptions of ethics can sometimes both be valid, and that community agreements about ethics often matter. Two economic systems need not have precisely the same view about the ethics of insider trading. Their views about what is wrong with insider trading may differ, yet both may be legitimate. Nor does every corporation have to follow exactly the same conception of fairness as it designs flextime or seniority rule. It follows from our view that all economic actors must recognize the critical role of social contracts in the communities they impact. To fail to do so, as many companies have done in the past, is to display moral blindness.

On our view, as social contracts change, so too do the challenges for business. The ethical "game" of business today is played by different rules, and harbors different penalties and benefits, than it did decades ago. Broad

Segments of this article first appeared in the book by Donaldson, T. and T. Dunfee (1999), *Ties that Bind: A Social Contracts Approach to Business Ethics*, Harvard University Business School Press, and in the article "*Précis for Ties that Bind,*" Donaldson, T. and T. Dunfee (2000), *Business & Society Review*, 104 (4). Copyright 2000 by Thomas Donaldson and Thomas Dunfee.

shifts of moral consensus have occurred. In subtle, far reaching shifts, managers and members of the general public have gradually redefined their view of the underlying responsibilities of large corporations. Half a century ago, companies were basically expected to focus on producing goods and services at reasonable prices; today, corporations are held responsible for a variety of issues involving fairness and quality of life. In companies throughout the world, gender issues, racial issues, and questions of the clash between work and family, are included in the agenda of corporate management.

The challenge that we accepted in TIES was to find a theory that accepts basic moral precepts, such as "Don't lie," "Be fair," and "Respect the environment," even as it refuses to pretend that these broad-brushed concepts provide full moral clarity. The challenge was to articulate an approach that holds fundamental truths to be relevant even as it accounts for legitimate differences in business communities and historical periods. We believe that ISCT is such a theory.

The concepts that inform ISCT are at the same time simple and complex. The simple idea, as stated already, is that implicit agreements constitute part of the basic software of business ethics. Without these "social contracts" knowing what ethically matters and what doesn't in a specific context is impossible. This very simple idea, however, needs explication and justification. Hence, ISCT is fitted with a more complex rationale and set of concepts.

In the extensive description of ISCT that we undertake in TIES, we begin with the same kind of thought experiment that was used to justify the traditional social contract arguments of Locke, Rousseau, Hobbes, and Rawls. While we utilize the approach of these classic contractarian thinkers, we add an important point. They asked about what citizens would require of the government and how they would define political justice. We, on the other hand, inquire about what economic participants would agree upon as defining *business ethics*. In the traditional manner, we begin with a thought experiment that envisions the terms of a contract for the foundation for economic ethics that would be acceptable to a diverse set of imaginary contractors (some greed driven egoists, some deeply religious altruists, most probably in-between) representing the varied attitudes of the modern world. We assume that these contractors are rational, i.e., not afflicted by inconsistency or logical confusion, and that they are knowledgeable, i.e., they know the range of facts accepted at the time as being true. We assume not, as Rawls does (Rawls, 1971), that these hypothetical contractors are ignorant of all facts concerning themselves. They may or may not know that they are Christian, Muslim, of a risk-adverse or risk-prone personality, etc. We assume only in this regard that they do not know in what economic communities they are members. For example, they do not know that they work for XYZ corporation, participate in country N's economic system, pay dues in worker union K, or ply their trade in profession P or industry Q. These facts about their economic membership are hidden to them. In a similar way, their level of personal wealth is obscured from them. They are ignorant of whether they possess a massive fortune, or nothing at all. Hence, one might envision all of rational humanity capable of voluntary choice afflicted with the partial amnesia just described, gathering for a global congress to construct an agreement that would provide a fundamental framework for ethical behavior in economic activities.

We do not assume, as again Rawls *would* assume, that the contractors are ignorant of their economic and political preferences. An individual may know her preferences, that she prefers to be rich rather than poor, wine to beer, employment in a worker-owned over employment in an investor-owned firm, a Libertarian to a Socialist form of government. The question then becomes what terms, if any, would be acceptable to these contractors?

We assume that the contractors do not come to the table entirely bereft of moral principles. They at least bring with them the underlying senses of right and wrong with which they have grown up. They bring with them these settled understandings of deep moral values. Because the contractors are unaware of other economic preferences and memberships, they lack detailed knowledge of their economic morality. Yet even as they lack such detailed knowledge, they know the basic values to which they subscribe. Some may profess philosophical utilitarianism. Some may profess philosophical Kantianism. Others may adhere to ethical principles articulated in their preferred religion (in Judaism or Christianity this might be the Ten Commandments; in Buddhism it might be the principles of the "Dhamapada"). And some may subscribe to the traditional principles that have been handed down to them historically through their family, their village, or their culture.

When these hypothetical yet rational global contractors confront the fact that it would be impossible to obtain an intellectual consensus concerning adoption of a single morality as the framework for global economic ethics, then how would they go about resolving their dilemma of finding a basis for agreement? We believe that they would nonetheless be motivated to find such a basis. First, we assume that many are driven by an innate moral sense which will lead them to seek and to recognize elements of a foundational morality. That is, most humans are "hardwired" to be ethical. Second, our focus is on *economic* ethics. In this domain there are special considerations that must be of concern to rational, knowledgeable contractors. For example, rational contractors would realize the vital importance of having a framework of morality as a foundation for economic interaction. Without a core common morality, the result would be the economic analogue to a Hobbesian state of nature. Economic life would be, using Hobbes's language, "nasty and brutish," if not also "short." Such chaotic economic conditions have prevailed from time to time in nations that lacked the social and political background institutions necessary to sustain an ethical framework. In such a state, promises are not kept. Property is not respected. Violence is used to obtain economic advantage. Capital markets either become distorted, or fail altogether owing to a fundamental lack of trust.

Finally, we believe that rational contractors would rely upon a limited set of core assumptions in framing their search for a common economic ethics, where "economic ethics" refers to the principles establishing the boundaries of proper behavior in the context of the production and exchange of goods and services.

These are as follows:

- All humans are constrained by bounded moral rationality. This means that even rational persons knowledgeable about ethical theory cannot always divine good answers to moral problems without being acquainted with community-specific norms.
- The nature of ethical behavior in economic systems and communities helps determine the quality and efficiency of economic interactions. Higher quality

and more efficient economic interactions are preferable to lower quality and less efficient economic interactions.
- All other things being equal, economic activity that is consistent with the cultural, philosophical, or religious attitudes of economic actors is preferable to economic activity that is not.

In virtue of these three propositions (above), individual contractors would desire the option to join and to exit economic communities as a means of leveraging their ability to achieve the benefits of either greater efficiency or greater compatibility with preferred religious, philosophical, or community norms.

The hypothetical members of the global economic community would be capable of considering which norms would be best to guide all business activity in a way that achieves fairness. In this hypothetical state of nature, we argue that such rational global contractors would agree to the following *de minimis* macrosocial contract to govern all economic actors and thereby setting the terms for economic ethics:

1. Local economic communities have moral free space in which they may generate ethical norms for their members through microsocial contracts (i.e., contracts based on local norms).
2. Norm-generalized microsocial contracts must be grounded in consent, buttressed by the rights of individual members to voice and exit.
3. In order to become obligatory (legitimate), a microsocial contract norm must be compatible with hypernorms (see definition below).
4. In cases of conflicts among norms satisfying macrosocial contract terms 1–3, priority rules or "rules of thumb" must be established through the application of rules consistent with the spirit and letter of the macrosocial contract.[1]

We use certain core definitions throughout the book as we discuss the implications of the ISCT macrosocial contract. "Hypernorms" are principles so fundamental that they constitute norms by which all others are to be judged. Hypernorms are discernible in a convergence of religious, political and philosophical thought. An "authentic norm" is one that is generated within a community's moral free space and which satisfies the requirements of terms 1 and 2 of the macrosocial contract. Authentic norms are based upon the attitudes and behaviors of the members of their source communities. A "legitimate norm" is an authentic norm that is compatible with hypernorms. A norm has to be established as legitimate before it may become binding for members of the norm-generating community.

TIES details these core concepts and suggests ways in which they can be applied to business decisions. For example, we describe at some length an example of a structural hypernorm that we call the "hypernorm of necessary social efficiency," or "efficiency hypernorm" for short. This hypernorm identifies duties to maintain the efficiency of societal systems, including economic institutions, designed to promote economic welfare and social justice. A norm, policy, or institution satisfies the efficiency hypernorm when it contributes to the efficiency of the provision of necessary social goods, that is, aggregate economic welfare or social justice. The hypernorm entails, among other things, that economic actors have duties to support efficient policies and institutions that promote liberty and due process, as well as minimal possibilities for health, food, housing, and education.

TIES emphasizes the role of communities as the source of authentic norms. The familiar concept of the corporate "stakeholder" is often useful in identifying relevant ISCT communities. Stakeholders of corporations usually also constitute ISCT communities. In the book we offer many proxies and presumptions for use in identifying relevant communities, authentic norms, and hypernorms. The type of evidence required for such identifications will often be commonly known and readily available.

In TIES we illustrate the application of ISCT to specific issues. For example, we discuss at length how ISCT can be used to unravel the phenomenon of bribery around the world. ISCT reveals that bribery is typically condemned by high priority authentic norms and that most forms of bribery also violate hypernorms.

Thus, we offer ISCT as a means to highlight the ethical relevance of existing norms in industries, corporations, and other economic communities, even as it also must limit the acceptable range of such norms. Our aim is to reach beyond the generality of, say, Kantian Deontology or "virtue" ethics to allow a more detailed normative assessment of particular ethical problems in business. It is a theory that accommodates the widely held intuition that different ethical precepts are sometimes appropriate for different industries, companies and professions. The ethics of professional doctors need not be precisely the same as the ethics of journalists. Nor do the gift and entertainment practices within a Japanese keiretsu need to conform to the practices for government contracting within the United States. In accommodating diversity, ISCT recognizes variety in individual and cultural values and preferences. Thus, it refuses to impose a broad conception of the "good" upon dissenters, even as it recognizes the relevance of transcultural moral understanding.

In sum, then, the same logic that sanctifies a handshake between two individuals turns out also to sanctify the implicit understanding of economic communities woven throughout the business world. These are the informal but critical agreements—or "social contracts"—that provide the warp and woof of economic life. These are the agreements that exist within industries, national economies, trade groups, and corporations, and, further, that are the implicit "contracts" critical for understanding business ethics. These, then, are the "ties that bind."

Notes

1. ISCT priority principles (also sometimes referred to as "rules of thumb") are:
A. Local community norms have priority unless adopting them harms members of another community.
B. Local community norms designed to resolve norm conflicts have priority unless adopting them harms members of another community.
C. The more global the source of the norm, the greater the norm's priority.
D. Norms essential to the maintenance of the economic environment in which the transaction occurs have priority over norms potentially damaging to that environment.
E. Patterns of consistency among alternative norms add weight for priority.
F. Priority is given to well-defined norms over less well-defined ones.

Reference

Rawls, J. 1971. *A Theory of Justice.* Cambridge, MA: Harvard University Press.

The United Nations Universal Declaration
of Human Rights

Now, Therefore, The General Assembly *proclaims*

This universal declaration of human rights as a common standard of achievement for all peoples and all nations, to the end that every individual and every organ of society, keeping this Declaration constantly in mind, shall strive by teaching and education to promote respect for these rights and freedoms and by progressive measures, national and international, to secure their universal and effective recognition and observance, both among the peoples of Member States themselves and among the peoples of territories under their jurisdiction.

ARTICLE 1

All human beings are born free and equal in dignity and rights. They are endowed with reason and conscience and should act towards one another in a spirit of brotherhood.

ARTICLE 2

Everyone is entitled to all the rights and freedoms set forth in this Declaration without distinction of any kind, such as race, colour, sex, language, religion, political or other opinion, national or social origin, property, birth or other status.

Furthermore, no distinction shall be made on the basis of the political jurisdictional or international status of the country or territory to which a person belongs, whether it be independent, trust, non-self-governing or under any other limitation of sovereignty.

ARTICLE 3

Everyone has the right to life, liberty and security of person.

ARTICLE 4

No one shall be held in slavery or servitude; slavery and the slave trade shall be prohibited in all their forms.

Adopted and proclaimed by General Assembly resolution 217 A (III) of 10 December 1948. On December 10, 1948 the General Assembly of the United Nations adopted and proclaimed the Universal Declaration of Human Rights the full text of which appears in the following pages. Following this historic act the Assembly called upon all Member countries to publicize the text of the Declaration and "to cause it to be disseminated, displayed, read and expounded principally in schools and other educational institutions, without distinction based on the political status of countries or territories."

ARTICLE 5

No one shall be subjected to torture or to cruel, inhuman or degrading treatment or punishment.

ARTICLE 6

Everyone has the right to recognition everywhere as a person before the law.

ARTICLE 7

All are equal before the law and are entitled without any discrimination to equal protection of the law. All are entitled to equal protection against any discrimination in violation of this Declaration and against any incitement to such discrimination.

ARTICLE 8

Everyone has the right to an effective remedy by the competent national tribunals for acts violating the fundamental rights granted him by the constitution or by law.

ARTICLE 9

No one shall be subjected to arbitrary arrest, detention or exile.

ARTICLE 10

Everyone is entitled in full equality to a fair and public hearing by an independent and impartial tribunal, in the determination of his rights and obligations and of any criminal charge against him.

ARTICLE 11

1. Everyone charged with a penal offence has the right to be presumed innocent until proved guilty according to law in a public trial at which he has had all the guarantees necessary for his defense.
2. No one shall be held guilty of any penal offence on account of any act or omission which did not constitute a penal offence, under national or international law, at the time when it was committed. Nor shall a heavier penalty be imposed than the one that was applicable at the time the penal offence was committed.

ARTICLE 12

No one shall be subjected to arbitrary interference with his privacy, family, home or correspondence, nor to attacks upon his honour and reputation. Everyone has the right to the protection of the law against such interference or attacks.

ARTICLE 13

1. Everyone has the right to freedom of movement and residence within the borders of each state.
2. Everyone has the right to leave any country, including his own, and to return to his country.

ARTICLE 14

1. Everyone has the right to seek and to enjoy in other countries asylum from persecution.
2. This right may not be invoked in the case of prosecutions genuinely arising from non-political crimes or from acts contrary to the purposes and principles of the United Nations.

ARTICLE 15

1. Everyone has the right to a nationality.
2. No one shall be arbitrarily deprived of his nationality nor denied the right to change his nationality.

ARTICLE 16

1. Men and women of full age, without any limitation due to race, nationality or religion, have the right to marry and to found a family. They are entitled to equal rights as to marriage, during marriage and at its dissolution.
2. Marriage shall be entered into only with the free and full consent of the intending spouses.
3. The family is the natural and fundamental group unit of society and is entitled to protection by society and the State.

ARTICLE 17

1. Everyone has the right to own property alone as well as in association with others.
2. No one shall be arbitrarily deprived of his property.

ARTICLE 18

Everyone has the right to freedom of thought, conscience and religion; this right includes freedom to change his religion or belief, and freedom, either alone or in community with others and in public or private, to manifest his religion or belief in teaching, practice, worship and observance.

ARTICLE 19

Everyone has the right to freedom of opinion and expression; this right includes freedom to hold opinions without interference and to seek, receive and impart information and ideas through any media and regardless of frontiers.

ARTICLE 20

1. Everyone has the right to freedom of peaceful assembly and association.
2. No one may be compelled to belong to an association.

ARTICLE 21

1. Everyone has the right to take part in the government of his country, directly or through freely chosen representatives.
2. Everyone has the right of equal access to public service in his country.
3. The will of the people shall be the basis of the authority of government; this will shall be expressed in periodic and genuine elections which shall be by universal and equal suffrage and shall be held by secret vote or by equivalent free voting procedures.

ARTICLE 22

Everyone, as a member of society, has the right to social security and is entitled to realization, through national effort and international cooperation and in accordance with the organization and resources of each State, of the economic, social and cultural rights indispensable for his dignity and the free development of his personality.

ARTICLE 23

1. Everyone has the right to work, to free choice of employment, to just and favourable conditions of work and to protection against unemployment.
2. Everyone, without any discrimination, has the right to equal pay for equal work.

3. Everyone who works has the right to just and favourable remuneration ensuring for himself and his family an existence worthy of human dignity, and supplemented, if necessary, by other means of social protection.
4. Everyone has the right to form and to join trade unions for the protection of his interests.

ARTICLE 24

Everyone has the right to rest and leisure, including reasonable limitation of working hours and periodic holidays with pay.

ARTICLE 25

1. Everyone has the right to a standard of living adequate for the health and well-being of himself and of his family, including food, clothing, housing and medical care and necessary social services, and the right to security in the event of unemployment, sickness, disability, widowhood, old age or other lack of livelihood in circumstances beyond his control.
2. Motherhood and childhood are entitled to special care and assistance. All children, whether born in or out of wedlock, shall enjoy the same social protection.

ARTICLE 26

1. Everyone has the right to education. Education shall be free, at least in the elementary and fundamental stages. Elementary education shall be compulsory. Technical and professional education shall be made generally available and higher education shall be equally accessible to all on the basis of merit.
2. Education shall be directed to the full development of the human personality and to the strengthening of respect for human rights and fundamental freedoms. It shall promote understanding, tolerance and friendship among all nations, racial or religious groups, and shall further the activities of the United Nations for the maintenance of peace.
3. Parents have a prior right to choose the kind of education that shall be given to their children.

ARTICLE 27

1. Everyone has the right freely to participate in the cultural life of the community, to enjoy the arts and to share in scientific advancement and its benefits.
2. Everyone has the right to the protection of the moral and material interests resulting from any scientific, literary or artistic production of which he is the author.

ARTICLE 28

Everyone is entitled to a social and international order in which the rights and freedoms set forth in this Declaration can be fully realized.

ARTICLE 29

1. Everyone has duties to the community in which alone the free and full development of his personality is possible.
2. In the exercise of his rights and freedoms, everyone shall be subject only to such limitations as are determined by law solely for the purpose of securing due recognition and respect for the rights and freedoms of others and of meeting the just requirements of morality, public order and the general welfare in a democratic society.
3. These rights and freedoms may in no case be exercised contrary to the purposes and principles of the United Nations.

ARTICLE 30

Nothing in this Declaration may be interpreted as implying for any State, group or person any right to engage in any activity or to perform any act aimed at the destruction of any of the rights and freedoms set forth herein.

Chapter 12

Business Values Away from Home

Case Study

Alchemist's Dream Come True

BARNABY J. FEDER

When the Great Lakes Chemical Corporation bought control of the world's biggest maker of lead additives for gasoline six years ago, the product itself was almost an afterthought.

After all, leaded gasoline was banned in Japan, it was in the last stages of being phased out in the United States and it was scheduled for elimination from Western Europe. The lead content of gasoline was under attack all over the world not only because it fouls the catalytic converters that reduce pollutants in car exhaust, but also because it is suspected of contributing to brain damage in children and other ailments.

What Great Lakes really wanted from Octel Associates was the British company's capacity to produce bromine, a chemical that Octel used to make the additives but that Great Lakes sells in other products ranging from fire retardants to color stabilizers. To get the bromine, Great Lakes was willing to take on the last years of the production of lead additives—as well as an ethical, and public relations, challenge.

It is a problem faced by many industries, including tobacco and asbestos producers and agrichemical and drug companies: under what conditions should legal products that are being phased out of the developed world to protect people's health or the earth's environment be sold to poorer nations?

For Great Lakes, that question has hung around longer and become more important to the company's image than it had anticipated. Far from petering out, demand for leaded gasoline, while shrinking, has remained far stronger than anyone predicted, especially in the third world. Meanwhile, every other major producer has stopped making the additives, known as tetraethyl lead, or TEL. That has left Great Lakes with an unexpected flood of profits and 90 percent of a market that no one else will enter because of the environmental problems associated with lead and the huge capital costs of building a new plant.

So far, Great Lakes has been able to deflect most critics by arguing that there are sound environmental and economic reasons for continuing to produce TEL. Meanwhile, the Octel cash cow has bankrolled a huge expansion that shows no sign of ending soon. Indeed, Great Lakes told Wall Street analysts early this year that it expects to more than double its size by the year 2000, to $5 billion in annual revenue, and to maintain healthy 15 percent operating profit margins while doing it.

"Octel was a good financial surprise," said David A. Hall, the senior vice president who oversees its operations for Great Lakes.

The latest indicator of just how good: Standard & Poor's this month raised its credit rating for Great Lakes to AA- from A+.

Wall Street had grown used to pleasant surprises during the years Great Lakes was led by the charismatic Emerson Kampen, who died this summer. The company grew from a chemical pipsqueak with $50 million in revenues when Mr. Kampen became chief executive in 1977 to a multinational with $1.8 billion in sales when health problems forced him to step aside in late 1993.

It was Mr. Kampen who in 1958 discovered the huge bromine-rich brine deposits in southern Arkansas that vaulted Great Lakes into the forefront of the bromine business, which had once been dominated by giants like Dow Chemical. The company processes bromine into a huge variety of industrial and consumer products. Its bromine compounds, for example, dominate the $600 million market for chemical additives that retard fires in plastics and textiles.

Mr. Kampen viewed Octel's unique process for extracting bromine from sea water in Wales as a beachhead for Great Lakes' further expansion into Europe. Those plans were quickly put on hold, though, when Great Lakes discovered the size of the TEL gold mine it was sitting on.

Octel has accounted for well over half Great Lakes' total operating profit every year even as its share of sales has declined. Last year, the contribution came to $259 million, or 59 percent, of Great Lakes' total operating profit of $439 million. In a recent research report, Mark Gulley of Morgan Stanley projected that Octel's share of profits from current operations would not fall below 50 percent before the turn of the century, despite an 8 percent annual decline in pounds of TEL sold.

The job of exploiting those profits to continue Great Lakes' growth record is now the primary challenge for Mr. Kampen's successor as chief executive, Robert B. McDonald.

The 58-year-old Mr. McDonald endorses Mr. Kampen's strategy of using a big chunk of Octel's profits for acquisitions. Some $375 million has been spent on 15 deals since 1989, including $90 million early last year to purchase an Italian producer of ultraviolet light-absorbing plastic additives. In 1993, about $72 million went to four acquisitions for Great Lakes' fast-growing water-treatment business.

"We are being treated as a vehicle to intelligently reinvest cash flow," said Marshall E. Bloom, chief executive of Bio-Lab Inc., a Decatur, Ga., subsidiary that makes recreational and industrial water-treatment chemicals. Some of the diversification is within Octel itself, which now gets about 15 percent of its revenues from non-TEL additives.

The availability of so much cash is also a morale booster for Great Lakes executives. "It's a fun place for managers to work because of the cash flow," Mr. Gulley said. "Managers have a rich uncle to fund growth in their groups while their competitors have to self-finance."

Shareholders are also getting their due. The company has spent $386 million on stock repurchases since April of last year, helping to calm Wall Street's jitters about the management transition and a slowdown in earnings growth that largely reflected heavier-than-normal capital investments in existing businesses. After falling by a third from a peak of nearly $75 in late 1993, the price has climbed back to $67.

So far, Great Lakes has capitalized on Octel without running into much flak from environmentalists. That probably is due in part to its much lower profile as an industrial middleman than Octel's former owners, a consortium of oil companies including such giants as the British Petroleum Company, Texaco Inc., Mobil Inc. and the Royal Dutch/Shell Group. The last major oil company partner, Chevron, owns a 12 percent stake that Great Lakes hopes to buy soon.

But Great Lakes is also working hard to avoid confrontations. Unlike tobacco companies, Great Lakes readily concedes that its biggest profit spinner can be harmful and ought to disappear eventually. But it argues that calls by some environmental groups for a world-wide TEL ban as early as the end of the century are unrealistic. To start with, Great Lakes says, there are too few refineries equipped to produce unleaded gas and too many cars outside the industrialized world without catalytic converters.

Great Lakes argues that such cars get fewer miles per gallon and spew out increased amounts of cancer-causing pollutants like benzene if forced to run on lower-octane unleaded gasoline. Thus, leaded fuel may be an "economic and environmental bargain" in many developing countries for years to come, according to Mr. Hall, the senior vice president in charge of Octel.

Some critics, like Dr. Joel Schwartz, a former Environmental Protection Agency official who is now a professor at the Harvard University School of Public Health, argue that Great Lakes and the oil refiners who use TEL underestimate its environmental impact. And the Alliance to End Childhood Lead Poisoning, a Washington-based group that sponsored an international conference on leaded gasoline last May, says Octel's suggestions that burning unleaded fuel may create even worse problems amount to a "disinformation campaign."

Such accusations are ignored on Wall Street, where Great Lakes is seen as one of the chemical industry's environmental white hats. Many of its products are substitutes for more noxious chemicals made by others; its largest nonbromine business recycles agricultural wastes into a metal processing chemical.

Case Study

Gift Giving and the African Elder

JAMES GATHII

Business executives from the United States, a recent signatory of the OECD Convention against bribery, plan to visit a senior cabinet minister in his office with regard to their plans to expand their business in a rapidly liberalizing sub-Saharan African economy.

In one of their advance briefing memos handed to them by the minister's assistant is some information of gift giving in African custom. The information states that it is an established African custom for visitors to give gifts to elders, as long as they are not in cash, or given in the expectation of a return of a favor, and they are understood to be a tribute to the seniority of the elder.

Asked to explain whether the business executives were expected to bring gifts for the minister (who is regarded as an elder), the minister's eloquent assistant says that African custom does not place mandatory obligations on gift giving since it is a courtesy acknowledging the elder's seniority and seeking his/her blessings in return. The minister's assistant then goes ahead to justify gift giving by analogizing it to the "professional courtesy" medical doctors extend to each other and to their families in advanced industrialized countries. According to the minister's assistant, just as doctors in advanced countries treat their colleagues and their families for free, or provide discounted services by forgiving their colleagues' insurance co-payments, so too do elders enjoy the courtesy of gift giving and subsequently blessing the fortunes of the gift givers.

The minister's assistant concludes by pointing out that just as medical doctors in the United States are resisting federal restrictions of this time-honored professional practice by labeling it a fraudulent practice, African elders are similarly entitled to defend gift giving from the intrusive policy of the OECD and the American corporations that wish to stop it. As long as gift giving is in accordance with the three conditions laid out above, the minister's assistant advises the American business executives it is perfectly permissible for them to bring gifts when they come to see the minister.

What would you do if you were in the position of the business executives?

"Gift Giving and the African Elder" by James Gathii. Reprinted by permission of the author.

International Business Ethics and Incipient Capitalism: A Double Standard?

RICHARD T. DE GEORGE

The term "international business ethics" is ambiguous, and this ambiguity leads to some confusion and to a number of disputes. It is ambiguous because its referent is not clear. It may refer to the ethical rules that govern all business everywhere in the world. But in that case it is arguably reducible to the general or basic ethical norms that govern human behavior, irrespective of society. For it is doubtful that there are special rules of business that are so general as to be applicable everywhere. International business ethics might refer to the ethical rules that ought to govern multinational corporations; or to the rules that apply to business as well as to nations in speaking of global problems, such as global warming and depletion of the ozone level; or to the different ethical norms applicable in different countries because of different social, economic, political, and historical conditions.

The term also leads to a number of debates, the chief of which is a debate about moral relativism. Moral relativism has a long tradition apart from international business ethics, and in the modern period stems from cultural relativism documented by anthropological studies. If mores and customs vary from society to society, what rules should one follow when one leaves one's own society and goes to another? Is one bound by the sexual moral rules of one's own monogamous society if one goes to another which allows polygamy or polyandry? If such relativism holds with respect to sex, does it also hold with respect to business?

In some ways the term "international business ethics"—like the term "business ethics"—is misleading, because both seem to refer to something that is modeled on general ethics. If general ethical theories of the standard kinds are correct, they are not dependent on particular circumstances, even though one must consider particular circumstances in applying them. But utilitarianism and Kantianism do not depend on particular circumstances for their defense.

Business ethics is an area of applied ethics. What distinguishes it from general ethics is its application to specific kinds of activity, namely business activity. As such it necessarily depends heavily for its content on the structures that define business and in which business operates. It gains its specificity by taking into account particular socio-economic circumstances; the political system and existing laws that are intertwined with these; the level of economic development and the standard of living of a country; the local traditions, beliefs, and expectations of the people in a given society; and a host of other similar considerations. These taken together form what can be called the background institutions or conditions within which business, and so business ethics, operate and make sense.

Presented to the Society for Business Ethics, May, 1994. Copyright © by Richard T. De George. Reprinted with the permission of the author.

Thus business ethics in a socio-economic-political system such as that found in the United States is very different from what might be called business ethics in a socialist system, to the extent that business is allowed in the latter.

What is allowed by legitimate legal structures varies from country to country and makes the practice of business vary accordingly. In a society in which social benefits for workers are mandated by law, the question of what ethics requires from employers with respect to the treatment of workers may be very different from a society in which such benefits are not mandated. If government provides health, old-age pension and other benefits to all its citizens, then the obligations of business in these regards are very different from a society in which these are not provided. If a country has a long tradition of business providing lifetime employment, the obligations of business are again different from a society which has no such tradition.

Business ethics as a movement and as an area of study had its birth in the United States. The issues that rose to the fore were those about which Americans were concerned. Business ethics in the United States developed within specifically American background institutions. As it was exported or as other countries followed America's lead in this area, business ethics texts written for America were often used as texts in other countries. It was not long before both business and those teaching business ethics saw the lack of fit in many areas. Because background institutions vary, so the issues of business ethics and specific applications vary. In a country such as Japan in the 1970s, when trading in the stock market was done almost exclusively by insiders, each of whom belonged to a system of interlocking companies, insider trading was not unethical, even though insider trading in the United States was both unethical and illegal. The same practice—or at least practices that went by the same name—was morally justifiable in the one case but not in the other. In Japan there was no unfairness, no one had advantages other traders did not equally enjoy, and the practice did not harm any of the participants. In the United States, however, insider trading did give insiders unfair advantage and did harm those who traded without access in principle to appropriate information. By the 1990s the situation had changed on the Tokyo exchange. Trading was done not only by insiders but significantly by small Japanese investors and by foreign investors. Hence the practice of insider trading came to be seen as unfair to non-insiders and the practice was eventually made illegal. Insider trading is neither ethical nor unethical in itself; it takes on a moral character only when considered in a specific social context.

Because background institutions vary to such a great extent, it is difficult to speak of international business ethics as if it were all of a piece. It cannot simply be American business ethics or German or Japanese or any other kind of business ethics, extended to an international level. But in one sense it is that. An American multinational must respect the ethical norms and values of the home company wherever the company is located. It must, of course, take into account local laws, traditions, and so on. But it cannot hire child labor, even if that is the local custom; nor can it discriminate against women, or follow apartheid laws, or buy goods made by slave labor, or fail to provide safe working conditions. The list goes on.

What might give one pause is my presenting these requirements as mandatory only for American companies, as if they were not required for all companies. After all, all companies must respect the human rights of workers, honor contracts, and not harm people by dumping toxic waste. Yet these are demanded not by any special ethics of business but by general moral norms, which apply in business as well as in every other realm in life.

As a test case for the thesis I have proposed, consider the differences, if any, between business in the United States on the one hand and in Russia at the present time on the other. The United States is the business leader of the world. It has a highly developed system of laws that control many of the socially negative tendencies of unrestrained capitalism. It has an educated citizenry conscious of its rights. It has critical and choosy consumers, who usually have the choice of which products to buy and which manufacturers to do business with. It has strong environmental protection groups. It has a tradition of business being expected to contribute to the welfare of the local community in which it operates. In sum, it has a host of well-defined background institutions, within which one can intelligently speak about business ethics and analyze practices from hostile buyouts to drug testing of employees to liability for dangerous products.

The background institutions in the United States did not come into place all at once. They developed slowly over time, often in response to abuses. The robber barons at the turn of the century are not a proud part of the history of American business, nor are the racketeers of the 1920s, or the sellers of snake oil, or the carpetbaggers in the South after the Civil War. Free enterprise is not as free as some of its early proponents would have wished. Government regulations aim to protect the public interest, promote health and safety, and keep competition fair. All of this developed within a democratic society with a free press. The history of capitalism in other countries with other background institutions is very different. Capitalism has been linked with dictatorships, with corrupt governments, with criminal elements, and with a variety of different background conditions and institutions. It is not all of a piece, and business ethics does not serve the same function or come up with the same evaluations of similar-sounding practices, often because the differing circumstances and legal backgrounds make the practices different in reality, despite the fact that they go by the same name.

What Americans consider just with respect to property transactions assumes the institution of private property, protected by law, and ethically justified within the system of free enterprise. In the former Soviet Union, in which private property was condemned as unethical and unjustifiable, there was no private ownership of the means of production and there was a very different notion of what justice with respect to property meant. A host of transactions that were legitimate and ethical in the United States were either not possible or were unethical in the former Soviet Union.

Because it is in transition between the state socialism under which it functioned for seventy years and some sort of still-to-be-defined free-market system, Russia at the present time makes for an interesting case study of the thesis that business ethics must take into account the existing background institutions in the societies in which business activities take place. Under existing conditions in Russia, which ethical rules can appropriately be applied to business?

In many instances the answer is not clear. But that does not mean that it is unclear in all instances. And I believe that with sufficiently careful analysis we can arrive at least at some tentative conclusions.

RUSSIAN BACKGROUND

Since it is essential to keep the background conditions in mind, let me briefly sketch some of them. Under Soviet socialism there was no private ownership of the means of production. All productive resources were state owned. No individual was allowed to be in business for himself or to hire others, since that would constitute exploitation. The state employed all workers, and all able-bodied citizens were required to work. The state provided subsidized housing, free education and health care, old-age pensions, and a variety of other social benefits. Often these were provided by the factories at which people worked.

Bureaucracy was the rule, and centralized control dominated industry. Inefficiency was widespread. Without a market to determine supply and demand, the prices of goods, resources, and labor were more or less arbitrary.

The government sought to undermine traditional bourgeois morality and to replace it with a collectivist and state-oriented socialist morality. It succeeded in undermining traditional morality but failed in replacing it with an effective social morality. As a result, many Russians adopted a dualistic approach to morals.[1] Family, friends, and those with whom one was closely associated—often fellow workers—were treated according to standard rules of decency, concern, and respect. The system and those who represented it were seen as "them"—nameless and faceless and deserving no moral respect. Rules, which were too rigid and numerous to follow, were ignored or circumvented whenever possible. Since all property belonged in theory to everyone, one took what one could when and where one could. Invoices meant little. They were simply internal accounting procedures. There was little work discipline, since everyone was guaranteed employment by law, and there was no incentive for innovation or hard work. Reports were often falsified at all levels so as to meet paper production norms. The people felt that the government was a master of fabricating, slanting, distorting and suppressing the truth, and they followed suit in dealing with the government. The people were taught (and many people accepted) the claim that private property was exploitative and unethical, that large discrepancies in wealth were anti-social and represented the fruits of unethical activity, and that capitalism, despite the wealth it produced, was built on ethically unjustifiable principles.

It is from this background that Russia emerged in 1991. It moved from a communist type government to one that at least in theory was democratic. It moved from a socialist type economy to something else that at least in theory allowed free enterprise. It started privatizing its industry. But all its steps were tentative. Although background institutions must be developed in order to support the new way of life, these institutions have been slow in coming. Many of the large enterprises are still state owned, and of those that have been privatized, many still operate essentially the way they did before, including receiving subsidies from the government. The legal system is in disarray. A new constitution has only recently been adopted. But the legislature is divided and has not followed through with much of the legislation needed for a functioning market economy. The laws governing private enterprise are in a state of flux: they have been frequently rewritten during the past three years, and they are still not settled. Without laws, the judicial system cannot be expected to settle disputes. The enforcement apparatus of the government is also in disarray, and crime has burgeoned.

The Russians tend to distinguish business, which they consider is entrepreneurial activity on a relatively small level, from the running of factories and large enterprises. Laws have tended to favor large enterprises. Entrepreneurial activity, prohibited under socialism, has consisted of people opening small businesses, and to a large extent of importing and selling goods from abroad, acting as middlemen. Some have made quick fortunes. Those with money—and Russian TV now carries ads for Mercedes Benz and BMW, indicating there are quite a few such people—are looked at askance by the masses without much, who now live at a lower level than under socialism. The latter, given their own experience, feel that the *nouveaux riches* must be gangsters or members of the mafia, or exploiters, or former communist officials who were able to take advantage of their special position. The people were taught that capitalism is unethical, and those who take advantage of the market to amass wealth are unethical. Although the switch from socialism has made goods available in a quantity and of a quality not previously available, wages have not kept pace with costs, unemployment is rising, and the standard of living is falling.

INCIPIENT CAPITALISM AND ETHICS

In such circumstances, what background institutions determine what is just, and how can one say what is fair or unfair, right or wrong, with respect to business? Failing to find any satisfactory answer, some claim that business ethics in this context is meaningless. Some characterize the situation as "wild" or primitive or incipient capitalism, reminiscent of conditions in the United States in the Wild West or under the robber barons. Many Russians, who were taught by their Marxist-Leninist teachers that capitalism is a rapacious system, think that the crime and corruption that has blossomed in Russia is a necessary price that goes together with the goods and higher standard of living that eventually capitalism will bring them. Is this so?

By way of response, I shall start with some broad generalizations. First, regardless of whether the characterization of wild or primitive or incipient capitalism is correct, the basic norms of morality apply to every society, whatever the background institutions. These norms are not dependent on particular background conditions. Murdering one's competitor, destroying the property of those who do not pay for protection, distributing poisoned food as pure—all such acts are unethical, no matter what the system. Hundreds of businessmen have been murdered by what has become known as the Russian mafia. This may resemble what took place as capitalism developed in 18th- and 19th-century Europe, but it is not a necessary stage on the way to a free-market economy today. Such behavior is clearly unethical. There are some acts that are wrong no matter what the background situation. Similarly, government officials who demand bribes to allow privileges that are legally restricted or who ignore violations of the law are unethical—no matter what the system. Such actions are generally and properly termed corrupt, no matter where practiced.

Second, although Russia will inevitably suffer the pangs of moving from a socialist economy to a free-market economy, it need not attempt to reinvent a market economy. Many rules necessary for its successful and efficient functioning have been developed elsewhere and need only be adopted. These include respect for private property and the honoring of contracts, among other norms. Without these, repeat business transactions will not take place or will be excessively costly. Efficient markets require rules, trust, enforcement mechanisms, and penalties for failure to perform.

Third, it is easier to control illegal and unethical behavior before it becomes a way of doing business, entrenched and powerful, than after it has become such. Hence there is no justification in terms of market development to allow unethical activity if it can be prevented.

Nonetheless, if we ask how Russia can move justly from a state-owned system to a privately owned system, the answer is anything but clear, and there may be no satisfactory answer. The reason is that what is just or fair depends in part on background institutions and assumptions, and these are systematically ambiguous in Russia with respect to privatization. Do the rules of socialism or of a free-market economy apply, for example, with respect to property rights? Under socialism, all property theoretically belonged to the people and was held and administered by the state. Property rights were not assigned to individuals. So if we ask who by right owns a particular factory or plant, the answer is not clear. Should the factory be turned over to the workers? But some factories were favored and are productive and worth a great deal, while others are for all intents and purposes worthless. Turning over a gold mine to the mine workers is different from turning over a university to its faculty. Should the rights to all state property be divided equally among all Russian citizens? An attempt to do just that consisted, in part, of giving each citizen vouchers worth 10,000 rubles ($40.00). But without a stock market to sell the vouchers and without information about how the system works, many quickly lost their share of Russian industry. Moreover neither approach brings in any new money, which is needed for many of the industries to function productively. To get new capital, some plants have been sold to non-Russian outside buyers. But such buyers are only interested in the more productive plants. No matter what method is chosen—and in Russia a variety of approaches to privatization have been used—each can be criticized as unjust to some group or portion of the population.[2]

Just as privatization cannot proceed justly because of different, changing and ambiguous background conditions, the difficulty spills over into other areas of economic life.

What then can we say about business ethics in Russia at the present time? As a start to answering this question I shall present and analyze four typical cases. I shall argue that these cases cannot be properly evaluated if we ignore the circumstances in which they are found, and that the evaluations that are justifiable may well be different from like-sounding cases in an American context. From the analyses I shall draw some tentative conclusions.

FOUR CASES

1.   Consider the case of Ivan Ivanovich, a Russian manager of a large formerly state-owned factory. Although he has the new responsibility of running his factory in order to make a profit for the shareholders, he takes upon himself the obligation of paying the company's workers all the benefits the workers received under the communist system. The factory supplies them with housing, health care, and old-age pensions. In order to do this and still stay in business, Ivan ignores a number of laws that are not strictly enforced, and falsifies the factory's records so as not to incur any taxes. This is similar to what he did under the communist regime.[3] For the factory to be at all efficient, he should fire at least ten percent of his employees. But because they would have to join the growing army of the unemployed, he refuses to do so.

Ivan does not run the company for his own profit or that of the shareholders. He breaks a number of Russian laws, which are not enforced anyway, in order to provide the kinds of benefits that the workers of the factory have traditionally received under communism, and which the state has not taken over. He chooses to keep people employed rather than make the company efficient. Are his actions ethically justifiable? In this case, what Ivan does is unethical if he has an ethical obligation to obey the law and an ethical obligation to run the factory efficiently and profitably. But arguably the ethical obligation to obey the law holds only when the law is itself ethically justifiable and equitably enforced. Since both are open to question in the given circumstances in Russia—the first because of the ambiguity and contradictory nature of many of the laws and the second because of the lack of any effective enforcement—the ethical obligation to obey such laws is questionable at best. Nonetheless, Ivan opens himself up to possible legal prosecution. What of his obligation to increase shareholder wealth, which he is not doing by continuing worker benefits that are no longer legally mandated? From a long-range perspective, is he not also delaying the transition of the society to a true market economy? From an ethical point of view, whether the obligations to shareholders and to develop the new system take precedence over former obligations of the firm to its employees depends on how one interprets the background assumptions. And it is these that are mixed. I would argue (although restrictions of space and time prevent my doing so here) that his actions are ethically justifiable, given the circumstances.

2.   Since I have implied that it may not be unethical to ignore the law in Russia, let us turn to Alexander Alexandrovich, a Russian manager of a large aluminum manufacturing company, *A*, who together with other managers of the firm forms an independent company, *B*, which they privately own.[4] Company *A* is state-owned and subsidized. It sells its aluminum to company *B* at subsidized prices, the same as it does to other Russian companies. The managers of company *B*, as is the custom, pay an official for an export permit. They then export the aluminum they buy at subsidized prices and receive much higher world prices for their product. They siphon off most of their earnings to private Swiss bank accounts, returning to Russia only enough funds to cover their next purchase.

In forming Company *B*, Alexander and his colleagues did nothing illegal, and were fostering the advent of a free-market economy. *B* pays *A* the government subsidized prices, legally exports the aluminum, sells it at world prices, banks the profit abroad, and brings back sufficient capital to make the next purchase. No laws are broken. Firm *A* continues in business, the workers receive the same pay they did previously, and the managers, in good entrepreneurial fashion, take advantage of a situation to become millionaires. Did they do anything for which they can be ethically faulted? If legality equaled ethical permissibility, the answer would be no. Yet some questions arise.

The workers of the aluminum firm feel that some injustice is being done them. The managers have used their position and experience to create an independent company that reaps great rewards for the managers, while the workers are no better off than they were before. Is this unethical? The workers are no worse off than they were, and unlike many of their fellow Russians they still have their jobs and their wages. Of course they would be better off if the managers of the firm did not create the trading company and shared their profits with the workers. The question is whether the managers were ethically required to do this or ethically precluded from doing what they did. Do the rules and expectations of socialism operate here, in which case we have a violation of socialist solidarity; or do we adopt the rules of capitalism, which ignore such claims? If we adopt the rules of capitalism, do we have a conflict of interest—a concept unfamiliar to many Russians—and a failure of Alexander in his capacity as the manager of *A* to manage it for the best interests of that company rather than of *B*? Would the situation be different if company *A* had been privatized and was owned by the workers? In a mixed situation must one choose which set of background assumptions apply or may one choose among them, more accurately reflecting the actual situation? More importantly, it is not outside observers but the Russians who decide what should apply. And there seems to be little consensus on this issue in the present state of flux.

The managers paid the government bureaucrat who issued the export license. Is this a bribe or a facilitating payment? In either case, is it justifiable? The managers did not pay the official to do anything that the official was not supposed to do or to break any Russian law. If the official required a payment to issue the export permit, the question is whether officials who require such payment are more to blame than those who pay them. Many Russians feel that the bureaucracy and many of the rules bureaucrats enforce exist solely for the benefit of those who enforce them. In this situation exactly who is unethical is not always clear. The government's purpose in permitting exports is to bring back hard currency into Russia for the benefit of the country. But the government has not been able to control companies that trade abroad, or to enforce any type of accountability. Is Alexander ethically required to follow the intent of export controls or may he take advantage of loopholes in the law?

Finally Alexander takes advantage of the fact that Company *A* is subsidized in various ways by the government. This provides the owners of *B* with a product that costs them relatively little, which they sell at a handsome profit. Clearly the state does not subsidize the aluminum industry so that managers can become wealthy. Yet what the managers do is not illegal. Rather than invoke ethics, both the market and the government are responding to the situation. The Russian aluminum firms over the past three years exported in such quantity that they created a glut on the international market. The price of aluminum dropped sharply, as did the profits of the Russian exporters. The government in the meantime stopped subsidizing the cost of electricity, thus forcing the producing firm to bear its real costs and raise its selling price to *B*, as well as to all other firms.

One might argue that Alexander exploits the workers, the country, and the legal loopholes that exist so that he can reap enormous profits. I am inclined to argue this position against those who claim that Alexander and his fellow managers are just acting as entrepreneurs do and so are justified in their actions. But making out the case that their actions are unethical is difficult in the given circumstances. The reason is that it is unclear which sets of rules—socialist or capitalist—form the background against which to evaluate the entrepreneurial actions.

3. An entrepreneur, Aleksey Alekseyevich, joins a private electricians' cooperative. They wire houses and provide all the services generally provided by electricians. Since copper wire is in short supply and electrical fixtures go first to large state-owned factories, Aleksey can operate only by getting wire and fixtures where and how he can. Sometimes Aleksey buys them from suppliers—no questions asked. Sometimes he can, for a fee, get a shipment of supplies rerouted from its intended destination to the cooperative. He pays the local protection agency (part of the Russian mafia) a monthly fee to be allowed to continue operating.

This case is typical of a considerable number of small firms in Russia. The transition from state-owned factories and shops to privately owned ones has taken place without the distribution and allocation system being effectively replaced by the market.[5] Large state-owned and formerly state-owned industries still have priority claims on many resources. Although small enterprises are allowed and sometimes verbally encouraged, it is often extremely difficult for them to get the supplies they need to function. To some extent this is not new and is similar to conditions under communism.

When everything is said to belong to everyone, as was the case under socialism, there is often little concern for exactly who gets what. If a shipment goes to one firm rather than another, the second firm in a sense owns it as appropriately as the first, since it is common property. Such an attitude is found in the U.S. military in which inventoried items that are lost or misplaced or stolen are frequently made up by trading among property officers and clerks from different units. With this sort of background, what the entrepreneurs are doing, as well as what those who supply the goods may be doing, fits in with the way of doing business under the former system. The allocation system has not caught up with the free-market thrust of the economy. From the point of view of a market economy, the allocation system is distorted, given a move to a partially developed private-ownership system. Under these circumstances a small entrepreneur like Aleksey must either operate as the situation describes or not operate at all. Let us suppose that this is an accurate characterization of the situation. In such a case, may the entrepreneur get the material he needs as he can, and may he pay extortion in order to be allowed to operate?

We can make several distinctions. First, it is unethical for the suppliers of protection to charge extortion. Extortion is unethical, no matter what the system. But paying extortion is less bad than charging it; and it may be justifiable, at least temporarily, under certain circumstances. It is an evil because it tends to perpetuate extortion, and helps it to escalate, to the detriment of society. Yet paying extortion is the lesser of two evils for Aleksey, if the alternative is for him and all small entrepreneurs to be driven out of business and for there either to be no such services available or for only those who have no ethical compunctions to operate businesses.

Similarly, if the goods sold to the small business are stolen, we can fault those who steal. If they are diverted from their intended receiver but the producer is paid, then the harm done to the system might be grounds for ethical complaint, except that the system is chaotic, and determining which recipient produces more good or harm may be difficult to determine. Even if we ethically fault the supplier (as we should), the fault of the receiver is certainly less, and operating in the same fashion as under the communist system may be preferable once again to leaving all enterprise to the criminal element.

Both of these justifications are justifications only insofar as they are truly necessary and temporary, given the current state of affairs, and only insofar as they are the lesser of two evils.

4. A U.S. multinational, represented by John Jones, purchases a portion of a formerly state-owned enterprise that has been privatized. Its Russian co-owners tell the U.S. company that if they are to succeed, they should be ready to pay bribes to a variety of government officials.

This case demands a different analysis from the other three. Although the American multinational operates in the Russian system in which the laws are ambiguous and often unenforced, in which bribery is rampant and extortion the norm for small businesses, none of this justifies American companies acting as Russian firms might justifiably act. The reason is that American companies are in a very different situation from the Russian companies.

First of all, no American company is forced to operate in Russia. It always has the option of not operating there, and many American firms, given the ambiguity of the laws, the ambiguous status of property claims, the uncertainty of adjudication of disputes and the prevalence of corruption on both the governmental and the criminal levels, have decided not to venture into those circumstances. Those who do venture, do so knowing that they take enormous risks in the hope of gaining equivalent returns. But unlike their Russian counterparts they operate from a position of power. They have hard currency, which is in great demand. They can successfully refuse to pay bribes that are prohibited by the Foreign Corrupt Practices Act, and they can successfully refuse to pay extortion. If in some instances the costs of protecting their property and employees from violence is too great, they have the option of leaving. Hence they are not in a position of either being forced to engage in corrupt practices, thereby helping to sustain and promote them, or of not operating at all—even though they will not operate in Russia.

To the extent that they do operate in Russia, because of their powerful position, they have the obligation to help bring ethical practices into the marketplace and to help make the market fair. They are potentially in a position to exploit the people and the country with relative impunity. But not only is that not in the long-term interest of the company or of the development of a market economy in Russia, it is exploitation of a gross kind.

Does this mean that there are two sets of ethical rules, one for Russian companies and one for American (and other) multinational corporations? The answer is no, but this must be properly understood. It is no because the actual circumstances of the Russian and of American firms operating in Russia are different, despite the fact that both operate in the same place at the same time.

Does this imply that because of their different circumstances less is expected of Russian companies, or more is tolerated from an ethical point of view than of American companies? The answer is a qualified yes. There is no special set of lesser ethical rules that applies to conditions of incipient capitalism. But ethics never demands more than can reasonably be expected of people, in business just as in other areas of life. Moreover, business itself embodies and presupposes certain ethical norms without which it cannot and does not function. The limits of corruption that it can tolerate are not great. Nor are the limits of intentional misinformation, deceit, and exploitation. As these increase, business tends to retreat, being replaced by barter and more primitive forms of exchange. We are presently seeing this phenomenon in Russia and in some of the other former Soviet and communist states.

Corruption is not justifiable simply because it is rampant. But operating amidst corruption is not easy. The actual alternatives that are open to one are frequently decisive in determining whether certain practices—such as paying extortion—are justifiable. The conditions are different for local and foreign firms. American and other multinationals can serve a positive function by being the exemplars and bearers of ethical business practices, and this is as important and perhaps more important to the developing system than the goods or services such firms might provide.

GENERALIZATIONS FROM THESE CASES

What conclusions can we draw from this discussion?

1. Some actions are wrong no matter which system of background institutions are in place. Hence whether Russia's background institutions are socialist, free-market, mixed or chaotic, murder, extortion, violence and theft are unethical. The longer they are tolerated and become de facto part of the way of doing business, the more difficult it will be to achieve a reasonably efficient market.

2. The U.S. business ethics literature and a U.S. perspective on particular business issues reflects American background conditions and cannot be superimposed on Russia. In the present circumstances in Russia some actions will appropriately be judged unethical when viewed from the assumption that socialist background conditions are operative, and will appropriately be viewed as ethically justifiable when viewed from the assumption that free-market conditions are operative. Since both are partially operative—or inoperative—it is not only practically difficult but in principle impossible to decide from some outside perspective the morality of some business practices.

3. The discrepancies between aspects of the socialist system that are still in place—such as state subsidies—and the opportunities for profit by selling subsidized goods abroad under free-market rules is being exploited by some

to their great advantage. Legislation and regulations that are rational, that are aimed at the common good, and that keep competition fair are essential. Russia can learn from the experience of developed countries what is required and need not learn only by trial and error.

4. The plight of the worker in Russia is worsening. Given the confusion about the role of the state in providing housing, health services, education, old-age benefits, and other social assistance, the obligations of industry and business to provide what was provided under the former socialist system are unclear. But business and industry cannot simply ignore the needs of their workers. How firms must treat employees, beyond respecting their basic human rights, is appropriately determined by considering the background conditions in which the firm operates. A pressing task is for Russia to determine and implement a clear policy. In the meantime Russian firms have some obligations to continue providing services that were formerly expected and considered entitlements.

5. American and other multinational corporations can serve an important function not only by economic joint ventures and economic activity, but also by adhering to the ethical standards that are expected at home and by helping guide the establishment of background institutions that are necessary for the long-run efficient and mutually beneficial development of business in Russia. Not only can they adhere to higher standards but they have the obligation to do so. This seemingly double set of ethical standards is justified by the fact that although operating in the same country, the circumstances of the foreign interest and of the local entrepreneur are different, and what is possible for each is different as well. Applying the principle of "ought implies can" yields different norms for foreign and for local businesses.[6]

Before closing, however, let me briefly extend the implications of my analysis to two other areas of international business ethics. I have discussed, first, business ethics within different countries (which one might call comparative international business ethics), and second, the possible difference between the obligations of multinationals and of indigenous businesses in a country like Russia. The third area is the area of mutual trade between or among countries.

If the thesis is correct that background institutions are necessary to the substantive norms of business ethics, then the background conditions of international trade and politics set the stage for international business and for international business ethics on this level. Here we frequently have negotiations not by multinationals but by the governments of countries. But in addition we have international codes, U.N. commissions, religious institutions, non-governmental organizations such as the Red Cross, and other similar groups and institutions that form part of the background. Expectations on the international level are also very different from on the national level. There is no effective redistribution mechanism among countries, no taxes for global redistribution, and so on. Issues of rich countries versus poor countries and of dependency versus independence form part of the background for trade negotiations, treaties, agreements, and the like for carrying on business. This area deserves more careful analysis and development for its ethical implications, problems, needs—especially the need for more effective background institutions—than it has received.

The fourth area is what I shall call the global area. There are some global issues—such as the depletion of the ozone level—that cannot be resolved and are not caused by individual companies or by companies from individual countries, but by countries and companies and people acting each in their own ways. With respect to the ozone level, to the extent that the problem is caused by chlorofluorocarbons, these are the results of modern chemistry, and are emitted by machines made by businesses—whether privately owned or government owned. No individual firm can solve the problem, nor can any individual country. The ethical responsibility falls collectively on all. Some contribute more to the problem than others. Some are able to do more to solve it than others. The background situation and conditions affect the obligations of different groups and different countries and different companies. The Rio Conference was a meeting of nations. Some American companies are ahead of the curve of the American government in their willingness to cut back on emissions; some poorer countries are unable to cut back as much as more affluent countries are. Are there two sets of norms here?

As in the case of Russia and incipient capitalism, it is possible to hold that some actions are simply wrong, no matter who does them; some actions are wrong, but may be tolerated in certain conditions as the lesser of two evils; and these same actions may be tolerated for some in certain conditions but not for others in other conditions. A greater burden falls on the industries in the developed countries than falls on the industries of developing countries both because the former are the greater cause of the degradation of the ozone level and because they have the financial and technological resources to do something to alleviate the problem. Similarly, affluent companies in developing countries have a greater responsibility to control their emissions than do struggling companies in such countries. The general rule to do no direct intentional harm plays out differently for different countries in different conditions. As we have seen, conditions may be different for two companies in the same country at the same time.

I started by noting the ambiguity of the term "international business ethics." It encompasses, I suggest, at least these four areas, although it is not exhausted by them. I also claimed at the start of this paper that even if general ethics had some claim to universality, business ethics, as an applied area, had much less, if any, such claim. As an applied area of ethics, it is always embedded in socio-economic-political conditions which form and engulf business. If this is correct, international business ethics is not more free from such constraints but equally tied to them, and is often more difficult because of the additional variables that one has to take into account.

Notes

1. See Richard T. De George, *Soviet Ethics and Morality*, Ann Arbor: Michigan University Press, 1969; Sheila M. Puffer, "Understanding the Bear: A Portrait of Russian Business Leaders," *The Academy of Management Executive*, Vol. 8, No. 1 (February 1994), pp. 41–54.
2. For a fuller discussion of privatization, see Richard T. De George, "International Business Ethics: Russia and Eastern Europe," *Social Responsibility: Business, Journalism, Law, Medicine*, Vol. XIX (1993), pp. 5–23.
3. Adi Ignatius, "Battling for Russia's Soul at the Factory," *The Wall Street Journal*, December 21, 1993, p. A6. In "Business Ethics of the Director of a Russian Industrial Enterprise," a paper presented at the 25th AAASS National Convention, Honolulu, November 12–22, 1993, Leonid Khotin describes such situations.
4. Ann Imse, "Russia's Wild Capitalists Take Aluminum for a Ride," *New York Times*, February 13, 1994, p. F4.

5. See, among other sources, Alexander Filatov, "Unethical Business Behavior In Post-Communist Russia: Origins and Trends," *Business Ethics Quarterly*, Vol. 4, No. 1 (January 1994), pp. 11–15.
6. A somewhat similar analysis yields greater obligations to U.S. multinationals than to indigenous firms in less developed countries. See Richard T. De George, *Competing With Integrity in International Business*, New York: Oxford University Press, 1993.

Values in Tension: Ethics Away from Home

THOMAS DONALDSON

When we leave home and cross our nation's boundaries, moral clarity often blurs. Without a backdrop of shared attitudes, and without familiar laws and judicial procedures that define standards of ethical conduct, certainty is elusive. Should a company invest in a foreign country where civil and political rights are violated? Should a company go along with a host country's discriminatory employment practices? If companies in developed countries shift facilities to developing nations that lack strict environmental and health regulations, or if those companies choose to fill management and other top-level positions in a host nation with people from the home country, whose standards should prevail?

Even the best-informed, best-intentioned executives must rethink their assumptions about business practice in foreign settings. What works in a company's home country can fail in a country with different standards of ethical conduct. Such difficulties are unavoidable for businesspeople who live and work abroad.

But how can managers resolve the problems? What are the principles that can help them work through the maze of cultural differences and establish codes of conduct for globally ethical business practice? How can companies answer the toughest question in global business ethics: What happens when a host country's ethical standards seem lower than the home country's?

COMPETING ANSWERS

One answer is as old as philosophical discourse. According to cultural relativism, no culture's ethics are better than any other's; therefore there are no international rights and wrongs. If the people of Indonesia tolerate the bribery of their public officials, so what? Their attitude is no better or worse than that of people in Denmark or Singapore who refuse to offer or accept bribes. Likewise, if Belgians fail to find insider trading morally repugnant, who cares? Not enforcing insider-trading laws is no more or less ethical than enforcing such laws.

The cultural relativist's creed—When in Rome, do as the Romans do—is tempting, especially when failing to do as the locals do means forfeiting business opportunities. The inadequacy of cultural relativism, however, becomes apparent when the practices in question are more damaging than petty bribery or insider trading.

In the late 1980s, some European tanneries and pharmaceutical companies were looking for cheap waste-dumping sites. They approached virtually every country on Africa's west coast from Morocco to the Congo. Nigeria agreed to take highly toxic polychlorinated biphenyls. Unprotected local workers, wearing thongs and shorts, unloaded barrels of PCBs and placed them near a residential area. Neither the residents nor the workers knew that the barrels contained toxic waste.

We may denounce governments that permit such abuses, but many countries are unable to police transnational corporations adequately even if they want to. And in many countries, the combination of ineffective enforcement and inadequate regulations leads to behavior by unscrupulous companies that is clearly wrong. A few years ago, for example, a group of investors became interested in restoring the SS United States, once a luxurious ocean liner. Before the actual restoration could begin, the ship had to be stripped of its asbestos lining. A bid from a U.S. company, based on U.S. standards for asbestos removal, priced the job at more than $100 million. A company in the Ukranian city of Sevastopol offered to do the work for less than $2 million. In October 1993, the ship was towed to Sevastopol.

A cultural relativist would have no problem with that outcome, but I do. A country has the right to establish its own health and safety regulations, but in the case described above, the standards and the terms of the contract could not possibly have protected workers in Sevastopol from known health risks. Even if the contract met Ukranian standards, ethical businesspeople must object. Cultural relativism is morally blind. There are fundamental values that cross cultures, and companies must uphold them. . . .

At the other end of the spectrum from cultural relativism is ethical imperialism, which directs people to do everywhere exactly as they do at home. Again, an understandably appealing approach but one that is clearly inadequate. Consider the large U.S. computer-products company that in 1993 introduced a course on sexual harassment in its Saudi Arabian facility. Under the banner of global consistency, instructors used the same approach to train Saudi Arabian managers that they had used with U.S. managers: the participants were asked to discuss a case in which a manager makes sexually explicit remarks to a new female employee over drinks in a bar. The instructors failed to consider how the exercise would work in a culture with strict conventions governing relationships between men and women. As a result, the training sessions were ludicrous. They baffled and offended the Saudi participants, and the message to avoid coercion and sexual discrimination was lost.

The theory behind ethical imperialism is absolutism, which is based on three problematic principles. Absolutists believe that there is a single list of truths, that they can be expressed only with one set of concepts, and that they call for exactly the same behavior around the world.

The first claim clashes with many people's belief that different cultural traditions must be respected. In some cultures, loyalty to a community— family, organization, or society—is the foundation of all ethical behavior. The Japanese, for example, define business ethics in terms of loyalty to their companies, their business networks, and their nation. Americans place a higher value on liberty than on loyalty; the U.S. tradition of rights emphasizes equality, fairness, and individual freedom. It is hard to conclude that truth lies on one side or the other, but an absolutist would have us select just one.

The second problem with absolutism is the presumption that people must express moral truth using only one set of concepts. For instance, some absolutists insist that the language of basic rights provide the framework for any discussion of ethics. That means, though, that entire cultural traditions must be ignored. The notion of a right evolved with the rise of democracy in post-Renaissance Europe and the United States, but the term is not found in either Confucian or Buddhist traditions. We all learn ethics in the context of our particular cultures, and the power in the principles is deeply tied to the way in which they are expressed. Internationally accepted lists of moral principles, such as the United Nations' Universal Declaration of Human Rights, draw on many cultural and religious traditions. As philosopher Michael Walzer has noted, "There is no Esperanto of global ethics."

The third problem with absolutism is the belief in a global standard of ethical behavior. Context must shape ethical practice. Very low wages, for example, may be considered unethical in rich, advanced countries, but developing nations may be acting ethically if they encourage investment and improve living standards by accepting low wages. Likewise, when people are malnourished or starving, a government may be wise to use more fertilizer in order to improve crop yields, even though that means settling for relatively high levels of thermal water pollution.

When cultures have different standards of ethical behavior—and different ways of handling unethical behavior—a company that takes an absolutist approach may find itself making a disastrous mistake. When a manager at a large U.S. specialty-products company in China caught an employee stealing, she followed the company's practice and turned the employee over to the provincial authorities, who executed him. Managers cannot operate in another culture without being aware of that culture's attitudes toward ethics.

If companies can neither adopt a host country's ethics nor extend the home country's standards, what is the answer? Even the traditional litmus test—What would people think of your actions if they were written up on the front page of the newspaper?—is an unreliable guide, for there is no international consensus on standards of business conduct.

BALANCING THE EXTREMES: THREE GUIDING PRINCIPLES

Companies must help managers distinguish between practices that are merely different and those that are wrong. For relativists, nothing is sacred and nothing is wrong. For absolutists, many things that are different are wrong. Neither extreme illuminates the real world of business decision making. The answer lies somewhere in between.

When it comes to shaping ethical behavior, companies must be guided by three principles.

- Respect for core human values, which determine the absolute moral threshold for all business activities.
- Respect for local traditions.
- The belief that context matters when deciding what is right and what is wrong.

Consider those principles in action. In Japan, people doing business together often exchange gifts—sometimes expensive ones—in keeping with long-standing Japanese tradition. When U.S. and European companies started doing a lot of business in Japan, many Western businesspeople thought that the practice of gift giving might be wrong rather than simply different. To them, accepting a gift felt like accepting a bribe. As Western companies have become more familiar with Japanese traditions, however, most have come to tolerate the practice and to set different limits on gift giving in Japan than they do elsewhere.

Respecting differences is a crucial ethical practice. Research shows that management ethics differ among cultures; respecting those differences means recognizing that some cultures have obvious weaknesses—as well as hidden strengths. Managers in Hong Kong, for example, have a higher tolerance for some forms of bribery than their Western counterparts, but they have a much lower tolerance for the failure to acknowledge a subordinate's work. In some parts of the Far East, stealing credit from a subordinate is nearly an unpardonable sin.

People often equate respect for local traditions with cultural relativism. That is incorrect. Some practices are clearly wrong. Union Carbide's tragic experience in Bhopal, India, provides one example. The company's executives seriously underestimated how much on-site management involvement was needed at the Bhopal plant to compensate for the country's poor infrastructure and regulatory capabilities. In the aftermath of the disastrous gas leak, the lesson is clear: companies using sophisticated technology in a developing country must evaluate that country's ability to oversee its safe use. Since the incident at Bhopal, Union Carbide has become a leader in advising companies on using hazardous technologies safely in developing countries.

Some activities are wrong no matter where they take place. But some practices that are unethical in one setting may be acceptable in another. For instance, the chemical EDB, a soil fungicide, is banned for use in the United States. In hot climates, however, it quickly becomes harmless through exposure to intense solar radiation and high soil temperatures. As long as the chemical is monitored, companies may be able to use EDB ethically in certain parts of the world.

DEFINING THE ETHICAL THRESHOLD: CORE VALUES

Few ethical questions are easy for managers to answer. But there are some hard truths that must guide managers' actions, a set of what I call core human values, which define minimum ethical standards for all companies.[1] The right to good health and the right to economic advancement and an improved standard of living are two core human values. Another is what Westerners call the Golden Rule, which is recognizable in every major religious and ethical tradition around the world. In Book 15 of his Analects, for instance, Confucius counsels people to maintain reciprocity, or not to do to others what they do not want done to themselves.

Although no single list would satisfy every scholar, I believe it is possible to articulate three core values that incorporate the work of scores of theologians and philosophers around the world. To be broadly relevant, these values must include elements found in both Western and non-Western cultural and religious traditions. Consider the examples of values in Exhibit 12.1, "What Do These Values Have in Common?"

At first glance, the values expressed in the two lists seem quite different. Nonetheless, in the spirit of what philosopher John Rawls calls overlapping consensus, one can see that the seemingly divergent values converge at key points. Despite important differences between Western and non-Western cultural and religious traditions, both express shared attitudes about what it means to be human. First, individuals must not treat others simply as tools; in other words, they must recognize a person's value as a human being. Next, individuals and communities must treat people in ways that respect people's basic rights. Finally, members of a community must work together to support and improve the institutions on which the community depends. I call those three values *respect for human dignity, respect for basic rights, and good citizenship.*

Those values must be the starting point for all companies as they formulate and evaluate standards of ethical conduct at home and abroad. But they are only a starting point. Companies need much more specific guidelines, and the first step to developing those is to translate the core human values into core values for business. What does it mean, for example, for a company to respect human dignity? How can a company be a good citizen?

I believe that companies can respect human dignity by creating and sustaining a corporate culture in which employees, customers, and suppliers are treated not as means to an end but as people whose intrinsic value must be acknowledged, and by producing safe products and services in a safe workplace. Companies can respect basic rights by acting in ways that support and protect the individual rights of employees, customers, and surrounding communities, and by avoiding relationships that violate human beings' rights to health, education, safety, and an adequate standard of living. And companies can be good citizens by supporting essential social institutions, such as the economic system and the education system, and by working with host governments and other organizations to protect the environment.

The core values establish a moral compass for business practice. They can help companies identify practices that are acceptable and those that are intolerable—even if the practices are compatible with a host country's norms and laws. Dumping pollutants near people's homes and accepting inadequate standards for handling hazardous materials are two examples of actions that violate core values.

EXHIBIT 12.1. What Do These Values Have in Common?

Non-Western	Western
Kyosei (Japanese): Living and working together for the common good.	Individual liberty
Dharma (Hindu): The fulfillment of inherited duty.	Egalitarianism
Santutthi (Buddhist): The importance of limited desires.	Political participation
Zakat (Muslim): The duty to give alms to the Muslim poor.	Human Rights

Similarly, if employing children prevents them from receiving a basic education, the practice is intolerable. Lying about product specifications in the act of selling may not affect human lives directly, but it too is intolerable because it violates the trust that is needed to sustain a corporate culture in which customers are respected.

Sometimes it is not a company's actions but those of a supplier or customer that pose problems. Take the case of the Tan family, a large supplier for Levi Strauss. The Tans were allegedly forcing 1,200 Chinese and Filipino women to work 74 hours per week in guarded compounds on the Mariana Islands. In 1992, after repeated warnings to the Tans, Levi Strauss broke off business relations with them.

CREATING AN ETHICAL CORPORATE CULTURE

The core values for business that I have enumerated can help companies begin to exercise ethical judgment and think about how to operate ethically in foreign cultures, but they are not specific enough to guide managers through actual ethical dilemmas. Levi Strauss relied on a written code of conduct when figuring out how to deal with the Tan family. The company's Global Sourcing and Operating Guidelines, formerly called the Business Partner Terms of Engagement, state that Levi Strauss will "seek to identify and utilize business partners who aspire as individuals and in the conduct of all their businesses to a set of ethical standards not incompatible with our own." Whenever intolerable business situations arise, managers should be guided by precise statements that spell out the behavior and operating practices that the company demands.

Ninety percent of all Fortune 500 companies have codes of conduct, and 70% have statements of vision and values. In Europe and the Far East, the percentages are lower but are increasing rapidly. Does that mean that most companies have what they need? Hardly. Even though most large U.S. companies have both statements of values and codes of conduct, many might be better off if they didn't. Too many companies don't do anything with the documents; they simply paste them on the wall to impress employees, customers, suppliers, and the public. As a result, the senior managers who drafted the statements lose credibility by proclaiming values and not living up to them. Companies such as Johnson & Johnson, Levi Strauss, Motorola, Texas Instruments, and Lockheed Martin, however, do a great deal to make the words meaningful. Johnson & Johnson, for example, has become well known for its Credo Challenge sessions, in which managers discuss ethics in the context of their current business problems and are invited to criticize the company's credo and make suggestions for changes. The participants' ideas are passed on to the company's senior managers. Lockheed Martin has created an innovative site on the World Wide Web and on its local network that gives employees, customers, and suppliers access to the company's ethical code and the chance to voice complaints.

Codes of conduct must provide clear direction about ethical behavior when the temptation to behave unethically is strongest. The pronouncement in a code of conduct that bribery is unacceptable is useless unless accompanied by guidelines for gift giving, payments to get goods through customs, and "requests" from intermediaries who are hired to ask for bribes.

Motorola's values are stated very simply as "How we will always act: [with] constant respect for people [and] uncompromising integrity." The company's code of conduct, however, is explicit about actual business practice. With respect to bribery, for example, the code states that the "funds and assets of Motorola shall not be used, directly or indirectly, for illegal payments of any kind." It is unambiguous about what sort of payment is illegal: "the payment of a bribe to a public official or the kickback of funds to an employee of a customer. . . ." The code goes on to prescribe specific procedures for handling commissions to intermediaries, issuing sales invoices, and disclosing confidential information in a sales transaction—all situations in which employees might have an opportunity to accept or offer bribes.

Codes of conduct must be explicit to be useful, but they must also leave room for a manager to use his or her judgment in situations requiring cultural sensitivity. Host-country employees shouldn't be forced to adopt all home-country values and renounce their own. Again, Motorola's code is exemplary. First, it gives clear direction: "Employees of Motorola will respect the laws, customs, and traditions of each country in which they operate, but will, at the same time, engage in no course of conduct which, even if legal, customary, and accepted in any such country, could be deemed to be in violation of the accepted business ethics of Motorola or the laws of the United States relating to business ethics." After laying down such absolutes, Motorola's code then makes clear when individual judgment will be necessary. For example, employees may sometimes accept certain kinds of small gifts "in rare circumstances, where the refusal to accept a gift" would injure Motorola's "legitimate business interests." Under certain circumstances, such gifts "may be accepted so long as the gift inures to the benefit of Motorola" and not "to the benefit of the Motorola employee."

Striking the appropriate balance between providing clear direction and leaving room for individual judgment makes crafting corporate values statements and ethics codes one of the hardest tasks that executives confront. The words are only a start. A company's leaders need to refer often to their organization's credo and code and must themselves be credible, committed, and consistent. If senior managers act as though ethics don't matter, the rest of the company's employees won't think they do, either.

CONFLICTS OF DEVELOPMENT AND CONFLICTS OF TRADITION

Managers living and working abroad who are not prepared to grapple with moral ambiguity and tension should pack their bags and come home. The view that all business practices can be categorized as either ethical or unethical is too simple. As Einstein is reported to have said, "Things should be as simple as possible—but no simpler." Many business practices that are considered unethical in one setting may be ethical in another. Such activities are neither black nor white but exist in what Thomas Dunfee and I have called moral free space.[2] In this gray zone, there are no tight prescriptions for a company's behavior. Managers must chart their own courses—as long as they do not violate core human values.

Consider the following example. Some successful Indian companies offer employees the opportunity for one of their children to gain a job with the company once the child has completed a certain level in school. The companies honor this commitment even when other applicants are more qualified than an employee's child. The perk is extremely valuable in a country where jobs are hard to find, and it reflects the Indian culture's belief that the West has gone too far in allowing economic opportunities to break up families. Not surprisingly, the perk is among the most cherished by employees, but in most Western countries, it would be branded unacceptable nepotism. In the United States, for example, the ethical principle of equal opportunity holds that jobs should go to the applicants with the best qualifications. If a U.S. company made such promises to its employees, it would violate regulations established by the Equal Employment Opportunity Commission. Given this difference in ethical attitudes, how should U.S. managers react to Indian nepotism? Should they condemn the Indian companies, refusing to accept them as partners or supplies until they agree to clean up their act?

Despite the obvious tension between nepotism and principles of equal opportunity, I cannot condemn the practice for Indians. In a country, such as India, that emphasizes clan and family relationships and has catastrophic levels of unemployment, the practice must be viewed in moral free space. The decision to allow a special perk for employees and their children is not necessarily wrong—at least for members of that country.

How can managers discover the limits of moral free space? That is, how can they learn to distinguish a value in tension with their own from one that is intolerable? Helping managers develop good ethical judgment requires companies to be clear about their core values and codes of conduct. But even the most explicit set of guidelines cannot always provide answers. That is especially true in the thorniest ethical dilemmas, in which the host country's ethical standards not only are different but also seem lower than the home country's. Managers must recognize that when countries have different ethical standards, there are two types of conflict that commonly arise. Each type requires its own line of reasoning.

In the first type of conflict, which I call a *conflict of relative development,* ethical standards conflict because of the countries' different levels of economic development. As mentioned before, developing countries may accept wage rates that seem inhumane to more advanced countries in order to attract investment. As economic conditions in a developing country improve, the incidence of that sort of conflict usually decreases. The second type of conflict is a *conflict of cultural tradition.* For example, Saudi Arabia, unlike most other countries, does not allow women to serve as corporate managers. Instead, women may work in only a few professions, such as education and health care. The prohibition stems from strongly held religious and cultural beliefs; any increase in the country's level of economic development, which is already quite high, is not likely to change the rules.

To resolve a conflict of relative development, a manager must ask the following question: Would the practice be acceptable at home if my country were in a similar stage of economic development? Consider the difference between wage and safety standards in the United States and in Angola, where citizens accept lower standards on both counts. If a U.S. oil company is hiring Angolans to work on an offshore Angolan oil rig, can the company pay them lower wages than it pays U.S. workers in the Gulf of Mexico? Reasonable people have to answer yes if the alternative for Angola is the loss of both the foreign investment and the jobs.

Consider, too, differences in regulatory environments. In the 1980s, the government of India fought hard to be able to import Ciba-Geigy's Entero Vioform, a drug known to be enormously effective in fighting dysentery but one that had been banned in the United States because some users experienced side effects. Although dysentery was not a big problem in the United States, in India, poor public sanitation was contributing to epidemic levels of the disease. Was it unethical to make the drug available in India after it had been banned in the United States? On the contrary, rational people should consider it unethical not to do so. Apply our test: Would the United States, at an earlier stage of development, have used this drug despite its side effects? The answer is clearly yes.

But there are many instances when the answer to similar questions is no. Sometimes a host country's standards are inadequate at any level of economic development. If a country's pollution standards are so low that working on an oil rig would considerably increase a person's risk of developing cancer, foreign oil companies must refuse to do business there. Likewise, if the dangerous side effects of a drug treatment outweigh its benefits, managers should not accept health standards that ignore the risks.

When relative economic conditions do not drive tensions, there is a more objective test for resolving ethical problems. Managers should deem a practice permissible only if they can answer no to both of the following questions: Is it possible to conduct business successfully in the host country without undertaking the practice? and Is the practice a violation of a core human value? Japanese gift giving is a perfect example of a conflict of cultural tradition. Most experienced businesspeople, Japanese and non-Japanese alike, would agree that doing business in Japan would be virtually impossible without adopting the practice. Does gift giving violate a core human value? I cannot identify one that it violates. As a result, gift giving may be permissible for foreign companies in Japan even if it conflicts with ethical attitudes at home. In fact, that conclusion is widely accepted, even by companies such as Texas Instruments and IBM, which are outspoken against bribery.

Does it follow that all nonmonetary gifts are acceptable or that bribes are generally acceptable in countries where they are common? Not at all. . . . What makes the routine practice of gift giving acceptable in Japan are the limits in its scope and intention. When gift giving moves outside those limits, it soon collides with core human values. For example, when Carl Kotchian, president of Lockheed in the 1970s, carried suitcases full of cash to Japanese politicians, he went beyond the norms established by Japanese tradition. That incident galvanized opinion in the United States Congress and helped lead to passage of the Foreign Corrupt Practices Act. Likewise, Roh Tae Woo went beyond the norms established by Korean cultural tradition when he accepted $635.4 million in bribes as president of the Republic of Korea between 1988 and 1993.

GUIDELINES FOR ETHICAL LEADERSHIP

Learning to spot intolerable practices and to exercise good judgment when ethical conflicts arise requires practice. Creating a company culture that rewards ethical behavior is essential. The following guidelines for developing a global ethical perspective among managers can help.

Treat corporate values and formal standards of conduct as absolutes. Whatever ethical standards a company chooses, it cannot waver on its principles either at home or abroad. Consider what has become part of company lore at Motorola. Around 1950, a senior executive was negotiating with officials of a South American government on a $10 million sale that would have increased the company's annual net profits by nearly 25%. As the negotiations neared completion, however, the executive walked away from the deal because the officials were asking for $1 million for "fees." CEO Robert Galvin not only supported the executive's decision but also made it clear that Motorola would neither accept the sale on any terms nor do business with those government officials again. Retold over the decades, this story demonstrating Galvin's resolve has helped cement a culture of ethics of thousands of employees at Motorola.

Design and implement conditions of engagement for suppliers and customers. Will your company do business with any customer or supplier? What if a customer or supplier uses child labor? What if it has strong links with organized crime? What if it pressures your company to break a host country's laws? Such issues are best not left for spur-of-the-moment decisions. Some companies have realized that. Sears, for instance, has developed a policy of not contracting production to companies that use prison labor or infringe on workers' rights to health and safety. And BankAmerica has specified as a condition for many of its loans to developing countries that environmental standards and human rights must be observed.

Allow foreign business units to help formulate ethical standards and interpret ethical issues. The French pharmaceutical company Rhône-Poulenc Rorer has allowed foreign subsidiaries to augment lists of corporate ethical principles with their own suggestions. Texas Instruments has paid special attention to issues of international business ethics by creating the Global Business Practices Council, which is made up of managers from countries in which the company operates. With the overarching intent to create a "global ethics strategy, locally deployed," the council's mandate is to provide ethics education and create local processes that will help managers in the company's foreign business units resolve ethical conflicts.

In host countries, support efforts to decrease institutional corruption. Individual managers will not be able to wipe out corruption in a host country, no matter how many bribes they turn down. When a host country's tax system, import and export procedures, and procurement practices favor unethical players, companies must take action.

Many companies have begun to participate in reforming host-country institutions. General Electric, for example, has taken a strong stand in India, using the media to make repeated condemnations of bribery in business and government. General Electric and others have found, however, that a single company usually cannot drive out entrenched corruption. Transparency International, an organization based in Germany, has been effective in helping coalitions of companies, government officials, and others work to reform bribery-ridden bureaucracies in Russia, Bangladesh, and elsewhere.

Exercise moral imagination. Using moral imagination means resolving tensions responsibly and creatively. Coca-Cola, for instance, has consistently turned down requests for bribes from Egyptian officials but has managed to gain political support and public trust by sponsoring a project to plant fruit trees. And take the example of Levi Strauss, which discovered in the early

1990s that two of its suppliers in Bangladesh were employing children under the age of 14—a practice that violated the company's principles but was tolerated in Bangladesh. Forcing the suppliers to fire the children would not have ensured that the children received an education, and it would have caused serious hardship for the families depending on the children's wages. In a creative arrangement, the suppliers agreed to pay the children's regular wages while they attended school and to offer each child a job at age 14. Levi Strauss, in turn, agreed to pay the children's tuition and provide books and uniforms. That arrangement allowed Levi Strauss to uphold its principles and provide long-term benefits to its host country.

Many people think of values as soft; to some they are usually unspoken. A South Seas island society uses the word *mokita*, which means, "the truth that everybody knows but nobody speaks." However difficult they are to articulate, values affect how we all behave. In a global business environment, values in tension are the rule rather than the exception. Without a company's commitment, statements of values and codes of ethics end up as empty platitudes that provide managers with no foundation for behaving ethically. Employees need and deserve more, and responsible members of the global business community can set examples for others to follow. The dark consequences of incidents such as Union Carbide's disaster in Bhopal remind us how high the stakes can be.

Notes

1. In other writings, Thomas W. Dunfee and I have used the term *hypernorm* instead of *core human value*.
2. Thomas Donaldson and Thomas W. Dunfee, "Toward a Unified Conception of Business Ethics: Integrative Social Contracts Theory," *Academy of Management Review*, April 1994; and "Integrative Social Contracts Theory: A Communication Conception of Economic Ethics," *Economics and Philosophy*, spring 1995.

Contemporary Business Themes

INTRODUCTION

Previous parts in this book have treated broad concepts and broad categories of business ethics issues. Because each historical period is confronted by a swarm of unique challenges, those issues also require attention. In Part 5 we look closely at contemporary issues of marketing, the environment, and leadership.

CHAPTER 13: MARKETING

What are the ethics of selling? We are daily bombarded by brochures, TV commercials, direct-mail solicitations, unsolicited phone calls, and the threat that our Internet activities may be monitored. But what kind of selling behavior, if any, steps over the ethical line? Also, consider what is being sold. Is it acceptable to sell products that are potentially harmful? Of course, automobiles are known to be some of the most harmful products, and yet we usually regard their utility as outweighing the disadvantages of their risk. But what happens when potential harm is not counterbalanced by substantial utility or when the harm falls upon a particular, vulnerable group of people? Is it acceptable to claim that "Sugar Beanies" (the name of an imaginary breakfast cereal) is the "fun part of a nutritious breakfast?" Is it ethical to make this claim even when over half of the weight of the cereal is sugar and when nutrition experts agree that too much sugar is harming today's children?

In their case study, "Fingerhut's Price Strategy," Lee Fennel, Gretchen Kalsow, and June West explore the case of a catalog merchandiser who targets the bottom one-third of America's economic strata. Fingerhut "bundles" the extension of credit with the sale of its goods. Often, Fingerhut is the only firm that will extend credit to this market segment. The NAACP, along with other influential organizations, is supporting a lawsuit filed against Fingerhut. Four customers have accused Fingerhut of charging usuriously high interest rates. The company had enjoyed significant growth by using its advanced customer database to target potential buyers of specific merchandise. Its catalogs display the small weekly or monthly payments in large type, while the total cost of the product is de-emphasized. Fingerhut's cash prices are significantly higher than its competitors, as its customer base is relatively price insensitive given the rare offer of credit. Is Fingerhut offering a valuable service to its customers—the opportunity to establish a credit record—or is it using deceptive advertising and framing techniques?

Roger Crisp, in his article "Persuasive Advertising, Autonomy, and the Creation of Desire," argues that advertising can negatively affect people's freedom or autonomy. Crisp delves into the issues surrounding the question of whether advertising constitutes manipulation. Does advertising manipulate people? Or, rather, are people sufficiently sophisticated to elude advertising's powers? Crisp questions the claim that advertising does not affect one's autonomy. Persuasive advertising in particular, he believes, creates desires, which in turn distract people from making clear choices. Advertising, he argues, can create images about lifestyles and values that at least peripherally affect one's self-image and choices.

In the ethics and advertising debate, subtleties abound. Experiments have shown that people are often economically irrational in responding to choice situations when framed in selective ways. For example, when asked whether they would attend a theater performance, having arrived at the theater after losing an amount of money equal to the purchase price of the ticket, a high percentage of people say that they would, indeed, go ahead and attend the performance. But when asked whether they would go ahead and attend the theater performance, having lost the ticket itself (but in a situation where they could easily repurchase the ticket), many fewer people say that they would attend the performance. This and other experiments show that it is not just economic rationality, but also psychological context, that often matters for customers.

This raises questions about how advertisers "frame" their message. A certain marketer may advertise a price in the newspaper, even as he fully intends to discount the price right away in order to "frame" the pricing attractively to the customer. The customer may not be directly misled, but she could be said to be indirectly misled insofar as she believes the price is below normal. Or, consider the practice of pricing with a "quantity surcharge" that relies upon the customer's expectation that if a pack is larger then the unit price is lower. Marketers have been known to exploit this presumption by selling larger packages while charging more per unit than for smaller packages.

CHAPTER 14: THE ENVIRONMENT

This section begins with the case of ExxonMobil's challenge to develop oil fields in Chad and run a pipeline through Cameroon, two of the poorest and most corrupt countries in Central Africa. Trying to learn from their own past mistakes, e.g., the Exxon Valdez oil spill on the Alaskan coast, and the public relations nightmare Shell Oil faced in the Ogoni oil fields of

Nigeria, ExxonMobil has developed a new model for thinking about global exploration of oil. Working with the World Bank, environmentalists, and nongovernment organizations, local tribes, and the governments of Chad and Cameroon, they now are trying to think through environmentally sustainable and socially responsible oil exploration. Whether they can succeed in this endeavor remains to be seen, but the partnership model they are engaged in may be a model for future environmentally and socially sustainable development in poor countries such as Chad and Cameroon.

A heated controversy has occurred during the past three decades between those who see environmental issues as potentially catastrophic and demanding of radical changes in corporate and government policies and those who believe that, however important, environmental issues have been exaggerated and are best addressed by market forces. Two essays in this section represent two starkly contrasting sides of this controversy. In his article, "Scarcity or Abundance," Julian Simon critiques key assumptions of the environmental movement, arguing instead for a better economic understanding of the environmental phenomenon. There is more reason for optimism, he believes, than the environmental "doomsdayers" would have us believe.

Much of the analysis of environmental degradation and improvement is conducted in terms of its costs and benefits. Stephen Kelman questions the cost-benefit analysis as a general rule for the evaluation of environmental concerns, in "Cost-Benefit Analysis." He argues that there are nonmarket values that cannot be measured quantitatively, such as life, health, and liberty. Thus, in approaching environmental issues, we must clarify what we value in order to calculate the risks of pollution, the harm to future generations, and questions of sustainability.

Responding to both these concerns William McDonough, a well-known architect, argues that both Simon's approach and Kelman's answer the wrong questions. Whether we live in a time of scarcity or abundance is not the central concern. Rather, McDonough is worried that we are wasteful and that we are wasting away our natural capital, the ecosystem, needlessly. Addressing the issue of how we can be environmentally conservative in a growing free-market global economy, McDonough suggests that we need to change our mindsets about environmental sustainability without sacrificing economic growth. Rather than think about costs and benefits of becoming cleaner or less polluting, McDonough's motto is "Waste equals food." That is, we should rid ourselves of the idea that we can throw away or discard what we no longer find useful. If instead we think carefully about reusing and recycling everything we buy, sell, and consume, so there is no longer an "away" where one can discard so-called junk, consumers and companies can create vast cost savings by recycling all products that are not biodegradable, thus reducing costs of new resources while preserving these resources for future generations.

CHAPTER 15: GLOBALIZATION

In the United States we thrive on low-cost goods, particularly clothing and shoes, much of which is manufactured in less-developed countries. It turns out that many well-known clothing and shoe brands do not manufacture good themselves. Rather, they contract with local factories in a variety of low-wage countries to produce goods to their specifications. As a result, much of what we buy and wear is made in sweatshops. These sweatshops are so named because of poor to dreadful working conditions, workers who are often paid poorly by their own country standards, productivity pressures, long hours, very few days off. Ian Maitland does not see that these are serious ethical issues. These workers are not forced to take these jobs and they can quit at any time. Our country had sweatshops in the nineteenth century, and it enabled us to develop as a strong economic machine. Sweatshops are part of the evolution to a high-growth free market economy. On the other hand, Baker, Hartman and Shaw discuss these problems. They find sweatshops intolerable even in countries where that is the only work available. Using Nike as an example, they offer solutions that benefit workers as well as consumers.

C. K. Prahalad introduces another approach to globalization and marketing in less developed countries. He points out that the poorest nations in the world have the largest populations—the bottom of the pyramid. Yet we ignore that market. If world economic growth is to continue, we have to heed what he calls the bottom of the pyramid. There are at least three approaches to these markets, all of which overlap. The first, developed by Hindustan Lever in India, is to market low-cost but necessary products such as soap to these populations. The second is to develop micro financing institutions lending small amounts of money to the poor so that those without access to capital can develop small entrepreneurial ventures and thus work their way out of abject poverty. The third is to pay a living wage so that these populations have money to buy more goods, thus decreasing the numbers below the poverty level and creating economic growth as a result of the demand for more products. All of these approaches are free-market approaches that both eschew welfare and international governmental aid and promote self-development and dignity.

Chapter 13

Marketing

Case Study

Fingerhut's Price Strategy

Lee Fennel ● Gretchen A. Kalsow ● June A. West

Businesses have target niches. Ours is the moderate-income consumer. We nei-ther apologize for, nor hide the fact that we serve this growing population—even when others won't.

—Ted Deikel, Chairman and CEO
of Fingerhut Companies, Inc.

Jane Johnson, director of corporate communication at Fingerhut, let her eyes swim over the legal pleadings and news clippings that lay before her. It was November 1996, weeks before the Minnetonka-based direct mar-keting company's holiday rush, and an unfavorable article had just ap-peared in a major Minneapolis paper, the *Star Tribune*. The article drew attention to a lawsuit pending against the company and suggested that Fingerhut made its profits by exploiting the poor. In January, four Min-nesota women had brought suit in Hennepin County District Court, al-leging usuriously high interest rates on merchandise they had purchased from Fingerhut's direct marketing catalogs. The lawsuit had gained the support of the Minneapolis Urban League, Minnesota COACT, and the Minneapolis chapter of the NAACP; these groups had filed a friend-of-the-court brief in support of the customers. Worse, the lawyers represent-ing the women were attempting to have the case certified as a class action.[1] If this move was successful, customers in at least 20 states might become involved.[2]

John Ellingboe, Fingerhut's vice president and general counsel, seemed convinced that the lawsuit had no legal merit and would be eventually dis-missed under Minnesota's "time-price doctrine," an exception to the usury law. Yet Jane found it deeply troubling that the customers had brought the lawsuit at all. One of the things that had attracted her to Fingerhut was the

This case was written by Lee Fennel under the supervision of Gretchen A. Kalsow, Assis-tant Professor of Business Administration, and June A. West, Assistant Professor of Business Ad-ministration. Copyright 2001 by the University of Virginia Darden School Foundation, Charlottesville, VA. All rights reserved.

high level of social consciousness exhibited at all levels of management. For example, CEO Ted Deikel was renowned for his philanthropy and environmental awareness. But this lawsuit painted Fingerhut as a predatory company that suckered low-income consumers by using unfair and deceptive marketing techniques. The fact that Fingerhut's advertising and credit policies might technically be legal didn't necessarily make them moral—or did it?

COMPANY BACKGROUND

The company began in 1948 when brothers Manny and William Fingerhut began selling seat covers to car owners through the mail. By 1996, Fingerhut had grown into a $1.8 billion direct marketing superpower, selling a smorgasbord of consumer goods—clothing, housewares, furniture, electronics, appliances, and more—through an array of specially-targeted catalogs. It had become the second-largest catalog company in the nation,[3] with more than 7 million loyal customers. The company had about 9,500 employees.

In 1996, it laid off 570 employees in Minnesota and opened two customer-service centers in Tampa, a move that allowed it to take advantage of a larger bilingual labor pool and better winter weather conditions.[4] Its earnings had been weak for the past two years, in part because of rising postal and paper costs and a failed TV home-shopping venture.[5] However, a co-branded Mastercard that it introduced in 1995 seemed to be catching on nicely, and the possibility of expanding into the financial services sector offered definite opportunities for growth.

THE TARGET MARKET

Fingerhut consistently distinguished itself from other direct marketing companies by explicitly targeting those customers with household incomes falling in the lowest one-third nationally. In 1996, this amounted to almost 89 million people, or 33.7 million families.[6] In that year, the median household income in the United States was $35,492.[7] Fingerhut's target market included most of the households in the bottom two quintiles, which had mean household incomes of $8,596 and $21,097 respectively. These two quintiles together received 12.7 percent of the total household income for the year.[8]

This segment of the market had been largely untapped by marketers and underserved by financial institutions. Many individuals falling into this category had no credit or poor credit, and they were typically unable to obtain credit from traditional lenders or credit card companies. Most were among the estimated 25 to 30 percent of U.S. households that live "paycheck to paycheck."[9]

A typical Fingerhut customer had a household income of about $18,000. Many customers were "empty-nesters" or people just starting families, and most were female—some 90 percent, according to a 1986 article.[10] In 1996, although only about five percent of Fingerhut's customers were Hispanic, they represented its fastest-growing segment.[11]

RISK, CHOICE, AND THE LOW-INCOME CUSTOMER

David Caplovitz stated that two options are available to the low-income consumer—foregoing major purchases or being exploited. While he admits that the marketing system that is targeted to the poor is a deviant one, it persists "because it fulfills social functions that are presently not fulfilled by more legitimate institutions. The poorest risks are shunted to a special class of merchants who are ready to accept great risk."[12]

In 1996, the picture was much the same, but some efforts were underway to improve the choices available to consumers. For example, in 1994 and 1995, a Minneapolis-based group called ACESS (Aggressive Consumer Education and Support Strategies) began offering credit cards for use in Dayton's and Target stores to low-income customers unable to meet traditional credit requirements.[13] However, the initial screening mechanism proved inadequate (almost half of the payments made by participants were late) requiring ACESS to revamp its eligibility criteria.

THE MARKETING APPROACH

Fingerhut attracted and retained its target market through strategies tailored to the low- or moderate-income consumer, including an installment payment option. Boldface monthly payment amounts and a smaller cash price accompanied each item. Exhibit 13.1 illustrates installment plan details. Virtually all of Fingerhut's customers purchased their merchandise through this installment plan.[14] Coupon books were delivered along with the merchandise rather than mailing consolidated statements. Typically customers had several "active" Fingerhut coupon books, representing different purchases at various stages of repayment.[15]

Many of Fingerhut's customers would not qualify for other credit options like credit cards and department store charges. A full 40 percent had so little credit history as to have no information available in a credit report. Thus Fingerhut was taking a risk with new, untested customers, selling them less expensive items. Customers who paid back the balance on time would then be "promoted"—made eligible to finance progressively larger purchases. They also would receive personalized mailings from the company with messages like "Congratulations! You've been selected to receive our exceptional customer award!" along with a certificate "suitable for framing."[16] Customers who fell behind on their payments were contacted by Fingerhut personnel, who attempted to arrange a viable repayment plan.

Fingerhut made extensive use of its database to "personalize" its mailings and target specific customers with specialty catalogs (in 1992, there were about 75 such catalogs, covering categories like outdoor living, electronics, and juvenile apparel and toys).[17] Personalized inserts making note of birthdays, "anniversaries" with Fingerhut, and recent purchases further enhanced customer's perceptions of personal service.[18] Fingerhut also relied on frequent contact with the customer to limit bad debt losses and ensure a steady stream of sales. Fingerhut's customers maintained, on average, a seven-year relationship with the company.

EXHIBIT 13.1 Fingerhut's Price Strategy

Fingerhut's Installment Plan

Payment Chart

How to use the Payment Chart: Reference the cash price and the shipping code (the letter in parentheses at the end of the paragraph) for each product you wish to order. Then, find that cash price and the letter in the Payment Chart below. For example, if you wish to order the 7-Pc, Tough-Tote Tweed Luggage Set on page 37 (see above) you should look for the cash price of $89.99 with the letter "c" next to it.

Fingerhut terms: No down payment required. Cash price plus shipping and handling. Total sale price includes a finance charge added to your purchase at the annual percentage rate of 24.9%, except for those items indicated with □ which will be at the annual percentage rate of 24.75%. Shipping and handling charges are included in the total sale price. See chart below and additional terms at end of Payment Chart.

Cash Price			Amount of Payments	Number of Monthly Payments	Total Sale Price	Total Finance Charge
9.99		a	7.99	2	15.98	.48
10.00	a		7.99	2	15.98	.48
12.99	a		7.99	2	15.98	.48
14.99	a		7.99	3	23.97	.96
15.99	a		7.99	3	23.97	.96
16.99	a		7.99	3	23.97	.96
18.95	a		7.99	3	23.97	.96
19.99	a		7.99	3	23.97	.96
		b	7.99	3	23.97	.96
24.95	a		7.99	4	31.96	1.59
24.99	a		7.99	4	31.96	1.59
		b	7.99	4	31.96	1.59
29.95	a		7.99	5	39.95	2.37
29.99	a		7.99	5	39.95	2.37
29.99	b		7.99	5	39.95	2.37
34.99	a		7.99	6	47.94	3.29
39.99	a		7.99	7	55.93	4.36
39.99	b		7.99	7	55.93	4.36
44.99	a		7.99	7	55.93	4.36
		b	7.99	8	63.92	5.57
49.98	a		7.99	8	63.92	5.57
49.99	a		7.99	8	63.92	5.57
		b	7.99	9	71.91	6.92
		c	7.99	9	71.91	6.92
54.99	a		7.99	9	71.91	6.92
59.98	b		7.99	10	79.90	8.40
59.99	a		7.99	10	79.90	8.40
		b	7.99	10	79.90	8.40
		c	7.99	11	87.89	10.02
64.99	a		7.99	10	79.90	8.40
69.96	c		7.99	12	95.88	11.76
69.99	a		7.99	11	87.89	10.02
		b	7.99	12	95.88	11.76
		c	7.99	12	95.88	11.76

79.98	b		7.99	13	103.87	13.64
79.99	a		7.99	13	103.87	13.64
		b	7.99	13	103.87	13.64
		c	7.99	14	111.86	15.63
84.99	a		7.99	14	111.86	15.63
89.99	a		7.99	15	119.85	17.75
89.99	b		7.99	15	119.85	17.75
		c	7.99	16	127.84	19.99
99.94	a		7.99	17	135.83	22.35
99.97	c		7.99	18	143.82	24.82
99.99	a		7.99	17	135.83	22.35
		b	7.99	17	135.83	22.35
		c	7.99	18	143.82	24.82
109.99	a		7.99	19	151.81	27.40
		c	7.99	20	159.80	30.09
119.97	c		7.99	22	175.78	35.79
119.99	a		7.99	21	167.79	32.88
		b	7.99	21	167.79	32.88
		c	7.99	22	175.78	35.79
129.98	a		7.99	24	191.76	41.91
129.99	a		7.99	22	175.78	35.79
		b	7.99	23	183.77	38.80
		c	7.99	24	191.76	41.91
139.99	a		7.99	25	199.75	45.12

If you order more than one item, we will combine shipments where possible and issue a single invoice for the combined items. The number of payments will be the same as it would have been for the item with the longest pay plan. For example, if you order a $29.99 Product at the "a" Rate and a $39.99 Product at the "a" Rate and we combine them into one shipment, the total cash price of the combined items is $69.98 plus $13.53 shipping and handling. On our Fingerhut terms, there is no down payment required. Total sale price of $90.58 ($12.94 per month for 7 months) includes a finance charge of $7.07 at the annual percentage rate of 24.9%.

Where required by local law, sales or use tax must be paid with the first installment. If any payment is more than 30 days past due, Fingerhut may, at its option, declare all remaining payments immediately due and payable. WI Residents: If an amount exceeding one full payment is more than 10 days past due, then subject to your right to cure any default, Fingerhut may, at its option, declare all remaining payments immediately due and payable.

Should you choose to add on to this order, the total price of goods or services covered by the Retail Installment Contract may then, at Fingerhut's option, be increased by the price(s) of any such additional purchase(s) and finance charges and installment payments will be increased proportionately. All terms and conditions of this Retail Installment Contract shall apply equally to the purchase of additional goods or services.

From time to time, companies and organizations ask to send their catalogs and brochures to our customers. If we find that they offer products or services that would be of interest to our customers, we allow it. If you prefer not to receive such mailings, please write your mailing address and customer number on a piece of paper (exactly as it appears on your Home Trial Form) and mail to: MAIL SERVICE, FINGERHUT CORPORATION, P.O. Box 200, St. Cloud, MN 56395.

We reserve the right to substitute similar merchandise of equal or better quality. If substituted merchandise is not acceptable, you can return it postpaid during your free trial period without further obligation.

© Fingerhut 5-060833-000

THE DATABASE

"It all goes back to the database."

—TED DEIKEL[19]

Central to Fingerhut's marketing strategy was its massive database system, which contained "more than 500 pieces of information on each of more than 50 million active and potential customers."[20] The information in the database had been compiled over more than 30 years, and kept up-to-date using state-of-the-art technology.[21] Deikel termed it the "world's most sophisticated database." The database application, Fingerhut's Customer Contact System, had been developed with Lincoln Software's Engineer toolset and was one of the largest client/server applications in the world.[22]

The detailed information Fingerhut gathered about each customer, including age, marital status, number of children, birthdays, and hobbies, enabled it to make predictions about the types of products each individual would be likely to purchase. It then sent each household the appropriate mix of targeted specialty catalogs.[23] Jim Bessen described the astounding degree to which Fingerhut collected and used computerized information about its customers to achieve marketing goals:

> Every catalog mailing and major promotional campaign at Fingerhut—there were nearly 150 in 1992—is based on statistically determined predictions about consumer behavior. . . . Fingerhut captures as many as 1,400 pieces of information about a household. These include typical demographic items like income and home ownership, appliance ownership, and purchasing histories for various categories of products.[24]

PRICING STRATEGIES

Fingerhut's focus on the coupon payment method required it to coordinate the pricing of two different types of commodities—the actual pieces of merchandise that it sold, and the closed-end credit which was "wrapped around" each item.[25] The installment payment plan bundled these two commodities together and offered customers a consolidated monthly price.

Pricing theory has recognized that the contextual and conceptual "frame" of a purchase decision can have profound effects on the perceived fairness of a price.[26] The tactic of breaking down a large purchase into smaller weekly or monthly payments alters the purchase context dramatically and has been successfully used by marketers to sell everything from encyclopedias to automobiles.[27] Instead of focusing the customer's attention on the weeks or months of work that would be required to save up the full purchase price of a particular good, the low monthly payment invites the customer to imagine enjoying the new purchase by making negligible day-to-day sacrifices on items of little or no lasting significance. Sometimes the insignificance of the necessary belt-tightening is made explicit, as in the Chevrolet advertisement that boasts, "[T]his Cavalier costs less a day than a burger, large fries and a shake—[just] $6.23 a day."[28] Reframing the purchase decision in this way is particularly attractive to low-income consumers, since it fits within their "paycheck-to-paycheck" frame of reference.[29]

The extension of credit, which allows the customer to "try out" the goods before making any payments, may also contribute to a perception of value. Because buyers quickly assimilate new merchandise into their frames of reference once it has entered the home, they are willing to pay for the goods rather than incur the loss associated with giving them up.[30]

Customers are also less price-sensitive if they believe that a particular retailer is offering them some uniquely valuable feature that is unavailable elsewhere.[31] Fingerhut was able to differentiate itself from its competitors by extending credit to customers who would not be able to obtain credit elsewhere. Fingerhut's willingness to wrap merchandise in credit created extra value for consumers and made them less sensitive to the prices of the commodities included in that package. Fingerhut also distinguished itself by fostering a socially responsible corporate image, leading the industry in recycling and other environmentally conscious practices and developing "personalized" relationships with its customers via its database.

Arguably, the low-income market is underserved—especially with respect to credit. "Typically, a small number of creditors serve low-income areas and many low-income buyers do not have the transportation or information necessary to shop intelligently."[32] A low-income consumer may find few alternative suppliers willing to extend credit, and this will make the consumer less sensitive to price. Moreover, in setting prices, the risk and costs associated with extending credit must be taken into account.[33] To the extent delayed payments are tolerated or expected, pricing must account for that as well.

THE COMPETITION

The goods retailed by Fingerhut were available from other sources, like K-Mart and Wal-Mart, as well as Sears and J.C. Penney, which sometimes offered the same items at a lower cash price. As Richard Tate, Fingerhut's senior vice president of merchandising explained, "We can't compete on price. We are the highest-priced guys in town. The value is not in the total price, it's in the total offer."[34]

Fingerhut's finance charge was 24.9 percent APR, and interest rates for credit cards ranged from low "teaser" rates to around 19 percent. Some charge accounts such as Sears typically fell in the 21 to 22 percent range. However, the interest rate could run higher on "closed-end" store credit arrangements similar to Fingerhut's installment plan. Fingerhut priced both elements of its "bundle"—the credit and the product's themselves—at higher rates than competitors. If this was the case, then why did Fingerhut continue to enjoy such a large share of the market?[35]

One explanation may be that many customers do not qualify for the types of credit that would make alternative purchase decisions attractive—or even possible. Caplovitz made a similar observation regarding low-income consumers who chose to patronize more expensive shops in their own neighborhoods: "Although some families may buy from neighborhood merchants out of ignorance of alternatives, others may do so because they fail to meet the credit requirements of the more "reliable" stores. In part, the low-income family is caught up in the choice of doing without or relying on

EXHIBIT 13.2 Fingerhut's Price Strategy

Product Cost Comparisons[65]
Product

Source	Hamilton Beach 48-oz 8-speed Blender[66]	Reebok Satellite 2000 Cross-Trainer (Men's)	Eureka 9 amp Upright Bravo II Vacuum Cleaner with free hand vac	Pentium 233 MHz MMX Computer with color Bubblejet Printer[67]
Fingerhut Cash	$49.99	$79.99	$99.99	$1,299.99
Fingerhut Installment Credit (includes Shipping & Handling)	$5.89/mo for 12 months = $70.68	$8.89/mo for 12 months = $106.68	$10.79/mo for 12 months = $129.48	$57.99/mo for 36 months = $2,087.64
Competitor's Price	(Sears) $19.99 (10-speed; does not include food processing attachment)	(Sears) $54.99	(Sears) $69.99	(Circuit City) $949.00 (266 MHz; price is after mfgr rebate) (Prime Time rental) $139.99/mo for 24 mo. = $3,359.76

credit and therefore paying more."[36] Fingerhut provides these families with an opportunity to purchase quality name brand products at affordable monthly payments (see Exhibit 13.2). The availability of credit has long been recognized as the single most salient factor in a low-income consumer's decision about where to buy.

If a customer cannot qualify for other forms of credit (e.g., a department store charge card or a credit card) the price of that credit becomes meaningless. If that customer has no cash on hand, the lower merchandise prices advertised elsewhere are likewise irrelevant. Such customers may save up for their purchases and pay a lower cash price at a competitor's store. But social and cultural factors make this option very unattractive to many consumers. While a savings fund earmarked for a particular item might be raided every time a short-term need or desire arose, the purchase of merchandise on credit represents an irrevocable commitment. Because the new purchase immediately becomes part of the buyer's frame of reference, the threat of losing it provides a powerful incentive for meeting the payments as they come due. Indeed, many low-income families do not maintain a bank account but choose instead to rely solely on check-cashing services and money orders for their financial needs, even though these services also exact hefty fees.[37] This behavior makes saving up for a major purchase even more difficult.

Layaway plans traditionally have offered a buyer a means for overcoming the difficulty in saving for a particular item, but they have costs and difficulties. Most significantly, a layaway item does not go home with the consumer and so cannot become integrated into his or her lifestyle. The consumer may lose enthusiasm for making payments. Further, there may be restrictions, time limits or fees which make layaway sub-optimal. For example, K-mart charges a $3 layaway fee and limits the payment period to ten weeks, far too short for most consumers. Wal-Mart does not charge a fee, but posts a lengthy list of rules and regulations which complicate the transaction and limit consumer choice (like a prohibition on laying away seasonal items more than a certain number of days in advance of the holiday to which such items relate).

NAACP VS. FINGERHUT

"Fingerhut targets poor and minority neighborhoods fairly aggressively," said Anne Bergman, an attorney who drafted an *amicus curiae* (friend-of-the-court) brief on behalf of several groups interested in the outcome of the lawsuit, including the NAACP and the Urban League. "Lenders like Fingerhut really siphon money from these areas."[38]

Two basic arguments seemed central to the attack on Fingerhut. First was the allegation that Fingerhut was charging an effective interest rate that exceeded the legal limit for transactions of the type in which Fingerhut was engaged. Minnesota's general usury statute prohibited lenders from charging interest rates in excess of 8 percent annually, but was riddled with exceptions and had limited applicability. Bill Crowder, one of the attorneys for the customers, said that "under Minnesota law, anybody can charge up to 8 percent interest. There are statutory exceptions for savings and loans, banks and credit cards. But Fingerhut doesn't fit within those exceptions."[39] Fingerhut's Ellerboe contended that the usury law was never meant to apply to financing that accompanied the sale of merchandise. Such sales, he argued, were covered by the common-law "time-price" doctrine which permitted merchants to charge a lower price for cash sales than for sale "on time."

The second prong of the attack on Fingerhut was the assertion that it was "preying on" low-income people through deceptive or misleading advertising. Critics noted that the low monthly payments were prominently displayed in the catalogs next to color pictures of the merchandise. The finance charge, effective interest rate, shipping and handling charge, and total cost of an item could only be found by referring to a tiny print in a multi-column table on another page. Bergman's brief accused Fingerhut of playing "hide-the-ball with bottom line information" to confuse and exploit "less-educated, less-sophisticated customers."[40] This argument, which depended to some extent on assumptions about the relative powerlessness and vulnerability of the target market, called into question Fingerhut's overall marketing strategy—indeed, even its choice of a target market.

Jane decided that the second argument was the one of primary concern for the company. She doubted that the public would base buying behavior or attitudes towards the company on the outcome of a technical legal argument—although she certainly hoped that Ellingboe was right in predicting the outcome of the case. Far more important, she thought, would be the public's perceptions of Fingerhut's practices. If Fingerhut were viewed as manipulative and sneaky, coaxing hard-earned dollars from the poor through tricks, fine print, and hide-the-ball credit terms, the blow to Fingerhut's image could be devastating.

FINGERHUT'S RESPONSE

Fingerhut CEO Ted Deikel had wasted no time in responding to the unfavorable news column that had appeared in the *Star Tribune*. In his response, which appeared in that same paper the following week, he asserted that Fingerhut's finance charges were legal under Minnesota's "time-price doctrine," which allows merchants to charge a different price for an immediate cash sale than for a purchase taking place over time. He also called the suggestion of unethical or predatory practices "an outrage."

"There is nothing 'tricky' about what we do," he wrote. "We provide our customers with purchasing options, and for those customers who do not have credit cards or enough free cash on hand to pay for items in a single payment, our in-house credit plans offer them the flexibility of buying merchandise in installments over time. And we make it easy. Unlike most retailers, Fingerhut will extend credit to customers who do not have a credit history, often without requiring credit applications or down payments. The risk is all ours." Deikel pointed out that by choosing to serve a riskier market segment, Fingerhut suffered a bad debt ratio "two to three times the industry average"—fifteen percent of sales.

Deikel also emphasized that Fingerhut enjoyed tremendous customer loyalty, and that many customers "remember when Fingerhut was the only company that offered them credit when no one else would."[41] Indeed, Fingerhut customer Marilyn Gnat, a retired salesclerk and mother of nine children, had expressed precisely that sentiment in a recent *Business Week* article: "When I started out, Fingerhut was the only place that would give me credit."[42]

SOCIAL FACTORS

Inner-city Chicago resident Jean Shelby paid over $1,100 for a TV/VCR combination on Fingerhut's installment plan, although the same item was available for a cash price of less than half that amount elsewhere. Her explanation was simple: "I want things right away."[43] Her attitude is not an uncommon one. In recent years, consumers at all income levels have been opting for costlier credit purchases because of the perceived comfort, convenience, and status advantages associated with immediately acquiring the goods. As Juliet Schor recently noted, "the fraction of Americans' disposable income that goes toward debt servicing continues to rise; it has now reached 18 percent. The total amount of debt held by the average household has increased relentlessly for decades, and it now equals just about what that household makes in any given year."[44] In a consumer guide, the American Bar Association declared credit "almost as American as apple pie."[45]

Obtaining certain consumer goods is extremely important across all sectors of society. Credit offers consumers a buffer against fluctuations in their income due to hardships or illnesses and provides the ability to make purchases that are commensurate with their lifetime earnings.[46] As the ABA consumer guide explains, "Only you can decide whether it is worth the cost of the finance charge to have a car or other goods and services now, rather than later."[47]

ALTERNATIVES TO TRADITIONAL CREDIT

Pawnshops and Title Pawnbrokers

Pawnshops are a traditional venue for short-term credit, dating back to the turn of the century, and they have recently experienced a resurgence of popularity. Between 1986 and 1996, listings for pawnshops increased 60 percent nationally.[48] They are exempted from general usury statutes and are often permitted to charge 20 percent or more per month, or 240 percent annually. "At least 11 of the 13 southern states allow pawnshops to charge 240 percent on loans; Georgia allows 300 percent."[49] While the consumer loses use of the goods and pays a high interest rate, the pawnbroker still benefits by gaining ownership of the merchandise for a fraction of its value.

Title pawnbrokers specializing in automobiles operate a bit differently: a car's title is taken as collateral for a small loan, often for only a few hundred dollars, and usually for no more than 10 percent of the vehicle's value.[50] The effective interest rate for such short-term loans may be over 900 percent.[51] The borrower maintains possession of the vehicle in the interim, but if the loan is not repaid on time and in accordance with the terms, the car is promptly repossessed. At that point, the car belongs to the title broker, who can resell it (perhaps even to its former owner) at a price close to its actual value—an amount that may be more than ten times the amount of the defaulted loan.[52]

One of the newest and costliest forms of short-term credit is the "lease-back."[53] Under this arrangement, a dealer buys merchandise from a consumer in need of short-term credit—a television set, for example—and pays the customer in cash. But instead of taking possession of the item, the dealer allows the customer to "lease it back" from the company at a high weekly or monthly rate. To get the merchandise back, the customer must pay not only any outstanding rental amounts, but also a buy-back price and sales tax. Lease-back dealers claim they are immune from attack under state usury laws because they are not actually making loans but merely buying, leasing, and selling merchandise. If, however, the customer's cost were computed as interest, the annualized rate would be about 900 percent.[54]

Secured Credit Cards

Secured credit cards offer an opportunity for consumers to establish or repair their credit by borrowing their own money—at a price. In order to set up a secured credit card, the customer must deposit cash to secure the credit line. The credit limit is usually equal to the amount on deposit, and interest rates are often higher than on unsecured cards. "The idea is that this will help them clean up their credit records and graduate to real bankcards," one commentator explains. "But they pay a high cost—application fees of $65, annual fees as high as $75, interest rates reaching

22 percent."[55] Meanwhile, the money left on deposit receives either no interest or a below-market rate. This differential between what the money could earn on the open market and what is paid by the secured credit card vendor is a very real cost of this option.[56] Because a secured credit card requires a large initial cash outlay, it has all the drawbacks associated with "saving up" for a major purchase, making it a difficult and unattractive option for many consumers.

Payday and Tax Refund Anticipation Loans

Some check cashing services offer an expensive form of short-term credit—loans using the customer's own post-dated check as collateral. "These loans, in small amounts, for terms of only a week or so at a time, may have effective interest rates of 700 to 2,000 percent."[57] Keest provides an example of how such a loan might work:

> Connie Consumer gives them a present or post-dated check for $256. In return, she gets $200. They withhold a fee of 28 percent of the amount advanced. The business agrees to hold Connie's check until a later date (usually her payday). When that date comes, Connie can either redeem the check for the full face value, or write another post-dated check to cover it, paying another service fee. The effective yield on this transaction? If she redeems the check after two weeks, it is 681% APR. If she redeems the check after ten days, it is about 1,000 percent; after five days, it is over 2,000 percent.[58]

Similarly, people expecting tax refunds can get short-term "refund anticipation loans" through commercial tax preparers like H&R Block. But the effective interest rate for these loans falls between 50 percent and 200 percent.[59] Bob Williams, a manager at Associates, offers a rationale for the high rates his loan company charges on short-term loans: "[A] lot of people need our services. All we're trying to provide is a service to people who might not be able to get credit elsewhere—and let them have the opportunity an upper class person might have."[60]

Rent-to-Own

Rent-to-own offers another alternative for low-income consumers. Most rent-to-own customers, like most Fingerhut customers, have household incomes of less than $36,000, and are unable to obtain credit.[61] Michael Hudson explained, "Rent-to-own customers routinely pay two, three, and four times what merchandise would cost if they could afford to pay cash. For example: A Rent-a-Center store in Roanoke, Virginia, recently offered a 20-inch Zenith TV for $14.99 a week for 74 weeks—or $1,109.26. Across town at Sears, the same TV was on sale for $329.99."[62]

In the past, rent-to-own dealers have been able to avoid state and federal credit legislation, since they claim to be leasing a product rather than extending any sort of loan. "Read literally, the TILA (Truth in Lending Act) definition of a credit sale does not include a RTO (rent-to-own) agreement, because the customer does not contract to pay the value of the goods he or she is acquiring, agreeing merely to pay for a week's or a month's rental."[63] By 1996, forty-three states had rent-to-own statutes regulating the disclosure of the full cost, although few placed limits on what the customer could be charged.[64] Where limits were attempted (for example, requiring that the total payments be no higher than twice the dealer's "cash price") they were unenforceable.

FINGERHUT'S DILEMMA

In the context of the other options available to its target market, Jane felt that Fingerhut's pricing strategy offered customers an affordable way of obtaining valued consumer goods on credit. Its tried-and-true installment pricing method had gained the loyalty of millions of satisfied customers. Viewed in this way, the allegations of four customers did not seem significant. But no matter how fair and reasonable Fingerhut's pricing strategy might seem to management, Jane knew that the lawsuit and its related publicity could damage Fingerhut's image as an ethical, socially conscious company. And there was always the chance that Minnesota could abolish the time-price doctrine through consumer protection legislation, as many other states already had. Was the lawsuit a wake-up call suggesting that Fingerhut's strategies targeted at the low-income market were ripe for revision? Jane picked up a legal pad and pen and began to write, her mind racing. She had to meet with Ted Deikel and Rachel O'Brien, vice president of customer relations, in a few hours to decide on a strategy.

Notes

1. Majorie Kelly, "Some Businesses Specialize in Capitalizing on the Poor; Fingerhut a State Firm that Targets Low Income Folks," *Star Tribune* (November 4, 1996), 3D.
2. Tim Gray, "Tampa Bay's Latest Catch Has Financial, Legal Problems," *St. Petersburg Times* (May 1, 1996), 1E.
3. Mark Albright, "Fingerhut Center is Symbol of Company's New Strategy," *St. Petersburg Times* (September 10, 1996), 1E.
4. Ibid.
5. Gray, op. cit.
6. Based on data in U.S. Department of Commerce, Bureau of the Census, *Money Income in the United States: 1996* (Washington, DC: Author, 1996) (P60–197) vii.
7. Ibid., v
8. Ibid.
9. Juliet B. Schor, *The Overspent American* (New York: Basic Books, 1998), 20.
10. Eileen Norris, "Fingerhut Gives Customers Credit," *Advertising Age* 57 (March 6, 1986): 19.
11. Albright, op. cit.
12. D. Caplovitz, *The Poor Pay More*, (London: Collier-MacMillan Ltd., 1967), 180.
13. S. Martin and N. Huckins, "Consumer Advocates vs. the Rent-to-Own Industry," 34 *American Business Law Journal* 385 (1997), 407.
14. A 1997 article reported that 99 percent of Fingerhut customers used the payment plan, in Paul Miller, "Fingerhut, to the Bone," *Catalog Age* 14:13 (December 1997): 5.
15. Sarah Brehm, "Catalog Shoppers Must Be Careful," Madison (Wisconsin) *Capital Times* (February 21, 1992), 1D.
16. Philip Kotler and Gary Armstrong, *Principles of Marketing*, 7th ed. (Upper Saddle River, NJ: Prentice Hall, 1997), 439.
17. Jim Bessen, "Riding the Marketing Information Wave," *Harvard Business Review* (September/October 1993), 150.
18. Ibid.

19. Quoted in Susan Chandler, "Data Is Power. Just Ask Fingerhut," *Business Week* (June 3, 1996), 69.
20. Ibid.
21. Harlan S. Byrne, "Shopping Made Easy," *Barron's* (July 25, 1994), 20.
22. Information taken from a case study on Lincoln software's website (http://www. ipsys .com/ fingerh. htm). 2001.
23. Chandler, op. cit.
24. Jim Bessen, "Riding the Marketing Information Wave," *Harvard Business Review* (September/October 1993), 150.
25. The setting of a service element such as an interest rate "is a pricing decision exactly like the pricing of a product purchased in a store," Kent B. Monroe, *Pricing: Making Profitable Decisions*, 2nd ed. (New York: McGraw-Hill, 1990), 403. Fingerhut also had to make pricing decisions concerning the shipping and handling incident to each sale.
26. Ibid., 72.
27. Tom Nagle and Reed Holden, *The Strategy and Tactics of Pricing* (Englewood Cliffs, N.J.: Prentice-Hall, 1995), 309.
28. Ibid.
29. James Agger, "Big Victory in N.J. Rent-to-Own Case," *The Legal Intelligencer* (October 31, 1996): 3.
30. Nagle & Holden, op. cit., 313.
31. Ibid., 80.
32. George J. Wallace, "The Logic of Consumer Credit Reform" *Yale Law Journal* 82 (1973), 461–82, 468.
33. See Monroe, op. cit., 347.
34. Ann-Margaret Kehoe, "Selling a Solution: Fingerhut Takes a Page from Supermarkets," *HFN, The Weekly Newspaper for the Home Furnishing Network* (December 8, 1997).
35. Jeff Bailey & Scott Kilman, "More Borrowers Appear to Be Wishing Up about Credit," *Star Tribune* (March 1, 1998), 5d.
36. Caplovitz, op. cit., 98.
37. Ibid.
38. Gray, op. cit.
39. Ibid.
40. Kelly, op. cit.
41. Ted Deikel, "Fingerhut Serves Its Customers Well," *Star Tribune* (November 11, 1996), 3D.
42. Chandler, op. cit.
43. Charles W. Lamb, Jr., Joseph F. Hair, Jr., and Carl McDaniel, eds., *Principles of Marketing*, Annotated Instructor's Edition, 2nd edition (Cincinnati: South-Western Publishing, 1994), 210.
44. Schlor, op. cit., 72.
45. American Bar Association, *You and the Law* (Chicago, 1993), 243.
46. Wallace, op. cit., 478.
47. American Bar Association, op. cit., 243.
48. Mary Kane, "Fringe Banks' Profit from Customers Without Banks" in Michael Hudson Ed., *Merchants of Misery* (Monroe ME: Common Courage Press, 1996): 55.
49. Kane, op. cit.
50. R. Robin McDonald, "Lawsuits to Decide Legality of Rates, Fees," *The Atlanta Constitution* (February 22, 1998), 5d.
51. K. Keest and E. Reuart, *The Cost of Credit* (Boston MA: National Consumer Law Center, 1966), 59.
52. McDonald, *op. cit.*
53. R. Robin McDonald, "Lease-back Schemes 'So Much Worse' than Pawning," *The Atlanta Journal-Constitution* (February 22, 1998), 5d.
54. Ibid.
55. Michael Hudson, ed., *Merchants of Misery: How Corporate America Profits from Poverty* (Monroe, ME: Common Courage Press, 1996), 7.

56. See Monroe, op. cit., 432.
57. Keest, op. cit.
58. Ibid., 240.
59. Hudson, op. cit., 10.
60. Quoted in "Signing Their Lives Away," in Hudson, op. cit., 45.
61. Shelly Branch, "Wayne's New World: Another Trashy Business," *Fortune* (February 2, 1998), 29.
62. Michael Hudson, "Rent-to-Own: The Slick Cousin of Paying on Time," in Hudson, op. cit., 146.
63. Susan Lorde Martin & Nancy White Huckins, "Consumer Advocates vs. the Rent-to-Own Industry: Reaching a Reasonable Accommodation," *American Business Law Journal* 34 (Spring 1997), 385–426, at 389.
64. Martin & Huckins, op. cit., 396 & n. 72.
65. Information compiled in August, 1998, from current advertising circulars, catalogs, and Internet sources.
66. The Fingerhut model includes a food processing attachment, which consists of a "work bowl" with a 3-cup capacity, and a "food pusher."
67. Both Prime Time Rental and Fingerhut include a Canon color bubble-jet printer. Circuit City includes a Lexmark color Jetprinter.

Persuasive Advertising, Autonomy, and the Creation of Desire

Roger Crisp

In this paper, I shall argue that all forms of a certain common type of advertising are morally wrong, on the ground that they override the autonomy of consumers.

One effect of an advertisement might be the creation of a desire for the advertised product. How such desires are caused is highly relevant as to whether we would describe the case as one in which the autonomy of the subject has been overridden. If I read an advertisement for a sale of clothes, I may rush down to my local clothes store and purchase a jacket I like. Here, my desire for the jacket has arisen partly out of my reading the advertisement. Yet, in an ordinary sense, it is based on or answers to certain properties of the jacket—its colour, style, material. Although I could not explain to you why my tastes are as they are, we still describe such cases as examples of autonomous action, in that all the decisions are being made by me: What kind of jacket do I like? Can I afford one? And so on. In certain other cases, however, the causal history of a desire may be different. Desires can be caused, for instance, by subliminal suggestion. In New Jersey, a cinema flashed sub-threshold advertisements for ice cream onto the screen during movies, and reported a dramatic increase in sales during intermissions. In such cases, choice is being deliberately ruled out by the method of advertising

Kluwer Academic Publishers, *Journal of Business Ethics* 6 (1987) 413–418. © 1987 by D. Reidel Publishing Company. Reprinted with kind permission of Kluwer Academic Publishers.

in question. These customers for ice cream were acting "automatonously," rather than autonomously. They did not buy the ice cream because they happened to like it and decided they would buy some, but rather because they had been subjected to subliminal suggestion. Subliminal suggestion is the most extreme form of what I shall call, adhering to a popular dichotomy, persuasive, as opposed to informative, advertising. Other techniques include puffery, which involves the linking of the product, through suggestive language and images, with the unconscious desires of consumers for power, wealth, status, sex, and so on; and repetition, which is self-explanatory, the name of the product being "drummed into" the mind of the consumer.

The obvious objection to persuasive advertising is that it somehow violates the autonomy of consumers. I believe that this objection is correct, and that, if one adopts certain common-sensical standards for autonomy, non-persuasive forms of advertising are not open to such an objection. Very high standards for autonomy are set by Kant, who requires that an agent be entirely external to the causal nexus found in the ordinary empirical world, if his or her actions are to be autonomous. These standards are too high, in that it is doubtful whether they allow any autonomous action. Standards for autonomy more congenial to common sense will allow that my buying the jacket is autonomous, although continuing to deny that the people in New Jersey were acting autonomously. In the former case, we have what has come to be known in recent discussions of freedom of the will as *both* free will *and* free action. I both decide what to do, and am not obstructed in carrying through my decision into action. In the latter case, there is free action, but not free will. No one prevents the customers buying their ice cream, but they have not themselves made any genuine decision whether or not to do so. In a very real sense, decisions are made for consumers by persuasive advertisers, who occupy the motivational territory properly belonging to the agent. If what we mean by autonomy, in the ordinary sense, is to be present, the possibility of decision must exist alongside.

Arrington (1982) discusses, in a challenging paper, the techniques of persuasive advertising I have mentioned, and argues that such advertising does not override the autonomy of consumers. He examines four notions central to autonomous action, and claims that, on each count, persuasive advertising is exonerated on the charge we have made against it. I shall now follow in the footsteps of Arrington, but argue that he sets the standards for autonomy too low for them to be acceptable to common sense, and that the charge therefore still sticks.

(A) AUTONOMOUS DESIRE

Arrington argues that an autonomous desire is a first-order desire (a desire for some object, say, Pongo Peach cosmetics) accepted by the agent because it fulfills a second-order desire (a desire about a desire, say, a desire that my first-order desire for Pongo Peach be fulfilled), and that most of the first-order desires engendered in us by advertising are desires that we do accept. His example is an advertisement for Grecian Formula 16, which engenders in him a desire to be younger. He desires that both his desire to be younger and his desire for Grecian Formula 16 be fulfilled.

Unfortunately, this example is not obviously one of persuasive advertising. It may be the case that he just has this desire to look young again rather as I had certain sartorial tastes before I saw the ad about the clothes sale, and then decides to buy Grecian Formula 16 on the basis of these tastes. Imagine this form of advertisement: a person is depicted using Grecian Formula 16, and is then shown in a position of authority, surrounded by admiring members of the opposite sex. This would be a case of puffery. The advertisement implies that having hair coloured by the product will lead to positions of power, and to one's becoming more attractive to the opposite sex. It links, by suggestion, the product with my unconscious desires for power and sex. I may still claim that I am buying the product because I want to look young again. But the real reasons for my purchase are my unconscious desires for power and sex, and the link made between the product and the fulfillment of those desires by the advertisement. These reasons are not reasons I could avow to myself as good reasons for buying the product, and, again, the possibility of decision is absent.

Arrington's claim is that an autonomous desire is a first-order desire which we accept. Even if we allow that it is possible for the agent to consider whether to accept or to repudiate first-order desires induced by persuasive advertising, it seems that all first-order desires induced purely by persuasive advertising will be non-autonomous in Arrington's sense. Many of us have a strong second-order desire not to be manipulated by others without our knowledge, and for no good reason. Often, we are manipulated by others without our knowledge, but for a good reason, and one that we can accept. Take an accomplished actor: much of the skill of an actor is to be found in unconscious body-language. This manipulation we see as essential to our being entertained, and thus acquiesce in it. What is important about this case is that there seems to be no diminution of autonomy. We can still judge the quality of the acting, in that the manipulation is part of its quality. In other cases, however, manipulation ought not to be present, and these are cases where the ability to decide is importantly diminished by the manipulation. Decision is central to the theory of the market-process: I should be able to decide whether to buy product *A* or product *B*, by judging them on their merits. Any manipulation here I shall repudiate as being for no good reason. This is not to say, incidentally, that once the fact that my desires are being manipulated by others has been made transparent to me, my desire will lapse. The people in New Jersey would have been unlikely to cease their craving for ice cream, if we had told them that their desire had been subliminally induced. But they would no longer have voiced acceptance of this desire, and, one assumes, would have resented the manipulation of their desires by the management of the cinema.

It is no evidence for the claim that most of our desires are autonomous in this sense that we often return to purchase the same product over and over again. For this might well show that persuasive advertising has been supremely efficient in inducing non-autonomous desires in us, which we are unable even to attempt not to act on, being unaware of their origin. Nor is it an argument in Arrington's favour that certain members of our society will claim not to have the second-order desire we have postulated. For it may be that this is a desire which we can see is one that human beings ought to have, a desire which it would be in their interests to have, and the lack of which is itself evidence of profound manipulation.

We have become desensitized to manipulation and no longer carefully consider purchase choices,

(B) RATIONAL DESIRE AND CHOICE

One might argue that the desires induced by advertising are often irrational, in the sense that they are not present in an agent in full possession of the facts about the product. This argument fails, says Arrington, because if we require *all* the facts about a thing before we can desire that thing, then all our desires will be irrational; and if we require only the relevant information, then prior desires determine the relevance of information. Advertising may be said to enable us to fulfill these prior desires, through the transfer of information, and the supplying of means to ends is surely a paradigm example of rationality.

But, what about persuasive, as opposed to informative, advertising? Take puffery. Is it not true that a person may buy Pongo Peach cosmetics, hoping for an adventure in paradise, and that the product will not fulfill these hopes? Are they really in possession of even the relevant facts? Yes, says Arrington. We wish to purchase *subjective* effects, and these are genuine enough. When I use Pongo Peach, I will experience a genuine feeling of adventure.

Once again, however, our analysis can help us to see the strength of the objection. For a desire to be rational, in any plausible sense, that desire must at least not be induced by the interference of other persons with my system of tastes, against my will and without my knowledge. Can we imagine a person, asked for a reason justifying their purchase of Pongo Peach, replying: "I have an unconscious desire to experience adventure, and the product has been linked with this desire through advertising"? If a desire is to be rational, it is not necessary that all the facts about the object be known to the agent, but one of the facts about that desire must be that it has not been induced in the agent through techniques which the agent cannot accept. Thus, applying the schema of Arrington's earlier argument, such a desire will be repudiated by the agent as non-autonomous and irrational.

Arrington's claim concerning the subjective effects of the products we purchase fails to deflect the charge of overriding autonomy we have made against persuasive advertising. Of course, very often the subjective effects will be lacking. If I use Grecian Formula 16, I am unlikely to find myself being promoted at work, or surrounded by admiring members of the opposite sex. This is just straight deception. But even when the effects do manifest themselves, such advertisements have still overridden my autonomy. They have activated desires which lie beyond my awareness, and over behaviour flowing from which I therefore have no control. If these claims appear doubtful, consider whether this advertisement is likely to be successful: "Do you have a feeling of adventure? Then use this brand of cosmetics." Such an advertisement will fail, in that it appeals to a conscious desire, either which we do not have, or which we realise will not be fulfilled by purchasing a certain brand of cosmetics. If the advertisement were for a course in mountain-climbing, it might meet with more success. Our conscious self is not so easily duped by advertising, and this is why advertisers make such frequent use of the techniques of persuasive advertising.

(C) FREE CHOICE

One might object to persuasive advertising that it creates desires so covert that an agent cannot resist them, and that acting on them is therefore neither free nor voluntary. Arrington claims that a person acts or chooses *freely* if they can adduce considerations which justify their act in their mind; and *voluntarily* if, had they been aware of a reason for acting otherwise, they could have done so. Only occasionally, he says, does advertising prevent us making free and voluntary choices.

Regarding free action, it is sufficient to note that, according to Arrington, if I were to be converted into a human robot, activated by an Evil Genius who has implanted electrodes in my brain, my actions would be free as long as I could cook up some justification for my behaviour. I want to dance this jig because I enjoy dancing. (Compare: I want to buy this ice cream because I like ice cream.) If my argument is right, we are placed in an analogous position by persuasive advertising. If we no longer mean by freedom of action the mere non-obstruction of behaviour, are we still ready to accept that we are engaged in free action? As for whether the actions of consumers subjected to persuasive advertising are voluntary in Arrington's sense, I am less optimistic than he is. It is likely, as we have suggested, that the purchasers of ice cream or Pongo Peach would have gone ahead with their purchase even if they had been made aware that their desires had been induced in them by persuasive advertising. But they would now claim that they themselves had not made the decision, that they were acting on a desire engendered in them which they did not accept, and that there was, therefore, a good reason for them not to make the purchase. The unconscious is not obedient to the commands of the conscious, although it may be forced to listen.

In fact, it is odd to suggest that persuasive advertising does give consumers a choice. A choice is usually taken to require the weighing-up of reasons. What persuasive advertising does is to remove the very conditions of choice.

(D) CONTROL OR MANIPULATION

Arrington offers the following criteria for control:

A person *C* controls the behaviour of another person *P* if

1. *C* intends P to act in a certain way *A*
2. *C*'s intention is causally effective in bringing about *A*, and
3. *C* intends to ensure that all of the necessary conditions of *A* are satisfied.

He argues that advertisements tend to induce a desire for *X*, given a more basic desire for *Y*. Given my desire for adventure, I desire Pongo Peach cosmetics. Thus, advertisers do not control consumers, since they do not intend to produce all of the necessary conditions for our purchases.

Arrington's analysis appears to lead to some highly counter-intuitive consequences. Consider, again, my position as human robot. Imagine that the Evil Genius relies on the fact that I have certain basic unconscious desires in order to effect his plan. Thus, when he wants me to dance a jig, it is necessary that I have a more basic desire, say, ironically, for power. What the electrodes do is to jumble up my practical reasoning processes, so that I believe that I am dancing the jig because I like dancing, while, in reality, the desire to dance stems from a link between the dance and the fulfillment of my desire for power, forged by the electrodes. Are we still happy to say that I am not controlled? And does not persuasive advertising bring about a similar jumbling-up of the practical reasoning processes of consumers? When I buy Pongo Peach, I may be unable to offer a reason for my purchase, or I may claim that I want to look good. In reality, I buy it owing to the link made by persuasive advertising between my unconscious desire for adventure and the cosmetic in question.

A more convincing account of behaviour control would be to claim that it occurs when a person causes another person to act for reasons which the other person could not accept as good or justifiable reasons for the action. This is how brain-washing is to be distinguished from liberal education, rather than on Arrington's ground that the brain-washer arranges all the necessary conditions for belief. The student can both accept that she has the beliefs she has because of her education and continue to hold those beliefs as true, whereas the victim of brain-washing could not accept the explanation of the origin of her beliefs, while continuing to hold those beliefs. It is worth recalling the two cases we mentioned at the beginning of this paper. I can accept my tastes in dress, and do not think that the fact that their origin is unknown to me detracts from my autonomy, when I choose to buy the jacket. The desire for ice cream, however, will be repudiated, in that it is the result of manipulation by others, without good reason.

It seems, then, that persuasive advertising does override the autonomy of consumers, and that, if the overriding of autonomy, other things being equal, is immoral, then persuasive advertising is immoral.

An argument has recently surfaced which suggests that, in fact, other things are not equal, and that persuasive advertising, although it overrides autonomy, is morally acceptable. This argument was first developed by Nelson (1978), and claims that persuasive advertising is a form of informative advertising, albeit an indirect form. The argument runs at two levels: first, the consumer can judge from the mere fact that a product is heavily advertised, regardless of the form or content of the advertisements, that that product is likely to be a market-winner. The reason for this is that it would not pay to advertise market-losers. Second, even if the consumer is taken in by the content of the advertisement, and buys the product for that reason, he is not being irrational. For he would have bought the product anyway, since the very fact that it is advertised means that it is a good product. As Nelson says:

> It does not pay consumers to make very thoughtful decisions about advertising. They can respond to advertising for the most ridiculous, explicit reasons and still do what they would have done if they had made the most careful judgements about their behaviour. "Irrationality" is rational if it is cost-free.

Our conclusions concerning the mode of operation of persuasive advertising, however, suggest that Nelson's argument cannot succeed. For the first level to work, it would have to be true that a purchaser of a product can evaluate that product on its own merits, and then decide whether to purchase it again. But, as we have seen, consumers induced to purchase products by persuasive advertising are not buying those products on the basis of a decision founded upon any merit the products happen to have. Thus, if the product turns out to be less good than less heavily advertised alternatives, they will not be disappointed, and will continue to purchase, if subjected to the heavy advertising which induced them to buy in the first place. For this reason, heavy persuasive advertising is not a sign of quality, and the fact that a product is advertised does not suggest that it is good. In fact, if the advertising has little or no informative content, it might suggest just the opposite. If the product has genuine merits, it should be possible to mention them. Persuasive advertising, as the executives on Madison Avenue know, can be used to sell anything, regardless of its nature or quality.

For the second level of Nelson's argument to succeed, and for it to be in the consumer's interest to react even unthinkingly to persuasive advertising, it must be true that the first level is valid. As the first level fails, there is not even a *prima facie* reason for the belief that it is in the interest of the consumer to be subjected to persuasive advertising. In fact, there are two weighty reasons for doubting this belief. The first has already been hinted at: products promoted through persuasive advertising may well not be being sold on their merits, and may, therefore, be bad products, or products that the consumer would not desire on being confronted with unembellished facts about the product. The second is that this form of "rational irrationality" is anything but cost-free. We consider it a great cost to lose our autonomy. If I were to demonstrate to you conclusively that if I were to take over your life, and make your decisions for you, you would have a life containing far more of whatever you think makes life worth living, apart from autonomy, than if you were to retain control, you would not surrender your autonomy to me even for these great gains in other values. As we mentioned above in our discussion of autonomous desire, we have a strong second-order desire not to act on first-order desires induced in us unawares by others, for no good reason, and now we can see that that desire applies even to cases in which we would appear to be better off in acting on such first-order desires.

Thus, we may conclude that Nelson's argument in favour of persuasive advertising is not convincing. I should note, perhaps, that my conclusion concerning persuasive advertising echoes that of Santilli (1983). My argument differs from his, however, in centering upon the notions of autonomy and causes of desires acceptable to the agent, rather than upon the distinction between needs and desires. Santilli claims that the arousal of a desire is not a rational process, unless it is preceded by a knowledge of actual needs. This, I believe, is too strong. I may well have no need of a new tennis-racket, but my desire for one, aroused by informative advertisements in the newspaper, seems rational enough. I would prefer to claim that a desire is autonomous and at least prima facie rational if it is not induced in the agent without his knowledge and for no good reason, and allows ordinary processes of decision-making to occur.

Finally, I should point out that, in arguing against all persuasive advertising, unlike Santilli, I am not to be interpreted as bestowing moral respectability upon all informative advertising. Advertisers of any variety ought to consider whether the ideological objections often made to their conduct have any weight. Are they, for instance, imposing a distorted system of values upon consumers, in which the goal of our lives is to consume, and in which success is measured by one's level of consumption? Or are they entrenching attitudes which prolong the position of certain groups subject to discrimination, such as women or homosexuals? Advertisers should also carefully consider whether their product will be of genuine value to any consumers, and, if so, attempt to restrict their campaigns to the groups in society which will benefit (see Durham, 1984). I would claim, for instance, that all advertising of tobacco-based products, even of the informative variety, is wrong, and that some advertisements for alcohol are wrong, in that they are directed at the wrong audience. Imagine, for instance, a liquor-store manager erecting an informative bill-board opposite an alcoholics' rehabilitation center. But these are secondary questions for prospective advertisers. The primary questions must be whether they are intending to employ the techniques of persuasive advertising, and, if so, how these techniques can be avoided.

References

Arrington, R.: 1982, "Advertising and Behaviour Control," *Journal of Business Ethics* I, 1.

Durham, T.: 1984, "Information, Persuasion, and Control in Moral Appraisal of Advertising Strategy," *Journal of Business Ethics III*, 3.

Nelson, P.: 1978, "Advertising and Ethics," in *Ethics, Free Enterprise, and Public Policy*, (eds.) R. De George and J. Pichler, New York: Oxford University Press.

Santilli, P.: 1983, "The Informative and Persuasive Functions of Advertising: A Moral Appraisal," *Journal of Business Ethics* II, I.

APPENDIX: SEVEN MARKETING PITCHES

Consider the following seven marketing techniques:

1. An ad claiming that the Honda Accord has high satisfaction ratings among first-year owners.
2. A TV commercial in which James Garner exhibits the sporty, fun experience of driving the Mazda RX-7.
3. An ad for the Chevrolet Camaro presenting it as enhancing sex appeal by displaying the car among a group of attractive young men/women (your pick) in bathing suits.
4. An ad for Allstate life insurance that pictures two houses, one of which is fully involved in a fire, with a voice-over informing us that the real tragedy has just happened in the other house: The breadwinner died without sufficient life insurance to cover the mortgage.
5. An ad for a device which can summon medical assistance in an emergency; the ad shows an elderly woman falling down a flight of steps. Unfortunately, she is not wearing the device, and help arrives too late.
6. A Saturday morning TV ad for Smurf dolls; it is broadcast during a cartoon show starring the cute little creatures.
7. A subliminal message "Buy Coke" shown before intermission in a movie theater.

Which of these ads do you intuitively feel is a violation of the consumer's autonomy? If you feel as most people do, you will find the first ad unproblematic and the last ad to be a violation. If this is your response, you must identify the features of the subliminal technique that make it objectionable from the point of view of autonomy. You must also be consistent and willing to accept the consequences of your analysis. For instance, if the feature that makes the subliminal technique unacceptable is also present in the ad aimed at children, you must make the same judgment about both ads.

The most common explanation of the usual reaction to the seventh case relates to the consumer's being unaware of the appeal. The subliminal technique is intended to manipulate consumers by making them less likely to resist the desire the ad may generate. (Note that this explanation makes the technique objectionable even if the consumer ultimately decides not to buy the product.)

Chapter 14

The Environment

Case Study

ExxonMobil and the Chad/Cameroon Pipeline

Jenny Mead ● Andy Wicks ● Patricia H. Werhane

In November 1999, ExxonMobil CEO Lee Raymond faced the potential collapse of the Chad/Cameroon Oil Pipeline project on which the company was about to embark. Both Royal Dutch/Shell and France's TotalFinaElf, ExxonMobil's partners in the Pipeline Consortium, had just withdrawn, citing environmental concerns among other things and leaving its future temporarily in doubt. This withdrawal delighted many environmental groups long opposed to the pipeline. A spokesperson for the Rainforest Action Network (RAN), a grassroots environmental organization and longtime pipeline opponent, said in a press release, "Based on its experience in Nigeria, Royal Dutch/Shell recognizes a bad situation when it sees one, and Elf Aquitaine will avoid becoming part of the tragedy. The human and environmental costs of proceeding with an oil pipeline that cuts through the heart of Africa's rainforest are simply too great."[1]

In 1996, after years of economic and environmental feasibility studies of accessing oil reserves in the Central African country of Chad, a consortium of oil companies that included ExxonMobil, Shell, and Elf signed a memoranda of understanding (MOU) with the governments of Chad and neighboring Cameroon. The Chad Development Project involved, over the span of 25 to 30 years, developing oil fields in southern Chad, drilling approximately 300 wells in the Doba Basin, and building a 650-mile underground

This case was prepared by Research Assistant Jenny Mead under the supervision of Patricia H. Werhane, Ruffin Professor of Business Ethics, and Andrew C. Wicks, Associate Professor of Business Administration, Darden Graduate School of Business, University of Virginia. It was written as a basis for class discussion rather than to illustrate effective or ineffective handling of an administrative situation. Copyright © 2007 by the University of Virginia Darden School Foundation, Charlottesville, VA. All rights reserved. *To order copies, send an e-mail to dardencases@virginia. edu. No part of this publication may be reproduced, stored in a retrieval system, used in a spreadsheet, or transmitted in any form or by any means—electronic, mechanical, photocopying, recording, or otherwise—without the permission of the Darden School Foundation.*

pipeline through landlocked Chad and the adjacent Cameroon to transport crude oil to the coast for shipping to world markets. Cost of the project was $3.5 billion; expected production was one billion barrels of oil; according to World Bank estimates, the project would generate $2 billion in revenues for Chad, $500 million for Cameroon, and $5.7 billion for ExxonMobil and its project partners.

Shell's and Elf's pull-out threatened to sideline the whole operation and seemed to give credence to those critics who thought that environmental and human risks of oil exploration and extraction in the extremely poor countries of Chad and Cameroon were too great. The project's many issues burned in CEO Lee Raymond's mind as he considered whether ExxonMobil should follow suit or proceed with the pipeline project.

EXXONMOBIL

At the time of their December 1998 merger, which some oil industry analysts called "seismic," Exxon and Mobil, each a multi-billion dollar operation, were the world's two largest oil companies. In 1997, Exxon had a net income of $8.5 billion; an "AAA" debt rating; revenues of $137.2 billion; and it sold 5.4 million barrels of petroleum products daily. Mobil had a net income of $3.3 billion; revenues of $65.9 billion; and total petroleum product sales of 3.3 million barrels a day.[2] Many analysts attributed the merger to tough times for oil companies, which in the 1990s faced lower prices, decreased demand, fierce competition, oversupply, and a general global economic weakness.[3] Indeed, just three months before this merger, Mobil had attempted, unsuccessfully, to merge with Amoco, which then merged with BP. (Ironically, the Exxon Mobil merger reassembled the legendary Standard Oil, John Rockefeller's company. In 1911, anti-trust authorities forced Standard Oil to break into two companies: Standard Oil of New Jersey, which later became Exxon, and Standard Oil of New York, which later became Mobil). Nonetheless, the two companies had very different images in the oil industry. Mobil was seen as having a "combative feistiness," while Exxon had a "relentlessly efficient stuffiness."[4] Because of the size of the companies, the merger was scrutinized by anti-trust regulators and, in order to complete the merger, both companies had to divest certain operations, including almost 2,500 service stations in the United States and Europe.

By the mere fact that the growing population of environmentally concerned people worldwide were skeptical of large oil companies and their promotion of fossil fuel use, both Exxon and Mobil had struggled with their public image. However, Exxon had the most damage to contain because of the 1989 Exxon Valdez oil spill in Alaska's Prince William Sound, when the single-hulled oil tanker, while dodging icebergs, hit a reef outside the shipping lanes. The tanker then spilled 53,094,510 gallons (equal to 1,264,155 barrels) of oil. The spill covered 460 miles; took four years to clean up (although some Alaskan shores still were covered with oil at the start of the 21st century); and killed an estimated 250,000 seabirds, 2,800 sea otters, 300 harbor seals, 250 bald eagles, approximately 22 killer whales, and billions of salmon and herring eggs.[5] Worldwide public outcry was fiercely negative and

Exxon's reputation severely tarnished.[6] After the accident, the Exxon Shipping Company, owner of the Valdez, was renamed Sea River Shipping Company and the repaired Valdez was renamed the Sea River Mediterranean. Prohibited from ever returning to Prince William Sound, the tanker began carrying oil back and forth across the Atlantic. Nonetheless, Exxon's handling of the Valdez episode and its subsequent appeal of a $5 billion jury award to spill victims "was derided as an example of how not to handle a public-relations disaster."[7] Exacerbating the situation was an Exxon representative's claim at a 1993 Atlanta symposium that some of the oil attributed to the Valdez spill actually came from other sources such as natural underwater fields.[8]

After the Valdez incident, Exxon tried to establish an environmentally friendly image (see Exhibit 14.1 for ExxonMobil's Environment Policy) and began using more tugboats and increasingly sophisticated navigational equipment, such as global positioning systems, to guide its tankers through

---

EXHIBIT 14.1. ExxonMobil Environment Policy: Safeguarding Our Environment

It is our policy to conduct our business in a manner that is compatible with the balanced environmental and economic needs of the communities in which we operate. We are committed to continuous efforts to improve environmental performance throughout our operations worldwide.
Our policy is to:

- comply with all applicable environmental laws and regulations and apply responsible standards where laws or regulations do not exist;
- encourage concern and respect for the environment, emphasize every employee's responsibility in environmental performance and ensure appropriate operating practices and training;
- work with government and industry groups to foster timely development of effective environmental laws and regulations based on sound science and considering risks, costs and benefits and effects on energy and product supply;
- manage our business with the goal of preventing incidents and of controlling emissions and wastes to below harmful levels; design, operate and maintain facilities to this end;
- respond quickly and effectively to incidents resulting from our operations, cooperating with industry organizations and authorized government agencies;
- conduct and support research to improve understanding of the impact of our business on the environment, to improve methods of environmental protection, and to enhance our capability to make operations and products compatible with the environment;
- communicate with the public on environmental matters and share our experience with others to facilitate improvements in industry performance;
- undertake appropriate reviews and evaluations of our operations to measure progress and to ensure compliance with this policy.

Source: http/www2.ExxonMobil.com/Corporate/Notebook/Footprint/Corp_N Policy.asp

the waters.[9] Many of ExxonMobil's website pages dealt with the issues of environment and sustainability. One webpage, "Safeguarding Our Environment" (see Exhibit 14.2), outlined the mechanisms put in place, including an Operations Integrity Management System (OIMS), which "provides the framework for our top-notch environmental management system that helps prevent all types of incidents." The webpage acknowledged damage done in the Valdez incident and confirmed that the company had developed an "Oil Spill Response Preparedness" program. ExxonMobil claimed that its concerns now lay not only with responding to spills, but in preventing them. There was also a link to the company's "Environmental Performance Indicators," which included: statistics on the company's marine spills, regulatory compliance (number of penalty assessments), cogeneration capacity, greenhouse gas emissions, and the reduction of NO_x (nitrous oxide), VOC (volatile organic compounds) and SO_2 (sulfur dioxide).

EXHIBIT 14.2. Safeguarding our Environment

ExxonMobil is committed to operational excellence in all we do including continuous efforts to improve environmental performance. Governance of environmental matters is overseen by Corporate directors and our comprehensive Operations Integrity Management System (OIMS) provides the framework for our top-notch environmental management system that helps prevent all types of incidents. As a result of our efforts, our environmental performance continues to improve.

OIMS is ExxonMobil's system that ensures environmental considerations are addressed in all our operations. OIMS has become a respected benchmark approach for incident prevention. Lloyd's Register of Quality Assurance (LRQA) attests that OIMS meets the intent and requirements of ISO 14001 (the recognized international standard for environmental management systems). LRQA also found "ExxonMobil to be among the industry leaders in the extent to which environmental management considerations have been integrated into ongoing business practices". We built into OIMS a culture of continuous improvement to make our environmental protection programs even stronger. We are currently strengthening systems to further integrate environmental planning into long-range business decision-making. Find out more about Lloyd's attestation.

We have learned from the events of the 1989 Valdez oil spill. It was a terrible accident everyone in our company regrets. As a result we committed to improve our accident prevention and incident response capabilities. Should an incident occur, our emergency response network would mobilize the appropriate resources. For spill response, we would capitalize on a worldwide network of oil spill cooperatives that we helped to establish and fund. We would also utilize our stockpile of emergency response equipment. Research efforts on dispersant and bioremediation techniques have expanded our abilities to reduce the impact of oil spills and speed recovery of impacted environments. Learn more about our Oil Spill Response Preparedness.

A responsible environmental approach involves much more than responding to accidents. Our scientists and engineers develop and apply technologies to continually reduce the impacts of our operations and products in many environmental media: air, water, and land. We apply these technologies to our own facilities and, in some cases, license them for broad application. Our strong focus on <u>energy efficiency</u> has helped reduce air emissions and is expected to continue to reduce pollutants per unit of production.

ExxonMobil's Global Energy Management System is an approach that has identified opportunities to reduce energy use and operating costs at refineries and chemical plants. Furthermore, we use cogeneration facilities that can supply 2,700 megawatts of electricity and reduce carbon dioxide emissions by almost seven million tons a year from what they would otherwise be using conventional electricity generation.

We continue pacesetter performance in limiting the number of spills from marine operations. Several outside organizations have recognized ExxonMobil facilities with recent <u>awards</u> for outstanding environmental management and performance. See more accounting of our <u>ExxonMobil Environmental Performance Indicators.</u>

Also available here is more about ExxonMobil and <u>sustainability</u>, <u>climate change</u> and <u>biodiversity</u>.

> **"Sea River (ExxonMobil's U.S. marine transportation company) has not only complied with Best Achievable Protection standards since their inception in 1995, but it remains the only company to date, to receive the ECOPRO (Exceptional Compliance Program)**
>
> **Award. Sea River's commitment to safe transportation of oil sets the industry standard."**
>
> **Director, Washington State Department of Ecology, March 2001**

Source: http://www.ExxonMobil.com/Corporate/Notebook/Footprint/Corp_N_FootprintDetails.asp

In part because it had no Valdez incident, Mobil's public image—on the surface at least—was different; the company, with a focus on support of the arts, sponsored *Masterpiece Theater* and ran full-page "advertorials," or discussions of timely issues. Aside from *Masterpiece Theater* and PBS programming, the company had funded community projects focusing on minorities, the handicapped, the elderly, and critical human needs.[10] Perhaps foreshadowing its eventual participation in the Chad/Cameroon pipeline, Mobil had sponsored "The Art of Cameroon," a traveling exhibition, in 1984. Mobil had also initiated some environmentally friendly programs, which included planting half a million trees around the United States in the mid-1990s and proposing the same for Peru and Indonesia (Exxon was a tree proponent, too, with its "Esso Living Tree Campaign," a reforestation project both in the United States and England). In smaller, more specific ways, Mobil had a softer image; in their service stations, the oil company had reinstated the practice of having employees clean car windows and offer coffee to drivers.[11] But the bottom line remained for Mobil, which in the early 1990s had exited the more environmentally friendly solar power business "because it was not economically attractive."[12]

Less visible to the public than Exxon's Valdez crisis was Mobil's involvement with some allegedly corrupt regimes. In an early 1990s attempt to enter the oil-rich Central Asian country of Kazakhstan, run by the brutal dictator Nursultan Nazarbayev, Mobil was involved with James Giffen, a corrupt

American "consultant," or go-between for countries wishing to deal with Kazakhastan. (In April 2003, Giffen was indicted by a New York grand jury on charges of bribing foreign officials.) Mobil also had dealt with the poverty-stricken Equatorial Guinea's oppressive ruler, Teodoro Obiang Nguema Mbasogo, in exploring and drilling the Zafiro Oil Field in 1995.

Exploration areas

By 1999, ExxonMobil, with almost sixty exploration projects worldwide, was considered one of the strongest oil companies in Upstream Operations.[13] Its exploration and production efforts were scattered throughout the world, with 58 major projects under way in various countries. Some of the emerging exploration areas were West Africa, South America, the Middle East, the Caspian region, and Eastern Canada.

Some of the major areas of exploration included:

North America	Gulf of Mexico
Eastern Canada	Nova Scotia, Newfoundland
Western Canada	Cold Lake Field
South America	Argentina, Venezuela, Brazil, Trinidad, Guyana
Europe	North Sea, Netherlands, Germany, Norway, United Kingdom
Africa	Nigeria, Equatorial Guineas
West Africa	Angola, Chad, Cameroon
North Africa	Egypt
Asia-Pacific	Malaysia, Australia, Indonesia (North Sumatra)
Caspian	Azerbaijan, Kazakhstan
Middle East	Abu Dhabi, Yemen, Qatar, Kuwait
Russia	Sakhalin Island

Source: ExxonMobil 1999 Annual Report.

Alternative Energy

Despite public pressure from environmental groups favoring alternative fuel sources, ExxonMobil remained firmly committed to fossil fuels. Other fuel sources such as solar, biomass, water and wind power, and electricity, were simply impractical, the company claimed, and were "economical only in niche markets."[14] To illustrate the impracticality of other energy sources, ExxonMobil utilized a Manhattan Institute Senior Fellow's estimate to power New York City on solar power alone would take four times the area of the city to hold the required solar panels, even on a sunny day.[15] Ethanol alcohol, another fuel source identified by environmentalists as more earth-friendly, was not as harmless as claimed, according to ExxonMobil, because of all the agricultural effort (and byproducts such as waste water) that grain production required.[16] Future efforts looked dim; in a 2000 corporate report publication, ExxonMobil claimed that despite significant efforts to develop alternative energy sources such as solar or wind, these sources comprised less than 0.25 percent of the world's energy supply and would not, in the foreseeable future, be economical without significant governmental subsidies.[17]

CHAD AND CAMEROON

In the late 20th century, Chad and Cameroon were two of the poorest countries in the world. Although Cameroon was more developed than its neighbor and had a higher literacy rate, many of the same problems assailed both countries. Both countries had rampant disease, poor nutrition, extreme poverty, and very little safe drinking water. Although three times the size of France, Chad could claim only 166 miles of paved roads, no rail system, a substandard telecommunications system (only two phones per thousand people), and overall insubstantial infrastructure and erratic access to electricity (see Exhibit 14.3 for maps of both countries).

Chad

Chad gained its independence from the French in 1960 (although the French stepped in four times over the next two decades to help the Chad government fend off coups). Almost immediately, the country was thrown into civil war, primarily between the Muslim northern rebel groups, called

EXHIBIT 14.3. Map of Cameroon

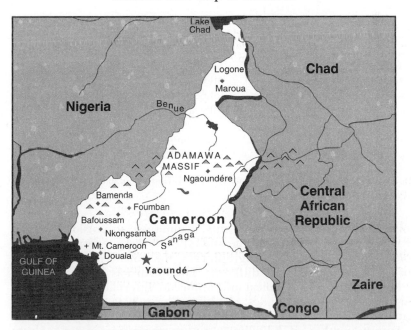

Source: http://www.compufix.demon.co.uk/camweb/

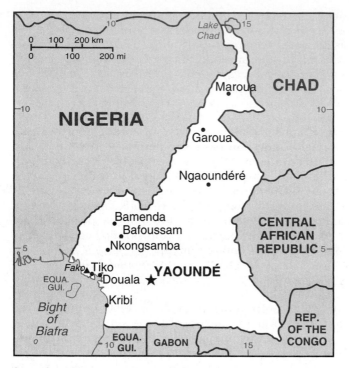

Source: http://www.cia.gov/cia/publications/factbook/geos/cm.html

	Cameroon	Chad	United States
Per capita GNP	$610	$230	$29,240
Life expectancy	54 years	48 years	77 years
Infant mortality	77 per 1000 births	99 per 1000 births	7 per 1000 births
Literacy Rate	80% men	49% men	97%
	67% women	31% women	(both sexes)
Country GNP	$8.7 billion	$1.7 billion	9,400.2 billion
Annual Exports	$2.3 billion	$328 million	

Source: Chad/Cameroon Development Project Fact Sheet 2001, Esso Exploration & Production Chad, Inc., p. 2.

by one journalist "an explosive ethnic mix," vulnerable to outside manipulation (from Libya and Sudan, among others), and the government in the south. Politically, culturally, and geographically, the northern and southern regions of Chad were immensely different. The north was arid, desert-like, primarily Muslim; the south tropical and animistic. Internal turmoil continued through the next three decades, resulting in over 20,000 deaths. As one analyst put it, "Undoubtedly Chad can pride itself as the African country with the largest number of rebellious groups since independence from France."[18]

In 1990, French-trained 38-year-old General Idriss Deby staged a coup, ousting President Hissene Habre. Deby, the fifth Chad head-of-state in the country's thirty years of independence, promised human rights, a multi-party system, and democracy; under his leadership, however, corruption and human rights abuses ran rampant. According to Transparency International, a global organization monitoring corruption levels globally, Chad and Cameroon repeatedly had one of the world's worst records for corruption.[19]

Skepticism about Exxon's dealings in Chad were exacerbated by a 1994 incident in Doba, where a local peasant, having taken his family to watch an airplane land at the Exxon exploration field, was shot to death by the security forces guarding the Exxon staff. Miscommunication was the cause; security forces claimed that the peasant was a rebel, while villagers claimed he was just a man who wanted to watch the "miracle" of a plane landing. Ultimately, the cause of the incident was assigned to "language problems." This incident was indicative of potential problems in the ExxonMobil project. "Language differences may indeed exacerbate tensions in the Doba region. The Chadian security forces, which protect the oil consortium, are mainly recruited from the ethnic group of Chad's president, Idriss Deby. Most of these recruits are Arabic speakers from the North who do not know the local languages of the South."[20]

Other tragic incidents occurred, most notably in 1998 when Chadian security forces allegedly killed 200 civilians in the Dobara and Lara villages in the Doba region, a massacre that was never investigated. "The Chadian government also utilized extrajudicial killings and disappearances, illegal searches and wiretaps, home demolition, threat of death or grave bodily harm, rape, and arbitrary arrest and detentions against its political opponents and their neighbors and family members."[21]

Cameroon

Cameroon achieved independence in 1960, after years of foreign domination by the Portuguese, Germans, British, and French. In World War I, the country was divided into French- and British-mandated regions. The French mandate was eliminated in 1960, giving the country independence, although part of the British mandate remained. The next twenty years saw a repressive government under President Ahmadou Ahidjou, which was nonetheless accompanied by investment in agriculture, education, health care, and transport. Ahidjou's Prime Minister, Paul Biya, succeeded him in 1982 and, with pressure from Cameroonians, instituted a multi-party system. Although the country's literacy rate was one of the highest on the African continent, its development was slow because of widespread corruption and huge military and security expenditures.[22] In 1972, the country was the United Republic of Cameroon; it became the Republic of Cameroon in 1984. This West African country was 475,400 square kilometers, roughly the size of California, with 402 kilometers of coastline. In the late 1990s, the population was approximately 16 million.

In the 1980s, Cameroon had severe economic problems because of the worldwide drop in prices for its staple products, coffee, rubber, and cotton, and because the country was dependent on French companies, which controlled almost half of the export market. There was also internal friction between ethic groups and regions as each fought for oil revenues.[23] Government repression increased in the 1990s, and while political parties were allowed to emerge, rampant fraud permeated the elections and the government arrested opposition leaders. In 1997, Biya was re-elected president, although half of the country's population was excluded from voting for various reasons.

The Pipeline

Working with oil companies from various other countries, the Republic of Chad began exploring its own oil resources in the late 1960s. By 1975, after many exploration wells had been drilled, it was clear that oil was abundant. Further exploration was halted by Chad's 1979 civil war and did not resume until the late 1980s. In 1988, an Exxon consortium signed an agreement with Chad that set the framework for the eventual pipeline project; Exxon had thirty years to develop the oilfields at Doba in southern Chad and produce and transport the oil to market. Since Chad was landlocked, the Exxon Consortium signed an agreement with neighboring Cameroon to build a 1,070 km (approximately 600 mile) underground pipeline to carry the crude oil to a shipping terminal just offshore from Kribi, on the Gulf of Guinea. In January 1995, Exxon, through its affiliates, Esso Exploration and Production Chad Inc., signed an agreement with Chad and Cameroon outlining the principal terms for the pipeline. In 1997, the Chad government enacted an amendment to the 1988 Exxon Consortium convention, outlining the relationship between the Consortium and Chad, "including the processes for environmental protection, land acquisition, and compensation, as well as royalty and tax payments that could approximately double the size of Chad's annual budget."[24]

World Bank Involvement[25]

The World Bank was conceived and founded in 1944, initially to help rebuild Europe after World War II. The Bank's first loan was to France: $250 million for post-war reconstruction. While reconstruction remained an important mission, over the years the Bank expanded to lending money for relief from "natural disasters, humanitarian emergencies, and postconflict rehabilitation needs." The 1980s was a critical period for the Bank, which had suffered from "macroeconomic and debt rescheduling issues," and faced criticism from many regarding its environmental and social positions. By the 1990s, the World Bank was focusing on stimulating economic development throughout the world, particularly in poorer countries. In 1999, the Bank lent approximately $15 billion to developing countries.[26] Before becoming involved in the Chad Cameroon Pipeline Project, the Bank had helped fund ten other pipeline projects around the world. Its return on earnings had averaged 22 percent over the years, although the returns on investments in Africa and oil and gas ventures were much lower.[27] By 1999, the Bank's worldwide staff of 10,000 included 250 environmental experts and 800 employees working on sustainable development issues.[28]

Although World Bank involvement in the Pipeline Project did not become official until 1997 (and a date for final project financing approval was not slated until 1999), the Bank originally took an interest in 1993. In 1995, to ascertain the various environmental and social risks, the Bank commissioned the governments of Chad and Cameroon, scientists, various NGOs, and environmental engineers to analyze the Pipeline's impact on the areas through which it would run and produce an Environmental Assessment plan. Many of the villagers in the path of the pipeline were consulted, primarily through village meetings. The Environmental Assessment plan covered a variety of topics including environmental management, compensation and resettlement, regional development, and waste management. The report, which was submitted to the World Bank in mid-1999, took five years to compile; at completion, it was a 19-volume, 3000-page study.

The environmental assessment report identified key problems and their potential solutions. The report acknowledged that the pipeline would cross over and thus affect "a number of ecological zones and a variety of socio-economic groups."[29] The report also identified the potential environmental and social costs to both Chad and Cameroon:

a) oil spill costs

b) health costs

c) agriculture production losses

d) livestock fodder losses

e) forest and bush product losses

f) small emission of greenhouse gases[30]

The report acknowledged the "uncertainty in estimating incremental environmental and social costs," but it claimed that "most of these potential costs will be mitigated and/or compensated for by the Private Sponsors, and any remaining impacts are expected to be negligible in comparison to the large benefits that both Chad and Cameroon stand to gain from the project."[31] A result of the report and the research was the Environmental Management Plans, country-specific documentation on construction and operations (see Exhibit 14.4 for the plan's key documents).[32]

On its website, the World Bank explained its participation:

> This project could transform the economy of Chad. The country is so poor at present that it cannot afford the minimum public services necessary for a decent life. By 2004, the pipeline would increase Government revenues by 45-50 percent per year and allow it to use those resources for important investments in health, education, environment, infrastructure, and rural development, necessary to reduce poverty.[33]

However, pipeline foes derided the World Bank's investment in the project. A RAN African Rainforest spokesperson was cynical, claiming that if the Bank were truly committed to the environment and ending poverty, it would fund non-oil-related projects with direct benefits to local communities rather than large corporations and "corrupt governments."[34] One World Bank official conceded the occasional collision between the Bank's goals and environmental responsibility: "The Bank can't run away from a project that might harm the environment when it is being put forward by 'a country which may not have many development options'. . . . Poverty alleviation and the environment often are at odds. There are some real trade-offs you have to make."[35]

EXHIBIT 14.4. Environmental Documentation Package

The Environmental Management Plans are country-specific documentation on how the project will be managed during construction and operation, six volumes for Chad and six volumes for Cameroon. Key documents contained in these Environmental Management Plans include:

- The Compensation Plan for Cameroon and the Compensation and Resettlement Plan for Chad.
- The Revenue Management Plan for the Republic of Chad, as described in the law passed by the National Assembly and signed by the President. The Revenue Management Plan codifies the utilization of project revenues for the benefit of that country's citizens and residents.
- The oilfield area Regional Development Plan, a plan for managing the development opportunity for the residents of the oilfield area in Chad and managing the indirect impacts associated with the project in the oilfield development area.
- An Indigenous Peoples Plan that will assist in ensuring positive project benefits reach the Bakola Pygmies of coastal Cameroon, as required under World Bank Operational Directive 4.20.
- The Offsite Environmental Enhancement Program, which will provide for habitat preservation and management in two designated national parks in Cameroon.
- The Environmental Foundation Plan, documenting the governances for the Foundation that will administer funds allocated to the Offsite Environmental Enhancement Program and the Indigenous Peoples Plan.
- The Environmental Alignment Sheets and Handbooks for Site-Specific Environmental Mitigation Actions for each country, specifying on a kilometer-by-kilometer basis the path of the pipeline and the environmental mitigation measures at each point along the way.
- Technical Requirements and Specifications as applicable to each country. This volume includes the performance standards for contractors working during construction.
- The Environmental Monitoring Plan, describing the process for measuring project performance and its conformance with technical requirements and specifications.
- The Waste Management Plan, providing for disposal or recycling of waste.

Source: "Chad/Cameroon Development Project: Environmental Assessment Executive Summary and Update," Section TOC, Chapter 8,. 81–82. [http://www.essochad.com/Chad/Library/Documentation/Chad_DO_Exec.as]

ENVIRONMENTAL/SOCIAL ISSUES

Beginning in 1993, during the pipeline's initial planning phase, ExxonMobil began an evaluation of the project's potential environmental and social issues. Company representatives met with Chad and Cameroon government officials at all levels and with residents in the pipeline area. By 1998, ExxonMobil had held many village meetings and met with approximately 20,000 people in 65 affected villages. ExxonMobil also consulted with NGOs, including Africare, Care, and the Worldwide Fund for Nature. The company set up informational reading rooms in Cameroon, distributed a survey questionnaire, and set up consultations with the Bakola Pygmies, many of whom lived along the pipeline route.

Cameroon's Indigenous People

In central African countries, there were an estimated 250,000 Pygmies;[36] Cameroon's Pygmies were primarily the Bagyeli (or Bakola) people, with a population of approximately 4,000; there were also the Baka and the Medzan in the southeastern section of the country. Although the history of the Pygmies in Cameroon was somewhat unclear—Were they the original inhabitants of the forest or did they move there with farmers and fishers from elsewhere?—their connection with the forest was strong and clear: "They see the forest as a personal god, fruitful and kind, and enact their relationship with it and with the spirits of the forest in ritual and song."[37] "What they do have in abundance is an intimate knowledge of the forest: the ability to read animal tracks, to know the flowering and fruiting cycles of plants, to locate a bee's nest from the flight of a bee. They know the individual properties of thousands of plants for food or medicine."[38] Pygmies' average height was 4'8"; each group had its own language, with some common words indicating that once there was a shared language; because they were hunters, not farmers, Pygmies had few possessions and were transient, moving around in groups of fifteen to sixty people. As the 20th century came to a close, however, the Pygmy lifestyle was becoming more sedentary, with more or less permanent villages springing up.

The Chad Export Project's Indigenous People's Plan (commissioned by the Cameroon Oil Transportation Company, the pipeline project's management) outlined the primary characteristics of the Bagyeli Pygmies. They were sensitive to the ecological environment and dependent on the forest resources; they had limited interaction with Cameroon's mainstream population, in large part because of "pre-existing socioeconomic prejudice based on their way of life and physical appearance." The Bagyeli were also highly susceptible to disease, a condition exacerbated by their poor access to health care and health facilities. The Bagyeli had little to no access to formal schooling, and little motivation to acquire an education anyway. Because of their hunting lifestyles and their lack of agricultural training, the Bagyeli were unable to farm for subsistence or a living. In addition, the Bagyeli's habitat had already been severely damaged by industrial logging, which started in the 1950s.[39]

Other reports, focusing more on the Pygmies' social situation, warned of the Bagyelis' fragile place in Cameroonian society as a whole.

> The Bagyeli are indeed a highly marginalized and vulnerable group. They are not recognized as Cameroonian citizens, have no identity papers, never participate in local elections, have no recognized collective land and property rights under . . . law. They are thus marginalized in all local decision making.[40]

Cameroon's Environment

By the mid-1990s, Cameroon was one of the world's top five exporters of tropical logs; however, the logging that had taken place for over forty years had decimated much of the country's forests. Between 1959 and the late

1990s, 81 percent of the country's unprotected forests had been logged. Although legislation to protect the forests was established in 1994, compliance with the legislation was problematic, with over half of the licensees ignoring the regulations (see Exhibit 14.5 and Exhibit 14.6 for statistics on world forest depletion). Cameroon's forests were some of the most diverse in the Congo Basin, but they faced the worst depletion. Experts agreed, "If managed properly, Cameroon's forests could offer long-term revenues without compromising the ecosystems' natural function,"[41] but that this safeguarding would require careful monitoring. The pipeline was slated to go through the pristine M'bere Rift Valley and Deng Deng Forest, home to rare plant life, endangered species, and several thousand Pygmies, with their hunting grounds, settlements, and sacred sites.

In the words of one of the Bagyeli people,

> Today, we don't recognize the forest any more, we don't understand it. The logging companies destroy the forest. . . . Our children have no future. Where will they find the animals to hunt? The bark, the leaves and the fruits for food and medicine? We ask the Government not to forget us, to do something so that our life today and tomorrow will not be as black as a night without stars. Protect us, protect the forest.[42]

The Rainforest Action Network (RAN), a major Pipeline foe, claimed in a November 1999 press release:

> [t]he African Rainforest Pipeline project will slice through the heart of pristine rainforests, and will put hundreds of millions of dollars into the pockets of Exxon and two corrupt governments. . . . southern Chad is so dangerous and politically unstable that neither Amnesty International nor the U.S. State Department was able to visit and confirm the massacre of hundreds of people. A 1999 U.S. State Department report on Chad shows a government engaged in indiscriminate human rights abuses.[43]

EXHIBIT 14.5

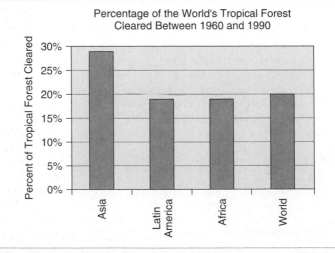

Source: Bryant, et al., *The Last Frontier Forests: Ecosystems and Economies on the Edge* (Washington, DC: World Resources Institute, 1997).

EXHIBIT 14.6. The Last Frontier Forests

Total Area in Original, Current and Frontier Forest

Region	Original Forest (000 Km²)	Total Remaining Forest (Frontier and non-Frontier Forest) (000 Km²)	Total Remaining as % of Original Forest	Total Frontier Forest (000 Km²)	Frontier Forest as a % of Total Original Forest	Frontier Forest as a % of Total Remaining Forest
Africa	6,799	2,302	34%	527	8%	23%
Asia	15,132	4,275	28%	844	6%	20%
North and Central America	12,656	9,453	75%	3,909	31%	41%
— Central America	1,779	970	55%	172	10%	18%
— North America	10,877	8,483	78%	3,737	34%	44%
South America	9,736	6,800	70%	4,439	46%	65%
Russia & Europe	16,449	9,604	58%	3,463	21%	36%
— Europe	4,690	1,521	32%	14	0.3%	1%
— Russia	11,759	8,083	69%	3,448	29%	43%
Oceania (i)	1,431	929	65%	319	22%	34%
World	62,203	33,363	54%	13,501	22%	40%

Notes: (i) Oceania consists of Papua New Guinea, Australia and New Zealand

Source: World Resource Institute website, Publication and Papers, http://www.wri.org/wri/ffi/lff-eng/index.html.

The African Forest Action Network (AFAN), a network of 60 West and Central African nongovernmental organizations, concurred with RAN's fears that the pipeline threatened biodiversity, forests, and the watersheds. An AFAN representative pointed out that, in its 670 mile route, the Pipeline would cross 17 rivers used extensively by local communities for bathing, drinking, and washing, as well as five habitat zones. As it approached the Cameroon coast, the Pipeline would run extremely close to a coastal national reserve with endangered marine life, as well as the Lob Waterfalls, one of the world's few falls flowing directly into the ocean.[44]

According to RAN and AFAN, the pipeline posed threats to "forests, mangroves and coral reefs," all of which played a vital role "in sustaining local communities, particularly for thousands of indigenous cultures around the globe that depend on them for their economic survival, cultural grounding and spiritual relations."[45] A combination of logging, air pollution, and climate change had led to extreme deforestation by the late 20th century. Deforestation then led to loss of biodiversity and the environmental benefits such as watershed protection, nutrient recycling, and climate regulation that forests provided.[46] Petroleum exploration only exacerbated the situation, since every stage of this exploration involved cutting down trees. In order to ascertain the path of petroleum, oil companies used explosive devices in the ground; these explosions added to the damage caused by deforestation, particularly in chasing away wildlife. The drilling process itself had enormous environmental fall-out, producing drilling wastes (water, fluid, mud, rock cuttings, all often toxic). Waste management processes to lessen the toxic waste generated were expensive and thus often ignored by the oil companies. Also, there was the infrastructure that needed to be built to support the drilling and pipeline communities; construction of these roads could affect both the surrounding environment and communities. Indeed, in the extreme poverty both of rural Chad and Cameroon, the simple loss of a piece of land or a fruit-bearing tree could severely affect a family's ability to survive.[47]

Mangroves trees were important parts of ecosystems, serving as spawning and nursery area for many species such as fish, waterbirds, crustaceans, and aquatic mammals. Groves of mangrove trees helped prevent erosion, mitigated climate change, and buffered land against storm-generated sea level rises. Because they were coastal trees, mangroves could suffer greatly from any marine oil spills or pollution generated by offshore rigs.[48] Studies showed that it could take over a century for mangrove trees (as well as coral reefs) to recover from damage caused by an oil spill, primarily because once their shallow roots were covered with oil, the trees could not breathe and consequently died off. Cameroon had large expanses of mangrove trees along the Rio del Rey and Cross Rivers estuary; these trees were important for the country's large fishing industry.

Although ExxonMobil had commissioned an "Environmental Impact Assessment" for the Pipeline Project in the mid-1990s, many critics, such as the Dutch Commission on Environmental Impact Assessment, claimed that the report lacked key information, particularly about the effect on the two countries' ecosystems and inhabitants (especially the Pygmies) and also lacked emergency response and compensation plans in the case of an oil spill.[49] Critics even derided Exxon's decision to place the pipeline three feet under ground to avoid tampering and protect its leak monitoring system.

> Even with the latest state-of-the-art technology, oil leaks in pipelines can go undetected until a huge amount of damage has been done. The most sophisticated technology has a detection capacity of a leakage of 0.002 percent of the oil passing through. [T]his means that under the best of circumstances 2,000 gallons could leak a day without being noticed.[50]

Other critics pointed out the dangers to Cameroon's Atlantic Littoral Forest, one of the world's most undisturbed classified rainforests, home to a myriad of plant and animal species, such as chimpanzees, elephants, gorillas, black rhinos, as well as the Bakola Pygmies.[51] As this forest was opened up to pipeline construction, critics argued, it would be more susceptible to logging and poaching, thus putting the forest's health and survival at risk.[52] This forest was home to the Bakola Pygmies. Still other opponents argued that the consortium's stationary offloading vessel, off the coast of Cameroon, was only a single-hulled tanker—not as protective as a double-hulled tanker.

HISTORY OF OIL DRILLING IN LESS DEVELOPED COUNTRIES (LDCs)

ExxonMobil faced another challenge: the history of oil company exploration in less developed countries. The most publicized case was Shell's operations in Nigeria. Shell had drilled for oil in Nigeria since 1937 and until the mid-1990s was the largest oil operation in that country. In the early 1990s its joint venture with Elf and Agip produced over 900,000 barrels of oil a day, mostly from a region inhabited primarily by the Ogoni people, one of Nigeria's 240 minority tribes. At the same time, between 1982 and 1992 approximately 1.6 million gallons of oil were spilled in the Nigerian oil fields, some precipitated by dissident Ogoni unhappy with the oil ventures, the environmental degradation, and the lack of improved social impact the drilling had on the local villages and communities. Although Shell claimed to have invested over $100 million in environmental projects in Nigeria, there was little to show for this investment. Even the *Wall Street Journal* described Ogoniland as "a ravaged environment."[53] Finally, when Shell did not try to intervene or protest the government's assassination of a number of prominent dissidents, including Ken Sari-Wiwa, worldwide media attacked Shell for what was perceived to be complicity in these deaths.[54] Despite $300 billion earned from oil since 1975, Nigeria's per capita income dropped 23 percent in that time period.

A similar controversy assailed Canadian Talisman Energy, Inc., which came under fire in 1999 for drilling oil in Sudan, Africa's biggest country and a place notorious for its human rights abuses. One journalist wrote that Sudan was "a place of epic misery. . . . In this largely arid and badly eroded land, rogue militias routinely enslave women and children. . . . At the centre of this conflict stands a fundamentalist Muslim government that has bombed hospitals, torn down Christian churches, and denied famine relief to its people."[55] To accommodate oil drilling, the government had displaced approximately 4.5 million of its 33 million inhabitants.

THE OIL INDUSTRY IN THE LATE 20TH CENTURY

In a report, "Changing Oil: Emerging Environmental Risks and Shareholder Value in the Oil and Gas Industry," the World Resources Institute (WRI) examined and evaluated the state of worldwide oil exploration in the late 20th century. In this 39-page assessment of the state of the oil industry, WRI presented some conclusions about the financial implications of restricted access to oil reserves:

- As traditional oil-producing regions mature and yield progressively less oil, the industry is increasingly choosing to explore and produce in new areas where environmental and social controversies may be significant.
- New information technologies and emerging networks between NGOs ensure that companies' activities become more transparent to their principal markets and shareholders.
- In environmentally and socially sensitive areas, access to reserves can be denied, restricted, or kept in limbo. Where access is permitted, opposition from local communities can constrain production operations, making them more costly. One prominent example is the case of Shell in Nigeria, where production has at times been cut to 40 percent of capacity and lower due to opposition and sabotage from local communities.[56]

The WRI report also touched on other issues facing the oil industry. Aside from increasingly limited access to reserves, companies must deal with the issues of climate change and environmental and social effects and how those would affect sales, operating costs, asset values, and shareholder values. In the late 20th century, environmental issues had already had an impact on oil companies and would hold even greater sway in how these companies conducted business and how profitable they ultimately would be. Investors were (and would be) increasingly eager to gauge the environmental "conscience" of a company, and any lack of transparency would affect investor relations.

CONCLUSION

If ExxonMobil did not proceed with the Pipeline project, undoubtedly another country or company would take its place. Two possibilites were neighboring Sudan, which had financed its own pipeline, and Libya, whose president Muammar Qaddafi had encouraged Chad to ignore the western oil companies and let Libya ship the oil. ExxonMobil certainly could look elsewhere for oil reserves both in Africa and other continents. As a World Bank press release pointed out, "Chad is not the only country with untapped petroleum reserves. Exploration is underway right across the continent to find new oil sources—which could prove cheaper and more accessible. If Chad does not seize this opportunity, it may well pass the country by."[57]

All these issues went through Lee Raymond's mind as he considered the course of action that ExxonMobil should take.[58]

Notes

1. "On Anniversary of Nigerian Executions, Shell, Elf Pull Out of African Oil Project," *Rainforest Action Network Press Release* (November 10, 1999), http://www.ran.org/news/newsitem.php?id=139&area=newsroom.
2. "Exxon and Mobil Sign Merger Agreement," *Business Wire* (December 1, 1998).
3. Tim Smart, "Increasingly, Size Counts; Falling Prices in a World of Plenty Drive Mergers Such as Exxon-Mobil," *The Washington Post* (December 4, 1998), D-01.
4. "From Mobil to Exx-Mobil: Pegasus Gets His Wings Clipped," *Petroleum Review* (The Institute of Petroleum) (January 1, 1999), 38.
5. Information taken from Alaska's website about the spill: http://www.oilspill.state.ak.us.
6. If there was a silver lining to the Valdez incident, it was that the spill prompted passage of the long-debated (14 years) Oil Pollution Act, 17 months after the spill.
7. "Merger Mixes Oil, Water: Aggressive Mobil Joins Stiff Exxon," *The New Orleans Times-Picayune* (December 3, 1998), C3.
8. Paul Leavitt, "Pa., Wis. Residents Boiling Tainted Water," *USA Today* (April 27, 1993), p. 3-A.
9. "10 Years After Valdez Oil Spill, Such Disasters are Less Likely, But Dangers Are Still There," *Houston Chronicle* (March 21, 1999), 1.
10. "American Business and the Arts," *Forbes* (Special Advertising Section) (October 28, 1985).
11. "Merger of Exxon and Mobil: Opposites Attracted; Must Mesh Different Cultures," *The Record*, Northern New Jersey (December 3, 1998), B01.
12. "Tree Lover," International Petroleum Finance (Energy Intelligence Group) (October 31, 1999).
13. Oil companies in general had four major divisions: Upstream Operations, for exploration and production of crude oil and natural gases; Downstream Operations for transportation and sale; Chemicals for the manufacture and marketing of petrochemicals; and Coal, Minerals & Powers, for mining exploration and the generation of power.
14. "An Anniversary to Celebrate," ExxonMobil Press Release, www. exxon. mobil. com, 2000.

15. Ibid.
16. Ibid.
17. http://www.exxonmobil.com/Corporate/Newsroom/Publications/shareholder_publications/c_fo_00/c_corporate_06.html.
18. Janet Matthews, Information Services, "Chad Review," *Africa Review* (Sidcup, Kent, United Kingdom: World of Information, August 23, 2001), 1.
19. See http://www.trans.de/index.html.
20. Korinna Horta, "Fueling Strife in Chad and Cameroon: the Exxon-Shell-ELF-World Bank Plans for Central Africa," *Multinational Monitor* 18, No. 5 (May 1, 1997), 10.
21. "Chad & Cameroon: Oil Pipeline Project Threatens Local Communities and Fragile Ecosystems," Amnesty International, www.amnestyusa.org/justearth/chad-cameroon.html.
22. Country Profile: Cameroon, *BBC News* (June 24, 2002), http://news.bbc.co.uk/2/hi/africa/country_profiles/1042937.stm.
23. http://gbgm-umc.org/country_profiles/country_history.cfm?Id=227.
24. http://www.essochad.com/Chad/Project/Development/Chad_Development.asp.
25. Much of the information in this material is taken from the World Bank website: http://web.worldbank.org/WBSITE/EXTERNAL/EXTABOUTUS/EXTARCHIVES/0,,contentMDK:20053333~menuPK:63762~pagePK:36726~piPK:36092~theSitePK:29506,00.html and http://web.worldbank.org/WBSITE/EXTERNAL/EXTABOUTUS/EXTARCHIVES/0,,contentMDK:20035653~menuPK:56305~pagePK:36726~piPK:36092~theSitePK:29506,00.html.
26. Benjamin C. Esty, "The Chad-Cameroon Petroleum Development and Pipeline Project (A)," Harvard Business School Publishing, Case # 9-202-010 (January 17, 2002) (Rev.), 6.
27. http://www.environmentaldefense.org/documents/465_Letter%20to%20World%20Bank%2C%20July%201998%2Ehtm.
28. Abid Aslam, "Environment: Taking the World Bank's Measure," Inter Press Service (September 26, 1999).
29. Project Appraisal Document-Chad/Cameroon Petroleum Development and Pipeline Project," Washington, D.C., The World Bank, Report # 19627-CM, Annex 14 (March 30, 2000) 139.
30. Ibid., p. 74.
31. Ibid., p. 76.
32. "Environmental Assessment Executive Summary and Update," Section TOC, Chapter 8, 81–82.
33. http://www.worldbank.org/afr/ccproj/project/pro_overview.htm.
34. "World Bank Approves 'Nightmare' African Oil and Pipeline Project," RAN Newsroom, http://www.ran.org/news/newsitem.php?id=118&area=newsroom.
35. Aslam, op. cit.
36. Many of Africa's indigenous people over time had grown to dislike the word "pygmy" because of its often derisive use.
37. "Peoples of the Forest: Pygmies in Central Africa," Background Sheet (London: Survival for Tribal Peoples Organization, 1998).
38. Ibid.
39. Information taken from the "Indigenous Peoples Plan, Environmental Management Plan, Cameroon Portion, Vol. 4, The Chad Export Project, May 1999.
40. Thomas Griffith and Marcus Colchester, "Indigenous Peoples, Forests, and the World Bank: Policies and Practice, World Rainforest Movement, August 2000, http://www.wrm.org.uy/actors/WB/IPreport2.html#box11.
41. "An Overview of Logging in Cameroon," Global Forest Watch & World Resources Institute, 2000, 5.
42. "Peoples of the Forest: Pygmies in Central Africa," Background Sheet, Survival for Tribal Peoples, London, 1998.
43. "On Anniversary of Nigerian Executions, Shell, Elf Pull Out of African Oil Project," Rainforest Action Network Press Release (November 10, 1999), http://www.ran.org/news/newsitem.php?id=139&area=newsroom.

44. Korinna Horta, "Fueling Strife in Chad and Cameroon: the Exxon-Shelf-ELF-World Bank Plan for Central Africa," *Multinational Monitor*, Vol. 18, No. 5 (May 1, 1997): 10.
45. "Drilling to the Ends of the Earth: The Case Against New Fossil Fuel Exploration," http://www. an.org/oilreport/ecosystems.html, 1998.
46. Ibid.
47. Horta, "Fueling Strife in Chad and Cameroon."
48. Ibid.
49. Drilling to the Ends of the Earth: The Case Against New Fossil Fuel Exploration, Offshore Boom, Onshore Impact: Central Africa, *Rainforest Action Network*, http://www.ran.org/oilreport/africa.html, 1998.
50. K. Walsh, "World Bank Funding of Chad/Cameroon Oil Project," Environmental Defense Fund (March 17, 1997), www.hartford-hwp.com/archives/32/031. html.
51. There were an estimated 1000 Bakola Pygmies in the entire Pipeline project area.
52. Rachel Naba, "Oil Exploited, Nature Disturbed," http://theearthcenter. com/chad.html.
53. Brooks, 1994, rpt. in Newberry and Gladwin, 2002, 526.
54. William E. Newburry, and Thomas N. Gladwin, "Shell and Nigerian Oil," (1997 report) in eds, Thomas Donaldson, Patricia H. Werhane, and Margaret Cording, *Ethical Issues in Business: A Philosophical Approach*, 7th Edition (Upper Saddle River, NJ: Prentice Hall, 2002), 522-40. In 1993, Shell shut down its operations in Ogoniland, but continued to drill for oil and gas in other parts of Nigeria. Shell then dramatically revised its Code of Ethics, invested at least $100 million in cleaning up Ogoniland, and pledged over ½ billion dollars in exploring alternate energy sources. (www.shell.com. 2003).
55. Andrew Nikiforuk, "Oil Patch Pariah," *Canadian Business Magazine* (December 10, 1999).
56. "Changing Oil: Emerging Environmental Risks and Shareholder Value in the Oil and Gas Industry," (Washington, D.C.: World Resources Institute, July 2002), 25.
57. "World Bank Group Approves Support for the Chad-Cameroon Petroleum Development and Pipeline Project," Washington, D.C.,World Bank, News Release No. 2000/AFR (June 6, 2000), 2.
58. When this news of Shell and TotalFinaElf's withdrawal became public on November 11, more than 10,000 Chadians took to the streets of capital city N'Djamena to protest the withdrawal. Protestors were mainly angry at France. Posters read "Elf's Withdrawal is Unworthy of the Common History of Chad and France" and "We congratulate the World Bank and Exxon." ["10,000 Protest Pullout of Elf, Shell from Huge Oil Deal in Chad," Agence France-Presse, November 16, 1999]. Chad's minister of communication threatened legal action over "an important breach of contract compromising the higher interests of the Chadian nation." [Abid Aslam, "Rights: Nigerian Oil Venture Targeted," Inter Press Service, November 11, 1999.]

Scarcity or Abundance?

JULIAN L. SIMON

Is a big wheat harvest a good thing? Sometimes we read headlines such as "Good harvest, bad news"—the bad news being for wheat farmers, who face low prices. On balance a big harvest surely is better for society as a whole than a small harvest. Still, the headline is negative, as if a bad thing has happened.

Is the trend of black infant mortality rates discouraging? Take a look at Figure 1 and make your judgment, please. My own judgment is that the overall picture is good for blacks as well as for the community as a whole, because many fewer babies are dying nowadays than in earlier years and many fewer parents need to grieve. Unless you focus only on the relative positions of the two groups, there seems slim basis for judging the situation as bad, unless you enjoy being morally indignant.

This is the point of these examples: viewing the same facts, one person may be optimistic while the other is pessimistic. The contradiction often happens because persons judge from different points of view. Frequently the root of the difference is the length of the period you focus on—the short run or the long run. For many issues—and especially issues related to economic and population growth—the long-run effect is the opposite of the short-run effect. More people are an economic benefit in the long run, though they are a burden in the short run.

My central proposition here is simply stated: Almost every trend that affects human welfare points in a positive direction, as long as we consider a reasonably long period of time and hence grasp the overall trend. . . .

I will first review some important absolute trends in human welfare. To repeat, my thesis is that just about every important measure of human welfare shows improvement over the decades and centuries.

Let's start with some trends and conclusions that have long represented the uncontroversial settled wisdom of the economists and other experts who work in these fields, except for the case of population growth. On that latter subject, what you read below was a minority viewpoint until sometime in the 1980s, at which point the mainstream scientific opinion shifted almost all the way to the position set forth here.

LENGTH OF LIFE

The most important and amazing demographic fact—the greatest human achievement in history—is the decrease in the world's death rate. We see that it took thousands of years for life expectancy at birth to increase from just over twenty years to the high 20s. Then, in just the past two centuries, the length of life you could expect for your newborn child in the advanced countries jumped from perhaps thirty years to about seventy-five years. It is this decrease in the death rate that is the cause of there being a larger world population nowadays than in former times. Is this not the greatest change that humankind has ever experienced?

Then, starting well after World War II, the length of life one could expect in the *poor* countries leaped upward by perhaps fifteen or even twenty years, caused by advances in agriculture, sanitation, and medicine. Are not these trends remarkably benign?

AGRICULTURAL LABOR FORCE

The best simple measure of a country's standard of living is the proportion of the labor force that works in agriculture. If almost everyone works at farming, there can be little production of non-agricultural goods. We see the astonishing

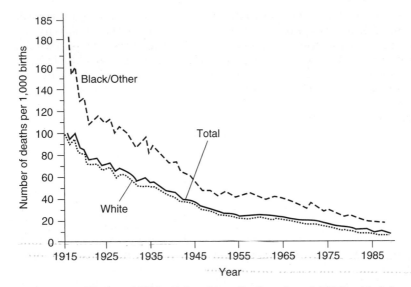

FIGURE 14-1 Black and White Infant Mortality Rate (per 1,000 live births)

Source: U.S. Dept. of Commerce Bureau of the Census, *Historical Statistics of the United States: Colonial Times to 1970* (GPO, Washington, D.C., 1976); U.S. Dept. of Commerce Bureau of the Census, *Statistical Abstract of the United States* (GPO, Washington, D.C., various years)

decline over the centuries in the proportion of the population working in agriculture in Great Britain to only about one person in fifty, and the same story describes the United States. This has enabled us to increase our consumption per person by a factor perhaps of 20 or 40 over the centuries.

RAW MATERIALS

During all of human existence, people have worried about running out of natural resources—flint, game animals, what have you. Amazingly, all the evidence shows that exactly the opposite has been true. Raw materials—all of them—are becoming more available rather than more scarce.

Data clearly shows that natural resource scarcity—as measured by the economically meaningful indicator of cost or price for copper, which is representative of all raw materials—has been decreasing rather than increasing in the long run, with only temporary exceptions from time to time. In the case of copper, we have evidence that the trend of falling prices has been going on for a very long time. In the eighteenth century BCE in Babylonia under Hammurabi—almost 4,000 years ago—the price of copper was about 1,000 times its price in the United States now, relative to wages. And there is no reason why this downward trend might not continue forever.

The trend toward greater availability includes the most counterintuitive case of all—oil. The price rises in crude oil since the 1970s did not stem from increases in the cost of world supply, but rather cartel political action. The production cost in the Persian Gulf still is perhaps 25–75 cents per barrel (1993 dollars). Concerning energy in general, there is no reason to believe that the supply of energy is finite, or that the price of energy will not continue its long-run decrease forever. I realize that it seems strange that the supply of energy is not finite or limited, but if you want a full discussion of the subject, I hope that you will consult another of my books.[1]

FOOD

Food is an especially important resource. The evidence is particularly strong for food that we are on a benign trend despite rising population. The long-run price of wheat relative to wages, and even relative to consumer products, is down, due to increased productivity.

Famine deaths have decreased during the past century even in absolute terms, let alone relative to population, which pertains particularly to the poor countries. Food consumption per person is up over the last thirty years. Africa's food production per person is down, but by 1993 few people still believe that Africa's suffering has anything to do with a shortage of land or water or sun. Hunger in Africa clearly stems from civil wars and the collectivization of agriculture, which periodic droughts have made more murderous.

HUMAN LIFE AND LABOR

There is only one important resource which has shown a trend of increasing scarcity rather than increasing abundance—human beings. Yes, there are more people on Earth now than ever before. But if we measure the scarcity of people the same way that we measure the scarcity of other economic goods—by how much we must pay to obtain their services—we see that wages and salaries have been going up all over the world, in poor as well as rich countries. The amount that you must pay to obtain the services of a manager or a cook has risen in India, just as the price of a cook or manager has risen in the United States over the decades. The increases in the prices of people's services are a clear indication that people are becoming more scarce economically even though there are more of us.

CLEANLINESS OF THE ENVIRONMENT

Ask an average roomful of people if our environment is becoming dirtier or cleaner, and most will say "dirtier." The irrefutable facts are that the air in the United States (and in other rich countries) is safer to breathe now than in decades past. The quantities of pollutants have been declining, especially particulates which are the main pollutant. The proportion of sites monitoring water of good drinkability in the United States has increased since the data began in 1961. Our environment is increasingly healthy, with every prospect that this trend will continue.

THE VANISHING FARMLAND CRISIS

The supposed problem of farmland being urbanized has now been entirely discredited, out-and-out disavowed by those who created the scare. This saga serves to illuminate many similar environmental issues.

THE GREENHOUSE EFFECT, THE OZONE LAYER, AND ACID RAIN

What about the greenhouse effect? The ozone layer? Acid rain? I'm not a technical expert on the atmosphere. I can say with confidence, however, that on all of these issues there is major scientific controversy about what has happened until now, why it happened, and what might happen in the future. All of these scares are recent, and there has not yet been time for complete research to be done and for the intellectual dust to settle. There may be hard problems here, or there may not.

Even more important for people is that no threatening trend in human welfare has been connected to those phenomena. There has been no increase in skin cancers from ozone, no damage to agriculture from a greenhouse effect, and at most slight damage to lakes from acid rain. It may even be that a greenhouse effect would benefit us on balance by warming some areas we'd like warmer, and by increasing the carbon dioxide to agriculture.

Perhaps the most important aspect of the greenhouse–ozone-acid rain complex, and of their as-yet-unknown cousin scares which will surely be brought before the public in the future, is that we now have large and ever-increasing capabilities to reverse such trends if they are proven to be dangerous, and at costs that are manageable. Dealing with greenhouse–ozone–acid rain would not place an insuperable constraint upon growth, and would not constitute an ultimate limit upon the increase of productive output or of population. So we can look these issues squarely in the eye and move on.

ARE THESE PREDICTIONS SURE ENOUGH TO BET ON?

I am so sure of all these upbeat statements that I offer to bet on them, my winnings going to fund new research. Here is the offer: You pick (a) any measure of human welfare—such as life expectancy, infant mortality, the price of aluminum or gasoline, the amount of education per cohort of young people, the rate of ownership of television sets, you name it; (b) a country (or a region such as the developing countries, or the world as a whole); (c) any future year, and I'll bet a week's or a month's pay that that indicator shows improvement relative to the present while you bet that it shows deterioration.

1.   Here is the overarching theory that I offer you to explain why things happen exactly the opposite of the way Malthus and the contemporary

Malthusians predict—and why I offer to bet that any measure of human welfare that you choose will show improvement rather than deterioration.

In 1951, Theodore Schultz published an article called "The Declining Economic Importance of Land." He showed that because of technological change, two related things were happening: Food production per person was going up, and the need for agricultural land was going down—even as population was growing very fast. In 1963, Harold Barnett and Chandler Morse showed that despite all the theory about limited quantities of raw materials, and reducing richness of the lodes that are mined, all the raw materials they studied had become less expensive and more available for the decades since the 1870s. A general process underlies these specific findings: Human beings create more than they use, on average. It had to be so, or we would be an extinct species. And this process is, as the physicists say, an invariancy. It applies to all metals, all fuels, all foods, and all other measures of human welfare, and it applies in all countries, and at all times. In other words, this is a theory of "everything economic," or really, a theory of economic history.

2.   Consider this example of the process by which people wind up with increasing availability rather than decreasing availability of resources. England was full of alarm in the 1600s at an impending shortage of energy due to the deforestation of the country for firewood. People feared a scarcity of fuel for both heating and the iron industry. This impending scarcity led to the development of coal.

> Then in the mid-1800s, the English came to worry about an impending coal crisis. The great English economist W. S. Jevons calculated that a shortage of coal would bring England's industry to a standstill by 1900; he carefully assessed that oil could never make a decisive difference. Triggered by the impending scarcity of coal (and of whale oil, whose story comes next), ingenious profit-minded people developed oil into a more desirable fuel than coal ever was. And in 1993 we find England exporting both coal and oil.

Another element in the story: Because of increased demand due to population growth and increased income, the price of whale oil for lamps jumped in the 1840s, and the U. S. Civil War pushed it even higher, leading to a whale oil "crisis." This provided incentive for enterprising people to discover and produce substitutes. First came oil from rapeseed, olives, linseed, and camphene oil from pine trees. Then inventors learned how to get coal oil from coal. Other ingenious persons produced kerosene from the rock oil that seeped to the surface, a product so desirable that its price then rose from $0.75 a gallon to $2.00. This high price stimulated enterprisers to focus on the supply of oil, and finally Edwin L. Drake brought in his famous well in Titusville, Pennsylvania. Learning how to refine the oil took a while. But in a few years there were hundreds of small refiners in the United States, and soon the bottom fell out of the whale oil market, the price falling from $2.50 or more at its peak around 1866 to well below $1.00.

We should note that it was not the English or American governments that developed coal or oil, because governments are not effective developers of new technology. Rather, it was individual entrepreneurs who sensed the need, saw opportunity, used all kinds of available information and ideas, made lots of false starts which were very costly to many of those individuals but not to others, and eventually arrived at coal as a viable fuel—because there were enough independent individuals investigating the matter for at least some of them to arrive at sound ideas and methods. And this happened in the context of a competitive enterprise system that worked to produce what was needed by the public. And the entire process of impending shortage and new solution left us better off than if the shortage problem had never arisen.

Here we must address *another crucial element in the economics of resources and population*—the extent to which the *political-social-economic system provides personal freedom* from government coercion. Skilled persons require an appropriate social and economic framework that provides incentives for working hard and taking risks, enabling their talents to flower and come to fruition. The key elements of such a framework are economic liberty, respect for property, and fair and sensible rules of the market that are enforced equally for all.

3. The world's problem is not too many people, but lack of political and economic freedom. Powerful evidence comes from pairs of countries that have the same culture and history, and had much the same standard of living when they split apart after World War II—East and West Germany, North and South Korea, Taiwan and China. In each case the centrally planned communist country began with less population "pressure," as measured by density per square kilometer, than did the market-directed economy. And the communist and non-communist countries also started with much the same birth rates. But the market-directed economies have performed much better economically than the centrally planned economies. This powerful explanation of economic development cuts the ground from under population growth as a likely explanation.

4. In 1993 there is an important new element not present twenty years ago. The scientific community now agrees with almost all of what you have just heard. My comments today do not represent a single lone voice, but rather the scientific consensus.

The earlier remarks about agriculture and resources have always represented the consensus of economists in those fields. And now the consensus of population economists also is not far from what I have said to you.

In 1986, the National Research Council and the National Academy of Sciences published a book on population growth and economic development prepared by a prestigious scholarly group. This "official" report reversed almost completely the frightening conclusions of the previous 1971 NAS report. "Population growth is at *most* a minor factor. . . . The scarcity of exhaustible resources is at most a minor constraint on economic growth," it now says. It found benefits of additional people as well as costs.

A host of review articles by distinguished economic demographers in the last three or four years have confirmed that this "revisionist" view is indeed consistent with the scientific evidence, though not all the writers would go as far as I do in pointing out the positive long-run effects of population growth. The consensus is more toward a "neutral" judgment. But this is a huge change from the earlier judgment that population growth is economically detrimental.

By 1993, anyone who asserts that population growth damages the economy must either be unaware of the recent economic literature on the subject, or turn a blind eye to the scientific evidence.

5.   There are many reasons why the public hears false bad news about population, resources, and the environment. Many of these matters are discussed in my earlier books. (E.g. Simon, 1984) But lately I have come to emphasize the role of unsound logic and scientific understanding.

These are some of the elements of bad thinking that predispose people to doomsday thinking: (a) Lack of understanding of statistical variability, and of the consequent need for looking at a large and representative sample and not just a few casual observations. (b) Lack of historical perspective, and the need for looking at long time series and not just a few recent observations. (c) Lack of proportion in judgments. (d) Lack of understanding of the Hume-Hayek idea of spontaneously evolving cooperative social systems—Adam Smith's "invisible hand." (e) Seduction by exponential growth and the rest of Malthusian thinking. (f) Lack of understanding of Frédéric Bastiat's and Henry Hazlitt's one key lesson of policy economics—that we must consider not just the short-run effects of an action that we might take but also the effects well into the future, and not just the local effect but also the effect on faraway communities. That is, we must take into account not just the immediate and obvious impacts, but also the slow-responding adjustments which diffuse far from the point of initial contact and which often have the opposite result from the short-run localized effects.

6.   In response to questions about species extinction, the World Conservation Union (IUCN) commissioned a book edited by Whitmore and Sayer (1992) to inquire into the extent of extinctions that appeared after the first draft of this book. The results of that project must be considered amazing. All the authors are ecologists who express concern about the rate of extinction. Nevertheless, they all agree that the rate of *known* extinctions has been and continues to be very low. This is a sampling of quotations (with emphasis supplied), first on the subject of the estimated rates:

> . . . *60 birds and mammals are known to have become extinct between 1900 and 1950.* (Reid, 1992, p. 55)

> [F]orests of the eastern United States were reduced over two centuries to fragments totalling 1–2% of their original extent . . . during this destruction, only three forest birds went extinct—the Carolina parakeet (Conuropsis carolinensis), the ivory-billed woodpecker (Campephilus principalis principalis), and the passenger pigeon (Ectopistes migratorius). Although deforestation certainly contributed to the decline of all three species, it was probably not critical for the pigeon or the parakeet (Greenway, 1967). *Why, then, would one predict massive extinction from similar destruction of tropical forest?* (Simberloff, 1992, p. 85)

> IUCN, together with the World Conservation Monitoring Centre, has amassed large volumes of data from specialists around the world relating to species decline, and it would seem sensible to compare these more empirical data with the global extinction estimates. In fact, these and other data indicate that *the number of recorded extinctions for both plants and animals is very small*. . . . (Heywood and Stuart, 1992, p. 93)

Known extinction rates are very low. Reasonably good data exist only for mammals and birds, and the current rate of extinction is about one species per year (Reid and Miller, 1989). If other taxa were to exhibit the same liability to extinction as mammals and birds (as some authors suggest, although others would dispute this), then, if the total number of species in the world is, say, 30 million, the annual rate of extinction would be some 2300 species per year. This is a very significant and disturbing number, but it is much less than most estimates given over the last decade. (Heywood and Stuart, 1992, p. 94)

. . . if we assume that today's tropical forests occupy only about 80% of the area they did in the 1830s, *it must be assumed that during this contraction, very large numbers of species have been lost in some areas. Yet surprisingly there is no clear-cut evidence for this.* . . . Despite extensive enquiries we have been unable to obtain conclusive evidence to support the suggestion that massive extinctions have taken place in recent times as Myers and others have suggested. On the contrary, work on projects such as Flora Meso-Americana has, at least in some cases, revealed an increase in abundance in many species (Blackmore, pers. comm. 1991). An exceptional and much quoted situation is described by Gentry (1986) who reports the quite dramatic level of evolution in situ in the Centinela ridge in the foothills of the Ecuadorian Andes where he found that at least 38 and probably as many as 90 species (10% of the total flora of the ridge) were endemic to the "unprepossessing ridge." However, the last patches of forest were cleared subsequent to his last visit and "its prospective 90 new species have already passed into botanical history," or so it was assumed. Subsequently, Dodson and Gentry (1991) modified this to say that an undetermined number of species at Centinela are apparently extinct, following brief visits to other areas such as Lita where *up to 11 of the species previously considered extinct were refound*, and at Poza Honda near La Mana where six were rediscovered. (Heywood and Stuart, 1992, p. 96)

. . . *actual extinctions remain low.* . . . "Many endangered species appear to have either an almost miraculous capacity for survival, or a guardian angel is watching over their destiny! This means that it is not too late to attempt to protect the Mediterranean flora as a whole, while still identifying appropriate priorities with regard to the goals and means of conservation." (Heywood and Stuart, 1992, p. 102)

. . . *the group of zoologists could not find a single known animal species which could be properly declared as extinct*, in spite of the massive reduction in area and fragmentation of their habitats in the past decades and centuries of intensive human activity. A second list of over 120 lesser-known animal species, some of which may later be included as threatened, show no species considered extinct; and the older Brazilian list of threatened plants, presently under revision, also indicated no species as extinct. . . . (Brown and Brown, 1992, p. 127)

Closer examination of the existing data on both well- and little-known groups, however, supports the affirmation that little or no species extinction has yet occurred (though some may be in very fragile persistence) in the Atlantic forests. Indeed, an appreciable number of species considered extinct 20 years ago, including several birds and six butterflies, have been rediscovered more recently. (Brown and Brown, 1992, p. 128)

And here are some comments from that volume on the lack of any solid basis for estimation:

. . . How large is the loss of species likely to be? *Although the loss of species may rank among the most significant environmental problems of our time, relatively few attempts have been made to rigorously assess its likely magnitude.* (Reid, 1992, p. 55)

It is impossible to estimate even approximately how many unrecorded species may have become extinct. (Heywood and Stuart, 1992, p. 95)

While better knowledge of extinction rates can clearly improve the design of public policies, it is equally apparent that *estimates of global extinction rates are fraught with imprecision. We do not yet know how many species exist, even to within an order of magnitude.* (Reid, 1992, p. 56)

. . . the literature addressing this phenomenon is relatively small. . . . Efforts to clarify the magnitude of the extinction crisis and the steps that can be taken to defuse the crisis could considerably expand the financial and political support for actions to confront what is indisputably the most serious issue that the field of ecology faces, and arguably the most serious issue faced by humankind today. (Reid, 1992, p. 57)

The best tool available to estimate species extinction rates is the use of species-area curves. . . . This approach has formed the basis for almost all current estimates of species extinction rates. (Reid, 1992, p. 57)

There are many reasons why recorded extinctions do not match the predictions and ex trapolations that are frequently published. . . . (Heywood and Stuart, 1992, p. 93)

---

7.   The most important difference between my and . . . the doomsters' approach to environmental issues is that I base my conclusions on the historical record of the past rather than Malthusian speculation that is inconsistent with the historical statistical record.

Note

1. See *The Ultimate Resource 2* (Princeton: Princeton University Press, 1998), chapters 1–3.

References

Barnett, Harold and Chandler Morse, 1963. *Scarcity and Growth* (Baltimore MD: Johns Hopkins Press).

Brown, K. S., and G. G. Brown, 1992. "Habitat Alteration and Species Loss in Brazilian Forests," in T. C. Whitmore, and J. A. Sayer, eds., *Tropical Forest and Species Extinction,* pp. 119–142.

Dodson, C. H. & A. H. Gentry, 1991. *Biological extinction in western Ecuador.* Annals of Missouri Botanical Garden 78: 273–295.

Gentry, A. H., 1986. Endemism in tropical versus temperate plant communities, in *Conservation Biology: The Science of Scarcity and Diversity* (ed. M.E. Soulé) Sinauer Associates, Sunderland, MA, pp. 153–181.

Greenway, J. C. 1967. *Extinct and Vanishing Birds of the World.* (N.Y.: Dover Press).

Heywood, V. H., and S. N. Stuart, 1992. "Species Extinctions in Tropical Forests," in T. C. Whitmore and J. A. Sayer, eds., *Tropical Deforestation and Species Extinction,* pp. 91–118.

National Research Council and Academy of Sciences, 1971. *Rapid Population Growth: Consequences and Policy Implications.* Baltimore: Johns Hopkins University Press.

National Research Council, Committee on Population, and Working Group on Population Growth and Economic Development, *Population Growth and Economic Development: Policy Questions* (Washington, D.C.: National Academy Press, 1986).

Reid, W. V., 1992. "How Many Species Will There Be?" in T. C. Whitmore and J. A. Sayer, eds., *Tropical Deforestation and Species Extinction.*

Reid W. V. and Miller, K. R., 1989. *Keeping Options Alive: The Scientific Basis for Conserving Biodiversity.* World Resources Institute, Washington, DC.

Simberloff, D., 1992. "Do Species-Area Curves Predict Extinction in Fragmented

Forest?", in Whitmore and Sayer, eds., *Tropical Deforestation and Species Extinction.*

Simon, Julian L., 1984. *Economics of Population Growth.* Princeton: Princeton University Press, 1977; translated into Chinese, Beijing: Peking University Press.

————, 1981. *The Ultimate Resource.* Princeton: Princeton University Press.

Schultz, Theodore W., 1951. "The Declining Economic Importance of Land," *Economic Journal,* LXI, December, pp. 725–740.

Whitmore, T. C., and J. A. Sayer, eds., 1992. *Tropical Deforestation and Species Extinction.* New York: Chapman and Hall.

Cost-Benefit Analysis: An Ethical Critique

STEVEN KELMAN

I

At the broadest and vaguest level, cost-benefit analysis may be regarded simply as systematic thinking about decision-making. Who can oppose, economists sometimes ask, efforts to think in a systematic way about the consequences of different courses of action? The alternative, it would appear, is unexamined decision-making. But defining cost-benefit analysis so simply leaves it with few implications for actual regulatory decision-making. Presumably, therefore, those who urge regulators to make greater use of the technique have a more extensive prescription in mind. I assume here that their prescription includes the following views:

1. [There] exists a strong presumption that an act should not be undertaken unless its benefits outweigh its costs.
2. In order to determine whether benefits outweigh costs, it is desirable to attempt to express all benefits and costs in a common scale or denominator, so that they can be compared with each other, even when some benefits and costs are not traded on markets and hence have no established dollar values.
3. Getting decision-makers to make more use of cost-benefit techniques is important enough to warrant both the expense required to gather the data for improved cost-benefit estimation and the political efforts needed to give the activity higher priority compared to other activities, also valuable in and of themselves.

My focus is on cost-benefit analysis as applied to environment, safety, and health regulation. In that context, I examine each of the above propositions from the perspective of formal ethical theory, that is, the study of what actions it is morally right to undertake. My conclusions are:

1. In areas of environmental, safety, and health regulation, there may be many instances where a certain decision might be right even though its benefits do not outweigh its costs.

Regulation (Jan., Feb., 1981), pp. 74–82. Reprinted by permission of the American Enterprise Institute for Public Policy Research, Washington, D.C.

2. There are good reasons to oppose efforts to put dollar values on non-marketed benefits and costs.
3. Given the relative frequency of occasions in the areas of environmental, safety, and health regulation where one would not wish to use a benefits-outweigh-costs test as a decision rule, and given the reasons to oppose the monetizing of non-marketed benefits or costs that is a prerequisite for cost-benefit analysis, it is not justifiable to devote major resources to the generation of data for cost-benefit calculations or to undertake efforts to "spread the gospel" of cost-benefit analysis further.

II

In order for cost-benefit calculations to be performed the way they are supposed to be, all costs and benefits must be expressed in a common measure, typically dollars, including things not normally bought and sold on markets and to which dollar prices are therefore not attached. The most dramatic example of such things is human life itself; but many of the other benefits achieved or preserved by environmental policy—such as peace and quiet, fresh-smelling air, swimmable rivers, spectacular vistas—are not traded on markets either.

Economists who do cost-benefit analysis regard the quest after dollar values for nonmarket things as a difficult challenge—but one to be met with relish. They have tried to develop methods for imputing a person's "willingness to pay," for such things, their approach generally involving a search for bundled goods that *are* traded on markets and that vary as to whether they include a feature that is, *by itself*, not marketed. Thus, fresh air is not marketed, but houses in different parts of Los Angeles that are similar except for the degree of smog are. Peace and quiet is not marketed, but similar houses inside and outside airport flight paths are. The risk of death is not marketed, but similar jobs that have different levels of risk are. Economists have produced many often ingenious efforts to impute dollar prices to nonmarketed things by observing the premiums accorded homes in clean air areas over similar homes in dirty areas or the premiums paid for risky jobs over similar nonrisky jobs.

These ingenious efforts are subject to criticism on a number of technical grounds. It may be difficult to control for all the dimensions of quality other than the presence or absence of the non-marketed thing. More important, in a world where people have different preferences and are subject to different constraints as they make their choices, the dollar value imputed to the non-market things that most people would wish to avoid will be lower than otherwise, because people with unusually weak aversion to those things or unusually strong constraints on their choices will be willing to take the bundled good in question at less of a discount than the average person. Thus, to use the property value discount of homes near airports as a measure of people's willingness to pay for quiet means to accept as a proxy for the rest of us the behavior of those least sensitive to noise, of airport employees (who value the convenience of a near-airport location) or of others who are susceptible to an agent's assurances that "it's not so bad." To use the wage premiums accorded hazardous work as a measure of the value of life means to accept as proxies for the rest of us the choices of people who do not have many choices or who are exceptional risk-seekers.

A second problem is that the attempts of economists to measure people's willingness to pay for non-marketed things assume that there is no difference between the price a person would require for giving up something to which he has a preexisting right and the price he would pay to *gain* something to which he enjoys no right. Thus, the analysis assumes no difference between how much a homeowner would need to be paid in order to give up an unobstructed mountain view that he already enjoys and how much he would be willing to pay to get an obstruction moved once it is already in place. Available evidence suggests that most people would insist on being paid far more to assent to a worsening of their situation. The difference arises from such factors as being accustomed to and psychologically attached to that which one believes one enjoys by right. But this creates a circularity problem for any attempt to use cost-benefit analysis to determine *whether* to assign to, say, the homeowner the right to an unobstructed mountain view. For willingness to pay will be different depending on whether the right is assigned initially or not. The value judgment about whether to assign the right must thus be made first. (In order to set an upper bound on the value of the benefit, one might hypothetically assign the right to the person and determine how much he would need to be paid to give it up.)

Third, the efforts of economists to impute willingness to pay invariably involve bundled goods exchanged in *private* transactions. Those who use figures garnered from such analysis to provide guidance for *public* decisions assume no difference between how people value certain things in private individual transactions and how they would wish those same things to be valued in public collective decisions. In making such assumptions, economists insidiously slip into their analysis an important and controversial value judgment, growing naturally out of the highly individualistic microeconomic tradition—namely, the view that there should be no difference between private behavior and the behavior we display in public social life. An alternate view—one that enjoys, I would suggest, wide resonance among citizens—would be that public, social decisions provide an opportunity to give certain things a higher valuation than we choose, for one reason or another, to give them in our private activities.

Thus, opponents of stricter regulation of health risks often argue that we show by our daily risk-taking behavior that we do not value life infinitely, and therefore our public decisions should not reflect the high value of life that proponents of strict regulation propose. However, an alternative view is equally plausible. Precisely because we fail, for whatever reasons, to give life-saving the value in everyday personal decisions that we in some general terms believe we should give it, we may wish our social decisions to provide us the occasion to display the reverence for life that we espouse but do not always show. By this view, people do not have fixed unambiguous "preferences" to which they give expression through private activities and which therefore should be given expression in public decisions. Rather, they may have what they themselves regard as "higher" and "lower" preferences. The latter may come to the fore in private decisions, but people may want the former to come to the fore in public decisions. They may sometimes display racial prejudice, but support anti-discrimination laws. They may buy a certain product after seeing a seductive ad, but be skeptical enough of advertising to want the government to keep a close eye on it. In such cases, the use of private behavior to impute the values that should be entered for public decisions, as is done by using willingness to pay in private transactions, commits grievous offense against a view of the behavior of the citizen that is deeply engrained in our democratic tradition. It is a view that denudes politics of any independent role in society, reducing it to a mechanistic, mimicking recalculation based on private behavior.

Finally, one may oppose the effort to place prices on a non-market system out of a fear that the very act of doing so will reduce the thing's perceived value. To place a price on the benefit may, in other words, reduce the value of that benefit. Cost-benefit analysis thus may be like the thermometer that, when placed in a liquid to be measured, itself changes the liquid's temperature.

Examples of the perceived cheapening of a thing's value by the very act of buying and selling it abound in everyday life and language. The disgust that accompanies the idea of buying and selling human beings is based on the sense that this would dramatically diminish human worth. Epithets such as "he prostituted himself," applied as linguistic analogies to people who have sold something, reflect the view that certain things should not be sold because doing so diminishes their value. Praise that is bought is worth little, even to the person buying it. A true anecdote is told of an economist who retired to another university community and complained that he was having difficulty making friends. The laconic response of a critical colleague—"If you want a friend why don't you buy yourself one"—illustrates in a pithy way the intuition that for some things, the very act of placing a price on them reduces their perceived value.

The first reason that pricing something decreases its perceived value is that, in many circumstances, non-market exchange is associated with the production of certain values not associated with market exchange. These may include spontaneity and various other feelings that come from personal relationships. If a good becomes less associated with the production of positively valued feelings because of market exchange, the perceived value of the good declines to the extent that those feelings are valued. This can be seen clearly in instances where a thing may be transferred both by market and by non market mechanisms. The willingness to pay for sex bought from a prostitute is less than the perceived value of the sex consummating love. (Imagine the reaction if a practitioner of cost-benefit analysis computed the benefits of sex based on the price of prostitute services.)

Furthermore, if one values in a general sense the existence of a non-market sector because of its connection with the production of certain valued feelings, then one ascribes added value to any non-marketed good simply as a repository of values represented by the non-market sector one wishes to preserve. This seems certainly to be the case for things in nature, such as pristine streams or undisturbed forests: for many people who value them, part of their value comes from their position as repositories of values the non-market sector represents.

The second way in which placing a market price on a thing decreases its perceived value is by removing the possibility of proclaiming that the thing is "not for sale," since things on the market by definition are for sale.

The very statement that something is not for sale affirms, enhances, and protects a thing's value in a number of ways. To begin with, the statement is a way of showing that a thing is valued for its own sake whereas selling a thing for money demonstrates that it was valued only instrumentally. Furthermore, to say that something cannot be transferred in that way places it in the exceptional category—which requires the person interested in obtaining that thing to be able to offer something else that is exceptional, rather than allowing him the easier alternative of obtaining the thing for money that could have been obtained in an infinity of ways. This enhances its value. If I am willing to say "You're a really kind person" to whoever pays me to do so, my praise loses the value that attaches to it from being exchangeable only for an act of kindness.

In addition, if we have already decided we value something highly, one way of stamping it with a cachet affirming its high value is to announce that it is "not for sale." Such an announcement does more, however, than just reflect a preexisting high valuation. It signals a thing's distinctive value to others and helps us persuade them to value the thing more highly than they otherwise might. It also expresses our resolution to safeguard that distinctive value. To state that something is not for sale is thus also a source of value for that thing, since if a thing's value is easy to affirm or protect, it will be worth more than an otherwise similar thing without such attributes.

If we proclaim that something is not for sale, we make a once-and-for-all judgment of its special value. When something is priced, the issue of its perceived value is constantly coming up, as a standing invitation to reconsider that original judgment. Were people constantly faced with questions such as "how much money could get you to give up your freedom of speech?", or "how much would you sell your vote for if you could?", the perceived value of the freedom to speak or the right to vote would soon become devastated as, in moments of weakness, people started saying "maybe it's not worth so much after all." Better not to be faced with the constant questioning in the first place. Something similar did in fact occur when the slogan "better red than dead" was launched by some pacifists during the Cold War. Critics pointed out that the very posing of this stark choice—in effect, "would you *really* be willing to give up your life in exchange for not living under communism?"—reduced the value people attached to freedom and thus diminished resistance to attacks on freedom.

Finally, of some things valued very highly it is stated that they are "priceless" or that they have "infinite value." Such expressions are reserved for a subset of things not for sale, such as life or health. Economists tend to scoff at talk of pricelessness. For them, saying that something is priceless is to state a willingness to trade off an infinite quantity of all other goods for one unit of the priceless good, a situation that empirically appears highly unlikely. For most people, however, the word priceless is pregnant with meaning. Its value-affirming and value-protecting functions cannot be bestowed on expressions that merely denote a determinate, albeit high, valuation. John Kennedy in his inaugural address proclaimed that the nation was ready to "pay any price [and] bear any burden ... to assure the survival and the success of liberty." Had he said instead that we were willing to "pay a high price" or "bear a large burden" for liberty, the statement would have rung hollow.

III

An objection that advocates of cost-benefit analysis might well make to the preceding argument should be considered. I noted earlier that, in cases where various non-utility-based duties or rights conflict with the maximization of utility, it is necessary to make a deliberative judgment about what act is finally right. I also argued earlier that the search for commensurability might not always be a desirable one, that the attempt to go beyond expressing benefits in terms of (say) lives saved and costs in terms of dollars is not something devoutly to be wished.

In situations involving things that are not expressed in a common measure, advocates of cost-benefit analysis argue that people making judgments "in effect" perform cost-benefit calculations anyway. If government regulators promulgate a regulation that saves 100 lives at a cost of $1 billion, they are "in effect" valuing a life at (a minimum of) $10 million, whether or not they say that they are willing to place a dollar value on a human life. Since, in this view, cost-benefit analysis "in effect" is inevitable, it might as well be made specific.

This argument misconstrues the real difference in the reasoning processes involved. In cost-benefit analysis, equivalencies are established *in advance* as one of the raw materials for the calculation. One determines costs and benefits, one determines equivalences (to be able to put various costs and benefits into a common measure), and then one sets to toting things— waiting, as it were, with bated breath for the results of the calculation to come out. The outcome is determined by the arithmetic, if the outcome is a close call or if one is not good at long division, one does not know how it will turn out until the calculation is finished. In the kind of deliberative judgment that is performed without a common measure, no establishment of equivalencies occurs in advance. Equivalencies are not aids to the decision process. In fact, the decision-maker might not even be aware of what the "in effect" equivalencies were, at least before they are revealed to him afterwards by someone pointing out what he had "in effect" done. The decision-maker would see himself as simply having made a deliberate judgment; the "in effect" equivalency number did not play a causal role in the decision but at most merely reflects it. Given this, the argument against making the process explicit is the one discussed earlier in the discussion of problems with putting specific values on things that are not normally quantified—that the very act of doing so may serve to reduce the value of those things.

My own judgment is that modest efforts to assess levels of benefits and costs are justified, although I do not believe that government agencies ought to sponsor efforts to put dollar prices on non-market things. I also do not believe that the cry for more cost-benefit analysis in regulation is, on the whole, justified. If regulatory officials were so insensitive about regulatory costs that they did not provide acceptable raw material for deliberative judgments (even if not of a strictly cost-benefit nature), my conclusion might be different. But a good deal of research into costs and benefits already occurs—actually, far more in U.S. regulatory process than in that of any other industrial society. The danger now would seem to come more from the other side.

A Boat for Thoreau

WILLIAM MCDONOUGH

One of the great leaders of the United States, Thomas Jefferson, saw himself primarily as a designer. This is evident from his tombstone, which he designed, and on which we can read three things: *"Thomas Jefferson, author of the Declaration of American Independence, author of the Statute of Virginia for Religious Freedom, and Father of the University of Virginia."* These were the three things Jefferson thought were worth mentioning on his tombstone. He did not record his various activities—that he had been president of the United States, minister to France, an architect. He recorded only what he had left behind for future generations: his creative legacy, to the world, his lasting contributions to prosperity. Consider looking at the world as a series of design assignments. How would we present the design assignment of the Declaration of Independence? Perhaps it could be framed like this: please prepare a document that provides us with the concept of "life, liberty and the pursuit of happiness free from remote tyranny." That would be the retroactive design assignment of the Declaration of Independence.

In Mr. Jefferson's case, "remote tyranny" referred to the King of England, George III: someone who ruled from a distant place, who was not sensitive to local needs and circumstance. Now, seven generations later, I believe we need to look at the concept of many Declarations of Interdependence, because we realize that some of the remote tyranny future generations will suffer—is us. Right now, we—as a culture—are imposing what I call intergenerational remote tyranny. I would like to focus on this tyrannizing effect from a design perspective and consider how we can design it out.

Thomas Jefferson clearly understood the idea of intergenerational remote tyranny. In 1789, he wrote a letter to James Madison, which I paraphrase here:

> The earth belongs to the living. No man may by natural right oblige the lands he owns or occupies to debts greater than those that may be paid during his own lifetime. Because if he could, then the world would belong to the dead and not to the living.[1]

In *Silent Spring,* Rachel Carson stated that the founding fathers who wrote the Bill of Rights—despite their intellectual gifts and foresight—could not have imagined that corporations, governments, and individuals would poison children downstream.[2] They did not protect us from this kind of tyranny in the Bill of Rights because they could not even conceive of such a problem. We have to remember that Jefferson and Madison were living in a world that was effectively solar-powered. Their homes, the original grounds of the University of Virginia, were built with local materials: local clay, local fuel

From *The Business of Consumption*, Patricia H. Werhane and Laura Westra, eds. (Totawa, MD: Rowman and Littlefield, 1998), pp. 297–317. Reprinted by permission of William McDonough, www.mcdonough.com.

sources, solar-driven fuel sources. These people inhabited a world of natural energy flows. At that time, you could look out to the West and see a vast expanse of natural resources. Petrochemicals had not yet been invented. Yet Jefferson's phrase "The earth belongs to the living" is a powerful commentary on the tyrannies we are now seeing due to poor design.

Regulations are signals of design failure. They can even be seen—in the case of regulated toxic emissions—as licenses to kill. Polluters are basically telling us, "You are going to be poisoned. The question is, how long will it take?" Regulation is a signal of design and ethical failure. So I agree with a lot of the discussion about removing regulations to liberate business, but I would like to do it for all generations, not just this one. And I would like to do it by design, on purpose, with intention.

Jefferson's design legacy still provides for us, his seventh generation, and it continues to offer profound benefits even as the world changes around us. To see the legacy he brought to the Bill of Rights more clearly, we have to consider what it promulgated over time and imagine what it might promulgate in the future.

Jefferson wrote, "No man may by natural right. . . ." "Natural rights" had become a fundamental concept for Jefferson, and he expanded on it often. In *The Rights of Nature,* Roderick Nash pointed out that the concept of rights has been expanding since the Magna Carta gave rights to white noble English males in 1215. In 1776, the Declaration of Independence gave rights to white American land-owning males. In 1864, we had the Emancipation Proclamation. In 1922, female suffrage. In 1964, the Civil Rights Voting Act. And then, in 1973, the Endangered Species Act: the first time in our history that human beings took responsibility for giving other living species the right to exist. We acknowledged the rights of nature itself. From our perspective, "natural rights" has now expanded to include the rights of nature itself.[3]

If we project this pattern out, it is clear that our next discourse must be about endangered ecosystems, because we are finally realizing our interdependent connection to the natural world, and it won't be enough that there's a snail here or a condor there. We now understand that we are all connected to the web of life. Our understanding of rights and responsibilities must expand to include the rights and responsibilities of all living things.

Many people question the use of the word *dominion* in the Book of Genesis, which states that human beings are given dominion over the earth. Some wish the word had been *stewardship,* because of the relationship that might imply. Yet stewardship and dominion are both still anthropocentric concepts and presume we are in charge of everything. The Native American question is really the most relevant: How do we find ourselves in kinship with nature? How do we recognize ourselves as a vital and responsible part of it? To see the world this way, and to begin creating things within that context, is an exciting prospect. We need to understand and design for a world of fecundity, growth, and abundance, not for a world of destruction, loss, and limits.

What is the natural world, and how are humans meant to inhabit it? In 1836, Emerson wrote an essay entitled "Nature" in which he reflected on these questions: If human beings are natural, are all things made by humans natural? For that matter, what is Nature? He concluded that Nature is all those things that are immutable—those "essences" unaffected by man. His examples were the mountains, the oceans, the leaves.[4]

Following Emerson, Thoreau contemplated the mutability of nature and the search for our rightful and meaningful place within it. Unlike Emerson, however, he understood that we can affect the natural world. Today, the notion that nature is immutable, that there are "essences" so powerful they are beyond our ability to *affect* them, is obsolete.

We used to be able to throw things away. Remember that? Things went "away." Where is "away" now? "Away" is here. "Away" is someone's backyard. There is no place to go from here. We now see that we inhabit a smaller and smaller planet. "Away" has become very close indeed.

In this context, we must again ask ourselves, "What is natural?" and, "What are our intentions as evidenced by our designs?" Early in the 1830s, Ralph Waldo Emerson went to Europe on a sailboat and returned on a steamship. Let me abstract this for effect: He went over on a solar-powered recyclable craft operated by crafts persons practicing ancient arts in the open air. He returned in a steel rust bucket putting oil on the water and smoke in the sky, operated by people working in the dark shoveling fossil fuels into the mouths of boilers. We are still designing steamships. Most buildings we design are essentially steamships. On any given day, the sun is shining and we're inside with the lights on causing the production of nuclear isotopes, carbon dioxide, nitrous oxides, and sulfur dioxide. Every time you find yourself in a building illuminated by electric light when the sun is shining, you should think, "I am in a steamship. I am in the dark." We need a new design. We need a boat for Thoreau.

Peter Senge, a professor at MIT's Sloan School of Management, works with a Learning Laboratory, a program where he discusses how organizations learn to learn. One of the first questions he asks the CEOs and chairs that attend his leadership program is, "Who is the leader on a ship crossing the ocean?" The responses he gets are *captain, navigator, helmsman.* But Senge tells them no: the leader of that ship is the designer of that ship, because you can be the best captain in the world, but if your ship is not designed to be seaworthy, you're going down.[5] From my perspective as a designer, the ship designed during the First Industrial Revolution is going down. I want to focus on the design of that ship, and I want us to imagine what the boat for Thoreau might be like—how it would work, what it would be made of, and what effects it might have. This boat is my metaphor for the design assignment of the Next Industrial Revolution.

What is the fundamental design principle of a steamship and most modern systems? The only one I can discover is, "If brute force doesn't work, you're not using enough of it." In fact, that's the design principle behind most modern architecture, behind what is known as the "International Style." You can build the same building in Reykjavik as in Rangoon, you simply heat one and cool the other. If you're too hot or too cold, just add more energy. If brute force doesn't work, you're not using enough of it. This principle kills culture. This principle kills society. This principle kills nature. And this principle kills diversity. It kills the richness of experience—the wealth of our relationship to the web of life and place.

I would like to posit the design principles for the Next Industrial Revolution, and I would also like to describe a new design assignment. But first, let me describe the retroactive design assignment of the First Industrial Revolution: Would you design a system of production and a system of commerce that

- produces billions of pounds of highly toxic hazardous material and puts them in your soil, your air, and your water every year?
- measures prosperity by how much of your natural capital you can dig up, burn, deplete, throw into holes in the ground and into the rivers and otherwise destroy?
- measures productivity by how few people are working?
- measures progress by how many smokestacks you have?
- requires thousands of complex regulations to keep you from killing each other too quickly?
- produces a few things so highly dangerous and toxic they will require future generations to maintain constant vigilance while living in terror?

That is the retroactive design assignment of the First Industrial Revolution. Is this an ethical assignment?

I am sure the framers of the Bill of Rights had no idea this could be posited as a design. In fact, I don't think it is a design, because it didn't happen by intention. The First Industrial Revolution happened incrementally, in a series of steps, as designers and engineers responded to single problems with the materials and information at hand. We have now reached the point where we can agree that this is not a design assignment we wish to accept in our time, and it is certainly not one we want to pass on to our children. It is time to look again at the horizon with delight and anticipation, with a new responsibility and a new design legacy in mind.

A magnificent example of true intergenerational responsibility is the great Peacemaker of the Six Nations of the Iroquois, who instructed all chiefs to make decisions on behalf of their seventh generation to come. Those of us here today are Thomas Jefferson's seventh generation: he designed the Declaration of Independence for us. So it's our turn now to make decisions on behalf of our seventh generation. Let's design a system for what I call the Next Industrial Revolution that

- introduces no hazardous material into the soil, the air, and the water every year
- measures prosperity by how much natural capital and how much solar income we can accrue in productive and fecund ways
- measures productivity by how many people are being gainfully and meaningfully employed
- measures progress by how many buildings have no smokestacks, no dangerous effluents, and no pipes
- does not require regulations to stop us from killing one another too quickly
- produces nothing that will require future generations to maintain vigilance and live in terror

I believe we can accomplish great and profitable things within that conceptual framework. But first, we must step out of the framework of guilt. Guilt does not help us. People who feel guilty often tell themselves, "I am guilty, I am guilty," and then they keep doing what they were doing. This is the way they compensate, by saying, "I am bad. I am bad. I am sorry." What we need is a much more productive concept: Negligence starts tomorrow.

If you recognize the tragic consequences of bad design and mindlessly continue to do what you are doing, then you are negligent. But what we want is change, not guilt. Because if you project the tragedy, as Jaime Lerner, the brilliant civic visionary and governor of Parana, Brazil, has pointed out, you have the tragedy. Unless you change immediately, you are unintentionally invested in watching the tragedy occur. As designers with intention, you have then adopted what Governor Lerner would call a "Strategy of Tragedy." As he would say, when you recognize the tragedy you have the tragedy.

The New York City Regional Plan Association just published a report entitled *A Region at Risk,* which indicated that a generation ago the impervious surfaces of the New York metropolitan region—the roads, the buildings, the parking lots—made up 19 percent of the city's surfaces. In 1996, they made up 30 percent. The projection for 2020? 45 percent impervious surfaces. Imagine this pattern continuing until the amount of impervious surfaces[6] rises to 70 or 80 percent. Where are the songbirds? What is the temperature? Where do the children play? What does the water look like? This is a tragedy. How do we deal with this tragedy? The only way to counter a Strategy of Tragedy is to adopt a Strategy of Change.

This Strategy of Change must go beyond what business and government have responded with, which we call "eco-efficiency." A primary response to the Earth Summit by the Business Council for Sustainable Development and the environmental organizations was eco-efficiency—do more with less. Although eco-efficiency is a noble and valuable concept, it is not going to save us for several reasons. First of all, its motivation is guilt. When we adopt eco-efficiency, we are basically telling ourselves, "I am bad. I am bad. I am using too much fuel and too much wood. I'm destroying cultures. I'm creating pollution. I've got to cut my energy consumption. I've got to go through all this tedious stuff because I'm bad."

When I gave the opening address at a conference celebrating the conclusion of the Environmental Protection Agency's 33/50 Voluntary Toxics Reduction Program last year, we found that people there were very excited—and rightly so—because they had achieved toxic reductions of 90 percent. But we have to wonder what we were doing before these reductions. Even more importantly, we have to realize that the 10 percent we have now becomes a new, negative 100 percent, because current scientific studies are telling us that even the smallest trace amounts of certain contaminants can have devastating effects—on our endocrine systems, for example. So this smaller amount of dangerous effluent becomes a new 100 percent to eliminate entirely. This isn't revolutionary; it's still a linear process headed for zero and never getting there, like Zeno's Paradox. What do we tell our children? "You're really bad. Try to feel better by being less bad. And your goal is zero." This is our legacy? I don't know any business person who thinks a goal of zero is very exciting.

From the "Third World's" perspective, eco-efficiency is simply the "First World" figuring out how to use the "Third World's" resources longer. Since our 20 percent of the world is using up 80 percent of the world's resources, they see eco-efficiency as a way for us to steal from the rest of the world for a longer period of time.

That's the problem with eco-efficiency from a designer's perspective: it tells us to leave the way we do things in the world the same—to just get better and more "efficient" at it. It's the same system that got us into trouble in the first place, slowed down. Paradoxically, this may make eco-efficiency even more insidious, because people are lulled into thinking the problem is being solved, when we're really just going in the same direction.

Let me borrow an analogy from Dave Crockett, a city councilor in Chattanooga: if you're driving out of Charlottesville, Virginia, you can go north to Washington, D.C., or you can go south to Lynchburg. If you find yourself going one hundred miles an hour toward Washington when you're supposed to be going to Lynchburg, it isn't going to help you to slow down to twenty miles an hour. We've got to turn around. We've got to be going somewhere else. But where? What principles do we use to get there?

A real Strategy of Change requires a new and inspiring vision of taking, making, using, and consuming in the world. We need massive creative imagination, with the design goal of imagining what perfect looks like. Then we can have a new, positive, 100 percent to work on. That's what I'm really interested in: redesign toward that 100 percent, so we can wake up in the morning and say, "I am only 20 percent sustainable. Tomorrow I want to be 21 percent. I'm trying to reach 100 percent sustainability. That's my chart." We've got to chart a new course and begin heading in a different direction. That means we have to start imagining what the new course looks like, and start framing the conditions required to achieve it.

I have developed some principles that we use in our work:

1. *Waste Equals Food.*[7]   In nature, there is no such thing as waste, so the first thing we must do is eliminate the concept of waste. I am not saying we need to minimize waste; I am saying we need to eliminate the entire concept of waste.
2. *Use Current Solar Income.*   Nature does not mine the past; it does not borrow from the future. It operates on current income. Most of us can't pursue our professional lives working out of capital reserves. We have to work with current income, and so should our designs.
3. *Respect Diversity.*   One size does not fit all. We are all different. Every place in the world is completely different; material flows, spiritual flows, character flows, cultural flows, energy flows—all of these vary in different places. We should celebrate our differences instead of trying to make us all the same.

These are the fundamental principles. But we also need new design criteria. The traditional design criteria used by designers until now are three: *cost, performance,* and *aesthetics.* Can I afford it? Does it work? Do I like it? Now we have to add three more characteristics: Is it ecologically intelligent? Is it just? Is it fun? How do I apply these principles to find out what is ecologically intelligent? How do I apply these principles to find out what is just? (The fun part I'm going to leave to you.)

If *Waste Equals Food,* we eliminate the concept of waste. If we eliminate the concept of waste, there is no such thing as waste, and everything becomes a product. So we need some guidelines to help us design these products. I have been inspired by a chemist named Michael Braungart from Germany, and he and I have developed a series of protocols that we use when designing products. We've identified a whole typology of products.

If *Waste Equals Food* and "food" implies nutrients, then we need to understand that nutrients work within a metabolism. What are the metabolisms we find in the world? What are the artifacts of human artifice, and what is their relationship to these metabolisms? Remember that question of Emerson's: If human beings are natural, are all things made by humans natural?

We now know that many things made by humans are not "natural." So there are two fundamental metabolisms in the world: one is biological, the world of biological systems, of which we are physically a part; the other is the metabolism of human industry that exists apart from natural systems. We need to design products to go into each of these metabolisms so that they nourish one metabolism without contaminating the other.

The things we design to go into the biological metabolism should not contain mutagens, carcinogens, heavy metals, persistent toxins, bioaccumulative substances, or endocrine disrupters. The things we design to go into the technical metabolism should circulate in a closed loop forever; they should not unintentionally contaminate the organic metabolism, because many materials we marshal into the technical metabolism can damage or kill the organic metabolism.

We need to design into these two metabolisms, and this will mean products are differentiated into three fundamental types: a *Product of Consumption,* a *Product of Service,* and an *Unmarketable Product.* A *Product of Consumption* is designed to return safely to the organic cycle. It is literally a consumable and goes back to the soil. A *Product of Service* is designed to go back into the technical cycle, into the industrial metabolism from which it came. An *Unmarketable Product* is a product that should not be made because it can't feed either of these two metabolisms; this category includes substances such as radioactive materials and currently indissoluble contaminated materials, like the chromium contained in shoes.

I spent most of my childhood in the Far East, in Hong Kong, and when I moved to America, I was amazed by the fact that we no longer seem to be people with lives; we've become "consumers" with lifestyles. When did we stop being people with lives? We are not "consumers." We are people. The media will tell us how many "consumers" bought television sets, but how do you consume a television set?

Imagine I had a television hidden behind my desk and I said, "I have this amazing thing. It's a *Product of Service* because you want the function, not the thing. You want the service the item provides, but you do not necessarily want the ownership of its complex and potentially hazardous materials. Again, you want the function, not the thing. Before I tell you what the thing does, which will interest you, let me tell you what it is: It is thousands of chemicals, it has toxic heavy metals, it has a potentially implosive glass tube, and we want you to put it at eye level with your children and encourage them to play with it." Do you want this in your house? Why are we selling people hazardous waste? What do you want with this thing? You want to watch television, you don't want to own hazardous waste. When you pay for a television set today you have the right (the "right") to take this combination of valuable heavy metals and miscellaneous toxins and dump it in a trashcan. Future generations are going to look back and say, "What were you thinking? What did you do with the mercury? What did you do with the chromium? You lost its quality! You put it in little holes all over the planet where we can never get it back! And it is persistently toxic! What were you thinking?"

Think about the redesign of this product as a *Product of Service,* because what happens is remarkable. When you have finished with the use of the machine, you ask yourself, "Whose food is this?" A television set is obviously food for the electronics and other industries.

My partner and I work with major corporations to redesign these products to be, in effect, leased by the manufacturer to the customer—not *consumer,* customer. Customers purchase the use of a machine, and when they are finished with it they can return it to the manufacturer and say, "Thank you very much for the use of this television. I would like a new one." The system is designed so that the old product goes back into what we call the "technical cycle" and becomes a *Product of Service* again—forever. This design for return we call our Eco-leasing concept.

We talk about recycling, but most of us don't recycle in the full sense of the word; we often do what Michael Braungart and I call "downcycling"—we reduce the quality of a material until its value is practically nonexistent. In other words, we slow its journey to the landfill. For example, when a high quality plastic like PET is "recycled" it may be mixed with other plastics to produce a hybrid of much lower quality, which is then used to make park benches. The original elevated quality can never be retrieved. So what we call recycling is still working with a *Cradle-to-Grave* life cycle.

Michael Braungart points out that the *Cradle-to-Grave* mentality is definitely Northern European. In Sweden, if you throw a banana peel on the ground it is going to be there a long time, because nothing rots quickly. Northern Europeans tended to bury everything. Western culture, then, tends to bury unwanted things. Consequently, our culture developed products in terms of a *Cradle-to-Grave* life cycle concept; once you finish with something you bury it because you don't want to look at it. In the abstract, one might say it's too bad the First Industrial Revolution didn't begin in a place like Mali. As Dr. Braungart notes, if you go to "primitive" places today, you might see a lot of aluminum cans lying on the ground outside a fence and think the people there are inconsiderate and slovenly. But those people once drank out of clay cups or gourds, and when they finished, they would simply toss the vessel over the fence and the goats, ants, or beetles would take it away. Its organic materials would nourish other organisms and go back to the soil. So these people are still doing what they've been doing forever; modern production just hasn't provided them with an intelligent design for a container that turns back into dirt—a design in what I call a *Cradle-to-Cradle* life cycle.

Plastic bottles could easily be redesigned so that they don't contain questionable substances and could safely replenish the soil. Right now they may contain antimony, catalytic residues, UV stabilizers, plasticizers, and antioxidants. What happens when the people in Mali throw that over the fence? Why not design a bottle so that when you finish with it you toss it into the compost or it biodegrades by the roadside, or it can be used as fuel for needy people to cook with? It should be safe fuel. If a clothing manufacturer wants to make clothing out of it, it should not contain potentially toxic substances. Plastic bottles were not originally designed to become clothing; they were designed to hold liquids. We have a fundamental design problem. We need to design things so they go into the biological or the technical cycle, safely, *Cradle-to-Cradle.*

Use Current Solar Income. I think we're going to resolve the energy problem, because we have current solar income. Energy from the sun is the only income the planet has (except for meteorites); all our other materials are already here. If you're in business, you understand that you must work from current income, not savings. Because we have that income from the sun, I think it won't be long before we find elegant solutions to the energy situation.

The University of Virginia's School of Architecture is about to build a building addition project designed to be a net energy exporter, a structure that produces more energy than it consumes. Why would we want to make a building that produces more energy than it needs? The reason is that *sustainability* may just be a shibboleth—the magic word that lets us into the temple of hope. A lot of people use the term *sustainability* as if it's going to save us. But sustainability as it's presently defined may be only the edge between destruction and restoration. Why would we want to simply sustain where we are now? We're in a depletive mode. We need to actually design things that are restorative. Think about the high-tech designs you see around you: airplanes, computers, space age stores. Imagine how much farther we can go, how wonderfully ambitious we can really be.

What is one of the best designs we know of for inspiration? How about a tree? How about a design that can accrue solar income, is fecund, produces habitat for all sorts of living things including people, provides fuel, food, and micro-climate, distills and transpires water, sequesters carbon, and makes oxygen? How many things do you know that do that? How many things have humans designed that make oxygen?

Why not make a building that produces oxygen? Why not make a building that produces energy? We're not very bright or ambitious designers if we can't even emulate a tree, which nature has put right there in front of us as an obvious model. Just compare a tree to most rooms. Right now, I'm in a room that sucks electrical energy from a grid, I'm responsible for the production of nuclear isotopes simply by turning on a light switch, and I'm probably breathing all sorts of chemical experiments I don't even realize I am undertaking. Compared to a tree, this is obviously primitive design. If I'm going to be a sophisticated designer, I had better start thinking more about trees—about buildings that produce more energy than they need and purify their water, and I had better start thinking about designing buildings and sites that absorb water quickly and release it slowly in a pure form like healthy soil. A building could be a restorative thing, a thing that is more fecund than destructive.

Do modern buildings absorb water quickly and release it slowly? Absolutely not. Water coming to human environments has been treated as if it is chemistry, H_2O suffering from physics, and falling, and we have got to get it away as quickly as possible. But water is the flux of life. Human beings are biology; we are where chemistry and physics conjoin. So our designs need to celebrate this flux and celebrate water, not just flush it, contaminated, away as fast as we can. We are now conceptualizing designs "without pipes." We are designing building materials and sites that absorb, filter, and transpire water, that keep buildings cool and provide habitat on site. Just like nature, they will release water slowly and cleanly.

One particular project we are designing right now is a new corporate campus for a large corporation in San Bruno, California, near San Francisco. The roof is a giant, undulating, grass-covered savannah. In the middle of the site there is an open-air courtyard around an established grove of oaks. So from the air a bird looking down might think, "Oh. That looks nice." Where are the songbirds in modern building? This roof is for songbirds.

When you're inside the building the ceiling looks like a cloud. The interior is fully daylit, so the sun illumines the workspace during the day. Workers spending their day indoors feel as if they've been outdoors. We've put in raised floors, which everyone wants for planning flexibility but no one can afford, and we've put them in because they allow us to run cool evening air from the San Francisco area against the concrete slabs all night long to refresh the air and cool the building down. This design means we don't have to pump foreign energy into the building during the day to cool it, and it also means there's fresh air individually directed into each person's breathing zone. Because of these strategies, we're able to cut energy equipment and energy consumption and pay for the raised floors. The building works just like an old hacienda, but goes even further with new techniques. From the air the roof is the earth. From the interior the roof is the sky. A building that's like a tree. A building that's like a meadow. Why not do this all the time?

We can do this all the time, but we need integrative thinking. We need new design principles, new aesthetics, and new engineering. Imagine what might happen if we applied our design principles to various things starting with the molecule and working up the scale to buildings, cities, and regions.

We were asked to design a fabric for a unit of the Steelcase Corporation, the largest office furniture maker in the country, and we told them we were honored to be among the famous designers they'd selected—Richard Meier, Aldo Rossi, Robert Venturi, Denise Scott Brown—these were all impressive architects. But we said we had one stipulation: unlike the others, we would not just design what the fabric looks like; we would design what it is. The company told us they expected we might say that, so they presented us with an option: what about a blend of cotton, which is natural, and PET soda bottles, which are recycled? If you put the two together, they said, you have natural, you have recycled—all the current eco-product buzzwords. You're all set. It's also durable and cheap.

But let's think about this for a minute: Is this blend an organic nutrient? Is this a Product of *Consumption?* Can it go back to soil safely? Not with the PET. Is it a product of service? Can it go back to technical cycles? Not with the cotton. Look again at our criteria: Is it ecologically intelligent? Is it just? Cotton currently occasions over 20 percent of the world's pesticide use, causes hydrological disasters, and has never been associated with social fairness. As I mentioned earlier, recycled fabrics from plastic bottles may contain antioxidants, UV stabilizers, and antimony residues from catalytic reactions. Does this belong next to human skin? Why would we want to help a company make this kind of product?

In this case, we decided to create a fabric that would be an organic nutrient, a Product of Consumption. Our client, Susan Lyons, the design director at DesignTex, arranged for us to work at Rohner Textil, a respected textile mill in Switzerland, with Albin Kälin, a director who had already made many advances at his mill. But when we arrived, Kälin told us that our project was fortuitous, because the trimmings of his bolts of cloth had just been declared hazardous waste by the Swiss government. He could no longer bury or burn it in Switzerland but had to pay to export the trimmings. Haven't you hit the wall of the First Industrial Revolution when the edges of your product are declared hazardous waste but you can still sell what's in the middle? With eco-efficiency, people contend, "My cadmium releases have been reduced and reduced," but if you look carefully, you realize that their new worst emission may be the product itself.

"Wouldn't it be nice," we told Min, "if the trimmings of your cloth became mulch for the local garden club?" So we got to work, and the first thing we reviewed was what it means to sit in a cloth-covered chair for extended periods of time. The fabric makers had interviewed people in wheelchairs, since they represent the worst case of extensive sitting, and we found out that they wanted dryness, because the biggest problem they have is moisture buildup. So we used wool, which absorbs water, and ramie, a plant similar to nettles, which provides a strong structural fiber that wicks water. The wool in the fabric absorbs moisture and the ramie wicks it away, so you're cool in the summer, warm in the winter, and comfortable all the time. Is it ecologically intelligent? Is it just? Ramie has been organically grown for thousands of years without any help from the chemical industry. And we hope the sheep in New Zealand are happy—they're free-ranging sheep.

Once we had developed the cloth, we had the finishes, the dyes, and all the rest of the process materials to consider. Remember the smokestack analogy: the filters have to be in our heads, not on the ends of pipes. Design filters. Our design filters told us that if this fabric were going back to the soil safely, it had to be free of mutagens, carcinogens, heavy metals, persistent toxins, bio-accumulatives, endocrine disrupters, and so on. Then we approached sixty chemical companies, and when we asked them to join us and put their products through this review, they summarily declined. Finally, the chairman of Ciba Geigy in Basel agreed to let us in.

Michael Braungart and our scientific colleagues reviewed *8,000* chemicals in the textile industry using this "design filter" and had to eliminate 7,962. This left 38 chemicals. We created the entire fabric line with those 38 chemicals. Everything we needed—dyes, auxiliaries, fixatives, et cetera—came from those 38 chemicals. The fabric has won gold medals and design awards and is a success in the marketplace. It is good business, and it is also creating a new standard for business excellence.

After the fabric was in production at the factory in Switzerland, a strange thing happened. Inspectors came to inspect the water coming out of the factory, and they thought their equipment was broken. They didn't find the things they expected to find. So they went to the front of the factory and checked the inflow pipes. As they expected, the water going in was Swiss drinking water. Their equipment was fine. It turned out that during the manufacturing process the fabrics were further filtering and purifying the water. Consider this concept: when the water coming out of your factory is as clean as the water going into your factory, and the water going into your factory is Swiss drinking water, that means you can cap the pipe. That means you would rather use your effluent than your influent. If you don't have anything bad coming out of the factory, there's nothing to regulate. Isn't that interesting: there are no more regulations implicit in this complete redesign. In fact, there are less! In this case, there may be none at all. This is not eco-efficiency—this mill is not "less" bad. It's not bad, period. We did not say we wanted to cut our cadmium or our mercury as much as we can. We completely redesigned this product based on a new set of principles. Welcome to the Next Industrial Revolution.[8]

What happened within the chemical industry as a result of all these efforts is also interesting. Naturally, your ordinary engineers who were using conventional materials got a little nervous, because implicit in what we were doing was an analysis of what had gone on before. Why were they using this chemical? Why all this cobalt? Why all this antimony? Why all these heavy metals? Why mutagens? Why carcinogens? The chemists told us that because their customers wanted something blue, their job was to figure out how to make it blue, not to solve environmental or health problems—just to make sure to tell customers to be careful handling the stuff and stay within regulatory limits. Is this ethical? Is this intelligent?

Regulatory structures cost a lot of money and require the government to tax their commerce in order to get the money to set up a regulatory structure. Then, the same people the government just taxed have to spend money to set up an anti-regulatory structure to respond to the regulatory structure. Now, have we made anything yet? How are we doing on competition in world markets? What does it mean when environmental regulation all of a sudden prevents you from being in the marketplace and competing with Taiwan, Korea, and the Philippines, where their environmental regulations are not so stringent and they can make things more cheaply? What ends up happening is that commerce, which is looking for the quickest, cheapest thing, goes to Taiwan, goes to Korea, and buys chemicals and dyes because they are much less expensive than the locally produced ones. But because these cheap materials are not produced as carefully, what customers get from them is what we call "Products Plus": you get the dye, plus, perhaps, PCBs, plus heavy metals, plus carcinogens, plus all of these other things you did not intend to buy but that come with the cheap product. Instead of going to someone who is working hard to be clean and good, commerce goes to companies that have figured out how to compete purely on an economic basis. That's a tough economic situation.

The Dutch realized that if their industries could police themselves, the government would not have to regulate them, and they would not have to place those compliance cost burdens on their industries. They could compete in world markets. So they created the Green Plan, which asks Dutch commerce to figure out the quickest, most effective solution to environmental problems, and if commerce doesn't do that then the government says it will have to step in to regulate. Now that all of this is taking place, imagine what would happen if the textile industry in Holland started to look around and ask, "How do we do this?" And suddenly, because of our redesign, here is Ciba Geigy with a package of thirty-eight chemicals that will make any color safely. To guarantee quality, all you have to do is specify their whole package. But you must use their package exclusively, or other chemicals reviewed with the same "design filter," because in order to guarantee quality you can't contaminate it with materials from some other supplier who has not been reviewed. As a result of using this exclusive protocol, you do not need special storage rooms for hazardous waste. You do not need to file with regulatory agents for handling hazardous material. Your workers are not wearing protective equipment anymore because there is nothing to fear. Within the textile industry this little revolution starts: "Wait a minute! I hear over there they're not exposing their workers to carcinogens. Why can't we do that?" And the chairman of a major chemical company looks pretty smart for having taken the obvious next step in Total Quality Management.

Let's look at the concept of Total Quality Management, at the ideas started by W. Edwards Deming. He began as a statistician who was sent into factories to monitor production during World War II. Since so many men were at war, women had gone in to work in the factories, and he was there to judge the statistical effect. Let's abstract this story for a moment to get the main point of his discovery: a statistician goes into the factory, and he notes that the men who had manufactured artillery shells before the women took over produced, say, approximately a thousand shells a day, with an inspector throwing out "rejects" at the end of the process. The men expected lemons, they expected failure. They anticipated it and planned on it.

After the men had gone to war, the statistician watched the women at work to see what would happen. He watched them make twenty shells in the first week, forty in the next, then eighty, then a hundred, then three hundred, then five hundred, then seven hundred, then nine hundred, then twelve hundred, then fourteen hundred. They leveled off at a thousand, and all the shells were perfect. Production was up, quality was up. The statistician investigated the system more closely to find out what had happened, and guess what he found out? The women talked to each other. They sat in the round and discussed their mutual problems and needs. There was no hierarchy, no inspection. They went about their business and shared the worst work. They also adopted the policy that they would not accept the concept of failure: the idea of making an artillery shell that would blow up in their husbands' faces in the middle of the war was absolutely unacceptable to them. They eliminated the concept of failure. They did not count on failure, and the result was Total Quality Management.

When the men came back after the war, the statistician explained what had happened, but the men told him they had hierarchies, they had quotas, they were inspection-based, and they had just won a major war. So the statistician moved on to a more hospitable audience in Japan, and the rest is history.

The United States eventually profited from his experience. I remember when you used to buy a car and you hoped it wouldn't turn out to be a lemon. No one expects a lemon today, but when I was a kid, you didn't want to be the one who got the lemon. You were expecting one to come off the line. Then "Quality" became "Job One" at Ford after years of being "Job One" in Japan, which captured huge pieces of the auto market. That was literally due to Deming.

The Total Quality Management concept started a revolution in production. Because those women rejected the concept of failure—the concept of a defective product—Total Quality Management can be seen as a working engagement to the concept of zero defects. Just-in-time delivery came along as a result of high interest rates, high handling costs, and expensive inventory, and can be seen as providing the benefits of zero inventory. Zero accidents have always been a noble goal, and now, with total redesign, we can have zero emissions and zero waste (of undesirable materials). As Gunter Pauli likes to say, this is the next step in Total Quality Management.

The organic fabric we designed is a *Product of Consumption*; after its useful life, it goes back into the organic metabolism and feeds the soil. We're also working with Guilford of Maine, a subsidiary of Interface Corporation, to design the *Product of Service* version of fabrics, and we're working with partners in the chemical industry to develop and redesign polyester products that eliminate concerns for heavy metal residues from catalytic reactions, so people will no longer be exposed to them. Then, if we actually do recycle these materials back into the human environment, we will not be recycling heavy metals. We're also designing new dye protocols. In fact, we've recently identified a whole new line of dyes to go with polyesters based on our "design filters." The resulting fabrics will be safe and recyclable forever. They will never need to go into a landfill.

Interface Corporation is a major U.S. carpet and textile manufacturer that wants to lead the way in the Next Industrial Revolution. Ray Anderson, Interface Inc.'s founder and chairman, read about our concepts in Paul Hawken's *Ecology of Commerce*,[9] and was moved by this important book to transform his business.

Interface Corporation is also adopting our *Product of Service* concept and the eco-leasing concept that goes with it for their large carpet business. They are calling it their *Evergreen Lease.* One way to understand how this concept has revolutionary economic implications is to think of it this way: If you buy a conventional carpet you buy a liability, not an asset. When you finish with it you're going to have to pay to get it removed. What does that mean to American business, to natural flows and materials, to prosperity? The chairman of Interface understood the problems of such a system. By adopting the Product of Service concept, his company will continue to own the material but will effectively lease it and maintain it for the customer that wants the use of it. When the customer has finished with the service of the carpet, Interface will take back their *technical nutrient.*

However, it's not enough to take a carpet back if it's not designed properly. The average carpet is nylon embedded in fiberglass and PVC. It was never designed to be recycled. You can really only "downcycle" it: you shave off some of the nylon material, and then you're left with a material "soup" that you can't use effectively. We've redesigned the actual carpet and its entire delivery system so a customer can say, "I don't like red anymore. I want blue," without feeling guilty. Right now, when you order a carpet you're contributing to the destruction of natural systems, because you're basically taking a bunch of petrochemicals the manufacturer compiled to make the product and then throwing them "away" in a landfill. Under the new protocol, your carpet order would create jobs and the negative material flows would go down or be eliminated. Consequently, when you want to change your carpet color you can have fun instead of feeling guilty. The old design process requires virgin or imperfect recycled material; the new design employs people to re-circulate technical nutrients. So you can trade throwing away petrochemicals for jobs.

What else does this new protocol mean to commerce? If our companies and countries expect to be wealthy in the future, why would they put the valuable nutrients of their industry into a landfill? The essence of our argument to Ray Anderson was simply this: If you'd been using this concept from day one, you would have four billion pounds of technical nutrients designed for use in your industry. That's how much carpet you've made since you started the company. Four *billion pounds,* and where is it? It's in holes in the ground, or on its way there. The street value of this? Over one billion dollars. This is how you could accrue capital over time and accrue assets: by designing carpet to constantly become technical nutrients for your own company. Michael Braungart and I can apply this thinking to almost any industry with similar results.

On the regional level, we helped create the concept of Zero Emissions Zoning for Chattanooga, "the Pittsburgh of the South." Chattanooga had what Dave Crockett called a "civic heart attack" in 1968. The city was rated as having the worst air quality in the country—even worse than Los Angeles. So the city's civic leaders looked at this problem and decided to clean up their own air. They've been doing this for the last thirty years. But when their eco-industrial concept was initially proposed, a lot of industry CEOs said, "Zero Emissions Concept? What are you talking about? No corporation is going to accept it. No one will come here and do business." Then Gunter Pauli, who worked with Ecover in Europe and is now at the United Nations University in Tokyo, arranged an international conference and announced one of the first companies to agree with the Zero Emissions Concept in Chattanooga: DuPont. The chairman of DuPont actually stood up in Chattanooga and declared zero emissions a goal for his entire company. This is not a marginal event. This is big business.

Many industrial leaders claim there is no such thing as a factory without emissions. What we are talking about is zero waste and unwanted emissions. But we did it in Switzerland, so we respond with Amory Lovins's famous phrase, "It exists, therefore it is possible." I think these new design assignments are the most exciting and revolutionary ways of approaching commerce. And I believe that commerce is the primary engine of change, which is why I am involved with and respect the power of commerce so deeply.

Paul Hawken introduced me to the book *Systems of Survival*, in which Jane Jacobs states that humans have developed two fundamental systems for their own survival: the syndrome of the guardian and the syndrome of commerce.[10] A guardian is, for example, the government, a system that is meant to preserve, protect, and maintain. We grow very nervous when our government officials get cozy with commerce, because the guardian is meant to shun commerce. You should not be able to buy a government official. And the guardian's biggest fear is a traitor, someone who has sold out—a commercial term. The government will kill a traitor. It will go to war, and it can incarcerate and even kill you if you threaten the state or society. It's the only system that can legally sanction murder and duplicity.

So the guardian is slow, serious, and reserves the exclusive right to kill. Commerce, on the other hand, is meant to be quick, creative, adroit, and honest. If you are dishonest, people will stop doing business with you; because it doesn't take them long to realize that their involvement with you is not profitable if you cheat, lie, or steal. Now, let me restate the characteristics of the guardian versus those of commerce: the guardian is simple, slow, direct and even brutal when it feels the need to be. Commerce is quick, clever, and honest. As Jacobs points out, every time you put the two together you get what she calls a "monstrous hybrid."

When a city or town calls for Zero Emissions Zoning, what are they saying? That's the guardian saying, "Don't try to kill us. We'll do transportation and schools, but don't try to kill us, business." Then business—It would be DuPont in Chattanooga's case—says, "We can do that. With no complex regulations, we can figure out how not to release anything that will kill you. That's our job." The guardian wouldn't need to regulate commerce, and commerce wouldn't have to figure out how to respond to detailed micromanaged regulations, but only if commerce designs comprehensive production systems that don't release toxic emissions. Commerce doesn't need to be in the killing business.

We must, by design, allow commerce to do what commerce does best: be creative, be inventive, be quick, be smart, and be honest. And let government do what government does best simple, important things like saying, "Don't kill us." Then our arrangements get less confused and complex.

Finally, I believe our primary design assignment, and the question we should ask ourselves in business in the future, comes down to this: How do you love all the children? Not some of the children. Not just your own children. All of the children.

Jaime Lerner has been working with the whole city of Curitiba, Brazil, around this precept. He has been developing systems that respect all the children's needs for safe shelter and food, health care, education, transportation, creative opportunity, dignity, and hope. When it was time for the city to build a public library, instead of San Francisco's response—a central 100-million-dollar mausoleum for books—Curitiba's leaders asked themselves how they could provide library services for every single child in the city, including the impoverished ones in the flavelas. They decided that with their limited budget, all they could afford was many tiny libraries, each the size of a small house.

In front of every library they put a "friendly beacon of knowledge," a brightly colored and illuminated lighthouse for visibility and security. A volunteer forester, teacher, or parent sits in a little room behind a window and watches the street, reads a book, and makes sure the children are safe going to and from the library. The library holds the reference books the children need for school, as well as books the poorest children can "buy" in exchange for compostible garbage. Curitiba's goal is to put one of these libraries in each neighborhood, within easy walking distance of every child in the city. The children will have all the books they need for school, and they'll also have access to the World Wide Web. That's how they decided to design a library in Curitiba.

How do you love all the children? Well, for one thing, imagine that your outlet pipes are immediately upstream of your inlet pipes, and you'll begin to understand. We have to take responsibility for all the children, for all the generations. We're all going to have to do this, not just those "in charge." It's going to require massive creativity—massive creativity. It's going to require a complete redesign of commerce itself.

Let's get creative and start redesigning a new kind of prosperity for ourselves, but let's make sure this prosperity includes everyone else, including our seventh generation to come. Design for all of our prosperity, not just your own prosperity. We can start by eliminating our destruction masquerading as consumption, and begin to enjoy the search for our rightful and responsible place in the natural world. Get prosperous. Get very prosperous, because then people will want to imitate you. But honor that thing in yourself, that creativity in your spirit and your place that is really the sacred trust for all generations. We need to design a system of production and consumption and a system of commerce that will allow everyone life, liberty, and the pursuit of happiness in their own place, free from remote tyranny— the remote tyranny that is us and our bad design.

Note

Adapted from a speech given by Mr. McDonough to the Darden Graduate School of Business Administration, December 17, 1996. Copyright 1997 by William A. McDonough. All rights reserved.

Notes

1. Thomas Jefferson, *The Political Writings of Thomas Jefferson,* ed. Merill D. Peterson (Woodlawn: Walk Press, 1993).
2. Rachel Carson, *Silent Spring* (Boston: Houghton Mifflin, 1987).
3. Roderick Nash, *The Rights of Nature: A History of Environmental Ethics* (Madison: University of Wisconsin Press, 1989).
4. Ralph Waldo Emerson, "Nature," *Selections from Ralph Waldo Emerson,* ed. Stephen E. Whicher (Boston: Houghton Mifflin, 1957).
5. Peter Senge, *The Fifth Discipline* (New York: Doubleday, 1991).
6. Tony Hiss and Robert D. Yaro, *A Region at Risk: The Third Regional Plan for the New York-New Jersey-Connecticut Metropolitan Area* (Washington, D.C.: Island Press, 1996).
7. Mr. McDonough has developed and trademarked certain terms to describe his product and systems design protocols. These terms include: *Waste Equals Food, Product of Consumption, Product of Service, Eco-leasing Concept, technical nutrient, downcycling, Cradle-to-Cradle.*
8. See Matthew Mehalik, Michael Gorman, and Patricia Werhane, "DesignTex, Inc.," *Darden Case Bibliography* (Charlottesville, VA: Colgate-Darden School of Business, 1996), and Matthew Mehalik, Michael Gorman and Patricia Werhane, "Rohner Textil, AG," *Darden Case Bibliography* (Charlottesville, VA: Colgate-Darden School of Business, 1997).
9. Paul Hawken, *The Ecology of Commerce: A Declaration of Sustainability* (New York: HarperCollins, 1993).
10. Jane Jacobs, *Systems of Survival: A Dialogue on the Moral Foundations of Commerce and Politics* (New York: Vintage Books, 1992).

Chapter 15

Globalization

Case Study

Global Profits, Global Headaches

Mark Baker   ●   Laura Hartman   ●   Bill Shaw[1]

K-PAN is a Fort Worth-based Nevada corporation that manufactures and markets textiles. It is a publicly traded firm whose name, for over 50 years, has been synonymous with men and women's work clothes. The last two decades brought great changes to the textile industry. Among other things, labor costs have been on a steep incline. In K-PAN's North Carolina and Texas plants, costs were squeezing profits to the point that K-PAN's board decided to follow its competitors overseas. Over a three year period, K-PAN phased out its domestic operations with a generous re-training and re-settlement program for former employees in need of help; built a $28 million state-of-the-art plant in Nicaragua (with $20.5 million in bonds placed by Dillion), and purchased its remaining needs through local agents in Pakistan and Indonesia.

Cost advantages of this globalization effort reflect international differences in labor market conditions, labor laws, producer constraints and environmental restrictions. A typical developing country has higher unemployment levels, lower wage rates, fewer effective labor unions, less effective labor laws, fewer producer constraints, and lower environmental standards. In short, many goods can be produced at a much lower cost in developing countries than in developed countries. By keeping production costs low, sweatshops provide a strong economic incentive for corporations to shift production from developed to developing countries. Increased exports bring jobs for the domestic economy and hard currency for international purchases. As a consequence, the developing county's economy improves along with its standing in world markets.

The worldwide popularity of one of K-PAN's articles of clothing, a pair of pants called "Hangins," put a welcomed spike in its earnings, but also

Mark Baker is Associate Professor, University of Texas-Austin; Laura Hartman is the Associate Vice President for Academic Affairs at De Paul University. Bill Shaw is Woodson Centennial Professor in Business Administration, University of Texas-Austin. Copyright © 1999. Reprinted by permission.

focused public attention on the corporation. In doing so, the company came under closer scrutiny, not only from the financial markets, but also from those whose avowed purpose was to monitor MNE's to assure conformance with modern ethical principals.

The adverse publicity that had stunned Nike,[2] The Gap[3] and Kathy Lee,[4] amongst others, began to haunt K-PAN with a vengeance. Ft. Worth residents, supported by a vocal group of former K-PAN employees and the Amalgamated Textile Workers Union, assailed the firm via informational picketing and through the media. In addition to a number of stories in the local media, a group of radical citizens, calling themselves Terrorists Against Multinational Suppressors created and circulated adverse e-mails, some of which had no basis in truth. After some inquiry it became apparent that K-PAN's "model" plant in Nicaragua exhibited a number of shortcomings traditionally associated with "sweatshops" (long hours, low pay, environmental, health, and safety problems). None of these concerns violated the laws of their host country and, in many ways, the plant greatly exceeded local minimum standards in all areas.

However, the negative publicity generated by its Central American operations paled in comparison to the outcry that stemmed from its link with sweatshops in Southeast Asia. Its purchases through local agents in Pakistan and Indonesia allegedly contributed to the perpetuation of atrocious working conditions and poor economic situation in those countries. This predicament was similar to that suffered by Nike in connection with its Indonesian suppliers. A study of Nike workers in Indonesia found that currency devaluation compounded the problems of low wages.

> While workers producing Nike shoes were low-paid before their currency, the rupiah, began plummeting in late 1997, the dollar value of their wages has dropped from $2.47/day in 1997 to 80 cents/day in 1998. Meanwhile, the prices of basic goods have sky-rocketed. Workers reported that they had received a 15 percent pay raise earlier this year, meaning that their base salary had increased from about Rp. 175,000 per month (approximately $17) to about Rp. 200,000 per month (approximately $20). However, they estimated that their cost of living had gone up anywhere from 100 to 300 percent. . . . We found that the cost for a single male worker is $33.20/month and $35/month for a female worker. The base pay for Nike workers, however, is $20/month—not enough to fulfill the basic needs for one worker, much less a family.[5]

K-PAN's insistence that it owned and operated no facilities in those countries couldn't begin to ward off attacks on its corporate policy. K-PAN's internal code of conduct, entitled "K-PAN Ethics," has been in place since 1980 and was patterned after codes of prominent MNE's. Each employee is given a copy of the code, asked to sign it, and subjected to a test on its principles. The central focus of its code had been untouched since it was carefully crafted by K-PAN's founder, Mr. W, as he was widely known. K-PAN ETHICS speaks of a "living wage," "shareholder satisfaction," "community responsibility," and "customer confidence"; these components of the code were met satisfactorily (or at least, they were un-protested) since their inception.

Members of the marketing team came up with the following background information regarding labor conditions in developing economies. Sweatshops are a product of the industrial revolution. Creative entrepreneurs realized that they could earn substantial profits if they could find low-cost labor to operate the new machines. The workers were found when new agricultural practices and the closure of the commons created provided factory owners a growing urban-based pool of workers that could no longer grow what they needed to survive. With few employment opportunities, workers were willing to work long hours under unhealthy conditions for very low pay.

Though business owners were quick to figure out how to keep labor costs low, lexicographers were slow in finding a term to define the owners' shops. The term "sweater" began to be used in the mid-1800s to describe an employer that paid workers very low wages for monotonous work.[6] "Sweatshop" came into use in the late nineteenth century to characterize subcontracting systems where profit margins were increased by "sweating" the workers—requiring employees to work long hours for very little pay.[7] The words sweating and sweatshop crossed the Atlantic as American employers adopted British labor practices.[8]

The Encyclopedia Britannica defines the term *sweatshop* based on a set of employment practices: "a workplace in which workers are employed for long hours at low wages and under unhealthy or oppressive conditions."[9] Several organizations define sweatshops based on compliance with national labor law. According to the U.S. General Accounting Office, a place of work with "an employer that violates more than one federal or state labor, industrial homework, occupational safety and health, workers' compensation, or industry registration law" is a sweatshop.[10] Other groups add to compliance the concept of labor rights. The AFL-CIO Union of Needletrades, Industrial and Textile Employees define sweatshop as a place of employment with "systematic violation of one or more fundamental workers' rights that have been codified in international and U.S. law."[11] Some would say that a variety of sub-standard labor practices needs to be present before a place of employment can be called a sweatshop. Others, such as the Interfaith Center on Corporate Responsibility, require only a single questionable practice: "[though] a factory may be clean, well-organized and harassment free, unless its workers are paid a sustainable living wage, it's still a sweatshop."[12]

The word *sweatshop* is emotive and carries prejudicial connotations. The undercurrent of invoked prejudicial emotions makes it difficult to engage in open, multi-party collaboration to improve working conditions in developing economies. In an effort to deal with these issues, the K-PAN Board of Directors called a special meeting.

"If we forego profits to raise working conditions in the developing world," remarked one board member, "we're just going to have to reduce our purchases and that's going to cost jobs. Who'll be better off?" "Yeah, and our customers won't be happy with the higher prices either. They could switch to Levis or Wranglers. It wouldn't be fair to our shareholders or workers for this to happen," said another. "I really wish all companies worldwide had to adhere to the same rules; that way we'd all be on a level playing field. I wonder if such a set of rules or a proposal exists."

Manuel Smith, a longtime employee who had worked his way up from the factory floor to the Board suggested that they devise a profit-sharing plan designed to keep costs low but to also return profits to every employee of the company. "Let's pay the minimum wage in each country and split the profits with the employees." He liked the incentives this offered.

Claire Harrera, the youngest member of the board and a person of color, reminded her colleagues that "good social work is good business; and a policy of helping workers in developing countries will encourage enlightened consumers to do business with K-PAN, thereby increasing sales; helping costs stay low and maintaining our profits." Her suggestion was to pay all employees at the plant 150% of the local minimum wage, let the world know of the good deed, and require all suppliers to sign and adhere to K-PAN Ethics. Manuel echoed the sentiment of the group when he said, "she's so young and naïve; consumers only care about the bottom line!"

Recognizing that some middle ground must be sought, Professor Dickinson, boyhood pal of the founder and the most recently elected board member, referred members to his recent speech on the topic that included the following remarks:

> Economic growth requires market expansion and market expansion depends on growing product demand. A developing country's export sector is the most likely source of market expansion since its domestic markets will likely not expand until the general economy becomes robust. The International Labor Organization found that the most successful economies have been "those who best exploited emerging opportunities in the global economy. An export-oriented policy is vital in countries that are starting on the industrialization path and have large surpluses of cheap labor."[13]

Whether wages are low, working hours are long, or working conditions are hazardous and unhealthy, the decision to accept employment by a worker in an MNE is not forced slavery but instead made by the employee.[14]

> [I]f the choice is between [meeting] subsistence needs and [having] 'decent' work hours, the work days will be very long. Or if the choice is between child labor on the family farm or a smaller harvest, children will work long and hard in the fields.[15]

Workers wouldn't accept employment if other jobs were more attractive. Research by Sargent and Matthews supports the economists' conclusion. After conducting more than fifty interviews with workers in *maquiladoras* in Mexico, the researchers found that there was no evidence that workers found their present jobs less attractive than other jobs in that economy.[16]

It is not that economists are against better working conditions *per se*. But they are extremely concerned about the manner in which improvements are sought. According to the neoclassicists, improved working conditions will not come from government controls that restrict child labor, raise minimum wage, improve health and safety conditions, allow unionizing, or protect employee rights. At best, governmental controls will improve the working conditions for only a few workers; however, workers in the export industries and throughout the rest of the economy will lose their jobs as exports decline and the economy falters.

Economists argue that the best way to improve working conditions is to leave markets alone.[17] In the short-run, sweatshops give workers a job and some income.[18] In the long-run, an improved economy will give workers the leverage they need to obtain better working conditions. When a developing country's economy grows, the demand for labor increases and provides workers with more employment opportunities. Producers must then offer higher wages, shorter work hours, and other improved working conditions if they want to retain existing workers or attract new workers.

"My God, is any option palatable?" groaned Manuel and the chief financial officer at the same time. The representative of Dillion rolled her eyes and remarked, "The bondholders are going to love us." "Well then," said the professor, "there does exist ethical and economic solutions to our quandary. We just need to be creative and innovative." Someone caught the Chairman's attention and asked, "Can we take a break now?"

The Chairman was about to grant the request, when Kim W. Robins, daughter of the founder interrupted. "I'd like for the Chairman to appoint my sister, my brother, and myself as a committee of the board to look into this matter further and report back at our next meeting."

"So ordered," said the Chair, "we'll hear your report at our West Coast retreat, schedule for the 18th of April in L.A. Meeting adjourned."

Notes

1. Authors names are listed alphabetically.
2. See Bob Herbert, "Nike's Boot Camps," *New York Times* (Mar. 31, 1997), A15.
3. Christian Task Force on Central America, "Urgent Action El Salvador," http://www/grannyg.bc.ca/CTFCA/act1295a.html (Nov. 29, 1995); National Labor Committee, "Gap Agrees to Independent Monitoring Setting New Standard for the Entire Industry," http://www.alfea.it/coordns/work/industria/gap.agrees.html; United Auto Workers, "The Gap Agrees to Improve Conditions in Overseas Plants," *Frontlines*, http://www.uaw.org/solidarity/9601/frontlinesjan96.html (January 1996), p. 1.
4. See Stephanie Strom, "A Sweetheart Becomes Suspect: Looking Behind Those Kathie Lee Labels," *New York Times* (June 27, 1996), D1.
5. Campaign for Labor Rights, *Labor Alerts* (Oct. 16, 1998).
6. http://members.eb.com/bol/topic?eu=72449&sctn=1#s_top. See also H. Braverman, *Labor and Monopoly Capital: The Degradation of Work in the 20th Century* (New York: Monthly Review Press, 1974). The creation of jobs where the primary tasks are routine and repetitive may be considered exploitative in itself.
7. Smithsonian Institution, "The Contracting System," in exhibition: "Between A Rock and A Hard Place: A History of American Sweatshops 1820–Present" (1999) http://www.si.edu/nmah/ve/sweatshops/history/2t35.htm (Subsequent citations to Smithsonian Institution are from same exhibit.) See also "Facts on the Global Sweatshop," *Rethinking Schools* 11, no. 4.
8. Mass migration to America provided factory owners an abundant source of inexpensive labor. Immigrant workers were easy to control because they had limited language skills and a lack of awareness of American labor laws. An Italian folk tale expresses the American immigrant's plight: "Well, I came to America because I heard the streets were paved with gold. When I got here, I found out three things: first, the streets weren't paved with gold; second, they weren't paved at all; and third, I was expected to pave them." http://www.si.edu/nmah/ve/sweatshops/history/2t34.htm (1999). See also Charles Krause, "Labors' Pains," *Online Newshour* (PBS, April 14, 1997) http://www.pbs.org/newshour/bb/business/jan-june97/sweatshops_4-14a.html; Smithsonian Institution, "Tenement Sweatshops" http://www.si.edu/nmah/ve/sweatshops/history/tenement.htm (1999); U.S. Department of Labor, *Dynamic Change in the Garment Industry*, http://www.dol.gov/dol/esa/public/forum/report.htm; L.J. Foo, "The Vulnerable and Exploitable Immigrant Workforce and the Need for Strengthening Worker Protection Legislation," *Yale Law Review* 103, no. 8 (June, 1994), pp. 2179–2212.
9. Encyclopedia Britannica Online Edition, http://members.eb.com/bol/topic?eu=72449&sctn=1#s_top (1999). For a virtually identical definition, see Merriam Webster Dictionary Online Edition, http://www.m-w.com/cgi-bin/dictionary?book=Dictionary&va=sweatshop.
10. http://www.sweatshopwatch.org/swatch/industry/.
11. http://www.uniteunion.org/sweatshops/whatis/infosheet.html.

12. Ruth Rosenbaum, David Schilling, *In Sweatshops, Wages are the Issue* (May 1997).

13. International Labour Organization, *World Employment Report 1995* (Geneva: International Labour Organization, 1995), pp. 75–76, cited in Ian Maitland, "The Great Non-Debate over International Sweatshops," *British Academy of Management Annual Conference Proceedings* (1997), pp. 240–265.

14. See John Sargent and Linda Matthews, "Exploitation or Choice? Exploring the Relative Attractiveness of Employment in the Maquiladoras," *Journal of Business Ethics* 18, no. 2 (Jan. 1999), p. 213. [After conducting more than fifty interviews with workers in *maquiladoras* in Mexico, the researchers found that there was no evidence that workers found their present jobs less attractive that other jobs in that economy.] See also Ian Maitland, "The Great Non-Debate over International Sweatshops," *British Academy of Management Annual Conference Proceedings* (1997), pp. 240–265.

15. Gary S. Fields, "Labor Standards, Economic Development, and International Trade," in *Labor Standards and Development in the Global Economy* (ed. Stephen Herzenberg and Jorge F. Pérez-López) (Washington, D.C.: U.S. Department of Labor Bureau of International Labor Affairs, 1990), pp. 19–20.

16. John Sargent and Linda Matthews, "Exploitation or Choice? Exploring the Relative Attractiveness of Employment in the Maquiladoras," *Journal of Business Ethics* 18, no. 2 (Jan. 1999), pp. 213, 221.

17. Ibid., p. 213 [After conducting more than fifty interviews with workers in *maquiladoras* in Mexico, the researchers found that there was no evidence that workers found their present jobs less attractive that other jobs in that economy.] See also Ian Maitland, *infra* note 14, pp. 240–265.

18. Stephen Golub, "Are International Labor Standards Needed to Prevent Social Dumping?" *Finance & Development* (Dec. 1997), pp. 20, 22.

The Market at the Bottom of the Pyramid

C. K. PRAHALAD

Turn on your television and you will see calls for money to help the world's 4 billion poor—people who live on far less than $2 a day. In fact, the cry is so constant and the need so chronic that the tendency for many people is to tune out these images as well as the message. Even those who do hear and heed the cry are limited in what they can accomplish. For more than 50 years, the World Bank, donor nations, various aid agencies, national governments, and, lately, civil society organizations have all fought the good fight, but have not eradicated poverty. The adoption of the Millennium Development Goals (MDG) by the United Nations only underscores that reality; as we enter the 21st century, poverty—and the disenfranchisement that accompanies it—remains one of the world's most daunting problems.

The purpose of this book is to change that familiar image on TV. It is to illustrate that the typical pictures of poverty mask the fact that the very

C.K. Prahalad is Harvey C. Fruehauf Professor of Business Administration and Professor of Corporate Strategy and International Business at the University of Michigan Business School. May 9, 2005. Sample Chapter from C.K. Prahalad, *Fortune at the Bottom of the Pyramid: Eradicating Poverty Through Profits*, © 2005, pp. 3–21. Reprinted by permission of Pearson Education, Inc., Upper Saddle River, NJ.

poor represent resilient entrepreneurs and value-conscious consumers. What is needed is a better approach to help the poor, an approach that involves partnering with them to innovate and achieve sustainable win–win scenarios where the poor are actively engaged and, at the same time, the companies providing products and services to them are profitable. This collaboration between the poor, civil society organizations, governments, and large firms can create the largest and fastest growing markets in the world. Large-scale and wide-spread entrepreneurship is at the heart of the solution to poverty. Such an approach exists and has, in several instances, gone well past the idea stage as private enterprises, both large and small, have begun to successfully build markets at the bottom of the pyramid (BOP) as a way of eradicating poverty.

The economic pyramid of the world is shown in Figure 15-1. As we can see, more than 4 billion constitute the BOP. These are the people who are the subject matter of this book.

THE BOTTOM OF THE PYRAMID (BOP)

The distribution of wealth and the capacity to generate incomes in the world can be captured in the form of an economic pyramid. At the top of the pyramid are the wealthy, with numerous opportunities for generating high levels of income. More than 4 billion people live at the BOP on less than $2 per day. . . .

[There are] companies fighting disease with educational campaigns and innovative products. There are organizations helping the handicapped walk

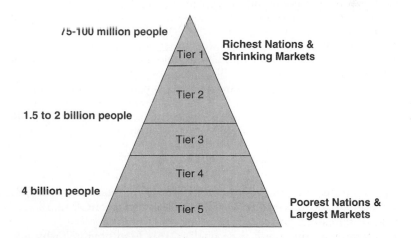

FIGURE 15-1   The economic pyramid.

Source: C. K. Prahalad and Stuart Hart, 2002. The Fortune at the Bottom of the Pyramid, *Strategy + Business,* Issue 26, 2002. Reprinted with permission from *strategy + business,* the award-winning management quarterly published by Booz Allen Hamilton. http://www.strategy-business.com.

and helping subsistence farmers check commodity prices and connect with the rest of the world. There are banks adapting to the financial needs of the poor, power companies reaching out to meet energy needs, and construction companies doing what they can to house the poor in affordable ways that allow for pride. There are chains of stores tailored to understand the needs of the poor and to make products available to them.

The strength of these innovative approaches, . . ., is that they tend to create opportunities for the poor by offering them choices and encouraging self-esteem. Entrepreneurial solutions such as these place a minimal financial burden on the developing countries in which they occur.

To begin to understand how all of this is remotely possible, we need to start with some basic assumptions:

- First, while cases certainly can be found of large firms and multinational corporations (MNCs) that may have undermined the efforts of the poor to build their livelihoods, the greatest harm they might have done to the poor is to ignore them altogether. The poor cannot participate in the benefits of globalization without an active engagement and without access to products and services that represent global quality standards. They need to be exposed to the range and variety of opportunities that inclusive globalization can provide. The poor represent a "latent market" for goods and services. Active engagement of private enterprises at the BOP is a critical element in creating inclusive capitalism, as private-sector competition for this market will foster attention to the poor as consumers. It will create choices for them. They do not have to depend only on what is available in their villages. If large firms approach this market with the BOP consumers' interests at heart, it can also lead to significant growth and profits for them. These characteristics of a market economy, new to the BOP, can facilitate dramatic change at the BOP. Free and transparent private-sector competition, unlike local village and shanty-town monopolies controlled by local slum lords, can transform the "poor" into consumers (as we illustrate with examples). Poverty alleviation will become a business development task shared among the large private sector firms and local BOP entrepreneurs.

- Second, the BOP, as a market, provides a new growth opportunity for the private sector and a forum for innovations. Old and tired solutions cannot create markets at the BOP.

- Third, BOP markets must become an integral part of the work of the private sector. They must become part of the firms' core businesses; they cannot merely be relegated to the realm of corporate social responsibility (CSR) initiatives. Successfully creating BOP markets involves change in the functioning of MNCs as much as it changes the functioning of developing countries. BOP markets must become integral to the success of the firm in order to command senior management attention and sustained resource allocation.

There is significant untapped opportunity for value creation (for BOP consumers, shareholders, and employees) that is latent in the BOP market. These markets have remained "invisible" for too long.

It is natural for you to ask this: If all of this is so obvious, why has this not yet occurred?

THE POWER OF DOMINANT LOGIC

All of us are prisoners of our own socialization. The lenses through which we perceive the world are colored by our own ideology, experiences, and established management practices. Each one of the groups that is focusing on poverty alleviation—the World Bank, rich countries providing aid, charitable organizations, national governments, and the private sector—is conditioned by its own dominant logic. Let us, for example, examine the dominant logic of each group as it approaches the task of eradicating poverty.

Consider, for instance, the politicians and bureaucrats in India, one of the largest countries with a significant portion of the world's poor. India is home to more than 400 million people who qualify as being very poor. The policies of the government for the first 45 years since independence from Great Britain in 1947 were based on a set of basic assumptions. Independent India started with a deep suspicion of the private sector. The country's interaction with the East India Company and colonialism played a major part in creating this mindset. The experience with the indigenous private sector was not very positive, either. The private sector was deemed exploitative of the poor. This suspicion was coupled with an enormous confidence in the government machinery to do what is "right and moral." For example, the government of India initiated a series of large industrial projects in the public sector (owned by the Indian government) in a wide variety of industries, from steel to food distribution and global trading in essential commodities. India's general suspicion of the private sector led to controls over its size and expansion. Some sectors of economic activity were reserved for small-scale industries. In textiles, for example, the "hand loom sector" dominated by small firms was given preference. There was no credible voice in public policy for nurturing market-based ecosystems that included the large and the small in a symbiotic relationship. The thinking was cleanly divided among the public sector (mostly large firms with significant capital outlay as in steel), the private sector with large firms strictly controlled by the government through a system of licenses, and a small-scale sector. The focus of public policy was on distributive justice over wealth creation. Because of the disparities in wealth and the preponderance of the poor, the government thought its first priority must be policies that "equalized" wealth distribution. Taxation, limits on salaries of top managers, and other such measures were instituted to ensure distributive justice. The discussion further polarized around the somewhat contrived concepts of rural poor and urban rich. The assumption was that the rural population was primarily poor and the urban population was relatively rich. However, the data increasingly does not support this distinction. There are as many rural rich as there are urban poor. Poverty knows no such boundaries. In the developing world, more than one third of the urban population lives in shanty towns and slums. These traditional views reflect the philosophy behind actions taken by bureaucrats and politicians. During the last decade, a slow but discernable transition has been taking place from the traditional to a more market-based outlook.

This much-needed and desirable transition is in its infancy. The dominant logic, built over 45 years, is difficult to give up for individuals, political parties, and sections of the bureaucracy. This is the reason why politicians and bureaucrats appear to be vacillating in their positions. Most thinking people know where they have to go, but letting go of their beliefs and abandoning their "zones of comfort" and familiarity are not easy. We also believe that it is equally difficult for a whole generation of BOP consumers to give up their dependence on governmental subsidies.

We have explicitly focused on ideology and policy and not on the quality of implementation of projects focused on the poor, be it building roads and dams or providing basic education and health care. The distinct role of corruption, which seems so endemic to developing countries in general, deserves separate treatment.

Private-sector businesses, especially MNCs (and large local firms that emulate their MNC competitors), also suffer from a deeply etched dominant logic of their own, which restricts their ability to see a vibrant market opportunity at the BOP. For example, it is common in MNCs to have the assumptions outlined in Table 15.1. These assumptions dictate decision and resource allocation processes for developing countries and BOP markets in particular.

These and other implicit assumptions surface in every discussion of BOP markets with managers in MNCs and those in large domestic firms in developing countries that fashion their management practices after those at successful MNCs. These biases are hard to eradicate in large firms. Although the dominant logic and its implications are clear, it is our goal in this book to challenge and provide counterpoints. For example, BOP markets enable firms to challenge their perspectives on cost. We will show that a 10 to 200 times advantage (compared to the cost structures that are oriented to the top of the pyramid markets) is possible if firms innovate from the BOP up

TABLE 15.1   The Dominant Logic of MNCs as It Relates to BOP

Assumption	Implication
The poor are not our target customers; they cannot afford our products or services.	Our cost structure is a given; with our cost structure, we cannot serve the BOP market.
The poor do not have use for products sold in developed countries.	We are committed to a form over functionality. The poor might need sanitation, but can't afford detergents in formats we offer. Therefore, there is no market in the BOP.
Only developed countries appreciate and pay for technological innovations.	The BOP does not need advanced technology solutions; they will not pay for them. Therefore, the BOP cannot be a source of innovations.
The BOP market is not critical for long-term growth and vitality of MNCs.	BOP markets are at best an attractive distraction.
Intellectual excitement is in developed markets; it is very hard to recruit managers for BOP markets.	We cannot assign our best people to work on market development in BOP markets.

Adapted from C. K. Prahalad and Stuart Hart, The Fortune at the Bottom of the Pyramid, *Strategy + Business*, Issue 26, 2002. Reprinted with permission from *strategy + business*, the award-winning management quarterly published by Booz Allen Hamilton. http://www.strategy-business.com.

and do not follow the traditional practice of serving the BOP markets by making minor changes to the products created for the top of the pyramid.

Most charitable organizations also believe that the private sector is greedy and uncaring and that corporations cannot be trusted with the problems of poverty alleviation. From this perspective, profit motive and poverty alleviation do not mix easily or well. Aid agencies have come full circle in their own thinking. From aid focused on large infrastructure projects and public spending on education and health, they are also moving toward a belief that private-sector involvement is a crucial ingredient to poverty alleviation.

Historically, governments, aid agencies, nongovernmental organizations (NGOs), large firms, and the organized (formal and legal as opposed to extralegal) business sector all seem to have reached an implicit agreement: Market-based solutions cannot lead to poverty reduction and economic development. The dominant logic of each group restricts its ability to see the market opportunities at the BOP. The dominant logic of each group is different, but the conclusions are similar. During the last decade, each group has been searching for ways out of this self-imposed intellectual trap. To eradicate poverty, we have to break this implicit compact through a BOP-oriented involvement of the private sector.

We have to change our long-held beliefs about the BOP—our genetic code, if you will. The barrier that each group has to cross is different, but difficult nonetheless. However, once we cross the intellectual barrier, the opportunities become obvious. The BOP market also represents a major engine of growth and global trade, as we illustrate in our subsequent stories of MNCs and private firms from around the world.

THE NATURE OF THE BOP MARKET

The nature of the BOP market has characteristics that are distinct. We outline some of the critical dimensions that define this market. These characteristics must be incorporated into our thinking as we approach the BOP.

There Is Money at the BOP

The dominant assumption is that the poor have no purchasing power and therefore do not represent a viable market.

Let us start with the aggregate purchasing power in developing countries where most of the BOP market exists. Developing countries offer tremendous growth opportunities. Within these markets, the BOP represents a major opportunity. Take China as an example. With a population of 1.2 billion and an average per capita gross domestic product (GDP) of US $1,000, China currently represents a $1.2 trillion economy. However, the U.S. dollar equivalent is not a good measure of the demand for goods and services produced and consumed in China. If we convert the GDP-based figure into its dollar purchasing power parity (PPP), China is already a $5.0 trillion economy, making it the second largest economy behind the United States in PPP terms. Similarly, the Indian economy is worth about $3.0 trillion in PPP terms. If we take nine countries—China, India, Brazil, Mexico, Russia, Indonesia, Turkey, South Africa, and Thailand—collectively they are home to about 3 billion people, representing 70 percent of the developing world population. In PPP terms, this group's GDP is $12.5 trillion, which represents 90 percent of the developing world. It is larger than the GDP of Japan, Germany, France, the United Kingdom, and Italy combined. This is not a market to be ignored.

Now, consider the BOP within the broad developing country opportunity. The dominant assumption is that the poor do not have money to spend and, therefore, are not a viable market. Certainly, the buying power for those earning less than US $2 per day cannot be compared with the purchasing power of individuals in the developed nations. However, by virtue of their numbers, the poor represent a significant latent purchasing power that must be unlocked. For example, all too often, the poor tend to reside in high-cost ecosystems even within developing countries. In the shanty town of Dharavi, outside Mumbai, India, the poor pay a premium for everything from rice to credit. Compare the cost of everyday items of consumption between Dharavi and Warden Road (now redesignated B. Desai Road), a higher income neighborhood in Mumbai. The poverty penalty in Dharavi can be as high as 5 to 25 times what the rich pay for the same services (Table 15.2). Research indicates that this poverty penalty is universal, although the magnitude differs by country. The poverty penalty is the result of local monopolies, inadequate access, poor distribution, and strong traditional intermediaries. Large-scale private-sector businesses can "unlock this poverty penalty." For example, the poor in Dharavi pay 600 to 1,000 percent interest for credit from local moneylenders. A bank with access to this market can do well for itself by offering credit at 25 percent. Although 25 percent interest might look excessive to a casual observer, from the point of view of the BOP consumer, access to a bank decreases the cost of credit from 600 percent to 25 percent. The BOP consumer

TABLE 15.2.   The Poor and High-Cost Economic Ecosystems

Item	Dharavi	Warden Road	Poverty Premium
Credit (annual interest)	600–1,000%	12–18%	53.0
Municipal grade water (per cubic meter)	$1.12	$0.03	37.0
Phone call (per minute)	$0.04–0.05	$0.025	1.8
Diarrhea medication	$20.00	$2.00	10.0
Rice (per kg)	$0.28	$0.24	1.2

Source: Reprinted with permission from Harvard Business Review. "The Poor and High-Cost Economics Ecosystems." From "Serving the World's Poor Profitably" by C. K. Prahalad and Allen Hammond, September 2002. Copyright © 2002 by the Harvard Business School Publishing Corporation, all rights reserved.

is focused on the difference between the local moneylender rates and the rates that a commercial bank would charge. The bank can make a reasonable profit after adjusting for risk (10 percent over its traditional, top-of-the-pyramid customers). We argue later that the BOP consumers do not represent higher risk.

These cost disparities between BOP consumers and the rich in the same economy can be explained only by the fact that the poverty penalty at the BOP is a result of inefficiencies in access to distribution and the role of the local intermediaries. These problems can easily be cured if the organized private sector decides to serve the BOP. The organized sector brings with it the scale, scope of operations, and management know-how that can lead to efficiencies for itself and its potential consumers.

The poor also spend their earnings in ways that reflect a different set of priorities. For example, they might not spend disposable income on sanitation, clean running water, and better homes, but will spend it on items traditionally considered luxuries. Without legal title to land, these residents are unlikely to invest in improving their living quarters, much less the public facilities surrounding their homes. For example, in Dharavi, 85 percent of the households own a television set, 75 percent own a pressure cooker and blender, 56 percent own a gas stove, and 21 percent have telephones. In Bangladesh, women entrepreneurs with cell phones, which they rent out by the minute to other villagers, do a brisk business. It is estimated that the poor in Bangladesh spend as much as 7 percent of their income on connectivity.

Access to BOP Markets

The dominant assumption is that distribution access to the BOP markets is very difficult and therefore represents a major impediment for the participation of large firms and MNCs.

Urban areas have become a magnet for the poor. By 2015 there will be more than 225 cities in Africa, 903 in Asia, and 225 in Latin America. More than 368 cities in the developing world will have more than 1 million people in each. There will be at least 23 cities with more than 10 million residents. Collectively, these cities will account for about 1.5 to 2.0 billion people. Over 35 to 40 percent of these urban concentrations will be comprised of BOP consumers. The density of these settlements—about 15,000 people per hectare—will allow for intense distribution opportunities.

The rural poor represent a different problem. Access to distribution in rural markets continues to be problematic. Most of the rural markets are also inaccessible to audio and television signals and are often designated as "media dark." Therefore, the rural poor are not only denied access to products and services, but also to knowledge about what is available and how to use it. The spread of wireless connectivity among the poor might help reduce this problem. The ability to download movie and audio clips on wireless devices might allow firms to access traditionally "media dark" areas and provide consumers in these locations with newfound access to information about products and services. However, this is still an evolving phenomenon restricted to a few countries.

The BOP does not lend itself to a single distribution solution. Urban concentrations represent a problem distinct from that of the distribution access to dispersed rural communities. Worldwide, the cost of reach per consumer can vary significantly across countries. A wide variety of experiments are underway in these markets to find efficient methods of distributing goods and services. One such experiment, Project Shakti at Hindustan Lever Ltd. (HLL) in India, is a case in point. HLL created a direct distribution network in hard-to-reach locales (markets without distribution coverage through traditional distributors and dealers). HLL selected entrepreneurial women from these villages and trained them to become distributors, providing education, advice, and access to products to their villages. These village women entrepreneurs, called Shakti Amma ("empowered mother"), have unique knowledge about what the village needs and which products are in demand. They earn between Rs. 3,000 and 7,000 per month (U.S. $60–$150) and therefore create a new capacity to consume for themselves and their families. More important, these entrepreneurial women are increasingly becoming the educators and access points for the rural BOP consumers in their communities. This approach is not new. Avon is one of the largest cosmetics operations in Brazil and has used a similar approach by leveraging more than 800,000 "Avon ladies" as distributors to reach even the most remote regions of Amazonia.[1]

The BOP Markets Are Brand-Conscious

The dominant assumption is that the poor are not brand-conscious. On the contrary, the poor are very brand-conscious. They are also extremely value-conscious by necessity.

The experience of Casas Bahia in Brazil and Elektra in Mexico—two of the largest retailers of consumer durables, such as televisions, washing machines, radios, and other appliances—suggests that the BOP markets are very brand-conscious. Brand consciousness among the poor is universal. In a way, brand consciousness should not be a surprise. An aspiration to a new and different quality of life is the dream of everyone, including those at the BOP. Therefore, aspirational brands are critical for BOP consumers. However, BOP consumers are value buyers. They expect great quality at prices they can afford. The challenge to large firms is to make aspirational products affordable to BOP consumers. These consumers represent a new challenge for managers with increased pressure on costs of development, manufacturing, and distribution. As a result, BOP markets will force a new level of efficiency in the MNCs. . . .

The BOP Market Is Connected

Contrary to the popular view, BOP consumers are getting connected and networked. They are rapidly exploiting the benefits of information networks.

The spread of wireless devices among the poor is proof of a market at the BOP. For example, by the end of 2003, China had an installed base of 250 million cell phones. India had an installed base of approximately 30 million. The Indian market is growing at about 1.5 million handsets per month. The expectation is that India will reach 100 million handsets by 2005. Brazil already has 35 to 40 million. Both the current market size and the growth rates suggest that the BOP market is a critical factor in worldwide wireless growth. Telecommunications providers have made it easier for BOP consumers to purchase handsets and service through prepaid cards. The proliferation of wireless devices among the poor is universal, from Grameen Phone in Bangladesh to Telefonica in Brazil. Further, the availability of PCs in kiosks at a very low price per hour and the opportunity to videoconference using PCs are adding to the intensity of connectivity among those at the BOP. The net result is an unprecedented ability of BOP consumers to communicate with each other in several countries. The technology of wireless and PC connectivity is allowing the BOP population to be actively engaged in a dialogue with each other, with the firms from which they wish to purchase goods and services, and with the politicians who represent them.

Connectivity also allows the BOP consumers to establish new patterns of communication away from their villages. With cell phones and TV, the BOP consumer has unprecedented access to information as well as opportunities to engage in a dialogue with the larger community. As a result, word of mouth among BOP consumers is becoming a very potent force for assessing product quality, prices, and options available to them. The spread of good bargains as well as bad news can be very rapid. For example, in India, it appears that some consumers found worms in chocolates sold by Cadbury, a large and very successful MNC. Ten years ago this would have been a non-event, but with access to multiple and fiercely competitive TV channels, wireless, and Internet, the news spread so rapidly across India that not just managers within Cadbury but all managers involved in the "fast-moving consumer goods" industry were surprised and worried.[2]

BOP Consumers Accept Advanced Technology Readily

Contrary to popular belief, the BOP consumers accept advanced technology readily.

The spread of wireless devices, PC kiosks, and personal digital assistants (PDAs) at the BOP has surprised many a manager and researcher. For example, ITC, an Indian conglomerate, decided to connect Indian farmers with PCs in their villages. The ITC e-Choupal (literally, "village meeting place") allowed the farmers to check prices not only in the local auction houses (called mandis), but also prices of soybean futures at the Chicago Board of Trade. The e-Choupal network allowed the farmers access to information that allowed them to make decisions about how much to sell and when, thus improving their margins. Similarly, women entrepreneurs in southern India, given a PC kiosk in their villages, have learned to videoconference among themselves, across villages on all kinds of issues, from the cost of loans from various banks to the lives of their grandchildren in the

United States.[3] Chat rooms are full of activity that none of us could have imagined. Most interestingly, in Kerala, India, fishermen in traditional fishing boats, after a day of productive work, sell their catch to the highest bidders, using their cell phones to contact multiple possible landing sites along the Kerala coast. The simple boats, called catamarans, have not changed, but the entire process of pricing the catch and knowing how to sell based on reliable information has totally changed lives at the BOP.[4] The BOP consumers are more willing to adopt new technologies because they have nothing to forget. Moving to wireless from nothing is easier than moving to wireless from a strong tradition of efficient and ubiquitous landlines.

THE MARKET DEVELOPMENT IMPERATIVE

The task of converting the poor into consumers is one of market development. Market development involves both the consumer and the private-sector firm. We consider the risks and benefits to the private-sector firm later. Here, we reflect on the incentives for the BOP consumer, who is so far isolated from the benefits of access to regional and global markets, to participate. What are the benefits to the BOP consumer? . . .

Create the Capacity to Consume

To convert the BOP into a consumer market, we have to create the capacity to consume. Cash-poor and with a low level of income, the BOP consumer has to be accessed differently.

The traditional approach to creating the capacity to consume among the poor has been to provide the product or service free of charge. This has the feel of philanthropy. As mentioned previously, charity might feel good, but it rarely solves the problem in a scalable and sustainable fashion.

A rapidly evolving approach to encouraging consumption and choice at the BOP is to make unit packages that are small and, therefore, affordable. The logic is obvious. The rich use cash to inventory convenience. They can afford, for example, to buy a large bottle of shampoo to avoid multiple trips to the store. The poor have unpredictable income streams. Many subsist on daily wages and have to use cash conservatively. They tend to make purchases only when they have cash and buy only what they need for that day. Single-serve packaging—be it shampoo, ketchup, tea and coffee, or aspirin—is well suited to this population. A single-serve revolution is sweeping through the BOP markets. For example, in India, single-serve sachets have become the norm for a wide variety of products, as shown in Table 15.3.

The number of products sold in the single-serve format is rapidly increasing. The format is so popular that even firms producing high-end merchandise have to adopt it to remain viable long-term players in the growing markets. . . .

Measured in tons, the size of the Indian shampoo market is as large as the U.S. market. Large MNCs, such as Unilever and Procter & Gamble (P&G), are major participants in this market, as are large local firms. Because the poor are just as brand-conscious as the rich, it is possible to buy

TABLE 15.3. Creating the Capacity to Consume: Single-Serve Resolution

Single-Serve Value
at Retail

Rs.	$	Typical Products
0.50	0.01	Shampoo, confectionary, matches, tea
1.00	0.02	Shampoo, salt, biscuits, ketchup, fruit drink concentrate
2.00	0.04	Detergent, soap, mouth fresheners, biscuits, jams, spreads, coffee, spices
5.00	0.10	Biscuits, toothpaste, color cosmetics, fragrance, bread, cooking oil, skin cream

Note: Shampoo and biscuits are shown under different price ranges because these items are available in multiple single-serve and low unit pack quantities.

Pantene, a high-end shampoo from P&G, in a single-serve sachet in India. The entrepreneurial private sector has created a large market at the BOP; the penetration of shampoo in India is about 90 percent.

A similar approach to creating capacity to consume is through innovative purchase schemes. More BOP consumers in Brazil are able to buy appliances through Casas Bahia because the firm provides credit even for consumers with low and unpredictable income streams. Through a very sophisticated credit rating system coupled with counseling, Casas Bahia is able to provide access to high-quality appliances to consumers who could not otherwise afford them. At the same time, the firm ensures that its consumers are not overstretched. The default rate is very low at 8.5 percent, compared to over 15 percent for competitor firms. Casas Bahia has also created a new pool of repeat customers. Cemex, one of the world's largest cement companies in Mexico, follows a similar approach in its "do-it-yourself" business focused on the BOP market. The idea is to help the consumers learn to save and invest. By creating a pool of three women who save as a group and discipline and pressure each other to stay with the scheme, Cemex facilitates the process of consumption by bundling savings and access to credit with the ability to add a bathroom or a kitchen to their homes.

Creating the capacity to consume is based on three simple principles best described as the "Three As":

1. Affordability. Whether it is a single-serve package or novel purchasing schemes, the key is affordability without sacrificing quality or efficacy.
2. Access. Distribution patterns for products and services must take into account where the poor live as well as their work patterns. Most BOP consumers must work the full day before they can have enough cash to purchase the necessities for that day. Stores that close at 5:00 PM have no relevance to them, as their shopping begins after 7:00 PM. Further, BOP consumers cannot travel great distances. Stores must be easy to reach, often within a short walk. This calls for geographical intensity of distribution.

3. Availability. Often, the decision to buy for BOP consumers is based on the cash they have on hand at a given point in time. They cannot defer buying decisions. Availability (and therefore, distribution efficiency) is a critical factor in serving the BOP consumer.

Of course, the ideal is to create the capacity to earn more so that the BOP consumers can afford to consume more. The ITC e-Choupal story illustrates how farmers with access to the Internet and thereby access to the prices of commodities around the world can increase their incomes by 5 to 10 percent. These farmers can decide when and how much to sell based on their understanding of the likely price movements for their products. Modern technology not only allows them to realize better prices, but also to improve their logistics. The aggregation of food grains allows for efficiencies for both the farmer and the buyer.

By focusing on the BOP consumers' capacity to consume, private-sector businesses can create a new market. The critical requirement is the ability to invent ways that take into account the variability in the cash flows of BOP consumers that makes it difficult for them to access the traditional market for goods and services oriented toward the top of the pyramid.

The Need for New Goods and Services

The involvement of the private sector at the BOP can provide opportunities for the development of new products and services.

Amul, a dairy cooperative in India, has introduced good quality ice cream at less than $0.05 per serving, affordable by all at the BOP. This product is not only a source of enjoyment; the milk in it is also a source of nutrition for the poor. Now, Amul is planning to introduce a natural laxative-laced ice cream called "isabgol-enriched." It is too early to tell whether the product can be a success. However, the experimentation is what the game is about. Similarly, the popularization of pizza by the same company allows the poor to obtain an adequate quantity of protein.[5] PRODEM FFP, a Bolivian financial services company, has introduced smart automated teller machines (ATMs) that recognize fingerprints, use color-coded touch screens, and speak in three local languages. This technological innovation allows even illiterate BOP consumers to access, on a 24-hour basis, high-quality financial services.[6] Cemex, as we saw earlier, provides access to good quality housing. Through Tecnosol, the BOP consumers in rural Nicaragua have access to clean energy from renewable sources—solar and wind power. Previously, these consumers did not have access to grid-based electricity and were dependent on more expensive sources, such as kerosene and batteries. Now they have energy that is affordable enough to run their households. Casas Bahia not only sells appliances, but has also introduced a line of good quality furniture oriented toward the BOP markets. Furniture has become one of the fastest growing businesses for the company as well as a source of pride and satisfaction to its consumers.

Dignity and Choice

When the poor are converted into consumers, they get more than access to products and services. They acquire the dignity of attention and choices from the private sector that were previously reserved for the middle-class and rich.

The farmers we interviewed at an ITC e-Choupal were very clear. The traditional auctioning system at the government-mandated markets (mandis) did not offer them any choices. Once they went to a mandi, they had to sell their produce at the prices offered on that day. They could not wait for better prices or haul their produce back to their villages. More important, the local merchants who controlled the mandi were not very respectful of the farmers. One farmer remarked, "They make rude comments about my produce. They also raise the prices in the auction by $0.02 per ton. It is as if they have already determined the price you will get and they go through the motions of an auction. It used to be very demeaning." Not any longer. Now, the same farmers can access information on the Web across all the mandis and can decide where, when, and at which prices they want to sell. Similarly, women in self-help groups (SHGs) working with ICICI Bank in India also have had their dignity restored. As a group, they decide which borrowers and projects will receive loans. This involvement of women in leadership development and in learning about finances and bank operations has given them a new sense of personal worth. The single-serve revolution has created a revolutionary level of choice for consumers at the BOP. For example, the "switching costs" for the consumer are negligible because she can buy a sachet of shampoo or detergent or pickles; if she is not satisfied with her purchase she can switch brands the next day. Firms must continuously innovate and upgrade their products to keep customers interested in their brands, thereby improving quality and reducing costs.

Trust Is a Prerequisite

> *Both sides—the large firms and the BOP consumers—have traditionally not trusted each other. The mistrust runs deep. However, private-sector firms approaching the BOP market must focus on building trust between themselves and the consumers.*

This is clearly evident when one visits a Casas Bahia store. BOP consumers here venerate the founder, Mr. Klein, for giving them the opportunity to possess appliances that they could not otherwise afford. Although the shanty towns of Sao Paulo or Rio de Janeiro can be dangerous to outsiders, Casas Bahia trucks move freely around without worry. The same is true for Bimbo, the provider of fresh bread and other bakery products to the BOP consumers in Mexico. Bimbo[7] is the largest bakery in Mexico and its trucks have become symbols of trust between the BOP consumers and the firm. The truck drivers are so trusted that often the small store owners in the slums allow them to open their shops, stock them with bread, and collect cash from the cash boxes without supervision. Both Casas Bahia and Bimbo believe that the truck drivers who deliver their products to the BOP consumers are their ambassadors and neither company will outsource the delivery process. In fact, all managers at Bimbo must work as truck drivers for the company to become better educated about their customers.

MNCs often assume that the default rate among the poor is likely to be higher than that of their rich customers. The opposite is often true. The poor pay on time and default rates are very low. In the case of ICICI Bank, out of a customer base of 200,000, the default rate is less than 1 percent.

The default rate at Grameen Bank, a microfinance pioneer in Bangladesh, is less than 1.5 percent among 2,500,000 customers. The lessons are clear. Through persistent effort and the provision of world-class quality, private-sector businesses can create mutual trust and responsibility between their companies and BOP customers. Trust is difficult to build after 50 years of suspicion and prejudice based on little evidence and strong stereotyping.

BENEFITS TO THE PRIVATE SECTOR

We have identified the immediate benefits of treating the poor as consumers as well as the poverty alleviation process that will result as businesses focus on the BOP. It is clear that the consumers (the poor) benefit, but do the private-sector businesses benefit as well? The BOP market potential is huge: 4 to 5 billion underserved people and an economy of more than $13 trillion PPP. The needs of the poor are many. The case for growth opportunity in the BOP markets is easy to make. However, to participate in these markets, the private sector must learn to innovate. Traditional products, services, and management processes will not work.

Notes

1. Helen Cha, Polly Cline, Lilly Liu, Carrie Meek, and Michelle Villagomez. "Direct Selling and Economic Empowerment in Brazil: The Case of Avon." Edited by Anuradha Dayal-Gulati, Kellogg School of Management, 2003.
2. Syed Firdaus Ashraf. "Worms Found in Chocolate Packet." *rediff.com*, October 3, 2003.
3. See multiparty video conferencing, http://www.n-Logue.com.
4. Saritha Rai. "In Rural India, a Passage to Wirelessness." *The New York Times*, August 4, 2001.
5. Harish Damodaran. "Try Amul's New Ice Cream and—Be Relieved." *The Hindu Business Line*, September 8, 2002.
6. Roberto Hernandez and Yerina Mugica. "What Works: Prodem FFP's Multilingual Smart ATMs for Micro Finance." World Resources Institute, Digital Dividend Website, *digitaldividend .com*, August, 2003.
7. http://www.bimbo.com

The Great Non-Debate over International Sweatshops

IAN MAITLAND

In recent years there has been a dramatic growth in the contracting out of production by companies in the industrialized countries to suppliers in developing countries. This globalization of production has led to an emerging international division of labor in footwear and apparel in which companies like Nike and Reebok concentrate on product design and marketing but

From Ian Maitland, "The Great Non-Debate Over International Sweatshops," *British Academy of Management Annual Conference Proceedings*, September, 1997, pp. 240–265. Reprinted by permission of the author.

rely on a network of contractors in Indonesia, China, Central America, etc., to build shoes or sew shirts according to exact specifications and deliver a high quality good according to precise delivery schedules. As Nike's vice president for Asia has put it, "We don't know the first thing about manufacturing. We are marketers and designers."

The contracting arrangements have drawn intense fire from critics—usually labor and human rights activists. These "critics" (as I will refer to them) have charged that the companies are (by proxy) exploiting workers in the plants (which I will call "international sweatshops") of their suppliers. Specifically the companies stand accused of chasing cheap labor around the globe, failing to pay their workers living wages, using child labor, turning a blind eye to abuses of human rights, being complicit with repressive regimes in denying workers the right to join unions and failing to enforce minimum labor standards in the workplace, and so on.

The campaign against international sweatshops has largely unfolded on television and, to a lesser extent, in the print media. What seems like no more than a handful of critics has mounted an aggressive, media-savvy campaign which has put the publicity-shy retail giants on the defensive. The critics have orchestrated a series of sensational "disclosures" on prime time television exposing the terrible pay and working conditions in factories making jeans for Levi's or sneakers for Nike or Pocahontas shirts for Disney. One of the principal scourges of the companies has been Charles Kernaghan who runs the National Labor Coalition (NLC), a labor human rights group involving 25 unions. It was Kernaghan who, in 1996, broke the news before a Congressional committee that Kathie Lee Gifford's clothing line was being made by 13- and 14-year-olds working 20 hour days in factories in Honduras. Kernaghan also arranged for teenage workers from sweatshops in Central America to testify before Congressional committees about abusive labor practices. At one of these hearings, one of the workers held up a Liz Claiborne cotton sweater identical to ones she had sewn since she was a 13-year-old working 12 hours a day. According to a news report "[t]his image, accusations of oppressive conditions at the factory and the Claiborne logo played well on that evening's network news." The result has been a circus-like atmosphere—as in Roman circus where Christians were thrown to lions.

Kernaghan has shrewdly targeted the companies carefully cultivated public images. He has explained: "Their image is everything. They live and die by their image. That gives you a certain power over them." As a result, he says, "these companies are sitting ducks. They have no leg to stand on. That's why it's possible for a tiny group like us to take on a giant like Wal-Mart. You can't defend paying someone 31 cents an hour in Honduras. . . ."[1] Apparently most of the companies agree with Kernaghan. Not a single company has tried to mount a serious defense of its contracting practices. They have judged that they cannot win a war of soundbites with the critics. Instead of making a fight of it, the companies have sued for peace in order to protect their principal asset—their image.

Major U.S. retailers have responded by adopting codes of conduct on human and labor rights in their international operations. Levi-Strauss, Nike, Sears, J.C. Penney, Wal-Mart, Home Depot, and Philips Van-Heusen now have such codes. As Lance Compa notes, such codes are the result of a blend of humanitarian and pragmatic impulses: "Often the altruistic motive coincides with the 'bottom line' considerations related to brand name, company image, and other intangibles that make for core value to the firm."[2] Peter Jacobi, President of Global Sourcing for Levi-Strauss has advised: "If your company owns a popular brand, protect this priceless asset at all costs. Highly visible companies have any number of reasons to conduct their business not just responsibly but also in ways that cannot be portrayed as unfair, illegal, or unethical. This sets an extremely high standard since it must be applied to both company owned businesses and contractors. . . ."[3] And according to another Levi-Strauss spokesman, "In many respects, we're protecting our single largest asset: our brand image and corporate reputation."[4] Nike recently published the results of a generally favorable review of its international operations conducted by former American Ambassador Andrew Young.

Recently, a truce of sorts between the critics and the companies was announced on the White House lawn with President Clinton and Kathie Lee Gifford in attendance. A presidential task force, including representatives of labor unions, human rights groups and apparel companies like L.L. Bean and Nike, has come up with a set of voluntary standards which, it hopes, will be embraced by the entire industry. Companies that comply with the code will be entitled to use a "No Sweat" label.

OBJECTIVES OF THIS PAPER

In this confrontation between the companies and their critics, neither side seems to have judged it to be in its interest to seriously engage the issue at the heart of this controversy, namely: What are appropriate wages and labor standards in international sweatshops? As we have seen, the companies have treated the charges about sweatshops as a public relations problem to be managed so as to minimize harm to their public images. The critics have apparently judged that the best way to keep public indignation at the boiling point is to oversimplify the issue and treat it as a morality play featuring heartless exploiters and victimized third world workers. The result has been a great non-debate over international sweatshops. Paradoxically, if peace breaks out between the two sides, the chances that the debate will be seriously joined may recede still further. Indeed, there exists a real risk (I argue) that any such truce may be a collusive one that will come at the expense of the very third world workers it is supposed to help.

This paper takes up the issue of what are appropriate wages and labor standards in international sweatshops. Critics charge that the present arrangements are exploitative. I proceed by examining the specific charges of exploitation from the standpoints of both (a) their factual and (b) their ethical sufficiency. However, in the absence of any well-established consensus among business ethicists (or other thoughtful observers), I simultaneously use the investigation of sweatshops as a setting for trying to adjudicate between competing views about what those standards should be. My examination will pay particular attention to (but will not be limited to) labor conditions at the plants of Nike's suppliers in Indonesia. I have not personally visited any international sweatshops, and so my conclusions are based entirely on secondary analysis of the voluminous published record on the topic.

WHAT ARE ETHICALLY APPROPRIATE LABOR STANDARDS
IN INTERNATIONAL SWEATSHOPS?

What are ethically acceptable or appropriate levels of wages and labor standards in international sweatshops? The following three possibilities just about run the gamut of standards or principles that have been seriously proposed to regulate such policies.

1. *Home-country standards:* It might be argued (and in rare case has been) that international corporations have an ethical duty to pay the same wages and provide the same labor standards regardless of where they operate. However, the view that home-country standards should apply in host-countries is rejected by most business ethicists and (officially at least) by the critics of international sweatshops. Thus, Thomas Donaldson argues that "[by] arbitrarily establishing U.S. wage levels as the benchmark for fairness one eliminates the role of the international market in establishing salary levels, and this in turn eliminates the incentive U.S. corporations have to hire foreign workers."[5] Richard De George makes much the same argument: If there were a rule that said that "that American MNCs [multinational corporations] that wish to be ethical must pay the same wages abroad as they do at home, . . . [then] MNCs would have little incentive to move their manufacturing abroad; and if they did move abroad they would disrupt the local labor market with artificially high wages that bore no relation to the local standard or cost of living."[6]

2. *"Living wage" standard:* It has been proposed that an international corporation should, at a minimum, pay a "living wage." Thus De George says that corporations should pay a living wage "even when this is not paid by local firms."[7] However, it is hard to pin down what this means operationally. According to De George, a living wage should "allow the worker to live in dignity as a human being." In order to respect the human rights of its workers, he says, a corporation must pay "at least subsistence wages and as much above that as workers and their dependents need to live with reasonable dignity, given the general state of development of the society."[8] As we shall see, the living wage standard has become a rallying cry of the critics of international sweatshops. Apparently, De George believes that it is preferable for a corporation to provide no job at all than to offer one that pays less than a living wage. . . .

3. *Classical liberal standard:* Finally, there is what I will call the classical liberal standard. According to this standard a practice (wage or labor practice) is ethically acceptable if it is freely chosen by informed workers. For example, in a recent report the World Bank invoked this standard in connection with workplace safety. It said: "The appropriate level is therefore that at which the costs are commensurate with the value that informed workers place on improved working conditions and reduced risk."[9] Most business ethicists reject this standard on the grounds that there is some sort of market failure or the "background conditions" are lacking for markets to work effectively. Thus for Donaldson full (or near-full) employment is a prerequisite if workers are to make sound choices regarding workplace safety:

The average level of unemployment in the developing countries today exceeds 40 percent, a figure that has frustrated the application of neoclassical economic principles to the international economy on a score of issues. With full employment, and all other things being equal, market forces will encourage workers to make trade-offs between job opportunities using safety as a variable. But with massive unemployment, market forces in developing countries drive the unemployed to the jobs they are lucky enough to land, regardless of the safety.[10]

Apparently there are other forces, like Islamic fundamentalism and the global debt "bomb" that rule out reliance on market solutions, but Donaldson does not explain their relevance.[11] De George, too, believes that the necessary conditions are lacking for market forces to operate benignly. Without what he calls "background institutions" to protect the workers and the resources of the developing country (e.g., enforceable minimum wages) and/or greater equality of bargaining power exploitation is the most likely result.[12] "if American MNCs pay workers very low wages . . . they clearly have the opportunity to make significant profits."[13] De George goes on to make the interesting observation that "competition has developed among multinationals themselves, so that the profit margin has been driven down" and developing countries "can play one company against another."[14] But apparently that is not enough to rehabilitate market forces in his eyes.

THE CASE AGAINST INTERNATIONAL SWEATSHOPS

To many of their critics, international sweatshops exemplify the way in which the greater openness of the world economy is hurting workers. . . . Globalization means a transition from (more or less) regulated domestic economies to an unregulated world economy. The superior mobility of capital, and the essentially fixed, immobile nature of world labor, means a fundamental shift in bargaining power in favor of large international corporations. Their global reach permits them to shift production almost costlessly from one location to another. As a consequence, instead of being able to exercise some degree of control over companies operating within their borders, governments are now locked in a bidding war with one another to attract and retain the business of large multinational companies.

The critics allege that international companies are using the threat of withdrawal or withholding investment to pressure and workers to grant concessions. "Today [multinational companies] choose between workers in developing countries that compete against each other to depress wages to attract foreign investment." The result is a race for the bottom—a "destructive downward bidding spiral of the labor conditions and wages of workers throughout the world. . . ."[15] Thus critics charge that in Indonesia wages are deliberately held below the poverty level or subsistence in order to make the country a desirable location. The results of this competitive dismantling of worker protections, living standards, and worker rights are predictable: deteriorating work conditions, declining real incomes for workers, and a widening gap between rich and poor in developing countries. I turn next to the specific charges made by the critics of international sweatshops.

Unconscionable Wages

Critics charge that the companies, by their proxies, are paying "starvation wages" and "slave wages." They are far from clear about what wage level they consider to be appropriate. But they generally demand that companies pay a "living wage." Kernaghan has said that workers should be paid enough to support their families and they should get a "living wage" and "be treated like human beings."[16] . . . According to Tim Smith, wage levels should be "fair, decent or a living wage for an employee and his or her family." He has said that wages in the maquiladoras of Mexico averaged $35 to $55 a week (in or near 1993) which he calls a "shockingly substandard wage," apparently on the grounds that it "clearly does not allow an employee to feed and care for a family adequately."[17] In 1992, Nike came in for harsh criticism when a magazine published the pay stub of a worker at one of its Indonesian suppliers. It showed that the worker was paid at the rate of $1.03 per day which was reportedly less than the Indonesian government's figure for "minimum physical need."[18]

Immiserization Thesis

Former Labor Secretary Robert Reich has proposed as a test of the fairness of development policies that "Low-wage workers should become better off, not worse off, as trade and investment boost national income." He has written that "[i]f a country pursues policies that . . . limit to a narrow elite the benefits of trade, the promise of open commerce is perverted and drained of its rationale."[19] A key claim of the activists is that companies actually impoverish or immiserize developing country workers. They experience an absolute decline in living standards. This thesis follows from the claim that the bidding war among developing countries is depressing wages. . . .

Widening Gap Between Rich and Poor

A related charge is that international sweatshops are contributing to the increasing gap between rich and poor. Not only are the poor being absolutely impoverished, but trade in generating greater inequality within developing countries. Another test that Reich has proposed to establish the fairness of international trade is that "the gap between rich and poor should tend to narrow with development, not widen."[20] Critics charge that international sweatshops flunk that test. They say that the increasing GNPs of some developing countries simply mask a widening gap between rich and poor. "Across the world, both local and foreign elites are getting richer from the exploitation of the most vulnerable."[21] And, "The major adverse consequence of quickening global economic integration has been widening income disparity within almost all nations. . . ."[22] There appears to be a tacit alliance between the elites of both first and third worlds to exploit the most vulnerable, to regiment and control and conscript them so that they can create the material conditions for the elites' extravagant lifestyles.

Collusion with Repressive Regimes

Critics charge that, in their zeal to make their countries safe for foreign investment, Third World regimes, notably China and Indonesia, have stepped up their repression. Not only have these countries failed to enforce even the minimal labor rules on the books, but they have also used their military and police to break strikes and suppress independent unions. They have stifled political dissent, both to retain their hold on political power and to avoid any instability that might scare off foreign investors. Consequently, critics charge, companies like Nike are profiting from political repression. "As unions spread in [Korea and Taiwan], Nike shifted its suppliers primarily to Indonesia, China and Thailand, where they could depend on governments to suppress independent union-organizing efforts."[23]

EVALUATION OF THE CHARGES AGAINS INTERNATIONAL SWEATSHOPS

The critics' charges are undoubtedly accurate on a number of points: (1) There is no doubt that international companies are chasing cheap labor. (2) The wages paid by the international sweatshops are—by American standards—shockingly low. (3) Some developing country governments have tightly controlled or repressed organized labor in order to prevent it from disturbing the flow of foreign investment. Thus, in Indonesia, independent unions have been suppressed. (4) It is not unusual in developing countries for minimum wage levels to be lower than the official poverty level. (5) Developing country governments have winked at violations of minimum wage laws and labor rules. However, most jobs are in the informal sector and so largely outside the scope of government supervision. (6) Some suppliers have employed children or have subcontracted work to other producers who have done so. (7) Some developing country governments deny their people basic political rights. China is the obvious example; Indonesia's record is pretty horrible but had shown steady improvement until the last two years. But on many of the other counts, the critics charges appear to be seriously inaccurate. And, even where the charges are accurate, it is not self-evident that the practices in question are improper or unethical, as we see next.

Wages and Conditions

Even the critics of international sweatshops do not dispute that the wages they pay are generally higher than—or at least equal to—comparable wages in the labor markets where they operate. According to the International Labor Organization (ILO), multinational companies often apply standards relating to wages, benefits, conditions of work, and occupational safety and health, which both exceed statutory requirements and those practiced by local firms.[24] The ILO also says that wages and working conditions in so-called Export Processing Zones (EPZs) are often equal to or higher than jobs outside. The World Bank says that the poorest workers in developing countries work in the informal sector where they often earn less than half what a formal sector employee earns. Moreover, "informal and rural workers often must work under more hazardous and insecure conditions than their formal sector counterparts."[25]

The same appears to hold true for the international sweatshops. In 1996, young women working in the plant of a Nike supplier in Serang, Indonesia were earning the Indonesian legal minimum wage of 5,200 rupiahs or about $2.28 each day. As a report in the *Washington Post* pointed out, just earning the minimum wage put these workers among higher-paid Indonesians: "In Indonesia, less than half the working population earns the minimum wage, since about half of all adults here are in farming, and the typical farmer would make only about 2,000 rupiahs each day."[26] The workers in the Serang plant reported that they save about three-quarters of their pay.

A 17-year-old woman said: "I came here one year ago from central Java. I'm making more money than my father makes." This woman also said that she sent about 75 percent of her earnings back to her family on the farm.[27] Also in 1996, a Nike spokeswoman estimated that an entry-level factory worker in the plant of a Nike supplier made five times what a farmer makes.[28] Nike's chairman, Phil Knight, likes to teasingly remind critics that the average worker in one of Nike's Chinese factories is paid more than a professor at Beijing University.[29] There is also plentiful anecdotal evidence from non-Nike sources. A worker at the Taiwanese-owned King Star Garment Assembly plant in Honduras told a reporter that he was earning seven times what he earned in the countryside.[30] In Bangladesh, the country's fledgling garment industry was paying women who had never worked before between $40 and $55 a month in 1991. That compared with a national per capita income of about $200 and the approximately $1 a day earned by many of these women's husbands as day laborers or rickshaw drivers.[31]

The same news reports also shed some light on the working conditions in sweatshops. According to the *Washington Post*, in 1994 the Indonesian office of the international accounting firm Ernst & Young surveyed Nike workers concerning worker pay, safety conditions and attitudes toward the job. The auditors pulled workers off the assembly line at random and asked them questions that the workers answered anonymously. The survey of 25 workers at Nike's Serang plant found that 23 thought the hours and overtime hours too high. None of the workers reported[32] that they had been discriminated against. Thirteen said the working environment was the key reason they worked at the Serang plant while eight cited salary and benefits. The *Post* report also noted that the Serang plant closes for about ten days each year for Muslim holidays. It quoted Nike officials and the plant's Taiwanese owners as saying that 94 percent of the workers had returned to the plant following the recent break. . . .

There is also the mute testimony of the lines of job applicants outside the sweatshops in Guatemala and Honduras. According to Lucy Martinez-Mont, in Guatemala the sweatshops are conspicuous for the long lines of young people waiting to be interviewed for a job.[33] Outside the gates of the industrial park in Honduras that Rohter visited "anxious on-lookers are always waiting, hoping for a chance to at least fill out a job application for [employment at one of the apparel plants].[34]

The critics of sweatshops acknowledge that workers have voluntarily taken their jobs, consider themselves lucky to have them, and want to keep them. . . . But they go on to discount the workers' views as the product of confusion or ignorance, and/or they just argue that the workers' views are beside the point. Thus, while "it is undoubtedly true" that Nike has given jobs to thousands of people who wouldn't be working otherwise, they say that "neatly skirts the fundamental human-rights issue raised by these production arrangements that are now spreading all across the world."[35] Similarly the NLC's Kernaghan says that "[w]hether workers think they are better off in the assembly plants than elsewhere is not the real issue."[36] Kernaghan, and Jeff Ballinger of the AFL-CIO, concede that the workers desperately need these jobs. But "[t]hey say they're not asking that U.S. companies stop operating in these countries. They're asking that workers be paid a living wage and treated like human beings."[37] Apparently these workers are victims of what Marx called false consciousness, or else they would grasp that they are being exploited. According to Barnet and Cavanagh, "For many workers . . . exploitation is not a concept easily comprehended because the alternative prospects for earning a living are so bleak."[38]

Immiserization and Inequality

The critics' claim that the countries that host international sweatshops are marked by growing poverty and inequality is flatly contradicted by the record. In fact, many of those countries have experienced sharp increases in living standards—for all strata of society. In trying to attract investment in simple manufacturing, Malaysia and Indonesia and, now, Vietnam and China, are retracing the industrialization path already successfully taken by East Asian countries like Taiwan, Korea, Singapore and Hong Kong. These four countries got their start by producing labor-intensive manufactured goods (often electrical and electronic components, shoes, and garments) for export markets. Over time they graduated to the export of higher value-added items that are skill-intensive and require a relatively developed industrial base.[39]

As is well known, these East Asian countries achieved growth rates exceeding eight percent for a quarter century. . . . The workers in these economies achieved essentially full employment in the 1960s. Real wages rose by as much as a factor of four. Absolute poverty fell. And income inequality remained at low to moderate levels. It is true that in the initial stages the rapid growth generated only moderate increases in wages. But once essentially full employment was reached, and what economists call the Fei-Ranis turning point was reached, the increased demand for labor resulted in the bidding up of wage as firms competed for a scarce labor supply.

Interestingly, given its historic mission as a watchdog for international labor standards, the ILO had embraced this development model. It recently noted that the most successful developing economies, in terms of output and employment growth, have been "those who best exploited emerging opportunities in the global economy."[40] An "export oriented policy is vital in countries that are starting on the industrialization path and have large surpluses of cheap labor." Countries which have succeeded in attracting foreign direct investment (FDI) have experienced rapid growth in manufacturing output and exports. The successful attraction of foreign investment in plant and equipment "can be a powerful spur to rapid industrialization and employment creation." "At low levels of industrialization, FDI in garments and shoes and some types of consumer electronics can be very useful for creating employment and opening the economy to international markets; there may be some entrepreneurial skills created in simple activities like garments (as has happened in Bangladesh). Moreover, in some cases, such as Malaysia, the investors may strike deeper roots and invest in more capital-intensive technologies as wages rise."

According to the World Bank, the rapidly growing Asian economies (including Indonesia) "have also been unusually successful at sharing the fruits of their growth."[41] In fact, while inequality in the West has been growing, it has been shrinking in the Asian economies. They are the only economies in the world to have experienced high growth *and* declining inequality, and they also show shrinking gender gaps in education. . . .

Profiting from Repression?

What about the charge that international sweatshops are profiting from repression? It is undeniable that there is repression in many of the countries where sweatshops are located. But economic development appears to be relaxing that repression rather than strengthening its grip. The companies are supposed to benefit from government policies (e.g., repression of unions) that hold down labor costs. However, as we have seen, the wages paid by the international sweatshops already match or exceed the prevailing local wages. Not only that, but incomes in the East Asian economies, and in Indonesia, have risen rapidly. . . .

The critics, however, are right in saying that the Indonesian government has opposed independent unions in the sweatshops out of fear they would lead to higher wages and labor unrest. But the government's fear clearly is that unions might drive wages in the modern industrial sector *above* market-clearing levels—or, more exactly, further above market. It is ironic that critics like Barnet and Cavanagh would use the Marxian term "reserve army of the unemployed." According to Marx, capitalists deliberately maintain high levels of unemployment in order to control the working class. But the Indonesian government's policies (e.g., suppression of unions, resistance to a higher minimum wage and lax enforcement of labor rules) have been directed at achieving exactly the opposite result. The government appears to have calculated that high unemployment is a greater threat to its hold on power. I think we can safely take at face value its claims that its policies are genuinely intended to help the economy create jobs to absorb the massive numbers of unemployed and underemployed.[42]

LABOR STANDARDS IN INTERNATIONAL SWEATSHOPS: PAINFUL TRADE-OFFS

Who but the grinch could begrudge paying a few additional pennies to some of the world's poorest workers? There is no doubt that the rhetorical force of the critics' case against international sweatshops rests on this apparently self-evident proposition. However, higher wages and improved labor standards are not free. After all, the critics themselves attack companies for chasing cheap labor. It follows that, if labor in developing countries is made more expensive (say, as the result of pressure by the critics), then those countries will receive less foreign investment, and fewer jobs will be created there. Imposing higher wages may deprive those countries of the one comparative advantage they enjoy, namely low-cost labor.

We have seen that workers in most "international sweatshops" are already relatively well paid. Workers in the urban, formal sectors of developing countries commonly earn more than twice what informal and rural workers get. Simply earning the minimum wage put the young women making Nike shoes in Serang in the top half of the income distribution in Indonesia. Accordingly, the critics are in effect calling for a *widening* of the economic disparity that already greatly favors sweatshop workers.

By itself that may or may not be ethically objectionable. But these higher wages come at the expense of the incomes and the job opportunities of much poorer workers. As economists explain, higher wages in the formal sector reduce employment there and (by increasing the supply of labor) depress incomes in the informal sector. The case against requiring above-market wages for international sweatshop workers is essentially the same as the case against other measures that artificially raise labor costs, like the minimum wage. In Jagdish Bhagwati's words, "Requiring a minimum wage in an overpopulated, developing country may actually be morally wicked. A minimum wage might help the unionized, industrial proletariat, while limiting the ability to save and invest rapidly which is necessary to draw more of the unemployed and nonunionized rural poor into gainful employment and income."[43] The World Bank makes the same point: "Minimum wages may help the most poverty-stricken workers in industrial countries, but they clearly do not in developing nations. . . . The workers whom minimum wage legislation tries to protect—urban formal workers—already earn much more than the less favored majority. . . . And inasmuch as minimum wage and other regulations discourage formal employment by increasing wage and nonwage costs, they hurt the poor who aspire to formal employment."[44]

The story is no different when it comes to labor standard other than wages. If standards are set too high they will hurt investment and employment. The World Bank report points out that "[r]educing hazards in the workplace is costly, and typically the greater the reduction the more it costs. Moreover, the costs of compliance often fall largely on employees through lower wages or reduced employment. As a result, setting standards too high can actually lower workers' welfare. . . ."[45] Perversely, if the higher standards advocated by critics retard the growth of formal sector jobs, then that will trap more informal and rural workers in jobs which are far more hazardous and insecure than those of their formal sector counterparts.

The critics consistently advocate policies that will benefit better-off workers at the expense of worse-off ones. If it were within their power, it appears that they could reinvent the labor markets of much of Latin America. Alejandro Portes' description seems to be on the mark: "In Mexico, Brazil, Peru, and other Third World countries, [unlike East Asia], there are powerful independent unions representing the protected sector of the working class. Although their rhetoric is populist and even radical, the fact is that they tend to represent the better-paid and more stable fraction of the working class. Alongside, there toils a vast, unprotected proletariat, employed by informal enterprises and linked, in ways hidden from public view, with modern sector firms." . . .

Of course, it might be objected that trading off workers' rights for more jobs is unethical. But, so far as I can determine, the critics have not made this argument. Although they sometimes implicitly accept the existence of the trade-off (we saw that they attack Nike for chasing cheap labor), their public statements are silent on the lost or foregone jobs from higher wages and better labor standards. At other times, they imply or claim that improvements in workers' wages and conditions are essentially free. . . .

In summary, the result of the ostensibly humanitarian changes urged by critics are likely to be (1) reduced employment in the formal or modern sector of the economy, (2) lower incomes in the informal sector, (3) less investment and so slower economic growth, (4) reduced exports, (5) greater inequality and poverty.

CONCLUSION: THE CASE FOR NOT EXCEEDING MARKET STANDARDS

It is part of the job description of business ethicists to exhort companies to treat their workers better (otherwise what purpose do they serve?). So it will have come as no surprise that both the business ethicists whose views I summarized at the beginning of the paper—Thomas Donaldson and Richard De George—objected to letting the market alone determine wages and labor standards in multinational companies. Both of them proposed criteria for setting wages that might occasionally "improve" on the outcomes of the market.

Their reasons for rejecting market determination of wages were similar. They both cited conditions that allegedly prevent international markets from generating ethically acceptable results. Donaldson argued that neoclassical economic principles are not applicable to international business because of high unemployment rates in developing countries. And De George argued that, in an unregulated international market, the gross inequality of bargaining power between workers and companies would lead to exploitation.

But this paper has shown that attempts to improve on market outcomes may have unforeseen tragic consequences. We saw how raising the wages of workers in international sweatshops might wind up penalizing the most vulnerable workers (those in the informal sectors of developing countries) by depressing their wages and reducing their job opportunities in the formal sector. Donaldson and De George cited high unemployment and unequal bargaining power as conditions that made it necessary to bypass or override the market determination of wages. However, in both cases, bypassing the market in order to prevent exploitation may aggravate these conditions. As we have seen, above-market wages paid to sweatshop workers may discourage further investment and so perpetuate high unemployment. In turn, the higher unemployment may weaken the bargaining power of workers vis-à-vis employers. Thus such market imperfections seem to call for more reliance on market forces rather than less. Likewise, the experience of the newly industrialized East Asian economies suggests that the best cure for the ills of sweatshops is more sweatshops. But most of the well-intentioned policies that improve on market outcomes are likely to have the opposite effects.

Where does this leave the international manager? If the preceding analysis is correct, then it follows that it is ethically permissible to pay market wage rates in developing countries (and to provide employment conditions appropriate for the level of development). That holds true even if the wages pay less than so-called living wages or subsistence or even (conceivably) the local minimum wage. The appropriate test is not whether the wage reaches some predetermined standard, but whether it is freely accepted by (reasonably) informed workers. The workers themselves are in the best position to judge whether the wages offered are superior to their next best alternatives. (The same logic applies *mutatis mutandis* to workplace labor standards.)

Indeed, not only is it ethically acceptable for a company to pay market wages, but it may be ethically unacceptable for it to pay wages that exceed market levels. That will be the case if the company's above-market wages set precedents for other international companies which raise labor costs to the point of discouraging foreign investment. Furthermore, companies may have a social responsibility to transcend their own narrow preoccupation with protecting their brand image and to publicly defend a system which has greatly improved the lot of millions of workers in developing countries.

Notes

1. Steven Greenhouse, "A Crusader Makes Celebrities Tremble." *New York Times* (June 18, 1996) p. B4.
2. Lance A. Compa and Tashia Hinchliffe Darricarrere, "Enforcement Through Corporate Codes of Conduct," in Compa and Stephen F. Diamond, *Human Rights, Labor Rights, and International Trade* (Philadelphia: University of Pennsylvania Press, 1996) p. 193.
3. Peter Jacobi, in Martha Nichols, "Third-World Families at Work: Child Labor or Child Care." *The Harvard Business Review* (January-February, 1993).
4. David Sampson, in Robin G. Givhan, "A Stain on Fashion; The Garment Industry Profits from Cheap Labor." *Washington Post* (September 12, 1995), p. B1.
5. Thomas Donaldson, *Ethics of International Business* (New York: Oxford University Press, 1989), p. 98.
6. Richard De George, *Competing with Integrity in International Business* (New York: Oxford University Press, 1993), p. 79.
7. Ibid., pp. 356–357.
8. Ibid., p. 78.
9. World Bank, *World Development Report 1995*, *"Workers in an Integrating World Economy"* (Oxford University Press, 1995), p. 77.
10. Donaldson, op. cit., p. 115.
11. Ibid., p. 150.
12. De George, op. cit., p. 48.
13. Ibid., p. 358.
14. Ibid.
15. Terry Collingsworth, J. William Goold, Pharis J. Harvey, "Time for a Global New Deal," *Foreign Affairs* (January-February 1994), p.8.
16. William B. Falk, "Dirty Little Secrets," *Newsday* (June 16, 1996).
17. Tim Smith, "The Power of Business for Human Rights," *Business & Society Review* (January, 1994), p. 36.
18. Jeffrey Ballinger, "The New Free Trade Heel," *Harper's Magazine* (August 1992), pp. 46–47. As in many developing countries, Indonesia's minimum wage, . . . is less than poverty level." Nina Baker, "The Hidden Hands of Nike," *Oregonian* (August 9, 1992).
19. Robert B. Reich, "Escape from the Global Sweatshop. Capitalism's Stake in Uniting the Workers of the World," *Washington Post* (May 22, 1994). Reich's test is intended to apply in developing countries "where democratic institutions are weak or absent."
20. Ibid.
21. Kenneth P. Hutchinson, "Third World Growth," *Harvard Business Review* (November-December 1994).
22. Robin Broad and John Cavanagh, "Don't Neglect the Impoverished South," *Foreign Affairs* (December 22, 1995).
23. John Cavanagh and Robin Broad, "Global Reach: Workers Fight the Multinationals," *The Nation* (March 18, 1996), p. 21. See also Bob Herbert, "Nike's Bad Neighborhood," *New York Times* (June 14, 1996).
24. International Labor Organization, *World Employment 1995* (Geneva: ILO, 1995), p. 73.
25. World Bank, op. cit., p. 5.
26. Keith B. Richburg and Anne Swarsdon, "U.S. Industry Overseas: Sweatshop or Job Source?: Indonesians Praise Work at Nike Factory," *Washington Post* (July 28, 1996).
27. Richburg and Swarsdon, op. cit. The 17-year-old was interviewed in the presence of managers. For other reports that workers remit home large parts of their earnings see Seth Mydans, "Tangerang Journal; For Indonesian Workers at Nike Plant: Just Do It," *New York Times* (August 9, 1996), and Nina Baker, op. cit.

28. Donna Gibbs, Nike spokeswoman on ABC's *World News Tonight,* June 6, 1996.
29. Mark Clifford, "Trading in Social Issues: Labor Policy and International Trade Regulations," *World Press Review* (June 1994), p. 36.
30. Larry Rohter, "To U.S. Critics, a Sweatshop; for Hondurans, a Better Life," *New York Times* (July 18, 1996).
31. Marcus Brauchli, "Garment Industry Booms in Bangladesh," *Wall Street Journal* (August 6, 1991).
32. Richburg and Swarsdon, op. cit.
33. Lucy Martinez-Mont, "Sweatshops Are Better Than No Shops," *Wall Street Journal* (June 25, 1996).
34. Rohter, op. cit.
35. Richard Barnet and Cavanagh, 1995. *Global Dreams,* N.Y. Simon and Schuster.
36. Rohter, op. cit.
37. William B. Falk, "Dirty Little Secrets," *Newsday* (June 16, 1996).
38. Richard Barnet and John Cavanagh, "Just Undo It: Nike's Exploited Workers," *New York Times* (February 13, 1994).
39. Saroh Kuruvilla, "Linkages Between Industrialization Strategies and Industrial Relations/ Human Resources Policies: Singapore, Malaysia, The Philippines, and India," *Industrial & Labor Relations Review* (July 1996), p. 637.
40. The ILO's Constitution (of 1919) mentions that ". . . the failure of any nation to adopt humane conditions of labor is an obstacle in the way of other nations which desire to improve the conditions in their own countries." ILO, *World Employment 1995,* p. 74.
41. World Bank, *The East Asian Miracle* (New York: Oxford University Press, 1993), p. 2.
42. Gideon Rachman, "Wealth in Its Grasp, a Survey of Indonesia, " *Economist* (April 17, 1993), pp. 14–15.
43. Jagdish Bhagwati and Robert E. Hudec, eds., *Fair Trade and Harmonization* (Cambridge, MA: MIT Press, 1996), vol. 1, p. 2.
44. World Bank, *Workers in an Integrating World Economy,* p. 75.
45. Ibid., p. 77. As I have noted, the report proposes that the "appropriate level is therefore that at which the costs are commensurate with the value that informed workers place on improved working conditions and reduced risk . . ." (p. 77)

Biographical Information

GEETA ANAND is an investigative reporter and feature writer for *The Wall Street Journal*. Formerly a political reporter for the *Boston Globe*, she now specializes in health and biotechnology. In 2003, she shared a staff Pulitzer Prize for explanatory journalism for a series of stories about scandals in corporate America. Born in Mumbai, India, Ms. Anand received a bachelor's degree from Dartmouth. She recently published a book entitled *The Cure* (2006) with HarperCollins.

MARK BAKER is an associate professor at the McCombs School of Business of the University of Texas at Austin. His research interests include international business, trade, and law.

FREDERICK BIRD is a professor and research chair at Concordia University in Montreal, where he teaches comparative ethics. He is the author of *The Muted Conscience: Moral Silence and the Practice of Ethics in Business*, co-author of *Good Management: Business Ethics in Action*, and co-editor of *International Businesses and the Dilemmas of Development, International Businesses and the Challenges of Poverty in the Developing World*, and *Just Business Practices in a Diverse and Developing World: Essays on International Businesses and Global Responsibilities*. Professor Bird has also written numerous articles on business ethics, comparative ethics, and contemporary religious movements.

SISSELA BOK was born in Sweden and educated in Switzerland, France, and the United States. She received her Ph.D. in Philosophy from Harvard University in 1970. Formerly a professor of Philosophy at Brandeis University, Bok is currently a Distinguished Fellow at the Harvard Center for Population and Development Studies. She is the author of numerous articles on ethics, literature, and biography, and of *Lying: Moral Choice in Private and Public Life* (1978); *Secrets: On the Ethics of Concealment and Revelation* (1982); *A Strategy for Peace: Human Values and the Threat of War* (1989); *Alva Myrdal: A Daughter's Memoir* (1991); *Common Values* (1996); and *Mayhem, Violence as Public Entertainment* (1998). In 2001, she received the St. Botolph Foundation Award for Distinction in Literature.

NORMAN E. BOWIE is the Elmer L. Andersen Chair in Corporate Responsibility at the University of Minnesota. He has written extensively on business ethics. His latest books are *Business Ethics: A Kantian Perspective* and *Ethical Theory and Business*, sixth edition, co-edited with Thomas L. Beauchamp. He has been a Fellow at Harvard's Program in Ethics and the Professions. He is past president of the Society for Value Inquiry, the Society for Business Ethics, and the former executive secretary of the American Philosophical Association. He also served a term as chair of the Department of Strategic Management and Organization at the University of Minnesota.

GEORGE G. BRENKERT is Professor and Director of the Georgetown Business Ethics Institute at Georgetown University. He received his Ph.D. from the University of Michigan. He specializes in the areas of business ethics, ethics, and social and political philosophy. He is currently writing a book on marketing ethics. His latest books are *Ethical Theory and Business*, seventh edition, co-edited with Thomas L. Beauchamp, and *Guide to Business Ethics*. Professor Brenkert serves as editor-in-chief of *Business Ethics Quarterly*.

ANDREW CARNEGIE was born in Scotland in 1835 and emigrated to the United States with his family in 1848. He worked in a cotton factory, was a telegraph operator, and introduced sleeping cars for the Pennsylvania Railroad. Foreseeing the future demand for iron and steel, he left the railroad, founded the Keystone Bridge Company, and began to amass his fortune. The Carnegie companies were incorporated into U.S. Steel in 1901, when Carnegie retired and devoted himself to philanthropy.

ALBERT CARR was born in 1902 and educated at the University of Chicago, Columbia University, and the London School of Economics. He was active in business and politics, serving as economic advisor to President Truman. He wrote numerous books and articles, among them *Truman, Stalin, and Peace*, and *Business as a Game*. In addition, he authored several films and television plays. He died in 1971.

JOANNE B. CIULLA holds the Coston Family Chair in Leadership and Ethics at the Jepson School of Leadership Studies at the University of Richmond. She was also the first UNESCO Chair in Leadership Studies at the United Nations International Leadership Academy. A Ph.D. in philosophy, she is author of *The Working Life: The Promise and Betrayal of Modern Work* (Times Books, 2000); *Ethics, The Heart of Leadership* (Praeger, 1998); *The Ethics of Leadership* (Harcourt Brace, 2001); and *Honest Work: A Business Ethics Reader* (Oxford University Press, 2006).

JOHN C. COFFEE, JR. is the Adolf A. Berle Professor of Law at Columbia Law School. He is a member or former member of numerous influential organizations, including the Economic Advisory Board to NASDAQ and the Legal Advisory Committee to the Board of Directors of the New York Stock Exchange. Professor Coffee's primary research interests are corporations, securities regulation, class actions, criminal law, and white-collar crime. He received his LL.B. from Yale and LL.M (in taxation) from New York University.

ROGER CRISP is a fellow and tutor in Philosophy at St. Anne's College, Oxford. He is the author of *Mill on Utilitarianism* and editor of *Utilitas*. He has edited two collections of papers on virtue ethics, translated Aristotle's *Ethics*, and has written articles in several areas of philosophy.

RICHARD T. DE GEORGE is University Distinguished Professor of Philosophy, Business Administration, and Russian and East European Studies, and Director of the International Center for Ethics in Business at the University of Kansas. He is the author of many books, including *Business Ethics* and *Competing with Integrity in International Business*.

THOMAS DONALDSON is the Mark O. Winkelman Professor at the Wharton School of the University of Pennsylvania, where he is the director of the Wharton Ethics Program. From 1990 to 1996 he held the position of the John F. Connelly Professor of Business Ethics in the School of Business, Georgetown University. Professor Donaldson has written broadly in the area of business values and professional ethics including *The Ties That Bind: A Social Contract Approach to Business Ethics*, co-authored with Thomas W. Dunfee (Harvard University Business School Press, 1999), and *Ethics in International Business* (Oxford University Press, 1989).

THOMAS W. DUNFEE is vice dean and director of the Wharton Undergraduate Division, University of Pennsylvania. He is the Kolodny Professor of Social Responsibility and professor of Legal Studies at Wharton. His current research interests focus on the role of morality in markets, how social contract theory can enhance ethical business practice, and global business ethics.

William J. Ellos, S.J., until recently held the Charles Miller Professorship, teaching professional ethics at Saint Mary's University in San Antonio, Texas, and is a Fellow of the MacLean Center for Clinical Medical Ethics at the University of Chicago.

Barbara Ehrenreich is a freelance journalist and the author of the bestseller *Nickel and Dimed: On (not) Getting by in America,* an insight into the plight of low-wage workers in America. She received a BA in Physics from Reed College, as well as a Ph.D. in Cell Biology from Rockefeller University. She has served as a guest columnist in periodicals such as *The New York Times* and *Harper's Magazine,* in which she published "Welcome to Cancerland," an article on her fight against breast cancer and the breast cancer industry.

Richard A. Epstein is the James Parker Hall Distinguished Service Professor of Law at The University of Chicago Law School, and the Peter and Kristen Bedford Senior Fellow at the Hoover Institution. He has been a member of the American Academy of Arts and Sciences since 1985 and a Senior Fellow of the Center for Clinical Medical Ethics at the University of Chicago Medical School, also since 1983. At present he is a director of the John M. Olin Program in Law and Economics. His books include, among many, *Skepticism and Freedom: A Modern Case for Classical Liberalism* (University of Chicago, 2003); *Cases and Materials on Torts,* 7th edition (Aspen Law & Business, 2000); *Torts* (Aspen Law & Business, 1999); *Principles for a Free Society: Reconciling Individual Liberty with the Common Good* (Perseus Books, 1998); *Mortal Peril: Our Inalienable Rights to Health Care* (Addison-Wesley, 1997); and *Simple Rules for a Complex World* (Harvard, 1995).

Barnaby Feder is a science and technology reporter for *The New York Times.* His current beat encompasses information technology, materials sciences, and environmental and biology-based innovations. He joined the *Times* in 1980 as a technology reporter covering subjects such as the early commercial stages of biotechnology and, while based in London, business news in the United Kingdom, Ireland, Scandinavia, and the Benelux countries. From October 1992 until August 1998, he was based in Chicago, where he handled most of the paper's coverage of agricultural biotechnology. He has also worked at *World Business Weekly* and *Energy User News.* He is a graduate of Williams College and the University of California at Berkeley Law School.

Lee Anne Fennell is a Professor of Law and Associate Director of the Illinois Program in Law and Economics at the University of Illinois College of Law. Her teaching and research interests include property, land use, housing, social welfare law, state and local government law, and public finance. Her work incorporates law and economics, including behavioral perspectives and strategic interactions. Professor Fennell's scholarship has appeared in the *Harvard Law Review, Yale Law Journal, Texas Law Review,* and *Northwestern University Law Review,* among other law journals. She is currently writing a book for Yale University Press with the working title of *Property Unbound: Strategy and Choice in Metropolitan Neighborhoods.*

Robert H. Frank is the Henrietta Johnson Louis Professor of Management and Professor of Economics in the Johnson Graduate School of Management and Department of Economics at Cornell University. His books include *Choosing the Right Pond, Passions within Reason, Luxury Fever,* and *The Winner-Take-All Society* (with Phillip Cook), which was named a Notable Book of the Year by *The New York Times,* and was included in *Business Week*'s list of the ten best books for 1995.

R. EDWARD FREEMAN is Elis and Signe Olsson Professor of Business Administration and director of the Olsson Center for Applied Ethics at the Darden Graduate School of Business Administration at the University of Virginia, and a professor of Religious Studies. His books include *Strategic Management: A Stakeholder Approach, Ethics and Agency Theory* (with Norman Bowie), *Business Ethics: The State of the Art, Corporate Strategy and the Search for Ethics* (with Dan Gilbert, Jr.), and most recently, *Environmentalism and the New Logic of Business: How Firms Can be Profitable and Leave Our Children a Living Planet.*

MILTON FRIEDMAN was a senior research fellow at the Hoover Institution, Stanford University, and the Paul Snowden Russell Distinguished Service Professor of Economics Emeritus at the University of Chicago. He was widely regarded as the leader of the Chicago School of monetary economics. He was the author of *Capitalism and Freedom* and co-author of *A Monetary History of the United States* and *Free to Choose.* He was awarded the Nobel Prize for Economics in 1976. He passed away in November 2006.

ANDREW GUSTAFSON is the Associate Professor of Business Ethics and Society at Creighton University. He received his Ph.D. in philosophy from Marquette University. Dr. Gustafson's research interests include John Stewart Mill, utilitarianism, and philosophy of religion.

STEWART HAMILTON is a Professor of Accounting and Finance at the International Institute for Management Development (IMD) in Switzerland. He combines a 20-year career in public accounting practice with teaching accounting, finance, and law at universities in Canada and the United Kingdom. Prof. Hamilton holds an MA degree in Economics from Edinburgh University and he has co-authored books on company law and taxation and written many articles for the professional and financial press.

EDWIN M. HARTMAN serves as Chair of the Department of Business Environment as well as Director of the Prudential Business Ethics Center, both at Rutgers Business School. He received a Ph.D. in Ancient Philosophy from Princeton University and an MBA from the Wharton School of the University of Pennsylvania. Professor Hartman is also a member of the board of the Society for Business Ethics.

LAURA HARTMAN is Associate Vice President for Academic Affairs at DePaul University and is responsible for coordinating the development of new academic programs. She is also a Professor of Business Ethics and Legal Studies in the Management Department in DePaul's College of Commerce. Hartman graduated *magna cum laude* from Tufts University and received her law degree from the University of Chicago Law School. She has engaged in ethics training workshops and presentations for a number of local and global companies and professional associations at the employee, executive, and board levels.

ROBERT JACKALL is Class of 1956 Professor of Sociology and Social Thought at Williams College. A much fuller account of the themes treated in this article is presented in *Moral Mazes: The World of Corporate Managers.* His most recent books are *Wild Cowboys: Urban Marauders and the Forces of Order* (1997); *Image Makers: Advertising, Public Relations, and the Ethos of Advocacy* (2000), written with Janice M. Hirota; and *Street Stories: The World of Police Detectives* (2005).

DEBORAH JOHNSON is the Anne Shirley Carter Professor of Applied Ethics at the University of Virginia School of Engineering and Applied Sciences. She is the author/editor of four books, including the popular textbook, *Computer Ethics,* Third Edition

(2001), and over 40 published papers. She received her Ph.D. from the University of Kansas. Dr. Johnson's research interests include ethical and policy issues surrounding technology, especially computer and information technology.

GRETCHEN KALSOW is a former Assistant Professor of Business Administration at the Darden Graduate School of Business at the University of Virginia. She received her Ph.D. from the California Institute of Technology.

IMMANUEL KANT was born in 1724 in East Prussia where he took his Master's degree at Konigsberg in 1755 and began teaching in the University as a Privatdozent, teaching a wide variety of subjects, including mathematics, physics, and geography, in addition to philosophy. Kant's publication during this period, primarily concerning the natural sciences, won him considerable acclaim in Germany, but he is most known today for his three critiques—the *Critique of Pure Reason*, the *Critique of Practical Reason*, and the *Critique of Judgement*—all of which were written and published after he obtained his professorship. Kant died in 1804.

ROSABETH MOSS KANTER holds the Ernest Arbuckle Chair as Professor at the Harvard Business School, where she has taught since 1986. Her 15 influential books include *When Giants Learn to Dance*, *The Change Masters: The Challenge of Organizational Change*, and *Evolve!: Succeeding in the Digital Culture of Tomorrow*. Her most recent book is *Confidence: How Winning Streaks and Losing Streaks Begin and End* (2004), which was a *New York Times* Business and number 1 *Business Week* bestseller.

ARTHUR L. KELLY is a graduate of Yale University and earned his M.B.A. from the University of Chicago. He was formerly a management consultant with A. T. Kearney, Inc., and later served as president and chief executive officer of LaSalle Steel Company. Currently Mr. Kelly is president of KEL Enterprises LTD., a Chicago holding and investment company, and serves as a member of the boards of directors of corporations in the United States and Europe, including Deere & Company and BMW A.G.

STEVEN KELMAN is the Weatherhead Professor of Public Management at Harvard University's John F. Kennedy School of Government. He is the author of many books and articles on the policymaking process and on improving the management of government organizations, including *Procurement and Public Management: The Fear of Discretion* and *The Quality of Government Performance and Making Public Policy: A Hopeful View of American Government*. From 1993 to 1997, Dr. Kelman served as administrator of the Office of Federal Procurement Policy at the Office of Management and Budget, where he played a lead role in the Clinton Administration's "Reinventing Government" effort.

STEFANIE A. LENWAY is the Dean of the College of Business Administration and Professor of Managerial Studies at the University of Illinois-Chicago. She formerly taught strategic management and organization at the University of Minnesota. Stefanie received her Ph.D. from the University of California, Berkeley, in business and public policy in 1982. Her current research focuses on how the global diffusion of technology requires companies to adopt global strategies to access cutting-edge technical and industry knowledge in leading markets. This research grew out of a long-term research interest in business-government strategic interaction. Her articles have appeared in the *Academy of Management Journal*, the *Strategic Management Journal*, the *Journal of Management*, and the *Journal of International Business*, among others. Her book, *Managing New Industry Creation*, published by Stanford University Press, chronicles the evolution of the flat panel display industry. The book is based on research sponsored by the Alfred

P. Sloan Foundation. Her most recent publication is *Revisiting the Obsolescing Bargain Model: International Business-Government Relations in the 21st Century* (2006), published by Cambridge University Press.

JOHN LOCKE was born in 1632 and educated in classics, near-eastern languages, scholastic philosophy and, later, in medicine. Active and influential in the political affairs of his time, Locke was forced to flee England and his position at Oxford after his close friend, the Earl of Shaftesbury, was tried for treason in 1681. After events turned to his advantage, he returned to England from exile in Holland and subsequently published his two most famous works, the *Essay Concerning Human Understanding* and the *Second Treatise of Government.*

IAN MAITLAND is Associate Director of the Strategic Management Research Center and an associate professor of Ethics and International Business at the Carlson School of Management at the University of Minnesota. He is a senior fellow of the Center of the American Experiment, a Minneapolis-based conservative think-tank. He earned his B.A. from Oxford and a Ph.D. from Columbia University. Most recently, he has written articles on how the market teaches virtues like honesty and considerateness and on Japanese–U.S. competition.

KARL MARX, the famous German political philosopher and revolutionary socialist, was born in 1818. His radical Hegelianism and militant atheism precluded an academic career in Prussia, and he subsequently lived the life of an exile in Paris and London. Financially supported by Friedrich Engels, he devoted himself to research, the development of his theory of socialism, and to agitation for social reforms. *The Communist Manifesto* was written in collaboration with Engels in 1847. His greatest work, *Das Kapital,* remained unfinished at the time of his death in 1883 and was carried to completion by Engels from posthumous papers.

BOWEN H. "BUZZ" MCCOY is a retired managing director of Morgan Stanley, a firm that he served for 28 years. For 13 years he was responsible for worldwide real estate finance activities at Morgan Stanley. He has served as president of the Urban Land Foundation and trustee of the Urban Land Institute. He has also served as president of the Real Estate Counselors, chairman of the Center for Economic Policy Research at Stanford University, and a member of the Executive Committee at the Hoover Institution.

WILLIAM MCDONOUGH is a world-renowned architect and designer and winner of three U.S. presidential awards: the Presidential Award for Sustainable Development (1996), the National Design Award (2004), and the Presidential Green Chemistry Challenge Award (2003). *Time* magazine recognized him as a "Hero for the Planet" in 1999, stating that "his utopianism is grounded in a unified philosophy that—in demonstrable and practical ways—is changing the design of the world." Mr. McDonough is the founding principal of William McDonough + Partners, Architecture and Community Design, and he is also the cofounder and principal, with German chemist Michael Braungart, of McDonough Braungart Design Chemistry (MBDC).

PEGGY MCINTOSH is associate director of the Wellesley College Center for Research on Women. She is founder and co-director of the National S.E.E.D. (Seeking Educational Equity and Diversity) Project on Inclusive Curriculum. She is the author of many influential articles on curriculum change, women's studies, and systems of unearned privilege. Dr. McIntosh is also the consulting editor to *Sage: A Scholarly Journal on Black Women* and is co-founder of the Rocky Mountain

Women's Institute. In addition to having two honorary degrees, she recently received the Klingenstein Award for Distinguished Educational Leadership from Columbia Teachers College.

JOHN MCVEA is an Assistant Professor at the University of St. Thomas, primarily teaching courses in entrepreneurship. Dr. McVea received his undergraduate education in Birmingham, England, and his M.B.A. and Ph.D. at the University of Virginia. His research interests and specialties include entrepreneurial decision making, science, entrepreneurship and ethics, ethical deliberation and decision making, and stakeholder management.

RS MOORTHY is Director, Research and Strategic Capabilities, Global Leadership and Organizational Development, Motorola.

JENNY MEAD is a freelance writer and Research Assistant at the Olsson Center for Applied Ethics, Darden Graduate School of Business. She taught high school English, was a Hollywood studio executive, has published numerous short stories as well as a novel in the Czech language, and worked as a journalist.

ROBERT NOZICK is the Pellegrino University Professor at Harvard University. In addition to *Anarchy, State and Utopia,* for which he won the National Book Award, he is the author of *Philosophical Explanations, The Examined Life, The Nature of Rationality, Socratic Puzzles,* and *Invariances.*

LYNN SHARP PAINE is the John G. McLean Professor of Business Administration at the Harvard Business School. Head of the general management area from 1997–2000, she currently chairs the school's initiative in leadership, ethics, and corporate responsibility. Author of *Cases in Leadership, Ethics and Organizational Integrity* (Irwin/McGraw Hill, 1997), Professor Paine has also published numerous scholarly articles and nearly 150 case studies. Her recent book, *Value Shift: Why Companies Must Merge Social and Financial Imperatives to Achieve Superior Performance* (McGraw-Hill, 2003), was named one of the year's top 10 business books by Soundview Executive Book Summaries and selected by *Library Journal* as one of the Best Business Books of 2003.

JEFFREY PFEFFER is the Thomas D. Dee II Professor of Organizational Behavior in the Graduate School of Business at Stanford University. He received a B.S. in Administration and Management Science, an M.S. in Industrial Administration from Carnegie-Mellon University, and a Ph.D. in Business Administration from the Stanford Graduate School of Business. He currently writes "The Human Factor," a column for the popular business periodical *Business 2.0.*

C.K. PRAHALAD is Harvey C. Fruehauf Professor of Business Administration and Professor of Corporate Strategy and International Business at the University of Michigan Business School. He is a globally recognized business consultant who has worked with senior management at many of the world's leading companies. He is the author of *The Fortune at the Bottom of the Pyramid: Eradicating Poverty Through Profits* (2004), which helped to launch a global movement toward private-sector solutions for global poverty.

PAUL L. PRESTON has written more than 200 articles, cases, films, and videocassettes on a wide range of topics, and is the author of 14 books on communication, management, and administration, including, most recently, *Leadership Strategies for Health Care Managers.*

JAMES RACHELS was a member of the philosophy faculty at the University of Alabama at Birmingham (UAB) since 1977. Previously he taught at the University of Richmond, New York University, and the University of Miami. From 1978 to 1983 he was dean of UAB's School of Arts and Humanities. He received his undergraduate degree from Mercer University and his Ph.D. from the University of North Carolina at Chapel Hill. Dr. Rachels is the author of *The End of Life: Euthanasia and Morality* (Oxford University Press, 1986); *Created from Animals: The Moral Implications of Darwinism* (Oxford University Press, 1991); *The Elements of Moral Philosophy* (McGraw-Hill, third edition 1998); and *Can Ethics Provide Answers? And Other Essays in Moral Philosophy* (Rowman and Littlefield, 1997). Professor Rachels passed away in September 2003.

TARA J. RADIN is an assistant professor of management and general business at Hofstra University. She earned her Ph.D. in management at the Darden Graduate School of Business Administration at the University of Virginia, where she also earned her J.D./M.B.A. and B.A. She has served as a consultant for companies such as Citicorp and was an editoral assistant for Prentice-Hall for *Management*, sixth edition, by Stoner, Freeman, and Gilbert.

JOHN RAWLS was the James Bryant Conant University Professor of Philosophy Emeritus at Harvard University and was among the leading moral and political theorists of this century. His book *A Theory of Justice* is a contemporary classic; it has prompted wide-ranging comment and discussion, not only by philosophers, but by economists, sociologists, political and legal theorists, and others. John Rawls also published *Political Liberalism* (1993), *The Law of Peoples, with the Idea of Public Reason Revisited* (1999), *Lectures on the History of Moral Philosophy* (2000), and *Justice As Fairness: A Restatement* (2001). He authored numerous articles as well, most of which are reprinted in his *Collected Papers* (1999). Professor Rawls passed away November 24, 2002.

DIANA ROBERTSON is a professor of Organization and Management at the Goizueta Business School of Emory University. She received an A.B. in Comparative Literature from Northwestern University, and an M.A. and Ph.D. in sociology from the University of California at Los Angeles. Robertson's specialties include business ethics, social responsibility, and corporate ethics initiatives.

BARBARA ROSE is a staff reporter for the *Chicago Tribune* and *Crain's Chicago Business.*

JUDY B. ROSENER is a professor at the Paul Merage School of Business, University of California at Irvine. Dr. Rosener has taught classes on several subjects in the business and business ethics fields, but her research focuses largely on cultural and gender issues in the workplace. She has served as a columnist for the *Los Angeles Times* and a commentator for PBS's *Life and Times* and is currently a columnist for the *Orange County Business Journal.*

AMARTYA SEN is currently the Lamont University Professor and professor of economics and philosophy at Harvard University. He was formerly master of Trinity College, Cambridge. He has written on welfare economics, social choice theory, development economics, economic methodology, and ethics and political philosophy. His most famous works include *Poverty and Famine: An Essay on Entitlement and Deprivation* (Oxford, Clarendon Press, 1982) and *Development as Freedom* (Oxford University Press, 1999). He is past president of the Econometrics Society, the International Economic Association, the Indian Economic Association and the American Economic Association. Professor Sen was awarded the Nobel Prize in economics in 1998.

KRISTI SEVERANCE worked for the Olsson Center for Applied Ethics at the Darden Graduate School of Business at the University of Virginia. She was a Fellow at the Central European and Eurasian Law Initiative (CEELI) for the American Bar Association where she conducted research on human trafficking and comparative legal systems. She holds a J.D. with honors from the American University, Washington College of Law. She also holds a diploma in international and European legal studies, with honors, from the University of Paris X.

BILL SHAW is a professor of legal environment at the University of Texas at Austin and recipient of the Woodson Centennial Professor award. His research areas include legal and ethical studies in business. Shaw is president of the American Business Law Association and chair of its Business Ethics section.

JULIAN L. SIMON was a professor of business administration at the University of Maryland, College Park. He was the author of *The Ultimate Resource* and *Population and Development in Poor Countries*, among other books, and co-editor, with Herman Kahn, of *The Resourceful Earth: A Response to the Global 2000 Report*. Professor Simon passed away in 1998.

MARK SKERTIC is an investigative reporter for the *Chicago Tribune* and was recently awarded the National Headliner Award for investigative reporting for stories he wrote in 2000 on poorly made tires. He graduated from the University of Indiana and is the author of the book *A Native's Guide to Northwest Indiana*.

ADAM SMITH, first known as a moral philosopher, is now famous as a political economist. He was born in 1723 in Scotland and was later elected professor of logic at the University of Glasgow. He published *Theory of Moral Sentiments* in 1759 to great acclaim. He resigned his professorship at Glasgow and after 10 years of work published *The Wealth of Nations*, for which his fame has endured. In 1778 he was appointed a commissioner of customs for Scotland. He died in 1790.

ROBERT C. SOLOMON was Quincy Lee Centennial Professor and Distinguished Teaching Professor at the University of Texas at Austin. He was the author of more than 30 books, including *A Short History of Philosophy, The Passions, The Joy of Philosophy in the Spirit of Hegel, About Love, Above the Bottom Line, Ethics and Excellence, It's Good Business, A Better Way to Think About Business*, and *In Defense of Sentimentality*. Professor Solomon died in January 2007.

ROBERT B. TEXTOR is Professor of Anthropology, Emeritus, at Stanford University, and Courtesy Professor of International Studies at the University of Oregon.

LESTER C. THUROW has been a professor of management and economics at MIT since 1968. He was dean of the MIT Sloan School of Management from 1987 until 1993. Thurow received his Ph.D. in economics from Harvard University in 1964. In his formal academic work, he focuses on international economics, public finance, macroeconomics, and income distribution economics. In addition, he writes for the general public in a number of U.S. and international newspapers. A prolific writer, Thurow is the author of several books, three of them *New York Times* bestsellers.

JAMES A. WATERS was dean of the Graduate School of Management at Boston College. His research interests concerned the process of strategy formation in complex organization, organizational change and development, and ethics in organizations. His work has been published in journals such as *Organizational Dynamics, Academy of Management Journal, Strategic Management Journal, California Management Review, and Journal of Business Ethics*, and in numerous anthologies.

PATRICIA H. WERHANE is the Wicklander Chair of Business Ethics in the Department of Philosophy and Director of the Institute for Business and Professional Ethics at DePaul University with a joint appointment as the Peter and Adeline Ruffin Professor of Business Ethics and Senior Fellow at the Olsson Center for Applied Ethics in the Darden School at the University of Virginia. Professor Werhane has published numerous articles and is the author or editor of 20 books, including *Persons, Rights and Corporations, Adam Smith and His Legacy for Modern Capitalism, Moral Imagination and Managerial Decision-Making*, with Oxford University Press, and *Employment and Employee Rights* (with Tara J. Radin and Norman Bowie) with Blackwell's. She is the founder and former editor-in-chief of *Business Ethics Quarterly*, the journal of the Society for Business Ethics. Professor Werhane is a member of the academic advisory team for the newly created Business Roundtable Institute for Corporate Ethics housed at the University of Virginia.

JUNE WEST is the Academic Director for the University of Virginia Partnership for Leaders in Education and an Assistant Professor of Business Administration at the Darden Graduate School of Business Administration. West has also served as director of the Philip Rauch Center for Business Communication at Lehigh University, clinical professor at the Stern Graduate School of Business at New York University, and assistant professor in the Master of Arts Program in Corporate and Public Communication at Seton Hall University.

ANDY WICKS teaches Business Ethics at the Darden School of Business of the University of Virginia as an Associate Professor of Business Administration and serves as Co-Director of the Olsson Center for Applied Ethics. Wicks's areas of expertise include business ethics and corporate social responsibility, as well as stakeholder theory, trust, health care ethics, total quality management, and ethics and entrepreneurship. Before joining the faculty at Darden, he taught at the University of Washington Graduate Business School.

THOMAS W. ZIMMERER is dean and professor of management in the School of Business at Saint Leo University. He was formerly the director of the Breech School of Business Administration at Drury University and professor of management at Clemson University. He is the author of numerous textbooks and more than 130 professional papers and articles in such prestigious journals as the *Academy of Management Review*. His most recent book is *Effective Small Business Management: An Entrepreneurial Approach* (2005), published by Pearson Prentice-Hall.